ADIN BALLOU

ADIN BALLOU (1803-1890) grew up on a farm in Cumberland, Rhode Island. When he was 11 his family was converted by the Christian Connexion, under whose auspices he began preaching at age 18. Shortly afterward he converted to Universalism. He served as Universalist minister in New York City and in Milford, Massachusetts, 1824-31. In 1831 he was one of a group of Universalists who seceded to form their own denomination, the Massachusetts Association of Universal Restorationists. While serving a Unitarian church in Mendon, Massachusetts, 1831-1842, he was for nearly a decade a leader of the Restorationist movement.

During the 1830s Ballou became increasingly interested in reform causes, notably temperance and abolitionism. In 1838 he was converted to the cause of peace and Christian non-resistance. His promotion of social causes was a major factor in the breakup of the Restorationists in 1839. In 1842 he organized Fraternal Community No. 1 (later called the Hopedale Community) in Hopedale, Massachusetts. This community, founded on non-resistant principles, repudiated participation in any government that relied upon ultimate recourse to coercive force. The people of Hopedale experimented with various forms of socialism, rejecting pure communism and eventually adopting a joint-stock constitution. The community survived and largely prospered for 14 years before the largest shareholders engineered its sudden collapse in 1856 and converted the community into a company town.

During the Hopedale years Ballou edited the community's newspaper, the *Practical Christian*, and wrote his major works, *Christian Non-Resistance* (1846) and *Practical Christian Socialism* (1854). During the Civil War he was nearly alone among abolitionists in maintaining his pacifist principles. He remained in Hopedale as minister of the Unitarian church, retiring in 1880. Late in life he wrote a number of historical books, including the *History of the Hopedale Community*, *History of the Town of Milford*, and his *Autobiography*. In the last year of his life he corresponded with Leo Tolstoy, upon whom Ballou's exposition of Christian non-resistance had a great influence.

Emil Otto Grundemann, 1885

Adin Ballou

Autobiography of Adin Ballou

ANNOTATED EDITION

Completed and edited by his son-in-law
William S. Heywood

Introduction and notes by
Lynn Gordon Hughes and Peter Hughes

Blackstone Editions

Blackstone Editions
Toronto, Ontario, Canada
www.BlackstoneEditions.com

Preface, introduction, and notes © 2016 by Lynn Gordon Hughes and Peter Hughes
All rights reserved. Published 2016
Second printing 2018

Printed in the United States of America

ISBN 978-0-9816402-4-2

*We spend our years
as a tale that is told.*

Psalms 90:9

Contents

EDITOR'S PREFACE *by Lynn Gordon Hughes* xv
EDITOR'S INTRODUCTION *by Peter Hughes* xxiii
A NOTE ON THE TEXT xxxiii

AUTOBIOGRAPHY OF ADIN BALLOU

INTRODUCTION *by William S. Heywood* 1
PREFACE *by Adin Ballou* 5

CHAPTER 1. 1803-1813 7
    Birth, ancestry, and family relationship – Place of nativity and vicinage – Unpromising infancy – Natural disposition and susceptibilities – Annoyances and casualties – Paternal discipline – Relation to employees – First appearance at church – Ancient burying ground – Early religious impressions – Prevailing indifference to spiritual things – Home and life there – Old-fashioned tavern – Military witchery – Intoxicating liquors – At school – Easy to learn – Episode in domestic affairs – Back again – War clouds and the opening storm

CHAPTER 2. 1813-1818 24
    Interest in public affairs – Opportunities for self-culture improved – A great "Reformation" – Parents and older brothers converted – Church of the "Christian Connexion" formed – Father made deacon and kept ministers' tavern – Personal experience – Baptized and received into the church – Self-revelation and self-conflict – A memorable year – Great September gale – General Conference – Death of brothers Cyrus and Arnold – Routine of employment – Intense love of learning – Hope for a collegiate education thwarted – Reflections – Singing-school privileges interdicted – Spiritual lapse and recovery

CHAPTER 3. 1818-1821 35
    Increased responsibilities – Lurch into asceticism – A formulated belief – Final destruction of the wicked held and maintained – All forms of Universalism deemed anti-Christian – Several clergymen mentioned – Eccentric Lorenzo Dow and his

lesson – Informed upon political questions – Favorable school privileges enjoyed and much benefit derived from them – Important commission undertaken and executed with much difficulty – Marriage of cousin – One such occasion leads to another – Betrothal – Apologetic comments – Manager of ancestral estate – Disastrous business venture

CHAPTER 4. 1821-1822 46
Life plans presumably settled – Undreamed-of changes subvert them – A startling vision – Call to the Christian ministry – Conflicting emotions awakened thereby – Many reasons for not responding favorably to the mysterious message – Yet it seemed sacredly imperative and could not be denied – Yielding, therefore, the work involved was soon made manifest – Unpremeditatedly, announcement to preach was made and a text in due time given – The result – The evil of sin – Invitations to conduct religious services – First authorship – Teaching – A refractory pupil and an angry father – Wedding feast interrupted, but with a satisfactory issue – Housekeeping

CHAPTER 5. 1822-1823 57
Preaching in the general vicinity – Winchester's Dialogues read – Discussion with Universalist neighbors – Self-satisfied, but conscious of one weak point – Doubts concerning destiny of the impenitent wicked arise – Thorough search of the Scriptures resulted in the conviction that they teach Universal Restoration – After an agonizing experience accepted that doctrine and announced change of belief – A stormy time followed – Denounced by relatives and friends, and excommunicated by the church – Entered Universalist fellowship, though not accepting the dogma of no future punishment – After another heart-searching experience fully confirming the new faith, began preaching it – Second visit to Boston – New friends under new auspices

CHAPTER 6. 1823-1825 70
Engagement to supply several pulpits – Disgraceful proceeding at Bellingham – "The furious priest reproved" – First born child – Candidacy in Boston – Ordained as a Universalist minister – Call to pastorate at Milford received and accepted – Entered upon work with diligence and zeal – A religious war of several years' continuance in the town – Causes and characteristics of the same – Incidents growing out of it – A stroke of good policy – A Freemason and military chaplain – Teaching again – Religious condition of Milford Society

CHAPTER 7. 1825-1828 83
Provision for a home – Ludicrous performances at a funeral in Franklin – More serious one near at hand – Personal bereavements – House completed and occupied – Celebration of American Independence, 1827 – Laughable incident – Received invitation to preach for Prince Street Society in New York City – Accepted, though under some misapprehension – After a brief candidacy was called to the pastorate – Removal to the new field of labor – Child lost and found – Work prosecuted vigorously, but with indifferent results – Expectations unrealized – New means of usefulness – Friendly messages and appeals from Milford

CHAPTER 8. 1828-1829 99
Return to former parish decided upon – Regrets of New York people expressed – Inquiries concerning a successor revealed a desire to obtain Rev. Hosea Ballou – Negotiations opened accordingly – Encouraging response received – Mr. Ballou's visit to the city to arrange details – Satisfactorily settled, then unsettled, then settled again with an if – Meanwhile the proposed return to Milford has been effected – Reflections on Rev. Hosea Ballou's proceedings – Some misapprehensions corrected – Universalism in New York – A singular marriage – A gloomy premonition – Treading the old paths – Visit from Origen Bacheler and a consequent theological debate – Birth of a daughter – Decline of wife's health and early death – Musings

CHAPTER 9. 1829-1830 111
Field of service enlarging – A student in theology – The use of tobacco – Its final abandonment after a desperate struggle – Extracts from diary – Sudden and serious illness – Recovery gratefully referred to in the first sermon thereafter – A re-established home contemplated – Engagement of marriage with the daughter of a parishioner – Her qualifications for the duties of wife and mother – The nuptial vows sealed, Rev. Hosea Ballou 2d officiating – A Wrentham funeral – Consolatory discourse attacked by a local clergyman – Pastoral duties divided between Milford and Medway

CHAPTER 10. 1830-1831 120
Eventful year – Attitude of early Universalists on Future Retribution – Radical change on the subject – Existing dominant belief accompanied by derision of Restorationism – The famous "Medway sermon" – Request for its publication granted and it was sent to the Trumpet *office accordingly – Before appearing in print it was severely criticized and disparaged by the editor, Rev. Thomas Whittemore – A new crisis reached – Review of the situation resulting in a determination to repel the attack and defend the truth – A vigorous Reply to Mr. Whittemore was written but refused publication – The Milford Society and its action – An uncompromising Restorationist thenceforth – The* Independent Messenger *started – Bitter hostility of so-called ultra Universalists – Discharged from Milford and invited to Mendon – Fourth of July, 1830 – Birth of a second son – Renewed assault on the* Trumpet *and rejoinder – Restorationist brethren timid*

CHAPTER 11. 1831-1832 135
Settled in Mendon – Condition of the parish – Revival of interest and continued increase in prosperity – Ecclesiastical gatherings – Massachusetts Association of Universal Restorationists organized – Occasion of a fresh assault on the part of the Trumpet *– Met with unabated vigor – Restorationism assailed from the opposite direction and defended no less vigorously – Rev. Amos A. Phelps – Independent Messenger moved to Boston – At the end of a year's service in Mendon was engaged for five years – Policy in regard to salary – Friendship with prominent Unitarians*

CHAPTER 12. 1832-1833 150
Installation by a council of Restorationists and Unitarians – Prevailing spirit of harmony and cooperation – Sermon of Rev. Bernard Whitman on Christian

Union – Courage and independence of Unitarians who sympathized with Restorationists – Espousal of the Temperance Reform – Curious conduct of Rev. J. M. S. Perry at a public meeting in aid of the cause – Benefits derived from the position taken – Calls to lecture – Resolutions of the Providence Association – Extracts from diary – Anxiety and sorrow – Death of two children – Consolatory thoughts

CHAPTER 13. 1833-1834 164
Installation of Seth Chandler, a former theological student – Whitman's "Letters to a Universalist" – Third son born, named Adin Augustus – Call to Watertown declined – Rev. Stephen Cutler and an unfortunate partnership – Review of Huidekoper's treatise on "The Destruction of the Wicked" – Discussion with Rev. Jonathan Farr – Abhorrence of the doctrine of endless punishment emphasized – Controversy with ultra Universalists continued – Challenge to a public discussion – Accepted by Rev. Daniel D. Smith – Report of what was said printed – Course of Mr. Smith and Universalists generally in regard thereto

CHAPTER 14. 1834-1836 177
Another student, Edmund Capron – Swords measured with distinguished champions of orthodoxy – Temperance work – Attendance upon public occasions – Death of Rev. Bernard Whitman – Family bereavements – Settlement of father's estate – "Omega" to Controversy with former associates – A long silence ensued concerning the main points in question, followed by an almost unanimous adoption of the views held and maintained by the Restorationists – Warfare with advocates of endless torments still raging – Debate with Rev. W. P. Apthorp – Improved condition of Mendon parish – Diary extracts

CHAPTER 15. 1836-1838 189
Ordination of George W. Stacy – Interesting visit to Concord–Mendon pastorate extended – Endeavors to promote the Christian life of the people – Total Abstinence – The Antislavery Movement – Its claims examined – Conclusions arrived at and stand taken – Fast Day sermon, 1837, and its consequences – Fourth of July oration – Blunder of Rev. Mr. Grosvenor at installation of Rev. Thomas Edwards – Ordination of Rev. Edmund Capron and death soon afterward – Reform resolutions passed by Massachusetts Association of Restorationists – The Touchstone published – Personal religion – Murder of Lovejoy – Dangerous illness of son

CHAPTER 16. 1838-1840 207
Personal memoranda – An unusual ceremonial – A parishioner elected to Congress – First Christmas celebration in Mendon – Claims of the cause of Peace carefully considered – Serious questions involved – Christian Non-Resistance – The logical outcome of Restorationism – Standard of Practical Christianity – Opposition by conservative brethren – Death of father – Quarterly Conferences – On the non-resistant platform – End of the Messenger *– A new organ provided for*

CHAPTER 17. 1840-1842 222
The Practical Christian *– Groton Convention – Requirements of the adopted Standard – Truth is to be lived – A new civilization demanded – The Fraternal*

Communion – Other social experiments – Brook Farm – Declaration of principles – Location of proposed Community selected and named Hopedale – Village site laid out – The outlook – Varied experiences – The Restorationist Association – Lectures – Afflictions – Letters of William Ellery Channing, D. D. and Rev. Paul Dean – Farewell to Mendon and removal to Hopedale – First religious meeting there – Visit of Frederick Douglass

CHAPTER 18. 1842-1845 236
Man, a moral and religious being – Deductions from that postulate – Hopedale statistics – Valuable lessons learned – Rev. David R. Lamson and his co-incompatibles – The real trouble – Change of policy required and effected – Withdrawal of Mr. Lamson and his subsequent history – Lectures on Social Reform and kindred topics – Second Advent discussions and True Scriptural Doctrine of the Second Advent *– Progress – Donation of Andrew H. Ernst of Cincinnati – Religious meetings – Difficulties and dangers – Heavy bereavement*

CHAPTER 19. 1845-1852 250
Personal reflections – Helpmeet in the household – Year of marked prosperity – Faint-heartedness, nevertheless – Withdrawal of Rev. George W. Stacy – Visit from Robert Owen, an English Communist – Reverses – The system simplified – Cemetery laid out – Small partnerships granted, with diverse results – Rectification of land titles – Resignation of Rev. Daniel S. Whitney – A new president – Death of Susan Fish – Death of the dear son, Adin Augustus – Christian Non-Resistance published – Debates with Origen Bacheler and Rev. Thomas Williams – Spirit manifestations examined – Education of children – Educational Home – Memoir of A. A. Ballou – Work on Spiritualism – Henry C. Wright and Oliver Johnson – The Practical Christian Ministry – Demise of wife's mother – Preaching for Theodore Parker

CHAPTER 20. 1852-1858 267
Enfeebled condition of body and mind – Sympathizing friends – Visit to Troy, New York – Relations to Spiritualism – Lectures on Spiritualism – Opening of 1853 – Tragic death of Butler Wilmarth, M.D. – Inductive Communion – Inquiries Answered and Errors Withstood – Practical Christian Republic – Work on Practical Christian Socialism *published – Journey to the West, with notes by the way, visits to noted places, and interviews with distinguished statesmen – Year of prosperity – New Communities proposed – Explorers in Western fields – Lecture tours – Call upon Hon. Gerrit Smith – The fatal crisis – Resolution for the future – Commune No. 1 – Vision of Thomas Lake Harris*

CHAPTER 21. 1858-1862 283
Promulgatory activities – Hopedale Home School – Lectures on the Bible – Pleasant memories – Hopedale church organized – Death of friends – The John Brown raid – Course of Anti-war Abolitionists condemned – Peace principles of the American Anti-Slavery Society stated – Stirring meeting of Worcester South Anti-Slavery Society – Position of William Lloyd Garrison criticized – Past and present utterances contrasted – Commentary on the Scriptures – Discontinuance of the Practical Christian *– Kindly words from Rev. Thomas Whittemore and*

response – Promulgation Society formed – New house of worship – Remarkable spirit seances – Discussion with Miles Grant – Mutterings of coming war – Birth of granddaughter – The Monitorial Guide – The Lord's freeman

CHAPTER 22. 1862-1872 302
Hopedale affairs – Business prospers, but Practical Christianity is in abeyance – Home School suspended – Discourses of William Lloyd Garrison – Discussion of objectionable points sought but declined – Reviewed in the pulpit – Case of conscription – Excursions and comments – Andrew Leighton of Liverpool, England – Discourses on Human Progress with Respect to Religion *– The Hopedale Parish formed – its first pastor – The Worcester Unitarian Conference joined – Work for coming generations prosecuted – Sketch of Milford –* Primitive Christianity and its Corruptions, *vol. I published – Long-standing misrepresentations corrected – Unitarians, Spiritualists, special reformers, etc.*

CHAPTER 23. 1872-1882 322
Primitive Christianity reviewed by Rev. A. St. John Chambré – Rejoinder – Ancient dogma rejected – Essay before Worcester Conference – Parochial Christian Union – Resignation of pastorate tendered and withdrawn – Primitive Christianity and its Corruptions, *vol. II in manuscript – Last scene in the drama of the Hopedale Community – Third volume of* Primitive Christianity *prepared –* The church as it is *– History of the Hopedale Community ready for the printer – Engaged to write a complete history of Milford – Termination of the Hopedale pastorate – The narrative broken, with note from the editor – Celebrations of the Centennial of American Independence – Letter from Mr. Garrison – Sermon before G. A. R. post – Serious illness of wife – Arranged to prepare a history of the Ballous in America*

CHAPTER 24. 1882-1890 341
The Ballou history – The family burial lot – Essays and reviews – The town of Hopedale – Dedication of the town hall – Ex-Governor John D. Long's oration and Mr. Ballou's correction of its disparaging statements and misapprehensions – Dr. Richard Eddy on the Restorationist secession – Count Leo Tolstoy's My Religion *read and criticized – Letter to Tolstoy and response – Answer to the last – Sermon of Rev. Lewis G. Wilson and* Arena *article – Deaths of William H. Humphrey, George Draper, and Ebenezer D. Draper – Relations of the latter to the Hopedale Community and its founder – Death of brother, Ariel Ballou, M. D. – Work on autobiography – Eighty-ninth birthday – Last public efforts – Funerals and marriages – Decline, illness, and death – Funeral*

APPENDIXES

A. Tributes and Testimonials 366

B. Funeral Sermon 379

C. The Adin Ballou Lectureship of Practical Christian Sociology 387

D. Lucy Hunt Ballou 391

E. Works of Adin Ballou 395

F. "An Epistle General to Restorationists" 401
   From the Independent Messenger, *January 1, 1831*

G. "The Restorationist Secession" 415
   From The Universalist, *February 11 and 25, 1871*

H. The Ballou-Tolstoy Correspondence 423

NOTES 431

INDEX 557

Editor's Preface
Lynn Gordon Hughes

I have been working on this book for more than twenty-five years. Or perhaps I should say that it has been working on me, for this book has had a powerful effect on the shape of my adult life.

When I first encountered the *Autobiography of Adin Ballou*, in 1990, I was living with my husband Peter and our two children in Woonsocket, Rhode Island, where Peter was the minister of the First Universalist Church. I worked as a computer programmer at Brown University, but still found time to run the church's small religious education program.

I had discovered Adin Ballou while searching for resources for a coming-of-age program for the church's teenagers. The search led me to Clinton Lee Scott's *These Live Tomorrow*, a collection of brief Unitarian and Universalist biographies written for young people. The chapter on Adin Ballou is only nine pages long, more than half of it about his childhood. It barely hints at his pacifism. Nevertheless, its short but stirring account of the rise and fall of the Hopedale Community captured my imagination. Peter had come upon Adin Ballou from a different direction: while researching the history of the Woonsocket church in preparation for the celebration of its 150th anniversary, he had found Ballou's name mentioned several times in the diary of the church's first minister, John Boyden.

Peter and I enjoy reading aloud. In the fall of 1990, the book we selected was the *Autobiography of Adin Ballou*. We were captivated by the voice of this wise old man: steady, compassionate, firm without being fanatical, looking back on the disappointments of his life with some self-deprecating humor, but with his ideals intact.

Issues of war and peace were very much on my mind that fall, as Operation Desert Shield gave way to Operation Desert Storm. I had been strongly attracted to pacifism since I was a teenager, but I remained unsure whether it was a sound philosophy, or mere wishful thinking. Then, in Chapter 16, I found this:

> It seemed to me clear that true Christian Non-Resistance was not mere *passivity*, nor sheer tameness and indifference in respect to evildoers, nor simple abstinence from physical force in the treatment of violent and wicked men, but abstinence from every kind of *injurious* and *unbeneficent* force ... All rebukes and restraints,

all preventives and resistances of wrong doing, which do not in any way harm but benefit those subjected to them, which are accordant with the friendship and good will towards them, are not only consistent with *Christian* Non-Resistance, but are absolutely dictated by that godlike love out of which it springs.

It seemed to me that Ballou's concept of uninjurious physical force was the missing piece I had been seeking – the key to resisting evil without doing evil. I was amazed that this was not better known. Why, in twenty years of reading and reflecting on the subject, had I never heard of it before?

We had come nearly to the end of the book before we read the Preface. "Times and generations are coming," Peter read, "that will justly estimate me and my work ... For them, as it has proved, have I lived and labored, rather than for my contemporaries. To them I appeal for vindication and approval." I said, "He is talking about us." I felt that we had a mission to make Adin Ballou and his ideas known to our generation – but how?

Around this time, in my capacity as a programmer at Brown, I was working on replacing the traditionally typeset course catalog with one formatted by a page layout program called FrameMaker. With such a program, I saw, books could be produced by ordinary people, using readily available software on a home computer. This gave me the glimmering of an idea. Adin Ballou's works were out of print and, though still available in libraries and the occasional used bookstore, they had a musty nineteenth-century look about them. Would it be possible to republish them in bright, clean, reasonably priced modern editions, with notes to explain the references that had become obscure with the passage of time?

Though we may not have been consciously aware of it at the time, Peter and I were ideally situated to bridge the gap between Adin Ballou's world and our own. For we were living in Ballou's world, as much it was possible for anyone in the late twentieth century to do so. Our home in Woonsocket was only a few miles from the site of the Ballou family farm. The Ballou Meetinghouse had burned down in 1962, but we could still drive out on Elder Ballou Meetinghouse Road to visit the old cemetery, looking much as Ballou had described it, with the graves "scarcely marked at all amid the wild grass and brush." The Social Manufacturing Company where Ballou had worked as a child was gone, but there were still old mill buildings on Social Street. Old textile mills were very much part of the landscape of Woonsocket when we lived there. Occasionally one would burn down, the oil-soaked timber going up in a spectacular blaze that could be seen for miles.

Our church provided us with another window into Ballou's world. Many of the members of the First Universalist Church were descendants of the Universalist families who had founded the church in the 1840s. Peter once made a genealogical chart showing how the various church members were related to each other and to the Ballou family; almost everyone in the church was on it, except us and another family who had recently joined. We had our coffee hours and potluck lunches under a large oil painting of Adin's cousin Latimer W. Ballou – a pillar of nineteenth-century Woonsocket, and one of my predecessors as director of the Sunday school.

Unitarian Universalists are typically affluent, well-educated, urban, religiously unorthodox, and politically liberal, but the working-class Universalists of Woonsocket were conservative, in the original sense of the word – loyal, proud of their heritage, and dedicated to preserving the values and the institutions they cherished. They were firmly rooted in their corner of Rhode Island – firmly rooted, too, in the Christian tradition. Every service included the Lord's Prayer and a reading from the Bible. At First Universalist I learned how it is possible to be unitarian, universalist, and Christian at the same time.

Peter and I were well placed to do the historical research that would be required for the annotations. Woonsocket is only an hour's drive from Boston, and even closer to Milford, Mendon, and Hopedale. As a local minister, Peter had borrowing privileges at the Andover-Harvard Theological Library. We used the library's microfilm machines to photocopy almost the entire run of the *Practical Christian*. The Unitarian Universalist special collection yielded masses of unpublished information on churches and ministers. We visited the three churches served by Ballou, all still extant. In Hopedale we consulted the archives in the Bancroft Memorial Library, paid our respects at Ballou's grave, and saw streets and buildings dating back to the days of the Hopedale Community.

As an employee of Brown University I could use the libraries to read up on such topics as the temperance and abolition movements, the early history of Providence, New York City in the 1820s, nineteenth-century education, steamboats, and textile mills. I spent many lunch hours at the John Hay Library, with its marvelous collections of printed sermons, speeches, memorial books, and old newspapers. When I read that Adin's father "took the leading Republican paper of the state," I was able not only to identify the newspaper, but to consult actual copies of the *Columbian Phenix: or Providence Patriot* from 1812, and admire the beautifully preserved rag paper.

The resources were available, but I was not yet ready to take full advantage of them. Peter had theological training and a lifelong interest in history, but I did not even have a liberal arts education. My bachelor's degree was in water resources engineering, and my courses had been almost exclusively technical. The one history course I had taken, to satisfy a distribution requirement, was on China and Japan. I was going to need more education before I could do what I had in mind.

I started in my comfort zone with some technical studies: a certificate program in graphic design and book production at the Rhode Island School of Design. Then I started taking courses as a special student in Brown's history and American Civilization departments. In 1999, I began work on a master's degree in history. Taking one or two courses a semester, I finished the course work in a couple of years, but it took me until 2007 to complete my master's thesis. (It was not on

Adin Ballou, but on another religious seeker with a complicated relationship to Universalism and Unitarianism, Orestes Brownson.)

Meanwhile, Peter's study of local church history had developed into a much more ambitious study of the history of Universalism in New England. His first published article, in the *Unitarian Universalist Christian* magazine in 1994, was on the theology of Ballou's Restorationist colleague, Paul Dean. This was followed by an article in the *Journal of Unitarian Universalist History*, "Quackery among the Clergy," which explored the homeopathic medical practice of our church's first minister. Over the next few years Peter became a regular contributor to the *Journal of Unitarian Universalist History*, with articles on the origin of New England Universalism in 1997 and 1999, and on the Restorationist controversy in 2000 and 2001.

Peter retired on disability in 1999, due to the late effects of childhood polio. When he left the ministry in Woonsocket, we had to look for another church to attend. After visiting each of the Unitarian Universalist churches in the area, we settled on the old Universalist church in Milford, where Adin Ballou had once been the minister. Through the Milford church we made the acquaintance of the Friends of Adin Ballou, a group that had recently formed in Hopedale for the purpose of studying Ballou's works and keeping his memory alive in the town he had founded. We began attending Friends of Adin Ballou meetings, and helped to develop a walking tour of historic sites in Hopedale.

All of this made us better qualified to annotate the *Autobiography*, but delayed the actual accomplishment of the task. In fact we were making negative progress, as our growing expertise made us dissatisfied with the work we had already done. By the turn of the century we had been engaged in the project for almost a decade, but seemed as far as ever from completing it.

Meanwhile I continued to move ahead with the idea of starting a micro-publishing company. In Adin Ballou's day, changes in printing technology had made it possible for individuals to publish newspapers; now the same thing was happening with books. Page layout software was improving and becoming easier to use. Digital printing made it economically feasible to produce books in small quantities. Most importantly, the Internet had sprung up, and with it came e-commerce. Now we were able not only to publish books, but to sell them worldwide, without the intervention of book distributors or retailers.

Our work with the Friends of Adin Ballou gave us fresh enthusiasm for the project of putting Ballou's books back in print. It also made us aware of how difficult some of Ballou's theoretical writings could seem, even to highly motivated and interested readers. I interrupted my work on the *Autobiography* in order to prepare a simplified version of *Practical Christian Socialism* for the Friends of Adin Ballou. They found it useful and encouraged me to publish it. When I launched Blackstone Editions in 2002, this work, retitled *Practical Christianity* at the suggestion of one of the Friends, became the first book I published.

By this time I was caught up in yet another project. One of my courses at Brown was a seminar on how to communicate historical information outside the narrow world of academic historians. Our assignment was to pick a historical event and come up with a creative, engaging way to present it to a non-specialist audience. My project was the first draft of a children's book about life in the Hopedale Community. When the semester ended, I decided to develop the idea into an actual children's book. I recruited an illustrator, Linda Rogers, who was enthusiastic about the project. She and I worked closely together for over a year, without ever meeting, except on the Internet. The result was the second Blackstone book, *To Live a Truer Life*.

The third book was *Christian Non-Resistance*. With minimal notes, and an introduction adapted from a paper I wrote for one of my history classes, it was the quickest and easiest publishing project I have ever done. I was able to release it in June 2003, only a month after *To Live a Truer Life*. In that year of the United States invasion of Iraq, the book was sadly relevant. A reader in the Netherlands emailed me, "It is good to know that not all Americans are warmongers." I received invitations to lecture about Adin Ballou and non-resistance from the Unitarian Universalist Historical Society and the New Massachusetts Universalist Convention.

Over the next few years the autobiography receded farther into the background as exciting new opportunities competed for our attention. Peter and I were becoming known in the small community of Unitarian Universalist historians. Peter became vice-president of the Unitarian Universalist Historical Society and editor of the online Dictionary of Unitarian and Universalist Biography. I was called upon to use my book-production skills to produce books for the Liberal Religious Educators Association, the Unitarian Universalist Women's Heritage Society, and the Unitarian Universalist Historical Society. Since 2005 I have been producing each year's issue of the *Journal of Unitarian Universalist History*. I published original works on Unitarian history by two elder statesmen of Unitarianism, Phillip Hewett from Canada and Leonard Smith from England. I did manage to publish one small Hopedale-related book, *Hopedale Reminiscences*, in 2006. But the book that had started it all remained stubbornly incomplete.

As time went on, we moved away from Adin Ballou's world. Peter resumed work on a topic that had interested him long before he ever heard of Adin Ballou, the Reformation roots of Unitarianism. And in 2007, with my degree finally completed and our children grown up and on their own, Peter and I carried out a long-cherished dream of returning to Canada, after twenty-nine years in the United States.

This might have spelled the end of our involvement with Adin Ballou and Hopedale, but it did not. With the perspective of time and distance, we came to see the two decades we had spent in Adin Ballou's world as a gift that had enriched our lives and conferred upon us a responsibility to complete the task we had begun so long ago.

Fortunately, by this time the Internet had grown into such a powerful tool that we were able not only to annotate the later chapters, but also to fill in gaps in the notes for the earlier ones, despite being miles away from our New England sources of information. Google Books gave us access to vast stores of out-of-print books that would previously have been available only via interlibrary loan, if at all. Genealogical web sites documented the lives of ordinary people who would otherwise have left little trace in history. The Internet enabled us to trace quotations that had eluded us for years, and to follow up such intriguing side issues as the history of silk manufacture in Kansas, the nature of Jesuitical reasoning, the bridges across the Niagara River, and the career of the piano prodigy "Blind Tom" Wiggins. We also had at our disposal the University of Toronto libraries, as well as the boxes full of notes and photocopies that we had brought with us from Rhode Island. With the help of these resources, we were able to publish our edition of Ballou's *History of the Hopedale Community* in 2010. It took us an additional five years to complete the notes for the *Autobiography*.

We have been asked why, after doing so much research, we chose to publish an annotated edition of Ballou's autobiography instead of writing a biography. A modern biography of Adin Ballou would certainly be welcome, but we are content to have amassed information for future biographers to use.

When I was a student at Brown I learned the maxim "In history, the answers come from the past, but the questions come from the present." If we had written a biography, we would have addressed the questions of our generation (now rapidly becoming the older generation) and discarded the information that was not needed for this purpose. Instead, we have chosen to pass along the information we have uncovered in this decades-long odyssey, whether we can see its usefulness or not.

In the course of our research we have come to appreciate those nineteenth-century town histories, such as Ballou's *History of the Town of Milford*, that are not really histories at all, but chronicles – collections of information stored up for use by later historians. We see this book as part of that tradition. There will always be more to discover, but there should be enough here to assist any number of future biographers, whatever questions they may ask in their generation.

Besides, this book has done enough for me. It has made me a historian, a Master of Arts, an author, a lecturer, an editor, a book designer, and a publisher. It is time to send it back out into the world, to work its magic on others. "To them," as Adin Ballou said, "I bequeath whatever is valuable and worth preserving of my possessions – the fruits of my toil while yet a dweller in the tabernacles of earth and time."

Acknowledgments

In pursuing this project over so many years, we have drawn on the efforts, resources, and generosity of numerous individuals and organizations, only some of whom we can acknowledge or even identify. We would particularly like to thank the librarians and archivists at the Brown University libraries, Andover-Harvard Theological Library, the Rhode Island Historical Society, and the Bancroft Memorial Library in Hopedale. We remember in particular the help we received from the late Frances O'Donnell, curator of the Unitarian Universalist collection at the Andover-Harvard Theological Library.

We have received help from local historians at the Mendon Historical Society and church historians at the First Universalist Church of Providence, First Parish in Berlin, Massachusetts, and the Unitarian Congregation of Mendon and Uxbridge. Hopedale historian Dan Malloy has been a steadfast and generous source of information and encouragement. Especially during the period when our research was being conducted largely on the Internet, we have benefited from the work of a great cloud of contributors, unknown to us but indispensable to this project, who compiled and posted family histories and genealogies, town archives, church histories, and nineteenth-century publications of all kinds.

Throughout the process, we have been supported in countless tangible and intangible ways by our friends and parishioners at the First Universalist Church of Woonsocket and the First Unitarian Universalist Church of Milford, by the Friends of Adin Ballou, and by our extended family. Special thanks are due to Marcia Matthews and Laurie Stearns for their care and dedication in editing and proofreading this long and complex work.

Editor's Introduction
Peter Hughes

In 1894, when the diplomat Andrew Dickson White asked Leo Tolstoy to name the foremost American writer, Tolstoy answered, "Adin Ballou." White was amazed. How could Ballou, whom he dismissed as merely an "excellent Massachusetts country clergyman," be the best author that the United States had to offer? And it was not that Tolstoy was unfamiliar with distinguished American authors. White and Tolstoy had just been surveying American literature together. During their conversation Tolstoy had expressed admiration for the work of Ralph Waldo Emerson, Nathaniel Hawthorne, John Greenleaf Whittier, Henry Wadsworth Longfellow, Theodore Parker, William Lloyd Garrison, William Dean Howells, and Felix Adler. Yet above all these Tolstoy placed Adin Ballou.[1]

Tolstoy was aware that this might seem to be an idiosyncratic choice. That same year, in *The Kingdom of God Is Within You*, he acknowledged that Ballou's work languished in obscurity, but claimed that this was due to a "conspiracy of silence" against pacifist writings. "One would have thought Ballou's work would have been well known," he wrote, "and the ideas expressed by him would have been either accepted or refuted; but such has not been the case."[2] By omitting Adin Ballou from the canon of American literature, Tolstoy thought, the world at large, and American readers in particular, had expressed a disinclination to come to grips with the ideas that Ballou so passionately promoted.

Adin Ballou was not a great writer, in the literary sense that Andrew Dickson White meant. He was not an outstanding prose stylist. His writing is workmanlike and unpretentious, always readable, sometimes eloquent, but occasionally homely or awkward. Nevertheless his works, especially *History of the Hopedale Community*, ought to be better known in the United States, and elsewhere. His economic and political account of Hopedale is the record of a great experiment in trying to find an American way of living that lies somewhere between the extremes of unfettered capitalism and authoritarian communism. It makes plain the difficulties inherent in creating a truly just, merciful, and practical democracy and hints at how the struggles between the competing ideologies of left and right might be worked out. In fact, although it is told very personally, it is the epic story of an endeavor to create a soul within the body of the American republic.

Ballou's *Autobiography* and *History of the Hopedale Community* were two of the four major works of his later years. The other two were *History of the Town of Milford* and *History and Genealogy of the Ballous in America*. Each of these was an ambitious volume (or, in the case of the town history, two). The town history and the genealogy were models of their kind, pushing the customary boundaries of their genres. The town history includes what amounts to a biographical dictionary of the inhabitants of Milford. The genealogy is full of descriptive biographical detail going well beyond the usual vital statistics. Accordingly, when evaluating Adin Ballou as a historian we should consider that he was, first of all, a practitioner of town history and genealogy. He brought the strengths and weaknesses of local historians and genealogists to the writing of his autobiographical works.

Many substantial American town histories were printed in the latter part of the nineteenth century. Unlike amateur local histories produced in the twentieth century, which tend to omit detail in order to summarize and analyze events, these earlier examples are much less processed. They include entire documents: lists of office-holders and of soldiers who served in wars; property records; and detailed stories of churches, organizations, and businesses. These publications may be criticized on literary grounds, for their content is rather miscellaneous and betrays its cut-and-paste origin, but they remain rich sources of primary and near-primary information. The same is to some extent true for genealogies. Family histories preserve a lot of data that is relatively inaccessible or no longer available – although caution must be exercised when taking biographical information from these works, because enthusiastic genealogists have not always asked critical questions when copying information from secondary sources.

As the writer of an exemplary town history and a model genealogy, Adin Ballou brought much of the best of the genealogist and of the local historian to the writing of his autobiography and showed himself able to move both of these forms in the direction of critical biography. Thus, although autobiography as a genre is notoriously apologetic and self-serving, a strong case can be made for the relative accuracy of this particular autobiography as a historical document. For this autobiography is not merely a memoir of a life recollected in old age. Ballou was plainly researching his own life by consulting a rich trove of documents.

Almost everywhere in the autobiography we find that Ballou pays careful attention to detail and is determined to remain close to primary records. He had a diary – unfortunately now lost – that he followed and occasionally quoted. He had an extensive archive of newspaper clippings, drawn largely but not exclusively from the newspapers that he edited or co-edited: *The Dialogical Instructor*, *The Independent Messenger*, and *The Practical Christian*. The organizational methods that he and his wife Lucy had developed while preparing *History of the Town of Milford* and the Ballou genealogy stood him in good stead as he worked on *History of the Hopedale Community* and the *Autobiography*. In writing his life story he stayed very close to the documents that he had collected, using his memory only to fill in the gaps.

The year-by-year chronicle form, and the archival documents that Ballou included, left him less room than is usual in an autobiography to bury anything that did not support his overall narrative or self-portrayal. In this regard, an interesting comparison might be made with the better-known autobiography of Ballou's exact contemporary Orestes Brownson (1803-1876). Brownson's autobiography, *The Convert*, tells the story of his religious journey through various forms of liberal and evangelical Protestantism and his conversion to Roman Catholicism.[3] In describing the period during which he was engaged in Universalist ministry (1825-30), Brownson offered almost no details of events, but instead wrote a kind of intellectual history, focusing on a critique of Universalist theology from his later Roman Catholic perspective. None of the many interesting doings of the young Brownson as a Universalist minister and journalist are related, and none of the embarrassments that were his lot during these years are so much as hinted at.[4] In describing Universalism, Brownson displayed much knowledge, and some penetrating insight, based upon wide reading and personal experience.[5] It is clear that the Catholic author had once been a Universalist. But the text also reveals that he was careless in verifying details. For example, in his discussion of early Universalist writers he credits to John Murray works that were actually written by Elhanan Winchester.[6] His description of the later career of Adin Ballou, while not actionable perhaps, is a bit of wanton mud-slinging: "When I last heard from him, he was a spiritualist, spiritist, or devil-worshipper, conversing with spirits, and believing in Andrew Jackson Davis, and the Fox girls."[7]

The difference between Adin Ballou's *Autobiography* and Brownson's *The Convert* ought not to be entirely attributed to a greater degree of forthrightness in Ballou, because their different approaches to autobiography reflect the divergent nature of their lives' paths. Brownson was, in effect, reborn in his rather sudden conversion to a faith apparently quite distant from his previous ones. From his later perspective, what had happened to him in his Universalist years was of little importance to the person he had become. Ballou, on the other hand, had quite a different trajectory to his spiritual and intellectual life. He was always being converted – to universalism, to openly-declared Restorationism, to the temperance reform, to abolition, to pacifism, to communitarianism, and to spiritualism, just to name a few. But beneath all these important changes there was an underlying continuity of belief. Ballou always emphasized that his basic theology had hardly changed at all, in spite of his changes in denominational affiliation and the radical social movements to which he was drawn. When his theology did change, it was a gradual enlightenment, one of many stages in the unfolding of his religious character. Given this evolutionary development, all of the epochs in Ballou's religious progress were of more or less equal importance to him. Since he considered himself to be, at bottom, fundamentally unchanged, he felt connection and sympathy with the self who existed in all of his earlier periods. Thus he was pleased to explore all of the chapters of his life in depth.

The theology of Restorationism, which taught that every soul would be saved after a period of salutary discipline and education in the afterlife – what was known to Universalists as "future punishment" – was not just a passing phase with Adin Ballou. It became the core of the theology he set down in *Practical Christian Socialism* (1855). When he ministered to a parish in Hopedale that, after the collapse of the Hopedale Community, eventually became Unitarian, he preached the same Restorationist religion that he had preached during the 1830s to his Unitarian congregation in Mendon. Even the spiritualism of his later years did not deflect him from his long-held theological beliefs. For Spiritualism, with its generally consoling reports of the afterlife, tended to confirm Restorationist views. In short, the *Autobiography* emphasizes the religious and sectarian side of Ballou's teaching much more than does the more political *History of the Hopedale Community* or the more ecumenical *Christian Non-Resistance*. This is the story of a Restorationist minister as much as it is the history of the leader of a Non-Resistant community.

If Ballou had written the kind of autobiography that Brownson did, he would have concentrated much more on the Hopedale period in his life, for the utopian community was his greatest and most celebrated achievement, and the project dearest to his heart. But that is not the book that Ballou wrote. In fact, he devoted far more space in the *Autobiography* to his religious development as a Universalist minister and to his role in denominational controversies than he did to the story of Hopedale. Since he had already written his history of the Hopedale Community, in the *Autobiography* he set about to narrate his life as a whole, and to discuss the trials and struggles of his pre-Hopedale life almost as if he did not know what was to come afterward.

Ballou's career divides into two parts, equally interesting, in both of which he left a substantial mark upon the world. In the first part he was a principal founder, chief sustainer, and leading theological controversialist of a new denomination. In the second part he was a social reformer and the creator of a fairly successful utopian experiment. The first part of the book, before pacifism is even mentioned, makes an interesting and complete story in itself. It contains over half of the text, enough material by itself for a substantial volume.

Thus, the first half of the book can be read simply as the story of the career of an early Universalist minister, comparable to the important but far less engagingly written autobiographical accounts of other Universalist ministers, such as the *Memoirs of the Life of Nathaniel Stacy*, the *Autobiography of Rev. Abel C. Thomas*, and *The Life of Rev. John Murray*. All of these works are indispensable contemporary accounts of events in the history of Universalism. Each provides information that is available nowhere else. Ballou's autobiography provides a uniquely detailed account of the rise and the fall of the organization created by the Restorationists who broke away from the Universalist denomination in 1831. It also records an engagement between these Restorationist Universalists and one wing of the recently organized Unitarian denomination, a union of fellowship that anticipated by well over a century the consolidation that took place between the American Unitarian Association and the Universalist Church of America in 1961.

To many Unitarians, the division that had taken place between them and the more conservative wing of the established Standing Order in Massachusetts seemed like a breakup of the Church universal. They longed to reunite the body of Christianity. In this context, the appearance of the Restorationists, some of whom, like Adin Ballou, served Unitarian congregations and were anxious for broader fellowship, seemed a God-sent opportunity. There were, however, obstacles standing in the way of this rapprochement. Most Unitarians were disdainful of Universalists. Unitarian clergy were almost all Harvard-educated, while most Universalist ministers were self-educated, as Adin Ballou was, or apprenticed. And, although with few exceptions Universalists had long since become unitarian, few Unitarians were willing to admit belief in universal salvation. But there was a group of Unitarian clergy, settled outside of Boston, who were able to rise above elitism and willing to engage in friendly theological discourse. These Unitarians extended their hands towards Adin Ballou and the other Restorationists.

The *Autobiography* highlights the importance of two Unitarians who changed the direction of Ballou's ministry: Bernard Whitman and Samuel J. May. Bernard Whitman's friendship with Ballou cemented the alliance between Restorationists and Unitarians, and his premature death in 1834 marked the end of Ballou's interest in these ecumenical and denominational matters. Whitman's preaching drew Ballou's attention to the term "Practical Christianity." Late in life Whitman became increasingly interested in social change. But it was almost certainly Samuel J. May who recruited Ballou for the antislavery and peace movements and thus set Ballou on the path to Hopedale. The events connecting these two men with Ballou come at the mid-point of the *Autobiography* and form a watershed in Ballou's career. Before 1835 Ballou's energies were directed towards theology and the fostering of denominational interests. Afterwards, his primary concern was the application of his religious message to the revolutionary improvement of society.

If one is interested in denominational history – of the Christian Connexion, the Universalists, the Universal Restorationists, the Unitarians – the lengthy narration of the first part of Adin Ballou's career will be of considerable interest in itself. Ballou is an important figure in many of the events he describes and his testimony is a vital part of the documentary record of these events. Without it our understanding of them would be unbalanced and incomplete.

If, on the other hand, one is principally interested in utopian history, the first half of the book, with its focus on religious and theological matters, should still be of great interest. For, as Ballou tells us, Practical Christianity was the application to social problems of the theology that he had developed during his Universalist and Restorationist years. This can be seen in the construction of his most comprehensive theoretical work, *Practical Christian Socialism*, the first third of which is devoted to his underlying theology. Thus the first phase of Ballou's career, in which he developed and refined his own version of Christianity, forms a long theological prelude to the founding of an explicitly religious utopian community.

In addition, for the reader interested in the story of Hopedale, the relatively modest section on the Hopedale Community in the *Autobiography* provides a useful and crucial supplement to the institutionally more important *History of the Hopedale Community*. The *Autobiography* reveals more of Ballou's personal feelings and relates family events – notably the death of his son, Adin Augustus – that affected Ballou's actions and, through him, the course of the community. It provides a different perspective on Hopedale than the earlier book. One might even say that, reading between the lines, it suggests a different answer to the mystery of why Hopedale so suddenly came to an end.

In *History of the Hopedale Community* Ballou offered two explanations for the community's failure, one economic and one moral. The standard economic explanation focuses on the flaws in the community's accounting practices and the opportunity that this created for George and Ebenezer Draper to force a takeover of the community's assets. Ballou did not believe that this was a sufficient explanation for the disaster. In the closing chapter of *History of the Hopedale Community* he expressed his belief that the community could not have survived because the members lacked the moral and spiritual maturity to bring their plans to fruition. He did not blame the Drapers for withdrawing their stock and precipitating the crisis, for he felt that, had that not happened, given the community's inability to raise itself to "a higher moral and spiritual level than it occupied at that time," some other event would have shortly brought it down. Although he granted that the people of Hopedale were among the very best that could be found, he concluded that the human material for such a community did not yet exist.[8] The *Autobiography*, with its forthright account of Ballou's "mentally and physically enervated and depressed" state after his son's death (p. 265), adds another layer of explanation to the other two. One wonders whether Hopedale's fate would have been different if Ballou had been emotionally able to be more actively engaged with the community in the early 1850s.

The *Autobiography* provides some insight into the dynamics of Ballou's own family – his eagerness for his son to succeed him as a leader at Hopedale, and his relative undervaluing of his daughter as a potential community leader. Ballou planned an ambitious Hopedale Educational Home to be headed by his son Adin Augustus, although the young man was just eighteen and had not yet completed his teacher training at the Normal School. This seems to be another instance of Ballou's tendency to push his son too hard, too fast, as when he had made the boy foreman of the Hopedale printing shop at the age of fourteen. (Ballou himself eventually realized that this was "an undue load of business" for an adolescent, and allowed Augustus to be "liberated from his *Foremanship*" after two years.⁹) Perhaps Ballou hoped, by placing his son in positions of responsibility and trust, to prevent his attention from straying to the world beyond the borders of Hopedale. For he recognized Augustus's interest in life outside Hopedale and "watched the indications of his maturing ambition with anxious solicitude lest the temptations of the prevailing civilization should allure him from the struggling cause of Christian Socialism" (p. 261). Augustus did, at last, formally join the community in November 1851, less than three months before he died. But had he lived, it is quite likely that Adin's conflict with his own father would have been played out again in the next generation.

In attempting to develop his son as a community leader Adin passed over consideration of his daughter Abbie, who was four years older than Augustus and already an experienced teacher. Though Abbie was also given a Normal School education, Ballou entertained no grandiose plans for her; she was expected merely to be a teacher. This seems like an injustice to Abbie as well as a missed opportunity for the community, for Abbie was devoted to the ideals of the community and by all accounts was an unusually gifted teacher. One of her students later recalled her as the best teacher he ever had, while another described her as "handsome and loving, with insight, originality, and personal power, the ideal teacher."¹⁰ In the event, Abbie and her husband, William S. Heywood, took over the Hopedale Home School – a scaled-down version of the Educational Home – around the time that the Hopedale Community was being disbanded. Together, Abbie and William administered and taught this progressive and innovative school for seven years, until the Civil War disrupted its student body. Abbie Ballou Heywood was in her late twenties, just entering her youthful prime, when Hopedale came to an end. Perhaps if Adin Ballou had nurtured the same kind of dreams for her that he had entertained for Augustus, he would not have let the community pass out of existence so meekly.

Looking back from a twenty-first-century vantage point, we may be surprised to find such traditional attitudes about gender in such a progressive community as Hopedale. Ballou claimed that his vision of Practical Christianity was generations, and perhaps centuries, in advance of the times. And to a large extent it was, if we consider his pacifism, his socialism, and his opinions on race. Yet in the area of gender relations he was quite conservative. To the extent that Ballou supported women's leadership it was generally within the special spheres that society traditionally allocated to women. Such leadership was exercised by Ballou's tireless wife, Lucy Hunt Ballou, and by Anna Thwing Draper, the wife of Ebenezer Draper. Hopedale could not have functioned without the organizational ability, as well as the willingness to work, of such women. But in his views on the roles of women and men in society, Ballou did not go beyond the average for a liberal man of his times. His views on gender roles were considerably behind those of his friends and mentors, William Lloyd Garrison and Samuel J. May.

The Hopedale Community as a whole was not particularly interested in changing the conventional gender-based division of labor. The community's most ardent feminist, Abby Hills Price, campaigned vigorously to liberate women from domestic drudgery by establishing communal dining and laundry facilities, but the scheme found little support. Price and her family eventually left Hopedale for a new utopian community, Raritan Bay Union in New Jersey, that offered a communal dwelling.[11] One wonders if Hopedale's communitarians might have achieved a better-known and more long-lasting result if they had tried to develop a feminist as well as a pacifist and socialist paradise.

We are surprised by Ballou's views on gender because this is one aspect of society that has changed radically between his time and ours. In retrospect we can see that, even as Hopedale struggled to develop the plan of a "new civilization," a movement was developing for the emancipation and development of the fuller potential of women that would, over the next century and more, truly begin to reshape society.

When the feminist dream of the 1840s began to develop into a mass movement in the later part of the century, Ballou still resisted adding his voice to the campaign. He did so not because he lacked sympathy for the growing aspirations of women, but because the women's movement had become increasingly focused on suffrage and Ballou, in accordance with his non-resistant principles, did not believe in voting or otherwise participating in a government that was willing and able to deploy deadly force. He had a similar objection to the direction taken by the temperance movement, when it began to focus less on moral suasion and more on legislation (p. 321).

Ballou's vision for the process of reform was quite different from that of those who sought to extend the franchise or prohibit the use of alcohol. He had no confidence in top-down reform, which, even if imposed by a freely elected government, would still have to be regulated by force. He had hoped to start a movement for change from the bottom up – to build a radically new society from the cumulative effect of small changes in the way ordinary people arranged and conducted their lives. The success of the women's movement in the twentieth century, and the spectacular failure of Prohibition, have shown that Ballou's instinct was a good one. Most social change does come about by changing people's hearts and minds, one at a time. Legislation can play a role, but it must follow rather than lead social change.

The history of the women's movement also demonstrates the uneven pace of change. Decades of unremitting effort seemed to have little effect. Then, when the moment was right, long-established patterns were rearranged faster than anyone could have predicted. This should give us hope that, at some point in the not too distant future, as Adin Ballou and many others have dreamed, the world may yet learn to more equitably share its resources and to live in peace.

Notes

1. *Autobiography of Andrew Dickson White* (New York: The Century Co., 1905), 2:82-83.
2. Leo Tolstoy, *The Kingdom of God Is Within You*, trans. Constance Garnett (1894; reprint, Lincoln, NE: University of Nebraska Press, 1984), 17.
3. Orestes A. Brownson, *The Convert* (1857; vol. 5. of *Works of Orestes A. Brownson*, ed. Henry F. Brownson, Detroit, 1884).
4. The story of Brownson's tumultuous career as a Universalist minister is told in Lynn Gordon Hughes, "Orestes A. Brownson, Universalist Infidel?" *Journal of Unitarian Universalist History* (2009-2010), 38-85.
5. One of the things Brownson says about the Restorationist controversy is that it was "formed mainly through the instrumentality of Adin Ballou" (*The Convert*, 63). This goes beyond what Ballou himself claimed, as well as what has been said in most Universalist history. The schism is more generally attributed to ministers of an older generation, such as Paul Dean and David Pickering. But the entry of Ballou into the Restorationist camp just prior to the schism was probably an essential element in the success of the breakaway group in establishing themselves, however briefly, as a denomination. See Peter Hughes, "The Second Phase of the Restorationist Controversy: Disciplinary Crisis and Schism, 1824-1831," *Journal of Unitarian Universalist History* (2001), 28-91.
6. Brownson, *The Convert*, 40.
7. Brownson, *The Convert*, 64.
8. Adin Ballou, *History of the Hopedale Community* (1897; reprint, Providence: Blackstone Editions, 2010), 232-234.
9. Adin Ballou, *Memoir of Adin Augustus Ballou* (Hopedale: Hopedale Press, 1853), 49.
10. Ellen M. Patrick, "Our Community School and its Teacher," in *Hopedale Reminiscences: Childhood Memories of the Hopedale Community and the Hopedale Home School* (1910; reprint, Providence: Blackstone Editions, 2006), 34-35.
11. The Price family left Hopedale after Abby was censured for being too sympathetic to a couple who were expelled for practicing "free love" (see *History of the Hopedale Community*, 324n.56). However, Colin Bossen argues persuasively that Price's writings show increasing dissatisfaction with Hopedale's gender politics during her last three years in the community. Colin Bossen, "Recovering Abby Price: Hopedale's Advocate for Women's Rights," *Journal of Unitarian Universalist History* (2014-2015), 33-55.
    Raritan Bay Union appealed to other women's rights advocates, including Elizabeth Cady Stanton and Paulina Wright Davis. In December 1852 Stanton wrote to Davis, "It did rejoice me to see your names appended to the Prospectus of the Raritan Bay Union, for I am resolved to go there." *The Selected Papers of Elizabeth Cady Stanton and Susan B. Anthony*, ed. Ann D. Gordon (New Brunswick, NJ: Rutgers University Press, 1997), 1:214-215.

A Note on the Text

The text of this edition is taken from *Autobiography of Adin Ballou 1803-1890: Containing an elaborate record and narrative of his life from infancy to old age*, published in 1896 by the Vox Populi Press –Thompson & Hill, Lowell, Massachusetts. In a very few places we have corrected obvious errors or inserted a year when necessary to clarify the sequence of events; these emendations are marked by square brackets and discussed in the endnotes.

The most significant change we have made is to structure and subdivide the chapters by inserting subheadings. The original text uses subheadings much more sparingly, perhaps a half dozen in the entire book. The selection and placement of the new subheadings is entirely our own. The actual text of the subheadings, however, is largely taken from the original book. In addition to the small number of existing subheadings, we have used language from the chapter summaries in the table of contents, from the running headers on the pages in the original edition, and from the text itself.

Appendixes A through D are from the original edition. Appendix E, the bibliography of Ballou's works, was prepared for this edition; it replaces a less detailed bibliography that was included in the original edition. Appendixes F, G, and H are new in this edition.

Introduction
William S. Heywood

This volume is one of several prepared by its author and left in manuscript at his decease, the publication of which was provided for in specific clauses of his will. Its appearance has been considerably delayed by pre-existing engagements and more urgent duties on the part of him to whose supervision the matter was entrusted, and by other circumstances that could not be easily avoided or overcome. Its contents have been condensed somewhat from the original in order to bring them within desirable limits, but nothing has been eliminated that was deemed necessary to the completeness of the work as a portraiture of the man whose life, character, and career it was designed to outline and illustrate. Save in the particular indicated, the narrative, up to the time when the hand of the writer became incapable of further service by reason of the illness that terminated his mortal life, is given in his own way and mostly in his own language. The plan of the work, the arrangement of topics, its literary style and mode of expression, are distinctively his own, and bear the impress of his marked individuality.

The subject of the autobiography was no ordinary personage, and he played no unimportant part in the drama of human affairs during the eventful period in which he lived. Springing from humble and obscure conditions, without ancestral or social prestige or the favor of influential friends; without more than very meager opportunities for self-improvement and for rising above the common level, he yet became a central figure in the community where most of his days on earth were spent, a great power for good in the world, a noteworthy man of his age. Wherever he was known, he was loved and honored for his elevated and pure spirit, for his many excellences of character, for his broad and disinterested philanthropy, and for his unremitting endeavors to promote the welfare and happiness of his fellow men.

Born in the early years of the nineteenth century and continuing until the opening of its last decade, he was not only an interested observer *of*, but an active participant *in*, those great progressive moral and religious movements which make that century memorable in the annals of the race. He appeared upon the stage of being when the stern dogmatism of the primitive New England theology was beginning to be permeated with the leaven of a more reasonable and a more liberal faith, and when the long-received beliefs of the fathers were made the themes of sharp and unrelenting controversy on the part of thoughtful religious people throughout the land. While yet a mere youth, he passed through certain profound spiritual experiences which gave bias and trend to his entire subsequent life – which foreshadowed, as they in large measure shaped, his whole earthly career.

Very naturally, in his immature and receptive state of mind, he imbibed at first the dominant views of his teachers and elders upon religious subjects, concerning which he formulated for himself a definite statement of doctrine which, to his mind, was impregnable. But presently, by reason of questionings and doubts from within as well as from without, he entered upon and went through a most searching investigation which resulted, much to his own surprise, in a complete reversal of his own previously cherished convictions upon some of the most fundamental doctrines of theology, and caused him to adopt those representing more cheerful and inspiring views of God and man – of life, death, and immortality – in which he rejoiced with exceeding joy, and of which he became an earnest, eloquent, uncompromising, life-long adherent and champion. Passing over from his former conception of the sovereignty of God, as expressed in His inexorable will and irresistible power, to that of the fatherhood of God, expressed in His infinite goodness and love, his idea of the whole vast economy of being and of the overruling divine providence was correspondingly transformed, as was also his idea of human duty and responsibility. The new thought of the great Author of all being and Disposer of all events engendered new emotions, as it appealed to new motives in his breast; gave, in his estimate, a new meaning and purpose to existence, and required a new type of personal character and a new order of life among men. It brought into distinct and commanding prominence the humanitarian side of religion. Out of the fatherhood of God comes, by logical and moral necessity, the brotherhood of man and the whole vast round of sentiments and obligations incumbent upon the co-equal members of one great family.

The author of this book saw this and, in the candor and loyalty of his mind and heart, accepted it, and with it all the issues it involved bearing upon human conduct and character. He was thus not only predisposed but compelled to espouse and advocate every salutary moral reform, and to lend a hand to every activity and enterprise calculated to benefit and bless the world. Nay, more. Deeming the principles of the gospel of Christ, in which he was a most devout believer, and the spirit of brotherhood applicable to human life in all possible circumstances and concerns, and beholding the injustice and wrong, the suffering and misery inseparable from the existing social order, he devised and, with the cooperation of sympathizing friends, put in operation a scheme for the complete reorganization of society, by which all special reforms should be united in one great comprehensive movement for the suppression of the ills that afflict humanity and the promotion of the welfare and happiness of all the classes and conditions of people; by which all human interests and affairs should be brought into harmony with the divine law of love to God and man – an attempt, in short, to inaugurate the kingdom of heaven on the earth.

Of one whose life was consecrated to such purposes and spent in the pursuit of such objects as have been indicated, this volume treats with all needful particularity of detail, showing how he went on, step by step, in his course, from childhood and youth to hoary age, animated and cheered by an unfailing faith in God and the eternal realities, and by the unbeclouded vision of a reign of righteousness, brotherhood, and peace, which shall some day come to emancipate, uplift, sanctify, and rejoice with exceeding joy, the children of men. And it is commended to those who would be glad to know something of such a man and of his varied and manifold experiences in the attainment of those qualities of mind, heart, and character which he so fully illustrated, and in the prosecution of the work by which his influence for good shall be felt by those coming after him unto many generations. It is commended also to his surviving relatives and friends, who hold his memory dear and who will be glad to have some memento bearing the impress of his own immediate hand, wherewith to be reminded from time of the lessons he was wont to give them while he was with them in the flesh, and to be kept in touch with his spirit and the purpose of his life. It is furthermore commended to the earnest and reverent students of sociological problems – to those who, in the present or some coming day, believe in the possibility of a divine order of society among men, and who are desirous of doing what they may to make that possibility a living and enduring reality upon the earth. In the hope that those to whom reference is made and many others disposed to peruse the pages that follow, may find in them a source, not only of pleasure and satisfaction, but of inspiration to noble living and to endeavors to advance the interests and subserve the ends which the author had so much at heart, this book is sent forth into the world and submitted to the considerate attention of all who seek to show forth their reverence and love for God by faithful service of mankind.

Preface
Adin Ballou

The world worships success and despises failure. It judges of success and failure chiefly according to outward appearance – according to material manifestations and tangible results. It concerns itself little with causes, motives, preliminary conditions or noiseless agencies and operations. Its eyes are carnal not spiritual. It condemns the prophets of any given age while they are yet alive – perhaps crucifies, stones, or starves them – but builds the tombs and garnishes the sepulchers of those of a former age who have passed away, and whose testimonies and sufferings have immortalized their memories. So it has ever been; so it is still. Nothing else is to be expected.

I have not been a man of much popular success, but in several respects of failure. Not because my intentions, principles, ideas, objects and plans were reprehensible and unworthy of success, but because they foreran the conditions and means indispensable to its acquisition. My hopes were too urgent and sanguine; my standard and aim were set too high for immediate realization. So have I been defeated in some of my noblest schemes; some of my most disinterested and earnest labors have been expended in vain, and my way has been overshadowed with disappointment and grief. The world has judged and will for some time longer judge of me and of my undertakings after its own ancient fashion, and I complain not. In the wisdom of God all is for the best, and nothing true and good is forever lost. The final verdict is not rendered yet, and my case and cause are adjourned to a more auspicious future.

Times and generations are coming that will justly estimate me and my work, and assign both to their proper place in the providential plan for the progress and redemption of humanity. For them, as it has proved, have I lived and labored, rather than for my contemporaries. To them I appeal for vindication and approval; to them I bequeath whatever is valuable and worth preserving of my possessions – the fruits of my toil while yet a dweller in the tabernacles of earth and time.

I have been repeatedly urged by some of my relatives and friends who seem to cherish for me a very earnest regard and to have great confidence in me, to write my biography. In my less buoyant moods I have shrunk from the task, feeling for the time being that I preferred to be forgotten, if possible, by posterity and to have all my seemingly illusory theories and abortive projects buried in oblivion. But in more lucid and thoughtful states of mind and heart, under cheering inspirations from the spiritual world which have always prevailed against impulsive and momentary despondency and gloom, I have been more inclined to undertake the task desired of me. Yielding to such inclination, I have at length set myself about the work involved, with a view of carrying it forward to completion as rapidly as possible without interfering with other duties to which I am pledged, making due allowance for hindrances and delays to which my position before the public and wide acquaintanceship expose me continually. I do this partly because I think that in this way I can still render some benefit to mankind; partly because no one else, moved to tell the story of my life after my decease, has at hand the data I can command for doing the subject justice; and partly because, if nothing more comes of it, the narrative will afford my surviving relatives and friends, to whom I owe a great debt of gratitude for all their kindness to me, something of personal satisfaction and delight.

I have many memoranda preserved among my private papers and a carefully kept diary covering the greater part of my active life, as well as much private matter accumulated through a long term of editorial service, from which I can draw to aid my memory in giving definiteness and authenticity to the facts of which mention will be made. I shall proceed, therefore, in the preparation of a volume for the press, with an unwavering confidence in the accuracy of all the details essential to a trustworthy and desirable narrative.

CHAPTER 1

1803-1813

I was born Saturday, April 23, 1803, in the town of Cumberland, Providence County, Rhode Island, on a farm inherited from my paternal ancestors, and lying, partly in the state named, and partly in Massachusetts. The dwelling-house and accompanying buildings were on the Rhode Island territory, about fifteen miles north-northwest from Providence, three in the same direction from Cumberland Hill, and four east of Woonsocket. The locality was then, as now, a comparatively obscure, rural one, remote from any populous center, and inhabited chiefly by plain, hard-working, economical tillers of the soil.

My parents were Ariel and Edilda (Tower) Ballou. The former was the son of Ariel, who was the son of James, who was the son of James, who was the son of Maturin Ballou, the immigrant ancestor of the family and a co-proprietor with Roger Williams in the first settlement of Providence Plantations, in 1646.[1] My mother was the eldest daughter of Levi and Mary (Whipple) Tower, natives of Cumberland, both of whom I remember well. She departed this life in my early youth; he, several years later. She was a woman of portly presence, natural dignity, strong common sense, and great benignity, without the slightest affectation. In her old-fashioned way she was at once commanding and genial. I have a vivid recollection of the affectionate hospitality which I always received from her in my childhood visits. My grandfather Tower was not her equal in all these excellent qualities, yet a respectable man and citizen. He had a tall, well-built frame, a somewhat excitable temperament, a mechanical genius for work in wood and metals, and a penchant for mineral discoveries and experimentation, though he gained thereby neither profit nor popularity.[2]

My paternal grandparents, Ariel and Jerusha (Slack) Ballou, had both finished their earthly course before my birth. I have therefore no knowledge of them except what has come to me in scanty records and traditions. They reared a large family, and, from all I can learn, deservedly enjoyed the respect of the social circle in which they moved. My grandfather had the misfortune to be sadly crippled during the latter portion of his life, in consequence of mercurial medication injudiciously administered in a severe illness. He was long unable to walk, and could only move about in a chair specially fitted to his case. My grandmother on that side survived him many years. They have always been represented to me as industrious, frugal, sensible, worthy persons, ranking with the better class of their rustic contemporaries. Whether or not they were members of the Baptist church in their neighborhood I have never learned, but think it probable.[3]

My father's children were eight in number: six by his first wife, Lucina (Comstock) Ballou, and two by his second, Edilda (Tower) Ballou. Those by Lucina were: Rosina, Abigail, Cyrus, Arnold, Sarah, and Alfred; by Edilda, myself and Ariel, M.D. Rosina married Nathan Arnold and died December 5, 1825, leaving one son and two twin daughters. Abigail married Davis Cook, both now deceased, having had numerous children and grandchildren. Cyrus married Susanna Ballou, a third cousin, and died March 7, 1816, leaving two sons who have had children. Arnold married Lorinda Bates and died November 27, 1816. A posthumous daughter married and became the mother of several children. Alfred married Matilda Cook, both having recently deceased, leaving children and grandchildren.[4] Ariel, my own younger brother, an eminent physician, married Hannah Horton and had several children, of whom only two daughters survive; their mother having passed away some years since.[5] Of my own family I shall speak at length in due time and place.

As yet I have been unable to trace my ancestry further back than Maturin Ballou, who was at Providence, as stated, in 1646. I have a faint hope of ascertaining his birthplace and progenitors. I find his Christian name and surname both spelled with a various orthography in the old Rhode Island records, but his descendants have for a long time written the two as above. Tradition holds him to have been of French extraction, belonging to a Huguenot family and coming to this country from England, whither many of that persecuted sect fled some generations since. There is little doubt that such was the case, but for lack of reliable information I must be content to commence my pedigree with him.[6]

I have often been taken or *mis*taken for a son of Rev. Hosea Ballou,[7] a distinguished Universalist clergyman of his time, and have frequently been asked what our relationship was. He was a third cousin of my father, our common immigrant ancestor, Maturin Ballou, having had three sons, who lived to rear offspring: John, James, and Peter. His descent ran thus: Maturin[1], John[2], Peter[3], Rev. Maturin[4], Rev. Hosea[5]. Mine was as follows: Maturin[1], James[2], James[3], Ariel[4], Ariel[5], Adin[6].

The Ballou Neighborhood

James Ballou, my great-great grandfather, settled in what was then Providence, later Smithfield, and now Lincoln, Rhode Island, and founded a homestead, still owned, I believe, by one of his descendants. It was less than a mile southerly from the village of Manville, on Blackstone River, and about a half mile west of Albion. He was a very capable, enterprising man, becoming a great landholder in his later years. He had five sons, viz. James, Nathaniel, Obadiah, Samuel, and Nehemiah. He endowed them all with handsome farms, or at least with tracts of land that became handsome farms. To Samuel he gave his home place, and to

Nehemiah an ample estate in what was then Gloucester, but is now Burrillville, Rhode Island. Each of his three older sons, James, Nathaniel, and Obadiah, he settled on wild or nearly wild lands, purchased by him, on the northerly side of Blackstone, then called Pawtucket River, within the boundaries of territory for a long time in dispute between the three colonies of Plymouth, Massachusetts, and Rhode Island. Neither of the colonies knew exactly where their respective lines were, but each laid strong claims to the section involved. After many years a settlement was effected, Attleborough Gore, as it was called, being surrendered to Rhode Island, the Legislature of which, in 1746, incorporated it with its inhabitants as a township bearing the name of Cumberland.

In 1713 James Ballou conveyed the lands specified by gift deeds to the three sons named, who soon after settled their families upon them – their several patrimonies lying adjacent to each other and constituting "the Ballou neighborhood," as it was for a long time designated. This was originally more than half a square mile in extent, and, with inherited rights in common lands adjoining, ultimately covered an area of nearly a whole mile square.

All this section of country and its landmarks were familiar to me in my youth, and are still fresh in my remembrance. Beacon Pole Hill received its name from a tall mast with a crane attached, from which was suspended a kettle designed to be filled with tar or other combustibles and lighted on occasions, as an alarm signal during the Revolutionary War and as a summons for Minutemen from far and wide to reinforce the Rhode Island army.[8] Iron Rock Meadow is supposed to have been originally a beaver pond. It contained forty acres and was the first purchase made by James Ballou, senior, in the vicinity. For many years it bore splendid crops of nutritious grass, which finally ran out or was supplanted by a comparatively worthless kind. Its name was derived from Iron Rock Hill, an elevation near by which is very much of a natural curiosity. It seems to have been raised to the height of a hundred feet or more by some volcanic upheaval, and is largely composed of a rich iron ore, with magnetic qualities, amalgamated with solid rock. Nothing of the kind is to be found within hundreds of miles of it.

A little north of this remarkable hill the early settlers built a small house of worship, known in all that region as the Ballou Meetinghouse.[9] It has undergone successive repairs from generation to generation, and though occupied only occasionally, in the mild season of the year, remains in its rude simplicity, an interesting memorial of the olden time and its characteristic piety. A few rods southeasterly from it is the ancient burying ground, where sleep the mortal remains of the original worshipers and many of their descendants, some with sculptured monuments, others with common stones from the field, while many are scarcely marked at all amid the wild grass and brush.[10] It is a place for the study of moss-covered inscriptions and for solemn meditation, especially to a Ballou of the lineage of James. There molder the ashes of my older kindred, and there my father, in my early youth, erected a family tomb, one of the first two built in the enclosure.

The Ballou Meetinghouse was designed for and long occupied by a church of the order called the Six Principle Baptists – a small sect hardly known out of Rhode Island, and now almost extinct even there.[11] Elder Abner Ballou,[12] son of Obadiah, was long pastor of this church. He had considerable local celebrity in his day, passing away January 4, 1806, and leaving behind him a venerated memory. In that old Meetinghouse, I first listened with awe to prayer and preaching from the lips of Elder Stephen Place[13] – the successor, and I think the last successor, of Elder Ballou. In my youthful veneration I worshipped him almost as God, certainly as one of God's best human representatives. But as I grew older, my reverential estimation became modified somewhat by the criticisms of middle-aged people who knew him in the common walks of life, and who were not too good to reveal their discoveries that he was not wholly above the general weaknesses of human nature. How few of us escape this judgment of our more intimate contemporaries!

In this immediate vicinity the descendants of James, Nathaniel, and Obadiah Ballou multiplied greatly and for a long time constituted a majority of the population. At length they began to scatter by emigration, till now but few families of the name remain. One of the first to leave was James, a brother of my grandfather.[14] He had many children, most of whom settled with him in Richmond, New Hampshire.[15] Among his sons were James, long famous in that region as an astrologer and fortune teller,[16] and Silas, the rustic poet.[17] Rev. Eli Ballou,[18] of Vermont, is the descendant of another emigrant family in the line of Nathaniel, the second in age of the three Cumberland patriarchs.

Infancy and Early Childhood

But I return from this digression to the main thread of my story. It was in the Ballou neighborhood above described, about a mile north of Iron Rock Hill, that I was born, as stated, on an estate derived by inheritance from James Ballou, my great grandfather and a grandson of the common ancestor. It is now owned by the heirs of my brother Alfred. My father at the time was about forty-three and my mother thirty-two years of age. My mother informed me that my birth was one of uncommon peril both to her and me; that I was a lean, feeble, unpromising babe; that for several weeks I seemed more likely to die than to live; and that I was six months old before she could have me seen without some feeling of motherly mortification. Thenceforth, however, I grew healthy, ruddy, and handsome, so that she was no longer ashamed of me. On the contrary, to use her own homely language, "I was proud to turn you out in company by the side of anybody's baby, and often got complimented for your comeliness."

Nevertheless, my early childhood, as I learned from the same source, was subject to frequent attacks of illness, some of them quite severe, seriously threatening at times my life. Moreover, I seem to have been anything but a lymphatic, quiet, good-natured child. I did my part at fretting and crying, and was indebted to my kind mother's indulgence in carrying me about the house while at her work, for escaping my father's hand of discipline, after he deemed me old enough to behave better than I sometimes did. So she laughingly told me in after years. He was of the old school in regard to family government, and believed in suppressing bad humor occasionally with a little wholesome severity. I have no doubt I sometimes tried his patience when he was weary with toil, for he was a very hard-working man. Besides, I remember when quite a small boy scarcely three years of age, being called by the housemaid, "a little mud-wasp."

It did not mend my temper much that the older members of the household were roguish enough to take delight in hectoring me. They could excite my mirth or my irritability at very little cost to themselves, and they were fond of opportunities. While still a mere frockling[19] their various pranks were often played upon me and became indelibly stamped on my memory. Among the worst I call to mind was that of being held under a bush covered with rose-bugs; the bush being meanwhile violently shaken till my hair, neck, breast, and, indeed, my entire body under my clothing, were alive with the hateful creatures. I had always felt and often evinced a great dread of these insects, and at the time referred to I screamed and ran for my mother's help in a very lively, and, to an observer, amusing manner. I was frightened and maddened to the utmost, while half a dozen of my tormentors shouted with merriment. It was exquisite sport to them, but intolerable vexation to me. Nothing malicious was intended by these mischievous teasings, but I am sure they made my excitable passions worse.

In those early years, I also had my full share of casualties. My father owned a sawmill and I barely escaped drowning one day in its flume. My brother, Alfred, four years older than myself, persuaded me to attempt following him over a tottling plank or slab from one of the mill doors across the flume to the dam beyond. The saw was running with my father in charge. I was a poor balancer and hence when part way over tumbled into the water. My father got the alarm just in time to save me. I was, at the moment, several feet under water and being drawn rapidly into the current that rushed through the open gate. The mill had a great head and fall, so that in a single minute more I should probably have been carried through the wheel, a lifeless mangled mass of flesh and bones. I was not so far gone as quite to lose my breath, and presently was able to be led home. I still wore long clothes and remember the sorrowful figure I cut as I draggled along tremulously some twenty-five rods, muttering as I went incoherent denunciations against that "plaguy old slab and flume." I was welcomed to the fond maternal bosom as a child rescued from the very jaws of death.

Not long afterwards, while sporting with a playmate, I fell into a stone sluiceway which my father was building and broke my arm. Dr. Abraham Mason, our family physician, who resided at Cumberland Hill, was sent for to set the fractured bone. By the time he arrived the process had been rendered painful by inflammation and swelling. I could not easily endure the operation or soon forget it, though it was so successfully done that I wholly recovered in a few weeks. As I grew older and was put to business in and about the farm buildings, I experienced plenty of throwings from horses, kicks from skittish cattle, and other mishaps incident to boyhood in that sphere of life.

Notwithstanding my natural sensitiveness and susceptibility to irritation by small provocations, I was generally easily governed. I was neither turbulent nor stubborn, but yielded prompt submission to authority and responded heartily to kind treatment. I was readily persuaded by reasonable appeals, but stung to the quick by personal taunt and reproach. My mother said that she never used the rod upon me but once and then very lightly. It was before my remembrance, in my second year. I seemed to have been seized with a strange freak of destructiveness in the way of throwing things into the fire. She had chided me again and again for my misconduct, but in vain. When left to myself, article after article went rapidly into the flames. At length, as she told me, she "got a little tingler," and, upon a repetition of the offense one day, gave me a few touches with it. I hopped about, screamed loudly, and was effectually cured. When a half-grown-up boy, I used to see a checkered linen handkerchief about the house with one corner gone. I was curious enough to inquire after a time, how that came to be. "It is a piece of your work," said my mother, and then told me the story with good-natured glee.

My father was stern and authoritative in his discipline, yet I can recollect only one whipping from him. This I shared with my brother Ariel when we had become old enough to drop corn, etc. in planting time. We had driven the cows to pasture one morning and instead of returning directly home where we were wanted for service in the field, strolled off to an old well and amused ourselves for a long time in throwing stones into the water below. Hearing the old conch shell blown, which we understood to be an extra summons to the house, we hastened thither and were told by our mother that she did not know what would happen to us, "for your father has been calling you at the top of his voice, and as you did not come has gone planting alone quite out of patience with you." We hastened into the field, a few rods distant, where he was doing our proper work, with a few apple tree sprouts stuck in his vest. He had not many words for us, but enough smart blows to make the impression that duty and business must take precedence of amusement in his family. There was no undue severity in this correction, but it was conclusive.

I generally found myself a favorite with my father's employees, indoors and out, of whom he had always more or less. I made myself agreeable, and sometimes serviceable to them, never having a particle of haughtiness or contempt to express towards them, even in childish ways, as of an inferior caste. In turn they liked me, and I received frequent acceptable proofs of their good will, either openly or slyly from manservants and maidservants. Earliest of them all I remember Reuben

Purchase, a sturdy, glossy-haired Indian, whose copper color was slightly bleached with the blood of the white race. He took a great liking to me, called me *his* boy, carried me about pick-a-back with him into the fields or woods, and made quite a big papoose of me. He must have been approaching middle age at the time, and had a family in the general neighborhood. He loved his mug of cider, and stronger drinks moved him occasionally. But he and I were on good terms and he gave me many a little token of his partiality. As I grew older I made successive friends in this line all the way up to manhood, and found my own trifling investments of kindness turn to good account in various ways, as, on a broader scale, I always have through life.

Early Religious Impressions
My first remembered attendance on public worship was soon after I donned boy's attire, perhaps as late as the summer of my fifth year. I was rigged out in a new suit of calico, the pants buttoned to the coat in the common fashion of that day, and was led by the hand of my mother a mile on foot to the Ballou Meetinghouse. I began to feel of some consequence in the world, but was too bashful to put on pompous airs, and paid reverential attention to the services of the occasion. Elder Stephen Place, mentioned on a preceding page, was the minister. He must have been sixty years of age, had a venerable aspect, and spoke in those sanctified tones of the old-time preacher, which, somehow or other, had a very solemnizing effect upon the younger hearers. I recollect nothing that he said, but he filled me with sublime, though vague, impressions of God, heaven, and hell, and made me feel for a long time afterward that he must be next to Deity.

My parents were not then professors of religion[20] and yet were partially religious. The ancient Six Principle Baptist Church was falling into decay, and the members were mostly elderly people. I recall distinctly their solemn countenances, whether in the Deacon's Seat or on the hard old pew seats – men and women occupying separate parts of the house – those fathers and mothers in Israel of a generation long since passed away.[21]

The old burying ground, too, was a place of almost dreadful solemnity to me. Thither the people resorted during the Sabbath intermissions, between forenoon and afternoon services, and thither I was sometimes led in my childhood by the maternal hand. My mother and others would read the epitaphs, and I instinctively moved with cautious tread lest I should do sacrilege to the silent abodes of the departed. Death was a strange and awful mystery to me for a considerable time, notwithstanding the patient answers to my inquiries concerning it. But at length I imbibed the inculcations given me that the souls of the dead had been taken away by God into some region of happiness or misery; that their bodies were asleep in the ground; and that at the great Judgment Day, or "morn of the resurrection," all would be raised to life again, body and soul be reunited, every one be judged according to his works, and then each be consigned to heaven or hell forever.

These religious ideas took early root in a susceptible and fertile soil. I had little special religious instruction, no Sunday schooling, no catechizing such as then prevailed in even the more popular churches – nothing in the way of spiritual culture but the suggestions which I incidentally stored up and the crude workings of my own busy mind. I had no doubt that there was a great and holy, yet awful, God in the form of a gigantic man, who was seated in a glorious chair above the blue arch of the sky. I imagined that he caused it to thunder by rolling a huge log with octagon corners from the convex center of the brazen firmament in various downward directions; that the sun, moon, and stars, the clouds, storms, and winds were all managed at will from day to day by his immediate interposition; and that all human actions were accurately recorded in a vast book for final judgment at the end of the world. Thus, with what I was taught and what I invented through my imagination, "I spake as a child, I understood as a child, and I thought as a child," until old enough "to put away childish things."[22] But neither then nor since have I lived without thinking, and thinking for *myself* in some fashion.

The remaining five years of this first decade of my life, as I call them to mind, witnessed very little religious interest in the Ballou neighborhood. Preaching in our meetinghouse grew irregular, the old church became colder in zeal and fewer in numbers, and a large majority of our Cumberland people spent the Sabbath in labor or rude sports and games. What followed will be noted in the next chapter. I certainly was not brought up thus far in a manner to be much injured or benefited by my religious training. Yet I was drawn into no very vicious or immoral courses of thought or conduct. Perhaps my industrial education and activity were the strongest safeguard against harm of that sort.

Work and Play

Work was the fundamental law in my father's household. He led off and all his forces had to follow. He allowed no idling and but a small modicum of amusement. This was confined to homely and simple kinds, such as hunting, fishing, wrestling, jumping, ball-playing, quoit-pitching, husking bees, quiltings, and the like, with neighborhood parties for the young folks and games appropriate to indoor arrangements and furnishings. Even these were few and some of them far between, and none of them wholly unrestricted and free. Card playing was utterly disallowed and anathematized. My father used to say that he once got bewitched with that sort of pastime, and, seeing its evils, forswore it forever. This was in his younger days. In my time, woe to every pack of cards smuggled by man or maid into his dominions. He had them in the fire instantly on discovery, and gave little quarter to the smuggler. Even simple countrified dancing was mighty scarce in my youthful days.

My father had over two hundred acres of land, including some woodlots nearly a mile away; also a sawmill, a cider mill, a large stock of cattle, and of course, there was no lack of employment indoors or out. Plowing, planting, harvesting, and all the multiform activities of farm life, with accompanying incidentals, kept all hands busy through the year. My mother used to say, when we of the younger brood complained of being hurried up in the morning and kept snug at work through the day, "You have a much easier time than your older brothers and sisters had, for your father has grown in years and does not drive ahead as he did when I first came to live with him." We thought it might be true, but that was no great comfort to us, as we still deemed ours a hard lot in the labor line.

We had a large, comfortable domicile, plenty of wholesome food, decent clothing, and the ordinary necessaries of an agricultural family; but luxuries, fineries, and gentilities were afar off. Brown bread and milk or porridge, different kinds of meat, rye or barley cake, coffee, cheap tea, cider, etc., were the staples of table fare, with plenty of butter, cheese, applesauce, and simple condiments. Cakes, pies, and other homemade delicacies had their occasions, but rarely was anything very rich or of outside manufacture furnished us. Our clothing was mostly of home production, spun and woven from flax and wool of our own raising – the woolen cloth being fulled and dressed at mills three or four miles distant. Some extra cotton and woolen stuffs from other sources supplemented what was made by the family, increasing rapidly as I grew up. In my early boyhood young women pulled flax and assisted sometimes in the hayfield, but this soon went out of fashion. The spinning wheel and loom were in vogue much longer, and their operations in my parental household were memorable.

We were shod in those days chiefly with leather tanned at an establishment two miles away, and made of skins from our own cattle or those obtained in barter for them. Once a year, not long before winter set in, a shoemaker came to the house with his kit of tools on his back to do the family cobbling. He had to stay several days, and to us younglings, at least, he was an important personage. New boots or shoes, and especially calfskin ones, which, however, were rare, inspired much interest, not only in anticipation and realization, but in the process of their manufacture. Wonderful manipulations were witnessed from the time of taking the measure of our feet to that of trying on the finished article to see if there was a good fit. Sometimes we were favored with a story or song, or whistled tune from the dignitary of the awl and lapstone as the work went on. This entertaining drama ended with a settlement between father and the craftsman, who usually received part or all his dues in some kind of farm produce.

The Tavern

As to places of dissipation, there was but one in the neighborhood. This was an old-fashioned tavern kept by Major William Ballou, a son of Rev. Abner, already mentioned. It was located a mile south of us and a short distance east of the meetinghouse. And a sorry establishment it was, especially for the proprietor and his family. Rum-selling was too largely its business. The concomitants and pernicious consequences need hardly be mentioned. It was a resort for the vicious, profligate, and sottish of the surrounding country, although it had some respectable phases of use. But it ruined the Major and all his family. They began life at the top of our Cumberland society as to wealth and general good standing, but most of them ended at the bottom, intemperate, poor, and more or less degraded.[23] But this dangerous resort was placed under a perpetual ban by my father so far as his household was concerned, or at least his children. We were kept entirely away from it, except on now and then a public holiday or a strictly business errand.

I shall never forget one occasion on which I was allowed to go there with older members of our family. There was a military training, a single company of militia under Captain Amos Cook[24] being out for regular parade. They had a kettledrum and fife for music, and their officers were arrayed in their accustomed toggery. I was perfectly bewitched with this, my first spectacle in the drama of war. I could not have been more than seven years old but I followed at the heels of this trainband all the afternoon, till compelled to go home. Swords, guns, colors, marchings, evolutions, and above all the music of that drum and fife (now disgusting to me), completely charmed me. If I had been of military age, and there had been a call to the wars, it would have taken neither the promise of a large bounty nor an eloquent appeal of patriotic oratory, to have made me "a brave soldier boy." I was effectually inoculated with the pro-war contagion, which fevered in my veins for long years afterward.

Recurring to the subject of using intoxicating beverages, I will remark that I was brought up to a very restricted indulgence, but not to total abstinence. My father laid in a supply of ardent spirits for haying time and furnished them more or less on special occasions; but for common use, cider was the staple drink. I got lightheaded once or twice on the stronger liquors, of which I could bear but little. I had grown to man's stature, however, before I presumed to call for a glass of intoxicating drink at any public bar. Indeed I was a stranger to such places.

Of cider, I was never fond, especially after it began to ferment or grow sour. But I had my fill of making it in my father's mill, and also of drawing and serving it, after it was stored in the cellar. This was boys' special business, and many a barrel had I to help empty, quart by quart. There must be cider on the table at mealtime, also in the mill or field or woods, wherever there were work-folks, at all seasons, and it was by no means to be omitted as a mark of hospitality to callers, whether they came on business or pleasure. Even the miserable sots of the general vicinity must not be denied it, unless absolutely intoxicated or dangerous. A few such there were who could pour down a quart at two or three draughts, and it is wonderful that they did not become twice as numerous as they actually were.[25]

First Steps in Learning

I will now take up the reminiscences of my earlier schoolboy days. The state of Rhode Island was very slow to adopt the common public school system of education. In my childhood the voluntary method prevailed.[26] But every considerable section of territory had some kind of a schoolhouse and more or less schooling, both in warm and cold weather. The Ballou district was not an inferior one in this respect. It had wealth and intellect enough to erect a small building for educational purposes, and to secure competent teachers for summer and winter terms, which were of about three months' duration each. A female was employed for the former, and a male for the latter. Our neighbors in Massachusetts, who prided themselves on being better provided for in this respect than we, were prone to reproach us as ignorant and heathenish Rhode Islanders, which begat no very amiable feelings on our side the line. As a matter of fact we had in our particular district more and better schooling than the adjacent ones in our neighbor state, though neither had anything of this sort to boast of. Only the rudimental branches were taught and these but imperfectly, as compared with what is done at the present day.

There were eight or ten proprietors of our schoolhouse and they managed all school affairs. They provided for raising money, for boarding the teacher, a fortnight in one family and a week in another, as circumstances would allow, for supplying fuel and other incidentals, and appointed such committees to act for them as were deemed needful. They had their yearly meetings which were characterized by some tedious deliberations and sharp figurings. I frequently attended these gatherings after I was old enough to long for the school to open, but so much time was consumed in irrelevant talk and close reckoning that I often went home, discouraged and disgusted at the proceedings. But they knew what they were about and brought preliminaries to an issue generally on or before the first of December. The children of non-proprietors were provided for at a stipulated price of tuition per week; or, if their parents were quite poor, they might attend free, though this was of infrequent occurrence.

I think it likely that I was sent to the summer school earlier than I can now remember. I have a dim impression that I learned my letters of a schoolma'am when about three years old, but I recall distinctly the first master I had. It was when I was in my *a, b, abs,* and the shortest monosyllables.[27] I was furnished with a new spelling book which was strongly covered with sheepskin by my mother that I might not soon injure it by careless usage. I was placed on the small boys' seat with others, a bashful, awkward little fellow, and ordered to keep still, but was very much at a loss what to do with myself or how to behave. For there was his majesty the master, and a whole houseful of scholars, many of them men almost and women grown. And who was I! The scene comes to me afresh. I dropped my head, stuck one corner of my book in my mouth, and unconsciously began to gnaw it. I had already done some mischief of this sort when I was discovered by the teacher and reprimanded. But I seemed fated to round off those book corners. Nor was I cured of the fault for some days, though frequently threatened with something dreadful if I did not desist. At length, after much harm had been done, I was called up, ordered to take off my coat and roll up my shirt sleeves, when the announcement was made that here was a boy with bad blood in his veins which must be taken out of him. The teacher then exhibited a fine sharp-pointed penknife as the lancet, and applied it to the skin of my arm with a slight prick. By this time the terror-stricken young culprit cried for mercy with such piteous penitence that, on solemn promise of amendment, he was spared further punishment and sent to his seat. He nevermore treated a book disrespectfully. But the nice new spelling book was irreparably damaged, and long remained a sad memento of my entrance upon my educational career.

Nevertheless, I soon began to love books, study, and learning, fondly. And from that time to the present, I have hungered and thirsted for knowledge with unsatisfied desire. My older brothers cared little for books till fifteen years of age, but I delighted in them from my sixth year. I liked to go to school, was easy to learn, had a good memory and an ambition to excel. I was generally docile, orderly, and disposed to be on the best of terms with my teachers, a point on which I seldom failed. The punishments I received were few and comparatively light. Most of them I incurred by yielding to the instigation of my roguish cronies who could easily make me laugh, or divert my curiosity, or swerve me into some infraction of the prescribed proprieties; into nothing very bad, but sufficiently out of order at times to require correction.

With my schoolmates, I maintained, for the most part, genial and harmonious relations. In scholarship I kept up with my rivals and left the majority of pupils in the rear. At play most of my mates excelled me, and the dullest of them would often leave me in the lurch. I was no match for many at wrestling, running, leaping, snowballing, etc., or any of the athletic exercises, unless it were some trial of mere strength, like lifting, pushing, or pulling. At skating, in which many of my companions were experts, and which I much admired as a beholder, I was nothing. Having once put on a pair of skates to try my capability, and suffered a fall backwards that made me "see stars," I renounced them forever. But in all matters where head work and tongue work came into requisition, I feared none of my associates. I was not fond of joking, punning, blackguarding, or hectoring in any way, and never began at "cutting up" my playfellows. But if attacked, I could give back principal and interest. I asked nothing more of the bravest than that they should keep their hands off. Unluckily, in a few instances, some of the older and stouter of my assailants, when silenced in speech, made up for their intellectual defeat by a resort to brute force, when I went under. I soon learned what I have since found generally true, that the sauciest jokers and blackguards could bear the least of their own ammunition in return.

I was unhappy in but one of my childhood schools. That, I think, was a private one. It was taught by a worthy young lady, a niece of my father's first wife, on whose instructions I had already attended in our Ballou schoolhouse and whom

I personally liked. But she was now teaching in her own neighborhood, in West Wrentham, Massachusetts. I was yet too young to be worth much at work, and so was sent to her school by my parents with the best of motives. But it was a mile and a half away, and nearly all the pupils were strangers to me. We belonged to different clans, of uncongenial peculiarities. Some of the older and rougher ones, whom I dared not answer back, taunted me with being a "Rhode Island Yankee," and called me in derision the "high priest." I was not able to bear all this with undisturbed equanimity and patience.

Moreover, there was a weird-looking, yet harmless, old lady, known as "Granny Grant," living on the road to the school, for whom I had conceived a superstitious aversion. My head had been filled with all sorts of ghost and witch stories, causing me many strange, imaginary apprehensions. What should possess me but the notion that this woman was a witch. She had a sinister lop of one eyelid, an imperturbable face, and a queer voice, what little there was of it. She walked abroad with a staff, wearing an old-fashioned, hooded cloak, whether of drab or bright scarlet, I forget. She was frequently on the road, trudging slowly along, and answered to my ideal of a witch completely. I had a great dread of her, and avoided meeting her whenever I could, by making a circuit outside of the highway near her residence, always keeping a sharp lookout for her from every eminence.

These repellent circumstances rendered the Wrentham school decidedly unpleasant for me. I frequently loitered and was behind time, for which I was reproved by my teacher, causing me to feel deeply mortified before my sneering schoolmates. Finally, I brought things to a head by skulking nearly all one day in the vicinity of the schoolhouse; but, being discovered by some of the older pupils, I was seized and marched into the presence of the mistress, my captors in loyal triumph exulting over me as a doomed truant.

Fortunately, my judge dealt with me "more in sorrow than in anger."[28] She deprecated my misconduct and said she should content herself with reporting me to my parents. She did so, and I was severely admonished. By this time I was sufficiently humbled and almost sick. My kind mother, after hearing my explanations, saw through the case, and had me remain at home a few days, till she could recruit my health and encourage me to brave out the undertaking. This being done, I resumed my school attendance and no further trouble ensued. But I could not love my associations, and derived little profit from that particular opportunity. Probably, however, my experience there was a wholesome discipline to me.

One other unpleasant affair I call to mind in this connection. It occurred one winter in our district school, when I was between eight and nine years old, I think. One Christopher Olney from Providence, or vicinity, was the teacher. He had been a brilliant student at Brown University, but, falling into some bad habits, was expelled. He was an excellent scholar and a genius at teaching. He delighted in his profession, won the affection of his pupils, and was remarkably successful, provided he let liquor alone. An appetite for the intoxicating cup was one of his fatal weaknesses, and made a wreck of him at last. I shall never forget the captivating assiduity with which he would drill me all through an evening. This was his custom with his scholars wherever he boarded, especially if they manifested any interest in their studies. We were mutually fond of each other and he would flatter me by saying he was proud of me. He was also fond of cider, and when he had finished an evening's tuition, would cry out with a significant shrug of the shoulders, "Now take the bright luminary, descend into the dark vault, and fetch me some *aqua vitae* in a minute." And many a time I did it, which was sufficient pay for his extra services.

Before my time, this teacher had taught the same school, and had given a dramatic exhibition in the old meetinghouse at the close, which won popular admiration and fame in the vicinity. He now proposed to repeat the experiment, and began to prepare for it, the pupils all being expected to participate in the exercises of the occasion. To me was assigned the poetic effusion entitled "An Elegy to Pity," commencing:

> Hail! lovely power, whose bosom heaves the sigh,
> When fancy paints the scene of deep distress.[29]

I easily committed it to memory, but I was troubled because it must be spoken to begin with before the school, with the usual oratorical accompaniments as to gesture, emphasis, intonation, etc. I felt so diffident and awkward that I utterly shrunk from this first appearance on the stage, though it was only in the presence of my teacher and schoolfellows. I had to be literally broken in by force. In spite of their mutual kindly regard, the teacher and his pupil had a falling out on account of this, though but for a short time.

When the rehearsal took place, I was called, in my turn, to the floor. I was slow to respond. My heart palpitated, my knees grew weak, a strange mingling of dread and shame seemed to possess me, and I had to be hauled into my proper position. Even then I could not or did not speak. My master, not expecting such conduct from his favorite pupil, flattered, urged, commanded me to begin, but all in vain. He then used threats, which proved equally ineffectual. Finally, he resorted to a droll, ignominious kind of punishment, more mortifying and vexatious than painful, unknown to me elsewhere before or since. It was a mock shaving, after the fashion of a barber, with a wooden razor, amid the laughter of the whole school. As he proceeded to put me through this process, I became *stuffy*, but neither struggles nor cries saved me. It was a ludicrous conflict, but I was subdued, and made to blubber out my rudimental oratory with more spunk than elegance.

Thenceforth I progressed to my teacher's entire satisfaction. He was quick to make up with me, professed to be sorry for the shaving episode, and almost begged my pardon. I was easily conciliated, and our relations were thenceforward as amiable as ever. The unfortunate man fell into some of his dissipations soon after, the meetinghouse exhibition was given up, and only an impaired schoolhouse program performed. But the teacher pronounced me the flower of the occasion, and lavished on me abundant commendation.

The round of school exercises in those days was comparatively simple, as the textbooks were few in number, and crude in method and arrangement. The teacher stuck closely to the letter of the books, seldom asking questions or submitting problems calculated to draw out the mind, or awaken and discipline thought. There was but little done by way of explanation or fresh analysis. What the books contained was deemed sufficient. Now and then a genius in the teacher's chair or among the scholars transcended this routine, but such innovations were rare in the sphere of my observation till I had passed my tenth year.

I learned to read and spell with ease, and in those branches excelled the majority of my schoolfellows. Spelling schools on winter evenings were customary, exciting great interest and a spirit of wholesome emulation. As a result, good spellers were, I think, as numerous then as now. We had readers, writers, and arithmeticians of very respectable attainments, chiefly by reason of the few departments of study then pursued. I began grammar before I was ten years of age, and soon memorized Alexander's elementary work,[30] and could parse plain prose after the old fashion very well. But it was some time before I really understood grammatical principles so as to enjoy the study. When I did it became my delight. In penmanship and arithmetic, I by no means kept pace with my other acquirements.

Our school district was prolific in teachers of its own production. Many of the sons and daughters of the populous Ballou families, as they grew up, took their turns in their native school with good acceptance; also in other neighborhoods on both sides the state line. Yet only one of them, Barton Ballou, received a college education.[31]

Episode in a Cotton Factory

I was withdrawn from summer school as soon as I was old enough to be of use on the farm, and I lost entirely the winter term next preceding my ninth birthday. This happened by a somewhat strange transfer to a cotton factory, whereof I will give a brief account.

After the celebrated Samuel Slater,[32] a native of England, had established cotton spinning by machinery at Pawtucket, Rhode Island, his success excited others to ambitious enterprise in the same pursuit. Money was to be made, it was thought, at a fabulous rate, and capitalists, large and small, became adventurers in the business. Even staid farmers caught the fever and formed companies for purposes of cotton manufacture.[33] One was started in our neighborhood with a capital of fifteen or twenty thousand dollars, in which my father became pecuniarily interested to the extent of two thousand dollars, a part of which he was obliged to borrow, much to his grief in the end. At the outset, however, everything was alluring and hopeful. The Blackstone (Slater's) establishment, then deemed gigantic, had already begun operations with a most promising outlook,[34] and fresh adventurers were encouraged to push forward their projects with all possible speed.

Early in the year 1811, an eventful one in the history of our family, a factory was erected by the company formed in the Ballou district, on Mill River, just above its junction with the Blackstone, about three miles due west of our residence. It was in the same town and only a short distance from Woonsocket Falls, the village bearing that name being then exceedingly small, rude, and unimportant. Near the mill a tenement house was put up, the construction of which was effected by my father. The proprietors of the establishment called themselves the Social Manufacturing Company, and their plant was known as the Social Factory, afterward nicknamed the Pistareen Factory.[35]

The grand climacteric of this whole scheme was that my father became one of the overseers of the mill and removed his family to one of the tenements in the house he had previously built. Renting his farm to my oldest brother, Cyrus, he transferred the rest of us to the new house late in the season, and the winter of 1811-12 was spent there. He had charge of the carding room and his children were distributed in various positions of service about the establishment.[36] I became what they used to call a "cotton bug."[37] In this way I lost the tuition of the schoolhouse for that term, but received another kind of education which was perhaps quite as valuable.

I was delighted with my new position for a time and rose rapidly from the roping to the throstle-frame.[38] But when spring opened my confinement grew irksome, and I sighed for my accustomed outdoor life. Great, therefore, was my joy when it was announced that father was disgusted with his situation and had arranged to return to the old home. This took place in April, and my ninth birthday found me once more a farmer boy.

War Clouds

For some time previous to this episode in our family history, the war clouds had been gathering in the usually peaceful sky, and a rupture between England and the United States became more and more probable as the weeks and months went by. The early part of the year 1812 was replete with martial excitement throughout the land. The crisis came on eighteenth of June, when war was declared by the United States government against the mother country. Hostile operations were soon after begun and continued through the year with varying results.

The press teemed with the reports of what was going on; the Republican and Federal parties were in bitter contention for and against the war, and all classes of the people were greatly agitated. Military companies of volunteers were formed all over the land, and our own neighborhood and family were not disposed to shirk any duty in the existing emergency. My two oldest brothers became lieutenants in their country's service, and I, silly child, regretted that I was not old enough to be in the ranks. As the young duck takes to water at the first opportunity, so was I predisposed to patriotism, politics, and war, from the start.

But more of this hereafter. I close the present chapter with the single remark that the routine of the year under notice, aside from what has been hinted at, consisted of the ordinary experiences of a lad in my situation at that period of history, and these were continued to the end of my first decade, April 23, 1813.

CHAPTER 2

1813-1818

Before the date at which this chapter opens, I had, as already intimated, begun to take a lively interest in public affairs. The war with England was now going on. Napoleon Bonaparte was descending from the zenith of his glory, and the civilized world was in great commotion.

My father took the leading Republican paper of the state,[1] published at Providence, and I read it with eagerness and delight. It was my oracle. The then Republican and Federal parties were hot and violent against each other, and, in our town, nearly balanced. My father had gone over from the latter to the former during the contest between Adams and Jefferson, and it was natural that I should be of the same political faith.

As the Republicans went all lengths for Madison and the war, also for Bonaparte and the French as against the British and their allies, my boyish sympathies ran strongly in the same direction. I not only read all I could find in the papers that related to the existing conflict, but the few books I could get hold of containing information upon the French Revolution, the rise of Bonaparte, his campaigns and strangely varying fortunes.

For some years my young head was as well filled with these and similar themes, as, in my obscure position, it well could be. Still there was room for religion, as I shall presently relate; but my dreamy reveries of political and military glory were legion. I always contrived in my surmisings to have a good cause and a brave army. Then such grand battles were fought, such victories achieved, and such a noble use was made of success, as never took place outside of a prolific imagination. It is well that they all originated, were carried through, and had their historic fame wholly within my own boyish mind.

Doubtless some will query how it came to pass that a rustic farmer lad of my age should occupy himself with matters usually entertained only by those more advanced in life. I was undoubtedly unlike others in some respects. My mental as well as physical development was early and rapid in a marked degree, even though external incentives were comparatively few, and opportunities small. I was held closely to the ordinary routine of useful industry, according to my capability.

I had barely common school advantages in winter, the weekly paper, and a very few books of any sort. To be sure, my father was a proprietor with others of a small library several miles distant which his family sometimes patronized; he had also a few volumes at home, and I could now and then borrow one of a neighbor. But the stock to which I had access was, all told, very scanty. Moreover, I was seldom brought into contact with persons above the common grade of country people.

There were a few "Revolutionaries," as they were called, in our neighborhood, to whose stories of adventure and perilous experience I delighted to listen. I was allowed to go to one or two town meetings a year and to general muster if not too far away; also, occasionally, to a Fourth of July celebration. These were about all the opportunities for self-improvement I enjoyed. But of these I made the most, getting out of them everything that one intensely interested could. Every school privilege, every newspaper, every book, every story, every town meeting, muster, or public celebration, was eagerly grasped, sedulously improved, remembered, and turned to good account. I went nowhere to play or kill time. At town meeting, for instance, I was not among the boys, engaged in or witnessing the sports, but with the men where business was going on, scrutinizing all that transpired. In this way I was continuously gathering facts, suggestions, items of information, sufficient to keep my intellect, ambition, and imagination always active. I have learned by experience as well as observation that small resources and opportunities, made the most of, produce greater results than an amplitude, indifferently improved. It is not so much what we have as how we use it that determines attainment. When the old domestic lights were not available to read by in the evening, I could and did read by firelight rather than not read at all. I made good use of what I read by thoroughness and fertile reflection upon it. The text might be brief, the suggestions few, but the comments and amplifications of thought were manifold.

A Religious Reformation

It was during the year 1813, if my memory is not at fault, that an extensive "Reformation," as it was called, or revival of religion, commenced in our vicinity. Elder Zephaniah S. Crossman[2] of the Christian Connexion[3] was the pioneer preacher and for a time almost sole manager of the movement. It spread over a region of country not less than fifty miles square, of which the Ballou neighborhood might be considered the center. My father, mother, brothers Cyrus and Alfred, and finally myself, became converts and were baptized by immersion. A large number of persons, nearly a hundred I should think, professed to have "experienced religion" during the three years of continued excitement.

A church of the order named was formed, of which my father was an active member and deacon. For a time it prospered wonderfully. Elder Crossman was not a profound man, but impulsive, magnetic, and insinuating. He did not deal so much in the terrific as in the pathetic and sentimental. He was full of touching anecdotes, illustrations, and appeals to the emotions of his hearers. He could sing, pray, exhort, in a manner well calculated to enlist the sympathies and move the feelings of those who had been living in comparative indifference to spiritual things, and had little intellectual discipline or insight. His matter, manner, and measures were novel and temporarily effective, but wore out with familiarity. Hence the period of his success, remarkable while it lasted, was brief, like that of most sensationalists in any one locality. After a few years he lost his influence and finally abandoned the ministry. Many of his converts fell away and even the church he had established in our midst ere long began to decline, becoming finally extinct.

The "Reformation" took deep and lasting hold of my father, who, from the time of his baptism through several succeeding years, devoted his personal efforts and property with almost Pentecostal zeal to the cause he had espoused. He kept a sort of Ministers' Tavern, not only opening his house for meetings at all times, but furnishing free entertainment for itinerant preachers, friends from a distance, etc., who flocked in to help on the "work of the Lord," as was claimed, or, as one might be tempted to say, to obtain their full share of "the loaves and the fishes." For it is a fact which gradually became stereotyped on my mind that religion and moral reform are not apt to spoil people's appetites when hospitality is offered them without cost, however eminent they may be as saints, or contrite and under "deep concern of mind as sinners," or devoted to the good of humanity. At length my father's patience with this kind of visitors gave out, as his resources were likely to do, and he rebelled, shutting down almost entirely the gates of his long-continued, lavish generosity. This phase of the great revival is, one might say, a ludicrous picture to look back upon with experienced and critical eyes, but one of not infrequent occurrence in the history of religious excitements in this country.

But there is a better side to the movement which must not be ignored. Many persons who had been living on in ignorance and sin, regardless of all obligation to God and their fellow men, were arrested in their worldly, carnal career and converted to a better life. A few, possibly, were disgusted with what was said and done, and hardened into scorners. Some, as stated, started off with good resolutions, but afterward fell back into their old ways. Yet a considerable number were really and lastingly benefited. Of these, I was one. True it is, we made a very crude beginning in what I now understand to be the real Christian life. But it *was* a beginning and one in my case, without which, I fear, I never should have been on my present religious plane. It was wrought out by solemn and rich spiritual experiences to which I look back with reverential gratitude to my Heavenly Father.

In another respect the revival was productive of good to the people affected by it. It was a wholesome agitation of thought. It moved the mental, as well as moral waters of the community. It awakened inquiry, investigation, and a progressive exercise of the understanding. It left people somewhat in advance, intellectually, of what they were before or probably would have been without it. This is undoubtedly true of all religious and moral excitements, none of them being utterly useless – all dross – though many of them have deplorable drawbacks and imperfections.

Beginnings of Christian Life

But to come back to my own personal experience, I remark that, seeing and hearing so much of what deeply impressed others around me, and especially those in my father's family, it was impossible for me not to become seriously affected. I was too young, however, to have it suspected in those days that I could be converted like older persons. Children of my age were then regarded by many as incapable of being religious in the deeper, experimental sense of the word. Therefore, little notice was taken of me in relation to the matter at first, and no one seemed to think I was a proper subject of conviction, repentance, and faith. Yet I felt that I was so, and it grieved me that I was not treated accordingly. How often I longed to have some minister or church member say something to me which would open the way for me to make known my feelings and desires! Nevertheless, I gave close attention to the meetings, watched the proceedings, heard the preaching, praying, singing, etc., and noted carefully every form of religious demonstration that was made.

I was intensely interested in all these things. I longed to be a Christian, and prayed and wept in secret places, seeking to be humble and penitent enough to receive some heavenly assurance of acceptance with God. I felt the same sense of imperfection and sinfulness which others described in narrating their experiences, but still no sense of divine pardon or approval was realized by me. Neither had I any human advisor or comforter. At length, when only about eleven years old, I retired one day, deeply distressed in mind, to my chamber and threw myself on my knees, in agonizing prayer. I gave myself up to the All-Father in the name of my Savior with the profoundest consciousness of submission, to be dealt with and disposed of as divine wisdom and love should determine. That moment my burden was removed; a heavenly light beamed upon me, and an inexpressible peace was diffused through my soul. I arose from my knees, believing that I was approved by Christ as one of his disciples. I rejoiced with exceeding joy and felt that I was entering upon a new life. I have ever recurred to that blessed hour as the decisive beginning of my Christian pilgrimage. It gave bent and direction to my character and career thenceforward to the present time.

It was not long before the matter began to be known to the church, and I received the sympathy I had so longed to enjoy. The result was that I was recognized as a true convert to Christ when about twelve years of age, was baptized by Elder Crossman, May 21, 1815, and registered as a member of the church in regular standing. My case called out divers comments from those who knew me, many deeming me too young to know what I was about, or to have any proper understanding of religious experiences, obligations, and professions. No doubt I was ignorant and of crude judgment, yet, I am sure, I was not far beneath the majority of those who have made a public profession of religion. I certainly knew that I was committing myself to Christian discipleship, and I think few of my seniors at the time acted more intelligently than myself.

If it be said that, according to my own showing, I mixed up my religion with politics, patriotism, and warlike reveries, it was in the same way that nominal Christians have been doing for sixteen hundred years[4] – in the same way that a vast majority of them are doing now. My theology and ethics were not clear and consistent, but quite as much so as is the case with most members of the so-called Christian Church today, even in the most enlightened denominations. Whatever my folly or imperfection, I have never regretted the step I then took, but have been devoutly thankful to the author of all good that thus early in life I committed myself to his service under the leadership of Jesus Christ.

For a year or two after uniting with the church, I was a constant attendant upon its meetings and established ordinances, and in a few instances ventured to take part in some of the more private and social gatherings, but was usually a silent listener and learner. As time went on and the enthusiasm began to abate, I was gradually brought to realize that I had undertaken a more difficult task than at first appeared obvious. I had pledged myself to a Christian life without counting the cost. I had presumed that my "change of heart" went a great deal further than was actually the case. This arose partly from my own ignorance and partly from the extravagant representations of the older professors and of my religious teachers generally. The notion that "experiencing religion" was a miraculously radical change led me, as it has others, to conclude that if the conversion was genuine, the natural propensities and passions would either be eradicated or so neutralized as to be harmless. The truth slowly forced itself upon me that the animal nature in my constitution remained essentially unchanged, and that what had been wrought in me was chiefly the germination of the spiritual element as a contestant against that nature for the throne of my being. Between these two forces or agencies there was to be a long and severe conflict – a warfare of many battles and of fluctuating successes and defeats. But it was a grand gain that the spiritual and divine had been born in my heart and had been unequivocally acknowledged as rightful heir to the kingdom.

The war indicated was not long in coming on. I had the same propensities and passions as before my conversion. If temporarily silenced by strong religious inspirations, they were awake and ready for action as soon as those influences subsided. This was proved in my subsequent experience. First, I was astonished at the strange coldness that crept over me – a sort of spiritual inertia, languor, listlessness, whereby I could neither pray fervently nor watch vigilantly. Then I was grieved to find my quick, irritable temper awake again and as sensitive and imperious as ever, gaining by degrees the mastery over me. It was a sad mystery how I, who had passed through such purifying seasons of thought, feeling, emotion, amounting almost to transfiguration, could be plunged into such depths of an opposite character.

As time passed by, all my natural propensities took their turns at tantalization and taught me of what stuff I was made. In manifold forms each asserted its claim, and in every direction some sort of battle seemed inevitable between the contending forces within. The good and the evil alternately prevailed for a season and the warfare of a long life was inaugurated, as described by the Apostle Paul, in Galatians 5:17 and Romans 7:18-24.

An Eventful Year

The year 1815 was one of memorable events in the affairs of the world. Peace was restored between the United States and Great Britain. Bonaparte was decisively crushed at Waterloo, and the old order of things was reinstated, as far as possible, on the continent of Europe. A thousand prophecies and interpretations of prophecy that had dazzled ardent, fanatical minds from the commencement of the French Revolution, vanished away or were indefinitely postponed, while the mysteries of Daniel's vision and the Apocalypse were bequeathed to another generation of expounders. Princes and nobles went into exile and those previously sent into retirement returned to the estates of their ancestors. Republican dreamers of equality and fraternity hid from the tempest of monarchical reaction and almost cursed their brilliant visions, so long cherished and now so apparently falsified. And yet there had been undoubtedly some progress made, some gain realized in behalf of justice and humanity. But at what cost of life, suffering, and treasure!

The Great Gale

Among the more eventful local occurrences of the year was the Great Gale,[5] as it is called in New England annals, which swept through Rhode Island and Massachusetts with terrific force at the time of the autumnal equinox, September 23. I recollect being engaged near my father's sawmill handling lumber with my brothers when the stocks of boards around us, piled up to season, began to be caught away by the rising wind and blown about strangely. We endeavored to pick them up and replace them for a while, but found ourselves borne along and almost lifted from the ground in spite of our utmost exertions. We were soon in danger of limb and life from the flying rubbish and lumber, and betook ourselves to a place of safety at the substantial farmhouse, which was built heavily and strong enough to resist the stoutest storm. The wind increasing, buildings began to be unroofed, smaller structures were moved out of place or completely demolished, apple and forest trees were upturned by the roots, and even the stoutest dwellings creaked and trembled before the mighty gusts that seemed to threaten destruction to everything that happened to be in their way.

The tempest, which began about seven o'clock in the morning, reached its height at noon, when it was little else than a hurricane. Multitudes of people were filled with terror and consternation. I confess that I was, and hastening to my chamber, obtained what relief and composure I could from the unseen world by earnest supplication. I gained something of trust and calmness, but hardly enough to overcome all my fearful apprehensions, for there seemed to be no place of refuge from impending danger and my faith was not of the surest type.

When the storm subsided, the inhabitants of southern New England looked with amazement on the devastations it had caused. Inland the noblest timber lots were covered with prostrate trees and upturned earth, the finest orchards were laid waste, rail fences, wood, and lumber were scattered far and wide, roads were rendered impassable by accumulated debris, and incalculable damage had been done to buildings on every hand, many of the lighter ones being wholly destroyed. In seaport towns and along the shore, still greater havoc, if possible, had been wrought. The ocean rolled in upon the coast its mountainous waves, which, in thickly settled localities, inundated the wharves, streets, and exposed places of business, filled the cellars and lower stories of dwellings and warehouses near the water line, causing the occupants to flee for their lives, and destroying immense amounts of property that chanced to be within reach. The wind drove before it all sorts of sea craft, even the largest vessels, sinking some, wrecking others, and landing many high on the beach, far away from tidewater. The remains of sloops and schooners, gradually dismantled and abandoned, appeared on the sand banks and along the coast for years, victims of the Storm King's insatiate power. Such was the Great Gale of 1815, the like whereof has never been seen by New Englanders since the Pilgrims landed on Plymouth Rock.

General Meeting of the Christian Connexion, 1815

Soon after this gale occurred, the Christian Connexion held one of their General Meetings at Assonet, in Freetown, Massachusetts. Thither my father and other members of our church, including myself, went. The convocation continued for several days and was replete with religious interest and edification. Elders Abner Jones and Elias Smith, then at the head of the denomination[6] were present, as were also Elder Frederick Plummer,[7] an eloquent revivalist; Elder Daniel Hix,[8] the solid farmer preacher; Elder Benjamin Taylor,[9] the John-like apostle; and a host of other zealous evangelists of that distinctive faith. Those were the palmy days of the "Christian" order in this section of the country, and we had much stirring exhortation, preaching, and other religious demonstration. Enthusiasm ran high and hopes of a good time coming were in the ascendant. The gathering was refreshing to the assembled hosts and passed off, as a kind of Pentecost, to general satisfaction.

Death of Brothers Cyrus and Arnold

About this time the health of my brother Cyrus began to decline and in spite of all efforts to restore it he gradually sank into an incurable consumption. He was failing during the entire winter following and died on the seventh of March, 1816. This was the first event of the kind in our family after I was old enough to remember it, the one last preceding having been the decease of a sister in 1803, the year of my birth. My brother was deeply religious and had been much exercised by impressions that it was his duty to enter the gospel ministry. But fatal illness ended all expectations in that direction. He departed in sweet hope of a blessed future and with the most perfect composure.

I did not witness the closing scene, but my father, who was with him during the night of his departure, perceiving a change in the countenance of the sick man indicating that death was at hand, said to him as he lay quietly before him, "Cyrus, do you know that you are dying?"

He answered distinctly, "No. Do you think I am?"

"Yes," father responded, "it seems so to me."

For a few moments the invalid was still; then of his own accord, said, "I believe I am dying. I feel differently from what I ever did before."

"Are you afraid to die?" he was asked.

"Oh, no!" was his reply. "I long to go and be with Christ; I am happy." He expressed a wish to be turned upon his other side, when, without a sign of pain, he breathed his last before the summoned family could reach the room.

This event could not fail to make a deep impression on us all. But to his youthful widow, left with two little boys, it was one of the heaviest of bereavements. My brother lacked a few days only of his twenty-seventh birthday, she being somewhat younger. Not many years afterward she married a second husband, who died in 1862, leaving her the second time a widow. She is still living in Franklin, Massachusetts. Thus roll on the ceaseless wheels of time, bringing changes to all human fortunes, but the divine providence faileth not.

This year, 1816, was one of sore visitation to our family, inasmuch as death invaded it a second time before its close. My next older brother, Arnold, an intelligent, amiable young man in the twenty-fifth year of his age, was summoned hence before winter set in. He was not a professor of religion, though always reverential towards it. In comeliness of person, sedateness of mind, urbanity of disposition, and propriety of deportment, he was the flower of our domestic circle. Wherever known, he was universally respected and loved. I had a strong and peculiar affection for him, though he was eleven years older than I. My father, who was beginning to feel that it was desirable to arrange his temporal affairs for old age and death, leaned confidently on this son. His plan was to settle one-half of his real estate on him and the other half on me when I should become of age, himself and my mother to be amply provided for by us, and suitable legacies to be paid in due time to the other children.

With this in view, Arnold, having married in April, brought home his young wife and entered at once upon the management of affairs. But in the autumn he was attacked by a fever which took on dangerous complications, and finally, in defiance of all medical skill, terminated his life on the twenty-seventh of November. He passed away in comparative unconsciousness and gave forth no memorable religious manifestations like those of Cyrus just recorded. And so another young heart was widowed, parental bosoms were deeply wounded, and the remaining family circle filled with mourning and distress. A posthumous daughter was born the following spring. By this second bereavement, my father's cherished plans and fond hopes went down to the dust.

Hopes and Ambitions

The time passed over by the foregoing narrative, from 1813 to 1817, brings me to the fifteenth year of my age. It will naturally be imagined what the general routine of my employment and experience was during this period. In the summer I was at work, as a lad in my circumstances might be expected to be, and indeed all through the year, except so much of the winter as I spent in school, of which I have spoken in preceding pages. And even while attending my usual three months' school, my time was much broken in upon by a variety of calls at home and abroad, incident to life on a large farm in those days, which, however necessary and unavoidable, resulted in serious hindrances to my educational progress.

Nevertheless, I made up, as far as I could, for deficiency of opportunities and systematic means of mental improvement in every possible way; so that I ripened in scholarship, such as mine was, every year, and stored up for future use all the fragments of general information that came within my reach. My thirst for learning grew with my growth, and before I was fifteen became intense, as is illustrated in the following incident of my experience.

My father had in Providence a considerable number of special customers for butter and other products of his farm which he marketed there from year to year. Among these was Rev. Dr. Messer,[10] president of Brown University, who would occasionally ask him, as he went his rounds, when he was going to send one of his sons to college, repeatedly urging him to do so. Upon his return home with reports of what Dr. Messer had said to him, I could not help having awakened in me the hope that somehow or other such a lot as was indicated might be mine. At length the hope became so strong and my desire in that direction so great that I begged my father to give me a collegiate education, proposing that the three or four hundred dollars it would cost in those days should be my sole inheritance out of his quite large estate, and confessing myself ready to quitclaim any right or title I might have to what might remain, for the sake of having this grand privilege granted me. So earnest was I in this matter that I believe I would have undertaken to crawl on my hands and knees to Providence, fifteen miles, if by so doing I could have secured my coveted object. My father was often moved in my behalf for the moment when I made my appeals to him, and would say he wished he was able to gratify me, but usually wound up with, "I am too much in debt." If I plead my case with great persistency and zeal, telling him how much better it would be for me to have the knowledge I would acquire than many times what it would cost in money, he would refer me to a distant kinsman who spent his little patrimony in getting a liberal education, but had been unsuccessful and poor all his days. In vain I endeavored to unclinch this nail; for the inexorable conclusion was, "I cannot send you to college as your all, and have you basking about in learned poverty." And so all my aspirations of this sort perished in the bud.

I have often in my later years pondered seriously over this matter and wondered what would have been my course and position in life if my ardent longing for a collegiate education had been gratified. In all probability they would have been radically different from what they have been and are. I should have been placed under influences quite dissimilar to those that have been brought to bear upon me, and at a period of life when I was supple and plastic and likely to yield to them. With my natural worldly inclinations and ambitions, heretofore adverted to, the chances are that I should have chosen the profession of law as most likely to open promising avenues to distinction and so-called success. Religion might have possibly become of chief importance to me; possibly literature. This would have depended much on my teachers and patrons, for I should have been easily led and molded by them. I should not have been drawn readily into the medical or clerical professions, as I had no natural inclination for either of them.

But whatever course or calling I had been persuaded to pursue, I should have become so trained and committed to it, as probably never to have broken away from its complicated attachments. In some popular, time-worn channel of respectability and renown, the current of my personal energies would very likely have flowed through life. The independent convictions, principles, and aims now so sacred to me, though so unpopular and, in worldly parlance, impracticable, if not contemptible, would either have found no welcome to my mind or been suppressed within it by the imperious dictates of a temporizing policy. I have hardly a doubt of this. Was it then a blessing or a bane that I was denied the training and culture I so longed to secure? Thousands would doubtless deem it a great misfortune. But I have come to regard it a benefit to myself and mankind. At any rate it was ordered or permitted by Him who overrules all things that my most earnest youthful wishes should not be gratified, nor the crowning ambition of my early years be encouraged. And if there reigns a God worthy to be revered and loved by his rational creatures, it was somehow all for the best.

The Singing School

When I was about fourteen years old, one Samuel Forest opened a singing school in our neighborhood – a rather uncommon event in that locality. The young people generally were delighted with the innovation and I hailed it as offering me a desirable privilege. I was gifted with not more than ordinary musical capability and could hope for only moderate attainments in that department of culture, even by dint of proper training. I had learned to sing many current tunes by rote, imperfectly, but greatly needed tuition in the principles and rules of rhythm and vocalization. In this, again, I was completely thwarted. My father was conscientiously opposed to choir singing as a part of divine worship, especially by the "unconverted" or "world's people." A singing school led directly to this "public mockery," as he called it. If he allowed me to join such a school, he would be an encourager and partaker of the assumed sin. So he peremptorily forbade my attending it. I quietly yielded but with great regret, and never afterward found a favorable opportunity to acquire even the rudiments of a musical education. My two brothers were less submissive and went to the school in spite of the same paternal prohibition. But I never regretted my filial obedience, though I deplored my loss and could not quite endorse my father's scruples or *prejudices*, as some would call them. Yet when I have witnessed the levity and almost impiety of some talented occupants of singing galleries, I have been compelled to think their performances were little better than public mockeries. But how much worse the shortcomings of the choir are in the sight of God than those of the pulpit and the press, I will not presume to judge. True worship is more sacred and rare by far than common minds have yet dreamed.

Spiritual Lapse and Recovery

The winter before I was fifteen, Mr. Noah Cook, a young man from Mendon, Massachusetts, taught our school and I attended for the last time in our own neighborhood. He was a live, ambitious teacher and succeeded well. I liked him and made commendable improvement in my several studies. He thought well of me, and amid the rivalries of the schools on different sides of the state line, offered to present me as a grammarian against some that boasted much greater privileges than I enjoyed, and were prone to speak of those less favored than themselves with contempt. Nothing, however, came of it except a little sharpshooting to and fro across the border with the pen.

Mr. Cook was not a religious man and my own spiritual tone was somewhat in decadence, for the revival had burnt out and the zeal of many waxed cold. In this state of things, the influence of Mr. Cook over me was not of the best, since he introduced me to pleasure parties and social gatherings where, though nothing vicious or immoral occurred, there was little to stimulate the better purpose and higher life of the soul. I soon, under some compunction, abandoned these assemblages and devoted much of my spare time to religious study, meditation, and prayer until I reached the anniversary of my birth, April 23, 1818.

CHAPTER 3

1818-1821

With the opening of the sixteenth year of my life, I entered on a period of increased personal responsibility. My oldest surviving brother, Alfred, was absent from home most of the time for the next two years, partly at school and partly in a factory counting-room, and I became my father's chief deputy in the management of the farm and collateral interests. Indeed, he signified his desire and purpose to settle me on the ancestral estate as his successor and the stay of his old age, and I began to shape my expectations accordingly. When winter came around work took precedence of schooling, causing it to be postponed to another year. It was hoped I might then be compensated for the loss of my ordinary privileges in our own district by securing more advantageous ones elsewhere, and this proved to be the case.

As to my religious state, I recovered from what I regarded my backsliding in the course of a few months, abandoned ordinary social gatherings and places of worldly amusement, and devoted my leisure hours largely to religious exercises and duties. I studied my Bible and books of devotion intently, prayed much in secret, had my seasons of fasting and self-examination, paid close attention to divine worship and subsidiary meetings, became clerk of our church, and gradually took on a phase of decided asceticism. I cultivated as stern a zeal for piety and righteousness as my nature was capable of, and subjected myself to a stricter self-discipline than at any other time of my life.

Theological Belief Formulated

Meanwhile my theology assumed a definite and positive form, its essential features being such, substantially, as prevailed in the Christian Connexion, whose leaders, though constantly denouncing creeds, had one, as a matter of fact, of pretty sharp points distributed through their preachings and published writings. I have generally found this to be the case with nominal anti-creedists, even down to nothingarians. By study and reflection, I had formulated the following items of doctrine in which I most firmly believed:

    1. The plenary inspiration of the Bible;
    2. The pre-existent divine sonship of Christ;
    3. The personal unity of God, the Father;

4. The impersonal agency of the Holy Spirit in working out the divine designs;
5. The fall of man in Adam and consequent universal but not total depravity;
6. The indispensable necessity of the new birth;
7. Man's free moral agency;
8. This life the only probationary state for eternity;
9. The resurrection of the body;
10. The final general day of judgment;
11. The special immortalization of the righteous, both body and soul, at the Judgment Seat;
12. The just punishment of the wicked, terminating in their utter destruction – absolute non-existence.

The controversy between the Trinitarians and Unitarians in this country was inaugurated about this time, and the "Christians" took sides against the former, though they clung to a sort of high Arianism and rather stiffly repudiated those forms of Unitarianism which questioned the personal pre-existence of Christ. I embraced this view of the subject and thought myself strongly entrenched therein behind the word of God.

Another grand question then in dispute was that relating to the final destiny of the wicked. Elders Elias Smith, Abner Jones, and other influential leaders in our order had come out against endless punishment and in favor of absolute, final destruction or annihilation of the doomed impenitent. This obliged them to deny the innate immortality of the soul, and contend that no one could ever be rendered immortal except by the special will and gift of God. These doctrines I readily embraced and made myself an expert in their scriptural defense. They and kindred topics furnished my ever active mind ample themes of inquiry and speculation in the department of theology.

The Restorationists,[1] as they termed themselves, of earlier times were only slightly known to me by general report, and it was a foregone conclusion that their distinctive doctrine could have no possible foundation in divine revelation. The Universalists, many of whom had rejected, as baseless, all belief in future punishment, were beginning to prevail in certain localities, and, through their preachers and published expositions, to make their influence felt in many places where they had no organized foothold. This was the case in our vicinity. We had several neighbors who professed to believe in the final salvation of all men, and ministers of that faith occasionally visited them, such visits growing at length frequent and conspicuous.[2] But I regarded all persons of that way of thinking as anti-religious in spirit, anti-Christian in doctrine, and practically no better than Deists. And I think, even now, that many of them gave me too much reason for regarding them as I did, though my prejudices made me unjust to them in a greater or less degree. The Universalists of later times and especially of this day exhibit very great religious improvement, both in theory and practice, on their predecessors of that period.

Changes in the Christian Connexion

Elder Crossman, the chief promoter of the great "Reformation," had now lost prestige and standing in the church and was fast receding from the ministry. He at one time professed Universalism, then recanted, then vacillated for awhile between different forms of faith – finally falling into some irregularities which terminated eventually his labors as a religious teacher. Later in life he became a book-peddler.

Elder Elias Smith, who had been regarded as one of the two chief apostles of the Christian Connexion, went over to the Universalists, in whose fellowship, after some vibrations to and fro, he finally died.[3] During his last years upon earth he devoted himself to the practice of medicine according to the Thomsonian system of therapeutics, which he claimed to have essentially improved.[4]

These and other unexpected developments rather shook the structure of the "Christian" denomination, but by no means destroyed it. The disturbed elements resumed their equilibrium and other leaders, older and younger, arose and moved forward in the van of the host. Little did I dream, when the defections referred to took place, that I should ever find sufficient reason for changing my general theological ground as related to the doctrines involved.

Of some of the new preachers who came forward to fill the vacancies that had been made in our "Christian" ministry, I will make brief mention. There was Reuben Potter Jr.,[5] a native of Coventry, Rhode Island, who first visited us as a youthful exhorter before the *revival* had subsided. He afterwards prepared himself for the ministry and at length became our pastor, leaving us finally for other fields of service. He was a scholarly, pleasant, fluent preacher, popular for a time and much esteemed. But he was not profound and did not excel in intellect, piety, or weight of character. After a gradual moral decadence of some years, he acquired intemperate habits, becoming at last a confirmed sot. He came to a sad end, being found dead in the street of a village not far from the place of his nativity.

Elder Dexter Bullard[6] was the next in order of our pastors, receiving ordination at Cumberland Hill. He was not a brilliant preacher, but a man of sound common sense, intelligence, candor, Christian principle, and moral integrity, sincere and faithful in all things. He married a respected cousin of mine, Juliana Sayles, had quite a numerous family of worthy children, most of whom settled in the West, whither himself and wife removed many years since, and where he died in 1865.

Among numerous itinerant preachers of our order and one of the ablest and best of them, was Elder Benjamin Taylor of Swansea, Massachusetts. He did not appear in our vicinity often, but was always welcome and his services were every way acceptable. He was not only a man of good natural abilities, but an upright, conscientious, exemplary Christian, combining zeal with knowledge and uncompromising fidelity to principle with a broad, deep charity. He was a John among our preachers, always entreating us to "love one another."

Elder Mark Fernald[7] of Kittery, Maine, was also a visiting preacher of creditable ability and reputation, but somewhat ascetic in his habits – a stern, blunt man, severe at times in speech, but possessing a kind heart and making himself useful in his sphere.

Lorenzo Dow

The celebrated and eccentric Lorenzo Dow,[8] who belonged to no sect, but was a sort of Methodist comet in the ecclesiastical heavens, visited us occasionally during the two years of which I am now writing. I first saw him in Providence. His fame was widespread, and I had read with much interest his published autobiography.[9] Learning that he was to be in an adjoining town, some of our people were anxious to see and hear him, myself being one of the number. I went to the house of a Methodist brother where he was stopping, but it was so thronged with callers that I barely got a glimpse of him. My only recollections of him are that he wore his hair and beard long (then an astonishing sight); that he was a lean, spare, dark-complexioned man; that his dress and general appearance were plain and simple, as of a pilgrim devotee; and that when he started for the chapel where he was to preach he could not find his hat and so went out bareheaded, but was soon supplied with the missing article by his consumptive-looking, devoted wife, Peggy, who came running after him with it in her hand, and shouting in shrill, tender tones, "Lorenzo, Lorenzo, here is your hat," which he rather indifferently accepted. Of his discourse, characteristic of him, no doubt, I, though hearing it, remember nothing.

After this he preached at different times in our neighborhood, stopping with us, and I became well acquainted with him, being charged with the duty of waiting upon him and of attending to his personal comfort, as occasion required. This I did with fidelity and discretion, carefully avoiding manifesting any surprise at his seeming eccentricities. He treated me not only with unaffected civility and kindness, but with confidential cordiality. It had been said that he was sometimes gruff and ungracious to those who served him, but I was led to believe that those complaining of such treatment provoked it by their ill-timed flattery and sycophantic fawning. He was a keen observer of human nature and scorned all affectation and obsequiousness.

We had unequivocal manifestations of his eccentricity amounting almost to breach of propriety or incivility sometimes during his several visits with us. Some of these may be mentioned. While preaching one evening in our large, old-fashioned kitchen, in his peculiar, impassioned style, an officious, elderly spinster, then an inmate of the family, disturbed him by repeatedly getting up and fussing with the fire – picking up the falling brands, replenishing the fuel, and otherwise setting things about it to rights. Seeing her start for the third or fourth time on the same errand, he left the thread of his discourse and broke out in an imperative tone,

"Woman, sit down, and don't be up trying to show off that new gown of yours any more." Spinster, in her fresh calico, subsided as if paralyzed and remained fixed in her chair till the meeting closed.

At another time he was seated with our family in the parlor after meeting, the center of a large circle, my mother being on his left and a worthy woman who was then working for us on his right hand. During a little lull in the conversation, he sat musing for a moment and then suddenly broke out, saying to my mother, as he pointed to the woman, who was a stranger to him, "Who is this? Whom have you here?" My mother gave the woman's name. "What is she good for?" he continued.

"Many things," replied my mother. "She is a good, honest woman, a member of our church, a devoted Christian, kind and helpful in sickness, and always quietly industrious."

"Perhaps, but how about her temper? If one should tread on her toes, wouldn't she feel something fluttering up in here?" shaking his skeleton-like finger significantly over his breast as much as to say, "Hasn't she a quick, irritable disposition?" This abrupt, queer incident took us all by surprise and shocked our demure servant well nigh into spasms. Meanwhile he looked the saint he was reputed to be.

The next day I was to take him in a sleigh (for it was winter) first to Cumberland Hill, where he was to preach at 11 A.M., and thence in the afternoon to Providence. Some delay about starting occurred, although there was ample time to reach the place of meeting in season for the service, at which he exhibited considerable uneasiness. When we were well seated in our vehicle and moving off at good speed, he turned to me and with a very earnest but kindly look, said, "Young man, I have a lesson for you. You may become a public character, perhaps a preacher. My lesson is this: *Always take elbow room.* Do you understand me? I mean keep a little ahead of your appointments. Be on hand some minutes before the set time. Make no one wait for you. Never be in a hurry at the last moment. Then you will not only avoid occasion for others to complain, but be in a calm, self-collected frame of mind to proceed with your own duties. Do you understand the lesson?"

"I do," said I; "it is a wise and wholesome one; I thank you for it; I will endeavor to lay it up and profit by it."

"So do," he responded, thus ending his admonition. I have never violated his rule, "Always take elbow room," without perturbation, regret, and shame.

Arriving at the little "Catholic Baptist Meetinghouse," so-called, in due season, the service was conducted in the usual form, the sermon being an exposition and application of the parable of the laborers in the vineyard, Matthew 20:1-16, laying the chief stress on the words, "They received every man a penny." After the meeting I went on with him to Providence, where we parted, never to meet again in this world. From what I saw and knew of him, I judged him to be a faithful, conscientious, Christian minister, notwithstanding he was so singular and erratic in many of his ways.

The Missouri Compromise

During the period of my youth now under review, though mainly occupied with manual labor on the farm and personal religious nurture and discipline, I kept myself posted in regard to public affairs and what was transpiring in the world at large, so far as the newspaper of the family and occasional conversation with well-informed townsmen could serve me in that direction.

When the "Missouri Compromise" excitement[10] prevailed, I recollect getting interested in it and being so patriotically devoted to the Union as to defend our Rhode Island congressman, who was severely denounced for voting in its favor. Without a particle of pro-slavery either in my nature or habits, I was at that time so utterly ignorant of the "peculiar institution" and its fatal evil tendencies, and so carried away with the cunningly-raised bugbear, "The Union in danger," that I readily took the wrong side from good motives – as many of my grave seniors then and afterwards did.

Last Schooling

During this same period a cousin of mine, Otis Mason,[11] some ten or fifteen years older than myself, taught what was called the "Academy" at Cumberland Hill. With him I fell into some intimacy and occasionally visited his school. At his solicitation I was induced to join a debating club connected with the institution, in which I a few times mustered courage enough to speak. There was a library in the same connection from which I took books to read at my convenience. By these means I made partial amends for the lack of regular educational advantages and gained some valuable intellectual culture which otherwise I should have missed.

Near the close of the year 1819, after the farming operations were for the most part suspended for the season, it was arranged that I should go to school ten weeks during the coming winter in the neighboring town of Franklin, Massachusetts. The school was nothing but a rural district one, but it was to be in charge of one Caleb Ward Wilson[12] of Mendon in the same state, a talented and successful teacher at that day, and was to have among its pupils some twenty or more young men and women who had attended sundry higher seminaries of learning under celebrated classical preceptors. So that the opportunity was an especially favorable one for me, much better than I had ever before enjoyed. I was to board in the family of my uncle, Daniel Sayles, a resident of the town, whose wife was a sister of my father. His oldest unmarried daughter, Avilda, had been an accomplished teacher, and his youngest daughter, Juliana, about twenty years of age, was an excellent scholar; while his sons, Orin and Ariel, about my own age, who had shared some superior educational advantages, were to be my fellow students. These circumstances rendered the opening additionally desirable and promising.

When I entered the crowded schoolhouse at the beginning of the term, I felt not only rusty in scholarship but a little awkward from the consciousness of being surrounded by proud-spirited associates who could not easily suppress their prejudices against a green Rhode Islander. It was therefore prudent for me to be modest – at least, not to expose my ignorance presumptuously or unnecessarily. Our teacher was really a superior one and handled his school in a manner worthy of his great reputation. In dealing with his large upper class, which made an imposing array upon the high seats, right and left, he treated them with marked respect, in consideration of their age and attainments, not only allowing but urging them to have opinions of their own, and to differ from him if their judgment so dictated, as well as from each other on all critical points, especially those of grammatical construction and analysis. Issue might be taken upon any question at any time, and the parties involved might give reasons for their opinion, each one arguing in proper order according to his best judgment and ability. There were several in the class who deemed themselves well advanced in scholarship and capable of criticism, and there were some exciting discussions both among the pupils and between pupils and teacher. If he happened to make a mistake, which rarely occurred, he was manly enough not only to hear himself foiled in argument without wounded pride, but to yield the point with open-hearted frankness and promptitude.

For my part, I listened with thoughtful attention to all that was said and done for five or six weeks, but did not venture a word of my own, waiting to have my scholastic rustiness well scoured off, and learn how bright and keen my fellow pupils were, before measuring lances with them. At length, finding that they were not altogether infallible, and thinking I was not wholly incompetent to cope with them in any case where our opinions might not concur, I cautiously submitted, now and then, some criticism of their conclusions. My bashfulness made this a severe trial to me – all the more so when I saw that I was regarded as one aspiring to a rank above my merits and antecedents. This, however, in the end proved to be an advantage to me, for it awakened in me a sense of self-respect and a determination not to be cowered into tame servility to those in no wise my betters.

So on one occasion I took the liberty of questioning the correctness of a certain analysis and the appropriateness of the rule given for it. My comrades stared with contemptuous scorn at what they assumed to be my presumption, and the teacher decided off-hand against me. "But stop," he said in his usual courteous way, "we must hear the reasons for objecting to the view presented." And turning to me, continued, "How, sir, do you make out your case?" My face crimsoned with timid blood and my heart leaped into my throat, but truth and pride put me through the struggle. I stated my position so clearly and gave my reasons so conclusively that the teacher was himself convinced and immediately responded, "He is right after all, and I am wrong." This "put the boot upon the other foot," as the saying is, and my learned sneerers looked as crestfallen as if I had robbed them of their fancied preeminence by magic.

Such experiences, when looked back upon from the far-off summit of advanced age, seem of little consequence if superficially regarded, yet they were in fact of great account to the novices immediately concerned – means of discipline, of progress and lasting enjoyment. They, too, are texts in the volume of human nature on which we can profitably moralize. They remind us that no one ever rises above the level of his supposed-to-be proper sphere without a struggle. His progress is obstructed and resisted by adverse surroundings, by jeering contemporaries, or envious rivals, and he must fight and conquer or be ignominiously overcome. Even those who from natural relationship or friendly consideration ought to cheer on the struggling aspirant, often frown contemptuously on his efforts and dissuade him from pressing forward in the line of his nobler purposes and aspirations. As Eliab said to David in the Bible story of Goliath, "Why comest thou down hither, and with whom hast thou left the few sheep in the wilderness? I know thy pride and the naughtiness of thy heart. For thou hast come that thou mightest see the battle." The undaunted youth only answered, "What have I now done? Is there not a cause?"[13] And he went on in his chosen way – went to conflict and to victory.

Having gained my point and a reputable standing in the school and wishing to avoid all unpleasant rivalry or whatever would occupy an undue proportion of my time and energy, I betook myself to those studies necessary to a well-rounded development in which I was particularly deficient, and where there was little or no emulation. I had always the best understanding with this teacher, and profited greatly by his instruction. His school proved to be my college of graduation. I did not "finish" my education there, as some seem to do in regularly organized institutions of learning, but I never again was a student in any strictly educational establishment of any kind or name.

An Important Trust

The same winter developed other interesting occurrences beside those connected with my school, some of which resulted in experiences of signal importance. It so happened that a mutual intimacy between Elder Dexter Bullard, already spoken of, and my cousin, Juliana Sayles, in whose father's family I was boarding, had ripened into a matrimonial engagement which was to be consummated by marriage before the school term expired. Preliminary to the legal solemnization of the union, there must be the usual *publishment* of the intentions of the parties on the part of the town clerk, either by "crying" the same in religious meeting on two successive Sabbaths, or by "posting" for two weeks in some place of public concourse. It was quite a desideratum with those immediately concerned to have this done as noiselessly as possible and to make it, since it must be known in due time, a surprise to outsiders, even to the family relatives. I was a special confidant in the matter, and to me was entrusted the necessary mission to the public official authorized to act in such cases, with the special charge to execute it with the utmost secrecy.

I was entirely ignorant of the details of such transactions, and undertook the task assigned only for friendship's sake and with great reluctance. Having accepted the trust, I was confronted with the double problem of how to fulfill it and how to do this with the desired secrecy. I must not take any of my school hours nor absent myself from my meals, nor engage a horse with which to ride to the residence of the town clerk, which was three miles away, since either of these would excite suspicion and lead to a discovery of the whole plot. So after supper one evening I slipped quietly out of the house and by an unfamiliar, unfrequented road reached, after much difficulty, the place I was seeking. Unfortunately, the clerk was not at home, being engaged in teaching some distance away and not returning except on Saturday evening for the Sabbath. Not knowing that I could accomplish the object of my visit by leaving the proper details with his wife, to be attended to when he was advised concerning them, I retraced my steps to my uncle's, weary and disappointed, to report my ill luck and to be told, to my great mortification, how easily all further trouble could have been obviated by the means just indicated.

I had not been missed or inquired for, and under a deep sense of humiliation, I resolved to try again on the ensuing Saturday evening, confident that I should then be able to make everything sure. I governed myself accordingly. But the gentleman I wanted to see had not arrived when I reached my destination. Nor did he come after long waiting, till time and distance admonished me that I must be on my way to my boarding-place again. So I left my errand in writing with his wife, but by further blundering failed to mention the proper residence of the groom. This, however, I did not find out until I reached my uncle's and reported progress. The omission was a greater mortification to me than my former misadventure, and I was as vexed with myself as I was tired, but, as there was no time to be lost, I determined, weary though I was, to go over the ground again immediately and finish my ill-starred performance before the dawning of another day. So I actually trudged those six miles (out and in) once more, awoke the now returned and sleeping official, gave him the lacking data, got back home again unsuspected, in season to have a short nap before morning, judging myself amply qualified by experience to act as agent for a couple wishing to have their intentions of marriage published according to law. I never had occasion, however, to undertake another commission of this sort, but was paid for executing this one in the consciousness of having served my beloved employers satisfactorily and in the lesson it taught me of understanding my errands before trying to deliver them. Much of my wisdom I have purchased in the same costly way, as my readers will not fail to see while tracing my subsequent history.

Betrothal

But something of greater consequence to me came from the event, one of the antecedent incidents of which has just been narrated. As arrangements for the approaching wedding were making, it was decided that I should be groomsman, and, after considerable canvassing of the claims and qualifications of several of the fair cousins of the bride on her father's side, of which I was more or less cognizant, that Abby, daughter of Smith Sayles of Smithfield, Rhode Island, should be bridesmaid. Though she was a comparative stranger to me, I readily acceded to the wishes of my friends in this respect as in others where I could serve them. The marriage was solemnized as provided for, February 1, 1820, and the foundation was laid for a long, useful, and happy union, under mortal conditions and in the order of the family, of two worthy, congenial, Christian souls.

One occasion of this sort often leads to another of a similar character. Very likely the arrangement concerning groomsman and bridesmaid in this case was entered into with some ulterior design respecting the parties brought together which did not appear to the casual observer, and which was not communicated to those more particularly concerned. Whether this were so or not, the acquaintance then formed between Abby Sayles and myself was by mutual agreement continued through occasional correspondence and personal interviews until it ripened, not many months afterward, into a definite hymeneal engagement, to be carried into effect at a then undetermined date of the future. So much was done in anticipation of marriage, soon after I had entered upon the eighteenth year of my age.

To the wise and prudent reader this early pledge of marital purposes and fidelities on my part may be deemed boyish and absurd, bespeaking my folly and want of sound judgment. Perhaps so. I cannot blame those who pronounce such a verdict upon me, but rather confess that, from my present standpoint of rationality, I was unfit to take such a step – unqualified to assume the contemplated responsibility. But I had no one to admonish or restrain me and was not wise enough to see, much less realize, my deficiencies. It had already been planned that I should settle down with my parents on the farm, see them through life, and inherit their domain. On that score I was favorably situated as to then present conditions and future prospects. What better could I do than take to myself a wife!

As to my affianced, I satisfied myself that she was every way worthy of my confidence and love. She was three years my senior, which, however objectionable in some regards, was really an advantage to me, her experience and more mature understanding acting as a counterpoise to my inexperience and unripeness. She was well qualified for the proposed relationship in all matters pertaining to domestic economy. She had been well trained to all womanly acquirements in a good home under wise parental influence, having a mother whose excellencies of character I shall never cease to love and revere. Her educational accomplishments, though comparatively small, were respectable for her rank and times. She was not a professor of religion, but eminently conscientious, virtuous, and exemplary. She was a woman of good sense, of sterling principles, and, above all, of an amiable disposition and an affectionate heart. The only serious drawback was her delicate health, which foredoomed our union to an early dissolution, as the sequel will show. That union, while it lasted, was a most cordial, harmonious, and happy one, and I trust it was best under the circumstances for both parties to it. And so, while I do not recommend my example to youths of my age and immaturity, I yet do congratulate any, young or old, who are fortunate enough to have entered a marriage relationship as well-matched, as rich in experience, as full of enjoyment, as abundantly blessed, as the one under notice.

An Unfortunate Business Venture
Passing my next birthday, I settled down to the various duties of my position as manager and prospective owner of the paternal homestead, where I confidently expected to spend my days. During the year upon which I had now entered, one incident occurred which was especially trying to me at the time, being, as it was, my first business venture outside of the calling to which I had been trained from my early years. It was, under the circumstances, an unfortunate and discouraging affair, but it reminded me that it was not wise for me to assume responsibilities for which I had no qualification, either by native aptitude or acquired skill.

My father had a tenant in a small dwelling house on his premises who manufactured on a limited scale what were called cotton-plush waterproof gentlemen's hats. He suggested to me the idea of becoming at certain leisure seasons of the year a traveling salesman of his goods about the adjacent country, and made me believe that I could make handsome profits on them. In my condition this was desirable, and I eagerly caught at a proposition which promised to fatten my inconveniently lean purse. I therefore closed a bargain with him for a goodly stock of hats, procured an outfit of a suitable team, and made preparations for starting on an expedition for which, the more I thought of it and the nearer I came to it, the stronger was my conviction that I was in no wise capacitated. While meditating on what I had undertaken and apprehending probable failure, the particular kind of hat which I had to dispose of was superseded by a better one and became almost entirely unsalable at any price. So my ambitious plans in that direction proved an utter failure and my lean purse grew leaner instead of more plethoric thereby. With this narration I close the present chapter, as I do the record of the eighteenth year of my life.

CHAPTER 4

1821-1822

At the opening of my nineteenth year, my general life work and field of activity seemed to be definitely marked out and permanently settled, as already indicated. I had entered upon my chosen vocation and my temporal interests had been satisfactorily provided for. The needful preliminaries to the founding of a home of my own had received due attention. My religious status, in respect to belief, practice, and associative position, was supposed to be fixed in essential respects for all coming time. Little dreamed I of the changes awaiting me – even of those close at hand.

A Startling Vision
It was early in the season that the first and most important of them occurred – the one that perhaps above all others turned my thoughts into new channels and caused me to recast the whole program of my future career. I had retired alone to my chamber on a certain night, gone to bed, and fallen asleep. Not far from midnight I awoke to consciousness in a state of mind such as I had never before and have not since experienced. I was taking cognizance of myself and surroundings with feelings of inward exaltation as unimpassioned as they were sublime and strange, when I distinctly beheld a human form, clad in a white robe, standing just outside of a window in front of me opening to the south, some twelve feet distant. I gazed upon the unusual object with a sense of profound amazement, but without the least fear or trepidation. Scrutinizing the features of the apparent personage, a sublimated resemblance to my deceased brother Cyrus became perfectly distinct. As I continued looking, he (for the appearance had now assumed personality to me) slowly entered the window, which was closed, as if there were no obstruction and approached my bedside. His countenance was moderately luminous, but not dazzling. Every lineament was perfectly defined. His aspect was calm and benign, but impressively solemn. When almost near enough to touch me, he paused, fixed his eyes upon me for a moment, inclined slightly forward, pointed with his right hand directly at my forehead, and in the most significant manner, said: "Adin, God commands you to preach the Gospel of Christ to your fellow men; obey his voice or the blood of their souls will be required at your hands."

I was filled with unutterable awe; my hair seemed to stand on end; I remained mute and immovable, but felt thrilled through and through with spiritual emotion, yet with no distraction of timidity or fright. The moment the words were spoken, the appearance turned from me, moved slowly back through the window, and vanished from my sight.

Memorable and ineffaceable vision! How often since have I yearned for similar ones to confirm or direct me in the path of duty, but without being gratified! How many times have I wondered at this manifestation and puzzled my rational power to account for it; to make myself sure whether it was real or illusory, objective or subjective, divinely ordained and sent, or mysteriously originated in the wilds of my own imagination!

But in whatever way the light of eternity may answer these inquiries, the vision was irresistibly effective and powerful on my own mind and subsequent life. When my first emotions had subsided a little, I tried to make myself sure whether or not I was "in the body" and in the full possession of my senses. I soon succeeded in this so far as everything material and normal was concerned. Time, place, circumstances, and my own consciousness were unmistakable. The vision itself alone was mysterious. Could it be a dream or anything of similar nature? If so, it was radically unlike anything of the kind I had ever had before. After revolving the matter deliberately in my mind, I could not resist the conviction that, somehow or other, it was a reality and was fraught with divine significance and authority.

Five years before, the spirit of my brother had left its earthly tabernacle, taking its departure from that very chamber. He had been profoundly impressed for some time that it was his duty to preach, but reluctantly shrank from doing so, and felt some compunction on account of such hesitancy. Had God sent or permitted him to incite me to the same mission?

All the day following my strange experience, I was quite unlike my ordinary self, and though I went about my customary labors, nothing seemed quite natural to me. I was in what is called a spiritualized or exalted condition. When this passed away, I was left to the most serious and trying reflections. What ought I to do? What *could* I do? What *must* I do? My cherished plans and expectations were threatened with annihilation in a moment and seemingly by a mandate from heaven. I shrank from communicating with any one and confined all my thoughts, reasonings, inquiries, and convictions entirely within my own breast. There it was that I must make the momentous decision forced upon me first of all for myself. So I pondered, prayed, and wept in secret for weeks.

My case was a peculiar one. There was not a single motive or inducement of a temporal nature in favor of my becoming a religious teacher – a preacher of the gospel. Moreover, I had no attraction or inclination to that profession whatever, but on the contrary, a strong repulsion from it. When I looked at the subject in a moral and spiritual light, the office of a true minister of Christ appeared to be so pure, sacred, unselfish, and renunciative of all worldly ambition – so replete with humility, service, and earthly emptiness, that I felt myself utterly unfit for it and unworthy to assume it. When I looked at the ministry *as it was*, I saw that a large proportion of its functionaries, as I had known them, were deficient in mental power or marked by moral delinquencies, or compelled to frequent change of residence, alike annoying and vexatious, through ever recurring dissatisfaction and inharmonies. They were a pitiable class, I thought, in almost every temporal respect. Even the popular and petted few afforded me no encouragement to the step proposed to me. The good were so far above all the probable attainments I could ever make in the conditions of success that it was useless for me to try for them; the bad were so un-Christlike in essential characteristics that their presence in the pulpit was an abomination to me.

Besides, I had no clerical education and no prospect of any. There was no theological school or professor of divinity within my reach. If I became a preacher at all, it must be in the most unpopular denomination extant or in the world at large, without name or prestige – where I must work my way against wind and tide under adverse circumstances and on very humble fare. At the same time I was young, inexperienced, diffident, and certainly far too unspiritual to delight in those heavenly contemplations and anticipations which all true ministers of Christ feast on amid their labors for the souls redeemed through their instrumentality. Moreover, I had contracted marriage without the most distant thought on the part of either myself or my betrothed that she was to become the wife of a poor preacher, and to make her such without her cordial approval would be alike presumptuous and dishonorable.

All these things taken into consideration made it impossible for me to decide upon the work of the ministry without an intense mental struggle. I could have been easily won to the profession of law, or perhaps to medicine; but preaching the gospel was utterly distasteful and fearful to me. There was nothing that could bring me to it except a most unwelcome sense of duty and the woe of disobedience to a call from heaven – considerations I could in no wise ignore or escape. That vivid and awfully impressive vision hung perpetually in my memory and the solemn echoes of the closing words of my celestial visitant – "Or the blood of their souls will be required at your hands" – would not cease to reverberate in my mental ears. It was this that finally conquered me and determined my subsequent career. In regard to the result of my decision, I can truly say in the language of another, "Though I preach the gospel, I have nothing to glory of; for necessity is laid upon me, yea, woe is me if I preach not the gospel. For if I do this thing willingly, I have my reward; but if against my will, a dispensation is committed unto me."[1]

I have known of persons animated by a fervent aspiration to become preachers, who qualified themselves for the profession with pleasing alacrity, and who were filled with delight when able to enter upon its appropriate duties. Alas! It was not my lot to know anything of such joys. On the contrary, I shrank from my call, as stated, to begin with, and often in my long life I have risen to preach with such reluctance, with such a sense of spiritual poverty and tremor (perhaps unsuspected by my hearers), that I would fain have vanished out of sight. Yet, when forgetting myself in my subject or borne along on some favoring breeze of inspiration, I have experienced unqualified enjoyment in prosecuting my mission. And now, after all I have passed through as a minister and as a man, I am so far from regretting my mysterious, imperative call to the work, that I feel profoundly thankful that the dispensation was forced upon me. For it has laid me under a wholesome discipline and wrought in me a spiritual regeneration and growth of character of inestimable value. I can but hope it has done some, though I fear too little, good to those around me and to the world of mankind; to me it has been of unspeakable and, I trust, eternal benefit. God knew how to use and bless me against my own will and to him be praise, worship, and glory forevermore.

The First Sermon

But to take up again the thread of my narrative. Having yielded to my inexorable convictions of duty, I communicated the conclusion I had reached to my intended wife. She was naturally astonished, but manifested no opposition or revulsion, and calmly acquiesced in the new phase of our probable future. I also opened my mind to my father, who was evidently pleased with the new aspect of things and saw nothing in my determination which need interfere with the plan previously arranged between us; his idea being that I might fulfill all stipulated obligations to him, reside on the old homestead, be pastor of our own little church, and make occasional preaching excursions abroad. How different was all this from what actually transpired with me during the long years that were then before me!

To others I was entirely reticent concerning the change that had come to me until compelled to reveal it on the Sabbath before I first occupied a pulpit. That occurrence was another notable feature of this eventful year – another crisis, and a most trying one, in my earthly career. How it came to pass is worthy of mention.

Our church had no pastor during the summer of 1821, and there was very little regular preaching in the Ballou Meetinghouse, but we held in lieu thereof a conference or deacon's meeting there from Sunday to Sunday. My father usually presided on these occasions and led off in the exercises, while the lay members followed in due form with prayer, singing, or exhortation, as they were moved by the Holy Spirit or a sense of personal obligation. I had refrained almost entirely from taking any active part in the proceedings, suffering as I did intensely from diffidence and dread of responsibility. On a certain Sunday, however, about the first of July, I was inwardly impelled to rise at the close of the exercises and announce that with divine assistance I should preach in that house on the Sunday following, naming the hour.

No language can describe the oppressive and almost suffocating sensations which at the moment agitated me. My knees smote together, my voice and even my whole frame trembled, and I sank back into my seat seemingly paralyzed, as soon as the words were out of my mouth. To the little congregation of men and women gathered there, my notification was like a sharp electrical clap from a cloudless sky – utterly unexpected and astonishing. They went their way in different directions and trumpeted the strange tidings far and wide on every hand. No alarm of war could have been more eagerly heralded abroad through all the surrounding region. The die was now cast; the announcement was made and could not be recalled. I must stand up when the time came and at least *attempt* to preach. And I must speak from inspiration, as thoughts and words should be given me at the moment. A written discourse, or even an abstract on paper, was almost sacrilegious in my estimation. My education and all my conceptions of a truly God-called preacher prejudiced me against everything of the kind. I must speak right out of the heart and soul, even if I broke down in the effort. Happily, my text and subject were given me in a dream, which seemed to be in accord with my former mysterious experience. The text was, "Necessity is laid upon me; yea, woe is me if I preach not the gospel" (1 Corinthians 9:16). The subject was easily deducible from that passage.

The momentous day arrived. The weather was fine and when the hour of worship drew near the ancient sanctuary was packed with expectant people – ministers, deacons, church members, my young friends and acquaintances more or less interested in me and in the things of the religious life, with a mixed throng of outsiders drawn to the place by curiosity. I occupied the old-fashioned pulpit alone, wrought up to the highest pitch of conscientious purpose, anxiety, and self-consecration. I almost agonized in silent prayer when I saw the multitudes surging in. But confidence and assurances of help from above seemed to possess my soul as I rose to begin the service. I opened with prayer and proceeded in the usual order to the sermon, which was, of course, the chief matter of interest and concern. I talked for three quarters of an hour, receiving the most respectful and profound attention. My youth, sincerity, and zeal no doubt atoned in good part for my lack of sound matter and coherency, so that those present departed with good impressions and an increased personal respect for me. Probably most of them were disappointed for the better by this my first effort at preaching. My discourse, little of which I now recall, must have been more hortatory than dialectical, and quite inspirational in some of its appeals. But whatever it was in substance and form, it discharged a solemn duty, as I then believed, and introduced me to a long ministry of religious teaching. I crossed the threshold of a public career whose varied experiences, often trying and repellent, have always seemed, like the first, providentially inevitable.

It is true that my subsequent change of theological faith from Destructionism to Restorationism naturally relaxed somewhat the intensity of my early concern about the ruin of souls, and the strain of my anxiety lest my unfaithfulness should occasion that ruin. But reflection has always impressed me deeply with the assurance that the wiles and dangers of sin are sufficiently dreadful to demand my most earnest efforts to avert them, however certain it may be that they are to be overruled, conquered, and finally terminated by the operations of omnipotent divine wisdom and love. Moreover, the ultimate triumph of good over evil cannot be rationally hoped for on the assumption that sin is not inherently malignant or hateful, or that its natural tendency is not poisonous and deadly, or that it works its own cure and must of necessity eventually extinguish or destroy itself. On the contrary, the only well-grounded expectation of its final extinction and of the deliverance of all sentient, moral beings from its miserable bondage, is the persistent, all-conquering will, wisdom, and grace of God, operating not only directly but through various intermediate instrumentalities and means, among which the faithful preaching of those great truths and duties embodied in the gospel of Christ is undoubtedly one, and a most important one. So if I am called to this work, I cannot be excused, but "woe" is unto me still if I refuse to do it. My better hopes of the ultimate universal reign of holiness and happiness in the universe of the great Creator, supplanting those of only a partial victory of the right, good, and true over the wrong, evil, and false – a victory darkly palled with despair of anything better than annihilation for countless incurable sinners, rationalizes my faith without changing my duty or excusing my neglect of it. Nay, rather am I encouraged and strengthened to greater fidelity by assurances of final success. My grand concern, therefore, is to stand fast in my lot and be faithful to my trust; otherwise just condemnation and punishment await me.

It was not long after my first attempt at preaching that I began to be called upon to speak at home and abroad, both on Sundays and week days, in public houses of worship and in private dwellings. I also was soon employed to conduct funeral services – a department of ministerial work which has commanded much of my attention and energy through my entire life.

Meeting of the Connecticut Christian Conference

To enlarge my acquaintance with the denomination to which I was attached and its leading representatives, and to open the way to greater usefulness, I attended a meeting of what was called the Connecticut Christian Conference, which included the churches of the Christian Connexion in Rhode Island and Connecticut, held at Hampton in the latter State in the autumn of the same year. There I was received into the fellowship of the entire body of believers known by the general name of "Christians," as attested by a certificate of which the following is a copy:

> *To all whom it may concern*: I hereby certify that Adin Ballou of Cumberland, R.I., is a member in good standing and fellowship of the Connecticut Christian Conference.
>
> REUBEN POTTER, JR., Standing Scribe
> Cumberland, R. I., Sept. 1, 1821.

General Meeting of the Christian Connexion, 1821

A few weeks later, the general conference of the denomination, including all subordinate local conferences, churches, and ministers, met at New Bedford, Massachusetts. This, also, I attended, having for a traveling companion thither Elder Ebenezer Robinson,[2] an enthusiastic young minister from Greenwich, Massachusetts. On the way we visited Elder Daniel Hix, a venerable farmer-preacher of our order in Dartmouth, Massachusetts, with whom we spent the night, holding an evening service at his request in his meetinghouse, with a goodly audience in attendance. At the conference there was a large representation of the talent and wisdom of the denomination – its greater and lesser lights shining with varied luster from pulpit and council room, much to my edification and encouragement and to the general satisfaction.

Thence Brother Robinson and I walked to Boston – fifty-six miles – where we spent a few days and where we separated, not to meet again for many years; both of us meantime having changed our doctrinal views and ecclesiastical relations. This was my first visit to the Athens of America, then wonderful to me, but hardly to be compared in magnitude, wealth, and magnificence with what it is today.

Review of Hosea Ballou's "The New Birth"

About this time my ambition and zeal betrayed me into the folly of appearing in print as a polemic author against modern Universalism. Several of my neighbors were of this persuasion and a few of them great debaters in its support. They plied me with their publications to read and with their arguments to answer. Willing to investigate and hear all sides, I perused their books and tracts, and, confident of my ability to maintain my own cause and defend my convictions, I did not shrink from the controversy to which I was invited. I felt, too, that I was in the way of my duty and that I could do something to put down what I deemed a dangerous and rampant error. Having met and refuted to my own satisfaction my Universalist assailants at home, I deemed myself qualified to enter the lists against more notable champions of false doctrines abroad, should occasion and loyalty to truth seem to require it, as was not long after the case.

Rev. Hosea Ballou of Boston, a distant kinsman of mine, was at that time the master spirit of Universalism in what was known as its "ultra" phase.[3] He had been delivering in his church fortnightly lectures expository of his peculiar views, which had been promptly published and disseminated far and wide throughout the country. These were pressed on my attention by my Universalist friends and I had sharply combated some of the positions taken by this author, in conversational discussion.

Among the lectures was one delivered in January, 1820, upon "The New Birth,"[4] from the text in John 3:3: "Except a man be born again, he cannot see the kingdom of God," and this was handed me and commended as a masterpiece –

conclusive and unanswerable. In that lecture the author gave some sharp thrusts at the prevailing theological notions of regeneration, and claimed that Christ in the passage under notice treated of a work "effected in the rational powers and faculties of man, by means of information which operates to change the sentiments and remove the errors of the mind, and, of course, the affections of the heart." And in illustration of that view the lecturer said: "The gospel as Jesus proclaimed it a system of impartial salvation to the world, is now performing the miracle of regeneration and thousands are born again from the partial systems and creeds of the church to the acknowledgment of the universal mercy and grace of Zion's King." Virtually and practically, this made the Christian new birth to be a turning from the old faith in endless punishment to a belief in Universalism. This was too much for me to swallow or patiently endure. So I must needs face Goliath in polemic battle array. I therefore wrote and published a review of the "Lecture Sermon," in which, after endeavoring to refute the author's reasoning, I gave my own exposition of the subject under consideration.

On general principles, this youthful exploit of mine was unwise, crude, presumptuous, and of little consequence. I was too unskilled in rhetoric to write for the press, too inexperienced in theological criticism to set up as a public reviewer, too immature in mental discipline to expound the great doctrine of regeneration, and too obscure and uninfluential an opponent to command the notice of my adversary or the community at large.[6] And yet I am constrained to declare that, judged from my present standpoint, my pamphlet contained more truth and less error on the main question at issue than the sermon whose theory and reasoning it condemned. It is true that I was then a Destructionist theologically, and changed not long afterward to a Restorationist, but my views of spiritual regeneration were essentially the same after the change as before. I became a believer with Hosea Ballou in the grand idea of universal salvation, but never a convert to his peculiar ideas of regeneration, or to his favorite doctrine of no future punishment. The assumption that conversion from Partialistic dogmas to the Universalist faith is the new birth taught by Jesus Christ, no more commends itself to my acceptance now than when I foolishly published my review of the "Lecture Sermon."

Marriage

When the winter of 1821-22 approached, I engaged to teach the school in my native district and did so, beginning at the usual date early in December. During the term my marriage was solemnized, to wit, on the seventeenth of January, 1822. Among all the pleasant and joyous experiences connected with my teaching and wedding were some exceedingly disagreeable and trying ones, one of which was of sufficient importance to justify a brief notice in this connection.

The school opened under favorable auspices and went on for a time harmoniously and prosperously. With one or two exceptions, the pupils were docile, teachable, obedient, and kind. There was the best feeling between them and their teacher; all were happy together and excellent progress was made in the studies pursued. But unfortunately an evil star after a while cast its baleful glare across my horizon. It was as unexpected as it was disagreeable and humiliating.

A lad some twelve years old, of apparently defective organization and subject to half-insane fits of sullenness and ill-temper, of which I was ignorant at the time, who had given me no trouble, became suddenly refractory, stubborn, insubordinate, and difficult of control, requiring all the tact, ingenuity, and wisdom I could command, together with some more distinctively disciplinary and punitive measures, to bring him to a state of submissiveness – the whole ending by my sending him home full of rebellious anger and vengeful spite. To his parents he had a terrible tale of woe to tell, making them think he had been unjustly dealt with – outrageously abused indeed. His father, an ignorant, intemperate man, took up the matter with a firm determination to be revenged for my supposed ill-treatment of his boy. He made clamorous appeals in all directions for sympathy and for help to bring me to justice, but to little purpose. Even the greatly exaggerated and baseless stories of my alleged cruelty, savagery almost, failed to arouse any interest in his case except among people of his own stamp, and those "lewd fellows of the baser sort"[7] to be found in every community, who are rife for mischief, and who delight in some sort of quarrel or tumult, the occasion of which matters little with them.

Of course I was to be prosecuted and made to suffer to the full extent of the law. An astute, unscrupulous Justice of the Peace was found to issue a warrant against me, the execution of which was entrusted to a constable of kindred spirit and character. And to crown all, the conspirators planned to have the warrant served on me on the day of my approaching wedding and while the nuptial festivities were going on; all of which was kept a profound secret from the parties immediately concerned.

The program thus arranged was punctiliously carried out. The memorable seventeenth of January arrived. The betrothed couple with a large company of their relatives and friends were at the residence of the bride's parents in Smithfield, Rhode Island, where ample provision had been made for the occasion. The marriage vows were acknowledged, the marriage pledges were given and received, and the marriage union was declared to be legally consummated and recognized by Rev. Reuben Potter, Jr., who officiated at the nuptial altar. Everything proceeded joyously. Congratulations were extended to the bridal pair, and the wedding feast was going on, when, lo! the ministers of the law appeared without previous announcement and demanded, "in the name of the State of Rhode Island and Providence Plantations,"[8] that I should accompany them as their prisoner to Cumberland Hill, three miles distant, to answer before Mr. Jillson, Justice of the Peace, for certain misdemeanors, specified in the legal document they carried, of which it was claimed I was guilty, and await his squireship's pleasure.

At first I was inclined to comply with the requisition without any delay. But upon taking counsel of some of our older and wiser guests who were amply competent to give it, I declined leaving the house. Whereupon the chief officer of the invading party grew pertinacious and intimated that he had the aid necessary to enforce his orders if they were not peaceably obeyed. I appealed to Hon. Thomas Mann,[9] Judge of the Court of Common Pleas, one of those present, who gave the person clothed with a little brief authority[10] to understand that he was exceeding his powers and had no grounds for compelling me to go with him, if I could only give bonds to appear before the justice named at a designated time, which I was entirely willing and ready to do. "You had better accept such guarantees," said the judge to the constable, "and go home." The latter, finding himself confronted by one greater in authority than he was, became at once supple and compliant, accepted the pledge, and with his fellow conspirators left; but not, however, till they had partaken of an undeserved portion of the wedding feast.

The issue of this tragico-comical affair was as complimentary to me as it was humiliating and condemnatory to my accuser and his abettors. I went, as agreed upon, before Justice Jillson, the constable and witnesses being present, but it was found that the charge against me was so groundless, so unsupported by requisite evidence, and so certain to be met by triumphant counter-evidence, that even he, the hitherto supple tool of the conspirators, refused to have the case come to trial, declaring that he would dismiss the complaint and consider the warrant annulled. The prevailing sentiment of the better citizens in the community was manifestly in my favor, deeming the proceedings against me malicious and shameful, and all parties to them worthy of abhorrence and contempt. This episode over, I took up again the duties of my position as teacher and carried the term of school through to a happy and successful conclusion.

Housekeeping

So well pleased were my friends and the general public with the results of my labors in the schoolroom that I was immediately approached with a proposition to open a private school in the same place and continue it for a few of the following months. As circumstances seemed to render it expedient that I should abandon the plan of settling down upon the old homestead with my parents and succeed to my father's estate and occupation, that plan was now given up and the contemplated private school was started, specific charges being made per week for tuition.

It was also deemed best that my wife and I should set up housekeeping on our own account, and we accordingly did so in a small dwelling owned by my father near the ancestral residence; my nineteenth birthday finding us happily installed in our new home. Our means were very limited, as my income was small, but our wants were comparatively few and our expectations in no wise extravagant, so that we probably enjoyed quite as much in our newly-begun domestic life as most of those at this day who start out under more auspicious worldly circumstances in general, and with abundant or perhaps princely resources at their command. I preached often here and there, but received little pecuniary compensation therefor; and teaching, my most productive source of supply, afforded me but a small revenue. Moreover, my *hat speculation* before mentioned, had imposed a heavy financial burden on me, which was increased by the publication of my "Review." I was getting ahead in dear-bought experience certainly (perhaps in useful knowledge), but not in the means of maintaining a family. We were comfortable so far as present necessities were concerned and hopeful for the future. Nor were our hopes wholly profitless and vain. Even our annoyances and trials were not without profit to us.

> There's a divinity that shapes our ends,
> Rough hew them as we will.[11]

This is something more than poetry; it is a universal truth. I realize it in my own case. I hewed awkwardly, but Providence shaped results. So it was in my youth; so it has been through my earthly pilgrimage. I have been led by a way I knew not and in paths of dubious aspect, but thus far, through every dark defile and fearful pass into bright and peaceful resting places.

This chapter has detailed the experiences of only a single year; the next one will be scarcely less replete with incidents for a similar period.

CHAPTER 5

1822-1823

During the continuance of my school, which closed about June 15, I preached on the Sabbath, either in the Ballou Meetinghouse nearby, or in the general vicinity, not farther away than Providence on the south and adjoining Massachusetts towns on the north. My discourses, doctrinally, were along the lines indicated in a former chapter, and yet my mind began to be exercised with some doubts whether, after all, Destructionism, as the final doom of the impenitent wicked, was really taught in the Bible.

Winchester's Dialogues
Some time before this, my wife's mother, one of the best of women and a sincere Restorationist withal, had asked me if I would read Winchester's *Dialogues on Universal Restoration*.[1] "Certainly," said I, "and I am sure such a doctrine can be easily refuted." She made no reply, but smiled at my self-confidence and handed me the volume. I went through it carefully, but with the persuasion that it was full of error and would make little impression on me.

I was surprised, however, to find it written in such a serious, religious, and candid spirit as to deeply interest and gratify me. Unlike most of the Universalist publications which had been urged upon my attention, there was not a sentence in it that seemed to denounce or ridicule what I called strictly religious convictions and feelings – regeneration, experimental piety, or consecration to God. Moreover, I was struck with the moral grandeur of the author's distinctive doctrine and the force of his answer to some leading objections to it. Yet I was not convinced that he was right, nor consciously shaken in my own belief. His argument seemed to be spent chiefly against the dogma of endless punishment, which I considered even then as indefensible as it was horrible. I flattered myself at the time that my own doctrine of the annihilation of those who died impenitent was so much stronger than that of never-ending misery or that of ultimate universal redemption that it must triumph over both in a fair contest. And I said so when I returned the *Dialogues* to my good mother-in-law. She was not disposed to debate the matter with me, but leave all to time and my own reflective mind. I now see what I was then unconscious of, that Winchester's ideas had imparted their leaven to my understanding too effectually to be wholly neutralized by my prejudices. And I would drop the hint to such religious inquirers as are determined never to embrace Restorationism that Winchester's *Dialogues* is too seductive and convincing a work for them to read, without jeopardy to their opposing faith.

Theological Questionings

The fact that I had published a review of Rev. Hosea Ballou's sermon on the "New Birth," naturally opened the way for further discussions with my Universalist neighbors. Several of them were fond of and skillful in debate and they missed no good opportunity of testing my ability in the same line. And on my part, I never declined to take issue with them. Foremost among these disputants were Lewis Metcalf, Luke Jenckes, and Levi Ballou,[2] the first two resident in Wrentham, Massachusetts, and the last in Cumberland, Rhode Island; all of them known by me from early childhood. They were elderly men, uneducated in the scholastic sense, but naturally strong-minded, shrewd, sharp reasoners, and well posted in all matters pertaining to Universalism. Winchester's opinions and claims they repudiated, cleaving with great tenacity and admiration to the new-school, no-future-punishment expositors and doctrinaires.[3] I thought myself competent to battle with these men, especially on their own peculiar platform. They argued mainly from Scripture and reason, both of which I could use to their frequent perplexity and discomfiture. But I found that I had one weak point to defend and that was that an all-perfect God, infinite in power, wisdom, and love, who really willed the final holiness and happiness of all humankind, and raised up Christ to redeem all, must needs ultimately annihilate most of them as incurable sinners and so practically confess his impotency and utter failure in that important behalf, so far as they were concerned. My opponents pushed me hard on this point whenever they could. And all I could do was to contend that the Bible taught the doctrine and that it was the best thing God could do without depriving mankind of moral freedom – an evil out of the question. When brought fairly to bay this was my only refuge.

At length, however, I began to have some doubts whether, after all, the Bible did, on the whole, teach what I claimed, and also whether it were absolutely certain that God must destroy man's moral freedom if he finally, by his saving might, regenerated all who left this state of existence unreconciled to himself. These doubts were too slight at first to affect me much, and especially so long as I firmly held the opinion that man's earth-life was his only probation for eternity. This opinion my ultra Universalist opponents did not attack with much force, for though they scouted it as groundless, their phase of Universalism led them to expend their strength in proving that the Bible taught no such thing as sinfulness and punishment after death under any possible circumstances. All this to me was labor lost, for I was just as certain then as now that if the Bible, particularly the New Testament, does not teach that a portion of mankind will wake up condemned sinners in the next life, it teaches nothing that common sense can understand. And I think now as I thought then, that many of the expositions whereby no-future-punishment Universalists explained away what are generally considered threatenings of future retribution, are specious, unsound, and some of them absurd. I should never have been converted from my old belief by any such interpretation of the sacred record.

But it was impossible for me to get over the weak point mentioned to my own satisfaction, however successfully I could confute my adversaries on their distinctive ground. Recurring to Winchester's *Dialogues*, I felt all the force of their reasoning and felt it against the doctrine of annihilation as well as against that of endless misery; for though the former was incomparably preferable to the latter, it was an alternative involving in less degree the same principles, difficulties, and objections, and was bound to go to the wall when it came to be submitted to the tribunal of my more enlightened, rational, and moral understanding, as was the case at an early day.

Meeting of the Southern Association of Universalists, 1822

I think it was in the month of June during the year now in review that the organization known as the Southern Association of Universalists held one of its sessions at West Wrentham, Massachusetts. My friend, Levi Ballou, kindly invited me to attend its public exercises. I accepted his invitation, but heard nothing from the preachers on the occasion that made much impression on me or exerted any appreciable influence in the way of effecting a change in my theological convictions.[4]

I was introduced to several of the ministers, among whom was Rev. Hosea Ballou 2d, as he was then called.[5] I had a conversation of much interest with him and took a decided liking to him at the time and thenceforth through life, though we did not sail in the same ecclesiastical ship except for a brief session. He was a candid and calm as well as a close reasoner and was more of a Restorationist than an ultra Universalist in his views, though he remained in continuous fellowship with the new-school men of the sect. Albeit he argued with me as one holding the idea of future retribution as well as that of final restoration and begged me to remember that the denomination embraced both believers and disbelievers in that view of the divine government, not making either a test of fellowship. I must therefore ponder the arguments on both sides and if I could accept the doctrine of universal salvation, do so on grounds that seemed to me reasonable and satisfactory. Should I adopt Restorationist views, I should not be obliged to endorse the other, and should be regarded the equal in every respect of those differing from me by all intelligent believers in the final redemption of all men.

Searching the Scriptures

I returned home under some conviction that I might be in error concerning the consummation of all things, but by no means converted from my former belief. I felt, however, that I must thoroughly investigate the whole subject, and at once set myself about the task, becoming a very close and anxious student. I took my

Bible and went through it carefully from Genesis to Revelation, noting down under three distinct heads, viz. endless punishment, final destruction of the wicked, and universal salvation, every text which seemed to favor each doctrine or which I knew to be quoted as such. I also noted the passages supposed to teach that this life is man's only probation for eternity or that there is no change from sin to holiness after death. The result was that I found the smallest numerical array of texts under the head of endless punishment, the largest under the head of the destruction of the wicked, and the next largest in favor of the final salvation of all. To my astonishment the word "probation" was not in the Bible, nor a single passage evidently intended to teach the doctrine that this life is man's only probationary state, and only about half a dozen passages from the letter of which that view could be plausibly inferred – none of these absolutely requiring such inference.

Respecting the texts seeming to favor endless punishment, I learned that their strength depended mainly on words often having a limited signification or on intensified forms of expression, employed in a figurative, impassioned sense, and that none of them were obviously designed to affirm that dogma as an article of faith; in fine, that they were highly-wrought, glowing descriptions of retribution in its general aspects, rather than positive and definite declarations of divine truth concerning it. The numerous passages apparently teaching the destruction of the wicked were also found to be of the intensive, figurative class, in which the mere sound of the words gave them force – words used elsewhere with a meaning altogether different from that of utter annihilation, and not one of them obviously employed to denote an item of doctrinal belief.

The passages that seemed to favor universal salvation were of various kind. Some commonly used in that behalf had no force whatever; others might be construed so as to support either of the three theories under examination; but there were none which I could be certain were designed to assert the doctrine absolutely as divinely revealed truth. There were, however, a large number, the principles and spirit of which would consistently harmonize with no other view. These related (1) to the nature, attributes, and moral character of God; (2) to his will, purpose, and design towards mankind; (3) to the mission, office, exaltation, and triumph of Christ; (4) to the essence and spirit of God-likeness, i.e. the moral imitation of God as the only true personal righteousness; (5) to the aim or purpose of divine rebuke, chastisement, judgment, and retribution, as beneficent and reformatory; and (6) to a grand prophetic era, in which there shall be no sin, evil, pain, but God "be all in all."[6]

I perceived that these six classes of Scripture testimony were of a different nature and scope from those seeming to teach the other two doctrines. They were not incidental statements, descriptions, or representations of divine retribution, nor figurative, intensified, impassioned forms of phraseology, but were declarations of great truths to be religiously held, and of fundamental principles demanding the broadest application both in faith and practice. Their weight did not depend on mere sound of words, it was intrinsic. They did not express a simple, positive, theological conclusion in respect to God's final disposal of the human race, but they necessitated the conclusion that it must be a disposal perfectly benevolent, impartial, wise, and good; perfectly accordant with his own will and purpose; and perfectly triumphant through Christ over all opposing forces, hindrances, and obstacles. I saw, therefore, that it was not warrantable to construe even the most intense, highly-wrought representations of sin and punishment as finalities, or as frustrating the ultimate divine purpose, or as rendering in any way doubtful the absolute moral perfections of God.

Conversion to Universalism

I was now in a tight place, with a flood of light beaming on my mind and a host of new ideas taking possession of my understanding. The whole subject presented itself in an aspect original and astonishing. The plain, unavoidable issue came home to me: Is the belief that God will finally blot out of existence all who die in sin reconcilable with the fundamental truths and principles unquestionably declared in those six classes of texts? And is any other belief than that he will sooner or later render all human beings holy and happy consistent with those testimonies? Regarded in the spirit of truth and unprejudiced reason, the case looked very much as if I must yield.

But why had I not seen the subject in this light before? I had been as sincere and honest in my desire for truth in the past as now. Why had so many millions of pious and learned Christians in all ages of the church held the final loss in some form or other of all that die out of Christ? I was then ignorant of the fact that many eminent Christian Fathers, including the great Origen, were unequivocal advocates of universal restoration.[7]

Furthermore, if I became a believer in the final holiness and happiness of all mankind, I should have to avow and preach it. In that case I must renounce all I had thus far professed and contended for to the contrary. I should shock, aggrieve, and alienate my fellow Christians, including my nearest and dearest friends. I should be denounced as a changeling and an apostate, as others had been. And with whom should I find myself presently in fellowship but those whom I had regarded as rejecters of experimental religion and whose phase of Universalism was radically repulsive to me? Then arose the strong internal suggestion: "You are a victim of Satanic delusion and that makes universal salvation look probable to you. Take care how you advance." I trembled and shrunk backward. Objections and doubts rolled in upon me. I wept, prayed, and reviewed the ground I had gone over again and again till I was well nigh distracted. I could not eat, drink, sleep, or appear like myself. I grew pale and wore an anxious, sickly look, to the serious concern of my wife and friends, who knew nothing of the conflict that was raging within me. My solicitude, doubt, and fear brought me to a poise of suspense and disquietude hardly to be endured.

In this dreadful condition I wandered off by myself one day to a retreat out of human sight (I can never forget the place), and gave full vent to my emotions, bordering almost on despair. A voice came to me, saying: "Kneel and pray."

"Alas!" thought I, "for what shall I pray?"

"For deliverance – for heavenly light and guidance. Pray that if this be a Satanic delusion it may be dispelled; but that if the Spirit of Truth is leading you into more glorious truth, you may not resist it; and that all doubts be banished from your mind."

I did as directed, breathing forth my petitions with all the fervor of which I was capable. In a moment the heavens seemed to open above my head; an inexpressibly sweet influence flowed in upon my soul; the whole subject became luminous, every doubt vanished, a vision of the final triumph of good over evil shone forth in majestic splendor, and my heart was filled with transports of joy. I was supremely blest and if I could have commanded an archangel's trumpet, the whole world would have heard the sublime gospel then and there revealed to me. My faith was conclusively sealed, and I have never since felt one serious doubt of the final universal holiness and happiness of all the immortal children of God. I returned to the house with a buoyant step and a joyful spirit, told my wife what had transpired, and she rejoiced with me.

A letter from Hosea Ballou 2d reached me about this time in reply to one addressed to him asking an explanation of certain of my strongest proof texts in support of Destructionism. But the work had been taken out of his hands and was already accomplished – more effectually than he possibly could have done it. His letter was an excellent one, but it would not have met my mental and moral wants as they had been supplied from the eternal world. It was valuable of its kind, as was also his then recently published discourse on Galatians 3:8, a copy of which he sent me. But neither of these would have overcome wholly my objections or removed my principal difficulties, because they did not deal so much with fundamental principles as they did in special expositions and polemic subtleties, some of which I should then have deemed unsound or at least inconclusive.

Excommunication

I had now a stormy scene to pass through with my brethren, relatives, and friends.[8] No sooner was it known that I had embraced the doctrine of Universal Salvation than they were filled with astonishment and overwhelmed with grief. All the fair promise I had given of gospel usefulness was to their minds blasted in the opening bloom. My own father was first and foremost among the aggrieved. I expected he would be, and thought it my duty to be prompt and frank with him and let him receive the painful news from my own lips. It was the bitterest cup he had ever been called upon to drink. I have no doubt that my death would have been more endurable to him. I was his favorite son and had flowered out into a promising minister of the gospel, as he understood and prized it. Profoundly sincere and firmly established in his religious convictions, he was no less so in his prejudices against Universalism in all its forms. He had not a doubt that it was of the Devil nor that I was the deluded victim of his Satanic majesty's wiles. He remonstrated, rebuked, denounced, pleaded, and deplored, but could not move me. Finally, in his impatient vexation, he threatened to disinherit me if I did not renounce such a damnable error. This had no effect whatever upon me. I was so insensible to such a motive that it did not even disturb my equanimity, for I had counted the cost and had received a special assurance from above that I should never be forsaken. I therefore replied in perfect kindness that I had no claim to any of his property, that he had a perfect right to give it to whomsoever he chose; but of this I was sure, that if I had no earthly father to provide for me, I had a heavenly one who would never fail me. He was sorely vexed by this answer and retorted, "You will find you have no father in heaven to do you any good in the way you are going."

I merely rejoined, "I can trust him implicitly." This was the last in a series of conversational debates I ever had with him. He had said and done all he could to save me and now gave me up as hopelessly lost. He, however, became sorry for his passionate threat of disinheritance and, some months after, wished my ever kind mother to tell me he should never cast off a child of his for difference of opinion. Meantime, he stood aloof from me and did not become fully reconciled till ten years had elapsed. My mother did not accept my new faith and probably regretted the change, but treated me with unaltered maternal affection and kindness. On the other side, my parents-in-law rejoiced in my conversion to their own cherished faith, and gave me nothing but sympathetic encouragement.

My father next felt it to be his painful duty to have me publicly disowned by the church and formally deposed from its membership as dangerous to its welfare. He dissuaded all he could from holding personal discussions with me, as it would be of no use to me and might unsettle their own minds; for, he said, I was very adroit and seductive in argument. Most of my friends were thereby deterred from coming to see me at all, but good Deacon Nathaniel Aldrich, who was once a member of our church, but who seceded on account of his strong Calvinistic views, had so much concern for me that he resolved upon a personal interview. My father, who never liked him very well, when he announced his intention, advised against it and signified that it would be labor lost. Yet the deacon was not to be deterred from his purpose; so he called upon me and gave me the full benefit of his counsel. Finding that I was unconvinced by his argument, and unmoved by his solemn admonition, he said he must leave me with grief to my chosen delusion. He deplored my apostasy and consequent doom, but could do no more for my salvation. I had taken pains to draw out his Calvinism in its baldest form, and now that he was about to leave with such despairing professions of sorrow for my fate, calmly said: "Why do you allow yourself to be so much distressed on my account?

If I am one of the elect, you cannot doubt my final salvation; and if I am one of the reprobates, it will be for the glory of God and the good of the universe that I should be lost. Why do you distrust the sovereignty of God, the wisdom of his decrees, or the certainty that my destiny will be just what you should rejoice in, whether I am consigned to heaven or hell?" His only response was a sigh!

He reported my case as hopeless to my father, who, after he left, said to my mother: "Aldrich has been talking with Adin and he got his mouth shut up pretty quick, as I knew he would." Father abhorred Calvinism almost as much as he did Universalism, and probably derived more pleasure from the recusant deacon's discomfiture than he could have done from his success.

At length I was summoned to appear before the church during the first week in August, 1822. The meeting was held in the same venerable house of worship in which I first heard preaching and where I delivered my first sermon. A full attendance of members was present and my father laid the case before them as one perfectly plain to them all and requiring no investigation or trial. To his heartfelt affliction and regret, I had become a Universalist. This I had openly avowed and persisted in, notwithstanding the most faithful admonition. The church could give no fellowship or countenance to that doctrine, my acceptance of it excluded me from the fold of Christ, and it was the solemn duty of the church to disown me. Discussions were unnecessary; action and record only were required. I asked the privilege of being heard in explanation and defense of my views, which I did not wish to disguise, but this was denied me, my father saying that he well knew my ability and skill at talking and should afford me no opportunity to unsettle and mislead the young and draw susceptible minds into my snare. The others concurring, I saw that the whole proceeding was a solemn farce and requested them to finish their work without the least delay. They did so and I became to them "as a heathen man and a publican."[9]

Whether the Connecticut Conference, whose letter of fellowship I held, ever took any action on my case, I do not remember. Probably not, as my disownment by the Cumberland church was deemed conclusive. For my part, I was so disgusted by that action that I did not care a straw for all the excommunications in the world. Good Elder Benjamin Taylor of Swansea was the only one of my old "Christian" brethren, who, to my knowledge, regretted and condemned the proceedings against me as utterly repugnant to the very foundation on which the denomination professed to stand, viz. "*No creed but the New Testament*, interpreted by each individual for himself, and a practical Christian life." Father Taylor was right – consistent with the often-boasted platform of the order and with his own large soul. He said: "Our young brother Ballou should have been treated tenderly, reasoned with kindly, borne with patiently, without ever being censured, much less disowned, except for un-Christian conduct." If I had been so treated, I should in all probability have spent my days as a minister of the Christian Connexion.

Objectionable Features of Universalism

For it was in some important respects an unnatural and most disagreeable transition for me to leave my old, fondly-cherished ecclesiastical relations and become identified with the Universalist denomination as it was at that period of its history. For while I had come to believe in what might be regarded the distinguishing doctrine of that body, there were many opinions, notions, theories, put forth and urged by its leading spirits as correlative deductions from, if not essential adjuncts of, that doctrine, with which I had not one particle of sympathy, but rather an instinctive repugnance to them. Those leading spirits were strongly opposed to the idea of any future disciplinary punishment; explained away, often by far-fetched interpretations, all the passages of Scripture which teach retribution after death; ridiculed revivals of religion; held all spiritual experience to be superstitious or fanatical; and expended nearly all their effort in proving, argumentatively, the naked tenet of universal salvation, as if that were the whole of the gospel of Christ. And this result was made to depend more on the arbitrary will and decree of God than on any searching process of regeneration whereby each soul must have a conscious struggle of choice or consent and be brought into a state of personal holiness. Death was to finish sin and the resurrection to inaugurate perfection of character and blessedness. These peculiarities of faith and practice were repulsive to my spiritual instincts and habits of thought. They had not exerted one particle of influence in aid of my conversion. During that whole experience, from inception to consummation, I had not had a single doubt that mankind would be called to judgment after death for the deeds done in the body; nor that most of the texts (not all), commonly understood to refer to retribution in the invisible world, did so refer; nor that death and the resurrection affected chiefly the mortal and immortal organisms inhabited by the soul in its different states of existence rather than its absolute moral character; nor that men must be born again out of animal selfishness into the love of God and man in order to enter the kingdom of heaven; nor that constant self-sacrifice must be practiced as a necessary condition of true holiness and happiness, here and hereafter. The much-vaunted notion that the destruction of Jerusalem was the grand crisis of divine judgment and retribution to which Christ and the apostles chiefly referred in their warnings against sin, did not commend itself then any more than it does now to my understanding. In short, I was not converted to the no-future-punishment phase of Universalism, nor by any arguments therefrom derived, but to pure Restorationism by reasons which had no affinity with those upon which that phase of the doctrine was based.

Welcome by the Universalists

But notwithstanding all this, I entered into the pale and fellowship of the denomination indicated – compelled to that alliance by stress of circumstances. I was driven out of the Christian Connexion by the honest narrow-mindedness of its members. The vast majority of them could not at that time tolerate the doctrines I had espoused. One must believe in destructionism or in endless torment, else in their judgment he could not be a Christian. On this ground, in spite of their declaration against all creeds save the Bible as each individual understood it and their boast that their sole test of fellowship was a Christian life, I was excluded from their Order. On the other hand, I was hailed and welcomed by the Universalists as a convert to their faith, although I scarcely held any views in strict accordance with what was generally believed among them except the single tenet of final universal holiness and happiness. I told them frankly how far I was in agreement with them and that on many points I differed from most of them. "All right," they said; "there are various opinions among our people upon those minor particulars, but we allow the largest liberty. Come with us, fear nothing, and feel at home." Thus behind me was the merciless outcry, "Begone from our midst," and before me a thousand greetings of hospitality and assurances of welcome.

As a religious outcast therefore, with no power to assume and maintain an independent position, I sought the only place of refuge open to me, and accepted the only proffered welcome and fellowship, casting in my lot with my new-found friends – the Universalists. In doing so, I did not feel that I was compromising any moral principle, or yielding any point of honor, all necessary explanations, positions, and concessions having been interchanged and clearly understood. Still I was unfortunately situated, inasmuch as the masses of my new allies, like most masses, were too indiscriminating to appreciate my peculiarities, while I was so placed as to be perpetually tempted to yield my scruples and conform to the prevailing sentiment of the body with which I had associated myself. And this temptation was all the more seductive and potent in that so much geniality and kindness were shown me. With ample liberty to differ, and with so many expressions of cordial friendship, it was much easier to agree and conform than to nurse dissent. Such was the course things took with me, and ere long I became to outward appearance completely amalgamated with the Universalists as a sect. Whatever dislikes and misgivings I had at first gradually diminished by closer intercourse till they ceased almost to exert any perceptible influence over me. In this I gained social power, but probably lost some religious stamina and strength of moral purpose. But whether, on the whole, more were lost than gained to me and to the world remains to be seen in the light of the great future.

A Universalist Minister

It may be asked what I was doing in other respects during this transition period. As soon as I began to doubt seriously the soundness of my theology, I suspended preaching altogether, and for a time gave myself wholly to study and investigation. This taxed my health and strength to the utmost. After passing the crisis and finding myself physically enfeebled, I began to have some anxiety in regard to my temporal affairs. My funds were low, I was burdened with debt, and the outlook, in a worldly point of view, was far from encouraging. I had many dark hours on this account, but in one of the darkest of them, when I was in secret deploring my dubious earthly prospects, a voice again came to me, saying: "Fear not, my child. I will never leave thee nor forsake thee."[10] The effect was electrifying and rapturous. My soul was thrilled to ecstasy and I felt the most perfect trust in divine providence and the most heartfelt joy.

The promise was soon after so fully verified to me, and has been through life, that I should deem myself basely ungrateful to doubt that it was from heaven. For I had hardly passed through this experience when an offer came to me from my uncle, Daniel Sayles of Franklin, Massachusetts, already mentioned, to work for him during haying time according to my strength, it being mutually understood that I was unable to render full service and should receive pay accordingly. This tided me over the shallow waters and enabled me to provide for myself and family until I could begin preaching again under new auspices and with assurances of a remunerative income equal to my necessities. And this good fortune visited me at an early day.

After becoming fully established in the belief of the final triumph of the all-redeeming grace of God, I wrote to my friend, Rev. Hosea Ballou 2d, in reply to his letter, referred to on a preceding page, announcing the fact and giving somewhat in detail the circumstances attending the change through which I had passed. The substance of my letter he published in the *Universalist Magazine*, Boston, of which he was one of the editors, the last week in August, 1822, I think, under the heading of "Another conversion in the ministry."[11]

This brought me before the public in my new ecclesiastical position, and advertised me far and wide among friends and foes as a Universalist minister. As a consequence, I immediately began to receive invitations to preach in the general region round about, which I was very glad to accept so far as health, time, and convenience would allow. My first discourse under new auspices was delivered in the Elder Williams meetinghouse, West Wrentham, Massachusetts, to a crowded audience, it having been extensively notified that "Young Ballou would give on the occasion the reasons for his change of theological faith." I also preached at Bellingham, Cumberland Hill, Woonsocket Falls, Providence, and other places in Rhode Island and Massachusetts, not far distant from my home, and officiated at several funerals in the same general vicinity, not lacking for employment in my adopted profession.

Visit to Hosea Ballou

During the autumn I made a second visit to Boston and its environs, being a guest for some days in the family of Rev. Hosea Ballou 2d, of Roxbury, where I was kindly received and treated with all the courtesy and hospitality I could desire.

Nor ought I to say less of his great-uncle, often called "Father Hosea," and other clergymen of the denomination with their families to whom I was introduced. I was invited to preach in each of the Ballou pulpits and perhaps one or two others near by. Of my impressions of the younger Hosea and my attractions to him, I have already spoken.

"Father Hosea," with whom I also visited, was a very genial man in the midst of his large family, and fond of pleasantry in common conversation. He was then in mid-life, being about fifty-one years old. His oldest son was already a clergyman in Vermont, his second son just entering the profession; while the youngest was a little boy in his frock, running about the house. One of his daughters was married and the others were at home, gracing the domestic circle.[12]

He was a man of sensible, plain habits; living comfortably, but not extravagantly. He was a great lover of children, and governed his household admirably, with a gentle but commanding discipline. He had a large store of anecdotes, and although not a great talker knew well how to keep up conversational discourse and entertainment when surrounded by his friends. He was not, however, inclined to intrude his theological peculiarities upon his visitors, much less to indoctrinate his juniors with them. So during this visit not a word was said to me on the subject of no future retribution, which, if broached, might have raised a discussion between us.

This pleasant visit had an indirect but strong tendency to blunt my convictions and scruples, or as might be said, soothe my prejudices against ultra Universalism. I was silenced, too nearly, by so much respect and kindness, and was drawn too far into acquiescence with men from whose teachings I was afterwards obliged strongly to dissent, much to my cost.[13] And what was worse, I became infected with an almost groundless prejudice against Revs. Paul Dean,[14] Edward Turner,[15] Charles Hudson,[16] and others – the defenders of Restorationism as opposed to ultra Universalism. A controversy had already been opened between the parties representing these two *isms*, in which some personalities appeared. And these, which were of trifling importance as related to the real point at issue, were magnified by the ultra leaders and made to seem the fundamental reasons or motives of their opponents in inaugurating and continuing the controversy. In fine, the Restorationist champions were represented as mere ambitious factionists and mischief-makers in the order, with no honest, solemn convictions of doctrinal faith or of Christian duty. This was a gross injustice to them, as I afterwards learned, for which there was no reasonable excuse. Nevertheless, this visit had the effect of making me for a time a sharer in that injustice to my subsequent regret and sorrow, causing me to think ill of the Restorationist party and their proceedings, when I ought to have sympathized and acted with them – at least on the main question at issue.

New Fellowship, New Friends

Returning from Boston, I preached from time to time during the autumn as opportunity in the surrounding towns offered, and in the winter had charge of a school in West Wrentham, adjacent to my home. New religious friends flocked around me from all directions and seemed anxious to make up for the loss of old ones, deserving, by numerous manifestations of regard and kindness to me and my wife, an indelible record of heartfelt appreciation and gratitude. Olney Ballou,[17] Levi Ballou, and Luke Jenckes, with their families, belong to this category, as do others of less prominence. My always first and foremost friend, my dear mother, never changed.

After the close of my school, perhaps in February, I received a request to preach one or two Sundays to the First Universalist Society in Boston. Their design seemed to be to hear different clergymen for short periods each, with a view of inviting the more acceptable of them to serve subsequently as candidates in anticipation of a call and settlement – their pastorate being already, or about to be, vacated by Rev. Paul Dean, who had filled it for several years most acceptably.[18] I occupied the pulpit as desired, then gave way to others, but was afterwards asked to supply it for six months, of which note will be made in the next chapter.

CHAPTER 6

1823-1825

My twenty-first year opened with an arrangement to preach regularly in several different places once or more in each month, viz. in West Medway, in Bellingham, and in different neighborhoods of Mendon, South Parish (now Blackstone), all in Massachusetts. I had warm friends and admirers in these several localities who were very desirous of sharing my ministrations as often as possible. My family residence still continued to be the tenement house of my father, already mentioned.

In the place first named, the Universalists owned a small meetinghouse jointly with the Baptists. In Bellingham Center our friends were striving to obtain the occasional use of the only house of worship there, the occupancy of which was in dispute between the town and the Baptist society.[1] Pending the settlement of the matter, our meetings, by my advice, were held in the hall of the adjacent tavern. At South Bellingham, services were in a schoolhouse. In the factory village of South Parish, Mendon, now East Blackstone, we occupied a store-loft furnished by my friend Col. Joseph Ray and his partners. I also spoke in the hall of the Henry Thayer tavern, Five Corners; in Capt. Aaron Burdon's hall, Chestnut Hill; or in some schoolhouse in that part of the town.[2] Occasionally I lectured in other neighborhoods of my general region.

In the principal of these places, my friends contributed to my support at the rate of five or six dollars per Sunday; in others, and for lectures, a smaller sum. As I never dictated prices or compensation for my religious ministrations, what I received was freely given, was the better enjoyed, and was all I had any right to expect under the circumstances. In other respects I was encouraged and cheered by the cordial interest manifested in my public exercises as well as in my private welfare.

The Furious Priest Reproved
On the third Sunday in May, 1823, a somewhat exciting and memorable occurrence transpired in Bellingham Center which it may be well to record. The town claimed to own and have rightful control of the meetinghouse, and had voted that the Universalists might occupy it one Sunday in each month. But the Baptists contended that it belonged wholly to them and were unwilling the others should use it at all. There had been much wrangling in the matter, and the case had been

submitted to the courts for adjudication, but was not yet settled.³ So the quarrel was still on between the home parties when I engaged to preach there. I told my friends that I should avoid all proceedings which savored of trickery, force, or indecorum, and occupy the disputed pulpit as a gentleman and a Christian or not at all.

On the third Sunday in April, large and excited crowds of both parties assembled to watch proceedings and see what would be the issue. The Rev. Abial Fisher was pastor of the Baptist church, a man of large combativeness, pluck, and obstinacy, and he determined that the Universalists should not occupy the house on that day, though the town had assigned it to them. But he and his people could not enter it, inasmuch as it was locked and the selectmen had the keys. So he collected his congregation about the doors of the edifice and preached from the steps, both morning and afternoon. My friends, by my advice, demanded as their right a peaceable entrance to the building, but not being allowed it, retired to the hall before spoken of, and held services there.

When the month came round again in May, matters were in a still more aggravated condition than before. During Saturday night some desperate Baptist entered the meetinghouse by a back window which he found unfastened, wrenched off the lock from the inner door of the entry, and set free the corresponding outside door which was rendered secure by a crossbar. Having done this, and, as he supposed, made access to the house easy for his Baptist friends on the following day, he withdrew. About this time, Mr. Foster of the public house, who had the keys to the place of worship in his possession, dreamed of what had been done; but upon awaking and thinking it over, concluded it was only a dream and went to sleep again; when the same dream was repeated with the same result as before. But when it occurred a third time, he deemed it of enough importance to be looked into a little. He therefore arose, much excited, dressed himself, lighted his lantern (for it was not yet daylight), and went and examined the premises, to find that what he had dreamed was literally true in all its details. He immediately procured another lock for the inside door, replaced the bar to the outside one, and returned home to await further developments.

As the hour of morning service drew near, the Baptist pastor and his flock collected about the house as four weeks before, those in the secret not doubting, probably, that they would obtain an easy entrance. Upon trying to open the supposed-to-be-unfastened door, they found, to their ill-concealed chagrin, that it was as firmly closed as ever. Nothing now remained for them to do but to go through the forenoon service outside again, I and my friends worshiping in the hall at the same time.

At the noon recess, several of the influential members of the Baptist society, becoming tired, if not ashamed, of such proceedings, approached some of my friends with assurances that if the house were opened in the afternoon we might occupy it in peace. But they either were unwarranted in giving those assurances or were deceived by their pastor. For when we approached the house, led by the selectmen with the keys, Mr. Fisher and his allies rushed forward and as soon as the door was unlocked both parties crowded in, filling the vestibule instantly, while considerable numbers remained outside. The padlocked inner door prevented further advance, and I, who was directly behind the selectmen, requested them not to permit entrance to the audience room till the situation could be somewhat discussed. I then demanded of Mr. Fisher what such conduct meant. The town had voted us the house and we had been promised the use of it by some of his leading men for the afternoon. He was furious with rage, declared the town had nothing to do with the house, and silently ignored the action of those who had made pledges to us. I remonstrated calmly but firmly, maintaining our rights and declaring that I should do nothing in violation of the true Christian spirit and rules of propriety. God could not be worshiped acceptably in the midst of such confusion and strife. Some of his people made a proposition to withdraw and leave us in possession of the place; but he and his more zealous supporters would not hear of it, determined as they were to force themselves in if possible. I then said: "Let the door be opened, and if Mr. Fisher does not conduct himself decently, I certainly shall and will publish his doings to the world."

The door was then unlocked, the selectmen entering first, with me immediately in the rear. We proceeded slowly and becomingly up the central aisle toward the pulpit, but Mr. Fisher crowded in as quickly as possible and rushed at rapid speed by one of the side aisles to the pulpit stairs, which he reached about the same time the head of our column did and, bouncing up them, cried out as he arrived at the top panting for breath, "Let us begin the worship of God by singing," etc. Some of his people had now entered their pews and, as the whole matter had been prearranged between pastor and flock, commenced singing. The whole scene was so ludicrous and withal such a mockery of public worship that I remained but a moment in the pulpit, which I had entered simultaneously with the breathless parson, then signified my purpose to retire to Mr. Foster's hall, which I did, followed by my part of the congregation.

What followed? Intensified excitement throughout the community and in all the neighboring region. I at once wrote and published a pamphlet letter to Mr. Fisher, entitled *The Furious Priest Reproved*,[4] in which I reviewed the whole case and characterized the proceedings in such terms of reprobation and censure as justice demanded. The pamphlet had an extensive circulation and a greedy perusal. By the affair I seemed to gain reputation and influence, while my opponent suffered in proportion. The question of the control of the meetinghouse was ere long decided by the court against the Baptists and they abandoned it altogether, building a new one for their own undisputed occupancy and use.[5] Mr. Fisher lost the respect and confidence of the people at large, and a few years after left the place for a more congenial home. In reading over, at this late period of my life, my only preserved copy of my letter to him and reviewing the whole strange scene it describes, I am confirmed in the truth, justice, and rectitude of my course, and can see nothing on my own part to be ashamed of or to reproach myself for, though I am obliged to regard all such religious squabbles as more or less pitiable and much to be deprecated. With my matured knowledge of human nature and of the workings of a perverted religious zeal, I make more allowances for my antagonist in this encounter than at the time of it, having learned that *conscience* and *will* may honestly fall into deplorable mistakes – mistakes oftentimes more to be pitied than blamed.

First-born Child

On Sunday, June 22 of this year, my wife brought forth our first-born child, a son, to whom was given my own name, Adin Ballou, Jr. This event was a joyous one in our marital experience, though the constitution of the mother was so frail that it taxed her physical energies to the utmost extent. The little one throve well as a babe and through its early childhood, awakening fond hopes in the parental breast for long years on its part, and great usefulness and honor in time to come. But these hopes were vain, for it was stricken with a fatal disease when in the tenth year of its age and was translated to the heritage of the immortals February 10, 1833, as will be more fully noted hereafter.

Candidacy in Boston

In the month following, as foreshadowed at the close of the preceding chapter, I received an invitation from the First Universalist Society in Boston, originally organized under Rev. John Murray,[6] the reputed founder of that faith in America, to supply their pulpit six months as a candidate for the vacant pastorate. Rev. Paul Dean had, during his ministry, gathered about him a large congregation from which a colony of his devoted friends had gone out, erected and dedicated a new house of worship on Bulfinch Street, and persuaded him to resign his position and take charge of the movement there.[7] Those remaining in the old association, whose meetinghouse was on Hanover Street, had heard as many other preachers as they desired and voted to give me the proposed six months' probation. I shared the good will of surrounding Universalist ministers, and had been favorably heard for several Sundays by those now extending to me the offer, as previously narrated; yet it was a somewhat presumptuous undertaking for me to engage in, considering the immaturity of my youth and the poverty of my qualifications. But I consented to make the trial. My friends in Medway, Bellingham, and South Mendon professed to be sorry to part with me, but acquiesced cheerfully in my decision and wished me success, it having been our mutual understanding that I was at liberty to accept any such call, should it come to me.

My Boston candidacy began on the last Sunday in July, 1823, and continued till the third in January, 1824. During that period (my wife and child being with me a part of the time) I gained many ardent friends in the congregation and outside, and succeeded in my pulpit labors quite as much to my own satisfaction and that of my hearers as I had a right to expect, though I finally failed in the object sought. A single competitor entered the field, who, being in many respects my superior at the time, carried off the prize. This was Rev. Sebastian Streeter,[8] who was willing to close his pastorate at Portsmouth, New Hampshire, where he had been eight years. He was then at the zenith of his ability, experience, judgment, and pulpit eloquence, and he very naturally triumphed, receiving a considerable majority of the suffrages. Nearly one-third of the society adhered to me with considerable tenacity, but, of course, submitted to superior numbers. If my ambitious hopes were somewhat dashed, I had no right nor disposition to complain. I had much more reason for thankfulness than for murmuring, for I had gained many friends and the preference was, on the whole, wise and best for all concerned.

Just before entering upon my Boston candidacy, I had been proposed and formally admitted to the fellowship of the Southern Association of Universalists, assembled in semi-annual session at Stafford, Connecticut, though I was not personally present on the occasion.[9] At the annual session, held in Milford, Massachusetts, the next December, I was regularly ordained with the usual ceremonies,[10] as is attested by the following certificate:

> This certifies that Brother Adin Ballou was ordained to the work of the ministry of reconciliation at the annual meeting of the Southern Association of Universalists convened at Milford, Mass., Dec. 10, 1823.
>
> JACOB FRIEZE, Clerk.

During my six months' engagement in Boston, I solemnized the first three of my marriages, now (1882) numbering over one thousand. At its close, on the evening of the third Sunday in January, 1824, I preached my final sermon from the text, "And now, brethren, I commend you to God and the word of his grace, which is able to build you up and to give you an inheritance among them that are sanctified" (Acts 20:32). Leaving the people with cordial good feeling and in a prosperous condition, I returned to my family.

Call to Milford

The call of the society, given soon after to Rev. Mr. Streeter, left me at liberty to find an available opening at my convenience and pleasure. Several invitations were in prospect, but without waiting for a more desirable location, I accepted the one coming to me shortly afterward from the Universalist society in Milford, Massachusetts,[11] whither I removed my family about the first of April. This society had had two pastors before me, viz. Rev. Thomas Whittemore,[12] then of

Cambridgeport, for one year, and Rev. Jacob Frieze,[13] who had just been called to Marlborough, for two years. Their salaries had been $330 per annum, and mine was to be the same. The society was comparatively small and deemed this sum a handsome one, since it was the same paid by the Milford Congregational parish to their minister, Rev. David Long.[14] The Methodist society in North Purchase,[15] the only other one in town at that time, was feeble and could not give their pastor anything like so good a pecuniary support.

The whole population of the place scarcely exceeded 1200, and its since large and thriving industries were then in their incipient stages of development. Tenements were scarce and crowded and it was with difficulty that I could find a place suited to the needs of myself and family. I finally obtained one that served us for a while until we could do better. It consisted of two rooms and a few exterior accommodations, three-fourths of a mile east of the meetinghouse, in the dwelling of Mr. Zebadiah Flagg,[16] one of my people. The quarters were more limited than we had been accustomed to, but we made ourselves comfortable in them, and there we found ourselves domiciled on my twenty-first birthday, April 23, 1824.

I now applied myself diligently to my pulpit, pastoral, and miscellaneous duties, preaching often three times on Sunday – twice regularly at home, and in the evening in some one of the neighboring towns; officiating at funerals within the same circuit, solemnizing marriages, and attending to incidental domestic affairs. My people received my services appreciatively and our mutual relations were pleasant and harmonious. Pearley Hunt, Esq., Col. Arial Bragg, Col. Sullivan Sumner, and others of prominent standing in the community were among the foremost of my people.[17]

The Parish and the Town

The town in which I was now located had been divided since 1819 into two very distinct and determined parties – the Parish party, so-called, and the Town party. The former consisted of persons attached to or sympathizing with the old or Congregational parish; the latter of Universalists, Methodists, and people having no religious affiliations – the promiscuous population.

This division originated in conflicting claims to the old precinct meetinghouse, or rather, perhaps, in a difference of opinion respecting the location of a new one. When the eastern part of Mendon was incorporated as the town of Milford in 1780, parochial affairs were assumed by the body corporate, and the existing house of worship was used for general public purposes. There was then only one religious organization in the place. In a few years the Universalist and Methodist societies were organized, while many persons signed off from the Standing Order or became indifferentists and refused to be taxed at all for the support of religions institutions, as formerly. This obliged the adherents of the old New England faith to reorganize, which they did under the name of the Congregational parish in 1815.

Four years afterwards it was deemed advisable to build a new meetinghouse, when a dispute arose whether the old site should be occupied by it or a new one selected, in which was involved the question of the ownership of the building. Those persons who favored the old site, under the leadership of John Claflin, Esq., claimed that it belonged to the parish, while those who contended for a new site near where Dr. Fay's office stood,[18] under the leadership of Pearley Hunt, Esq., claimed that it was the property of the town. Hence the names – Parish party and Town party.

In the vote on the location, the Parish party prevailed, as they did finally on the matter of proprietorship before the courts, and proceeded to erect the new house accordingly. The minority of the parish then withdrew and joined the Universalists, the combined forces in due time setting about building a brick meetinghouse, which they planned to be one foot larger on the ground than that of the parish, with a bell five hundred pounds heavier, and with a clock in its tower, which the other did not have. The Congregationalist house was dedicated November 19, 1819; the Universalist, January 10, 1821. By this time the conflicting parties were well-defined and belligerent to the highest degree. And the conflict thus inaugurated continued some fourteen years, entering more or less as a troublesome factor into all town affairs – into the consideration and decision of all public questions. Then a truce was sounded on both sides, a more peaceable era opened, and a growing spirit of mutual respect, unity, and cooperation sprang up, which has continued unto this day.

This conflict was at its highest pitch of intensity of purpose when I entered on my pastorate in 1824. I had no disposition to aggravate it and little power to mollify it. What I had, I found, after acquainting myself with the situation, must be exercised indirectly, prudently, and quietly. I took care not to add fuel to the flame, not to excite anyone by word or deed to greater partisan violence, but rather to moderate passion where I could, and above all, to set an example of courtesy, forbearance, and kindness in my personal intercourse with everybody. Two trifling incidents will illustrate my success in that direction.

I had been in town but a short time when a prominent leader of the parish, who enjoyed a joke and thought the newly-come Universalist minister a proper subject for one, was called upon by a colored wanderer from Connecticut and asked where he could get a night's lodging gratis, as he had no money. "I belong to the hospital at home," said he; "is there any hospital in these parts?"[19]

"Oh, yes," answered the honorable wag, "there is one down street kept by a Mr. Ballou." And turning to his clerk, said "Write this man a note of introduction," at the same time dictating it as follows: "Rev. Mr. Ballou: Please keep the bearer over night and charge the same to him." No signature was appended.

After some trouble, the poor fellow found me in the midst of a crowd on the common and handed me the note. I saw that there was some trickery in the matter and inquired who gave him the paper. "A fleshy man they called the squire in the store near the other meetinghouse. He said you kept a hospital and would let me stay with you over night."

"Well," I replied, "I keep no hospital, as the squire very well knows. This is an imposition on both of us. But you shall be cared for. I cannot lodge you in my own house, but I will pay for your entertainment with my good friend, Colonel Sumner, the tavern-keeper near by, and will introduce you to him at once." He was astonished, but full of thanks to me and indignant at the trickery played upon him. He was well provided for till the next morning, when he posted back to the squire and scolded him sharply in his rude way for imposing on a poor wayfarer and on so kind a gentleman as he found Mr. Ballou to be.

As the matter had already been pretty well ventilated in town and as several persons were listening to the talk, the discomfited joker handed him a twenty-five-cent piece and told him to go along, which he at once did, taking the road to Boston. I lost nothing by this performance and never received another insult from the Parish party.

A second incident, of an entirely different character, but redounding equally to my credit, occurred not long afterward in connection with the annual town meeting in April. The ancient custom of opening the proceedings with prayer was still observed from year to year. Since the quarrel had been going on, the Town party being all the while in the ascendant in public affairs, Parson Long, the Parish clergyman, had not been invited to conduct that service, but it had been assigned to the Universalist and Methodist ministers alternately. At the time under notice, it fell to the former, and when the proper moment came, my friend, Col. Bragg, who was presiding, called upon me for the usual ceremonial. I was much surprised, being wholly a stranger to such a usage, and in nowise prepared for it. Moreover, it was as repugnant to my feelings as it was unexpected, for I knew in what an unprayerful, pugnacious state the minds of most of those present were, making the formality very much of a pious farce. My first impulse was to excuse myself outright, but I saw at once that this would hardly do. Instantly the thought flashed into my mind: "There stands Rev. Mr. Long, who would be glad of the chance; decline the honor and nominate him." In a moment this was done, and with proper deference to all present. Doubtless the moderator and people generally, as well as Mr. Long, were astonished; but the invitation was promptly accepted, and the service satisfactorily rendered.

If I had carefully studied and devised a stroke of good policy, I could not have made a happier hit than was this unpremeditated act. It softened prejudice and won golden opinions in the Parish party, without disturbing the feelings of their opponents. I did not dream that it would have any effect beyond the passing occasion. But it did, and much to my advantage. It not only pleased Mr. Long at the time, but secured his personal respect (which lasted, I believe, to the end of his days) and conciliated many of his people, who thereafter spoke of me as a gentleman and treated me accordingly. I never, before or since, received so much compliment and good will in return for so small an investment of makeshift civility.

Pulpit Supply and Exchanges

During my first year in Milford, I ministered a considerable number of Sabbaths, either in person or by supply, to the society in Medway. This was pursuant to a mutual understanding between me and my people and was satisfactory to all parties concerned. I also made frequent exchanges with my ministerial brethren, some of whom occupied a high position and had an enviable reputation in the denomination. Among these were Revs. Hosea Ballou and Paul Dean of Boston,[20] Hosea Ballou 2d of Roxbury, and David Pickering[21] of Providence, Rhode Island. At the same time, my lectures and funeral addresses, which were then elaborate and carefully prepared sermons of an expository and argumentative character, were abundant at home and abroad.

Freemasonry

In the summer of the same year I became a Freemason, passing through the first three degrees in Charity Lodge, Milford, of which I was, in orderly succession, a member, subordinate officer, and finally master.[22] That lodge surrendered its charter and jewels a few years later to the Grand Lodge of Massachusetts, by reason of the violent anti-Masonic excitement which swept through the country,[23] and other depressing circumstances. Before the close of 1825, I ascended through the Royal Arch degrees in Mount Lebanon Chapter in West Medway to those of knighthood in the Worcester County Encampment at Holden, since removed to Worcester and now known as the Worcester County Commandery.

I had come to be much interested in the Masonic Order and its institutions, and especially in the broad fundamental principles of the fraternity therein represented. These commanded my reverence both in their theoretical and practical aspects, whatever might seem exceptional or doubtful in some incidentals. And although my interest abated somewhat in maturer age and under the pressure of more engrossing matters of thought and action, I still cherish a profound respect for the intrinsic essentials of Freemasonry, notwithstanding the furor of anti-Masonic denunciation which at one time threatened its existence. There are few persons, institutions, or movements that have not their shady as well as their bright side. This has its defects and shortcomings in common with all human inventions.

But its escutcheon is resplendent with "faith in God, hope in immortality, and charity to all mankind;" with "brotherly love, relief, and truth;" with "temperance, prudence, fortitude, and justice;" and with significant emblems of righteousness. It inculcates many great individual and social virtues, which, if they were faithfully practiced by its professors, would render it pre-eminently illustrious.

But with all their failures, the Fraternity have not fallen so far below their acknowledged standard as has the nominal Christian Church. They have steered almost entirely clear of all mean proselytism, lust of dominion, monopolizing selfishness, and sanguinary persecution. On the other hand, they have done much to assuage intolerance, violence, and cruelty; to liberalize, genialize, civilize, and humanize mankind. The world has grievously needed the influence of the Order and still needs it. Therefore, it is not likely to be crushed out by its enemies nor to die out at any very early future of itself. When human society shall have fairly transcended it in absolute Christlikeness, doubtless its mission will terminate. Meantime, let anti-Masonic zealots demonstrate individually and socially that they have superseded its excellence and are therefore worthy to minister at its funeral.

A Military Chaplain

On the third of August, 1825, my friend, Lebbeus Gaskill of South Mendon, colonel of the Second Regiment, First Brigade, Sixth Division Massachusetts Militia, did me the honor of placing me on his staff as chaplain. I received my commission as such August 9, and continued in the office till formally discharged July 13, 1837. I accepted the position with pleasure and officiated on various occasions to the best of my ability – always, I believe, to general satisfaction. Many a pleasant interview I enjoyed with my fellow officers at their various meetings and refreshment tables.

My first service in this new capacity was rendered at the autumnal muster of the regiment at Mendon on the ancient Hastings training field. An old Congregationalist deacon, not knowing me, was somewhat taken with my prayer and warmly commended it. But when told upon inquiry who I was, uttered an exclamatory "Oh!" in blank astonishment and at once subsided. A prejudiced Calvinist, who knew me, commenting upon it, said it sounded more like an oration than a prayer, which was probably a fair hit; for a military prayer ought to be more oratorical than reverential to be in good keeping with its surroundings.

The reader may wish to know how I now view that military chaplainship and its duties. With little admiration and self-complacency, yet not with profound compunction and shame. For I was acting up to my then highest light. I had not at the time a thought or a scruple against war *per se* as un-Christian and wrong, and of course not against training and preparation for war. Like all others, I claimed to be opposed to wicked wars, under the presumption that there were sometimes righteous ones which I could approve. I simply acted according to my education and predilections. The all-important truth that Christ moved on a higher moral plane than that of civil society and national government as they now are, and called his disciples to rise and act with him on his distinctive plane, had not at that day shot its faintest ray into my murky understanding. I had no more doubt that civil government, backed by necessary deadly force, was consistent with genuine Christianity, and that Christian ministers and people ought to act in it in both political and military capacities, than I had that they ought to be Christians. I took it for granted, as most good people do, that there is no plane or position distinctively higher than existing governmental civilization, which can be occupied to any practical advantage by eminently advanced minds, whether claiming to be Christians, or progressionists of some other name; as I also did that no Christianity can be organized above and in the lead of the prevailing civilization of the world. On this ground, Christianity must play the part of handmaid of such civilization, but attempt little or nothing more. On this ground, war must be provided for with all its requisites till the necessity for it shall cease by the universal prevalence of wisdom, righteousness, and love on earth – an era inconceivably remote under the reproductive genius of the politico-military system. In this view, chaplains of the army, navy, militia, etc., are as necessary, salutary, and respectable as voting citizens or any class of functionaries that cooperate in sustaining the existing institutions of civil society. So thinking in my youth, I acted accordingly. Besides, I had, as already indicated, the military, political, and civic instincts in my very nature, and it is no wonder that a regimental chaplaincy was congenial to my taste. The wonder is that such stock was ever fashioned into a conscientious, uncompromising, Christian Non-resistant. But so it was and is.

Teaching

I spent the winter months of 1824-25 in teaching what was known as the North Purchase school, two miles out of the village of Milford, in addition to my pulpit and pastoral labors. I had some eighty pupils under my care, ranging from those four and five years of age, just entering upon their educational tutelage, to grown-up young men and women, expecting to finish their common schooling with that term. My duties, so varied and multitudinous, kept my heart, head, and hands full, and I wrought persistently at my different posts of service. It was impossible for any one teacher to do full justice to such a throng of pupils as I had in charge, many of whom were poorly equipped and imperfectly classified. But all went prosperously on to the closing examination, which elicited flattering commendations from the superintending town committee. I won the respect, love, and general obedience of those under me and had little occasion to employ harsh corrections.

One case of discipline which had passed from my recollection has recently been recalled by an elderly matron, then a little girl in the school. The peculiarity of it, reminding one of the methods employed by the philosopher, A. Bronson Alcott, in his far-famed Boston school,[24] justifies a description of it in these pages.

It seems, according to my informant's statement, that I had among the rest a somewhat troublesome boy whose misbehavior evoked repeated reproofs on my part, but to little purpose. One day, after some fresh violation of the rules, I summoned him to my desk in unusually stern tones of voice, saying to him as he stood before me that I plainly saw that he meant to have some one whipped and the matter must be settled forthwith. "Now," said I, "here is my rod and I suppose it must be used or you cannot be cured of your misconduct. I cannot bear to whip you; perhaps it will do you more good if you whip me. At any rate, I have concluded to try it." Whereupon I took off my coat and having laid it aside, handed him the rod and told him to use it on me long enough to make him a good boy. Refusing to take it, I insisted that he should, inasmuch as it was necessary for him to do so in order to teach him obedience to the rules of the school. The boy broke down, wept bitterly, and promised that he would not repeat his offenses. I then sent him to his seat amid the amazement of the whole school, and he gave me no further trouble.

Religious Condition of the Milford Society

After the termination of my winter engagement, I gave myself with renewed zeal to the current duties of my home and pastorate, reaching, while busily engaged in them, the end of the twenty-second year of my life.

At this stage of my narrative, which finds me well settled under Universalist auspices in my new field of labor and active in my professional work, it may reasonably be asked "What was the religious condition of your society in Milford at that time and what thus far were the fruits of your ministry as an ambassador for Christ?" Not very flattering in either respect to the ambition or reputation of a devoted, faithful, Christian pastor. In the estimation of so-called Evangelical religionists, I was not such a pastor, nor scarcely was I according to my own then best ideal, and much less according to my present theoretical standard.

I was, however, sincerely desirous of preaching divine truth and of promoting human righteousness, as I then understood them, and current circumstances seemed to afford me favorable opportunities for doing so. And I have no doubt that in both of the particulars named, I exerted on the whole a salutary and effective influence. But I do not think my own intellectual, moral, and spiritual state was high enough to accomplish much in the way of raising the people of my charge to the true Christ-plane of thought and life.

There was then no church organization among them, no meetings for social Christian culture, and no Sunday school for the religious training of children and youth. Nor was there much, if any, perceptible desire for these institutions and helps to virtue and holiness. On the contrary, many were prejudiced against and adverse to them as savoring of "orthodox" superstition, craft, or bigotry. Even my own mind had been so repelled and sickened by the excommunicative and damnatory spirit of the dominant church religionists that I was in no haste to re-embrace their forms, modes, and expedients. Though in themselves good and perhaps necessary to human welfare, they had become so associated with irrational faith, terrorism, spasmodic emotionality, superstitious pietism, and sanctimonious cant, that I was not in a mood to separate them from their abuses and urge upon my hearers their right uses.

I had swung off into a sphere of theological protest against the dogma of endless punishment and all kindred notions derogatory to the moral character of God. I was in the midst of a polemical war with vast hosts of bitter antagonists whose watchword was *No quarter to Universalists of any school*. I neither asked nor expected any, and fought accordingly. The whole denomination of which I had become a member was at that time in the same combative sphere – one not very conducive of personal and social piety of the constructive type. How it could have been otherwise in the then warlike stage of theological opinion is hardly conceivable. If we had been ever so devotedly intent on the cultivation of strictly personal religion, the whole solid phalanx of our opponents was inflexibly resolved that we could not and should not have anything of the sort except on their platform and after their fashion. For a person to repent, become regenerated, and enter into church relations while in full belief of universal salvation was in their view not only impossible, but absurd and ridiculous. Men must believe that God loved only his friends and hated his enemies, certainly in the next life, and that his merciless vengeance awaited all who died in their sins, else there was no adequate motive or reason for any one to try to be personally and experimentally a disciple of Christ. But that folly and bigotry was destined to be overcome by valorous conflict and give place to better theories and convictions.

I must also state that nearly all my congregation, seldom exceeding 150 persons, had grown up as outsiders of the old churches; that some of them had been more or less skeptical with respect to revealed religion; and that as Universalists they were of the *ultra* school, with scarcely a Restorationist, properly so called, among them. Even my own Restorationism had receded into the background, becoming faint and feeble in its abeyance to the then predominant no-future-punishment doctrine of the denomination. In view of such a peculiar and complicated state of things, the nature and success of my ministry in those days must be judged. The special reforms which afterwards agitated the pulpit and public mind – temperance, antislavery, peace, etc. – had not then been sufficiently developed to attract attention. So the old social habits, customs, and ideas remained undisturbed among the people of Milford, as elsewhere throughout the country.

Nevertheless, all things considered, I cannot but persuade myself that my preaching, pastoral labors, and personal influence not only rendered no one morally and spiritually worse for this world or the next, but were salutary to some positive and appreciative extent and accomplished considerable good in the way of establishing religious opinions on a more rational basis than before in the community, commending practical Christian righteousness to my hearers as of inestimable worth, diffusing the spirit of charity and good will among the people at large, and making divine truth and love a power of redemption in the hearts and minds of men.

CHAPTER 7

1825-1828

The labors of a duly settled minister of the Christian religion, though many and various, are much the same, generally speaking, from year to year, and to mention them in chronological order and detail would involve wearisome and needless repetition. Only those, therefore, of special interest and importance in themselves considered, or in their relation to the personality of the writer or to the thought and life of the world at large, will be chronicled at length or more than hinted at in these pages, although months and even years may be passed over without reference to anything transpiring in them. In a narrative like this one here given, the omitted particulars are so well known as to be easily supplied, if necessary, by the reader.

Building a Home
Passing over, then, the first half of the twenty-third year of my life, I come to the autumn of 1825, when I purchased of my friend, Col. Sullivan Sumner, an acre of land in the village of Milford, for the purpose of building upon it at an early day a suitable and permanent home. It was the lot on which now stands house number 28 Main Street, owned wholly or in part by George B. Pierce.

I soon afterwards planned a dwelling thirty-eight feet in length by thirty-two in width, two stories high and nine feet between joints, fronting the north, with a sufficient yard between it and the road. On the first floor were a parlor, dining room, and kitchen of large size, with the needful halls, pantries, and other smaller apartments desirable for domestic uses; while on the second floor were two large chambers in front, and one of still greater measurement in the southeast corner designed for a schoolroom. The remaining area was divided as necessity and convenience seemed to dictate. A contract for the erection of the structure above the underpinning was made with Colonel Sumner, who was to have the whole completed according to specifications and ready for occupancy on or before the first of the following August. The cellar and foundations were to be otherwise provided for and made ready for the superstructure in due season.

This undertaking, entered upon with fond expectations, was rather a wild and extravagant one for a young minister with little capital, a meager income, and no certainty of a permanent residence in the town. But various considerations weighed with me in deciding to enter upon it. I was very much in need of a more eligible and commodious residence than the one I occupied; the estate, it was said, would be salable at any time without loss; a part of it might be rented, if I desired; it was so arranged that I could open a select school in it and so increase my annual receipts; my principal creditor, Colonel Sumner, was a very kind and indulgent man and would favor me in the matter of payment for the land and building, while other friends would give me an occasional lift; and, to cap the climax, I had a large amount of hope. So I went ahead with my project and took the consequences, some of which proved to be good, others indifferent, and yet others – the pecuniary ones – bad. None of my creditors lost anything by the affair, though it was some seven years before the last installment of the indebtedness incurred was paid. Circumstances so changed that I occupied the premises only about half of that period. So far as they furnished me a home, they added to my convenience, comfort, and happiness; otherwise they occasioned me many outlays, anxieties, and vexations. I rented them at much disadvantage and finally sold them at considerable pecuniary loss. My experience, I think, was that of the general average in analogous cases. I do not advise others, though like myself well-disposed and over-hopeful, to follow my example.

Notable Funerals

Other occurrences of quite a different nature took place during the year 1825, which left a lasting impression on my memory. Two of these were connected with my funeral ministrations. The first to be mentioned is almost laughable in its leading incident. Mr. Darius Morse of Franklin, a Universalist in faith, invited me to conduct the services upon the death of his mother. The celebrated Dr. Emmons,[1] then far advanced in years, was still pastor of the old church of that town, and they were few who dared dissent from his distinctive theological teachings. Mr. Morse was one of these, and so, when his mother passed away, he turned from the venerable champion of the ancient beliefs to one of the larger hope touching the plan and providence of God; but invited two of the elderly members of the Doctor's church, to which the deceased had belonged, to assist as bearers at the burial. When they learned that a young heretic was to officiate on the occasion, they refused to act as desired unless they could be roomed out of hearing of the preacher while the service was going on. Mr. Morse accommodated them by assigning them to a chamber in a remote part of the house. Thither they repaired in season to prevent contamination and there remained till all danger of that sort was over.

In untroubled ignorance of this arrangement, I went through with what devolved on me to do, opening with a brief invocation, then preaching a regular sermon from Isaiah 25:7-8, and closing with a funeral prayer and benediction, as was my custom in those days. When all was over, the two self-secluded bearers appeared to perform, with others, the duty belonging to them. Of their exploits

I was informed not long after, as I was also in due time of the light in which their conduct was regarded, both by individuals in the community and by Dr. Emmons himself. Laughed at by those of less religious turn of mind, they repaired to the house of their pastor to tell him how bravely they had stood by their creed, and to obtain his commendation, as they no doubt believed they would. But Dr. Emmons was not the man to relish their sort of tactics. And so after questioning them closely and getting all the information he wanted in the matter, he exclaimed: "What! What! Shut yourselves up in a chamber during the services! I am ashamed of you! You'll make people think your own faith is pretty weak if you act so cowardly as that! I don't advise you to run after such preaching, but if you have to go to a funeral, don't hide away from it as if you were afraid to trust your creed in its presence." They undoubtedly retired from the interview with more mortification than comfort, well cured of all such errantry.

About a month after this ludicrous affair took place, another of a more serious nature and of more immediate concern to me transpired, which taught me a salutary lesson. Within my own proper field of pastoral labor there had lived a family, consisting of the two parents and several children, indirectly connected with my parish. The husband and father, though possessed of a handsome estate, was penurious and miserly, living shabbily himself and denying his family the comforts and even the necessaries of life. The wife and mother, a most estimable woman, discharged the duties devolving upon her conscientiously and faithfully for many years, but finally by overwork, privation, neglect, and abuse, broke down in health and became a victim of consumption. Under these distressing circumstances, her husband made less provision for her comfort and happiness than before. At length her parents took her home to care for and nurse during her evidently few remaining days on earth. I frequently called to see the suffering woman, as her life was slowly ebbing away. In one of my last conversations with her, after referring sorrowfully to the cold and cruel treatment she had received from her husband, she spoke of her funeral (at which I had already engaged to minister) as soon to take place, and expressed the hope that I would so admonish and reprove him on that occasion as to make him realize his blameworthiness and guilt. It seemed to be a charge given me on her dying bed and I promised to fulfill it. She soon passed through the gate of death and arrangements were made for her obsequies in the Universalist house of worship.

The occasion was one that imposed unusual responsibility upon me, as a discourse was expected suited to the well-known circumstances of the case. I therefore prepared myself with great care, writing out in full what I had to say, which I was not accustomed to do except in extraordinary emergencies. The manuscript I have preserved – the oldest of its kind that ever came from my pen. To indicate the fidelity with which I discharged the trust committed to me from a dying bed, I subjoin a few disconnected extracts.

Taking a text from Job 21:23, 25-26, I first unfolded the subject there brought to notice in its general aspects, and made an application of it to the life, character, and trials of the deceased in such a way as to commend and honor her name and memory. I then proceeded to address the mourners directly, and particularly the husband, who sat cowering among the family relatives in the midst of a large promiscuous congregation, gathered for various reasons, no doubt, from all classes of the town's population. The passages which I deem it proper to reproduce are as follows:

> I commence with you, my friend, who claim the first and nearest relationship – that of husband – to the deceased woman who lies in silence before me. I beseech you in the name of Almighty God to hear patiently the solemn admonition of one who feels for you nothing but kindness and pity such as cannot be uttered. You never injured a hair of my head personally, but by a strange course of conduct, to me altogether unaccountable, towards your deceased wife, you have inflicted a grievous blow on my humane feelings and thereby laid me under the painful necessity of counseling you in the name of Jehovah for your good this day. Friend, bear with me and pardon my plainness, for I must be no flatterer or hypocrite towards you; otherwise, my God, who hears me, would smite me with a just condemnation.
>
> I must tell you what you can but already know, that you have lost one of the best of wives – one of the most devoted and faithful of bosom companions. She lives no longer yours – no longer the victim of sickness and death, or, what is still worse, ingratitude. But though silent in death, she still speaks to you through me. She solemnly asks why you treated her as you did; why you neglected her after she had been so faithful to you; why you abandoned her in her last sickness and in the hour of expiring agony! Did she deserve all this at your hands? Was she unworthy to receive your kind attention; unworthy to be benefited by the abundance of your wealth; unworthy to die in your house and in your arms? . . . Alas, my wretched friend, how can you answer these solemn questions? Have you done what you have in secret? No; but openly, before all the world, as it were, as well as under the inspecting eye of that God who is full of justice and judgment, who brought you into existence and has mercifully bestowed upon you all that you call yours, who has wept, if such a thing could be, at your doings, and whose warning voice has so often reproved you and called on you to turn from your errors.
>
> Let me ask you if a great sin lies not at the door of your heart, unrepented of and big with impending woes. Flee, oh, flee, friend, from them. Repent and seek shelter in the pardoning mercy of that God to whom thou art answerable, but who is a compassionate and sin-forgiving God. Bring forth fruits meet for repentance.[2] Then God and good men will forgive thee. Thou canst not undo altogether what thou hast done, but thou canst do what remains to be done. Break off thy inordinate love for the treasures of this vain and transitory world, for thou, too, must die and leave them all in a few more passing years. Let not another day go by before thou confessest unto God, unto thy father- and mother-in-law, unto all this circle of mourners whose feelings thou hast injured, and unto the whole public before whose eyes thou hast done this great wrong. Go and pay the uttermost farthing[3] of the expense incurred by reason of the sickness and death of her whose remains we are about to house in the tomb. Take these motherless children and be both a

father and mother to them. Withhold nothing from them that can tend to make them comfortable... Let them be trained up in the nurture and admonition of the Lord – in the love of virtue and truth. Do all this, and the *manes*[4] of thy departed wife will be appeased. God will smile mercifully upon thee, prosperity and happiness will attend thee, and all will believe thee to be a sincere penitent for sin, and a good man.

O that God might sanctify unto thee this event of his providence for thy good! If thou turn unto him with thy whole heart, thou wilt be safe – thou shalt be blest before him. But if not... I can hold nothing before thee but the blackness and darkness of woe. For the chastising hand of God will be heavy upon thee, and thou canst never escape till by salutary correction he has brought thee back to the ways of righteousness. Think, friend, seriously, of all I have said and lay up no hardness against me for uttering what has been so trying and painful to me, what I should never have said had I not felt that God had laid the duty upon me. It is my fervent prayer that thou mayst follow my counsels and enter into rest. I leave thee in the disposing hand of God. May he be gracious unto thee according to the multitude of his mercies.

I have made these quotations as a funeral curiosity and as suggestive of a lesson to be pondered and taken solemnly to heart. My whole discourse and especially the portion thus given was listened to with profound attention and mingled emotions that cannot be described. Many of those present expressed approval of my testimony as just, though some no doubt questioned silently the wisdom of it. One heart was deeply grieved by it, that of a sister of the inculpated man, who acknowledged the painful facts in the case and their wrongfulness, but pleaded that her brother was insane and so not responsible for his conduct. At first I could give no credence to this plea, but time proved it to be substantially true. His mental aberration, then unknown save by a few who were brought into close contact with him, increased as the years went by until he became a confirmed lunatic, not of the violent type, but of so pronounced and positive a character as to necessitate the appointment of a legal guardian to have constant charge of him and of his affairs. He lived, however, to a good old age, and when he at length passed away I was called upon to minister at his obsequies.

My course in this matter, which had been suggested and even enjoined by the suffering victim of neglect and abuse on her deathbed, and pursued under a profound sense of duty and with the conviction that some good would come of it to the offender and possibly to others, was subjected to a very careful and searching review on my part not long afterward, whereby I was brought to the conclusion that I had acted unwisely, and to no such salutary effect as I had anticipated. I therefore never again allowed myself on a funeral occasion to sit in judgment on sinful mourners, nor administer special personal rebuke even to notorious evil-doers. I had become convinced that such is not the time, place, and method for serving the cause of truth or promoting the moral and spiritual improvement of my fellow men. Neither the guilty nor the innocent are made better thereby. Very likely, in my purpose to avoid a recurrence of the mistake I made in this instance, I may have gone many times to the other extreme and estimated the virtues of both the departed and their survivors too highly, without intending to justify or palliate anything wrong in human conduct or character. But a fault in this direction, especially when proceeding from kindness of heart, seldom does moral harm.

Personal Bereavements

Three other deaths of more than ordinary personal interest to me occurred during the year 1825, subjecting me to a deep sense of bereavement and producing a lasting impression upon my heart and memory. The first of these took place March 27, removing from the scenes of earth and time the oldest member and one of the leading supporters of my society – the venerable and worthy Wales Cheney in the ninety-third year of his age. He was a man of good common sense, rigid justice, true to his word, outspoken to bluntness, strictly temperate, exemplary in all his habits, scrupulously conscientious, a little eccentric in some of his ways, but of kind and generous sympathies. Both he and his son Alexander, who cared for him in his declining years, were earnest Universalists and steadfast friends of mine, and his decease was a great grief to me.

Near the close of the year my half-sister, Mrs. Rosina (Ballou) Arnold, the oldest of my father's children, died in childbed at the age of forty-two – a great and sad bereavement to her family and a large circle of relations and friends. She was a woman of many excellent qualities and a noble heart, but sensitive to adverse experiences and subject to great depression of spirit and over-anxiety amid the trials through which she was called to pass. The loss of a greatly beloved and tenderly cherished daughter just blooming into youthful womanhood in the summer of 1824 was a terrible affliction to her and nearly crushed out her life. She recovered in a measure from the shock which so utterly prostrated her, but not sufficiently to rally from the exhaustion incident to the birth of twin daughters a year and a half later – a few days after which event, in which she greatly rejoiced at the time, her spirit passed on to the unseen world. She was the fourth of my father's children to enter that world and shares the rest and reward that there await all true and loving souls. Clouds and darkness seemed to hover over her departure hence, and to her husband and little ones it was indeed shrouded in gloom, but divine love and wisdom meant it for good – sometime to be understood and gratefully acknowledged.

Still another visitation of a similar kind occurred about the same date as the one just named. It was the decease of Mrs. Joanna (Sayles) Sweet, wife of Jesse B. Sweet of Providence, Rhode Island, a favorite sister of my wife, next older than herself. The two had grown up in loving intimacy from childhood, and their marriages were consummated not far apart. My wife felt this bereavement most keenly, as also did the whole family circle. The departed left infant children needing a mother's care and love. She was an amiable, excellent woman, whose spirit home must be a blessed one.

New Home Occupied

Little of a personal, professional, denominational or general nature transpired during the year 1826[5] that I deem worthy of record. During the spring and summer months, my house, contracted for late the previous season, had been in process of erection, the foundations having been prepared, and the grounds put in proper order under my own immediate supervision, though I received substantial help in executing the work from kind friends who rendered me gratuitous service and from hired jobbers or day laborers employed as they seemed to be needed. Much of the work, however, was performed by myself at such times and in such a manner as my other regular duties allowed. I was naturally ambitious to have the oversight of these outside matters and to take an active part in carrying them forward to completion according to my own choice and taste. I had been brought up to rough manual labor such as is incident to the care and management of a large farm, and deemed myself competent to judge fairly well how the task in hand ought to be accomplished. The result justified my confidence in my own ability in that direction – at any rate, I was satisfied and contented with what was done.

At length the house was finished, its surroundings were put in decent condition, and the premises were ready for occupancy. About the first of September, I and my little family were nicely settled in the new home and the machinery of our domestic life began to move under more agreeable conditions and with better prospects than ever before. I immediately opened a private school, as provided for in the original plan of my dwelling, and found myself encompassed and burdened with cares and duties many and various, which taxed to the utmost my time, strength, and energy of body, mind, and soul. I seemed to be firmly established in my lot and dreamed little of the changes that awaited me at an early day.

Fourth of July Celebration, 1827

For the greater part of a year, all things went smoothly on without jar or disturbance of any kind, and without premonition or expectation of what was soon to come to pass. As the anniversary of American Independence, 1827, drew near, the Republican citizens of Milford resolved to celebrate the day in some becoming manner, and I was favored with an invitation to deliver the oration in my own church, more commonly known as the "brick meetinghouse." Patriotism – civil, military, and religious – was then an essential part of my Christianity and I cheerfully accepted the proffered honor.

The occasion was one of unusual importance and one long remembered by those participating in it. Extraordinary preparations were made for it. Besides the oration, the dinner, and a grand military display, with martial music and other accompaniments, there was to be a formal presentation of a "splendid standard" by the ladies of the town to the long-famous Artillery Company, which had been organized in 1803 under Pearley Hunt, Captain, as a testimonial of respect and admiration. Announcement was duly made in all the neighboring towns of what was to be done and such a time was provided for and expected as Milford had never seen before.[6]

Nor were the promise and anticipation unfulfilled. The day was ushered in not only by bells and cannon, but by a resonant and copious thunderstorm, the last of which, however, soon passed away, leaving as clear a sky and atmosphere as mortals could desire. The program was carried out in full and everything went off to universal satisfaction. The streets were thronged with people from all the surrounding region, eager to share in the festivities and keep in patriotic fashion the nation's holiday.

The more formal proceedings began with the presentation of the flag. The company to be honored was out in full numbers and bright uniforms, Capt. Clark Sumner commanding it, with Lt. Isaac Davenport second officer, and John Corbett, Jr., third or standard bearer. A suitable platform had been erected on the common where the exercises were to take place, and where in due season the principal actors in the scene were gathered, surrounded by interested multitudes of people. A prayer having been offered, Miss Lucy Hunt, eldest daughter of Pearley Hunt, Esq., (with Miss Laura Ann Adams on her right and Miss Harriet Hunt on her left, all tastefully attired), came forward bearing the elegant gift, and partially unfurling it, presented it with an appropriate address to Second Lieutenant Corbett.[7] He received it with an appreciative response, at the close of which the band struck up one of their liveliest airs, amid whose inspiring strains and the plaudits of the delighted populace, the ladies were escorted back to Colonel Sumner's hotel, whence they came.

A long civic procession was immediately formed, and began its march through some of the principal streets to the meetinghouse, led by an imposing array of soldiery. The auditorium of the building was crowded to the full, many desiring entrance being obliged to remain outside. The oration, which was the principal feature of that part of the celebration, was delivered at the proper time, being preceded and followed by anthems, prayers, odes, and other customary accompaniments. There was nothing unique, profound, or eloquent about it, but it probably compared favorably with the old-style productions of that sort. A copy of it was asked for the press, and the request being granted, a considerable edition was at once printed and widely distributed, a few numbers of which are still in my possession, and will be preserved wholly or in part with the complete set of my published works.[8]

The services at the church having been concluded, such of the audience as were disposed, with others of like mind, repaired in processional order to the dinner tables – those for the ladies being spread in the hotel, the others under spacious tents or awnings outside where the post-prandial exercises were held. These were presided over, if my memory serves me, by Pearley Hunt, Esq. assisted by Newell Nelson, Esq. as toastmaster – most of what transpired consisting of regular and volunteer toasts, which, as they were announced, were washed down after the old ante-Temperance fashion, and responded to by cannonry and strains of martial music.

Without going into much further detail in regard to what took place on this occasion, I must speak of one laughable incident connected with the after-dinner festivities. Among those present was Mr. Timothy Walker, an elderly citizen of Hopkinton, who had distinguished himself somewhat during or soon after the war of 1812, by publishing several magniloquent letters to Gen. William Hull, of ignoble fame arising from his surrender of Detroit to the British.[9] Opportunity being given for volunteer sentiments, Mr. Walker rose, saying to the toastmaster that he had one to offer which he hoped would be received without local offense. Whereupon Esquire Nelson in strong, sonorous voice, called out, "Citizens, please give attention to a volunteer toast from Mr. Timothy Walker, author of letters to General Hull." Mr. Walker in sharp, age-cracked tones started off in a long sentiment, prepared no doubt with much care for the occasion. When about halfway through it he paused for a moment to take breath. The director of the artillery, supposing he had finished, signaled the cannoneer accordingly, when *boom* went the six-pounder and up struck the band, to the great merriment of those who understood the situation. But Mr. Walker, not in the least disconcerted, kept his standing, and when the music ceased cried out: "Mr. President and fellow citizens, you have been too fast for me; I hadn't got half through." This increased the mirth, which in no wise subsided when, re-announced by the toastmaster and given full sway, the speaker began anew and went through to the end as follows: "*Party Spirit* – that wicked and baneful party spirit, by which empires, kingdoms, and republics have been overthrown, and by which too many of the good people of this town have been greatly led astray: may this noxious party spirit be torn up by the roots, transported to the island of Java, and there placed in battle array with the bohon upas tree,[10] till it shall be demonstrated which is most poisonous to humanity, that deadly upas or party spirit." Then came another gun, more music, and deafening shouts of applause from the greatly amused assemblage. This closed substantially the more formal proceedings of the day.

Invitation to New York
A few days subsequent to the Fourth of July celebration just described, I received an unexpected visit from Asa Holden, Esq., an entire stranger to me and a leading trustee of the First Universalist Society, Prince Street, New York City.[11] He had come as a special messenger to New England for the purpose of looking up a minister to fill the vacant pastorate of that body. I had been mentioned to him

by some of my older clerical brethren and recommended as a suitable person for the position, and he had called upon me to engage my services at an early day as a candidate for it.

There were good reasons why I should at once have declined the proposition. I had a nice field of usefulness where I was, and the unanimous good will of an increasing number of friends, though in a rural community, which could afford me but a moderate compensation for my labors. I was well established with my family in our pleasant new home, and it was annoying, if not unwise, to leave it without great certainty of a better location elsewhere. There was no such certainty in the case presented me, for the society in question had just been sadly weakened by a division which resulted in the withdrawal of a considerable number of its members. The famous Abner Kneeland[12] had been its pastor, and being in that unsettled, transitive state of mind which not long after landed him in open infidelity, his preaching had so alienated from him a majority of his people that they voted his discharge from the pulpit. Thereupon his friends, considerable in number, seceded, hired a public hall, set up a rival organization, and employed him as their minister. All this must render my position in the Prince Street pulpit, if I occupied it, not only a delicate and trying one, but one of problematical success. New York was not as sensational then as now, and not easily moved by aspirants for popular favor of my moderate type and caliber. But I was probably too ambitious, vain, and shortsighted to weigh all these considerations judiciously, and so was inclined to yield to the solicitations urged upon me.

Nevertheless, I argued against the proposed change for some time with ambassador Holden, and requested him to consult some of my leading supporters, get their opinion, and learn their feelings about the matter, which he consented to do. He was a stirring, sanguine man and made quick work of his conferences, returning very soon and reporting that the few he could find thought I was fully competent to fill the proffered pastorate, and had better go to it if called, though it would be a great loss to them. He represented in particular that such were the views expressed by Esquire Hunt, my most influential parishioner. I was rather taken aback by this statement, inasmuch as it caused me to infer that possibly there was a willingness to have me leave, founded as much on indifference to my continuance in Milford as on a conviction of my fitness for the prospective place in New York. I was therefore much more disposed by this representation to listen to these new overtures than before. I ascertained afterward, however, that Esquire Holden had no warrant for saying that any willingness existed that I should leave the Milford parish, though I was not informed of this till too late to profit by it. I suppose that his zeal to have me comply with his wishes either warped his veracity or caused him to misconstrue expressions which seemed to favor his suit, though not intended to do so. Suffice it to say that I was persuaded to be a candidate for the vacant pastorate and engaged to preach as such the last two Sabbaths in July and the first in August. So much being settled, Brother Holden returned home with joy to report his success.

Pursuant to the above-named arrangement, I took my wife and little boy to Smithfield, Rhode Island, about the middle of July, to remain with relatives during my absence from Milford, and proceeded directly to New York to fulfill the terms of my candidacy there. A letter written to the former soon after my arrival detailed my experiences on the way and after reaching my destination to date, and also my first impressions of the people to whom I ministered and of the city. It has been preserved, and the major portion of it may not be inappropriate to the purpose of this volume, nor uninteresting to its readers. I therefore give it insertion here.

New York City, (Monday) July 23, 1827

Dear Wife: I embrace an early opportunity to write you a few lines agreeably to promise, and certainly according to inclination. Through the providence of God, I am well and hearty in the midst of this great and bustling metropolis. I did not arrive here till Sunday morning, just in time to attend divine service. The reason why was a disappointment at Providence. I reached that place about 10 o'clock on Friday morning. But on going to the steamboat wharf – behold, no boat was there! They told me none went on that day, but that a stage started soon for New London, where I could take a steamer for New York. On inquiry, however, I learned that the coach had gone, and of course I must wait till the next day and make the best of my ill fortune. Meanwhile, I came across Brother Pickering [then pastor of the First Universalist Church in Providence], who comforted and encouraged me, inviting me to spend the intervening time at his house, which I did very agreeably. I feel much indebted to him, for he was very kind . . . He acted the part of an able and warm friend throughout, of which I shall speak more fully to you hereafter.

On the passage, we had good wind, weather, and luck. The boat went much faster than usual, so that I reached the city in season for the morning service.[13] Mr. Holden, to my great joy, was at the landing, looking with eager eyes for me. He received and welcomed me with great kindness, took me in a coach to a friend's house, not far from the church, etc. I was much fatigued, but preached three discourses notwithstanding.

I am treated with much respect by the brethren here, who are plain, intelligent, kind people. There was double the number present at meeting I had expected, so that I was happily disappointed. I am also happily disappointed in the place. Those who have spoken against this city have misrepresented it. It is superior to Boston. The streets, if not so clean, are much more spacious and airy; the water is fully as good, if not better; and the people are less stiff and starched than in most large New England towns.[14] But I can add no more now. As to my being settled here, I can say nothing yet, for neither party is fully prepared to decide. The probability is that it will depend on my consent and pleasure.

Your affectionate husband,
ADIN BALLOU

The above language indicates that the candidate was rather captivated by his surroundings and prospects, and quite likely to take the new position. So it proved. After preaching three Sabbaths, I received and accepted the society's call on a salary, I think, of $800 per annum, to be raised as the society grew. During his visit I was pleasantly boarded in the family of Brother Sylvanus Adams, one of the trustees, and was introduced to most of the members. I also solemnized one marriage.

It being settled that I was to remove to New York, affairs made haste with me. My installation was arranged for the twenty-sixth of September, the Rev. Hosea Ballou to be invited to preach the sermon. But my pastorship was to date from the sixteenth of that month, the third Sabbath; and I was to make an exchange with Brother Hosea for that day and the Sunday following, arrangement for which was agreed upon and carried into effect.[15]

Close of Milford Pastorate

I returned to my home in Milford, taking my little family from their three weeks' visitation with me, and set about the necessary preparations for removal. My friends seemed deeply aggrieved at my leaving them, but blamed the New York strategist rather than myself, as having seductively robbed them of their minister in an unfraternal manner. I was sorrowful for them and also for myself, fearing that I had done wrong and that the change I was to make might turn out an unwise one for all concerned. But the die was cast; nothing could be undone. I must go ahead and do my best.

On the five Sabbaths that remained before the close of my pastorate, I preached morning and afternoon in my own pulpit to interested and anxious audiences, and on successive days at 5 P.M. lectured in Blackstone, Hopkinton, and Bellingham. My afternoon discourse September 9 was in the nature of a valedictory, from the text, "Finally, brethren, farewell; be perfect, be of good comfort, be of one mind; live in peace and the God of love and peace shall be with you" (2 Corinthians 13:11). It was an affecting and impressive occasion. A large audience was present, composed mostly of deeply interested friends, though some outsiders were there, drawn by curiosity or otherwise. I could ask no more unmistakable demonstrations of personal respect and attachment, nor of regret at my departure than were there manifest. And it was substantially the same with friends in neighboring towns where I was accustomed to lecture and officiate at funerals.

On the third Sabbath in September I commenced fulfilling my engagement to supply the pulpit of Rev. Hosea Ballou in Boston, while he went on to occupy what was now mine in New York. I spoke in the morning in his School Street church; in the afternoon in that of the First Society, Hanover Street, in exchange with Rev. Sebastian Streeter; and in the evening, by request of Rev. Hosea Ballou 2d, in his desk at Roxbury. The next Sunday morning I exchanged with Rev.

Brother Thompson[16] of Charlestown, and in the afternoon preached again in School Street, thus concluding my engagement and with it my ministry in New England for the then present.

Removal to New York

Meanwhile preparations had been going on rapidly for transferring myself, family, and belongings to the new home and field of service in the country's metropolis. Some household and other articles not likely to be needed had been disposed of at auction, and the rest were carefully packed and shipped in proper order. Our dwelling house was put in good hands, to be rented or sold, as might be deemed most desirable.

All things being ready, we left Milford on Tuesday, September 25, for Providence, where we boarded a steamer, expecting to reach our destination the next forenoon in time for the installation services at three o'clock p.m. But various things transpired to delay our boat, and we had a long, dismal passage, terminating about five o'clock, when we landed, in poor plight (by reason of seasickness, broken rest, etc.) for appearance before the public in any form. The installation had been postponed till evening and came off accordingly, though at a later hour than hoped for, and with much less than the customary display of parts.[17] I have neither memoranda nor recollection of details further than that the sermon was by Rev. Hosea Ballou, who took for a text Romans 1:14-16. The subject of discourse was treated with the well-known ability of the preacher, a respectable congregation was present, and the exercises were appreciatively satisfactory. Thus my pastoral canoe was once more launched on the uncertain waters.

After temporary accommodation in the family of Brother Holden, we rented a tenement and set up housekeeping at No. 99 Thompson Street,[18] though it was some time before our domestic affairs were comfortably reconstructed so that we felt really at home. We were subjected to serious disappointment at an early day in our New York life, in that our matronly friend, Miss Joanna Cook, who had come on with us to be an assistant in household cares and a companion more particularly for my wife, became so decidedly homesick and otherwise ill that she insisted upon returning to the friends she left behind her, and did so within a month of our arrival. After her departure we supplied the place thus vacated as best we could – sometimes readily and satisfactorily, but frequently quite otherwise.

Child Lost and Found

While getting settled in our new quarters we were one day thrown into a spasm of fearful anxiety and alarm by the sudden disappearance of our son, then a little over four years old, for whom a careful search of several hours throughout all the neighborhood and repeated calls in all directions proved fruitless and vain. I went hither and yon, hoping to find him in some of the streets or alleys; friends and neighbors were rallied to assist in looking him up; but the mystery grew deeper and deeper, and our apprehensions more and more distressing, till at length our good Brother Holden appeared, leading the tired and trembling wanderer into our presence. It may be imagined what relief came to our burdened hearts when we caught sight of him again and with what emotions of grateful joy we once more had him in our arms. It seemed that he ventured some distance from our dwelling place, lured by strange and pleasing sights – so far that when he came to himself and wanted to return, he could not find the way. Realizing very soon that he was lost, he began to cry and moan piteously, saying, "I want to go home." A watchman hearing him, took him in charge, and not being able to learn where he lived, carried him, agreeably to city regulations, to the public almshouse, where such stray ones are kindly taken care of until called for. When Brother Holden heard of his disappearance, knowing the course pursued in such cases, he at once repaired to the institution named where he found the lad a short time only after he had been brought in by the officer. The little fellow recognized Mr. Holden, whom he had seen repeatedly before, sprang to meet him, seized his hand eagerly, and was happy to be led by him back to the home from which he had thoughtlessly strayed and to the fond embraces of parental hands and hearts.

Pastoral Labor in New York
Having been duly inducted into my new field of labor, I addressed myself to my pulpit and pastoral duties with all the ability and zeal of which I was master, but with less evident success than I had hoped for. I had good friends who did what they could to assist and encourage me, but Mr. Kneeland and his adherents seemed to prosper, drawing into their support and fellowship many wavering and susceptible minds. My society had been seriously weakened by the division, and the faithful were anxiously looking for an increase of numbers and renewed thrift under my administration. But circumstances were unpropitious, and with all my diligence and zeal, I could not realize my own expectations, and what was a greater trial to me, I felt that I was not realizing the expectations of my people. After several months of earnest effort to little purpose, as I thought, I began to suspect that I was not the "right man in the right place"!

Still I persevered and cast about in my thought for some new means of usefulness and influence. In my anxiety and desire to accomplish the most I could for myself, my society, and the cause of truth, I devised a plan or scheme for starting and editing a small, semi-monthly paper to be called the *Dialogical Instructer*, and made arrangements for carrying the project into effect.[19] I secured a few personal friends as financial backers, and prepared and put to press my first issue, which bore date January 5, 1828. This gave me my first experience in editorship, of which I have had much since that day.

Appeals from Milford

My removal from Milford, though determined upon somewhat abruptly, and, as I afterward found, much against the judgment and earnest wishes of the principal members of my society there, awakened no unkindly feelings on their part toward me, and called forth from them no expressions of blame or condemnation. On the other hand, they still seemed to hold me in profound respect, manifested toward me a truly friendly spirit, and hoped the change would prove advantageous, both for me personally and for the cause of Universalism, which both I and they had so much at heart. This was evinced by the correspondence carried on between me and some of their leading representatives, which was always characterized by the utmost cordiality, frankness, and good will.

Somehow or other, perhaps by some casual remark of mine or by the general tone of my letters, or in some other way, it began to be suspected among my former parishioners ere many months had passed by, that things in New York were not going altogether to my mind; that my expectations were not fully realized; and that consequently there was a growing uncertainty in regard to what my future was to be. This suspicion appeared in letters of friends inquiring particularly into my pastoral affairs, whether or not I was satisfied with my position and work, etc., reminding me of my promise to return to Milford if all did not go well, and signifying that they all would be very glad to see me back again. As early as January 11, 1828, Esquire Hunt wrote me as follows:

> We are one and all anxious to hear how you are situated, what society you have, of your prosperity or adversity. I wish you to write me plainly and truly. I have a letter from Esquire Holden, who states that he was mistaken in his communication to me respecting your wishing to be considered a candidate for their society, but quite the reverse; therefore he takes the blame upon himself. Please give my compliments to him and tell him I thank him for the pamphlets he sent me, but am sorry that he should be the means of separating you from our society. We are at this time without any meeting except visiting each other, all waiting to hear from you.

It was evidently understood among my Milford friends that I was struggling against wind and tide, with little prospect of any change for the better. Probably I said as much as this in my letters to them from time to time. And so on February 25, Mr. Hunt wrote me again:

> You have the same opportunity, and I think, greater reason to return to Milford than you had to leave it; but you must and will be your own judge. Here are Milford, Bellingham, and Medway with meetinghouses; and Hopkinton, Mendon, Upton, Uxbridge, and many other societies you used to labor with, all destitute at this time. We, as well as our neighboring brethren, still feel anxious for your return. I do hope and trust you will not disappoint so many of your good friends here as to deprive them of your labors in the ministry without, after due trial and just experience, you are fully persuaded you can be far more useful in New York than in Milford.

And once more, March 17:

> Since I wrote you last I have not heard anything from you, etc. I am requested by the Universalist Committee to say to you that it is their desire you should inform them on what conditions you will return to Milford and settle with us for seven or ten years, provided there is a printing office set up and a schoolhouse built for you. For our society still believe it is best for them, as well as yourself, that you should come back as soon as possible.

About the first of April I sent a response to these earnest appeals of Esquire Hunt, confessing that I felt somewhat disappointed by my New York experiences, that I appreciated the good feelings and wishes of my Milford friends, and that I might ultimately think it best to return; but that there was likely to be a severe struggle in my mind before I could decide to abandon my situation. At this point all correspondence was suspended for a few weeks, during which period thoughtful deliberation was going on with both parties concerned, in order that a wise decision might be reached in regard to the matter in hand. Meanwhile I was brought to the end of the twenty-fifth year of my life.

CHAPTER 8

1828-1829

The urgent appeal from my former Milford society, quoted near the end of the last chapter, made a profound impression upon me, partly, no doubt, on account of the unpropitious circumstances in which I was placed. And hence, after much reflection, I concluded to signify to the trustees of my New York parish that I was not satisfied with the result of my labors in their behalf, and felt that I had better return to the place whence I came. They seemed to be astonished and sorry when I communicated my decision to them and expressed the hope that I would reconsider it. Finding me persistent in my purpose, they at length consented to give me up, provided I would assist them in obtaining another preacher of satisfactory talents and character. I replied that my influence was small in such matters, but what I had would be exerted to their advantage.

The Prince Street Society and Rev. Hosea Ballou

On inquiring if they had anyone particularly in view to succeed me, they named, to my great surprise, a no less distinguished personage than Rev. Hosea Ballou. I told them I had no faith whatever that he would entertain such a proposal as was suggested, but added that if his services could be secured it would be the making of the society and I would gladly do anything in my power to promote so desirable a consummation. They replied that they had good reasons for believing that he could be induced to come to New York, for he had signified as much when he was last in the city in a conversation with Mr. James Hall, an eminent Universalist merchant. I was still incredulous, thinking there must have been some misunderstanding on the part of the gentleman. They were sure there was none and asked me to open a correspondence with Mr. Ballou, which for want of faith in the thing I declined to do.

Thereupon Mr. Henry Fitz,[1] chairman of the board of trustees (who were more confident than I), was delegated to address him upon the subject. An answer to his letter of inquiry was soon received, which we all understood to be favorable to the contemplated negotiation. I confessed myself happily disappointed and immediately addressed an urgent appeal to my venerated brother in the ministry to come to New York and take charge of the Prince Street society. I had then unbounded confidence in him, both as to intellectual ability and moral integrity and honor. He responded, saying that in a few days he would see our trustees and confer with them face to face.

Mr. Ballou came on accordingly and a meeting was held when the whole matter in hand was thoroughly considered. During the interview, the reverend gentleman was asked what salary he should expect were he to take the position proposed. His reply was in substance this: "I am now very happily situated in Boston, my society there is large and respectable, I am in the midst of numerous friends, my children are settled at no great distance from me, my salary is ample – about $1600 – as large as my supporters are well able to pay; all I need or would willingly receive. Now if I come to New York, the good of the cause, not pecuniary advantage, would be the chief inducement. I shall therefore ask only such compensation as to be no loser in a monetary point of view." Nothing could be more just, honorable, or satisfactory than this and the conference closed.

A full meeting of the board was soon after held for final action in the case. The whole ground was traversed again, all the circumstances of expense of removal, comparative cost of living, distance from friends, etc., were carefully and frankly discussed, resulting in an agreement that my honored kinsman should come to New York upon a salary of $1800 – the expense of getting his family and goods from Boston to be paid by the brethren here. In regard to the time when the new pastorate should begin, Mr. Ballou said he was not sure his Boston society would release him, but thought there would be no great difficulty about it, and if he was released, he could enter on the new engagement in a few weeks. The interview closed satisfactorily and the trustees were joyous for the future. The tidings of what had been done and of the new prospects opened to the society gave great satisfaction to the members and their friends, exciting the liveliest anticipations – alas, never to be realized.

Mr. Ballou was to preach in Philadelphia the ensuing Sunday[2] and in my Prince Street pulpit the one following. Before leaving my house for the Quaker City, having been my guest during his stay in New York, he began to think he had been too moderate in his demands upon the brethren here, telling me in private conversation that he deemed it very doubtful if his Boston friends would consent to his leaving them on the terms named. After a long talk with him with a view of finding out what offers would be necessary to induce his people to give him up, he told me that if $200 were added to the sum agreed upon, making it $2000, he had no doubt they would release him, though, he added, he could not be absolutely ertain of it. On the strength of what he said, I promised to submit his new proposition to the trustees, hoping for the best.

I fulfilled this promise immediately after he started for Philadelphia, though it was an awkward and disagreeable task for me. The trustees were astonished at this new phase of the matter and some of them almost incredulous as to my having a correct understanding of Mr. Ballou's views and feelings; the increased demands, after what had been definitely agreed upon, being wholly unexpected, not to say exorbitant. But they were not long in finding out that even greater exactions were to be laid upon them and that if their object was to be attained, it would be upon still harder terms. For when the candidate returned and negotiations were opened anew, all former action was reconsidered and annulled, and an entirely new arrangement was consummated, to wit: the annual salary should be $2000, to be specially guaranteed by pecuniarily responsible individuals, the settlement to be for life, with the understanding that a colleague should be provided when necessary without reducing the salary more than $800 per annum, and all the expenses of removal to be paid. This being settled, an ardent epistle was sent by the trustees to the Boston society, beseeching them to concur in the contemplated change and a glorious consummation seemed now to be fully assured. All this transpired about June 1, 1828.

The final outcome of the protracted effort to secure the pastoral services of the most distinguished preacher in the denomination, with all the maneuvering and apparent craft connected therewith, was that in due time word came from Boston announcing that Mr. Ballou's society there refused to release him on any terms, and therefore he could not remove to New York. The Prince Street society were greatly disappointed, as well they might be, in thus having all their earnest endeavors prove fruitless and their plans for the future utterly frustrated; and they were thrown for the time being into a state of consternation, bewilderment, and almost despair.

Recall to Milford

While these things were going on with reference to my New York parish and its prospective pastorship, I had been negotiating with my old society in Milford for a return thither. In response to a letter written by me about the first of April, to which allusion has already been made, I received, after the lapse of a few weeks, the following communication:

Milford, May 3, 1828

Dear Rev. Brother: –
The Committee of the Universalist Society in Milford have had the pleasure of perusing your favor, through the politeness of Brother P. Hunt, to him of the first of last month. We thought we discovered a willingness in you to take up your residence and preach with us once more on some conditions or other. There are certain facts connected with this business which we think it proper to state, viz: Our Society are more than anxious that you should come and will not be satisfied with an answer in the negative; yet with the present numbers they are unable to pay you more yearly than before. We do not doubt that some would give almost all they have. We should be willing to add to the amount as the Society increases. We have a desire, should you return, even in our present circumstances, that you should have a barn and a horse and chaise as soon as possible. Should you be so kind as to come back, we will build you a barn suitable for your use immediately, and give the old salary – prompt pay; also as much and as fast towards a horse and chaise as our means will admit. In fact,

we will do all we can and more than we would for any other man. We understood you that there must be a conflict in your mind before you could decide. If it must be so, we hope it will soon begin, and soon end by your being placed in the bosom of your friends, where, if you have but a morsel of bread, you will eat that in love and quietness. All which we humbly submit for your candid consideration and for ourselves and Society anxiously await your answer.

From your most devoted friend,
per order of the Committee,
ARIAL BRAGG

On the twelfth of May I answered this letter, communicating my decision to comply with the committee's invitation and return to Milford in the course of a few weeks. To this Colonel Bragg cordially rejoined a week later, expressing for himself, the committee, and society, the most fraternal love and satisfaction.

So much being settled, the New York trustees, elated with the expectation of having Rev. Brother Ballou for a minister at an early day, consented to the removal of my family and effects to Milford as soon as I found it convenient, provided that I would supply the pulpit till my successor's arrival, which, it was understood, would be the first Sunday in July. During the week that he was in Philadelphia, therefore, we packed up whatever we desired to take with us to our old home, started it on its way, while we ourselves left in season to reach there before the following Sunday, when I was to preach again to the people of my former charge.

Having stored my goods for a few weeks and placed my wife and child among friends, I returned the next week to New York to fulfill my engagement there and close up a few matters that remained unsettled. I had the good fortune to find an old friend, Mr. Noah Cook, who was ready to take my house off my hands for the remainder of the time for which I had rented it, in order to occupy it himself. It was also necessary to make some disposition of the *Dialogical Instructer*, which had reached its thirteenth number, and an arrangement was entered into with Revs. Thomas Whittemore and Russell Streeter,[3] then about to start the *Trumpet and Universalist Magazine*,[4] by which its subscription list was transferred to them.[5]

I preached for the last time as pastor of the Prince Street society June 29, 1828, giving my friends an informal farewell with the least possible ado. My position at the time was a somewhat anomalous and trying one. I had pledged myself to supply the pulpit there till my successor was ready to take my place, which, it was supposed, would be on the next Sunday. And now word had just been received that Mr. Ballou, who had been relied upon to follow me, was not coming at all. The people were perplexed beyond measure, inconsolable almost, by their disappointment, and nothing that I could say was likely to soothe their feelings.

All my plans were laid with reference to the closing of my pastorate there and resuming the one at Milford immediately. No reasonable objections could be made to my leaving at once and I acted accordingly. And so on the first of July I bade my New York friends a final goodbye, taking a steamer to Providence, going thence to Smithfield where my family was, and proceeding with them to Milford. I was received with outstretched hands and warm hearts, and recommenced my pastoral labors the Sunday following, July 6, 1828.

Reflections on Rev. Hosea Ballou

In closing the record of my experiences in New York I deem it proper to indulge in a few reflections which they naturally suggest. The question has often arisen in my review of the matter just narrated whether or not there was anything wrong or dishonorable in the course I pursued with reference to it. I have never been able to see that there was, but have always felt myself justified and unworthy of blame at the bar of my own conscience and before my Maker.

I have not, however, been able to render the same exculpatory verdict in the case of Father Hosea Ballou. I thought at the time and I still think in the serenity of old age that his treatment of the Prince Street society was discreditable and blameworthy, derogatory to his character and standing as a man and as a minister of universal grace and salvation. It seriously shocked my previously entertained reverence for and confidence in him. Indeed, it destroyed much of these and they were never restored to me. There seemed a worldly shrewdness, a sort of mercantile foxiness in his conduct, which was repugnant to my notions of Christian duty and honor, and which I had thought to be morally impossible in him. My feeling in the matter was intensified by ascertaining soon after, on what I regarded good authority, that his maneuver resulted in securing some hundreds of dollars addition to his yearly stipend from his Boston friends. Nor does the fact that this is the way of the world and of many clergymen render it less culpable in my judgment, or more innocent and Christlike.

I do not censure Mr. Ballou for not going to New York. It would have been unwise for him to have done so on *any* salary. I censure him for demanding so much of the society there, repeatedly increasing his figures, and then accepting a premium for remaining in Boston, while making all the time the highest professions of disinterestedness and devotion to the cause of Universalism.

One good effect was produced by the revulsion that took place in my own mind at the transaction under consideration. My former great respect for Rev. Brother Hosea had drawn me far towards his peculiar doctrine that all sin, suffering, and punitive discipline end with man's earthly life; also into the evil persuasion that those Restorationists in the Universalist denomination who had publicly controverted that doctrine had done so not from honest convictions of truth and duty, but mainly from personal ambition, envy, spleen, and pique. I had never been converted to the no-future-punishment hypothesis, yet I was so strongly attached to the leading apostles and devotees of this hypothesis that I was silently acquiescing in it and as near embracing it as one could be who wished to find some convincing reason for doing so, but had wholly failed in the attempt. Moreover, by the same subtle influence, I had become greatly prejudiced against the "factious" Restorationists, as they were designated, which made the matter still worse. But here had come a shock to my feelings which suggested that I might have been too credulous and facile, and which led me to examine the ground on which I was standing and correct the mistakes into which I had been unwittingly led.

Another incident which occurred, I think, while the negotiations spoken of were going on, contributed largely to the same result. One day while Father Hosea was stopping at my own house, I tried to draw from him the main reasons for his distinctive view of the restriction of sin and misery to the present state of being. I addressed him in substance as follows: "I am perfectly persuaded of the final holiness and happiness of all human souls; as I am that there can be no such thing as God's inflicting any vindictive, cruel, or useless punishment on men here or hereafter. But if there are those who leave this mortal state in a sinful condition, hating the heavenly Father and one another, and dying perhaps in the very commission of some wicked act, how can they possibly enter into happiness in the next life without first experiencing more or less shame, sorrow, and penitence?"

This was a question of profound interest to me, and I expected he would give me, in view of my youth and of our mutual relations to each other, his strongest arguments in support of his theory, and so do something to enlighten me on so vital a subject. To my utter disappointment, he waggishly evaded the issue and with a smile and a shrug, said: "So then, Brother Adin, you think they'll have to be smoked a little, do you?" I was profoundly in earnest, but he chose to be facetious and, as he thought, witty. I did not like it and concluded, after reflecting upon the matter, that he could not give even a plausible answer to my inquiry. Nor have I ever had occasion to change that opinion. This was the first, last, and only conversation we ever had upon the subject.

Not far from this time, Rev. Charles Hudson, an able exponent of the Restorationist theory of life, death, and destiny, published in book form a series of letters in defense of the doctrine of limited future retribution addressed to Rev. Mr. Ballou, which were of great value and had a wide circulation.[6] Although designed especially for the latter's consideration, he, instead of giving them the attention they deserved, or which common courtesy even would have prompted, gravely announced to the Universalist public through its Boston organ, that he had not read the work and should not answer it, as he was told it contained nothing new upon the question involved.[7] This did not tend to check the declining respect I had for him. It rather led me to decide that men and doctrines alike ought to stand or fall, not on mere assumptions, but on their respective intrinsic merits or demerits, as determined by an enlightened and candid judgment.

State of Universalism in New York

Passing from these more immediately personal matters, I am moved to remark that the general conditions and prospects of Universalism in the nation's metropolis, as I was obliged to see and study it while there, were at best somewhat dubious. Rev. Edward Mitchell, an eminent champion of the doctrine of the final redemption of all men, and his society worshiping in Duane Street, were Restorationists and stood almost entirely aloof from the mass of those bearing the Universalist name.[8] Moreover, he was far along in years, with failing health, and his people were not large in numbers. Rev. Abner Kneeland in his new movement was riding a high horse down hill into atheism, with a motley train of admirers at his heels. The Prince Street society, of which he previously had charge, was greatly crippled by the withdrawal of so many who followed him in his wild career. Furthermore, with the exception of a few choice spirits, it was difficult to tell what the majority of professed Universalists believed or were aiming at – only that they had cut loose from the endless-misery sects and were adrift somewhere on the high seas of liberalism, with less of sound faith than of volatile skepticism. Of fraternal unity, cooperation, and fellowship, there was little. Thus my first favorable impressions proved illusory, and I left New York "a sadder, though a wiser man."[9]

The prevailing aspects of moral and social order, or rather of disorder, in the city, did not brighten much upon closer acquaintance. The place was a Babylon, composed of all peoples and tongues, high and low, rich and poor, fortunate and unfortunate, in one vast whirl of good and evil enterprise – a heterogeneous compound, which I will not attempt to describe.

During my ministry there, I was called upon to officiate but a few times either on funeral occasions or at the nuptial altar, though I solemnized enough marriages to give variety and uniqueness to my experience. As the laws of the state then were, few restrictions or safeguards were established for the governance of those proposing to enter the marital relation; no publishments, no registration, no certificates of intention being required of the parties concerned. Those conducting the ceremonial – magistrates or clergymen – must do so on their own responsibility, at least so far as mutual fitness was taken into account. In my youthful inexperience, I made some grievous mistakes. In one instance, the groom proved to be an unprincipled bigamist. In another, when two couples came to my house for the ceremony, there had been a mutual unmarrying of parties previously united, and swapping of mates. On the following Sunday, as I descended the pulpit stairs, I was met by a finely appearing lady dressed in mourning, who claimed to be the sister of one of the brides, and who stated that the family were greatly troubled about the affair and desired me to call at their house, giving me the street and number, and assist in straightening things out. I took the matter under advisement, and after reconnoitering the place designated and its neighborhood, concluded that it was the more discreet course not to risk any intimacy with the inhabitants of the premises indicated, but leave them to adjust their affairs without my aid. These experiences led me to believe that matrimonial alliances were liable to more uncertainty and erraticism than I could at that early period comprehend.

A Gloomy Premonition

While fulfilling my engagement to supply the New York pulpit for a few Sundays succeeding the removal of my family to New England, I boarded with Mr. N. Rose and wife, members of the Prince Street congregation and devoted friends of mine. During my sojourn with them I received in a dream one night a solemn premonition of coming bereavement. I saw, or seemed to see, as in a vision, the dead body of my wife lying before me, and nearby a new-born, living infant. The impression was so distinct and dreadful that it awoke me in a "horror of darkness,"[10] and thenceforth the memory of it haunted me more or less ominously until some months later it was literally fulfilled. I concealed the dream in my own bosom, hoping it might be only a barren and harmless freak of the mind, yet fearing all the while that it would prove true, and watching sedulously the signs that might in any way foreshadow or indicate the fatal issue it portrayed.

Return to Milford

About the first of July we were once more domiciliated in Milford, my opening sermon under the new arrangement being delivered on the morning of Sunday, the sixth of that month. As our own house had been rented to families that could not readily vacate it, we occupied rooms temporarily in an adjoining dwelling, but ere many months elapsed we were fairly established again in our old quarters, with none to molest or make afraid.[11] A new barn was erected during the summer, and in due time a horse and chaise were added to our domestic equipment, not only that they might contribute to our personal convenience and pleasure, but that I might more easily and faithfully discharge the pastoral duties of my office – the people of my charge, though not very many in number, being distributed in all directions over a wide extent of territory. Moreover, the many calls I had for miscellaneous services of one kind or another within driving distance of Milford, rendered it a part of wisdom and economy for me to have means of conveyance of my own and be independent of neighbors, parishioners, etc., however kind; and of livery stables, however ready to serve me, for a consideration, in that respect.

Very soon after my return, I found myself not simply going my old round of ministerial duty, but more in demand and more actively engaged otherwise than ever before. I received several invitations to occupy vacant pulpits as a candidate for settlement over parishes of more distinction in various respects than that of Milford, but felt myself in honor bound under the circumstances to decline them all. I attended and participated in the services of numerous ecclesiastical gatherings – ministerial associations and ordinations, dedications of houses of worship, religious conferences and the like, and made frequent exchanges far and near with my clerical brethren.

At the dedication of the Universalist meetinghouse in Pawtucket, Rhode Island, in December of the year now in review, at which time Rev. Jacob Frieze was installed pastor of the society, I met my elder brother, Rev. Hosea Ballou, but nothing passed between us concerning the New York affair, neither on that occasion nor indeed ever afterwards.

Meanwhile, my wife's health perceptibly declined, necessitating the giving up on her part of all manual labor and the employment of domestic help continuously. Very naturally, my dream would often recur to me and with ever-increasing vividness, awaking anew in my breast and torturing me with the most fearful apprehensions. I could do no otherwise than maintain unbroken silence about it, suppress and conceal as far as possible my feelings, and await the issue with such calmness and composure as my reason, conscience, and faith in the infinite perfections of my Heavenly Father enabled me to command. Nevertheless, the cloud still hung in the sky above me, and sent its chilling shadows into my heart.

Debate with Origen Bacheler

In the autumn of 1828, I was visited by Mr. Origen Bacheler[12] of Providence, Rhode Island, editor of a small periodical entitled the *Anti-Universalist*,[13] which, as its name indicates, was devoted to the controverting of the doctrine of the salvation of all men in its every form and feature. He had been canvassing the town for subscribers, he said by way of introduction, and so dropped in on me. I acknowledged his courtesy in some general reply in no wise calculated to provoke discussion or suggest even religious conversation. But he soon broached his favorite topic of thought, rather in the spirit of controversy than of candid discussion, for he loved debate as he loved his victuals. As my disposition has been through life not to seek nor shrink from polemic warfare, I met his assaults on my cherished faith promptly in a long and earnest argument. He was keen, forcible, persistent, and I was not slow to ward off his blows at every turn, and give, as well as receive, sharp shots of dialectic musketry. A severe toothache on his part and an equally severe headache on mine, brought the interview to a premature end, neither yielding a hair's breadth of ground assumed in the debate. But he conceived so much of a liking to me, as he said (with the notion, perhaps, of helping his paper), that before leaving he proposed a discussion of the subject at issue between us in its columns. I could not well refuse, and so consented to a public correspondence with him in a series of articles, pro and con, of a polemic character. To show how anxious he was for the fray, I copy the following letter received from him shortly afterward:

> Providence, Oct. 18, 1828
>
> Rev. Mr. Ballou: The public are on tiptoe with expectation. They feel great solicitude in relation to our proposed discussion. Already have some political papers noticed it and among the rest the National Gazette, Walsh's paper in Philadelphia. Some have subscribed for the Anti-Universalist solely on account of this expected controversy, and even some Universalists. What remains for me to observe is that after having excited public expectation, we proceed to gratify it without delay. Please, sir, forward me the introductory number as soon as possible. It is necessary that I receive it early next week in order to its insertion in our next.
>
> Very respectfully I am, etc.,
>
> ORIGEN BACHELER

Before this urgent prompting reached me, I had received an anonymous letter from a conspicuous Universalist layman in Providence, entreating me to have nothing to do with Bacheler and his *Anti-Universalist*. He said that "Universalists should treat that paper and its editor with silent contempt... Its publisher and patrons aim merely to vilify and abuse... Your character may suffer by coming in contact with such a low and contemptible vehicle... Saving a few bigots in this town, it is execrated by the whole community," etc. Nevertheless, having committed myself as far as I had, and never fancying a dainty dignity that refuses to notice ungenteel opponents for fear of getting besmeared, I went ahead. Quite a long series of articles followed,[14] the merits of which I can hardly pass judgment upon at this late day, the papers containing them having been lost or mislaid. Probably more good than harm was done, but not much of either.

Birth of Daughter and Death of Wife

During the ensuing winter I had charge of the school in North Purchase, the same taught by me the first year of my residence in Milford. I rode three miles to it in the morning, returning to my family at night, the health of my wife being such as to require more than usual attention and care. All my other duties were performed in regular order, and none of the interests entrusted to my keeping were consciously neglected or allowed to suffer detriment.

On the thirtieth of January, 1829, another child was born to us; a daughter who, notwithstanding the early loss of her mother and in spite of many threatened dangers, has survived to the present time – the only one of my four children now remaining in the flesh. The patient passed through the trying ordeal as well as could be expected in view of her previously debilitated condition, and for some days seemed so comfortable that I hoped for an escape from the portended fatal issue.

It was not long, however, before there appeared in the case marked symptoms of failing vitality and strength, ultimating in what was called quick consumption in those times, from which there was no release except in death. Oh, the sad and anxious days and nights through which I then passed! My feelings can be imagined only by those who have been visited by similar calamities. Everything possible was done for the sick and suffering one. The best of nursing was secured and there was all needful kindly, sympathetic helpfulness on the part of the women of my congregation. Our family physician, Dr. G. D. Peck,[15] in whom we had great confidence, called in as counsel Dr. Daniel Thurber[16] of South Milford, the most experienced, skillful, and eminent practitioner in our general region, so that there was no lack in that regard. But all in vain. Nothing could check the ravages of the destroyer.

When the fast-sinking patient became aware of her critical condition, she conversed with me freely about it and about her approaching dissolution. She desired me to pray with and for her (which I did as best I could with my anguish-stricken spirit and quivering lip), assured me of her unabated dying love for me, confided the children and her personal effects to my care, and expressed the wish that her body might be buried in some place where mine at last could rest by its side. She said but little about the future, but manifested an undoubting trust in her heavenly Father and an assurance that all would be well with her spirit beyond the river of death. She was calmly resigned but could not talk at any length, her eyes and countenance telling what her organs of speech were unable to articulate. In just three weeks from the birth of her child she breathed her last and passed into the world of spirits, leaving me her lifeless body and a little infant, just as had been shown me in that dream-vision some months before. Thus about seven years after marriage I was bereaved of a most affectionate, devoted, and exemplary wife, whom I had every reason to love, confide in, cherish, and hold in perpetual and ever precious remembrance. Our brief union had, I can but feel, the sanction of the Divine Father, as it certainly received abundant blessings from his guardian hand.

My beloved wife died on the twentieth of February, 1829, at the age of twenty-eight years, ten months, and twenty days. The funeral took place in the brick meetinghouse on the twenty-fourth, having been postponed one day on account of a terrific snowstorm that rendered the roads almost impassable. For this reason, but few relatives on either side were able to be present, but of sympathizing friends, parishioners, and neighbors there was a large attendance. The services, consisting of prayers and a sermon, etc., were conducted by Rev. Hosea Ballou 2d, of Roxbury, for whom I cherished a peculiar fraternal regard, and were appropriate and consolatory. What was mortal of the dear departed was interred in the old burying ground at Milford Center, and monumental stones with suitable inscriptions were soon after erected at the head of the grave. Some twelve years later the whole was removed to our burial lot in the Hopedale Cemetery.

A brief obituary notice from the pen of Rev. H. Ballou 2d, as I suppose, appeared in the *Trumpet and Universalist Magazine* of March 7, 1829, from which I transcribe the following passages:

> Throughout her short but painful sickness, amidst the rapid decay of a quick consumption, she uttered no complaint; nor was she alarmed on receiving a tender intimation from her husband that her disease threatened to prove mortal. As her

life wated away, she maintained a steady and serne confidence in the Father of Universal Grace, and when the last hour arrived and the torpor of death came upon her, she bade her husband farewell with composure.

From her childhood she was brought up in the doctrine of Universal Salvation; and in mature age her character, mild, benevolent, and conscientious, seemed to comport well with the sentiments she had received. Naturally attached to domestic life, its duties were the principal objects of her care and application; and if her religious professions were not loud and imposing, it was because her disposition as well as her belief inclined her to show her faith by her works.

My parochial and other duties, which had been somewhat interrupted by the sickness and death of my wife, were resumed after the funeral solemnities were over, and proceeded thenceforward with tolerable regularity. My thoughts were thereby turned away from the great sorrow through which I had passed, and I was somewhat relieved of the burden of grief and pain which otherwise would have seemed too heavy to be borne. At the same time I had the strongest reasons for gratitude to God, not only for spiritual consolation during all my afflictive experience from the great fountain of all good, but for a multitude of sympathetic demonstrations from my earthly friends. I remember "the wormwood and the gall"[17] and also, I trust, "the wine and the oil"[18] of those far-off days. The outlines of my troubled dream remain and of what it seemed to prognosticate, but the light and shade thereof grew more and more indistinct with the receding years.

Where, now, I can but ask, are the relatives and friends that then mourned with and comforted me? Nearly all gone over to the spirit continent, a scattered remnant only remaining, like myself, on the mortal shores, and we are awaiting the summons hence. But how has it fared with the departed? Are they lost in oblivion or only gone before?[19] Not lost, but translated to immortal fields – their spirits rehabilitated in bodies and garments suited to their present mode of being – each one in proper order progressing towards a celestial destiny of ineffable good and glory; some more slowly than others, but all surely. They have greeted each other on the eternal shore and congratulated each other upon their triumphant deliverance from the power of death and the grave, and upon the unfolding goodness of the Infinite Parent in all the dispensations of his ever-faithful providence. So may they greet us and we them, as we in God's own time shall emerge from the shadows of earth into the glorious sunlight of immortality.

CHAPTER 9

1829-1830

As I entered the twenty-seventh year of my life, I found new fields of service opening before me and new opportunities of advancing the cause of truth and righteousness, of which I felt myself to be the friend and champion. Not only did calls to lecture in surrounding towns on Sunday evenings and to officiate at funerals and on marriage occasions increase, but also invitations to preach in other pulpits than my own, both far and near; sometimes in exchange with a resident minister, and sometimes to fill a vacant place, in which latter case, if accepted, I had to provide for my own people as best I could.

Theological Student, Seth Chandler

Moreover, I took about this time under my care and tuition a young man who had been living at Lowell, Seth Chandler[1] by name, for the purpose of educating and training him for the work of the Christian ministry in the interest and fellowship of the Universalist denomination. He had in some way conceived a liking for me, and for some time a correspondence had been carried on between us in regard to his becoming my student. It resulted in an arrangement whereby his wishes were to be gratified, but sickness and death in my family had prevented it from being carried into effect. After the interruptions and changes occasioned by my bereavement had passed by, however, and I was fairly settled again in my plans and work, having secured board at the table of Mr. Adams Perry, Sr., to whom I had rented my house, Mr. Chandler came to Milford to enter upon his proposed course of study. This was in the month of June, 1829. He obtained an abiding place with Mr. Perry, so as to be with me as much as possible, receiving instruction from me and all the guidance and information I could impart to him in the way of equipping him for his chosen calling. This opened a new page of duty and responsibility for me to fill out.

He was about twenty-two years of age, a young man of excellent principles and moral character, with respectable talents and a moderate preliminary education, yet of laudable ambition, willing and anxious for improvement. His general knowledge was somewhat extensive and he was well posted in the literature of Universalism. I put him under such drill as I thought suitable, finding him an apt scholar, but so sensitive to criticism that it took me some time to make my correction and discipline fit his peculiar organization. We soon, however, came to understand and to adapt ourselves to each other, and his progress was rapid and satisfactory to a high degree. He remained under my tuition and influence till he was ripe for the pulpit – some three years. Soon after closing his engagement with me he was settled as pastor of the First Church and Society of Shirley; a position which he held and honored through a long and useful ministry.

A Bad Habit Conquered

About this time I was much exercised respecting the pernicious habit of using tobacco, which I formed not long after I entered the ministry of the Christian Connexion, by reason of the example and influence of the older clergymen with whom I was associated and for whom I entertained profound respect. In those days nearly all the ministers of every denomination were "hail fellows well met" in the filthy, harmful, and reprehensible practice of smoking, and many of them yet belong to the same shameful category. By continued indulgence I became a slave to the habit; so much so that I had a cigar or pipe in my mouth most of the time during my waking hours. I was so charmed and beguiled by what I was doing that I verily imagined that I could read, study, meditate, and write much better under the inspiration thus engendered than otherwise. At length my eyes were opened to the injury I was doing myself in this particular. There were unmistakable signs that I was undermining my health and waging war against my physical well-being. My reason and conscience were finally aroused and became faithful monitors and witnesses against me. I was convinced that I was abusing as well as defiling the temple in which God had for this present life installed my soul. Yet when I tried to escape from my thralldom, I found that in this as in other cases, my appetites, whether natural or artificial, when once enthroned were exceedingly pertinacious and obstinate. But could I not subdue them and reform? If not, I ought to be ashamed to preach repentance and reformation to others. And if I could, but did not do this, I was no true minister of the cross. I pondered this aspect of the case; I prayed for divine help and at last resolved to place my tobacco and pipe on a shelf within reach and see how long I could let them alone. I tried this expedient and, through grace from above strengthening me, triumphed with comparatively little struggle. The harmful, dangerous appetite was broken and I have abstained from its indulgence for more than forty years. And now, whenever I see an old or young tobacco slave, I am profoundly grateful to God for my own emancipation, and prayerful that all other such sinners may experience the like deliverance.

Extracts from Diary, September 1829

As an indication of the multiplicity of my cares and labors at this period and of the extent to which I was unconsciously overtaxing my physical and mental energies, I take the liberty of making a few extracts from my diary for the year 1829.[2]

[September 3-6.] Attended and took part in the dedication of the new Universalist meetinghouse in Marlborough, Massachusetts, September 3. Remained there over the Sabbath and preached three times. Also dedicated three children as a part of the afternoon service. Brother Chandler supplied the Milford desk for me.

[September 13.] At home on the next Sabbath.

[September 15-17.] Traveled the same week to Winchester, New Hampshire, to attend the general convention of the Universalist denomination, before which I delivered a discourse on Wednesday. Much annoyed and displeased at that convocation by the interference of Rev. Hosea Ballou with an arrangement whereby Rev. David Pickering, of Providence, was to offer the principal prayer in connection with the preaching of a sermon by Rev. Paul Dean, of Boston. There had been some ill-feeling engendered between the objector and Brother Pickering by reason of the vigorous and unanswerable protest which the latter had made on different occasions against the former's pet hypothesis of no future retribution. The assignment of the part referred to was before the brethren for approval and seemed likely to receive it. Whereupon Rev. Hosea peremptorily said, "If this convention has any regard for my feelings, it will not allow this man to pray before it." This silenced all debate and secured unresisting submission at once! I resolved in my own mind not to attend another convention of that sort, and I never did.[3]

September 20. Preached two discourses at Chestnut Hill [Mendon], A.M. and P.M.; another at 5 P.M. in Millville; and a fourth at 7:30 P.M. in Uxbridge.

[September 27.] On the next Sabbath exchanged with Rev. Massena B. Ballou, of Charlton, Massachusetts.

[September 30.] On the following Wednesday preached three times at Chepachet, Rhode Island, being entertained at the residence of Mr. Sabin Smith. Thence home almost sick, having stopped on the way and spent an hour with my friend Clark Cook, in Mendon, who was confined to his bed with a fever.

Serious Illness

On Sunday, the fourth of October, I had arranged an exchange with Rev. Paul Dean, Bulfinch Street, Boston, where I was expected to deliver three discourses, the last to be an anniversary one before the Sabbath School Association. But this expectation was not realized. My morning sermon was cut short and the services for the day abruptly closed by a sudden attack of illness which forbade all further effort on my part. I was much exhausted and feverish when the exercises commenced and I proceeded with difficulty. At length in the midst of my discourse my sight failed me and faltering, I summoned strength to announce my inability to go on further, then sunk back almost helpless upon the pulpit sofa. The congregation was much alarmed, friends flocked to my relief, and presently a devoted brother, one of my warmest adherents when a candidate for the pastorate of the First Universalist society in 1824, had me in a coach conveying me to his humble but most hospitable home. Arriving there, himself, wife, and the whole family did all in their power to soothe and recruit me during the ensuing afternoon and night. They besought me to remain with them, have a physician, and get better before attempting to return to Milford. But I instinctively felt that I must by all means get home. So with ardent thanks for their great kindness, I almost tore myself away from them the next morning and being lifted into my chaise, started on my journey. The day was cold and blustering, and when I had completed my ride of thirty miles I was chilled through and felt myself to be a sick man. I went directly to my chamber, utterly prostrated with what resulted in a severe and protracted lung fever.

I passed the night of October 5 in unalleviated distress, and on the morning of the next day sent for Dr. Peck, my regular physician, who at once saw what my disease was and said it must have its usual run. He, however, applied such palliatives and antidotes as seemed necessary to render me as comfortable as possible and secure a favorable issue. My brother Ariel Ballou Jr., then a student with Dr. Thurber (before mentioned) at South Milford, was sent for to come and minister to me as best he could in various ways, since there was no one else on whom I felt at liberty to call in my emergency. He hastened to my bedside and proved a brother indeed, watching over me and attending to my wants with all vigilance and faithfulness, scarcely leaving me till the crisis was passed and I was out of danger. My theological student, Mr. Chandler, also favored me with much kind and efficient service. During my convalescence, I was cared for by my beloved mother whose presence was a comfort and support to me and whose experience enabled her to render me most valuable assistance; and by the daughter of one of my most respected and worthy parishioners, Miss Lucy Hunt, between whom and myself there had already sprung up a very strong and tender attachment – an attachment which some months later ripened into marriage, as will be noted in due time and place.

Under the ministrations of such devoted, faithful, and efficient attendants, and of the most competent and scrupulous physicians, my disease was held much in check and successfully overcome, and my progress in the way of recovery, after my fever had passed its turning point, was rapid and sure, without serious hindrance or relapse. So that in five weeks from the day I was stricken down in Boston, I was in my own pulpit again engaged in the active duties of my ministerial office. I however preached but one sermon on that second Sabbath in November, and that a written one – one of the few in those days which I committed to manuscript. In it I referred to my recent illness and recovery in terms which I am moved to reproduce in these pages. It was prepared specially for the occasion and had for a text Psalm 116:18: "What shall I render unto the Lord for all his benefits towards me?" After the introduction, consisting chiefly of the context with a few incidental suggestions, I came to my own case:

My friends, I stand before you as one rescued from the cold prison-house of death. A few days ago it was by no means an improbability that the icy hand of the destroyer would soon be laid upon your minister and you be called to follow his remains in sad procession to yon dormitory of the dead. But the burning fever was arrested, the ravages of consuming disease were made to cease, and the dawn of returning health smiled calmly upon me. But by whom, above well-directed and kind human exertions, have I been restored to life and health? Who blessed the means used for my recovery, and whose hand hath brought me back from the borders of the grave? Do I not stand before you a monument of the unfailing compassion of Him that liveth forever and ever! Yes, it is of the mercy of the Most High that I am permitted again to utter my voice from this desk. I called upon him when sickness had almost swallowed me up and he hearkened to my supplication. He answered me with peace and returning strength; he lifted upon me the light of his countenance and the dark clouds were dissipated. He said, "Let him walk again in the land of the living, for I will have mercy upon him." And now, lo, I stand before you this day to make my grateful acknowledgments amid the congregation of my people for the loving kindness of God toward me. He hath restored me that I might watch over my tender children; that I might again bear testimony to the great salvation and proclaim the final redemption of a lost world. He hath preserved me to come in and go out before you, my friends, and that I might take sweet counsel with you again on the shores of mortality. He hath restored me to the enjoyment of all that may reasonably be expected to fall to the lot of favored man, and I will venture to hope that many years of prosperity and usefulness yet remain to me in the appointments of indulgent Heaven. Oh, how great and precious are the blessings and benefits of our Heavenly Father! Let us all praise and magnify His name from henceforth even forevermore![4]

Domestic Life Re-Established

As winter came on, I found myself so fully restored to health and strength as to warrant me in engaging to assume charge of the school in the first district in town for the approaching term, a new schoolhouse having been recently erected and made ready for use only a quarter of a mile from my place of residence. This engagement I was able to carry into effect without detriment to myself, and to the satisfaction of teacher, pupils, parents; in fact, of all concerned.

Having closed my school and being comparatively free from outside responsibilities and labors, I turned my attention more immediately to the rehabilitating of my own home and the renewal of my own distinctive family life by entering a second time into the marriage relation. The young lady spoken of on a preceding page and I had already become affianced to each other by mutual attraction and pledges of affection and constancy, and there seemed to be good and sufficient reasons why the formal and legal marital union should be consummated at an early date. I longed for the independence and freedom which exist only in one's own household. I yearned for the companionship, the sympathy, the sweet heart-repose which can be found only in the domestic circle. I sighed for my dear children, separated from me and from each other, and earnestly desired that they might be with me, under my constant supervision and care, where proper parental influence might be exerted upon them and where they might contribute more directly and effectively to my comfort and happiness. I was fully persuaded that she whom I had selected to be the partner of my future joys and sorrows was not only worthy of my confidence and love, but every way competent to fill a mother's place toward my little ones and to discharge a mother's sacred responsibilities. Though young in years and just ripening into womanhood, yet was she much more mature in experience and judgment than many farther advanced in life. She was sedate, modest, circumspect, sensible, and discreet in her general deportment, intelligent, thoughtful, well trained in household affairs, affectionate, kind of heart, and obviously disposed to solid usefulness. I was satisfied with her and she professed to be with me, and we were mutually agreed upon uniting our fortunes and our destinies at an early day.

The third of March, 1830, was finally determined upon as the date when our marriage should be solemnized and preliminary preparations were made accordingly. The ceremony took place in the meetinghouse in which I ministered, in the presence of a large concourse of people. My favorite clerical brother, Rev. Hosea Ballou 2d, was the officiating clergyman on the occasion. He preached an appropriate sermon and our choir furnished interesting musical accompaniments. Everything passed off pleasantly and satisfactorily to the wedded pair and to the whole congregation, and the day closed with a wedding banquet at the house of the bride's parents, at which there were present only the immediate relatives of the bride and groom and a few invited guests.

We very soon commenced housekeeping in the home that for more than a year had been so sadly broken up and troubled. My little boy, Adin Jr., was immediately brought from his year's sojourn with my good friends, Clark Sumner and wife of North Purchase, but his infant sister had caught the whooping cough and could not safely join us for some weeks afterward. In due time, however, we were all together and the bark of our new domestic life, fairly launched upon the waters of time, glided calmly on towards the great future that stretched out before us.

Scene at a Funeral

Near the close of the twenty-seventh year of my mortal pilgrimage, on the twentieth of April, I had a very singular funeral experience, which in itself and in its accompanying circumstances illustrates a certain type of religion and of religious sense of duty much more prevalent in my younger days than at the present time. A little daughter of my good friend Capt. William Grant, of West Wrentham, was burned to death – an event which almost overwhelmed the family with grief and awakened heartfelt, sympathetic sorrow throughout the entire neighborhood. As on previous similar occasions in the household, I was summoned to officiate at the funeral.

The principal services were to take place in what was called the Elder Williams Meetinghouse, which, though originally a Baptist sanctuary, had come to be owned in part and to be occasionally occupied by the Universalists of the vicinity, of whom my friend was one. The edifice was thronged with the relatives, friends, and sympathizing acquaintances of the deeply bereaved ones. The acting minister of the Baptist society at the time, a Rev. Mr. Reed, of English birth and training, had, out of courtesy, been invited to go into the pulpit with me and offer the concluding prayer. We were utter strangers to each other, and I suppose, from what transpired before the close of the exercises, he was as thoroughly prejudiced against my general religious faith as a man could be.

In opening my discourse, which was in the form of a sermon, I took a text from Lamentations 3:32-33: "But though He cause grief, yet will He have compassion according to the multitude of His mercies; for He doth not afflict willingly nor grieve the children of men." The general drift of my remarks may be inferred from the passage quoted, what I said being based upon the infinite goodness of God and his unfailing kindness and love to his human offspring, whence might be deduced the consolatory lesson that under his divine government in the universe of souls, the trials, misfortunes, and afflictions to which we are subject in this mortal state must and will be overruled for good and made to work out the final holiness and happiness of those experiencing them. I illustrated my subject with appropriate examples and applied the lesson inculcated to the case of bereavement and distress which had awakened such widespread sorrow and called together so large a congregation.

Good Brother Reed was not at all pleased with my discourse, but deemed it delusive and dangerous. Therefore, instead of proceeding at once with his prayer when he arose to take the part asked of him, he stated that he had a burden of duty upon his mind which be could not forego, and that was "to protest against the sentiments that had just been expressed and to warn the people present of the danger involved in them." It can be imagined how such an unusual proceeding would, under the circumstances, affect the congregation. They were in a state of solemn, intense, yet measurably suppressed excitement. Nevertheless, they listened quietly while the reverend gentleman went on to state that the preacher had falsified and perverted the gospel, that he had flattered his hearers with the notion that God loves and is merciful to his sinful creatures, and applied the promises of grace to them without the condition of their faith and repentance, etc.

"I tell you," he continued, "that as sinners you have nothing to expect from God but fiery wrath and indignation. You are his enemies and he is your enemy till you make him your friend by turning to him with all your heart. Thus only can you secure his love and mercy, whatever may be your calamities, afflictions, sufferings, and bereavements." Having gone on in this strain for several minutes, he closed with a corresponding prayer.

I immediately responded. "Bereaved and sympathizing friends," I said,

> it is very disagreeable to my feelings to hold a theological controversy on a funeral occasion, and especially one so sad and distressing as the present, but since it has been forced upon me by the extraordinary remarks of our reverend friend, you will pardon me a brief rejoinder. You are all my witnesses that I have not preached to you unbelief, rebellion, and impenitence before your Heavenly Father, nor underrated the necessity of faith, submission, and loving trust toward him as indispensable to your welfare and happiness in this world or the world to come. But I have preached that God is your all-perfect friend, whether you are his friends or not, whether you love him or not, whether you are thankful or unthankful, good or evil. And on the ground of his eternal goodness, I have counseled and exhorted you to obedience, penitence, and reconciliation to him. On the ground that he first loved you, I have besought you to love him and give him the unreserved confidence of your hearts. The real point at issue between the brother and myself is whether God loves mankind because they first loved him or the reverse. Whether God first is merciful and seeks after sinners, or they first seek after him and implore his mercy in order to make him good, kind, tenderly affected, savingly disposed to them. Now in this case our brother has much more important personages to contend against than I am. His quarrel is not with me but with Jesus Christ and his chief apostles.

I then went on to quote the parables of the lost piece of silver, the wandering sheep, and the prodigal son, remarking that the lost sheep did not first return to the shepherd, nor the wayward boy's confession of penitence inspire his father's compassion and forgiveness.[5] I also repeated such passages from the Savior's lips as the following:[6]

> God so loved the world that he sent His only begotten son, etc.

> Love your enemies, bless them that curse you . . . that ye may be the children of your Father in Heaven. For He maketh His sun to rise on the evil and on the good, and sendeth rain upon the just and the unjust.

> Be ye therefore merciful as your Father in Heaven is merciful.

> He is kind to the unthankful and the evil.

Also from the words of Paul:[7]

> God commended His love toward us in that while we were yet sinners Christ died for us.

> God, who is rich in mercy, for His great love wherewith He loved us even when we were dead in sins, hath quickened us together in Christ.

And from John's Epistle:[8]

> Herein is love; not that we loved God, but that He loved us and sent His son, etc.

> We love Him, because He first loved us.

These and other texts of similar import which I quoted I accompanied with appropriate remarks as a sort of running commentary upon them, closing as follows:

I shall leave our friend to contend with and denounce the Savior of the world, the great apostle to the Gentiles, and the beloved St. John. If he can silence them, he will have silenced me, for I have only echoed their testimony upon the matter in question between us. Even John Calvin, his great theological father, he opposes, for that distinguished champion of the old faith taught positively that the elect were chosen from the fallen race of Adam "without the least foresight of faith, good works, or any conditions performed by the creature."[9] Yet here today, over this charred body, in the presence of these afflicted mourners, whom I have tried to console with words of hope and trust, he could not even pray without denouncing and warning this whole congregation against the doctrine on which all I had said was based, that God's aboriginal, perfect, unchangeable, eternal love, so clearly affirmed in the Christian Scriptures, renders him the adorable refuge of all the afflicted, sorrowing children of men. His controversy is not primarily with me, but with the oracles of divine and everlasting truth.

I then pronounced the benediction. My opponent left the house in agitated confusion, his own brethren and friends deploring his fatuity and want of wisdom, and the multitude rejoicing in the triumph of the truth.

Pastoral Duties at Medway

Early in the spring of 1830, arrangements were made between the Universalist societies of Milford and Medway, by the terms of which I was to divide my services between the two, preaching alternate Sundays in each, and during the summer delivering five o'clock lectures in each on the days I was absent at the regular hours of worship.[10] Brother Chandler, who had been away teaching in the winter months, had rejoined my family and was making rapid progress in his studies, having already become an acceptable preacher in the pulpits of the general vicinity. My time was crowded with professional and other labors and responsibilities, the religious community was greatly agitated, and important developments were at hand.

CHAPTER 10

1830-1831

I now enter upon a review of one of the most eventful and stirring years of my life history – a year in which momentous questions were canvassed as never before, ecclesiastical changes made, and a new future opened to my advancing feet. All this came about by reason of the attitude of the Universalist denomination as a body, in respect to the dogma of no future punishment and my own growing convictions touching both that attitude and the dogma itself. I could in reason and conscience abide neither of them. Nor could I do otherwise than disapprove and scorn the contemptuous tone of the general Universalist press and pulpit towards nearly everything, however right and good in itself, which bore the stamp and characterized the action of the so-called evangelical sects. All such manifestations were an offense to me from the beginning.

Although the early advocates of the final redemption of all souls believed and taught that the consequences of sin extended into the future state of being, and although the Universalist Convention at Philadelphia[1] in 1791 emphatically disclaimed the theory that the good and the bad, the believer and unbeliever, are equally happy at the dissolution of the body,[2] yet had it come to pass at the time of which I am writing that this latter view had gained overwhelming ascendancy among the class of Christians bearing the Universalist name. Those who were deemed leaders – the ablest and most aggressive preachers – were of that way of thinking, and more than nine-tenths of the laity were in sympathy with them;[3] while the few Restorationists, as those of the opposition were called, especially if at all outspoken in their opinions, were scarcely treated with common civility. Their only chance for respectful consideration from the dominant party was to keep silence on the subject of difference and serve in the common ranks obsequiously.

It was authoritatively proclaimed by those in the ascendant that not a single passage of Scripture, justly interpreted, taught the doctrine of sin, punishment, reward, or corrective discipline beyond this mortal life.[4] Floods of absurd and wretched exegesis rolled forth and swept away assumptively every text which old-time Universalists, as well as believers in endless punishment, had always construed to teach future retribution. All believers in the final restitution of all things, ancient and modern, were claimed as Universalists, but those holding to retributive rewards and penalties beyond the grave were set down as crude in their notions on the subject, and not to be recognized as trustworthy expositors of the sacred oracles. The title "American Universalists" was assumed for those who were deemed sound and consistent representatives of the doctrine and who were the only true Universalists in what had become the proper denominational forms of speech. The positive and proscriptive declaration was made that "Universalists now know of no condition for man beyond the grave but that in which he is as the angels in heaven."[5] At the same time, limited future retributionism was odiously represented as "an old heathen notion," and "a remnant of superstition akin to the delusion of Salem witchcraft."[6] In addition to all this, almost every conceivable form of derisive and censorious expression was bandied about, in public and private, at the more spiritual, devout observances, customs, and socially religious instrumentalities of the "orthodox." These were characterized and sneered at as superstitions, or hypocritical pretenses, or inventions of priestcraft. There seemed to be an absolute infatuation in such matters among the prominent Universalists of that period. And that infatuation was accompanied by so much self-conceit, dogmatism, intolerance and scorn towards any in their own ranks who dissented from such invidious characterization, that if they had any staunch mental independence or honest convictions or sense of justice, it was impossible for them to be otherwise than repulsed and outraged thereby. Certainly I was.

The Medway Sermon

Under these circumstances, and in the state of mind indicated, I wrote a sermon on "The Inestimable Value of Souls," which I preached at Medway on Sunday, the twenty-fifth of April, 1830.[7] It was prepared in no spirit of controversy, and with no design of antagonizing any of my Universalist brethren. But it proved to be the first gun of a protracted and somewhat violent war.

My Medway friends, pleased with it, kindly asked it for the press. I consented to the request, and the manuscript was sent to the *Trumpet* office to be printed in pamphlet form, with little thought of the opposition it was destined to provoke. Its chief offense to those decrying it was that it interpreted and applied certain important passages of Scripture in such a way as to derive from them support for the doctrine of future retribution, which was contrary to the *ex cathedra* expositions of Rev. Hosea Ballou and kindred doctrinaires.[8] Such interpretation and application were made innocently on my part, from honest conviction and incidentally to the main drift of the discourse, which was to advocate and defend the doctrine of Universal Restoration in opposition to that of endless punishment, my text being Matthew 16:26: "What is a man profited if he gain the whole world and lose his own soul? or what shall a man give in exchange for his soul?"

Though the sermon was sent to the *Trumpet* printing office soon after it was delivered, with the expectation that it would be at once put to press and made ready for distribution at an early day, it yet suffered considerable delay and was not permitted to get into the hands of its readers until it had been heralded abroad and denounced by an extended notice from Rev. Thomas Whittemore, the editor of the paper mentioned. My self-constituted censor arraigned me as worthy of reprobation on six counts, which were substantially as follows: That I had inculcated the heathen notion of future rewards and punishments; that I had used certain texts of Scripture in support of that notion which leading Universalists and some others interpreted and applied differently; that I had done this without showing that they were in the wrong; that I had aggrieved and insulted some of my elder clerical brethren by saying that many divines, both orthodox and heterodox, tortured particular passages to no other purpose than to show their ingenuity; that I had injured and abused Rev. Hosea Ballou especially,[9] by discarding his expositions and charging him with making "egregious mistakes"; concluding his arraignment by declaring that I was "far behind the orthodox in rescuing the sacred writings from perversion." He was moved to notice my errors and offenses, he said, by a sense of duty "lest, if this sermon be read where the views of American Universalists are not known, it should be supposed they interpret the Scriptures in the same manner," and for the purpose of preventing the public from thinking that the sentiments of my sermon were embraced by Universalists generally.

The unreasonableness and injustice of all this carping criticism appear from the following facts: (1) The Universalist denomination had been founded and mostly built up by believers in a limited future retribution. (2) It still embraced a respectable minority who held to that doctrine. (3) There was no denominational creed or standard of faith giving the no-future-punishment view any precedence of its opposite. (4) It was acknowledged by all parties that the Restorationists and the Ultras, as they were respectively called, had co-equal rights in advocating and defending their distinctive views, without restriction or censure. (5) My Medway sermon contained nothing but what was perfectly consistent with these facts, professions, rights, and mutual understandings. Yet this editor, assuming to speak for the whole body of Universalists, took upon himself to denounce me as a notable offender for advocating universal salvation on the old ground occupied by Murray, Winchester, Chauncy,[10] and all the early champions of that form of faith.[11]

A New Crisis

By what had now transpired, I was unwittingly brought face to face with one of the leading spirits of the denomination to which I belonged and with whose distinguishing doctrine I was in hearty accord. In the ordinary discharge of my duty as a minister of Christian truth and an advocate of God's impartial and all-saving grace, I had provoked the hostility and the denunciatory judgment of the principal editor of the denominational organ, who, without doubt, in his attack upon me reflected the sentiment of a large majority of those holding the Universalist faith, and especially of those who had a controlling influence in its counsels and in the general administration of its affairs.

And now what was I going to do about it? What could I do? I must either sit down quiescently under the denunciation launched against me and let everything go as it might chance to do, or I must stand up manfully in defense of my cause. Had no great principle been involved – nothing but merely personal considerations, it might have been politic for me to keep still and "crook the pregnant hinges of the knee where thrift may follow fawning."[12] But as it was otherwise in my judgment, I was impelled to pursue a different course. If I were to act according to that impulse, I had nothing to expect but a bitter and unequal contest, in which the triumph of my cause, of which I was sure in the end, would cost me many a pleasant friendship, ejection from my pastoral office in Milford, grievous aspersions of my motives, and numberless other discomforts and privations. Of merely temporal advantage there was nothing in that direction to gain, but seemingly much to lose. The main current of feeling and opinion in the Universalist denomination was unmistakably with my opponents. Few professed Restorationists were outspoken and resolute in behalf of their distinctive tenets. Nearly all the pulpits and periodicals were either positively ultra or in some sort of abeyance to that arrogant influence. And the dominant policy was to decry every independent-minded defender of future disciplinary retribution, as a factious, ambitious, mischief-making disturber of the order. As to honest conviction, devotion to principle, and conscientious love for truth and righteousness, they were all claimed for those who had transcended the old swaddling-clothes of infant Universalism. They might contemn and denounce the doctrines of their opponents on the issue under notice as an "old heathen notion," "the wildest of all reveries," or however else they pleased,[13] and do so from the purest of motives, for they were not only honest and disinterested, but superiorly enlightened. So it verily seemed to them as it does generally to new-fledged speculatists, iconoclasts, and superficial radicals. They were honest and zealous, driving their chariot, Jehu-like through their ecclesiastical Israel,[14] and evoking deafening shouts from their admiring sympathizers. And yet I could not then, nor can I now, see one single plausible, much less valid, reason for their peculiar assumptions.

A new crisis had now arrived in my career as a minister of the gospel of Christ, and my decision in regard to it must be made. For several days I had a painful mental struggle upon the question whether to keep silence or to boldly meet the issue that had so unexpectedly been forced upon me. Very grave consequences, I was aware, must follow either course. I contemplated them on either hand with dread. I had no personal grievances to redress, wrongs to avenge, ambitions to gratify. But I had a position to maintain, a cause to defend, a consistency of life, character, and teaching to preserve and make clear before God and the world. I was a sincere, firm, devoted believer in the doctrine of the final universal holiness and happiness for the entire human race. That doctrine was sacred to me as the apple of my eye. I could not deny it, hide it under a bushel, nor in any way ignore it. To me it involved everything in theology and ethics worth preaching or living for. I had come into the belief of that doctrine by a never-to-be-forgotten experience which affected and agitated me to the very depths of my being. I had continued in that belief at great sacrifice of personal friendship, of social advantage, of religious fellowship, of promised worldly success. I had been thrust out of the Christian Connexion on the urgent motion of my own father because that body could not tolerate my honest convictions in that respect, though professing to have no creed and to fellowship all who lived a Christian life, regardless of theological belief. I had come into the Universalist denomination at the earnest solicitations of some of its foremost representatives rather than by my own importunity. And when I frankly stated that I was a Restorationist and not an ultra Universalist, so-called, I was assured of as hearty a welcome as if it were otherwise, and of being accorded an equal right to hold and preach limited future retribution with others cherishing different views upon that point. I believed this, joined the order, and found everything pleasant and cordial till I began to use my stipulated liberty of dissent from the prevailing orthodoxy of the denomination. Then, instead of kindly salutations and fraternal fellowship, there came coldness, detraction, harsh accusation, invective, denunciation.

Thus out of harmony and sympathetic union with my fellow Universalists, whither could I look for that cordial, hearty friendliness and spirit of cooperation so much to be desired in the pursuit and promulgation of religious truth and the things of the religious life? I could not quietly withdraw from existing ecclesiastical relations and offer myself to one of the so-called evangelical sects, except by stealth and cowardice. They had their honest convictions, I had mine; and the two, on certain vital points, were fundamentally irreconcilable. They knew this as well as I. They must do their duty and I mine, each as we respectively understood it. They wanted nothing of me as I was, nor I of them as they were, except to wish them well and honor them for whatever good they might do.

As to the Unitarian denomination in this country, it had, through its acknowledged leaders and advocates, manifested no approval of outspoken Restorationism at that day, though a few of its adherents professed a *quasi* belief in it. The general attitude of the body was one of aversion to that form of faith rather than of hospitality. I could not therefore, with honor, think of gaining entrance into that fold. Much less was I morally capable of accepting any form of philosophical materialism or of nebulous transcendentalism[15] with its hazy dreams of the Great Absolute and of a doubtful immortality, even though I might be allowed to entertain and promulgate my views unchallenged and without hindrance of any sort.

There was for me no alternative so far as I could see but to remain where I was and either yield tamely and obsequiously with a padlock on my lips to the autocratic majority, or accept the issue which confronted me, and in an honorable, manly, Christian way defend myself, my views, and my line of action from the attacks of my adversaries. To my apprehension there was much more involved in the question that arose between me and my ultra brethren than one at first would be inclined to think. "Why," it might be asked, "inaugurate what promised to be a long and acrimonious conflict with your opponents about the time, place, and continuance of divine retribution – whether all before or partly after death – so long as you were agreed upon the great distinguishing subject of the final salvation of all the children of men?" To my mind the question between me and my assailants was not simply one of "time, place, and extent" of retributory visitation, but one of far more radical and vital importance – one comprehending, as it then was stated, interpreted, and applied, the moral nature and accountability of man; the intrinsic relation of the present state of existence to that which is to come; the equity and impartial justice of retribution for wrong-doing; and the correct exegesis and use of the Scriptures. It was not enough for me that the advocates of no future punishment professed the highest devotion to the doctrine of universal salvation if at the same time they held it and interpreted it in such a way as to annihilate or undermine the idea of the moral agency and personal responsibility of mankind; or virtually break the thread of continuity between this life and the next, and so make existence to consist of two lives, instead of one and the same life extending through two stages of being; or misrepresent the divine government in its practical administration as absolutely just and righteous in all respects; or falsify and pervert the Hebrew and Christian sacred books by unwarrantable and absurd interpretations. It was on these grounds and for the reasons thus indicated that after deliberate, conscientious, prayerful canvassing of the situation, I resolved to take up the gauntlet that had been thrown at my feet and enter at once upon the warfare that I could not in good conscience avoid or turn away from except in cowardly disgrace.

I had consecrated myself to the unconditional service of God and His eternal truth. I was solemnly bound to maintain and defend what I sincerely believed to be the fundamental principles of moral order in the universe of souls. I was no less solemnly bound to stand up bravely for that freedom of utterance without which truth cannot be proclaimed or sustained against error, or divine principles be extended far and wide among men. I had no doubt that my cause was just and could be triumphantly vindicated on an open platform at the bar of enlightened reason. And in resolving upon a contest in its behalf, I was equally resolved that it should not be a half-smothered family quarrel, nor a series of sham fights, but one of open field, pitched battles. I had seen enough of cautious, politic, temporizing resistance to ultra Universalism on the part of Restorationists. It had only irritated their opponents, excited their animosity, aroused their scorn, and provoked more aggravated aggressions. I therefore solemnly determined to proclaim and enter upon a square fight on all the issues involved, as the only just, honorable, and rational course to pursue. And having so determined, there was no longer on my part the least hesitation or vacillation. Whatever the consequences might be, the die was cast and cast irrevocably. There were to be no discharge and no retreat in that war.[16]

Reply to Whittemore's Review

The decision made, I sat down and wrote a detailed and exhaustive "Reply to Mr. Thomas Whittemore's Review of a Sermon delivered in Medway, Mass. by Adin Ballou." It was addressed "to the clergy and laity of the Universalist faith throughout the United States." In my opening paragraph I quoted verbatim the several definite charges made against me in the Review, as in substance presented on a preceding page, saying at the close, "A sense of duty to myself and the cause of truth requires that I should meet and repel these charges with a sober and dignified answer." This I proceeded to do in an argument or series of arguments covering some fifteen large pages of manuscript, equal to about the same number of pages if transferred to this volume and hence too long for insertion in it. The final paragraph of the document was as follows:

> In closing this reply, it is incumbent on me to declare in the most solemn terms that I consider Mr. Whittemore's strictures upon my sermon an unjustifiable infringement of my inalienable rights, a deliberate violation of the obligations of fellowship, and a declaration of hostilities against both me and my doctrine. And I do furthermore solemnly declare that I consider myself outlawed and alienated from all fellowship with Rev. Thomas Whittemore and all persons who shall be found to have approved, justified, and encouraged him in this act of persecution. With these declarations clearly understood, I now submit this my defense to the candid contemplation of the clergy and laity of the whole denomination of Universalists, conjuring them to pass a righteous judgment upon my case and appealing to God in Heaven for the interposition of His justice and wisdom in bringing all difficulties to a happy conclusion.

The Reply was accompanied by this reasonable request:

> Mr. Editor: I ask at your hands the justice to insert in your paper the following vindication of myself from your recent attack. I desire you to publish it immediately, or if you decide not to do so, to return it within four days.
>
> With regret,
> ADIN BALLOU

Did Mr. Whittemore grant this request and publish my reply in the *Trumpet*? No. Did he open the columns of his paper to the free discussion of the points at issue? Never. Did he render any excuse, apology, or reason for not giving my article a place there, as he was desired to do? Not a word. Did he ever inform his readers that I had attempted an answer to his charges? No. What did he do? Returned my manuscript to me by mail in about a week without note or comment. And the most I ever heard from the *Trumpet* office on the subject was that he said my communication was "of a nature to disgrace [me] before the public" and he withheld it from his readers "out of compassionate regard for [my] reputation." This may have been more kindly meant than I was capable of understanding or being thankful for. However this may be, it was evidently deemed best that my article should be treated with silent contempt, presuming doubtless *that* would be the end of the matter. But I was not made of the stuff to cower and subside under such proceeding, as will appear in subsequent pages.

An Uncompromising Restorationist

My next step in this matter was to present the controversy now inaugurated and my relation to it frankly to my society in Milford. I knew the majority in it were ultras or prejudiced strongly in that direction. The notice of my Medway sermon in the *Trumpet* had already aroused the more excitable of them to contemptuous remarks about my "purgatory," "little tophet,"[17] "hell junior," etc. I also knew that there were some solid, considerate members who were disposed to see me treated honorably, and a few who sympathized with my distinctive views. But I felt that I ought not to continue my pastoral relationship with my people without a fair mutual understanding. So on the second Sabbath in July, at my five o'clock service I laid the whole matter before my congregation in a discourse having for a text, "Men, brethren and fathers, hear my defense, which I make now unto you" (Acts 22:1). I distinctly stated my views, feelings, and course of action in the past; how the case now stood in consequence of the public denunciation issued against me on account of my honest sentiments, with no chance of exculpating or explaining myself allowed me; that I was determined to be henceforth an outspoken Restorationist at all hazards; that I knew the general predilection of my hearers for the doctrine of no future retribution; that I could not ask them to retain me as their minister contrary to their convictions and choice; that I should be glad to continue with them if they could bear with my honest independence and desired me to remain; but if otherwise disposed, I should make no complaint for being openly and honorably discharged at their discretion. The discourse was well received by the nobler-minded of the society, and my friend Arial Bragg very kindly said to me that he saw no reason why my outspoken sentiments should render me less acceptable, useful, or desirable as their minister. Others concurred. But a different class of minds went away with confirmed dissatisfaction which subsequently manifested itself in decided hostility, the results of which were soon to be made known to their associates and to the community at large.

From that day forth I stood before the public an independent, uncompromising Restorationist, in contradistinction from the ultra Universalists on the one hand as well as from the advocates of endless punishment and the Destructionists on the other. For some months I continued preaching under prior arrangement, half the time in Milford and the other half in Medway – lecturing at convenient intervals in various other places. To complete my divorcement from the no future retributionists, it was only necessary for me to unite ecclesiastically with the Providence Association, which was under their ban of outlawry on account of its declared opposition to their favorite dogma.[18] This I did at an early day, casting in my lot with its Restorationist separatists, for such they virtually were, and thus practically severing my connection with the General Universalist Convention.

The Independent Messenger

A new movement had now actually begun among those rejecting the doctrine of endless punishment. An important desideratum as a means of promoting that movement was an organ of publication. Upon surveying the field and finding no one prepared to establish such an organ, I concluded to assume the responsibility myself, relying on such pledges of assistance as my sympathizing brother ministers were willing to offer. At a meeting of the Providence Association, held in Oxford, Massachusetts, August 19, 1830, the subject of a weekly periodical was introduced, discussed, and approved, and a title, suggested, I think, by Rev. Charles Hudson, *Independent Messenger*, was adopted.[19] The following document, drawn up by myself, was then submitted to those present and duly signed:

> We, the subscribers, do hereby solemnly bind and obligate ourselves to Adin Ballou that, in case he shall within one year commence the publication of a weekly periodical to be called the *Independent Messenger*, we will be responsible for the prompt payment of our respective subscriptions according to the number of copies noted opposite our several names.
>
> PAUL DEAN, Boston, 100 copies; DAVID PICKERING, Providence, 100 copies; LYMAN MAYNARD, Oxford, 50 copies; CHARLES HUDSON, Westminster, 25 copies; PHILEMON R. RUSSELL, Halifax, 25 copies; SETH CHANDLER, Milford, 25 copies.

These 325 copies were all I could depend upon as a subscription list outside my own personal influence and exertions – not a large outfit for such an undertaking. Evidently the prospect was by no means flattering, but I was in earnest and not to be easily intimidated or discouraged. It was readily seen that the venture must be conducted with the most rigid economy or it would fail, and that right early. I therefore concluded to enlist a practical printer with an inexpensive establishment, form a co-partnership with him, and open an office in Milford, where the paper could be published, and more or less job work be done in order to reduce expense.

An opportunity for such an arrangement soon presented itself. Mr. George W. Stacy,[20] a young Restorationist brother, had been publishing the *Groton Herald* at Groton, Massachusetts, in partnership with a Mr. Rogers, but the undertaking had proved unsuccessful and was to be abandoned. He had a fairly-equipped plant, was well recommended to me by those who knew him, and being approached with the proposition indicated, responded favorably. Articles of co-partnership between him and myself were drawn up and signed September 24, 1830; the office and its belongings were removed to Milford, and business began about October 1, under the firm title, "Ballou & Stacy." This was the first printing establishment in Milford and was domiciled in an old building long since removed, situated between the Congregationalist meetinghouse and Water Street, fronting the parish common.

During the month of October, I issued a prospectus of the *Independent Messenger*, to be published once a week on a neat, royal sheet of good paper at the price to subscribers of $1.50 per annum in advance and $2.00 after sixty days. The purpose and character of the new journal were clearly indicated in the opening paragraph, which is copied entire.

> Through the medium of this publication, we shall disseminate, illustrate, and defend the ancient doctrine of the "Restitution of all things;" explain, enforce, and vindicate the Holy Scriptures as the grand rule of Christian faith and practice; advocate the doctrine of limited future rewards and punishments; inculcate repentance towards God, faith in the Lord Jesus Christ, and good works among men; endeavor to promote piety, morality, charity, and social order; encourage free inquiry; contend for civil and religious liberty, and cultivate useful literature.

As was to be expected, the ultra Universalists did all in their power to hedge up the way[21] of this new venture and render it abortive. Not one of their periodicals (to my knowledge) gave my prospectus a favorable notice, several of them ignored it altogether, and one or two spoke in opposition to it. The old cry was raised in many quarters, "he is making difficulty in the order"; "stirring up disunion, discord, and strife among brethren"; "he cares nothing for doctrines or principles – it is all from ambition, envy, personal pique, and revenge." No means were spared to prejudice all susceptible persons against the proposed paper – to influence the public not to subscribe for it or in any manner countenance its publication.

Epistle General to Restorationists

Nevertheless, on the first day of January, 1831, I issued No. 1, Vol. I of the *Independent Messenger*. Its leading article was entitled, "An Epistle General to Restorationists," and occupied about two pages of the issue, beginning thus:

> To all sincere believers in the doctrine of Universal Restoration, whithersoever dispersed – Wisdom and grace be with you from God the Father and his Son Jesus Christ.
>
> BELOVED BRETHREN – Having been called by the God of our fathers to the defense of that ancient truth, whereof he hath "spoken by the mouths of all his holy prophets since the world began," I deem it my solemn duty to submit to your consideration an undisguised exposition of the motives and feelings with which I enter upon so responsible an undertaking. In order to render such an exposition more clear and forcible, I have chosen to present a brief historical sketch of my life and experience during the last eight years.

I then proceeded to state and explain everything necessary to illustrate the whole case. And I did so with entire honesty and frankness from beginning to end. The article is too long to insert in this autobiography, but I have taken care to collate it, with many kindred writings belonging to this controversy with the ultra Universalists, in a volume which may, if deemed advisable, be published at some future day.[22]

What was the effect of this *pronunciamento* on my part? It aroused the indignation of the Ultras in all directions. Its bold, trenchant, uncompromising disclosure of their aggressions and my expressed determination to resist them on every issue provoked their hostility to the utmost. But my onset was so unexpectedly impetuous and powerful that they were uncertain at first what course to pursue. But after taking counsel with each other, they decided that "their strength was to sit still"[23] in their chosen retreats and operate in secret ways to my detriment. By this policy they hoped I might ere long exhaust my energies and resources, and retire from the field. But they were soon obliged to break their silence by the unanticipated effect of my frank and fearless utterance in another quarter. My statement commanded such respect from the Orthodox and more conscientious and devout liberalists of all shades, that they manifested at once their approval and gratification. The *Boston Recorder*, then the leading Trinitarian journal in New England, commended exceedingly my "Epistle General," and reproduced copious extracts from it in its own columns.[24] This galled the editor of the *Trumpet* greatly and impelled him to speak out in the matter. But in doing so, he took pains to have it understood that he took notice of my slanders (as he characterized my declarations), not on my account, but solely because the *Recorder* had copied and endorsed them. The implication was that I was too insignificant and contemptible a foe to waste ammunition upon, but the *Recorder* was an old, respectable, and formidable enemy, with whom to do battle was honorable.

Close of Milford Pastorate and Call to Mendon

Meanwhile matters were ripening to a final issue in my society at Milford. The Ultras in it were much disturbed at my doings and resolved to get rid of me in a quiet way at as early a date as possible. So at a meeting held, without notice of what was designed, January 22, 1831, it was "voted to dispense with the services of Rev. Adin Ballou as to supplying [their] pulpit in [their] meetinghouse any more." This was objected to by some of my friends as having been done without any article in the warrant or other announcement providing for such action, and a motion to reconsider the vote was made, to be acted on at an adjourned meeting a week later. At that time it was readily "voted not to reconsider the vote dispensing with the services of Rev. Adin Ballou," and a committee was chosen to notify me accordingly. This was done immediately afterward by the chairman, Mr. Otis Parkhurst, causing my relations to the Milford people to come to a speedy termination. There was a striking and unpleasant contrast between this dismissal and the warm, urgent recall which brought me back to Milford from New York less than three years before. But circumstances alter cases, and I was prepared for anything that might arise.

Just at this juncture of affairs an incident occurred which I can scarcely regard otherwise than an ordering of divine Providence in my behalf, giving me renewed assurance that my heavenly Father had not forsaken me, but was opening the way before me to new fields of service and to larger opportunities of usefulness in the world than I had previously enjoyed. At about the same hour I was voted out of my Milford charge, the First Congregational parish in Mendon had taken action preparatory to inviting me to its vacant pastorate; and the Milford committee had hardly discharged its duty of informing me of the act by which my labors in that town were to terminate, before a committee from Mendon waited upon me for the purpose of offering me the pulpit at its disposal. The offer was accepted, and the details of my removal to the neighboring town and of my entrance upon my new duties there were arranged to the satisfaction of both parties.

Thus it came to pass that on the last Sunday of January, 1831, I closed my labors with the Universalist society in Milford, and on the following Sunday entered upon corresponding labors as pastor of the First Society and Church in Mendon. At as early a date thereafter as was practicable, my family and printing press were transferred to my new field of labor, and I was fairly settled in my re-established home, in my editorial work, and in the activities of my ministerial office, at the expiration of the twenty-eighth year of my life, April 23, 1831.

Fourth of July, 1830

Before proceeding to record the events and experiences of a new year, however, it seems advisable to go back a little in the order of time and briefly note a few facts that transpired during the period just passed in review, but could not be mentioned in their proper place, chronologically considered, without abruptly breaking in upon the continuity of the narrative in hand. The first of these is that on the fourth of July, 1830, I delivered my second oration commemorating the Declaration of our National Independence. It took place in the manufacturing village (now town) of Blackstone, in the then South Parish of Mendon, before a large, respectable, and apparently gratified audience. An honorable committee of the citizens of the village and vicinity waited upon me after the exercises of the occasion were over, and solicited a copy of my address for the press. Their request was granted, and the production soon after appeared in print and was widely circulated in the general community. It may be found by interested parties in the library of the town of Hopedale, with most of my printed works, and will show my political and patriotic status at that date.[25]

Birth of a Second Son

On the twenty-eighth of November, 1830, we had a son born to us, whom we named, in honor of his maternal grandfather, Pearley Hunt Ballou. He brought great joy into a household which was passing through trying experiences, and awakened many ardent and precious hopes for the future in the breasts of his parents and of all who held him dear. But his life was of but a few brief years' continuance here, being cut short by a fearful malady, which swept him and his elder brother into an early grave.

Reaction to the Epistle General

I have already spoken briefly of the effect produced by the issuing of the first number of the *Independent Messenger* upon my ultra Universalist brethren and especially on the editor of the *Trumpet*, who, after resolving evidently upon a policy of silence, was goaded to publish a rejoinder to my "General Appeal to Restorationists" by the use made of that article on the part of the *Boston Recorder* and other orthodox journals of the day. It is worth while to state that the paper mentioned declared "the Restorationist ministers concerned in the new movement to be the most respectable of the Universalist clergymen," which was too bitter a pill for the Rev. Thomas Whittemore to swallow with composure. His equanimity was greatly disturbed, and he must speak out, as he did in an issue of the *Trumpet*, January 29, 1831, in which he opened fire, not on me, for I was beneath his notice, but on the Orthodox who had committed a grievous offense by quoting my slanders and misrepresentations, and so making them their own. What he had to say at the date named, however, was mostly explanatory and predictive of what was to come in the next issue of the paper, when big guns were to be leveled against the offending Orthodox brethren and their chief instigators, the leaders in the Restorationist movement; myself, puerile and unworthy of notice as I was, among the number.

The appearance of the next number of the *Trumpet and Universalist Magazine*, to give the full title of the publication, was awaited with earnest expectation and fond desire, and when received its long editorial treating of the matter in hand was read with intense interest, but with equally intense repugnance and detestation.[26] The article opened with dark assaults on the moral character of Revs. Paul Dean and David Pickering, two of our leading ministers, with scarcely less accusatory ones against Rev. Charles Hudson and other Restorationist divines. These assaults were not open, frank, specific allegations, but vague assertions, implications, insinuations, and threats of contingent exposure.[27]

I replied to them in the *Messenger* as follows:

> The aspersions with which they [the conclave which spoke through Mr. Whittemore] have endeavored to destroy the reputation of such men as Revs. Paul Dean, David Pickering, and Charles Hudson will only rebound, and, like barbed arrows, pierce their own bosoms. These men will in due time reply to the defamatory charges with which they have been individually assailed.
>
> With regard to the vile insinuations against Brother Dean [who was then on a preaching tour in the southern states], and the threat that certain "certificates" now in the possession of Rev. Hosea Ballou, together with "a full history of the

faction from its beginning, shall go before the public," we feel authorized to speak in language that cannot be misunderstood. And therefore, in our own name, in the name of Mr. Dean, and of all independent Restorationists, we solemnly demand of Rev. Hosea Ballou and Thomas Whittemore, the immediate publication of said "certificates" and of all other documents alluded to, as affecting the case now pending at the bar of public opinion. We know the purport of those wonderful documents, and we also know that the private use of them by their very compassionate possessor has soured more minds against Brother Dean, and injured his reputation more than their publication ever can do, allowing them to be as frightful as Mr. W. intimates. The friends of Brother Dean may rest assured that the papers referred to will prove, *upon explanation*, injurious chiefly to those who hope to turn them to the gratification of their revenge.

Furthermore, we inform the public that we know of papers in safe keeping which relate to Rev. Hosea Ballou – papers which in a great measure have been hid from the public eye in order to save the subject of them from justly deserved reproach and blame. Should occasion require, these papers, under the hand of a justice, will be made known to the world.

This response was more than had been bargained for. It silenced the great gun of the enemy. No more was ever heard of those "certificates," nor of that "full history of the faction." Brothers Dean and Hudson waited for the threatened exposures before appearing in self-defense. But the occasion for such appearance never came. Brother Pickering submitted his case to the trustees of his society, who immediately demanded of Mr. Whittemore specific charges against their minister, if he had any, instead of the secret stabs with which he had assailed his character and reputation. He responded in a private letter, making no definite accusations, but only repeating the former vague insinuations. The trustees replied, telling him that he had no case, that his attacks were wholly unjustifiable, that they had full confidence in their pastor and were entirely satisfied with his character and conduct, closing with a request that the correspondence between them and him be published in the *Trumpet*. With his usual unfairness, he refused. It, however, appeared in the *Independent Messenger* of March 18, 1831. To this was added in the next number a communication from Brother Pickering in triumphant vindication of himself, which left nothing more to be said, and which silenced his accusers thenceforth and forevermore.

So much relating to the first part of the article of Rev. Thomas Whittemore, in response to my "Epistle General to Restorationists." The remainder of it consisted of a desperate cannonade designed to demolish my statements and professions in that "Epistle" against ultra Universalism. His principal efforts were expended in an endeavor to nullify my testimony and make it appear unworthy of credence by representing and denouncing me (1) as a weak-minded young man, ambitious of a distinction wholly beyond my capacity to reach; (2) as the mere tool of certain unprincipled designing men, chiefest of whom was Paul Dean, who had flattered and cajoled me into joining their cabal in order that they might use me for the furtherance of their own perfidious schemes; and (3) as a pretentious, unscrupulous liar and hypocrite in a bad cause, incapable of speaking the truth in the matters at issue, and unworthy of belief or confidence. These several points he attempted by most fallacious and excruciating special pleadings to demonstrate, and to make it appear that I exemplified in my personality the compound qualities of both fool and knave. I found no difficulty in meeting the charges preferred against me, in defending myself at every point of attack, and in putting aside and shielding myself from all the enemy's vituperation. I suffered nothing but gained much by this encounter, both in my own self-respect and, so far as I could judge, in the esteem and confidence of the general public.

Another aspect of the case now in review ought not to pass unnoticed. While the boldness of my utterance aroused the indignation and provoked the animosity of my opponents of the ultra school of Universalists, it awakened the fears and apprehensions of some of the prudent, conservative, and politic of my Restorationist friends. One of the most respected and active of them[28] immediately after the reception of the first issue of the *Messenger*, wrote me, chiding me somewhat for what he feared was my ill-timed though good article, and advising me that we must be "wise as serpents and harmless as doves."[29] He also suggested that in order to mollify the sharpness of my rebuke and prevent needless ill-feeling, I insert an editorial in the next number something like the following: "Our object is to defend our views rather than assail others. We intend to build up the cause of pure religion, not by a petty warfare with those who differ from us, but by presenting what we consider to be the truth. In our first issue, we felt it to be our duty to present to our readers a true, unvarnished tale of what we had felt, seen, and heard. Having done this, we shall not seek a controversy with the *Trumpet*, *Recorder*, or any of our neighbors. We shall commence no attack any further than it is necessary to vindicate our own sentiments. Being bent on truth, we shall not go out of our way to attack error, but if we are attacked, we shall endeavor to maintain our own ground."

Similar deprecatory expressions came from different sources, all kindly meant, and I could not do otherwise than give them thoughtful consideration. But they were for the most part lost upon me, for I viewed things from a standpoint quite different from that occupied by my kindly advisers and was in no mood to be governed by what seemed to them a wise expediency. So after duly canvassing the pro and con of their counsels, I decided to put them all aside and follow the dictates of my own best judgment and understanding – a conclusion which I never had reason to regret.

CHAPTER 11

1831-1832

At the opening of the twenty-ninth year of my life, I found myself fairly well settled in the town of Mendon and busily engaged in the discharge of the duties incident to my new pastorate and in the management of the editorial and financial affairs of the *Independent Messenger*, most of which had, by force of circumstances and my own choice, been entrusted to my keeping. Myself and family were snugly domiciled in the dwelling house belonging to what was then known as the Judge Rawson estate, located on high land overlooking the village from the west, near the junction of the Uxbridge and Chestnut Hill roads. Though not far from the center of the town, which was at that time one of the largest and most thriving in the southern part of Worcester County, and though pleasantly situated in many respects, commanding a fine view of the surrounding country, especially to the east and south, yet it seemed to us the most dreary and lonely abode we had ever occupied, contrasting most unfavorably with the comparatively new and attractive one we had left behind. The fact that we were the nominal owners of the Milford house and could in some proper sense call it our own, while the one we now occupied was the property of another, may account in some measure for the unhomelikeness and cheerlessness which characterized the latter and made it far from satisfactory as a permanent residence. Nevertheless, it was not in us to look backward with regret, murmuring, and complaint. The tide of events was onward and forward, and towards the future we were bound to press our way with courage and with hope.

Mendon Parish

The First Parish and Church in Mendon at the time I took pastoral charge of them, were in a depressed and unpromising condition. The church proper had been reduced by a recent secession to eight members, mostly superannuated persons, and the attendance on public worship was discouragingly small. Yet my predecessor, Rev. Simeon Doggett,[1] was an educated, scholarly man with a benignant heart, who for sixteen years had sustained a generally respectable pastorate. But the Calvinists had come in with their fiery zeal and impassioned appeals, drawing many away from the staid formalities of the ancient sanctuary of the town. They had organized a new church, built for themselves a house of worship, gathered in a large congregation, and were in an apparently prosperous condition.[2] Scattered through the territorial limits of the parish, however, were many heterogeneous elements which had drifted away from the established institutions of religion, but which, if they could be attracted to and combined with the substantial constituency that remained at the old center of church life, would presently change the aspect of things most essentially.

And this was evidently the work for me to do – a work for which I deemed myself well equipped and qualified. I was of vigorous age, earnest zeal, and competent abilities, and was charged with doctrines and principles as positive and unequivocal as the most orthodox. To the task thus set before me I at once addressed myself and with most successful and gratifying results.[3] Two discourses were preached every Sunday, which, with a reconstructed and active Sunday school, various special religious meetings during the week, and frequent parochial visitation, gave me enough to do in my proper ministerial field of service and yielded abundant fruit. My congregation increased greatly; the church membership soon began to be replenished, and the vacant places to be supplied, and an encouraging prosperity prevailed in all the borders of our Zion.

To these more strictly pastoral and home duties were added many lectures, funeral sermons, etc., outside my conventional field of service in the general vicinity. Moreover, my editorship and business oversight of the *Independent Messenger* occupied all the time I had to spare, keeping me in the harness oftentimes until midnight or the small hours of the morning. I was continually beset with controversial attacks from two classes of opponents – the ultra Universalists, who were in determined hostility to the Restorationist movement, and the believers in endless punishment, who were equally in earnest against the views I sought to promulgate in the pulpit and elsewhere as opportunity offered. Moreover, I had an extensive correspondence with persons desirous of information upon various points of doctrine which I was known to hold and advocate. So that between open assaults on the one hand and professed inquiries after truth on the other, my pen had all it could do to answer the demands made upon it. But these demands were promptly and frankly met, as the preserved files of the *Messenger* duly attest.

All this work was done and all these calls were answered under circumstances that necessitated the most rigid economy and the most scrupulous care of my material resources and expenditures, with more frequent resorts to credit than I wished. My paper, the pecuniary responsibility of which I had assumed, was not self-supporting, and my salary for pastoral service was only about $400 for the year, with but little, if any, income from incidental sources. Such was the general condition of my affairs, financially considered, in the year 1831-32.

Meeting of the Providence Association

During this year, as in the preceding one, important events and interesting personal experiences marked my career. To these I must briefly recur, in the order which seems most advisable, though not always in precise chronological succession.

The annual meeting of the Providence Association of Universalists, with which I had become identified, was held in Westminster, Massachusetts, then the pastoral home of our reverend brother, Charles Hudson, on the third Wednesday and Thursday of May. It was attended by the following ministerial brethren: Reverend Brothers Dean of Boston; Pickering of Providence, Rhode Island; Hudson of Westminster; Maynard[4] of Oxford; Wright[5] of Attleboro; Russell[6] of Winchester, New Hampshire; Chandler of Medway; and myself. I was chosen moderator of the session, and Brother Maynard, clerk. Two full days were spent in profitable private consultation and public religious services, at which earnest discourses were preached by Brothers Chandler, Pickering, Dean, and myself, to good congregations, on which salutary impressions seemed to have been made.

Among the proceedings of the meeting in council was the passage of a resolution pledging cordial support to the *Independent Messenger* and recommending it to the patronage of friends and the public. Also was there provision made for the printing in the *Messenger* of a "Circular letter to our brethren scattered abroad," to be prepared by myself.[7] A few extracts from it will show its character and spirit.

> To all their Christian brethren and especially those who cherish the hope of Universal Restoration, the Providence Association sends salutations of fraternal love, wishing you grace, truth, and peace from God the Father and Jesus Christ the Lord.
>
> We rejoice exceedingly in that divine goodness which hath shielded us from the fiery darts of the wicked and wrought our deliverance from the hand of them that sought our destruction. With deep-felt gratitude and joy, we announce to you that our most sanguine expectations have been more than realized in the success with which God hath crowned our cause.
>
> And now, beloved brethren, we exhort you to gird up the loins of your minds and take courage. With a cheerful and understanding zeal, persevere in the work of righteousness. Be not carried about with every wind of doctrine; neither listen to those who turn the grace of God into a strife of words, but setting your faces steadfastly Zionward, "Let your light so shine before men that they, seeing your good works, may glorify your Father in heaven." Remember always that "the grace of God which bringeth salvation to all men teacheth us that denying ungodliness and worldly lusts, we should live soberly, righteously, and godly in the present world."[8] We recommend that you be constant in your attendance upon the service of the sanctuary, that you confer often with one another, that you pray in your families and in social meetings with each other, but above all in secret – making supplication for us and for all men that the word of truth may have free course, and that the salvation of the human family may be consummated by the appointed means according to the purpose of God. Endeavor to become a peaceable, friendly, temperate, charitable people, that you may thereby adorn the doctrine of divine grace, promote the happiness of your fellow men, secure your own eternal welfare, and enjoy the approbation of the Most High. And now we commend you to God and the word of His grace, which is able to build you up and give you a place with the sanctified forever. Farewell.

Founding of the Massachusetts Association of Universal Restorationists

The second and most important of the ecclesiastical meetings of the year took place at Mendon, on the sixteenth, seventeenth, and eighteenth days of August. It commenced with a regular session of the Providence Association, which held council meetings and public services for two days, sermons being preached by Brothers Russell, Hudson, Dean, and Pickering to respectable and deeply interested audiences.[9]

On the last day of convocation, a certain number of us, members of that body, formed the Massachusetts Association of Universal Restorationists, thus consummating our separation from the Universalist denomination. The following is the document which announced to the world the step we had taken.

> Forasmuch as there has been of late years a great departure from the sentiments of the first Universalist preachers in this country by a majority of the General Convention, the leaders of which do now arrogate to themselves exclusively the name of Universalists; and whereas we believe with Murray, Winchester, Chauncy, and the ancient authors who have written upon this subject, that Regeneration, a General Judgment, Future Rewards and Punishments, to be followed by the Final Restoration of all men to holiness and happiness, are fundamental articles of Christian faith, and that the modern sentiments of no future accountability connected with materialism are unfriendly to pure religion and subversive of the best interest of society; and whereas our adherence to the doctrines on which the General Convention was first established, instead of producing fair, manly controversy, has procured for us contumely, exclusion from ecclesiastical councils, and final expulsion, and this without proof of any offense on our part against the rules of the order or the laws of Christ; it is therefore
>
> *Resolved*, that we hereby form ourselves into a religious Community for the Defense and Promulgation of the doctrines of Revelation in their original purity, and the promotion of our own improvement, to be known by the name of the *Massachusetts Association of Universal Restorationists*.
>
> *Resolved*, that the annual meeting of this body be holden in Boston on the first Wednesday and following Thursday in January.
>
> CHARLES HUDSON, President
NATHANIEL WRIGHT, Secretary

Eight ministers and several laymen composed the convention that adopted the foregoing preamble and resolutions.[10] These were originally drawn, I think, by Rev. Paul Dean, of Boston. They were unanimously adopted and sent out to the public as the climax of our independence and the herald of our cause. How they were treated by our former brethren of the ultra school will appear further on.

Installation of Seth Chandler at Medway

The third of our distinctive ecclesiastical meetings this year was a conference held in Medway village, so called, on the second Wednesday and Thursday in October. A small society had been formed there, and had invited Brother Seth Chandler to become their minister. The principal object of this gathering was to confer the rites of ordination upon the pastor-elect and install him in his office. He had been my student in theology and I was much interested in his success. The occasion was a pleasant and edifying one. Four sermons were delivered at as many public services by Revs. George Bradburn,[11] Paul Dean, Charles Hudson, and myself, respectively – the last being an ordination sermon from Acts 20:27: "I have not shunned to declare unto you the whole counsel of God." The ordaining prayer was offered by Brother Dean, the charge and delivery of the Scriptures by Brother Hudson, the right hand of fellowship by Brother Wright; all of which parts were printed with the sermon in an early issue of the *Independent Messenger*.[12]

"The New Sect"

The controversy with the ultra Universalists, the opening battles of which were portrayed in the preceding chapter, continued with more or less vigor during the present year. In the later spring and early summer months it assumed a guerrilla form of attack and was met at every point with promptitude and decisiveness. At any rate, if the assailants did not realize their discomfiture, they deemed discretion the better part of valor and withdrew at length from the field. But after the organization of the Restorationist Association in August, as narrated, and the issuance of our "Proclamation of Independence" soon afterward, a fresh campaign was inaugurated against us by the editor of the *Trumpet*, which was carried on for several months with no lack of energy or intensity on either side.

The renewal of hostilities occurred September 17, when Mr. Whittemore opened fire upon us as set forth below:

> THE NEW SECT
>
> The following article has been going the rounds of the Boston papers, and we cannot permit its further circulation, without exposing the misrepresentations of which it is composed.[13]

He then quoted our preamble and resolutions as herein before given, and proceeded to declare that nearly every statement of the former was a falsification of the facts of the case; a declaration which he attempted to make good by as groundless an argument as was ever framed in support of a weak and desperate cause.

To the sophistry and special pleading of the *Trumpet* editorial, I immediately prepared a reply, taking up the several charges of misrepresentation one by one and answering them at length – said reply appearing in the two succeeding numbers of the *Messenger*, issued September 23 and 30, 1831, to the files of which in the Hopedale public library those interested in the details of the discussion are hereby referred.

Nevertheless, it seems desirable that I should give my present readers a general outline of the argument on both sides as it was carried on between Mr. Whittemore and myself, from which they may be able to judge, with a considerable degree of accuracy, what were the real merits of the case, and whether or not the Restorationists were justified in the course they saw fit to pursue and in the defense I was moved to make in their behalf.

Mr. Whittemore, in considering the first reason given by the Restorationists for the formation of a new order, to wit, "that there had been of late years a great departure from the sentiments of the first Universalist preachers in this country by a majority of the General Convention," did not deny the fact that such was the case, but asserted that it was "not a reason for their separation," and as a proof of the assertion said that "these men themselves have departed as widely from the early American Universalist preachers, as any Universalists have ever done."

To this I replied that his assertion "is a high and insulting charge of dishonesty" on their part, and that his assumed proof of such dishonesty is his personal *ipse dixit* without one particle of evidence being adduced by him or anywhere existing in support of it. I therefore openly and emphatically denied the charge.

I then quoted from my opponent's own work, *Modern History of Universalism*, in which the author says of Winchester and Murray, the early Universalist preachers referred to, "They both held to the existence of misery in the future state";[14] and adds that the Restorationists entertain the same view, and furthermore that "they all believe as Winchester and Murray did, that this misery will grow out of the sinner's unbelief, sin and guilt, commenced in his life, persevered in through death, and remaining with him upon his entrance into the world to come." This, with those I represented, I declared to be an essential doctrine – a peculiar feature of the faith of the original Universalists, which separates them from modern ones generally, and which ought to separate them entirely from the Universalist denomination as it then existed and was controlled.

As to the Universalist leaders at the time of the controversy – Hosea Ballou, Walter Balfour, and Thomas Whittemore, who assumed to dictate the faith and polity of the denomination – they had renounced utterly this important theological position of their predecessors, as the author of the *Trumpet* article well knew when he penned it. To substantiate this statement, I presented, in full, passages from the writings of each of the men named, in which they repudiated unequivocally the views of Murray and Winchester, and other passages in which they stigmatized those views as "Salem witchcraft delusions," "old heathen notions," etc.

"Here, sir," I said, "your *ipse dixit*, omnipotent as you may imagine it, is overwhelmed with irresistible counter evidence. You have verified the ancient truth – 'the wicked is snared in the work of his own hands.'"[15]

The preamble to the resolutions of the Restorationist Association further set forth that its framers

> believe with Murray, Winchester, Chauncy, and the ancient authors who have written upon this subject, that Regeneration, a General Judgment, Future Rewards and Punishments, to be followed by the Final Restoration of all men to holiness and happiness, are fundamental articles of Christian faith.

In noticing this declaration, Mr. Whittemore undertook to parry its force and make us appear guilty of misrepresentation and deceit by saying, "They [the

Restorationists] do not hold to regeneration as Murray did – nor to the general judgment as he did – nor to future punishment as he did."

To which I replied that, whether this were so or not, the claim we made in our manifesto was not invalidated in the least. We did not profess to hold views upon the doctrines specified precisely as the fathers did. I said, "We intended to speak in general terms, not to split hairs; and we are well understood by those who care to understand us correctly." The preamble represents us as being in substantial agreement with Murray and others named upon certain great Christian truths, which the leading Universalists of the present day and most of their followers either deny or virtually abandon and ignore, as no part of their theological system. And this point I went on to demonstrate by ample quotations and illustrations.

Our cavilling critic, referring to another clause in our preamble, said, "Universalists are represented as not holding to future accountability. This is a misrepresentation." In meeting this charge, I inquired how our statement was a misrepresentation. By the phrase "no future accountability" we meant what all the world must understand, *no liability after death to retribution for the deeds done in the body*, and in support of our declaration copied Mr. W.'s own words, "Universalists now know of no condition of man beyond the grave, but that in which he is as the angels of God in heaven," with references to similar testimonies from Rev. Hosea Ballou and Walter Balfour.

"You may say," I continued, "that Universalists *do* hold to future accountability – they hold that people will be accountable in a future state for what they do in that state, though not for what they may have done in a former state." This is a mere quibble, for it does not meet the case presented by us at all. It changes most essentially the meaning of the phrase "no future accountability" as we used it and as the public generally understand it, and instead of making good the charge of misrepresentation against us, proves our censor guilty of misrepresenting us in his attempt to invalidate our testimony.

Again, the editor of the *Trumpet* said, "They [the Universalists] are represented as Materialists – another misrepresentation."

"Another misrepresentation!" I exclaimed in my rejoinder. "These Restorationists must be horrid creatures!"

I then produced extracts from the writings of Walter Balfour, one of the big guns among our opponents in those days, as follows:

> I deny that the soul is immortal.
> All who have read my books will bear witness I have invariably contended it [the soul] means life.
> How does the soul survive after men have killed the body? Have not I said, until I am tired in repeating it, that it returns to God who gave it? But have you [Mr. Hudson] shown that the soul is immortal in the sense essential to your system; that it exists after death in a state of consciousness in happiness or misery? No Sir; this you have not done, and I am confident you never will be able to do it.

> Man cannot kill the soul or life. It is God only who can do this. He breathed into man at first the breath, or life; at death, the life, or breath, he gave returns to him who gave it.[16]

"What, then," I asked, "is rational man on Mr. Balfour's scheme, but matter – mere matter animated with breath?"

> Here, sir, is Mr. Balfour's Materialism, the Materialism deprecated in our preamble, the Materialism which you disavow as belonging to your sort of Universalism. I will ask if you, who deny future punishment, even the American Universalists (generally), do not stand on Balfour's ground? Is not his *your* favorite system? If not, why have you not, like honest men, disclaimed his tenets concerning the soul, and concerning man's unconsciousness for a while after death? Why have you lauded the merits of his works with such unqualified praise? Say you in your *Trumpet* – "These works are written in the spirit of candor, and are replete with forcible argument and sound criticism."

In his animadversion on this point, Mr. Whittemore referred to Rev. Hosea Ballou's "perfect distinction between the human spirit and body," upon which Mr. Hudson had formerly commented. To this I replied:

> All that related to the *old* no-future-punishment scheme, as held before Mr. Balfour's *new* system came into vogue. That old system has been lost in silence since Mr. Balfour's has been promulgated. In fact the two schemes are utterly irreconcilable. The essential doctrine of the former – the soul's immortality – Mr. Balfour sets down as a *mere heathen notion*. You knew all this, sir, when you wrote your charge of misrepresentation. Your allusion to writings against H. Ballou's old scheme of no future punishment had nothing to do with the present state of Universalism, unless you meant the public should think that you and your confreres are still believers in the immortality of a distinct soul. But will you insinuate this? Will you revive the former views and discard Mr. Balfour's? Only be honest and consistent; you will then stand much better in the opinion of the public.

Upon the fourth reason given by the Restorationists for their action in forming an independent Association, which was that "our adherence to the doctrines on which the General Convention of Universalists was first established, instead of producing fair, manly controversy, has procured for us contumely, exclusion from ecclesiastical councils, and final expulsion," etc., Mr. Whittemore made a two-fold accusation against those concerned.

In the first place, he said, "The General Convention never was established on the doctrine of punishment in a future state; the subject was left untouched, and each member made up his mind as he understood the word of God."

In my reply I stated that this declaration of my opponent implied that among those who founded the General Convention at Oxford, in 1785,[17] were believers in the doctrine of no future punishment as well as Restorationists, which was not the case, and that the reason why the subject of future retribution was left alone was because there was such entire unanimity in its favor that no one deemed it in any way important to include it in their platform. In support of my position I quoted largely from Elhanan Winchester, the leading spirit in the movement, who, upon learning that some persons professing to hold the doctrine of the final restitution of all things believed that all men would be happy at death, publicly preached against it, and not only disclaimed all fellowship with it, but denounced it outright as utterly intolerable and pernicious.[18]

I further more stated that there was no evidence within my knowledge that John Murray (whose views upon the question of future limited punishment have been referred to) was any more ready to sacrifice his convictions in this matter than was Mr. Winchester. "There is scarcely room to doubt," I added, "that the founders and early members (whether clergy or laity) of the General Convention believed and took for granted, as an unquestionable doctrine of revealed religion, that those who left this life sinful and unreconciled to God must be miserable for a limited space beyond the grave." And for Mr. Whittemore to represent, even by implication, that it was otherwise – that ultra-Universalists as well as Restorationists were concerned in establishing the General Convention – was an act of dissimulation and Jesuitry unworthy of a man who stood before the world as a teacher of the principles and precepts of the Christian religion.

In order to show still more clearly the unreliability – not to say duplicity – of my reverend opponent, I reminded him that in his *History of Universalism* published the year before, he did not venture to date the difference between Universalists concerning future punishment earlier than "about twenty years since," and that Rev. Hosea Ballou, who was, in fact, the first great expositor of the modern ultra school, had affirmed, as quoted by Mr. Whittemore himself, that he was not fully satisfied that the Bible taught no future punishment until he examined the subject with Rev. Edward Turner of Charlestown. This examination took place in 1817.[19] Previous to that date the doctrine of the Restorationists had been the recognized orthodoxy of the Universalist denomination, only here and there an individual claiming to hold to the idea of no future punishment, and then on his own personal responsibility. The charge that Universalists, as such, entertained that notion was denied by the Philadelphia Convention of 1791 (as I have before said) and denounced as an "unjust slander."

"From all this," I observed, in closing this part of the discussion, "our readers can judge pretty conclusively whether the General Convention was established on the doctrine of future retribution, and whether the Restorationists are guilty of misrepresentation on this point or otherwise – whether you [Mr. Whittemore], in charging them with misrepresentation, have not stood forth a *false accuser*."

In the second place, under the same general head, our editorial combatant stoutly denied the assertion of the Restorationist Association that their adherence to the views of the fathers had procured for them contumely, exclusion, and expulsion, etc. As a refutation of this denial, I brought to notice the declarations of our opponents in public print and elsewhere, which likened our views to the superstitions that produced the Salem witchcraft, to the Catholic notions of Purgatory, calling them "heathen chaff," "wildest vagaries," etc. Also the use of such terms as "Little Tophet," "Hell Junior," bandied about in connection with our names and convictions, and the sarcasm and ridicule with which Walter Balfour and others were wont to speak of us, and of the truths which we solemnly believed ourselves called of God to maintain, defend, and promulgate to our fellow-men. If such treatment was not justly characterized by the term "contumely," we knew of no way in which it could be properly designated. Our opponents might call it kindness, but we did not so understand the meaning of words, and our readers would judge who of us were right.

Exclusion by Ultra Universalists

As to our statement that we had been excluded and expelled from ecclesiastical councils, our contumacious censor affirmed that it was "a gross and wilful misrepresentation." Worse than anything that had gone before!

In rebuttal of this allegation, I cited and explained at length the refusal of the General Convention at Winchester, New Hampshire, in 1829, at the dictum of Rev. Hosea Ballou, to allow Rev. Brother Pickering to offer prayer introductory to the sermon of Rev. Paul Dean, although he had been formally assigned to the discharge of that duty; also the abrogation of my own right to a seat in the same body by a vote passed in September, 1830. Rev. Seth Chandler was denied recognition as a Universalist, though a member of the Universalist society in Lowell, which was in fellowship with the General Convention, though he commenced preaching as a Universalist and was admitted into the pulpits of the order as one of its ministers, and though Mr. Whittemore himself had enrolled him in the catalogue of minsters of the denomination in his *History of Modern Universalism* [sic]. The same was true of Philemon R. Russell. It was stated that he never belonged to the Universalist denomination *in any way*. But he received the fellowship of the Eastern Association bearing the denominational name, and as a member of that body belonged to the General Convention. No doubt if we had all obeyed the orders and conformed to the wishes of those who assumed to be our rulers, we should have been neither censured nor expelled. But we *were* censured and expelled, if there be any such thing in ecclesiastical parlance.

In June, 1830, several members of the Boston Association, with other ministering brethren, held a meeting of what was called the Southern Association, in Berlin, Connecticut, where a preamble and resolutions were passed to the effect that independent associations (such as the Providence Association, composed mostly of Restorationists, was known to be) tended to promote division in the order and must therefore be discountenanced, and that ministers connected with such associations ought not to be allowed a seat in the General Convention, unless they withdraw fellowship from the former.[20]

At a meeting of the General Convention in September following, the authors of the Berlin resolutions secured the passage of a vote excluding from a seat in that body all of us who were members of the Providence Association, so long as we retained such membership.[21] The plea was that this organization held itself constitutionally independent of the General Convention. When those urging this plea were told that the Maine and New York conventions occupied the same independent position, they secured the appointment of committees to confer with those bodies and thus preserve friendly relations with them. But no committee was appointed to confer with our association, for the evident reason that the managers in the matter did not desire to preserve friendly relations with us, but rather to break up our body, or failing in that, to shut us out of the General Convention. We would not abandon our own fraternity and hence were cut off from the main body. It was said of us that we thus excluded ourselves from our former fellowship. Nevertheless, we maintained that by the carefully planned action of our opponents we were excluded from the Universalist Ecclesiastical Councils as we had affirmed, and we believed and felt that we had the support of the intelligent public in that position.

So ended, virtually, the direct controversy with our ultra Universalist brethren growing out of the formation of the Massachusetts Restorationist Association, though the same ground essentially was re-trodden by corresponding parties, at a meeting of the General Convention held in Barre, Vermont, soon afterward. There our opponents put in ecclesiastical form, with slight modifications, the same charges, aspersions, and insinuations against the Restorationists previously set forth in the *Trumpet*.[22] This reiteration of their special pleading and casuistry was, upon being made public, promptly repelled, partly by myself in the *Independent Messenger* of October 14 and November 18, and partly by Brother Charles Hudson, in the same paper of November 4, November 25, and December 9, 1831.

As a further illustration of the disingenuous, contemptuous treatment shown the Restorationists by their former brethren in the fellowship of the Universalist denomination, I am impelled to state, in passing to other topics, that while the columns of the *Independent Messenger* were always open to our opponents, and while we invited communications criticizing our distinctive views and exposing our fallacies of doctrine or argument, if any were thought to be found, never in a single instance were our refutory articles allowed to appear in their chief organ, the *Trumpet*, nor in any other of their publications. Neither justice nor magnanimity on their part gave us one solitary chance for self defense in their columns, or for a frank and manly exposition of our views as in any way opposed to those of the leading influences of the Universalist denomination in doctrine and polity at that time. Whether or not this was fair, manly, and honorable, I left my readers then, as I leave my present ones, to judge.

Controversy with Orthodox

I have already adverted to the fact that during this year (1831) I was beset with controversial attacks, not only from my Universalist opponents but from believers in endless punishment, each of whom I, in proper time and place, endeavored to repel and overcome. Most of the latter were merely newspaper thrusts and sallies to which I responded with such small shot as their unimportance required. A somewhat notable discussion, however, was carried on in the columns of the *Messenger* between an orthodox clergyman, who chose to write over the name of "Inquirer," and myself, the first onset being made by him. The wordy conflict continued through a series of fourteen articles in as many numbers of the publication, each of them being answered consecutively as it appeared.[23] My inquiring assailant proved to be the pastor of the Congregationalist church and society in Hopkinton, a conscientious and zealous young man, who had been educated in Dr. N. W. Taylor's New School Theological Seminary at New Haven, Connecticut,[24] and who felt himself called upon to defend against all adversaries the faith delivered to that sort of orthodox saints.[25] His name was Rev. Amos A. Phelps,[26] subsequently distinguished as an Abolitionist of the Liberty Party school.

Independent Messenger Moved to Boston

The first noticeable event of the calendar year 1832 was the disposal of my pecuniary interest in the *Independent Messenger* to Brother E. M. Stone,[27] who afterward became one of our most active and useful Restorationist ministers, and its removal with the allied printing establishment to Boston. This change, which was effected in the month of January, was deemed advisable by the concurrent judgment of those most interested in the paper and in the cause it was designed to promote, and my own convenience seemed to render it expedient. The office of publication was thenceforward for a considerable time at 40 Court Street in the city named, at which place the printing was also done. No change, however, occurred in the character of the sheet, inasmuch as I remained its senior editor, with essentially the same assistants as before. Its financial affairs were in other hands, and I was wholly relieved of its business management, much to my satisfaction, as I was thereby enabled to devote more time and energy to my proper ministerial and editorial labors.

Invitation to Permanent Settlement at Mendon

About the same time the people of my Mendon parish, to whom I had been preaching and rendering other pastoral services for more than a year, initiated measures preliminary to a more formal and permanent relationship between me and them than had hitherto existed. My labors had been so satisfactory that at a meeting held to consider and act upon the continuance of them after the term of my engagement had expired, it was unanimously voted to give me a call to a regular pastorate, according to ecclesiastical usages, and to have me publicly installed in that office. The parish committee were instructed to communicate to me what had been done, and take such other action as was necessary for carrying the wishes of their constituents into effect. The committee discharged the duty assigned them at once, so far as I was concerned, and to their letter informing me of the vote of the parish I made the following response:

Mendon, Feb. 6, 1832

To the Committee of the First Parish in Mendon, etc.

GENTLEMEN: The undersigned, having received through you, as the organs of the First Parish in Mendon, a copy of the votes and doings of said Parish unanimously inviting him to settle with them in the work of the gospel ministry, begs leave to return the following answer, to wit: That the undersigned, grateful for the confidence and respect evinced toward him by the invitation of the First Parish in Mendon to become their permanent minister, and relying on the blessing of God to prosper his well-meant labors in their service, respectfully accepts their invitation on the terms expressed in their several votes, and will endeavor to discharge the duties of the station to which they have called him, according to the best of his ability. In communicating this answer, you, gentlemen, will please accept for yourselves, the thanks of the undersigned for the kind manner in which you have discharged the duties of your appointment, and rest assured of the sincere respect with which he remains the humble servant of yourselves and the parish you represent.

ADIN BALLOU

To Messrs. WILLIAM S. HASTINGS, AMARIAH TAFT, JABEZ ALDRICH, *Committee*.[28]

The terms of settlement were: For five years, commencing April 1, 1832, a salary of $400 per annum; the connection dissolvable at the expiration of said five years, or at any time thereafter by either party, upon giving the other three months' notice. To professionally educated people in more extravagant times, such a salary as was stipulated for me must of course seem a meager one. It was indeed small, and would have but poorly served my needs but for the most watchful care and economy in the management of my personal and family affairs. Not only was I fortunate in this respect, making me content with a moderate pecuniary support, but there were other reasons why I should not murmur, repine, or object to the compensation I received.

In the first place, I was in no proper sense a *professional* clergyman. For as Paul said of his message, "I neither received it of man, neither was I taught it but by the revelation of Jesus Christ" (Galatians 1:12). I have told in a previous chapter how and why I became a preacher of divine truth and righteousness; not of my own will, nor by my own free choice, but because a dispensation of the gospel was committed to me, and a sacred necessity seemed laid upon me. And when I was spiritually constrained to enter on this, to me, self-renunciative calling, I did so under an inward assurance that I should be provided for, so far as my material needs were concerned, without ever making my ministerial labor a salable commodity – wholly by the free-will offerings of those to whom I ministered. It has accordingly been the inflexible rule of my clerical life, now over sixty-seven years long, never to dictate or demand any given price for my services as preacher, pastor, or conductor of any religious exercises whatsoever, but to accept only what has been voluntarily offered me – not even exacting repayment for unavoidable cash expenses in any given case. Under this rule, I have never been called to suffer for want of the necessaries and comforts of life, nor to be a burden on the shoulders of charity, and I confidently trust I never shall be, while my earthly life continues. Therefore when my Mendon friends named the salary specified above, I accepted it without hesitation or objection.

In the second place, had I demanded a larger sum, it would hardly have been granted me in the then existing circumstances of the parish. They had been long accustomed to paying but a small compensation to their minister; a recent secession of considerable numbers had sensibly reduced their financial resources, and newcomers from the indifferent outside public could not be relied on to contribute generously to an experimental and possibly temporary pastorate. Under such a condition of things, a demand for an unusual amount in those days would have been dangerous if not fatal to the contemplated union, and to all the good results hoped to be gained by it. Hence both principle and policy dictated to all parties concerned moderation of pecuniary expenditures and obligations. And the end justified what was done in this regard.

Friendship with Unitarians

Having formally accepted the call extended to me by the First Parish in Mendon, and arranged satisfactorily the terms upon which I was to become their duly settled pastor, the next thing to be done was to provide for a proper observance of the rite of installation. According to custom and the fitness of things the participating actors on such an occasion should be, as they usually are, persons largely in theological sympathy and spiritual fellowship with the one to be inducted into the pastoral office. I had broken away from the great body of my former Universalist brethren, and the sharp controversy I had carried on with some of their foremost men rendered it inappropriate, as well as repugnant to my feelings, that they should have seats in the installing council. But I had a goodly number of Restorationists whom it would be pleasant to have present on the occasion, and from among whom all the parts could, if deemed advisable, be filled.

The parish, however, had been connected with the Unitarian body, and its leading members would naturally incline in that direction. Happily my course had attracted the attention of several prominent ministers of progressive tendencies in that denomination, and a strong friendship had sprung up between me and them. Among these were Revs. Bernard Whitman[29] of Waltham, Samuel J. May[30] of Brooklyn, Connecticut, Daniel Austin[31] of Brighton, Charles C. Sewall[32] of Danvers, all long since passed on to the heavenly world.

The names of Bernard Whitman and Samuel J. May, I inscribe on these pages with most tender and reverential affection. I had exchanged and corresponded freely with both, and to some extent with others of the same household of faith, but these were especially congenial and dear to me. Between them and the Restorationist clergy there was so much in common and such sincere good feeling, that it was not difficult to secure an installing council that would be harmonious in itself and satisfactory to both me and my people. But before this could be fully accomplished and the services of installation take place, I had passed my twenty-ninth birthday, and the detailed account of that event belongs to the next chapter and may be found on its opening pages.

CHAPTER 12

1832-1833

The necessary measures preparatory to my installation having been taken, as intimated on a preceding page, the event was auspiciously consummated on the third day of May, 1832. Letters missive from the First Church in Mendon had been cordially responded to by the several Restorationist and Unitarian Congregationalist churches to which they were addressed, and their pastors and delegates in coequal numbers united in the exercises of the occasion. The subjoined notice of what transpired, from my editorial pen, appeared in the *Independent Messenger* of May 10, 1832.

Installation at Mendon

The installation of Adin Ballou as pastor of the First Church and Congregation in Mendon was solemnized agreeably to public notice on Thursday last, the 3d inst. The preliminaries having been arranged in an orderly and harmonious ecclesiastical council composed of ministers and delegates from four Restorationist and four Unitarian churches, public services were performed as follows: Introductory prayer by Rev. Samuel Barrett[1] of Boston; reading of the Scriptures by Rev. Charles C. Sewall of Danvers; Sermon by Rev. Bernard Whitman of Waltham, from John 13:34 – "A new commandment I give unto you that ye love one another"; Consecrating prayer by Rev. Charles Hudson of Westminster; Charge by Rev. Paul Dean of Boston; Right Hand of Fellowship by Rev. Samuel J. May of Brooklyn, Ct.; Address to the Church and Congregation by Rev. David Pickering of Providence, R.I.; Concluding prayer by Rev. Nathaniel Wright of Attleboro; and benediction by the Pastor installed. These services were accompanied and interspersed with appropriate and very delightful sacred music by the choir.

It is not easy to speak of this occasion and its exercises in a manner corresponding to the deep interest and felicity excited in the minds of all present. Clergymen and Christian brethren of different names and religious opinions hitherto separated in a greater or less degree by sectarian walls of partition, took sweet counsel together,[2] walked in company to the house of God, and there participated in a feast of intellectual dainties which caused all to *feel* and some actually to *exclaim*, "It is good for us to be here!"[3] All met on the level of enlightened Christian liberality, not to compare creeds and conform non-essential religious opinions to one standard formula; not to surrender the rights of private judgment or public profession of honest faith; not to discuss the relative value of sectarian names; not to concert measures of hostility against other Christian denominations; not to multiply causes of contention in the church of Christ – but to exemplify true brotherly love by Christian union on Christian principles; to enlarge and strengthen the influence of charity; to bear a united testimony against religious bigotry on the one hand and licentious skepticism on the other; to rally around the ancient standard of the "Stem of Jesse"[4]; and thus evince to the world that Christians may love one another in sincerity without agreeing precisely in all the items of their faith. Every exercise and indeed every circumstance of the occasion tended to the promotion of these happy results. Everything was done decently and in order, with cordial affection, in perfect harmony, with distinguished ability, and to universal acceptance. A pleasant day, a large congregation, and generous hospitality on the part of the society, were happy accompaniments to the ecclesiastical and religious felicities of the occasion. The very able and interesting sermon of Mr. Whitman will be published at the request of the Parish, and thereby, we hope, diffuse its truths widely among an inquiring religious public.

Finally, we cannot but rejoice before God with humble thanksgiving for the blessings of this occasion, and while we exclaim in the language of Israel's royal poet, "Behold, how good and how pleasant it is for brethren to dwell together in unity,"[5] we shall indulge the precious hope that this is the opening dawn of a new and blessed era for liberal Christianity – the beginning of a union on truly Christian principles, which, while it effectually guards against mock religion and skepticism, will widen and extend itself over Christendom till all who truly fear God, love Christ, and work righteousness shall come into that unity of spirit whereof the bonds are peace.[6]

Rev. Mr. Whitman's sermon was very scholarly, elaborate, and instructive. Its grand theme was *Christian Union*. It was published as stated, but owing to sickness and pressing avocations, he could not prepare it for the press till nearly a year after it was delivered. Meantime, he carefully revised and amplified it, so that when it appeared, it covered nearly seventy-eight pamphlet pages. There were appended to it Rev. Paul Dean's "Charge to the Pastor" and Rev. David Pickering's "Address to the People," both able and impressive utterances – all making eighty-four pages.[7] It was intended to have Rev. Samuel J. May's "Right Hand of Fellowship" appear in connection with the other parts, but for some unknown reason the manuscript failed to reach the printers.

The sermon was planned to show: (1) What is *not* necessary for Christian union; (2) What *is* necessary for it; and (3) The great importance of laboring to promote it. These points were treated exhaustively and followed out to a practical application with devout earnestness. The preacher stated forcibly his own theological and ecclesiastical position, recognized clearly that of the pastor and his flock, and warmly congratulated all parties represented in our services on the exemplification of Christian union they were that day illustrating before the world. Copies of the pamphlet are preserved in the town libraries of Mendon and Hopedale.

It is proper to observe in this connection that in those days it required no little moral courage for Rev. Mr. Whitman and his Unitarian brethren to unite with the Restorationists in a public religious service like that of my installation – a courage now hardly conceivable as having any occasion for its exercise. But such occasion then existed and for two prominent reasons.

(1) A large majority of the Unitarians at that time had a great dislike, amounting almost to contemptuous disgust, towards Universalists of every kind and name, few of them making any distinction between "ultras" and Restorationists, or if they recognized a difference, they had little respect for the latter so far as concerned any Scriptural authority for their distinctive belief. They insisted that though some mild form of endless punishment might or might not be true, the Bible, in their opinion, did not teach universal restoration but left the final destiny of the wicked in hopeless obscurity. Moreover, they generally believed that this obscurity was wholesome in its moral and religious influence upon mankind. Therefore, duty and expediency required them to preach the promises and threatenings of the sacred record according to the letter of the text as traditionally understood and not "to be wise above what was written"[8] – at the same time explaining away or ignoring the letter of texts that plainly favored the doctrine of the final restitution of all things. In this state of opinion, they deemed it sufficiently burdensome to defend their own special Unitarian tenets against the denunciations of the self-styled orthodox sects without fathering other heresies. And they were very sensitive about being charged by their theological enemies with any leanings toward Universalism. They were sure of being so charged if they affiliated with the Restorationists. They, therefore, dreaded and avoided all fellowship with them.

(2) The Unitarians were largely a well-educated class of people, and nursed the pride of having a highly educated ministry. But the Restorationists, tried by their standard, were "unlearned and ignorant"[9] – only a trifle better schooled, perhaps, than the humble Nazarene himself and his original twelve apostles, without a D.D. among them, and little better than barbarians when compared with the graduates of Harvard College, and other polished literati. This was quite as objectionable to many of the "grave and reverend signiors"[10] of the denomination as our peculiar theology. And I learned from my brave and kind Brother Whitman that, after the installation, he was sharply rebuked by one of his titled elders of the profession, for having assisted in introducing unlearned men into the clerical office.

I mention these things to show that our Brothers Whitman, May, and others had to take up no little of a cross and incur considerable reproach from their more numerous and dignified associates for keeping company with us and extending to us the courtesies of ecclesiastical and Christian fellowship. Let them receive credit accordingly from all who honor courage, honesty, and fair dealing.

The Temperance Reform

A somewhat memorable experience of the year in review was my open espousal of the Temperance Reform,[11] all the more so by reason of the circumstances attending such action on my part. My neighboring clerical friend, Rev. John M. S. Perry,[12] then pastor of the North Congregational church of Mendon (Orthodox), had become much interested in the cause, and, with a few of his people who sympathized with him, desired to inaugurate a movement for promoting its interests in our general vicinity. He accordingly came to me with a prepared preamble and pledge which he offered as a basis for a temperance society in the town.

In the multiplicity of my cares and labors, I had not previously given the subject much attention and so begged leave for a little time to consider it and act advisedly in regard to his proposition. After due deliberation, I became satisfied that the reform was essentially a righteous one and greatly needed in the community. But I had good reason to anticipate that it would disturb the harmony of my congregation if I embarked in it with honest zeal, and perhaps alienate some of my parishioners and hitherto ardent friends. Many liberalists of that day looked upon the organization of societies like that contemplated as a scheme of the so-called Evangelicals for making sectarian capital and gaining to themselves some special advantage, and upon that ground regarded all such action with distrust. I had myself some reason in this case to suspect that my neighbors of the other church and society hoped the project might prove an apple of discord in my parish, whose rising prosperity they deprecated, and in that or some other way redound to their profit.

Nevertheless, I resolved, whatever might be the motives and wishes of Mr. Perry and his allies, (1) that I would not allow myself to turn my back upon so good a cause; and (2) that my evangelical co-workers should secure no sectarian ends by my espousing it. I therefore told my clerical neighbor, upon further consultation with him, that I would take hold of the work as he desired, but that the proposed society must be thoroughly guarded against all sectarian and partisan misdirection or entanglement, by specific stipulations to that effect in the preliminary papers about to be circulated. He rather coolly assented, and the documents were re-drafted in conformity with my wishes.

The next thing deemed necessary to be done was to hold a public meeting, and have an expository lecture given, presenting the whole subject clearly to the people. Upon broaching the question where and by whom this lecture should be delivered, Mr. Perry and his friends were prompt, decided, and urgent, that my church must be the place, and I the lecturer. Seeing their persistency, I accepted the responsibility thus thrust upon me, but gave my ministerial brother to understand that I should expect him to sustain me by going into the pulpit with me, offering prayer, and otherwise cooperating on the occasion. This I knew would pinch in the bud whatever religious exclusiveness he might cherish, and test his devotion to the temperance cause. To this arrangement he reluctantly consented.

The time of the meeting was fixed on a given Sunday at 5 o'clock P.M. The day and hour arrived, and, due notice having been given throughout the town, a large audience assembled, composed of Mr. Perry's people and my own with some outsiders. I remained in the vestibule of the church during the tolling of the bell before the opening of the service, waiting for my clerical brother that I might courteously direct him to the pulpit, as customary in such cases. But no such brother appeared. I at length ordered the tolling stopped, still remaining in the vestibule. After a little further delay he came in, when I cordially greeted him, and signified my expectation that he was ready to go with me and participate in the exercises of the occasion. He immediately began to make excuses, saying that his labors had been very hard during the day, and consequently that he was very much fatigued and unable to take any part with me, etc., etc. I declined to excuse him and insisted that he should accompany me to the desk, which he made a pretense of doing, many of the people hearing the conversation and watching us, as we walked up the aisle together, with interest and amazement. At length he suddenly broke from me, darted into a pew, took a seat, and I proceeded to the duty of the hour without him. I went through the various exercises by myself, according to my best judgment and with evidently good effect.

In answering the objections that were sometimes urged against temperance organizations, I at length reached the one, based on sectarian grounds, which made such organizations unworthy of liberal Christian support. I stated that however this might be generally or in other cases, it would not apply in the present instance. I then read the clauses in our plan of action, which explicitly declared that nothing sectarian or partisan should be allowed in our proceedings, following the same with very pointed and emphatic comments in explication and application of the same. In closing under that head, I remarked that if anything contrary to the stipulated unsectarian character of the movement had been manifested on the present occasion, I trusted the blame would be laid where it belonged. A thrill of suppressed excitement ran through the audience, which vented itself freely after the service was over. Mr. Perry's leading parishioner was mortified and indignant at his pastor's course, and administered to him a scathing rebuke for having done the worst possible thing to damage the cause of temperance in its local infancy. None of his religious friends approved his course, while mine, of course, denounced it. He was himself greatly surprised, abashed, and humiliated. The next forenoon he called on me, apologized for his conduct, and promised never to repeat it. And he never did. He was cured and I was amply vindicated. Our relations thereafter, while he remained in town, were pleasant and harmonious. He left his pastorate in 1835, and went with his wife as missionaries to Ceylon, where both ere long died of cholera, within an hour of each other.

At this point it seems proper for me to confess my great indebtedness to the temperance reform for the inductive lessons it gave me, and for its salutary discipline of my mind, heart, and character. It was to me a primary school from which I went forth to all my later moral and social reform attainments. I had been brought up a moderate drinker, regarding drunkenness – an abuse of intoxicating liquors – alone a sin. So I believed, so I preached, so I practiced. And I deemed all temperance pledges and societies as supererogatory and useless. But I had come to a new view of the matter. The evils of intemperance were forced upon my attention wherever I went. Their terrors and the woes connected with them appalled me – wrung my very soul. And the great question how they could be removed confronted me whenever I thought of the matter, demanding not only consideration, but decision and action. I was a rational and accountable being. I was more than that – a public moral and religious teacher. There was no justifiable excuse for neutrality upon a subject of such magnitude, upon a question so closely related to the welfare and happiness of multitudes of my fellow men. I ought manfully to say *Yes* or *No* upon it; plant myself unequivocally and firmly on one side or the other; be for or against the reform. I thoroughly investigated the subject, weighing its claims in the scales of reason and conscience. I saw its merits and mastered its arguments. I became qualified to teach, defend, and successfully commend it to others, both by precept and example. I was rendered a better, a truer, a nobler man thereby. My whole being was enriched, my whole life was made a greater power for good for the stand I took at that early day in regard to this great movement.

Moreover, it suggested to me three great practical data in ethics, which have grown more and more important in my estimation ever since as means of promoting human progress and redemption: (1) that righteousness must be taught definitely, specifically, and practically to produce any marked results, not in vague generalisms; (2) that professed receivers and adherents of any given righteous cause must be unequivocally and uncompromisingly pledged to the practice of definitely declared duties pertaining to such cause, and not be left in a state of irresponsible non-committalism; (3) that such pledged adherents and receivers must voluntarily associate under explicit affirmations of a settled purpose to cooperate in exemplifying and diffusing abroad the virtues and excellences to which they are committed, and not act at random in disorganized and aimless individualism, often antagonistic to each other and detrimental to the interests involved.

Another great good which I derived from the temperance reform was that, under its influence, I was enabled to save myself, my family, and a multitude of friends (to say nothing of others whom I may have reached), if not from drunkenness, yet from all danger of it, and from innumerable foolish expenditures, wastes, and damages – pecuniary, physiological, and intellectual – while at the same time gaining more or less elevation of moral tone and character. My interest in it was a defense against many temptations in life and a help to many virtues, as well as a great means of usefulness to my fellow men.

I had no firmly rooted appetite for strong drink to overcome, and whatever inducements to break my pledge were presented to me after taking it were of a social and festive nature. It was the custom in those days, among family relatives and special friends when visiting or calling upon each other, to *treat* and *be treated*, as the phrasing was. A generous and warm-hearted hospitality demanded this, and even common civility, in some circles. To drink together was a badge or token of kindly regard. I remember visiting a venerable and much esteemed relative soon after committing myself to this cause and to abstinence from the use of all intoxicants. He knew nothing of the step I had taken in the matter, and, as he had previously done, brought out from his well-stored larder his choice liquors and concomitants for the usual treat. I, of course, had to decline his proffered glass. He was utterly astonished and deeply grieved, exclaiming, "What have I done that you refuse to drink with me?" I explained my position as well as I could, but he was hardly able to understand the reasons for my course. He looked so sorrowful that, but for my pledge, my good feelings would have impelled me to yield to his generous and kind-hearted solicitations.

Another result of my espousal and championship of the temperance cause, more trying and painful in many respects, though not without its salutary and helpful aspects, was the alienation of personal admirers, accompanied by a new baptism of vituperation and reproach. Some few of those who called me to Mendon, and who, up to this time, had been liberal in their plaudits and commendations, now turned their backs upon me as a disturber of their peace, and a meddler with what they deemed their personal rights. "Could they not eat and drink what they pleased without being called to account as sinners? Had they hired me to preach upon such subjects? No, indeed." And so they vented their indignation and spite upon me. These persons were chiefly wedded to the intoxicating cup. Only a few of them boldly gave utterance to their angry scurrility, but quite a number muttered their sullen dislike of my attitude in the matter.

I knew what it was aforetime to be scorned and hated on account of theological and ecclesiastical offenses, but now I must endure ill-will and denunciation as a moral reformer, seeking only the personal good of my assailants. I very likely needed this discipline, not only to wean me from the love of human praise, but to strengthen me to endure much sorer experiences of the same sort in the not far distant future. It was a wholesome medicine, which, though bitter to the taste, did me substantial good and resulted to my advantage. If I lost a few seeming friends, I gained many new and better ones. My heart was purged of some of its impurities, a wider sphere of usefulness opened before me, and multiplied opportunities were afforded me to labor for the uplifting and redemption of my fellow men.

It was no sooner noised abroad that I had enlisted in this great reform and was prepared to devote myself somewhat to the proclamation and diffusion of its principles in the general community, and wherever an opening should be made for me, than I began to have calls to lecture upon the subject. These I was happy to answer affirmatively, so far as home duties and circumstances otherwise would allow, and was thereby enabled to gain and exert a moral influence in behalf of truth and righteousness, which I had not before possessed. As a further encouragement, I had the great satisfaction of seeing my ministerial brethren of the Restorationist faith engage in the movement and unite heartily in efforts to carry it forward to successful issues. At a meeting of the Providence Association, held June 6, 1832, which I had the pleasure of attending, the following resolutions were unanimously passed:

> *Resolved*, That this Association take a deep and lively interest in the great *Temperance Reformation* now in progress throughout the United States, and that while we congratulate the friends of this reformation everywhere on their success in this laudable and praiseworthy cause, we will not cease to cooperate with all our ability in the accomplishment of its grand and fundamental objects.
>
> *Resolved*, That we recommend to our friends throughout the country to use their influence in arresting the progress of intemperance and in rearing up a generation who shall be temperate in all things.

Extracts from Diary, August-September 1832

As may be easily imagined, I had in those days no idle time. Besides my regular pastoral duties – preaching twice each Sunday at home or on exchange, overseeing the Sabbath school, administering church ordinances in their season, and visiting among my people – I delivered frequent lectures at near or more distant places, ministered at many funerals outside as well as inside my parish, solemnized numerous marriages in my own and neighboring towns, wrote week by week important articles as principal editor of the *Independent Messenger*, attended various religious and reform meetings here and there, kept up an extensive correspondence, discharged the duties of a member of the town school committee, and, of course, took some care of ordinary domestic affairs. Little opportunity had I for rest and recuperation.

Perhaps the best possible inside view of my various activities at this period may be presented by quoting somewhat from the fragmentary memoranda I kept, and I therefore submit a few extracts:[13]

Friday, August 24, 1832. Hired my friend Lewis Boyden's horse and sulky and made a forenoon's inspection of the district school near Mr. Robert Allen's, taught by a Miss Morse. With only a single cracker for my dinner, I rode thence to the southeast part of Bellingham, near Franklin, to officiate at the funeral of friend Martin Cushman. He had been an eccentric man and somewhat misanthropic. He was quite intellectual, but had strong passions not easily controlled, which rendered him disagreeable to many people, and prompted him to frequent lawsuits with his fellow citizens. He had been an ultra Universalist in opinion, and held me in great esteem till I broke with my brethren of that school, when he repudiated me and denounced me outright. Yet when mortal sickness prostrated him he relented, became prayerful, and sent for me to visit him, which I did, ministering in my way to his spiritual needs. When near his end, he requested that I should attend his funeral, and I was there on the date mentioned, accordingly. I preached from

2 Chronicles 21:13: "Let me fall now into the hand of the Lord," etc. The house was small and could not contain nearly all who had assembled, and so, the weather being favorable, the services took place in the yard outside, beneath some large shade trees. I spoke with a good degree of spiritual freedom, unction, and effect.

Sunday, August 26. Usual services in the church. In the morning gave an exposition of the first part of seventh chapter of Matthew. Afterward attended the examination of the Sunday School, which was good. Brother Fisher Ames Tyler[14] addressed the scholars. At night called on Mrs. Elizabeth (Mellen) Torrey, widow of Stephen, aged 95 years, now nearing the end of her mortal pilgrimage, and ripe for the heavenly granary.

Monday, August 27. At home. Prepared for the *Messenger* a Review of Rev. Lucius R. Paige's[15] "Letters to my devoted friend, Rev. Bernard Whitman,"[16] and wrote to the managing editor, Rev. E. M. Stone.

Tuesday, August 28. Attended a meeting of Revolutionary soldiers convened before our county judge of probate to certify to their ages and war services, in order that they might obtain pensions from the United States government. Fifty applicants were present from Mendon and vicinity. I dined with the company, and took home with me my venerable friend, Benjamin Pickering, who remained through the night and most of the next day, in the evening of which I went with wife and daughter to a considerable party at Mrs. Mary (Hastings) Hayward's, widow of Caleb, formerly a prominent citizen of the town.[17]

Thursday, August 30. Took tea with others at Col. Warren Rawson's.[18] On returning home found my parents awaiting us, having just arrived from Cumberland, Rhode Island for a two days' visit.

Friday, August 31. Went to Milford to invite my wife's father and mother to come and double the parental company. They complied, and we had a memorable visit – one never repeated in this mortal state.

Saturday, September 1. Letters received from two brother clergymen requesting early answers had to be laid aside for a less busy season. Rode 27 miles in the afternoon to Southbridge, where I had engaged to preach on the morrow. Arrived at 6:30 P.M., and stopped with Frederick W. Bottom, Esq., by whom I was agreeably entertained.

Sunday, September 2. Preached three discourses to good acceptance: (1) A written one from the text: "Draw nigh to God, and He will draw nigh to you";[19] (2) On universal restoration, *extempore*; (3) On Christian charity and union. Full and attentive audiences.

Monday, September 3. Dined with my kind and cordial friend, Josiah Snow,[20] publisher of the Southbridge *Register and Mirror*. He is a warm sympathizer and a zealous helper of the cause of universal restoration. Before starting for home, it was reported that a man in town had died of Asiatic cholera.[21] Our whole country in a state of great alarm on account of this disease, which is causing many deaths in certain localities. Arrived home about sundown, finding Rev. James W. Hoskins,[22] from Hampden, Maine, with my family. He is an able and devoted Restorationist, and has, in my absence, supplied my Mendon pulpit acceptably.

Friday, September 7. Troubled somewhat with sick headache, my frequent ailment. Off to Milford, with wife and two children.

Saturday, September 8. Answered junior editor's letter, but sent no article for the *Messenger*. A call from friend Arnold Buffum,[23] a pioneer Abolitionist, who proposed to lecture in our church tomorrow at 4:30 P.M. Went with him to consult Col. Rawson and Mr. Jabez Aldrich. Not much encouragement, but no opposition. Not a ripple of antislavery has yet reached Mendon. But friend Buffum thought it was high time to stir the waters, and he was not a man to be put off. So the appointment was made.

Sunday, September 9. Preached A.M. and P.M., as usual, and announced friend Buffum's lecture. It came off accordingly. Important truths uttered to a very small audience, with no striking effect, and the contribution box circulated in vain. Evening, rode to Uxbridge and solemnized marriage of Mr. Moses T. Murdock and Miss Dorinda W. Grout.

Monday, September 10. A call from my ever estimable Christian brother, Rev. Samuel J. May, of Brooklyn, Connecticut. He brought with him Rev. Mr. Brooks,[24] of Hingham, and we had a pleasant interview.

Tuesday, September 11. Plenty of household duties, but the important event of the day was an unexpected call from my brother, Ariel Ballou Jr., M.D., of Woonsocket, Rhode Island, and his bride, Miss Hannah Horton, for marriage. He could wait for no preparation, and desired the ceremony to take place at once. We conformed to his urgency. The marriage was solemnized and they left within an hour. This was less agreeable to us than to them. Just at night had a call from Benjamin Davenport, Esq.,[25] one of my prominent parishioners, with a request from a niece of his wife, Mrs. Freeman Fisher, to have me come to Milford and christen a dangerously sick child.

Wednesday, September 12. Went to Milford to find Mrs. Fisher's child a corpse. Just as safe in the Savior's bosom as if formally baptized. Dined at Father Hunt's. Returned to Mendon. Mr. Smith Sayles and wife, my good parents-in-law by the first marriage, arrived from Smithfield, Rhode Island to make us a visit. Excellent relatives these, and worthy of our kindest attention.

Thursday, September 13. Entertaining company, who left for home about 2 P.M.

Friday, September 14. Funeral service of Mrs. Allen Chase in Bellingham.

Saturday, September 15. Started with wife at half-past eleven A.M. for Brooklyn, Connecticut, to preach on the morrow in exchange with Rev. Brother S. J. May. Arrived at 8 P.M. and were quietly entertained by his family during our sojourn.

Sunday, September 16. Preached A.M. *extempore* from Acts 12:24-26: "God, who made the world," etc.; and P.M., a written sermon from James 4:8: "Draw nigh to God," etc. Before close of service published intentions of marriage for a couple, according to Connecticut law and usage. How much spiritual impression my performances made on the people, I know not – probably small. Took tea at 4 P.M. and departed for Thompson, Connecticut, where we spent the night. When nearing the place in the evening, we were suddenly surprised by the momentary flash of a brilliant meteor.

Monday, September 17. Remained at Stiles hotel through the forenoon. About 11:30 o'clock, Brother May arrived on his return from Mendon, and we dined together and enjoyed a delightful conversational conference upon high and sacred themes. He is an advanced thinker, a whole-hearted philanthropist, and a most genial Christian gentleman. We parted at 2:30 P.M., he going home, and wife and I turning our faces towards Winchester, New Hampshire, where a conference of Restorationist ministers had been appointed for the ensuing Wednesday and Thursday.

Tuesday, September 18. Left Leicester, our tarrying place for the night, early, and rode all day, reaching Warwick in the evening, and taking lodging in the public house.

Wednesday, September 19. Off soon after sunrise, arriving at our place of destination about 8 A.M. The Universalist society there, one of the oldest of that faith in New Hampshire, was strongly inclined to Restorationism, having then for a pastor Brother Lyman Maynard, a member of our Massachusetts Association. Myself and wife were hospitably cared for in the family of Brother Asa Alexander, a devoted layman of the society. The conference opened auspiciously, and proved to be an interesting and profitable occasion. I preached on both Wednesday and Thursday mornings; Brother Charles Hudson, Wednesday afternoon; Brother Paul Dean, Thursday afternoon and evening. Exhortations followed the discourses of Thursday morning and evening, and appropriate devotional and musical exercises were enjoyed at every session.[26]

Friday, September 21. Bade our Winchester friends a grateful farewell early in the morning and started for home with Brothers Dean, Hudson, and Stone. Dined at Templeton, having for a fellow guest at table a celebrated theological professor and D.D., who was remarkable for his eating powers and intemperate consumption of strong green tea, while descanting on the subject of temperance and exemplifying a coarse type of manners generally. His saintliness was quite below the standard of his reputation in Evangelical circles. Rode to Westminster in the afternoon and shared the kind hospitality of Brother and Mrs. Hudson for the succeeding night.

Saturday, September 22. A good day's ride to Mendon, taking dinner at Worcester. A safe and enjoyable journey of a week was thus completed.

Sunday, September 23. In my own pulpit again. Preached A.M. from Psalms 100:2: "Serve the Lord with gladness," and P.M. from Romans 2:11: "There is no respect of persons with God." At 5 P.M. attended the funeral of Miss Polly Corbett at the house of her mother in South Milford, preaching from Psalms 124:8: "Our help is in the name of the Lord, who made heaven and earth."

The foregoing passages from my journal, covering about four weeks of time, will indicate imperfectly to the reader the manner in which the wheels of my private and public life were kept in motion during the latter part of the year 1832, and there is no need for further particularization.

Meeting of the Massachusetts Association of Universal Restorationists, 1833

On the first Wednesday in January, 1833, the Massachusetts Association of Restorationists held its annual meeting in Boston.[27] The occasion proved a busy one, several matters of importance coming up for consideration, in which I was much interested, and in the discussion of which I took an active part.[28] The Annual Sermon, as it was called, was preached by me from Philippians 4:6: "Be careful for nothing, but in everything, by prayer and supplication, with thanksgiving, let your requests be made known unto God." I was housed and fed kindly by Bro. Dean, and the public services were held in his church in Bulfinch Street. Several discourses were delivered to interested audiences, and the proceedings of private sittings were cordial and harmonious. The weather was remarkable for the season, being more like May than January. I returned home by way of Waltham, calling there on my excellent friend and brother, Rev. Bernard Whitman, with whom I had a brief, but most elevating and soul-satisfying interview.

Death of Two Children

A dark cloud of anxiety and sorrow gathered without warning and hovered over our household towards the close of this month of January, 1833. Before the end of February its lurid bolts had bereaved us of two out of our three children. The scarlet fever, then nowhere prevalent in the vicinity, developed itself in our family and scathed, more or less severely, every member.

On the twenty-sixth of January, our eldest son, Adin Jr., a lad in the tenth year of his age, was sent on an errand about a mile distant, and while away became so ill that he had to be taken in and put to bed by one of our kind, motherly parishioners. We received word of this in the early evening and I hastened to bring him home. We did not suspect anything serious, and the pressure of my various duties occupied my utmost attention. But my sick boy, instead of improving, became gradually worse. We summoned our family physician, Dr. John G. Metcalf,[29] who at first thought the disease might be measles, but at length pronounced it scarlatina or canker rash, though, so far as we knew, he had been exposed to neither.[30] The case soon proved desperate and we were appalled at its aspect. Time had been inconsiderately lost and vigorous treatment delayed. In our distressed anxiety we called in the venerable and celebrated Dr. Daniel Thurber, but it was too late. The patient grew weaker and weaker in spite of all that was done for him, suffering intensely till relieved by death at half-past nine P.M., February 10.

Before this occurred our other children and young housemaid had come down with the same malady, and we, the parents, were half sick, worn, and debilitated. The neighborhood was in a state of more or less alarm and the funeral must take place under forlorn and gloomy circumstances. We were favored, however, with all needed sympathy and assistance. The obsequies were sadly but consolingly solemnized on Tuesday, February 12. Relatives from Milford; Cumberland, Rhode Island; and Woonsocket, Rhode Island were in attendance on the mournful occasion, as also were a goodly number of our parishioners and personal friends. Rev. J. M. S. Perry, the Orthodox minister, and Mercy Thayer,[31] a Friends preacher, met with us, manifesting a sympathetic spirit. The religious services, consisting of discourse and prayers, were rendered by Brother Seth Chandler, then ministering to the Restorationists of Oxford. The day was stormy, neither parent leaving the house, but its duties and experiences transpired as favorably as could be expected.

We were then hopeful of the other invalids, who seemed to be in a fair way of recovery. But, alas, another bitter cup was awaiting us. In the evening of February 22, our other little son, Pearley H., aged two years and three months, who had been improving, apparently, up to that time, suddenly showed signs of a relapse. Medical aid was again called in and our best efforts were put forth to save him, but all in vain. Dropsy on the brain[32] was soon developed, his case became hopeless, spasm succeeding spasm till February 27, when he expired. He was a bright and loving child, but of slender health, and during this last painful illness, as well as before, gave forth very tender and affecting little utterances, which still linger in the memory of those who gave him birth.

Another funeral darkened our home, drew around us condoling relatives and friends as before, and elicited needful religious consolation. It took place February 28, at one o'clock P.M., Rev. Samuel Clarke[33] of Uxbridge being our religious counselor on the occasion, his words breathing the soothing perfume of comfort and Christian consolation upon all our hearts.

In recalling these trying experiences with their concomitants and disciplinary lessons, how many sacred memories enthrong us! What anxieties, cares, vigils, devoured our energies! What pains and distresses, sighs and moans, from the sick couches of our suffering ones harrowed our parental sensibilities! What pitying kindnesses flowed in upon us from helpful neighbors, friends, and relatives! What mercies, consolations, and sanctifications, distilled from heaven, bedewed our stricken, aching souls! What a moral training for compassionate sympathy with other mourning families in after years! What longing aspirations swelled our breasts for perfect assurances of immortal life and blessedness!

"Do the departed loved ones still live on?" we asked. Was it indeed true that they were "not lost but gone before"? Or must our hearts freeze amid the chilling blasts of doubt and skepticism? Nay, we believed that

Where immortal spirits reign,
There shall we all meet again.[34]

No other cases of scarlatina occurred in our general neighborhood during the season. Those in our family were probably generated by local conditions, of whose deleterious influence we were then ignorant. The causes, preventives, and cure of disease will no doubt be better known in future ages than at present, and such knowledge will, I believe, deliver our human race from most of the ills to which it is now subject, and from most of the pain, suffering, and premature death that now afflict it.

CHAPTER 13

1833-1834

The pressure of duties and cares, though interrupted by the visitation of sickness, mentioned at the close of the last chapter, continued unabated. Indeed, it seemed to increase as time went on, so that I had little opportunity to sit down and brood over our afflictions, desolating and painful as they were. Pastoral and other public labors incident to my ministerial calling, oversight of the town schools, editorial and correspondential writing, with more or less secular occupation, demanded constant activity on my part. Occasional calls for service abroad, as well as at or near home, came to me, and under circumstances that I could not very well refuse them, inasmuch as they usually related to the cause of universal restoration, of which I had become an acknowledged champion.

Installation of Seth Chandler at Oxford

On the twenty-fifth of May, 1833, I attended the installation of Rev. Brother Seth Chandler, my former theological student, at Oxford, Massachusetts, as pastor of the Universalist society there, one of the oldest of that persuasion in the country, having been established under the ministry of Rev. Adams Streeter in 1785.[1] A fraternal ecclesiastical council united in the services of the occasion according to the following order: Introductory prayer by Rev. Thomas J. Greenwood;[2] Reading of the Scriptures by Rev. Charles Hudson; Sermon by Rev. Samuel J. May; consecrating prayer by Rev. David Pickering; Charge by myself; Right Hand of Fellowship by Rev. Ebenezer Robinson; Address to the people by Rev. John Goldsbury;[3] Concluding prayer by Rev. Nathaniel Wright; Benediction by the pastor elect. Proceedings in the council, composed of Unitarian and Restorationist clergymen, harmonious, the several exercises appropriate, hospitalities of the society generous, and the communion of saints pleasant.[4] My accompanying delegate from the Mendon church was Mr. Stephen Albee,[5] one of my lifelong friends.

Bernard Whitman's Letters

About this time, my esteemed brother, Rev. Bernard Whitman, published his able work, entitled *Friendly Letters to a Universalist on Divine Rewards and Punishments.*[6] It was a duodecimo volume of 366 pages – candid, lucid, pertinent, conclusive against the theory of no future retribution, and in support of the true

Christian doctrine upon that subject. His sympathy and cooperation with me had procured for him the coarse denunciations of the ultra Universalist press,[7] which I promptly repelled through the columns of the *Messenger*. I gave in that organ the high commendation of the volume which it deserved, and did all I could to promote its circulation. Its opponents affected to despise it and to disdain answering it. They were politic enough to make no attempt to refute its conclusions.[8] It was one among the effective efforts of those controversial days which gradually paralyzed the arrogant hypothesis that "knew of no condition for man beyond the grave but that in which he is as the angels of God in heaven." That hypothesis has for many years slumbered in an undisturbed tomb and many of the Universalist denomination today seem to have forgotten, if they ever knew, that it once claimed to be the orthodoxy of their order.[9]

Birth of a Son

On the thirtieth day of June, the same year, we had born to us another son, whom we named Adin Augustus. The season of anxiety and sorrow through which we had a few months before passed seemed to have made its impress upon his very nature. His early infant wailings were like echoes of those moans of his languishing brothers, which still vibrated in the memories of bereaved parental affection. But these characteristics were slowly outgrown and he became a joyous child, a sprightly, winsome lad, a promising youth, and a model young man. But, alas, at that auspicious climax, as will be told in its season, he was translated to the invisible realm, whither the others referred to preceded him.

An Unfortunate Partnership

During the ensuing month of August, I received a call to the pastorate of a church and society of our faith in Watertown, Massachusetts, which, though offering me sundry increased temporal advantages, I did not feel at liberty to accept. Immediately afterward I added to my already superabundant labors the care and responsibility of a private school opened in my own house. This enterprise succeeded very well with the exception of occasional interruptions caused by calls to funerals, etc., which I could not well decline, accommodating matters to them as well as I could, without serious inconvenience or complaint from any quarter. But the turn of a new leaf in the volume of my affairs obliged me to terminate the undertaking in October. For early in that month the *Independent Messenger* and its accompanying printing establishment came back into my hands. The Boston proprietor had become weary of the duties incident to its management, and urged me to resume them and so grant him the relief he desired.[10]

I was induced to yield to his wishes, partly, at least, by the offer of aid from a proposed co-partner, Rev. Stephen Cutler[11] of Cumberland, Rhode Island, who would share the pecuniary burdens of the concern equally with me, and attend to all its business affairs, excepting those of editorship, which I thought I could execute without serious difficulty. I had reason to suppose that my contemplated co-laborer was competent and trustworthy, and the partnership was accordingly formed under the name of "Cutler and Ballou," October 3, 1833. Four days afterward we went to Boston together, purchased the property in question, and completed all needful arrangements for its speedy removal to Mendon. This was effected October 18, and everything was soon in readiness for its designed use.

The experiment of forming a co-partnership in this matter proved to be a serious misfortune to me. Mr. Cutler, notwithstanding his pretensions and much show of ability, turned out to be wholly unfitted for his new position in three months, and our relations were dissolved, everything pertaining to the affairs of the company coming into my hands for care and management. Nor was this all, nor the worst, of the matter. For by false representations on his part he had induced me to enter into bonds with him to his Cumberland creditors to the amount of several hundred dollars, most of which I was ultimately obliged to pay. I found him not only without business capacity, but destitute of capital and unreliable in moral integrity. So I gained nothing by my connection with him, but lost considerable of my much needed funds. The settlement of matters between us was long pending, the details and result of which restored neither my confidence nor my money. He came from the Baptists through the Universalist into the Restorationist fold, whence he returned to the bosom of the church from which he first set out, and in which he ended his career.

Thus it came to pass that at the close of the year 1833 I found myself more heavily burdened than ever before with professional duties, editorial responsibilities, and business demands and obligations incident to the management of a printing office. Moreover, I had become so involved financially by the transactions of the few preceding months that I was obliged to resort to my credit in order to keep the wheels of all the machinery under my care in good working order. I learned thereby how true was the saying "He who goeth a-borrowing goeth a-sorrowing,"[12] but happily I neither then nor afterward broke my bond nor my word to any one to whom I owed money, and so through life have I had all the accommodation of the kind indicated that I needed.

Theological Discussion with Unitarians

The third volume of the *Messenger* closed with the year specified [1833]. I had furnished many strong articles for its columns, most of which I deem worthy of continued preservation. The controversy with the ultra Universalist brethren was prosecuted with unabated vigor on my part, and the dogma of endless punishment was opposed with some of the ablest argumentative expositions I ever wrote. My own doctrine of Restorationism I defended to my own satisfaction and that of my co-religionists, against all classes of assailants, and carried on interesting discussions with several doubting, but friendly querists.

Among the articles was a series near the end of the year, in review of a then recently published essay of H. J. Huidekoper,[13] of Meadville, Pennsylvania, on the final destruction of the wicked.[14] The author was a learned, able, and candid Unitarian layman, born in Germany, but long a resident in this country and thoroughly Americanized, and a most excellent man. He was virtually the founder of the Unitarian society in the place named, and of the theological school there,[15] now so widely known throughout the land. My friend, Bernard Whitman, knowing that I had been a convert from Destructionism to Restorationism, sent me a copy of the essay, with an urgent request that I should examine and answer it. I was glad to do so. When I had completed my review, I mailed the numbers of my paper containing it to Mr. Huidekoper, who, in due time, made a rejoinder, to which I in turn replied.[16] This discussion is preserved with other published writings of mine, as elsewhere stated.

During the same year, I was drawn into another friendly argument with Rev. Jonathan Farr,[17] of Harvard, Massachusetts, an intelligent and amiable clergyman, also of the Unitarian faith. It was upon the general subject of Restorationism and its correlative doctrines, and was carried on in the form of letters between us two, the opening one having been written by him. A few passages from my reply to his original communication will indicate the nature, drift, and spirit of the discussion, and so be of interest to the thoughtful reader.[18]

> Permit me to say, kind sir, that I am exceedingly glad to find a Unitarian like yourself, at once well qualified by temper and talent, and willing to meet the Restorationists in a friendly discussion of the principal points which hinder their fellowship with the denomination you represent. It seems to be clear either that the Restorationists are carrying things *too far*, or that their Unitarian brethren are not carrying them *far enough*.
>
> You say,
>
>> The proofs which you bring in favor of a Final Restoration are very familiar to me. It may be prejudice, it may be ignorance, but still I am obliged to confess that the passages which are so frequently adduced, do not to me seem to prove the doctrine in question. It seems to me that the doctrine is nowhere plainly taught in Scripture. From what I have read and heard on the subject, I have supposed that many who embraced the doctrine considered it rather one of inference than of revelation. It harmonized with their benevolent feelings and with their views of the goodness of God. I believe that many will own to you that this doctrine, important as it is deemed, is nowhere clearly, certainly, and directly taught in the gospel, and yet they receive it as reflecting more honor on the character of God and not inconsistent with his word.
>
> I am willing to concede that some passages of Scripture have been adduced in support of our doctrine, which, in my judgment, have nothing to do with the subject. Can you tell me of a single doctrine in your theology of which the same is not true? Was there ever a cause so good as to avoid all unworthy support? I am willing to concede that there are no passages of Scripture which declare in so many

unequivocal words, that *all men will finally be restored to holiness and happiness.* But I contend that there are several striking passages which necessarily involve this meaning and which cannot be explained consistently with the rules of just exegesis without recognizing the support they give to our doctrine. I will quote you three from St. Paul, who, as apostle of the Gentiles, would, of all others, be most likely to inculcate the truth upon the matter in question.

> For it pleased the Father that in Him should all fullness dwell; and having made peace through the blood of His cross, by Him to reconcile all things unto Himself; by Him, I say, whether they be things on earth or things in Heaven (Col. 1:19-20).

> Wherefore, God also hath highly exalted Him and given Him a name which is above every name; that at the name of Jesus every knee should bow, of things in heaven and things in earth, and things under the earth; and that every tongue should confess that Jesus Christ is Lord to the glory of God, the Father (Phil. 2:9-11).

> And when all things shall be subdued unto Him, then shall the Son also himself be subject unto Him that put all things under Him, that God may be all in all (1 Cor. 15:28).

If these passages do not involve the doctrine of universal restoration, I grant it is not the doctrine of the Bible. I could name many others, but will not cover too much ground. These passages mean something. What is it? I have stated in general terms what *I* think they mean. You are confident they mean something else. You will now frankly explain what *you* think they mean.

As to those Restorationists to whom you allude as acknowledging that our doctrine is not plainly revealed in the Scriptures, but who hold it rather as an indirect inference from their teachings, I think that either you have misunderstood what they mean by the term *inference*, or else, like the blind man at his first gaze, they "see men as trees walking."[19] Such will ere long see more clearly. The light shines upon them through a dense mist, but it will by-and-by shine unobscured. I profess to regard the doctrine as essentially a *necessary* inference – first, from several very remarkable texts like those just quoted, to which I can give no tolerable significance without it; and second, from the fundamental truths of divine revelation, which cannot be carried out harmoniously to any other result. I consider this sort of inference the principal basis upon which the conclusions of human faith are founded. It is the ground upon which, in nine cases out of ten, civil, medical, and moral jurisprudence renders a verdict. In everything but religion the common sense of mankind is perfectly satisfied with this principle of attaining conclusions. But here, strange to say, the generality of minds is wholly unwilling to trust it.

Ask one whether God is benevolent, and he will say, "Yes, God is love." Ask him if God loves all his human children, and he will say, "Yes." Ask him if love seeks the highest good of its object, and he will say, "Yes." Ask him if pure misery, tending only to misery, is an evil to its subject, and he will answer, "Yes." Ask him if misery, gradually increasing itself and continuing to all eternity, would not be the greatest conceivable curse that one could experience, and his reply would be, "Yes." Ask him if perfect hatred could contrive a greater curse, and he would admit it could not. Then ask him if the fact that "God is love," warrants the conclusion that he will so govern the moral universe as to render all finally holy and happy, and he will be off in a moment. He will see no necessary connection between the premises and the conclusion, but will tell you at once that God has no mercy for sinners except in this life; that all who die unsaved will be cast off forever as to any regard of their Creator for their welfare, and more likely than not will quote Scripture gravely to prove that God has threatened all this. At least, he will call upon you with an air of incredulity to prove from the Bible that God will not be malevolent after death; that he will not be cruel, that he will not be unjust, that he will not be the reverse of himself, for it amounts to this.

I have stood with astonishment to hear men lay down and define all the first principles of religion correctly, and then set themselves soberly at work to prove that God, the author and upholder of those principles, will so govern the universe as to violate every one of them. They will give just expositions of wisdom, benevolence, justice and mercy; they will urge them very powerfully upon the consciences of mankind; they are almost sure to decide upon the merits of human actions agreeably to these first principles of religion; they revolt at everything in human laws and usages which looks like cruelty, injustice, malevolence, etc. And yet, by holding the doctrine of endless punishment, they ascribe to the Almighty such horrible treatment of his creatures as finds no parallel in the annals of mortal tyranny and cruelty. Then, as if to cap the climax of inconsistency, they contend that this view of God's character is the only one that will sustain vital religion and save the world from utter moral corruption.

What can be done with so much strange inconsistency? The Restorationists have made up their minds: first, to rejoice in all the good that men are doing, because that good is from heaven and tends to human happiness; secondly, to labor with all their strength to remove from the character of Jehovah every imputation which tends to alienate the hearts of his creatures from him, because they expect thereby to help forward the consummation of universal holiness and bliss.

You say again:

> I should be glad if our brethren of the Restorationist denomination could feel justified in giving their distinguishing doctrines a less conspicuous place – in dwelling on them with less frequency, and in considering them of less importance. They might insist on the doctrine of a future righteous retribution, without defining the duration of it, neither asserting nor denying its eternity in their daily instruction.

In reply to this, I shall speak for myself and endeavor to explain the principles by which I regulate my ministerial conduct. I consider it the great end of preaching to render men good, that they may be happy. I regard all true moral goodness as divine – as learned and copied from God. When men love with such love as God exercises – when they are just as God is just – when they are merciful as their Father in heaven is merciful, *then* they are truly holy, truly good. Therefore I propose God as the perfect exemplar, and call upon mankind to strive with all their power to imitate him. I tell them that this is the only genuine holiness and the only method of rendering themselves perfectly happy.

Now, when I go forth to preach these truths, in what condition do I find the minds of my fellow men? Are they believers in a God whose example it will do for them to imitate? Are they relieved of all notions of God which destroy the perfection of his character? No; the reverse of this. Trained from infancy to regard God as a great and terrible being – an omnipotent despot, who seeks only his own glory whatever becomes of his creatures, they have learned merely that he must be obeyed, because he cannot be resisted. They entertain no just idea of a benignant Father, who has no glory in view independent of the good and happiness of his children. They do not perceive that his parental solicitude for their welfare led him to lay on them the restraints of the moral law; that he commands, rewards, punishes, and does all things which pertain to the administration of his moral government out of love to his creation. No; their minds are enveloped with a gross darkness[20] which shuts out all the light of a truly religious appeal to their hearts. That veil must be rent away. That darkness must be dissipated, or there is no use in exhorting them to be holy, as God is holy.

Besides all this, when I go forth to my ministry, I find my path hedged up before me.[21] I find the most unjust prejudices against the truth as I understand it reigning even in good minds. People will not suffer me to be silent concerning my peculiar views. Their religious teachers have set them all awry in regard to my heresy. I, therefore, upon entering the obstructed field, must clear away the hindrances, and after preparing men's hearts to feel the force of my preaching, bend all my efforts to their enlightenment and reformation. I do not then need to keep harping on the doctrine of final restoration. I have made myself understood. My hearers know I have discarded the doctrine of endless punishment and its concomitant notions. Then I can show them a perfect God at the head of a perfect moral government, accomplishing by a sure process perfect good. Then I can make them feel their obligations to love and obey such a God. I can make them understand that to be holy and happy, they must imitate this God. I can make them perceive the magnitude and utter inexcusableness of their guilt in disobeying this blessed Father of all men. I can warn them with tears to repent, and, like the prodigal, return to their Father's house. I can appeal to them as their own judge, and ask them how dreadful a punishment they will deserve if they contemn such a gracious Father's authority and counsels and mercies – if they abuse the infinite kindness of this greatest and best friend, and despise their own welfare. I can point them to the future and show them that they have no promise of finding anything but woe, while they remain rebel sinners. They know that I do not limit punishment to this life nor to any definite period in the next, but leave all to the wisdom of our God, who will punish neither too much nor too little, but render to every man according to his deeds and moral needs.

If this kind of preaching will not promote reformation of character, and extend the empire of holiness over the human heart, my ministerial labor is vain. There are those who have sat under Unitarian preaching – under that very preaching which holds up a future retribution without either affirming or denying its strict eternity – and which, of course, the common mind regards as endless. These persons now sit under my preaching. Ask them whether, with my final restoration all understood, I do not preach as much punishment and make it as much to be dreaded as the Unitarians. Still, I perceive that many Unitarians hesitate to cooperate with me and my brethren because they consider us as offering up strange fire[22] – as letting loose the restraints which they believe God has laid in the fear of endless punishment. Well, let them act conscientiously; we will not complain. Time will do us and our sentiments justice. We are willing and anxious to meet all Christians, however different from us in opinion, on a level of brotherly love, and while we claim and allow perfect freedom in matters of faith, to treat them as we wish to be treated. If we can have such fellowship and cooperation, we shall rejoice, not as a sect, but as Christians. If we cannot have such fellowship, we want none, for we are determined to be entangled with no yoke of bondage, but to "stand fast in the liberty wherewith Christ has made us free."[23]

Our controversy on these and kindred points was carried on to considerable length in the *Independent Messenger*, but, much as I desired it, nothing I wrote ever appeared in the Unitarian publication where Mr. Farr's first letter to me was found.[24] Probably it was deemed impolitic by the "wise and prudent"[25] manager of the paper to agitate such a theme at that date, but the denomination has since then gradually drifted out of its *quasi* indefiniteness into a more positive faith concerning the final destiny of the wicked.[26]

My object in quoting so largely from my argument in this case is mainly to present a sample of the willingness, frankness, and independence with which I have always avowed and defended my convictions upon any subject when fidelity to myself and to the truth demanded it. I have seldom sought a public controversy with tongue or pen, yet never shrank from one when it was urged upon me. I have always believed in free discussion, especially when the parties thereto had co-equal rights and privileges, and have always been ready to give a reason for the hope and faith I had espoused.

Another motive prompts me to quote so freely from the columns of the *Messenger*, and that is to emphasize anew my abhorrence of the doctrine of endless punishment. This abhorrence does not arise chiefly from my sense of the injustice, cruelty, and worse than useless misery to which, it alleges, God will subject countless hosts of his sinful creatures through all eternity, though these are unspeakably horrible and revolting to me. But it arises rather from the destructive falsification of the Infinite Father's moral character which it necessarily implies, and which, were it true, would render the Divine Being unworthy of the reverence, homage, love, and imitation of any rational, right-hearted, moral creature on earth or in heaven. The doctrine blasphemes God, the Father; Christ, the Son; and the Holy Spirit of both. It assails the foundation principles of the only religion which seeks the universal highest good of all mankind. The longer I live, the more profoundly I loathe and eschew it. Many of its nominal adherents have been good men and women, not by its influence, but by other influences in spite of it; and never one such loved it or prayed in accordance with it, or acted from its dictates in the treatment of their fellow human beings. It has been modified, softened down, and reduced to its mildest possibilities in later days by those who could not wholly renounce it, but in doing this they have removed its original foundations and prepared for its final overthrow.[27] Any form of it rests on a finality of incurable human wickedness and woe, which a God of love and all beings born of his spirit must forever deplore. It ought to perish utterly from the faiths of men, and it will, and the places that now know it will know it no more,[28] while the earth wheels in its circling orbit around the sun.

Discussion with Rev. Daniel D. Smith

While carrying on the friendly, argumentative correspondence with Rev. Mr. Farr, my controversy with the no-future-retributionists continued with unabated vigor. My course in this matter seemed unaccountable to many people in view of my well-known agreement with these antagonists as opponents of the doctrine of endless sin and misery. But I had my own distinctive faith (which was exceedingly dear to me) to defend against the attacks of both the ultra Universalists and the champions of the last named doctrine, who vied with each other in treating that faith with misrepresentation, reproach, and abuse, and in seeking its extermination. Therefore, my hostility to both was justified, and I contended against both (not on personal grounds, but by reason of my abhorrence of the errors they maintained) conscientiously and with unflinching resolution. Both preferred controversy with each other rather than with the Restorationists, open debate with whom on equal terms they sedulously avoided, each seemingly conscious that more was to be lost than gained thereby. They were both brave to falsify and denounce Restorationism in private circles and in pulpits and denominational organs, from which all replies were uniformly excluded. Otherwise, their policy was "to sit still,"[29] in their dignity and self-satisfaction.

On the other hand, the Restorationists invited inquiry, argument, and the most searching scrutiny of their position and theories. They never shunned debate, free discussion, public exposition and rejoinder, when opportunity occurred, deeming such means of upholding and promulgating truth as not only laudable and effective, but indispensable almost to the progress and triumph of their cause. As an exponent and promoter of that cause, I desired nothing so much as a fair and open field for canvassing *pro* and *con* all the important points at issue between myself and those differing from me. Under this prepossession, I kept the columns of the *Independent Messenger* always free to opponents of my distinctive views, and to a full hearing on both sides of controverted questions. But, as I have already stated, my frank and friendly course in this respect was never reciprocated on the part of any of my assailants or co-disputants.

In consequence of this artful policy pursued from the beginning by my ultra Universalist brethren, I was tempted to deviate from the general rule of my life in such matters, and to publish in my paper of February 8, 1834, the following:

CHALLENGE
"COME, LET US REASON TOGETHER"[30]

Reverend fathers and teachers in the Israel of Universalism –

I believe what you disbelieve – that the Holy Scriptures teach the doctrine of future righteous retribution. You consider my belief a relic of heathenism; I consider your disbelief a species of anti-Christian skepticism. A great controversy has commenced and will be prosecuted to an issue between yourselves and those who hold, with me, the doctrine of future retribution. Thousands of people need to be enlightened on the subject who cannot be induced to plod through the pages of elaborate works, but who would, nevertheless, be interested in an investigation carried on in the way of a public oral discussion. Now, therefore, I invite you to a friendly debate of the following question: *"Do the Holy Scriptures teach the doctrine of future rewards and punishments?"* And I respectfully propose the following terms of arrangement, viz.:

(1) The discussion to be holden in some commodious hall or edifice in the city of Boston.

(2) Thirty days' notice of its commencement to be given in the public papers.

(3) Three moderators to preside, with full power to enforce the most wholesome and approved rules of debate, the parties respectively choosing one moderator each, and these two, the third.

(4) In the affirmative of the question, myself alone; in the negative, as many of your clergymen as you please.

(5) The parties to occupy alternately thirty minutes' space of speech.

(6) Two experienced reporters to be employed, with full instructions to prepare for press a faithful report of the whole discussion, as nearly verbatim as possible, without submitting any part thereof to the previous inspection of the disputants or any other persons.

(7) The debate to commence on Tuesday and be continued, with suitable intermissions, till the close of Friday; and so on from week to week till the parties are mutually willing to terminate it, or till one of them shall absolutely decline its further prosecution.

(8) All expenses properly incident to the discussion (time, labor, and mere personal expense excepted), and all income arising from the sale of the Report, if any, to be equally shared by the parties.

(9) The printing of the Report, whether by the affirmative or negative party, to be decided by lot, under the direction of the moderators.

All which is respectfully submitted, with the humble hope that you will accept my invitation, proposals, and terms; and that by a friendly, fair, and full discussion of the question at issue, we may mutually contribute to enlighten and satisfy many thousand inquiring minds.

ADIN BALLOU

Two days after the publication of this challenge, I received a letter from Rev. Daniel D. Smith,[31] accepting it on condition that the form of the question be so changed as to read: "*Do the Scriptures teach the doctrine that men will be punished and rewarded subsequently to this life (or after death) for the deeds done in this life?*" The writer also suggested the wisdom of having but one reporter instead of two, in order to reduce the expenses to the lowest possible figure. The letter was cordial, respectful, and friendly, and solicited an early response.

I replied at once, saying that I was happy to receive the acceptance of my challenge provided a specified change could be made in the wording of the question for discussion, to which change I cheerfully consented. I also yielded to my friend's proposition that but one reporter be employed, if we could find a person competent to fill the position. I furthermore, at his suggestion, named Tuesday, the eighteenth of March following, as the time for commencing the discussion, the place to be determined and made known at a later date.[32]

So far everything was satisfactory and promised well for the fulfillment of my fondly-cherished desire. Shortly afterward, the standing committee of the First Universalist society of Boston generously tendered the disputants the free use of their church edifice on Hanover Street, which offer was gratefully accepted. Other arrangements were speedily completed. Rev. Bernard Whitman consented to act as my moderator, Rev. Linus Everett[33] as Mr. Smith's, and by their agreement Rev. Joshua V. Himes[34] was the third, who was to occupy the position of chairman. The services of Richard Hildreth, Esq.,[35] of Boston, as reporter were happily secured, and everything was ready for the fray.

The discussion opened at 9 A.M. on Tuesday, March 18, and closed on Thursday, March 20, about 5 P.M., having been held for three successive days with two sessions per day of three hours each – in all six sessions or eighteen hours. Of its character and progress from beginning to end, I gave a description and estimate from my standpoint in the issue of the *Messenger* for March 29, which I still believe to be truthful and just. I will not reproduce the article here, but refer to the preserved files of the paper in which it appeared.

I may, however, observe that the discussion, so far as my own side was concerned, gave me unqualified and grateful satisfaction, as it did also the friends of the doctrine which I sought to vindicate and maintain. My Restorationist brethren were enthusiastic in their commendation of my labors, and manifested their appreciation of what I had achieved for the cause of truth by presenting me, on Thursday evening after the debate was concluded, Dr. Adam Clarke's *Complete Commentary upon the Scriptures* in six large, handsomely bound volumes.[36]

As to my antagonist, I would state that although several Universalist clergymen disclaimed having counseled or encouraged him to enter the arena with me, yet he deserves the thanks of all Restorationists for doing so. He certainly thereby gave evidence of being an honest man in the matter, and though saying some things he probably afterwards had occasion to regret, yet I believe he did as well on the whole for his cause as any of his older and more experienced brethren could have done. If he made a poor fight of it, the fault was in his cause, and not in his lack of ability. In general he was calm and dispassionate, and preserved a respectful bearing. It was predicted, report said, that the disputants would soon lose their temper, become greatly irritated with each other, and finally outrageous. These prophecies, like many others of a like nature, did not come to pass. Alas, for the prophets!

The debate went on smoothly and in good order, with little hesitation or incoherency, during the first two days, but during the forenoon of the third day Mr. Smith showed signs of being weary of it and of wishing it were at an end. He complainingly remarked that he did not know but his opponent intended to keep him there till his locks were gray with age. I had compassion for him and when at noon some of his friends proposed to close the discussion with the afternoon session, I agreed to conclude my argument, if possible, before night, leaving it optional whether or not we should meet again the following day. He decided against doing so and the end came accordingly.

The conduct of Mr. Himes, who presided at all the sessions, and of our friend, Mr. Whitman, was such as became the dignity and responsibility of their position. With that of Mr. Everett, the moderator chosen by my opponent, I was not so well pleased. His manifest partisanship and desire for the success of his side of the case were apparent and provoked not a little unfavorable comment. As to the audience that listened to the discussion, it was respectable in numbers, general appearance, and deportment, throughout. Those comprising it were evidently interested in the subject under consideration and gave both the disputants candid, thoughtful, earnest attention. Everything in this particular was satisfactory and gratifying.[37]

The lot to print the report of this affair fell to me, and an edition of five thousand copies in pamphlet form was mutually agreed upon and ordered. In due time it was issued, making an octavo work of eighty-six pages, and offered to the public.[38] The Universalists did nothing to promote its circulation, but, on the contrary, all they could to discourage it. Their journals took no pains to advertise it and never recommended their patrons to read it, that they might be informed in regard to the merits of the discussion or to the nature and force of the arguments on either side of the question at issue. Even my co-equal disputant, Mr. Smith, notwithstanding the definite terms on which we entered the field of conflict, when he found that the report was not likely to redound to the honor and glory of himself and his cause, slunk dishonorably out of his engagements, refused to bear his equal share of the burden of disposing of the work, and to crown all, left me to shoulder nearly all the pecuniary cost of the undertaking, including the expense of its publication and the payment of Mr. Hildreth's large bill for reportorial labors. I bore the wrong patiently, met all incurred obligations as soon as I was able, scattered copies of the pamphlet often gratuitously up and down the country, my Restorationist associates and sympathizers cooperating with me in this distribution. What I lost in dollars and cents, I gained in a knowledge of no-future-retribution ethics, in the later satisfaction of learning that the leaders of "the order" were convinced that nothing could be gained for their *ism* by denouncing Restorationism and suppressing free discussion, and finally in seeing their peculiar dogma give way in their own denomination to the faith it was my privilege and duty to uphold, disseminate, and help to make perpetual among men.

Meeting of the Massachusetts Association of Universal Restorationists, 1833

But few additional events occurred during the then current year, worthy of description. I was present at several ecclesiastical convocations, such are likely to be held at irregular intervals under the general administration of the affairs of a Christian denomination, participating more or less in the public exercises incident to them. Among these was the meeting of the [Massachusetts Association of Universal Restorationists][39] in Westminster, Massachusetts, on the eleventh and twelfth of September [1833]. At that gathering, Brother Hudson's house of worship, which had been removed from its original site a mile and a half away to the central village and thoroughly renovated, was dedicated anew with appropriate services.

On the same occasion, Brother Edwin M. Stone, a native of Beverly, was ordained as a Christian minister and an evangelist of our Restorationist faith. He continued in our fellowship until the disbandment of the Massachusetts Restorationist Association in 1841, then entered the Unitarian denomination, under whose auspices he labored acceptably as pastor in various places, the last years of his life being devoted to the work of the "ministry-at-large" in Providence, Rhode Island, in which he rendered most important service.[40]

Regimental Muster

On the twenty-sixth of the same month, I again officiated as chaplain at a regimental muster in Uxbridge; the last time, if I remember rightly, that I appeared before the public in that capacity, though it was some years later that I became a convert to peace principles and received my official discharge. I dined, as was customary, with the officers: Col. Peter Corbett, Lt. Col. Horace Emerson, Maj. Putnam W. Taft, etc., at several of whose funerals I subsequently ministered.[41]

Having at that time become a devoted temperance man and so keenly observant of the evils of intemperance, I was enabled to see how many of the numerous attendants, as usually is the case on such occasions, needed salvation from inordinate artificial appetites and bad habits engendered thereby. I had been diligent in this field of reform for some time and measurably successful, but the field was of vast extent and I had gathered only a few sheaves into the granary of redemption.

CHAPTER 14

1834-1836

In entering upon the thirty-second year of my life, I found myself charged with extraordinary labors, cares, and responsibilities. In addition to those usually incumbent upon one occupying the position I did in the general community as a minister of the gospel and an expositor of divine truth, I had on my hands the entire proprietorship of the *Independent Messenger* printing establishment, the oversight of its weekly publication, its sole editorial management, and just at this time, the special burden of getting out five thousand copies of the Boston discussion report.

Moreover, in order to render myself still further useful to our Restorationist cause, I received into my family and under my tuition, another theological student, Brother Edmund Capron,[1] a very worthy and promising young man, anxious to devote himself to the work of the Christian ministry under the auspices of the Massachusetts Association. He was an earnest, faithful student, and successful in his endeavors to qualify himself for his chosen vocation. He remained with me until he had essentially completed the course of instruction requisite therefor – some two or more years.

The files of the fourth volume of the *Messenger*, then being issued under my sole care and supervision, bear witness to the industry, vigor, and zeal with which I continued to expound the doctrine of Universal Restoration, and defend it against all classes of assailants. I had still the leading Universalists of the ultra school to combat on the one hand, and the dogmatic champions of endless punishment on the other. Among the latter with whom I measured swords were such notables as Rev. Dr. Nathaniel W. Taylor, of New School Divinity fame; Rev. Dr. Bennet Tyler, of Old School Divinity fame;[2] and President Charles G. Finney, D.D.,[3] of Oberlin Seminary. My opponents of this class had the great advantage over me of access to many journals through which to reach the public, all closed against me, and of a vast multitude of sympathizing partisans; while I had but one small paper of limited circulation, with comparatively few supporters. But I had the strong consciousness and assurance that I was the advocate of divine truths which must at last prevail, and I wrote and wrought accordingly.

Ministerial Settlements

I had at this time become actively engaged in temperance work, delivering lectures at numerous points and attending meetings and conventions held in the same behalf. I also attended ecclesiastical gatherings, taking part in several, some of which were noteworthy by reason of the prominence in the religious world subsequently attained by the principal participants. I take the liberty of mentioning a few of these.

On the fourteenth of May, 1834, I was present at the installation of Rev. Orestes A. Brownson[4] as pastor of the First Congregational church and society in Canton, Massachusetts, in the exercises of which I had been assigned an important part. The council was composed mostly of members of the Unitarian denomination, the sermon being preached by Rev. George Ripley[5] of Boston, from Hebrews 13:8: "Jesus Christ, the same yesterday, today, and forever."[6]

Mr. Brownson was a ripe scholar, an able preacher, and a writer of rare ability. But in theology, metaphysics, ethics, and ecclesiasticism, his convictions, positions, and associations underwent strange vicissitudes. Soon after his settlement at Canton, he became a Transcendentalist, subsequently espousing the Workingmen's Movement (of which he was for awhile a distinguished champion), and later went over to the Roman Catholic church, resting there from his religio-philosophical journeyings, and rising to eminence as the author of several works devoted chiefly to the defense of the doctrines, polity, and traditions of the papal hierarchy. Rev. Mr. Ripley afterwards acquired a wide notoriety as the leader of the Brook Farm community, and later still, as literary editor for a generation of the New York *Tribune*.

The installation of Rev. Philemon R. Russell as pastor of the Liberal Congregational church and society of West Boylston, occurred on May 24, the council consisting equally of Unitarians and Restorationists.[7] The Restorationists having part in the proceedings were Rev. Paul Dean of Boston, who preached the sermon; Rev. Seth Chandler of Oxford, and myself, who gave the charge; the Unitarians were Rev. Joseph Allen[8] of Northborough; Rev. Peter Osgood[9] of Sterling; Rev. John Goldsbury of Hardwick; and Rev. Ebenezer Robinson of Hubbardston.

Mr. Russell was a zealous, enthusiastic man, with considerable natural and acquired ability, and much executive push. But his pastorates among us, of which there were several, were all brief. Either he did not wear well, or was himself a lover of change. After a time he left our body and joined the Christian Connexion. Later, he espoused Second Adventism, becoming its ardent advocate. When that illusion subsided, he abandoned the pulpit and rostrum, devoting himself thereafter to secular pursuits, in which he acquired a handsome property, ending his days at length in comparative wealth.

On Wednesday, June 18, Brother David R. Lamson[10] was ordained and installed pastor of the First church and society in Berlin, Massachusetts, with a union council as before. Rev. Joseph Allen of Northborough delivered the sermon, and Rev. Charles Hudson of Westminster gave the charge.[11] Of Mr. Lamson's ability, character and life career I shall have occasion to speak at a later period of this narrative.

Another union installation occurred a week later, June 25, when Rev. William Morse,[12] recently of Quincy, was inducted into the office of pastor of the Second Congregational parish in Marlborough, Massachusetts. I officiated in the opening exercises; Rev. James Walker[13] of Charlestown preached the sermon; Rev. Paul Dean offered the consecratory prayer; Rev. Joseph Allen gave the charge; Rev. Charles Hudson extended the right hand of fellowship; Rev. Isaac Allen[14] of Bolton addressed the society; and Rev. Mr. Sweet[15] of Southborough made the final prayer. A fine day, harmonious communion of souls, able and impressive services, hospitable entertainment, and all the incidents of the occasion remarkably pleasant.[16] Mr. Morse was well qualified for his office in all respects and had a satisfactory pastorate in Marlborough of ten years. He was subsequently settled in Tyngsborough and afterwards supplied in Chelmsford, going thence to Franklin, New Hampshire, where he finally departed this life at the ripe age of more than fourscore years.

I participated in one other ordination during the year 1834, that of Rev. Richard Stone[17] at West Bridgewater, Massachusetts, on the twentieth of August. I was the only Restorationist member of the council, being invited through the influence of several lay friends in the parish, all the others being Unitarians. The introductory prayer was offered by me; Rev. Jason Whitman,[18] brother of my dear friend, Rev. Bernard Whitman, and secretary of the American Unitarian Association, delivered the sermon, and neighboring Unitarian clergymen took the several other parts – all the exercises passing off pleasantly and auspiciously.[19]

Meeting of the Massachusetts Association of Universal Restorationists, 1834
The semi-annual meeting of the Massachusetts Restorationist Association was held at Attleboro, on the tenth and eleventh of September. Twelve of our ministerial fellowship were present, seven of whom preached during the several sessions of the convocation, which closed with great solemnity and sanctifying impressiveness by the administration of the ordinance of the Lord's Supper. An affecting incident of this gathering was the mutual farewell interchanged with our beloved brother, Nathaniel Wright, for some years secretary of the body, who had just closed his Attleboro pastorate and was about to remove to the far-off West. A testimonial of personal and professional regard for him was presented by Rev. Brother Dean, and adopted with hearty unanimity.[20] Brother Wright spent the remainder of his earthly life in the town of Tremont, Illinois, where he soon after located, and rarely made visits to his native state. How long or how successfully he prosecuted the work of the ministry in his new home I am not informed, but remember that later in life he was drawn into secular pursuits, attaining therein considerable success.

Death of Rev. Bernard Whitman

This faithful minister of Christ, this child of God and brother of man, this eminent champion of Christian liberty, truth, justice, and charity, this uncompromising opponent of bigotry, pseudo-liberality, and infidelity, passed through the shadow of death to the realm of the immortals on Wednesday, November 5, 1834, at the meridian age of thirty-eight years, four months, and twenty-seven days. He was the thirteenth child of Deacon John Whitman, of East Bridgewater, Massachusetts, who lived to be 103 years old. Though he inherited a strong constitution from his father, yet by overwork and exposure his native energies became early enfeebled, and he fell a victim to consumption, which resulted fatally, after several months of suffering decline, in his pastoral home at Waltham, Massachusetts.

Hewing his way through a forest of difficulties up to a well-equipped manhood, he had been an indomitable worker for religion and human progress, and had devised a host of plans for future usefulness which he longed to carry into effect; yet he bore his wasting sickness with Christian meekness and resignation, passing peacefully away from earth and leaving behind an admirable example of patient faith and of triumphant assurance of a welcome to the angelic mansions. Whether I regarded him as a personal friend, as a sympathizer with our Restorationist movement, or with reference to those public relationships which he sustained with honor to himself and spiritual profit to mankind, I felt it a sacred privilege to rank myself among his mourners and to welcome to the columns of the paper under my charge at the time numerous commemorative obituary testimonies celebrating his translation to the higher life.[21]

Family Bereavements

Two deaths in our respective domestic circles threw their shadows across the threshold of our home during the closing month of this year 1834. The first was that of an estimable and noble-hearted sister of my wife, occurring on the second day of December; the other that of my beloved and revered mother, which took place on the twenty-seventh. The *Independent Messenger* paid tender and affectionate tribute to each of them in turn as follows:

> In Milford, on the 2d inst., after a distressing illness of several months, Miss Chloe Albee [Hunt], daughter of Pearley Hunt, Esq., in the 20th year of her age.[22]
>
> Under this bereavement, the surviving family mourn the loss of a most worthy, kind-hearted, and estimable daughter and sister. Endowed with those better feelings which adorn human nature, the deceased endeared herself most to those who knew her best. She was rich in the noblest of social affections and virtues. To sympathize with and aid others, and render them happy by helpful ministrations, was her delight. She has vacated a sphere of kindness in the midst of her family connections which they will long contemplate with sincere grief. She leaves many friends, too, and no enemies in the youthful circle in which she was accustomed to move. They will all miss one from their number who was among the first in that substantial worth which ensured lasting esteem.

> In Cumberland, R.I., on the 27th ult., after a prostrating illness of eight days, Mrs. Edilda Ballou, wife of Deacon Ariel Ballou and mother of the editor of this paper, in the 64th year of her age.[23]
>
> Though this obituary notice is inscribed by the hand of filial affection, let it not be regarded as the exaggeration of bereaved fondness. It registers in general terms the excellence of a woman mourned by all who knew her, "full of good works and alms-deeds."[24] Her memory challenges not the honors rendered those who have moved in the fashionable walks of life. She was born and bred in the midst of the constant domestic cares belonging to the household of a New England farmer. Her mind, gifted with sound native sense and a strong thirst for improvement, was always restricted to scanty means, and, of course, gathered up only the fragments of general knowledge. These she employed to the great end for which she lived, the happiness of those around her. Here centered the distinguished virtues that adorned her character. She was naturally kind, sympathetic, generous, unassuming; by Christian grace eminently contrite, devout, meek, and charitable. She had that mind which was in Christ Jesus[25] – the mind that sees itself only in others, which loves to serve rather than be served, to give rather than receive, to suffer rather than see others suffer; which places its own chief good, glory, and happiness in the welfare of others. Poverty, sickness, sorrow, and misfortune never appealed to her in vain. Without the least seeming desire to show herself, she fed the hungry, clothed the naked, visited the sick, entertained the stranger, comforted the despondent, and pitied all the unhappy.[26] Her religion and morality were of the same stamp.
>
> The good she loved of every name,
> And prayed for all mankind.[27]

The death of my mother was soon followed by a general settlement of my father's estate. He was too old and infirm to bear the burden of managing his large farm, especially now that his faithful companion had passed away. So he summoned his three sons to the parental home and desired them to come to some terms of agreement satisfactory to all concerned. We met, conferred with each other and with him, and soon arrived at an amicable understanding. Whereupon, specific legal writings were drawn and in due time executed.

Change in Ownership of Independent Messenger

Another important change in matters of interest to me occurred about the same time. I had assumed duties and obligations which I learned were too onerous for me to bear for a great length of time, and some kind of relief was not only desirable but absolutely necessary. After careful deliberation, I concluded to unload myself essentially of the burden of the *Independent Messenger*, the entire responsibility of which, pecuniary, editorial, managemental, etc., rested upon me. And as a practicable way out of the difficulties besetting me, I conceived the project of making the proprietorship of the paper and its correlative printing house a joint stock concern, and of distributing the labor of furnishing matter for its columns among a staff of editors.

Having duly digested the plan and brought it into proper form, I announced it to the public and appealed earnestly to my clerical and lay brethren to aid me in adopting it and in carrying it out to a successful issue. They responded promptly and cheerfully, and a joint stock company was soon organized, Rev. Paul Dean (whom I always found to be the soul of honor in such emergencies) taking the leading part in the contemplated enterprise.[28] About the middle of March, 1835, circumstances under the new arrangement rendered it expedient to remove the *Messenger* and its appurtenances and belongings once more to Boston, the reasons for which, with sufficiency of detail, were given to the public in its issue of the fourteenth of the month. Thenceforward, it was published at the corner of Tremont (Court) and Howard Streets, its printing and the general supervision of all business matters pertaining to it being entrusted to Messrs. H. B. and J. Brewster. Its editorial staff was Rev. Paul Dean, resident editor; Revs. Charles Hudson, William Morse, Philemon R. Russell, and Adin Ballou, corresponding editors.

Move to New Home

For greater convenience and comfort to myself and family, I, in the spring of 1835, relinquished the tenement we had occupied since coming to Mendon four years before, which was quite out of the village, and hired what was then known as the Dr. Thayer house, at the very heart of the town, where we remained for seven years, or until I closed my official labors with the First Church and Society there. The location and internal arrangements of the building were much more pleasant than those we vacated and much better suited to the needs and circumstances of a clergyman's household.

Dedication at Uxbridge

Several public occasions occurring during the year 1835 in which I was a more or less active participant, are worthy of brief mention. The first was the dedication, January 13, of the new, commodious, and elegant church edifice of the First Congregational parish in Uxbridge, Rev. Samuel Clarke, pastor. The day was charming and a large congregation attended the services. The sermon was by Mr. Clarke, with a text from Exodus 12:26: "What mean ye by this service?" The venerable Aaron Bancroft, D.D.[29] of Worcester, offered the prayer of dedication. Everything passed off harmoniously, pleasantly, and auspiciously. The officiating clergymen, with the single exception of myself, were of the distinctively Unitarian faith.[30]

Restorationist Meetings, 1835

I shall do little more than make note of the several convocations of our Restorationist brethren during this year (1835), without entering much into details concerning those participating in them, the exercises, etc.

The first was a special conference held in Mendon on the seventh and eighth of May. In addition to the usual public religious exercises, there were sessions of a semi-business character, at which affairs pertaining to the *Independent Messenger* transfer were canvassed and adjusted. Brother Dean, in his editorial comments on the meeting, characterized its religious features as "happily adapted to excite and perpetuate a healthy tone of devotional feeling."[31]

On the third and fourth of June, the annual meeting of the Providence Association took place at Providence, Rhode Island, a full attendance of ministers and laymen being present. Important business was transacted, interesting and impressive religious services, including the administration of the Lord's Supper, were held, to the edification and spiritual profit of the participants.[32]

The Massachusetts Restorationist Association met at East Medway, September 2 and 3, the occasional sermon being delivered by Rev. Lyman Maynard, then of Amherst, New Hampshire, from 2 Corinthians 4:42: "Therefore, seeing we have this ministry, as we have received mercy, we faint not; but have renounced the hidden things of dishonesty, not walking in craftiness, nor handling the word of God deceitfully; but by manifestation of the truth, commending ourselves to every man's conscience in the sight of God." A special sermon was preached by myself from Acts 3:19: "Repent ye therefore, and be converted," etc. Rev. Orestes A. Brownson, before spoken of, was present and took an active part in the exercises of the occasion.[33] An interesting feature of one session was the approbation and reception, as members of the body, of four young ministers – William H. Fish,[34] Edmund Capron, George W. Stacy, Henry B. Brewster[35] – the first and third of whom were long and successfully engaged in the work to which they were then consecrated.

"Omega" to Controversy with Ultra Universalists

The controversy with our ultra Universalist brethren was prosecuted vigorously by me till February 7 of this year, when I voluntarily closed it, so far as the public press was concerned. My determination (which was arrived at after a careful survey of the whole matter) I announced through the columns of the *Messenger* in an article entitled "Omega," some extracts from which I submit to my present readers.

> *Omega*, the last letter of the Greek alphabet, was anciently employed to denote the end of any matter or thing. And I use the word to indicate that with this writing I terminate all newspaper controversy on my part with Universalist editors and their adherents, relating to the doctrine of future retribution. My opinions and feelings in respect to the subject are well known. My stand has been taken; my testimony has been recorded; my course for the future is marked out. I am inflexible.
>
> As I have believed, so have I spoken. I have opposed what is called Universalism with an indefatigable and uncompromising zeal. I have challenged its advocates to discussion and met them whenever I had an opponent. I have reasoned against, repelled, and controverted whatever in Universalist doctrine, spirit, or practice, I deemed essentially erroneous. I have regarded, and still regard, their prominent tenets, their style of preaching and writing, their tone of feeling towards other denominations, and the general drift of their sectarian policy, hostile to genuine Christianity. If I am wrong in this, God enlighten and forgive me.

> But while there is a time to speak and to act, there is also a time to pause, to be silent, to cease from contending, even for "the faith once delivered to the saints."³⁶ After one has said and done enough in the way of opposition and reproof, after he has been wrongfully accused, without stint or limit, and conjured again and again to let the subjects of his reprobation alone, it is time to suspend his labors and leave his antagonists to themselves. I feel that such a time has come with me in relation to the leaders of the Universalist denomination. They may believe, write, publish, manage, in their own way. But from me, so far as concerns newspaper controversy, they shall hear no more. The residue of my life shall be devoted to other matters.³⁷

So I thenceforth let them alone. What was the sequel? A notable change in a few years began to take place in the doctrines, spirit, preaching, writing, and general policy of the denomination, ultimating in a complete revolution in regard to every one of the points at issue at the time of the Restorationist secession and subsequent controversy. There was a radical reform both in theory and practice, which saved the denomination from its downward trend and led it upward and onward to its present condition of commendable excellence, usefulness, and prosperity. If its leaders in 1830 had stood where their successors now do, as evidenced by the action of the Universalist ministers of Boston and vicinity in 1878, there would have been no secession and no controversy.³⁸

Debate with Rev. W. P. Apthorp

But though my warfare with my Universalist brethren had come to an end, it was not so with that carried on between me and the advocates of endless punishment. That continued without abatement. My antagonists were numerous, persistent, and unrelenting. They represented the great mass of the nominal Christian church in all its popular denominations. To Restorationism they were unanimously and implacably opposed and neither truce nor quarter was to be expected from them. They were sincere and believed they were doing God service in trying to crush out what they regarded as a great heresy. But I was no less sincere and as confident and determined as they. They had great external advantages over me, but I had one condition of success not shared by them – I understood both sides of the question between us. I had been through the mill of investigation thoroughly and knew all the arguments they could command. In fact, I could defend their case at any moment as well or better than themselves, but they knew not the strength of Restorationism till discussion revealed it to them, sometimes to their manifest confusion. So this particular conflict went on from month to month, through the columns of the *Messenger*, through written correspondence, through sermons, special lectures, personal conversation, and public oral debate.

An instance of the last named method occurred in my own town. Rev. W. P. Apthorp,³⁹ provisional minister of the North Mendon Congregational church (orthodox), deemed it his duty to attempt the conversion and salvation of some of my "deluded" hearers by visiting, catechizing, and warning them against my dangerous views. On the street and in their houses, he improved convenient opportunities of pushing his crusade. He was not a man of large mental or moral caliber, but made up for other deficiencies by zeal and self-assurance. He had a professional outfit of theological scholarship after the fashion of his sect, was thoroughly imbued with the animus of his creed, and cherished an ignorant contempt for Restorationism. He soon learned that those he undertook to proselyte were not to be seriously affected by his endeavors. They received his exhortations and warnings calmly and intelligently. Some of them suggested that he had better call on me, get acquainted, and inform himself of my doctrines before arraigning and denouncing them. This he at first disdained to do, intimating that he knew all he wished to in that direction.

After receiving the same suggestion repeatedly, he finally said he intended making me a visit, signifying to one of my good women, whom he had plied his arts upon in vain, that he should do so on a specified evening. She informed me of his intentions, and asked the privilege of being present, which I cheerfully granted. When the time came, he appeared without previous announcement on his part – a gentleman parishioner having come in incidentally a little before him. I greeted him cordially, told him I was happy to see him, as I had heard of his conversations with several of my people, and referred to some of his reported sayings. He seemed a little embarrassed, but I soon put him at his ease and our conversation went on freely. He at first affected the role of an inquirer concerning my views and opinions, but soon assumed the attitude of a disputant. At the close of our interview he was not satisfied with the situation in which he had left his doctrine and solicited another opportunity to explain it. This I consented to and an evening was agreed upon when he was to call again. Meanwhile the matter was noised abroad in town, awakening considerable interest, resulting, when the time arrived, in my house being crowded with eager listeners.

At the end of the second evening's disputation, he was no better pleased with the aspect of his case than before, and hence must meet me again. The hotel keeper of the village, one of his parishioners, seeing how my family was incommoded by the large company present, kindly offered his hall to us for the third conference and we went there accordingly, having a larger auditory than before. The discussion was chiefly conversational but waxed warm. At the close my antagonist was still dissatisfied and demanded further opportunities to defend himself and his cause. I agreed and it was arranged that we meet in his house of worship to accommodate the still increasing crowd. It was also decided that the disputants occupy ten minutes alternately in orderly discussion, and that the innkeeper should act as moderator of the occasion. At the end of this fourth interview, Mr. Apthorp had not succeeded, as he thought, in doing full justice to his subject and requested another. I was quite willing to grant him all the time he wanted and consented to his wishes. By this time his friends began to think it was best for the discussion to be brought to an end, as no advantage was likely to accrue to himself or them by continuing it, and so advised him. He prudently yielded to their judgment and accordingly announced when we again came together that the debate would close with that session. It fell to my lot in the order of speaking to make the last address, and I took good care it should be conclusively my strongest. It told with such effect that Mr. Apthorp, greatly excited, sprang to his feet, exclaiming, "I cannot leave this subject so; I must discuss it further; I will meet Mr. Ballou again next Tuesday evening." But his brethren suppressed him and his appointment was reluctantly and sullenly relinquished.

The dates of our several meetings were October 13, 15, 16, 20, and 22, 1835.[40] In the discussion, which was chiefly a scriptural one, I rested my cause on the answer which the Bible furnishes to these inquiries: What is the character of God? For what end did he create man? For what end did he reveal the moral law? For what end was Christ sent into the world? For what end did he teach, suffer, and die? For what end has he been exalted to the Mediatorial throne? Finally, what do the holy prophets and apostles predict will be his success in accomplishing his undertaking?

My opponent conceded that the Bible taught that the character of God was essentially and perfectly benevolent; that he created men for happiness; that the revelation of the moral law was designed to discipline man for holiness and bliss; that Christ was sent into the world to restore it; that he died for all men; that he was exalted to the Mediatorial throne to reign over and subdue all things unto himself; and that many of the prophetic and apostolic predictions of his final triumph were in their literal sense favorable to the doctrine of universal restoration. While conceding all this in a certain way, he yet sought to disprove that doctrine by the help of what he called a *double sense* in the scriptures, and qualifying reservations. Being a "New School" man, he was neither a Calvinist nor Arminian all the way through, but by turns both, as best served his purpose. He steered as clear as possible from committing himself unqualifiedly upon any of the points raised, except that of believing in the absolute endless duration of punishment. To maintain this position he adduced the principal threatenings of scripture, emphasized their phraseology – such as the terms *everlasting, unquenchable*, etc., alleging that they ought to be understood in their most literal sense, and that from this point of view we ought to interpret all the rest of the Bible, and to understand the nature of the divine benevolence.

The discussion of the entire five evenings centered in and was an elaboration of the several points thus indicated, the details of which need not be given. It began, progressed, and terminated just as I could have desired. It did great good in the community and justified my conviction that such public debates subserve the triumph of truth. Moreover, it left me and my people free in the exercise and enjoyment of our own chosen faith. Neither I nor they were ever afterward troubled by the intermeddling of proselyting adventurers.

An extended report of this debate from my pen in the *Messenger* called forth a rejoinder by Mr. Apthorp which was followed by one article each from me and him respectively – the last appearing January 15, 1836, when the whole matter passed into history.[41] Not long after he left Mendon and nothing further is known of him.

Death of Theological Student, Cyrus Morse

During the autumn of 1835 I conducted another private school, carrying it through to a successful issue before winter set in. I also gave instruction to a young theological student, Brother Cyrus Morse, whose health, however, soon failed, obliging him to relinquish his studies and causing his death a few months afterward; his fond hopes of Christian usefulness in the world thus vanishing forever. He found a loving home in the family of Brother E. D. Draper[42] in Rogerson's Village, Uxbridge, where he received the kindest of ministrations and where he breathed his last on the ensuing twenty-eighth of March. He bore his illness with patience, meekness, and resignation, and departed in the full assurance of a blissful immortality. Appropriate funeral services were held in the Unitarian church, Uxbridge, in which I was assisted by the pastor, Rev. Samuel Clarke, and Rev. Mr. Ellis, Methodist minister at Rogerson's Village. I had a written sermon from the text, "Rejoice with them that do rejoice and weep with them that weep" (Romans 12:15).

New Year, 1836

The year 1836 came in with a special greeting of appreciation from the ladies of my pastoral flock, who presented me with a fine blue broadcloth cloak. The garment was a very elegant and substantial one, of ample proportions, and is still extant, though in a somewhat modified form, but is capable of much service yet. Accompanying it was a paper, still preserved, containing the names of the forty-five donors with the amount of their respective offerings appended, and certifying that the gift was made "as a testimony to the esteem and respect we entertain for his individual and pastoral character."

Resignation of Rev. David Pickering

Rev. Brother David Pickering having recently resigned his pastorate in Providence, Rhode Island and removed to New York City, I went by special invitation of the authorities of the church and society left without a minister, to supply the pulpit and administer the communion on Sunday, the first day of January. Three services were held – morning, afternoon, and evening, according to the custom in those days in large towns and cities. That society, after a time, renewed its connection with the Universalist denomination, and I never again occupied its pulpit in the order of ecclesiastical fellowship. Nor did I ever again meet Brother Pickering. He left the ministry a few years later, settled in western New York, where he encountered a series of adverse experiences, from which he happily emerged, removed thence to Ypsilanti, Michigan, and there died January 6, 1859, aged 70. He was largely a self-made man, of superior natural ability, an eloquent speaker, an author of considerable note, and a distinguished minister of liberal Christianity.

Reconciliation with Father

In the early part of April, my aged father, Deacon Ariel Ballou, then in the seventy-ninth year of his age, came to reside in our family. He was quite worn out with the continuous hard labor of a long lifetime, had various infirmities otherwise incident to old age, and was evidently nearing the grave. He remained with us only a few months, enjoying himself tolerably well, and seeming to take great delight in his little grandson, about three years old. Though I had departed widely from the strict path of doctrine in which he had trained me, thereby incurring his displeasure at the outset, yet he had laid aside all his unkindly feelings, and was pleased (when his health and strength would permit) to attend public worship, and apparently was able to extract considerable edification and spiritual profit from my ministrations.

Improved Condition of Mendon Church

I had now been the incumbent of my Mendon pastorate about five years. My church and society, which were in a greatly depressed condition when I assumed charge of them, had gradually improved, until they had attained a degree of prosperity unknown for a long time before. The Sunday School had taken to itself new life and was steadily increasing in numbers, discipline, and influence. I sought to elevate its religious tone and character by preparing a little manual of several opening and closing exercises in the form of a brief liturgy, with responsive readings and hymns – simple and impressive, such as any denomination might adopt and use to their moral and spiritual advantage.

Birthday Reflections

I close this chapter with the following extract from my diary:

> April 23, 1836. My thirty-third birthday. Went into serious scrutiny of last year's experiences, my present spiritual condition, and what improvements I ought to make in the future. As on preceding birthdays, I had to lament many shortcomings, form many resolutions of amendment, and implore divine strength to act more worthy of my high calling. My ideal is always far above my highest attainments, and (what is humiliating) I stand convicted before my own internal judgment seat of repeating sins against even former lower ideals. But I desire not to let down the divine standard to my frailties. Therefore will I welcome every bright ray of light, and strive on and hope on, ever girding up my loins with the encouraging assurance: "My grace is sufficient for thee; for my strength is made perfect in weakness."[43]

CHAPTER 15

1836-1838

On May 4, 1836, I, in company with Mr. E. D. Draper as lay delegate with me, attended the installation of Brother George W. Stacy as pastor of the First Congregational church and society in Carlisle, Massachusetts. He, as will be remembered, had formerly been associated with me in the printing of the *Messenger*, and becoming deeply interested in personal religion and in the principles of Restorationism, had resolved to devote himself to the work of the ministry under the auspices and as a member of our Massachusetts Association. His theological studies had been directed by Rev. Paul Dean, and he was deemed duly qualified for the office to the duties of which he had been called.

The installing council met as per request, and organized by the choice of the venerable Dr. Ezra Ripley[1] of Concord, moderator, and Rev. Lyman Maynard of Amherst, New Hampshire, clerk, after which the customary preliminaries for the public service of the occasion were harmoniously settled. Rev. David Damon[2] of West Cambridge offered the introductory prayer, and Rev. William Andrews[3] of Chelmsford read the Scriptures. The sermon was delivered by myself from Matthew 5:48: "Be ye therefore perfect," etc. The ordaining prayer was by Rev. Paul Dean; right hand of fellowship by Rev. William Morse; address to the people, by Rev. Dr. Ripley; and concluding prayer by Rev. William White[4] of Littleton.

A Memorable Journey

Arrangements having been made with Brother Stacy for an exchange of pulpits, I remained at Carlisle through the three intervening days. On Thursday he took me to the then new, but already wonderfully precocious, city of Lowell, nine miles distant. It was well started on its prosperous career, exhibited signs of great thrift, was growing rapidly in all directions, though, of course, buildings, streets, etc., were for the most part in a coarse, unfinished condition; all of which gave place in due time to that order, neatness, symmetry, magnificence even, which have commanded my admiration in my later visits there.[5]

The following day we walked five miles to Concord, chiefly for the purpose of visiting Dr. Ripley, above mentioned, a remarkably vigorous old man, eighty-five years of age. We were greeted with a most cordial welcome and received unstinted attention, courtesy, and hospitality. He conducted us before dinner to different parts of his estate, pointing out the several localities on and near it where occurred incidents connected with one of the first battles of the American Revolution. The spot where the firing and slaughter began was shown us, as was also the place where the two British soldiers that fell in the encounter were buried – a monument to whom, he said, had been contracted for and was soon to be erected there. A few years before Dr. Ripley had written an authoritative account of the Concord fight on the nineteenth of April, 1775, which was printed in pamphlet form, and a copy of which he presented each of us.

After a sumptuous dinner, presided over by his accomplished niece, his wife having been some years in the immortal realm, he took us about the town, going through the more important public buildings and acquainting us with whatever he thought would interest and instruct us. We were much impressed, when in the county jail, by his conversation with and advice to the prisoners there. Some of them seemed more unfortunate than criminal, and only one or two appeared hardened and calloused through vice. One was held in confinement under the old barbaric law[6] for a debt of twelve dollars, which he promised to pay his creditor if allowed twenty-four hours' time. This he alleged was brutally denied him, and "Now," he said, defiantly, "I shall stand it out."

We also went with our guide to call on his colleague, Rev. Mr. Goodwin,[7] an intelligent, amiable, refined and scholarly gentleman, but a suffering invalid. He was in the morning of life, had just launched upon what promised to be a career of pastoral usefulness, and was cheered by the affectionate confidence of his people. But all hopes of such a nature were soon blasted, for about two months later his spirit was translated to the home of the redeemed.

Returning to the hospitable mansion of our kind father in Israel, we were once more regaled at his table with a generous supply for our bodily needs and with pleasant and profitable conversation, after which, as the shades of evening came on, we retraced our steps to Carlisle. A memorable visit.

On Saturday, Brother Stacy left with his family for Mendon, while I was entertained at the house of his worthy deacon, John Green, the only surviving male member of the First Church after the orthodox secession of some years before – an intelligent, devout, substantial citizen of the town. On Sunday I preached *extempore* in the morning from Acts 17:25, and in the afternoon from Philippians 2:5. At 5 P.M. I gave a temperance lecture in the meetinghouse with apparently good effect. Rev. Dr. Ripley and Rev. Mr. Andrews of Chelmsford, who had exchanged pulpits that day, met at Deacon Green's on their return home and attended the lecture, giving it and the cause their encouragement. The Doctor remained over night and on Monday morning, after a delightful interview, we parted in gospel love to meet no more on earth. Five years afterward, in 1841, he entered his heavenly rest, aged about ninety years. I came home via Boston the same day, reaching my family at 9 P.M. after an absence of just a week.

Pastorate Extended

On the following Saturday, May 14, I was waited upon by two of my parishioners, Jabez Aldrich and Benjamin Davenport, a committee of the society, who presented me with the following document:

> At a parish meeting holden May 2, 1836, *Voted* unanimously, that we cordially approve the conduct and pastoral services of the Rev. Adin Ballou during the four years that he has officiated as the minister of this parish, and we earnestly hope and desire that he may continue with us for another term after the expiration of his present contract. Therefore, *Voted*, that Jabez Aldrich, Benjamin Davenport, and William S. Hastings be a committee to wait upon the Rev. Mr. Ballou and ascertain from him upon what conditions and for what time he will engage to officiate as minister of this parish from and after the expiration of his present contract and to report at an adjourned meeting.

I promised an early answer in writing, which I soon forwarded to the committee. The substance of it was that I gratefully appreciated the confidence reposed in me by the parish, and should be happy to renew my engagement for the term of five years, from and after the first of April, 1837, on condition that my annual salary be raised from four to five hundred dollars. The proposition was acceptable to the parish, and a mutual agreement was in due time ratified.

Endeavors to Promote Christian Life

The days through which I was passing at this period of my life were days of intense intellectual, moral, and religious activity. I zealously and scrupulously endeavored to improve my understanding in useful knowledge, to discipline my spiritual capabilities into true Christian holiness, to promote personal religion among my people, and to help forward the great moral reforms which had begun to command public attention. I read advanced books of the best quality, I studied the ancient languages somewhat, and in all possible ways sought to invigorate and enrich my mind. For religious quickening and culture, I familiarized my mind with Thomas à Kempis[8] and other devoutly-minded authors, and subjected myself to strict rules of prayer, watchfulness, and self-examination.

In trying to increase experimental piety among those to whom I ministered, I gave special lectures to the children and youth of the Sunday School, exhorting them earnestly to be conscientious, reverent, and prayerful, and to seek communion with their Heavenly Father and his son Jesus Christ; while with the adults, I labored to bring them into the church through serious convictions, conversion, and consecration, by preaching, social religious meetings, and personal counsel, and thus have them committed to acknowledged principles of righteousness and to a truly Christian life. So I pushed religion as urgently as I could, after the old methods modified by my revised theological views. The recent fashion of bringing people into the kingdom of heaven by social festivities and amusemental gatherings had not then been invented. My vineyard was not preeminently feasible and productive, nor was I the most skillful of husbandmen; but I did what I could.

As to the great moral reforms, only three had yet been born – Temperance, Antislavery, and the Peace Movement, others having only an embryotic existence. The first two assumed so much importance and entered so largely into my personal and ministerial experience during the period covered by the present chapter, that they require special consideration.

Total Abstinence

The Temperance Reform in its first phase I had earnestly espoused, as heretofore set forth, and was its ardent advocate; but it had taken on a new and more radical character about the time now in review. The disuse of distilled liquors alone, which was the original basis of the movement, while those resulting from fermentation were allowed, had proved insufficient to overcome or essentially lessen the evils against which warfare was waged. Drunkards were multiplied by indulgence in the milder intoxicants – wine, beer, cider, etc. And sharp discussions had arisen among temperance reformers upon the question of putting these under the same ban as so-called ardent spirits. This was strongly opposed by a considerable party of those who clung to the use of them. Nevertheless, logic and the permanent success of the cause imperatively demanded *total abstinence* – abstinence from the use of *all* intoxicating beverages. I was fully convinced of this, as was a large majority of the adherents and advocates of the reform. The only practical course for the more radical party was to leave the conservatives in a peaceable manner and start a new movement whose central principle should be the entire disuse of all that can intoxicate, forming societies in accordance with that principle to carry forward the work. And this was what was done in many localities throughout our general vicinity. We organized under the new regime in our town, the organization being entitled "The North Mendon Young Men's Temperance Society," for which I, with others, labored energetically. This society prospered, as did similar ones in surrounding towns. Those remaining attached to the old system did little thereafter to make converts to it, and finally allowed it to die out.

My position in reference to this great reform has been the same from the beginning until now. I never placed the duty of total abstinence from all intoxicating liquors on the ground that it was a sin *per se* to use them moderately – like murder, robbery, etc.; but only as a wrong done to humanity and an offense against sound morality, when social conditions and dominant circumstances rendered it dangerous as a habit or as an example to others. Such conditions and circumstances then, as in later days, existed in a marked degree. The sale of all kinds of strong drink had become general and civilization was greatly demoralized by personal indulgence and social custom. Drunkenness increased to an alarming extent, and poverty, disorder, crime, and misery prevailed on every hand. The evils consequent upon the use of alcoholics came to be intolerable. Something must be done.

After much study and experimentation, a remedy for the deadly contagion and the ruin it wrought was discovered: *Total Abstinence*. It was demonstrated that intoxicating beverages were not necessary for persons in health, that they were more or less perilous to those using them, and that the utter renunciation of them was not only a cure for, but a safeguard against, the manifold evils of intemperance. We who made ourselves sure of this worked on the lines thus indicated for the cause, and looked for its early triumph. But appetite, interest, fashion, and habit, have proved stronger with vast multitudes of people than reason, philanthropy, or religion, down to this year of grace, 1889. Yet I swerve not one iota from my original temperance principles, convictions, faith, and hope. The cause will some day triumph, and the blessings it has in store for a humanity redeemed from its curse will be enjoyed. "Fly swifter round, ye wheels of time, and bring the welcome day."[9]

The Antislavery Movement

Strange as it may seem to most of my readers, I was more than thirty years of age before the thought entered my mind that I was in any way responsible for chattel slavery in my country. I had no pro-slavery in my constitution, training, or habitual feeling. I had by nature no prejudice against color, no spirit of caste, and no disposition to estimate any of my fellow men higher or lower in the scale of being on account of nationality, race, birth, rank, wealth, sex, or any standard but personal merit and demerit. I was a born democrat, and never had to take up any cross in order to treat any one kindly and justly, as I would be treated. Of other sins and shortcomings I had enough, but none of this sort. The wrongs, abominations, and outrages of chattel slavery were out of my sight and so out of my mind. A thick veil of reverent patriotism in those early days shut out the vision of many things I afterward came to see. I was brought up to idolize my country, its constitution and laws, as a rich and sacred patrimony, earned and consecrated by the heroic blood of Revolutionary sires, whom I was accustomed to glorify as the wisest and noblest of mankind. The national union they had formed was sacred to me, to be preserved inviolate and transmitted as an invaluable heritage to posterity.

But all this self-complacent regard for the fathers and their work was destined to be sadly disturbed by the outcry of the Abolitionists that slavery as it existed in the land was a monstrous national sin of which we were all more or less guilty, and that immediate emancipation of the bondmen was an indispensable duty to God and man. That outcry grew louder and louder and was echoed by multiplying voices on every hand. It called in question the sacred guaranties of our fathers and laid violent hands on the ark of our national covenant. My blind patriotism was shocked and I deplored the agitation that had been raised. I did not desire to see the agitators harmed, nor to have their rights of free speech abridged, nor to oppose them by any other means than those of calm reason and earnest persuasion.

But presently their opponents of various sort began to assail them, not only with hard words but with threats of violence, and from threats they proceeded to flagrantly abhorrent deeds. Prices were set on the heads of their leaders, their meetings were broken up, their lecturers maltreated, their printing presses demolished, and their editors murderously hunted down and killed.[10] While such outrages were being enacted it became impossible for honest, conscientious people not to think upon the subject lying back of them all – back of the agitation provoking them – and not to investigate it; and equally impossible after such thought and investigation to be indifferent to or remain neutral upon it. At any rate, so it was with me. I yielded to the necessities of the case; I did a vast amount of solid, earnest thinking, more, perhaps, than in any equal portion of my life, and from indubitable evidence I came to the following conclusions:

(1) That slavery was what John Wesley had characterized it, "The sum of all villainies,"[11] that what I had regarded as its abuses were its natural fruits; and that from its inception to its consummation it was utterly wicked.

(2) That as it had to begin by violence and cruelty, it must be maintained by the same means; and that the enslaved must be kept in ignorance and held in bondage by brute force, or they would, out of their natural love of liberty, of themselves go free.

(3) That our Revolutionary fathers (whom I had been taught to revere) notwithstanding their sacrifices for their own liberty, inflicted on their fellow men, as Thomas Jefferson said, "a bondage, one hour of which was fraught with more misery than ages of that which they rose in rebellion to oppose."[12] Also that, by certain guaranties of the United States constitution,[13] they rendered all co-governing citizens of the country more or less responsible for the sin of American slavery.

(4) That the slave power had acquired such influence in Church and State, in commerce and finance, as to vitiate deplorably the whole moral status of the nation – millions being so perverted as to think wrong is right and right wrong; evil good and good evil.

(5) That Church and State, though nominally separate from and independent of each other, were yet so sympathetically and practically in harmony, as far as regarded subserviency to the slave power, the support of the guaranties of the Constitution to oppressors, and the imposition of unrighteous obligations in the interest of injustice and tyranny upon all citizens, as to demand withdrawal from both on the part of every enlightened, conscientious opponent of the gigantic crime, and entire separation from the fellowship of those who, with happy accord, were accustomed to treat the Abolitionists and their allies as *pestilent fellows*.

It took me some time to learn these important lessons, but when I had mastered them, I wondered that I had not seen, appreciated, and accepted them long before – especially in view of the theological progress I had made and the ethics logically derived therefrom. For the universal Fatherhood of God, and the universal brotherhood of man, which were among my settled fundamentals of religion, ought to have made me a thorough-going Abolitionist the moment the question of chattel slavery was presented to my thought and conscience for consideration and moral judgment. They ought also to have made me understand and take home to myself, theoretically and practically, the several lessons just enumerated. Such, however, was not for a long time the case.[14]

Nevertheless, light came to me before the spring of 1837, and both truth and duty in regard to the great national sin were clearly revealed to my mental and moral understanding. Of the essential wickedness of slaveholding I was thoroughly convinced, as I was also thoroughly convinced that I was under solemn obligations as a teacher of religion to make open proclamation of my views and to do what in me lay to oppose and overthrow the monstrous wrong. But such a course was obviously against my temporal interest, ambition, and comfort. Abolitionism was an element of discord in every social body it had entered thus far, and threatened to become more so as time went on.

How would it affect the new Restorationist denomination I had worked so hard and spent so much to get launched? There were serious reasons for apprehending damaging consequences if it was allowed to come within the borders of our body. Though small, it contained both conservative and radical minds, equally honest and nearly equal in numbers. We were well agreed in regard to our theological and ecclesiastical tenets and policy. We had all committed ourselves to the growing temperance reform. But radical antislavery – Abolitionism – was a very different thing to deal with. It struck at what we all had been accustomed to deem venerable, sacred, and patriotic in our national life, at solemn covenants of the Federal compact, at time-honored customs, at commercial interests, at political and religious affiliations and preferments – at a multitude of concerns affecting our personal, social, ecclesiastical, and civil well-being and happiness. It had already provoked popular prejudice and violent outbreaks in different denominations. What would it do to our little branch of the Christian church? We shall see.

And there were with me matters nearer home to be considered – questions to be answered, problems to be solved, difficulties to be met, trials to be borne. Were I to pursue the path that duty pointed out to me, what results to me personally and as a minister would be likely to ensue? Probably more or less disaffection towards me in my parish, withdrawal of support, loss of friends, perhaps ill-will, animosity, and bitter hate. Such had been the consequences to me hitherto of departing from the old ways, of adopting new truths, of proclaiming new principles of faith and conduct, of espousing unpopular causes, and going forward in the path of reform. Was this to be forever my fate? Why not remain quiet, let needed changes come without worrying myself to hurry their advance, thus giving Providence a chance to work out the problems of human progress and destiny without any of my aid? Worldly prudence and personal ease obviously dictated this policy. But duty would not be compromised with after this fashion and the voice of conscience said: *Follow thy highest light; be faithful to thy best convictions; bear witness to the truth; stand up for the right; be no laggard in the strife for God and man.* I heard, trembled, hesitated, and by divine grace obeyed.

So on the sixth of April, 1837, our annual State Fast-day, I preached my first distinctly outspoken antislavery discourse in my Mendon pulpit from Isaiah 58:5-6: "Is it such a fast that I have chosen? A day for a man to afflict his soul? Is it to bow down his head like a bulrush and to spread sackcloth and ashes under him? Wilt thou call this a fast and an acceptable day unto the Lord? Is not *this* the fast that I have chosen? To loose the bands of wickedness, to undo the heavy burdens and to let the oppressed go free, and that ye break every yoke?"

The doctrine of this text I applied faithfully to the great system of American oppression, setting forth the manifold evils it represented and engendered and the manifest duty of all good men and women in regard to it. What were the effects? Such an excitement among the people at large as the staid old town of Mendon had never experienced before. The unanimity of my parishioners in my favor, so emphatically declared within a year, vanished in a moment. A dozen families were irreconcilably disaffected, and at once left my congregation; some of them previously among my best friends and largest contributors to the parish treasury. Many hard things were said and some discreditable ones done. I tried to appease the malcontents by all honorable means, but in vain. In the midst of the commotion I gave up my pastorate; but at the earnest request of numerous devoted parishioners, who approved in the main my course and who assured me that more new members were ready to come into the society than there were old ones likely to depart, I ere long recalled my letter of resignation.[15] This seemed to irritate those who had seceded and inflame their ire against me. One of the wealthiest of them, to whom I had become indebted for pecuniary aid in some former time of need, in order to make me sensible of my dependence on him and humiliate me as much as possible, sent me, immediately after this occurrence, the following significant note:

> To Adin Ballou:
> Sir: I request you forthwith to pay me what you are owing me, or procure a satisfactory endorser therefor.
>
> Yours, etc.,
> ———— ————

I made known the position in which I was placed to some of my friends, who were ready to stand by me to the end and to help me in the emergency where I found myself, and within twelve hours after the imperative demand was made upon me, my disgruntled creditor was paid in full, and he never troubled me afterward. Such experiences are not pleasant, but they come sometimes and have to be endured. Happily, the main body of my people remained faithful to me, though probably some preferred that I should have kept silent on the subject of slavery, and the losses of hearers and pecuniary support occasioned by my fidelity to principle in this particular were soon more than supplied by newcomers, my congregations being larger than ever before. So I lost nothing in the end on that score. None of the seceders were happier for going away, and some of them ultimately returned to their ancestral religious home.

My labors were considerably increased by reason of the position I had taken with respect to the antislavery reform. I not only felt called upon to awaken interest in and secure cooperation for the much-maligned and struggling cause in my own town and its immediate neighborhood, but I was soon in considerable demand as a lecturer, platform speaker, and general helper of it in more remote and distant places. Its leaders were kindly disposed towards me and glad to welcome me as a fellow-laborer with them in their public gatherings, and interested personal friends were solicitous to have me heard upon the great question that was agitating the public mind, in their respective localities.

On the fourth of July of the same year as that in which the incidents narrated above took place, I delivered an elaborate and carefully prepared antislavery address[16] in my Mendon church to a large and deeply interested concourse of people, deeming this a most appropriate and profitable way of celebrating the anniversary of American independence. The production was very long and as complete in form and argument as I could possibly make it. It was printed and had an extended and influential circulation in this country;[17] also reprinted in England and spread broadcast throughout the dominion of Queen Victoria, then just entering upon her long and illustrious reign.

After the delivery of this discourse, on the evening of the same day, we formed a strong antislavery society in Mendon, as auxiliary to the American society organized in Philadelphia four years before,[18] and entered upon active work in behalf of universal freedom. Later on, we established an antislavery library, and these two instrumentalities wrought effectually for many years in the community to keep alive an interest in the cause, to disseminate the truth upon the subject for which they stood, and to hasten on the day when at length liberty should be "proclaimed throughout the land to all the inhabitants thereof."[19]

A Vexatious Episode

In addition to my multiform legitimate labors and responsibilities as a man and a minister of religion, I became about this time very unwisely involved in a matter wholly extraneous and foreign to my proper line of activity, from which I derived only trouble, perplexity, vexation, and a fool's tuition. Two Mendon citizens, both professing at the outset to be my friends, fell into a controversy in regard to the boundary line between their two wood-lots, lying side by side. They had referred the case to the courts, but before it came to trial obtained leave to withdraw it and submit it to the judgment and decision of three mutually agreed-upon arbitrators. Both wished me to act as chairman of this private board of judication, each choosing one of the other two. To this I foolishly consented. I and my associates had several meetings, canvassed the matter submitted to us, but accomplished very little; for, in spite of all the records we could find and of all the evidence brought before us, the true line of division seemed to us exceedingly obscure and uncertain. At length I unearthed the minutes of a long-forgotten survey which appeared to be well attested and conclusive both to me and my two comrades, and we decided pursuant to its plain statements. But our decision did not satisfy the chief claimant, and he declined to accept it, asking for another hearing, at which he said he could bring additional testimony in his favor and so cause us to change our verdict. So urgent was he that, upon my strong plea for him and against their own judgment, the others yielded, and another hearing was granted, though not till he solemnly promised that if he could not convince us that we were in error, he would freely quitclaim all right and title to the land we had assigned to his competitor. At the new hearing he failed utterly in presenting evidence calculated to induce us to change our opinion, and we therefore reaffirmed our former finding. This greatly incensed the dissatisfied contestant, who angrily refused either to abide by our decision or to fulfill the pledge to quitclaim the land in question which he had solemnly given at the last meeting. And no argument or appeal on the part of the referees could make him yield one iota of his dogged and unjustifiable determination. I was personally greatly humiliated and chagrined, not only because it was by my efforts that this additional hearing was granted, but also because by having it we had passed the date at which our decision was to have been reported to the court under its rescript and thereby rendered ourselves censurable at its bar.

But this was only the beginning of sorrows experienced by me on account of this case. For this man, who, under professions of the greatest friendship, had enticed me into the position of arbitrator, and in whose behalf I had yielded my own best judgment and persuasively and appealingly had induced my coadjutors to yield theirs also, became my bitter and relentless enemy from that day on. He dogged my footsteps for years with false accusations, calumnies, and scurrilous epithets and insinuations, letting no opportunity slip for annoying and tormenting me by attempts to blacken my character and injure my reputation. I was harassed by lawyers whom he had suborned for that purpose; I was summoned before a private council to answer libelous charges; I was brow-beaten, threatened, denounced, anathematized, and maltreated in a multitude of ways by this man, whom I had always dealt kindly and justly by, and whom I had never wronged or harmed, till his health failed him in his old age and his power of abusing me had gone forever. I never met a person who so baffled my understanding – who was such a moral puzzle to me. With respectable natural qualities, good judgment, executive ability, and some commendable traits of character, he yet allowed himself to be so mastered by self-interest and self-will that his conscience seemed utterly paralyzed and oblivious to all considerations of justice and equity; to all claims of truth, honor, and the eternal law of God. And yet when confronted and brought to bay by those whom he had abused and persecuted (for I was not the only one thus treated) he would assume the most guileless and inoffensive air, and the tears would course down his cheeks as if he were the victim of the most bitter injustice and cruelty. At such times I would look at him in amazement, doubtful whether to count him honestly insane or a brazen pretender. I never quite satisfied myself in regard to the matter, but concluded finally to refer such an enigma to Him who knoweth all things and who judgeth righteously. I have ever regretted the injustice done to the other party in this unfortunate affair by my improper and mistaken indulgence of his grasping and unscrupulous competitor, whereby the first verdict of the board of referees was withheld from the court beyond the time fixed for its return, thereby failing of judicial ratification and enforcement; as I have also the trouble and expense to which he was put in consequence. But it is due him to say that he never to my knowledge or from trustworthy report uttered against me one word of reproach, complaint, or blame. Such is the difference in men.

Meeting of Massachusetts Association of Universal Restorationists, 1836

And now to go back somewhat in the order of time, I will mention the more significant ecclesiastical and religious happenings of the two years in review. And I begin with the annual meeting of our Restorationist Association, held at Millville (then Mendon South Parish, now a part of Blackstone),[20] September 14 and 15, 1836. As usual, I was present at this meeting, participated in its proceedings, and took a lively interest in all that was said and done. It organized by the choice of Rev. Charles Hudson, moderator, and Rev. Alanson St. Clair,[21] clerk. An extract from the report of its transactions in the *Messenger* will indicate its spirit and character:

> During its session it was agreed that henceforth at each meeting there should be selected a subject for an essay or dissertation at the next session, and a person appointed for its preparation; that letters of license and fellowship be given to Brothers Emmons Partridge[22] and Daniel S. Whitney[23] as preachers of the gospel; and that the superintendents of the Sabbath schools connected with our churches be requested respectively to make returns to the annual meetings of the association. There were also six public services attended, and discourses were preached by Brethren George W. Stacy, Lyman Maynard, Alanson St. Clair, Edwin M. Stone, Paul Dean, and William Morse.
>
> In the council, harmony of sentiment and action with the best feelings prevailed. In the public services, solemnity, fervency, and deep attention, characterized the speakers and the hearers. And the season will be long remembered as one of refreshing and joy from the presence of the Lord. The following address to the churches[24] was ordered.
>
> ALANSON ST. CLAIR, CLERK

CHAPTER 15

Millville, Sept. 15, 1836

BELOVED BRETHREN: We desire to impart unto you the spirit and joy of this happy occasion, that your joy may be full, your gratitude ascend to God, and your praise be given to the Redeemer of the world. We desire you to realize more fully what heavenly peace there is in believing; what hope there is in Christ; what bright prospects are opened to you in the gospel. It is yours to know the fellowship of the saints; to taste the heavenly gift; and to press toward the mark for the prize of your high calling; to grow up daily into a holy and happy meetness for the kingdom of God; and to let your light shine before men.

It has pleased God greatly to bless you in the views which He has given you of the character, design, and tendency of Christianity – the great instrument by which He will overthrow idolatry and error, and enlighten and reconcile the world to Himself; in your views of that Divine providence under whose superintendence all things shall be conducted to a happy issue; and of that destiny assigned to all men and to all holy intelligences, of glorifying God and enjoying Him forever.

These pure and lovely sentiments which God has committed to you in trust have been believed and proclaimed by holy prophets, early Christians, and many great and good men in all ages. They, at this moment, have the sympathy of many devout souls in this and distant countries, some of whom express that sympathy freely, and others are only waiting to judge the tree by its fruits and to see whether these views will make you good, active, zealous, spiritual Christians. The eyes of thousands are turned on you to observe the result of the experiment now making – the effect of your doctrine on your lives.

Brethren, how high and solemn are the responsibilities under which we act, to God, to our fathers, and to the world! Leave to others the question of your success. It is yours to work, and trust the success to God, to be given in His own time. Let us forsake the vanities of the world, abandon all narrow and selfish feelings, and adorn the doctrine of God our Savior in all things, regarding alike a good profession and a good life as twin cherubim in the service of God. It behooves us to be valiant for the truth in which the glory of God and the good of man are concerned; but to be mild, gentle, and charitable to those who dissent from us; to guard the truth from being mixed with the error of no future responsibility – no future hopes or fears on the one hand, and on the other from the soul-chilling error of endless torments, which, as far as it extends, annuls the merits of Christ and defeats the gospel of His grace.

Let then the heavenly spirit of Christ dwell richly in your hearts by faith; and let your light shine before men in acts of justice and mercy, in deeds of piety and benevolence. Honor the name, word, and worship of God; bless and cherish the social, moral, and civil relations of life, that the truth of God be not blasphemed.

Finally, brethren, consider that in the order of His providence and grace, God gives His kingdom to those who will best improve it, and lets His vineyard to those who will render Him the fruit in His season. Remember, also, that Jesus, our Great Master, sought His glory by saving the world, and that we can never gain His kingdom but by that piety and benevolence which delight in doing good to mankind.

By thus doing may we obtain an abundant entrance into the everlasting kingdom of the King of kings, to share His grace and see His glory.

PAUL DEAN

Ordination of Rev. Thomas Edwards

Though out of the line of my ecclesiastical fellowship, I attended, on the twenty-eighth of December, 1836, the ordination of Rev. Thomas Edwards and his installation as pastor of the North Congregational Church in Mendon, which was established a few years before by those who had withdrawn from the old First Church, over which I now presided. Rev. Dr. Jacob Ide[25] of Medway preached the sermon of the occasion, the other exercises being rendered by clergymen of neighboring towns. I was interested in the several utterances, many good things being said and fewer offensive ones than I anticipated. A serious blunder was made by Rev. Mr. Grosvenor[26] of Uxbridge – a young man to whom was assigned the part of extending the right hand of fellowship to the minister-elect. In doing this, he emphasized the fact, as he claimed, that the church he represented was, 106 years before, a colony from that of the new pastor, when in truth neither his church nor the other was ten years old; both being recent seceders from the original churches of their respective towns. Whether this fiction was due to the young man's ignorance or unscrupulous sectarian assumption I know not, and it matters little at this late day, but it indicates a habit of those times prevalent among certain persons who withdrew from the established churches on account of their liberal tendencies and founded new ones on a more rigid theological basis. Mr. Edwards, who was an Englishman by birth, remained in Mendon till February, 1840, and proved to be an agreeable clerical neighbor.

Installation and Death of Theological Student, Edmund Capron

My young student friend and brother, Edmund Capron, having completed his preparatory studies and passed a satisfactory examination before an ecclesiastical council convened at Millville, Massachusetts, May 3, 1837, was on that day ordained and settled as minister of the Restorationist society in that flourishing village. As his pastor, instructor, and spiritual guide, I was invited to deliver the ordination sermon, which I did from 1 Timothy 1:5: "Now the end of the commandment is charity," etc. The other parts were taken mostly by ministers of our association, Rev. Samuel Clarke of Uxbridge being the only outsider. Everything passed off creditably, harmoniously, auspiciously, eliciting reciprocal congratulations from all concerned.[27] A second service was held in the afternoon, when Brother E. M. Stone preached, and in the evening the newly-ordained pastor and Miss Abby Pitts, daughter of the late Esek Pitts, Esq., were married, most of the council, with family relatives and friends, being present.

Brother Capron entered upon his work in this new field of labor under most happy circumstances and with great promise of usefulness and honor. But alas for him, for his most amiable and fitting companion, their friends and the world, the auspicious aspects of the situation proved deceptive and vain. In the early autumn of this same year, a fearful pestilence swept through Millville, carrying off many lamented victims, he being among the number. He was stricken with the prevailing disease in the midst of his labors, and in spite of the best of medical skill, tender nursing, and yearning prayers, after a distressing illness of two weeks, on the twenty-fourth of September, he passed away, leaving his wife a heartbroken widow and his devoted flock pastorless. He was in the twenty-ninth year of his age. Then was there mourning indeed in that newly-founded home of his and in that Zion of our faith. Then I wept with them that wept, as once I had rejoiced with them in their joyfulness, and from the same pulpit where, a few months before, I had discoursed amid most cheerful, inspiring surroundings and abundant demonstrations of gladness and delight, I now ministered Christian consolation to a great concourse of sorrow-stricken sufferers and their sympathizing neighbors and friends. So are sunshine and shade, smiles and tears, joy and grief, mingled in the experience of mortals here below. A few extracts from the published obituary of this beloved brother will indicate his state of mind in view of his approaching dissolution:

> Though enduring great distress of body, he remained calm, patient, and resigned in spirit to the last. As he drew near the end, his mind became clearer and stronger, and the sun of his Christian hopes shone in a cloudless sky. Being asked if he remained firm in his distinguishing religious doctrines, he answered with cheerful promptitude, "Yes; they give me happiness in death. How can one die happy without such hopes?" Having expressed his satisfaction and gratitude to his physician and attendants and taken leave of his heartriven consort and relatives, endeavoring to comfort them in the extremity of their anguish, he commended himself to his Redeemer and fell asleep without a struggle. Neither his strength of reason, of speech, nor of Christian confidence failed him to his expiring moment. All who witnessed his exit were deeply impressed by such manifest triumphs of mind over the elements of mortality, and can testify to the blessedness of his death.[28]

Meeting of Massachusetts Association of Universal Restorationists, 1837

The annual meeting of the Massachusetts Restorationist Association for the year 1837 was a memorable one, and marked an epoch in the history of that body. It was held in Milton at the Railway Church, so-called, on the evening of September 29, and through the two following days. The first session was devoted mostly to business pertaining to the proceedings of the occasion and to the polity of the association; the six other sessions were given up to public religious services, after our usual custom. Sermons were preached by Revs. David R. Lamson (Occasional), Charles Hudson, Lyman Maynard, Philemon R. Russell, Paul Dean, and myself. In council, William H. Kinsley[29] and Alexander T. Temple were admitted to fellowship; I was appointed to prepare a dissertation on "The Intermediate State"; Revs. Charles Hudson, E. M. Stone, and William Morse were chosen a committee to present an address on the Sabbath; reports on Sunday schools were made; and a resolve was passed approving and recommending the "Restorationist Tract Society," recently established.

Thus far all went off harmoniously and to united satisfaction. But the harmony was sadly disturbed, if not fatally injured, by the introduction of three resolutions which I had drafted, on Total Abstinence, Moral Reform, and Antislavery, respectively. These were met and opposed by an influential minority of our members, and a very unpleasant discussion followed, which made me regret that I had introduced them; not because there was anything improper in them, but because my brethren were not far enough advanced to appreciate and endorse them.[30] They evidently deemed them wholly uncalled-for, if not wrong in principle and detrimental to the growth of our denomination in the existing state of public sentiment. In this respect I saw that they were wise and prudent for the time being; but I was looking beyond immediate outward success, and had an ambition to build up a church that would lead, not follow, public sentiment in true righteousness. This, I saw reason to fear, was a task too onerous to be accomplished. The association, as a body, was not ready to take so radical a position as the resolutions involved, and the discussion upon them was closed by an agreement that those who pleased might sign them on their individual responsibility without in any wise committing their contesting brethren to them, and that they should be published in our journal accordingly. This was subsequently done, as follows:[31]

> *Whereas*, it has pleased God in these latter days to awaken the special attention of this people to the prevailing vices, iniquities, and corruptions of the age, and to incite them to extraordinary efforts for the reformation and improvement of their fellow men,
>
> *And whereas,* the benevolent and purifying truths held by Restorationists urgently demand their zealous cooperation in every Christian enterprise for the reformation of the vicious, the recovery of the outcast, the deliverance of the oppressed, the maintenance of virtue, and the promotion of human happiness; Therefore, *Resolved*:
>
> (1) That the undersigned cherish a hearty interest in the cause of temperance, as based on the salutary doctrine of total abstinence from all intoxicating liquor.
>
> (2) That we cherish a hearty interest in the cause of moral reform, as judiciously prosecuted against all manner of libertinism, lewdness, impurity, and connubial faithlessness.
>
> (3) That we deeply deplore the existence of slavery in the metropolis, territories, and states of our country, as a foul reproach to the nation; that we are constrained to express our unqualified reprobation of any and every form of bondage which empowers one man to hold and treat another as mere property; that we deem the laws, customs, and usages which support or countenance the system of American slavery utterly sinful in the sight of God, utterly anti-Christian, and utterly hostile to the moral and religious welfare of mankind; and that we cordially approve of all laudable efforts for the promotion of immediate emancipation throughout the United States and the world.
>
> (4) That we do earnestly and affectionately recommend to all the ministers, churches, and people of our fellowship prayerfully to consider their duty in respect

to these great enterprises; to give them their unequivocal and uncompromising support so far as they conscientiously can, and by no means to speak or act in a manner calculated to obstruct their progress.

ADIN BALLOU   ALANSON ST. CLAIR
CHARLES HUDSON   WILLIAM H. KINSLEY
GEORGE W. STACY   DAVID R. LAMSON
A. T. TEMPLE   WILLIAM SPARRELL
LYMAN MAYNARD   LEONARD BULLARD
EBENEZER D. DRAPER
Members of the Massachusetts Association of Restorationists, met at Milton, Mass., Sept. 29, 1837

The Touchstone

In the line of religious controversial writing during the two years now being traversed, I did considerably less than previously. A few articles of mine appeared in the *Messenger* in support of Restorationism as against endless punishment, and I also preached a few special discourses of the same nature. My "Omega," noticed in a former chapter, had foreclosed all further newspaper discussion with the ultra Universalists, but at the urgent request of my faithful friend, Samuel W. Wheeler[32] of Providence, Rhode Island, I prepared a concise statement designed to present in vivid contrast the two systems of doctrine represented by myself and them respectively. It so pleased him that he caused it to be printed in pamphlet form at his own expense and to be widely circulated. The publication was entitled *The Touchstone*.[33] It is the only one of my works, I think, not bearing my name.

Soon after this pamphlet was given to the public, it was noticed at some length by the editor of the *Christian Advocate*, a leading Methodist organ, who endeavored to disparage it, and to show that there was no essential difference between the two parties which it put in contrast. I publicly answered the article, exposing its absurdities, and showing that the disparity claimed by me was greater than that existing between the Methodists and Calvinists, the latter of whom the former had been bitterly denouncing for a hundred years.[34] Believers in endless torments had a special interest in taking the position indicated, lest that some of their number who had a strong prejudice against the Universalists should be won over to Restorationism. But "truth is mighty, and will prevail."[35] Restorationism will some day be the common orthodoxy of Christendom and all controversy regarding it will cease.

Conflicting Claims of Personal Piety and Social Reform

Before bringing this chapter to an end, I desire to enlarge upon and emphasize one feature of my ministerial work at which I hinted in one of its opening paragraphs. I have always realized more or less vividly the importance of awakening, cultivating, and promoting the distinctively religious life – personal piety and holiness in those to whom I preached – so that while honoring and exemplifying ordinary morality of all kinds and the external decencies of good society, they should not rest contented with such attainments of virtue as a sufficient equipment for eternity, or even for this world, without a spiritual force behind them generated by the proper activity of the religious faculties. Christ taught and insisted upon an inward experimental piety or sense of divine realities in each individual soul, which derives constant inspiration from the Heavenly Father and manifests itself in the outward conduct by fruits of righteousness and true holiness. And his ministers should teach, act, and live accordingly. To this phase of ministerial work, and to the development of the corresponding side of the Christian character and life, I addressed myself with unfaltering energy and zeal, as it has been my aim to do through life.

But my efforts in behalf of personal religion were more or less interfered with, and the work I would gladly have done in that direction hindered, by reason of the calls increasingly made upon me in the interest of the two great reforms – temperance and antislavery – whose importance and claims I was by no means disposed to forget or ignore. With respect to them, as with respect to spiritual concerns, "Necessity was laid upon me; Yea, woe was mine,"[36] if I did not do what I could to carry them forward on their mission of uplifting and redemption to a successful issue. The victims of strong drink, the wrecked characters, the ruined homes, the wretchedness and suffering of wives, mothers, and children, all resulting from the indulgence of perverted appetites and the use of intoxicating liquors, made appeals to my reason, conscience, and heart, which I could not and must not resist nor suffer to go unanswered.

Moreover, the aggressions of the slave-power and the outrages committed by the myrmidons of tyranny and oppression, together with the wailings of the suffering bondmen, were continually forced upon my attention, urging me in the name of God and humanity to "cry aloud and spare not; lift up my voice like a trumpet and show the people their transgressions and the house of Jacob its sins."[37] The pro-slavery murder of Rev. Elijah P. Lovejoy in Alton, Illinois, in November, 1837, which startled the conscientious, liberty-loving people of the North by its bloodthirsty atrocity, occasioned numerous demands for commemorative addresses, and for instruction upon the lessons to be derived from the event, of which I had a prominent share in my general neighborhood.[38]

All these things made it difficult for me to provide for personal Christianization as I felt I ought to do, and to so divide the word of divine truth that none of the great interests of the heavenly kingdom should suffer detriment by any neglect or unfaithfulness on my part. Yet I realized in some good degree the diversified responsibilities resting upon me, and endeavored by help from on high to acquit myself acceptably in respect to them all, beginning with the least and reaching out unto the greatest. True Christianity I felt then as now, requires a loyalty on the part of all its subjects and professors at once particular and universal – a righteousness starting in the utmost recesses of the individual soul and extending through the family and neighborhood into general society and seeking the holiness and happiness of all mankind; yea, of all moral intelligences in all states of existence. It aims at the rectification of the minutest violations of the divine law, as it also does of the more flagrant wrongs, the giant crimes of individuals, families, communities, states, nations, races. It never overlooks or passes by the least or greatest duties – the particular or universal good.

Domestic Burden of Reform Interests

The multiform interests that I had, at this date, come to represent before the general public, theologically, morally, and socially, not only increased very largely my correspondence (which laid an extra tax upon my time and energy) but also added greatly to the number of visitors calling for purposes of consultation and advice respecting ways and means of advancing those interests and making them serve most effectually the beneficent ends contemplated by them. My home became a sort of cabinet or place of resort for all kinds of reformers in which to discuss the various schemes proposed for the bettering the condition of mankind, and formulate plans for carrying such as were approved into effect; as it was also for a considerable swarm of inquirers into the principles and methods of human melioration and redemption. By unavoidable necessity, this made it at the same time a kind of public hostelry, in which entertainment of suitable sort – food, and not infrequently lodging – was to be provided. Myself and wife endeavored to act the parts of host and hostess with proper civility and liberality, showing due hospitality to all, though at considerable expense of money, time, and strength. The chief burden of it all, however, fell upon her, who, at the best, was ill-fitted to bear it, but who nevertheless discharged the duties and endured the trials thus thrust upon her with a patient, unmurmuring, heroic diligence and fidelity, worthy of record and of grateful commemoration.

Dangerous Illness of Son

In the autumn of 1837, the more strictly private cares and labors of our household were very much augmented and intensified by painful anxiety and fear on account of the dangerous sickness of our little son, Adin Augustus, who was brought to the brink of the grave by scarlatina. He had been with us on a preaching visit to Hillsborough, New Hampshire, and the returning journey (made in great haste, and probably without sufficient precautions against exposure and fatigue) seemed to overtax his rather delicate constitution, rendering him an easy prey to this insidious and debilitating disease. He was in imminent peril of his life for several weeks, but happily, after a long period of convalescence, recovered, bringing the thirty-fifth year of my life to a close under circumstances calculated to awaken in the hearts of all the members of our household the most profound emotions of gratitude and joy.

CHAPTER 16

1838-1840

As time passed by and I came to understand more fully the practical meaning and value of the theological and ethical principles I had deliberately and conscientiously espoused, and their adaptability to human conduct in all the departments and relations of life; and furthermore, as the absolute necessity of applying those principles as ruling forces to human conduct everywhere in order to secure the welfare and happiness of mankind became impressed upon my mind and heart, I found myself morally and religiously bound to recast in some important respects both my preaching and practice, so as to bring myself into harmonious accord with the new responsibilities thereby imposed on me.

Extracts from Diary, April-June 1838
Some of the changes I then felt impelled to make have already been noted at length, and others will be later on. Meanwhile, the more common and uneventful course of my life, after passing the thirty-fifth milestone, moved on (according to my diary) as follows:

Thursday evening, April 26. Lectured in a schoolhouse at West Medway, Massachusetts, upon "Universal Restorationism," from Job 32:10.

Sunday, April 29. Preached at home A.M. on "The Fidelity of Christ as a Teacher," from Mark 12:14; P.M. on "The Sunday School," from Proverbs 22:6. Also presided at the election of Sunday school officers for the coming year.

Monday, April 30. Ministered at funeral of Mrs. Otis Scott (South Mendon), preaching from Psalms 103:8-9.

Sunday, May 6. At home. Preached A.M. from Matthew 19:14; P.M. from 1 Corinthians 7:31. Lectured at 5 P.M. in schoolhouse at North Bellingham. Text, Luke 6:36.

Tuesday, May 8. Attended funeral of a third cousin, Charles Ballou,[1] Woonsocket, Rhode Island, preaching from Psalms 39:4.

Wednesday, May 9. Attended Young Men's Temperance Union meeting afternoon and evening. Home past 11 o'clock.

Sunday, May 13. At home. Communion day. Preached A.M. from Galatians 5:1; P.M. from Luke 17:17. Lectured at 5 P.M. in New England Village[2] on Matthew 24:46. Great attention and interest.

Sunday, May 20. At home. Preached A.M. from Ezekiel 36:37. Doctrine: "The promises of God to men are coupled with the requirement that they pray, seek, strive after, and fit themselves for, his gracious gifts"; P.M. from Luke 9:55. Subject, "Christ forbids the imprecation of the divine vengeance on enemies and the retaliation of injuries." 5 P.M. Lectured at North Bellingham on Matthew 25:46: "The severest threatenings against evil-doers are not in contravention of the sublime, far-reaching promises of God."

Thursday, May 24. Participated in the installation of Rev. Brother Lyman Maynard as pastor of the Second Congregational church and society in Hingham (South Hingham), an occasion of much spiritual interest and edification.[3] Rev. Paul Dean preached the sermon and I offered the consecratory prayer. Unitarian and Restorationist clergymen united cordially in the other parts of the service. The congregation was large and attentive; the several exercises were replete with ability, solemnity, and appropriateness; and every aspect of things was auspicious. In the evening, by particular request, I preached from 1 John 4:21, endeavoring to demonstrate that true piety and philanthropy are inseparable excellences of pure Christianity.

Sunday, May 27. Exchanged with Rev. Paul Dean, Boston, preaching A.M. from Ezekiel 18:23, and P.M. from Matthew 25:19. Lectured in evening from John 3:3, on "Regeneration, or the need of being born out of the animal life and earthly loves into the spiritual life and heavenly loves."

Sunday, June 3. At home. Preached A.M. and P.M. from the same texts as in Boston a week before. At 5 P.M. lectured in Baptist meetinghouse, West Medway, from Matthew 12:31-32; the text being left in the pulpit by some unknown person with the accompanying request that I speak upon it, which I was happy to do. The subject to be considered was "The sin against the Holy Ghost," or "The unpardonable sin." I discussed it under several heads: (1) What is the Holy Ghost? It is the manifestation of God's presence as a spirit, adapted to the comprehension of finite minds and revealing to them what is absolutely true, right, and good. (2) What is the peculiar nature and wickedness of sin against the Holy Ghost? It is the known transgression of the divine law, ascribing to Beelzebub what one understands belongs to God, or putting that which is false, wrong, wicked, with evil intent, into the place of what is true, right, and good. This is willful blasphemy. (3) What is the nature and effect of forgiveness? It is the merciful softening of the rigors of a just penalty for wrong doing by reason of the ignorance, frailty, or otherwise excusable characteristic of the offender, whereby he is exempt from more or less of the punishment which would ordinarily be visited upon him. (4) When is a sin not forgiven? When, by reason of its perverse and heinous character, he who commits it is condemned to suffer its entire punishment under the awards of absolute and unrestrained justice. (5) Can one thus unforgiven, and punished to the full extent of the penalty for his wrong doing, ever be redeemed from his iniquity and reconciled to God? Without doubt. Numerous instances of that sort are given in Scripture, to which I referred my hearers. If a man subject to the full penalty of the law is either by his suffering or in any other way made humble, penitent, and contrite – if he be brought by whatsoever means into a state of submission to the divine will and of trust in the divine mercy, God's favor will not be withheld from him, nor the smiles of His approbation be denied him. Neither reason nor scripture furnish any ground for believing otherwise, nor for believing that those who thus suffer will never abandon their sins and turn to God in true penitence and faith, but much to the contrary. The text, therefore, has a meaning perfectly consistent with the doctrine of the final triumph of good over evil and of the ultimate redemption of all mankind. The people were interested, instructed, and many of them, I think, convinced.

Sunday, June 10. At home. Communion service. I preached A.M. from John 13:17; P.M. I had a funeral discourse commemorative of the venerable Abigail Russell, the oldest of our church members, who departed this life May 30, in the ninety-third year of her age. She was a woman of excellent abilities, moral qualities, and social charms. She had been many years a widow, bore the increasing infirmities of old age with uncommon cheerfulness, and was held in high esteem by all who knew her. She was the mother of Hon. Jonathan Russell,[4] who was distinguished as a member of the United States Commission which negotiated the treaty of Ghent, whereby peace between this country and England was secured at the close of the war of 1812-1815. At 5 P.M. on the same day I delivered a temperance lecture at Holbrookville, in Northbridge.

Thursday evening, June 14. I gave an antislavery lecture in Upton and on the following evening, June 15, at East Medway.

Sunday, June 17. Exchanged with Rev. Luther Bailey[5] of East Medway. Preached A.M. from Ezekiel 18:23; P.M. from Hebrews 12:6; 5 P.M. a lecture appointed at Baptist meetinghouse, West Medway, was postponed on account of rain.

Sunday, June 24. At home. Preached A.M. from Luke 6:33. A sermon strongly impregnated with the doctrine of peace and non-resistance, the truth of which was rapidly growing to prominence in my mind. P.M. 2 Kings 8:13. The exclamation of Hazael, servant of the king of Syria, to Elisha, the prophet, upon being foretold of his own murderous cruelty to the Israelites when he should ere long rise to the throne. Moral: Few people know what powers of evil slumber within them, or suspect how wicked they may become under a change of circumstances, especially if elevated to positions of great worldly wealth and power. 5 P.M. Lectured in Farnumsville, Grafton, from Galatians 5:13: Lesson: "Prove by your lives that your liberty is not license; that your faith works by love, purifies the heart, and blesses mankind."

Thursday, June 28. The ordination and settlement of Brother William H. Fish at Millville, as successor of the lamented Rev. Edmund Capron, took place. The ecclesiastical council, consisting of eight ministers and two laymen, met at the residence of Col. Moses Buffum[6] in the morning, and after organizing, arranged the usual preliminaries of the public service, which was held in the house of worship, commencing at 2:30 o'clock, P.M. At that service Rev. William H. Kinsley offered the opening prayer; Rev. Isaac A. Pitman read the Scriptures; Rev. Charles Hudson delivered the sermon from 2 Timothy 2:15: "Study to show thyself approved unto God, a workman that needeth not to be ashamed, rightly dividing the word of truth." The consecrating prayer was by Rev. Samuel Clarke; charge, by myself; right hand of fellowship by Rev. A. St. Clair; address to the society, by Rev. Paul Dean; concluding prayer, by the same; and benediction by the new pastor.[7]

The whole ceremonial passed off satisfactorily, and a good degree of prosperity prevailed under the leadership of Brother Fish for some years. After the dissolution of the relation thus formed, by reason of changes incident to a manufacturing community in these later times, the church and society became extinct. The worthy pastor then ordained has done much general missionary work since, has had various settlements under Unitarian auspices, and still survives at this writing (1889), venerable in age and highly esteemed by all who know him. Through more than half a century of faithful service, he has proved true to his ordination vows and to the principles he then professed, "a workman needing not to be ashamed," "a good minister of Jesus Christ."[8]

Sermon Summaries

After the manner set forth in the preceding pages, I went on from week to week through the year and through the several years then passing, usually preaching morning and afternoon each Sunday, and delivering a lecture later in the day, with a lecture or two, or some ecclesiastical or reform convocation or funeral at which I always delivered a sermon, on intervening days. It is not desirable that I detail these labors in their order further. I will only, in passing to other matters, speak of certain special utterances of mine showing the state of my mind at the time and the general drift of my thought, theologically, morally, socially, etc., upon questions arresting the attention of the public on every hand.

Self-sacrifice. Text: Galatians 6:14. "God forbid that I should glory, save in the cross of our Lord Jesus Christ," etc. Self-sacrifice is the heavenly genius of pure Christianity. Jesus was the prince of self-sacrificers. The genius of the world is self-gratification, which degrades and disappoints all its votaries. But as self-sacrifice exalted and glorified Christ, the Savior of all lost souls, so it ennobles and glorifies all his faithful disciples. There is nothing else worthy to be gloried in. Let us learn, like Paul, to glory in nothing else and to seek nothing else as our highest good.

God's moral attitude towards sinners. Text: Ezekiel 18:23. "Have I any pleasure at all that the wicked should die," etc. God's infinite desire is that all sinners should turn unto Him and live, a desire which has given His beloved Son to the world to regenerate it and subdue it unto himself, and which will never rest satisfied till it be fulfilled – till through mercies and judgments, universal righteousness, peace, and joy prevail: till the divine kingdom come and the divine will be done on earth as it is in heaven. Let us cherish to the utmost the same desire, praying, laboring, and hoping confidently for the same glorious consummation.[9]

God's Repentance. Text: Jonah 3:10. "And God saw their works that they turned from their evil way; and God repented of the evil he said he would do unto them and did it not." A merely human manner of expressing the principle on which God invariably acts in forgiving sinners when seasonably and heartily penitent; because he delighteth in mercy and in the restoration of the lost. Let us therefore repent early of our own sins, and in imitation of our Heavenly Father delight in forgiving those who trespass against us, as soon as they manifest sincere sorrow therefor.[10]

The fountain of living waters. Text: Jeremiah 2:12-13. "Be astonished, etc., for my people have forsaken me, the fountain of living waters, and hewed them out cisterns, broken cisterns that can hold no water." God is indeed the fountain of living waters to his moral offspring. If they forsake him, expecting happiness in following their own flattering devices, whether as individuals or nations, those devices will prove to be broken cisterns that can hold no water of happiness. They utterly disappoint all who trust in them. All sin is suicidal to him who commits it, as it is contemptuous and rebellious towards the Great Creator.

Evil-doers left to themselves. Text: Psalms 81:12. "So I gave them up to their own hearts' lusts," etc. Thus God dealt with ancient Israel when they would not hearken to his voice, and thus he sometimes deals with people of these days – with individuals and nations – when they willfully cling to their iniquities in spite of wholesome counsel and reproof. Then they make haste to be miserable and wantonly prepare for themselves bitter punishments; as it is written, "Thine own wickedness shall correct thee and thy backslidings shall reprove thee!" Woe unto them that mingle wormwood and gall in the cup of their own sinful intoxication! Yet thanks be to God for overruling even this unto good.[11]

Prayer. Text: James 5:16. "The effectual prayer of a righteous man availeth much." That extraordinary results, in the physical world even, are recorded in the scriptures as having taken place in answer to prayer, we all know. Modern rationalism doubts the record and the possibility of any such answer to prayer on the ground that God governs the universe by fixed laws and never by special interposition. But there may be and probably are spiritual laws regulating the uses and effects of prayer, as there certainly are regulating the exercises and effects of human will-power. The so-called laws of nature or of God are not arbitrary rules by which the Supreme One is obliged to administer his government in the realm of matter, but orderly methods according to which men have learned that he usually acts. He is not a bondservant of law beyond his own control, but a free moral agent, operating according to his own choice and judgment. He may therefore modify or direct the movement of his laws in such a way as to answer prayer, not only in an ordinary, but in what seems to us an extraordinary manner. Otherwise, our petitions are superfluous and absurd. Let us pray fervently for what we think is best and reverently leave our Heavenly Father to answer as he deems fit. I cannot distrust the good effect of fervent prayer.

The Resurrection of Christ. Text: Luke 24:39. "A spirit hath not flesh and bones, as ye see me have." We are taught to believe in Christ's corporeal resurrection – that his spirit, which had not flesh and bones, re-entered and re-animated his crucified body, which had flesh and bones. This was an extraordinary manifestation of superhuman, God-given power, exercised in fulfillment of Christ's promise to His disciples for the confirmation of their faith. We are called upon to believe that the grosser elements of his body had been eliminated, leaving the organism so etherealized that he was able to render it visible or invisible, tangible or intangible to the external human sense, at will. Is this miraculous? Certainly, as we use words. We must believe in miracles of some sort if we believe in the credibility of the New Testament and in the claims of Christ to divine power as the Son of God, according to that record. Otherwise, we put ourselves outside of Christianity.

But I have made selections enough to serve the purpose for which I have quoted them, and now turn for a while to more miscellaneous topics and events.

Meeting of Massachusetts Association of Universal Restorationists, 1838

On Wednesday and Thursday, September 19 and 20, 1838, the Massachusetts Restorationist Association held its annual meeting in Brother Paul Dean's church, Boston, a preliminary session for more distinctively business purposes occurring on Tuesday evening, with a public service in the church afterward, at which a sermon was delivered by Rev. Matthew Harding,[12] temporarily in our fellowship. Discourses were preached as usual with accompanying devotional exercises on Wednesday, and a praise service took place in the evening. Thursday morning was devoted to Sunday School interests, and an association for the special furtherance of those interests was formed. At 3 p.m. I read my announced dissertation on "The Intermediate State." At 6 p.m. a prayer meeting was held in the vestry, and at 7 in the audience room. Brother Charles Gallagher, who had pursued his preparatory studies with Rev. Sylvanus Cobb,[13] Universalist minister at Malden, well known in after years, was ordained as an evangelist, the sermon being preached by Brother William Morse and the charge made by myself. The entire proceedings of the convocation passed off effectively and to the gratification of all, no further inharmonies arising in respect to the widely agitated reform movements of the time.[14]

An Unusual Ceremony

A somewhat unusual ceremonial – unusual in the ranks of liberal Christians – was observed on the thirtieth day of September at South Wilbraham, whither I had gone on a Restorationist missionary tour at the request of friends residing there. Having preached both morning and afternoon, I baptized by immersion, in the presence of a large concourse of people, two worthy disciples of our Restorationist faith, Joshua Stanton and John Calkins,[15] who thus desired to testify before God and men their belief in the principles which that faith stood for, and their consecration to a Christian life such as those principles required and were calculated to produce. The service was simple but reverent and impressive, and seemed to have a deeply religious effect upon those who witnessed as well as those who participated in it.

A Parishioner Elected to Congress

At the November election in 1838, Hon. William S. Hastings,[16] a leading citizen of the town and one of my most devoted and reliable parishioners, standing by me through all the excitement growing out of my espousal of the antislavery cause, was elected a member of Congress on the Whig ticket over his Democratic competitor, the distinguished Alexander H. Everett,[17] a minister to Spain under President John Quincy Adams. Mr. Hastings was eminently worthy of the honor thus conferred upon him, and proved to be so well qualified for the position that his constituents re-elected him in 1840 for a second term, during which he died.

First Christmas Celebration in Mendon

I presume that the reputed anniversary of the Savior's birth was never celebrated in my ancient Mendon parish, nor elsewhere in the vicinity, until the year 1838. Traditionary prejudice, an inheritance from our Pilgrim and Puritan ancestors, was strongly against it. But I suggested and encouraged a change from the long-prevailing custom, to which my people readily consented. Our sanctuary was accordingly appropriately and gracefully trimmed and well lighted for the evening of December 24, when I delivered a specially prepared discourse to a large and deeply interested congregation. My text was Isaiah 9:6-7: "For unto us a child is born, unto us a son is given," etc. Since that time celebrations of the event have prevailed more and more in the churches of this general region and indeed throughout the land, the descendants of the founders of New England of all shades of belief, vying with their Episcopalian and Roman Catholic brethren in making them attractive, significant, and impressive.[18]

Claims of the Cause of Peace

Early in the year in which the occurrences just noted took place, my attention was called to the claims of the cause of peace as opposed to the great war system of the world, in the more radical form it had lately assumed under the name of "Non-Resistance." This resulted in part, I suppose, from the general influence upon me of the two great reforms in the promotion of which I had become actively and earnestly engaged, and in part from the testimonies and appeals of those who had come forward as adherents and champions of the new movement, some of whom I knew to be persons of high character and of a generous, noble, philanthropic spirit.[19]

I did not have to consider the subject a great while before I saw very clearly that something of the kind had a basis in the scriptures of the New Testament and in the suggestions of an enlightened and spiritualized understanding. But I did not feel quite satisfied with the form in which its advocates presented it to the public, nor with the sweeping conclusions which they declared it logically and morally involved and even necessitated. And yet when I came to investigate the matter thoroughly in all its relations to and bearings upon human conduct, I was convinced that they were right and I wrong. I was also convinced that if its professed friends and receivers were consistent they would have to withdraw from all governmental society constitutionally committed to the war principle or to the use of deadly force in any case. As logical consistency was a part of my religion, I should be opposed to acting inside of any government as a coordinate factor therein while abjuring all responsibility for the execution of its constitutional provisions, among which was the carrying on of war and the visiting of penal vengeance upon offenders. I must be honestly inside or outside of all such governments. Here I paused and pondered.

Ought I to take a stand outside of the body politic as represented by the state and nation, and have nothing whatever to do with the administration of public affairs? This question was a serious one with me at the outset, and it was some time before I could answer it to my satisfaction. I went over all the arguments *pro* and *con* that had ever been presented to me or that I could frame out of my own earnest thought, but without definite result.

I finally looked to Christ to see if he did not provide a way of escape from my difficulty. I found that he nowhere inculcated, by precept or example, the duty of managing political concerns, of directing matters of state, of exercising the functions of citizenship in the existing governments of men. His kingdom was "not of this world." This fact he magnified and emphasized. And to the spirit and laws of the heavenly kingdom be enjoined uncompromising fidelity, even unto death. In subordination to that kingdom and as its earthly representative, he instituted a voluntary, fraternal association – the church – in which there were to be no titled magistrates or crowned sovereigns, but only chieftains and rulers who were *the servants of all*.[20] And this association was to transcend the righteousness of this world, rise above and supersede all human governments, abstain from all carnal strife with and violent resistance to established civil authority, even when tyrannical and cruel, submitting rather to its exactions meekly and thus proving itself true to the principles of Christ's gospel in the spirit of holy martyrdom. When I came to see and comprehend this, I stood in awe of its sublime wisdom and goodness. I bowed before it in adoring reverence; I yielded to my highest convictions; I became a Christian Non-Resistant.

But I did not become a blind, irrational one. It seemed to me clear that true Christian Non-Resistance was not mere *passivity*, nor sheer tameness and indifference in respect to evildoers, nor simple abstinence from physical force in the treatment of violent and wicked men, but abstinence from every kind of *injurious* and *unbeneficent* force whatsoever – from every act, word, feeling, towards evildoers which harms their bodies, minds, or spirits, or disregards their highest good and happiness as individual and social beings, for time and for eternity. All rebukes and restraints, all preventives and resistances of wrong doing, which do not in any way harm but benefit those subjected to them, which are accordant with the friendship and good will towards them, are not only consistent with *Christian* Non-Resistance, but are absolutely dictated by that godlike love out of which it springs. Such non-resistance is not abject submission to injustice and wrong – it is not recompensing evildoers with evil-doing, with harm, detriment, injury. It is radically different from the maxims, customs, usages, and laws of the different nations of the earth, whether savage or nominally civilized, and though greatly stigmatized and flouted by the worldly wise, is yet in my judgment an essential article in the orthodoxy of primitive Christianity, as it is a conclusion of the most enlightened reason.

Standard of Practical Christianity

In embracing this doctrine, it was a great satisfaction to me to know that it was logically and morally in harmony with my Restorationist theology and even requisite to its practical exemplification in individual and social life. It only required me to love my enemies and treat them in all regards as my Heavenly Father does, seeking their highest welfare in all my dealings with them, now and forever. Nevertheless, to my deep regret and sorrow, I found that this doctrine was offensive to some of my Restorationist brethren who were wedded to the popular opinion and practice upon the subject it involved, and I was the more grieved in that the new step I had taken seemed likely to break that bond of fellowship in which we had labored and sacrificed so earnestly and happily together for a common great and noble cause.

But I could not be false to my honest convictions, nor refrain from acting according to their dictates. An irresistible spiritual impulse within me seemed to set all ecclesiastical and worldly prudence at defiance. Under its guidance I called around me the few brethren who had manifested a sympathy with my views, and after much prayerful and deliberate conference we adopted and published the subjoined statement, to wit:

STANDARD OF PRACTICAL CHRISTIANITY[21]

Humbly desirous of promoting Christian piety and morality in their primitive purity, the undersigned do solemnly acknowledge the Principles, Sentiments, and Duties declared in the following Standard, viz.:

We are Christians. Our creed is the New Testament. Our religion is love. Our only law is the will of God. Our grand object is the restoration of man, especially the most fallen and friendless. Our immediate concern is the promotion of useful knowledge, moral improvement, and Christian perfection. We recognize no Spiritual Father but God; no master but Christ. We belong to that kingdom of "righteousness, peace, and joy" which is "not of this world";[22] whose throne is holiness, whose scepter is truth, whose greatness is humility, whose preeminence is service, whose patriotism is love of enemies, whose heroism is forbearance, whose glory is self-sacrifice, whose wealth is charity, whose triumphs are salvation. Therefore, we can make no earthly object our chief good, nor be governed by any motive but the love of *Right*, nor compromise duty with worldly convenience, nor seek the preservation of our property, our reputation, our personal liberty, or our life, by the sacrifice of Conscience. We cannot live merely to eat, drink, sleep, gratify our sensual appetites, dress, display ourselves, acquire property, and be accounted great in this world; but to do good.

All that we are and have, with all that God shall ever bestow upon us, we unreservedly dedicate to the cause of universal righteousness, expecting for ourselves in the order of divine providence only a comfortable subsistence until death, and in the world to come eternal life.

Placing unlimited confidence in our Heavenly Father, we distrust all other guidance. We cannot be governed by the will of man, however solemnly and formally declared, nor put our trust in an arm of flesh.[23] Hence we voluntarily withdraw from all interference with the governments of this world. We can take no part in the politics, the administration, or the defense of those governments, either by voting at their polls, holding their offices, aiding in the execution of their legal vengeance, fighting under their banners, claiming their protection against violence, seeking redress in their courts, petitioning their legislatures to enact laws, or obeying their unrighteous requirements. Neither can we participate in any rebellion, insurrection, sedition, riot, conspiracy, or plot against any of these governments, nor resist any of their ordinances by physical force, nor do anything unbecoming a peaceable submission to the existing powers; but will quietly pay the taxes levied upon us, conform to all innocent laws and usages, enjoy all righteous privileges, abstain from all civil commotions, freely express our opinions of governmental acts, and patiently endure whatever penalties we may for conscience' sake incur.

We cannot employ carnal weapons[24] nor any physical violence whatsoever to compel moral agents to do right, or to prevent their doing wrong – not even for the preservation of our lives. We cannot render evil for evil, railing for railing,[25] wrath for wrath, nor revenge insults and injuries, nor lay up grudges, nor be overcome of evil,[26] nor do otherwise than "love our enemies, bless them that curse us, do good to them that hate us, and pray for them that despitefully use us and persecute us."[27]

We cannot indulge the lust of dominion, nor exercise arbitrary authority, nor cherish bigotry, nor be egotistical, nor receive honorary titles, nor accept flattery, nor seek human applause, nor assume the place of dignity. We cannot be pharisaical, self-righteous, nor dogmatical. We cannot do evil that good may come.[28] We cannot resent reproof, nor justify our faults, nor persist in wrong-doing.

We cannot excommunicate, anathematize, or execrate an apostate, heretic, or reprobate person otherwise than withdrawing our fellowship, refusing our confidence, and declining familiar intercourse.

We cannot be cruel, even to the beasts of the earth. We cannot be inhuman, unmerciful, unjust, unkind, abusive, or injurious to any being of our race. We cannot be indifferent to the sufferings of distressed humanity, nor treat the unfortunate with contempt. But we hold ourselves bound to do good, as we have opportunity, unto all mankind; to feed the hungry, clothe the naked, minister to the sick, visit the imprisoned, entertain the stranger,[29] protect the helpless, comfort the afflicted, plead for the oppressed, seek the lost, lift up the fallen, rescue the ensnared, reclaim the wandering, reform the vicious, enlighten the benighted, instruct the young, admonish the wayward, rebuke the scornful, encourage the penitent, confirm the upright, and diffuse a universal charity.

We cannot go with a multitude to do evil,[30] nor take part with the mighty against the feeble, nor excite enmity between the rich and the poor, nor stand aloof from the friendless, nor abandon them that take refuge with us, nor court the great, nor despise the small, nor be afraid of the terrible, nor take advantage of the timid, nor show respect of persons,[31] nor side with a friend in what is wrong, nor oppose an enemy in what is right, nor forbid others to do good because they follow not us,[32] nor set up names and forms above personal holiness, nor refuse to cooperate with any man, class, or association of men on our own principles in favor of righteousness, nor contemn any new light, improvement, excellence, which may be commended to our attention from any direction whatsoever.

We cannot make a trade or emolument of preaching the gospel, nor be supported therein by unwilling contributions, nor keep back any truth thereof which ought to be declared, nor consent to preach anything more or less than God directs us, nor encourage religious devotion in mere worldly show, nor pursue any course of conduct whereby the *money*, the *smiles*, or the *frowns* of corrupt men may overrule the divine law and testimony. We cannot surrender the right of serving God according to the dictates of our own conscience, nor interfere with others in their exercise of the same liberty.

We hold it impossible to cherish a holy love for mankind without abhorring sin. Therefore, we can give no countenance, express or implied, to any iniquity, vice, wrong, or evil, on the ground that the same is established by law, or is a source of pecuniary profit to any class of men, or is fashionable in high life, or is popular with the multitude; but we hold ourselves bound so much the more to testify plainly, faithfully, and fearlessly against such sins. Hence, we declare our utter abhorrence of war, slavery, intemperance, licentiousness, covetousness, and worldly ambitions in all their forms. We cannot partake in these sins nor apologize for them, nor remain neutral concerning them, nor refrain from rebuking their various manifestations; but must forever abstain from and oppose them.

We cannot promote our own advantage at the expense of others by deceiving, defrauding, corrupting, degrading, overbearing, or impoverishing them. We cannot take away their good name by defamation, nor by retailing the scandal of their enemies, nor by spreading abroad evil reports on mere hearsay authority, nor by wantonly publishing their failings. We cannot be busybodies in other people's affairs, nor tale-bearers of domestic privacy, nor proclaimers of matters unsuitable for the public ear. We cannot rashly judge men's motives, nor raise evil suspicions against them, nor join in condemning the accused without a hearing, nor delay reparation to the injured, nor make any one's necessity our advantage, nor willingly render ourselves burdensome to others, nor cause any one a single unnecessary step for our mere gratification; but we will always deem it "more blessed to give than to receive,"[33] to serve than to be served – sacrificing *nothing of holy principle*, though, if need be, everything of personal convenience.

We cannot live in idleness, nor be careless or extravagant, nor on the other hand avaricious, parsimonious, or niggardly. We cannot indulge a feverish anxiety in any of our temporal concerns, nor fret ourselves under disappointment, nor repine at anything that marks our lot. We cannot be austere, morose, or rude; nor capricious, ungrateful, or treacherous. We cannot practice dissimulation, nor offer fulsome compliments, nor use a flattering courtesy. We cannot follow pernicious fashions, nor encourage theatrical exhibitions, nor join in frivolous amusements, nor countenance games of chance, nor array ourselves in costly apparel, nor wear useless ornaments, nor put on badges of mourning, nor distinguish ourselves by any peculiar formalities of raiment or language.

We cannot indulge to excess in eating, drinking, sleeping, recreation, labor, study, joy, or sorrow, nor permit our passions to tyrannize over our reason. We cannot harbor pride, envy, anger, malice, wrath, ill-will, sullenness, or peevishness; nor cherish any unholy lusts, imaginations, or tempers.

We cannot swear by any manner of oath, nor make any rash vows, nor offer any extraordinary protestations of our innocence, sincerity, or veracity; nor utter any blasphemy, imprecation, falsehood, obscene expression, foolish jest, or profane exclamation.

We cannot enter into the state of matrimony without grave deliberation and an assurance of divine approbation. We cannot neglect or abuse our families, nor evince any want of natural affection towards our bosom companion, our aged parents, or our helpless offspring. We cannot imbrute our children by disregarding their education, nor by setting them an evil example, nor by over-fondness, nor by harshness and severity, nor by corporeal punishment, nor by petulance and scolding.

We cannot neglect our brethren in their adversity, nor call anything our own when their necessities demand relief, nor be silent when they are unjustly accused or reproached. We cannot speak of their faults in their absence without first having conferred with and admonished them; nor then if they have promised amendment.

We cannot over-urge any person to unite with us, nor resort to undignified artifices of proselytism, nor seek debate with unreasonable men, nor protract a controversy for the sake of the last word, nor introduce sacred subjects for discussion in a company of scorners. Yet we will hold ourselves ready to give an answer to every one that asketh of us a reason for our faith, opinion, or conduct, with meekness, frankness, and patience.

Finally, as disciples of Jesus Christ, before whose judgment seat all must appear,[34] we acknowledge ourselves bound by the most sublime, solemn, and indispensable obligations to be perfect as our Father in heaven is perfect,[35] in all possible respects; and whereinsoever we come short thereof to take shame to ourselves, confess our sins, seek divine pardon, repair to the utmost our delinquencies, and bring forth fruits meet for repentance.[36] And for all this, our sufficiency is of God,[37] to whom be glory, world without end. Amen.[38]

ADIN BALLOU, DAVID R. LAMSON, GEORGE W. STACY,[39]
DANIEL S. WHITNEY, WM. H. FISH, *MINISTERS.*
CHARLES GLADDING,[40] WM. W. COOK,[41] *LAYMEN CONCURRING.*

This "Standard," when originally presented to the public, was accompanied by numerous references to those passages of scripture which were understood to teach the truths and duties set forth in its specifications. Also by an explanatory statement indicating the relation, practically, which those accepting it stood to existing churches, ecclesiastical bodies, and moral and social reform associations, and to the persons and parties composing them, all professedly working to the same great end of human elevation, redemption, and happiness. Furthermore, there was appended to it a series of resolutions taking strongly radical ground against the giant evils of human society – war, slavery, intemperance, licentiousness, covetousness, and sectarian bigotry – and in favor of their opposites, together with one recognizing, commending, and rejoicing in the many indications of a better time coming to the world – an era when sin and misery shall be known on earth no more forever.[42]

Whether we who put forth this manifesto fully understood what we were saying and realized our responsibilities, I have now serious doubts. And these doubts are confirmed by remembering how little we accomplished, and above all how far we fell short of our sublime ideal. Nevertheless, I believed when we adopted it that the principles, sentiments, and duties it embodied and inculcated were substantially true and obligatory, and I have never changed my mind, except with respect to a few comparatively unimportant declarations and phrases. I know that as a whole, it is not in accord with the popular Christianity of Christendom, but I am confident that it is in accord with the Christianity of the New Testament. And I am no less confident that it is indispensable to the regeneration and absolute happiness of mankind. If this made me a fanatic in 1839, I am a still greater one in 1889, though doubtless a wiser one by disciplinary experience.

The adoption and publication of the "Standard" widened the breach already opened between the conservative and progressive wings of our Restorationist body and hastened its dissolution. The former retained their places in the old order of society while the latter were impelled forward, entering alliances and taking up activities looking to a more Christlike type of civilization and leading more or less directly to the movement which two or three years later culminated in the Hopedale Community.

It may be proper to mention the fact that in connection with the consideration and adoption of the pronunciamento to which attention has just been directed, our Brother Daniel S. Whitney, another student of Rev. Paul Dean, was ordained as an evangelist, himself preaching the sermon, the other ministering brethren present taking part in the service. He was afterward settled as pastor at Middlesex Village,[43] West Boylston, and Berlin, and later became a participator in the enterprise at Hopedale alluded to.

Death of Father

I had but just passed the thirty-sixth anniversary of my birth in April, 1839, when I was summoned to the dying bed of my venerable father, who was nearing his end on the ancient homestead where he and all his children were born. I watched anxiously with him through one long night, but he was too far lost to the things of time to know me. The following day, April 28, his spirit was released from its mortal thralldom and ascended to the realm of the immortals. His age was eighty-one years, two months, and seven days. His funeral was solemnized May 1, with becoming ceremonial. He was an honest, conscientious man, served his day and generation well, and merited the grateful remembrance of his children.

Meeting of Massachusetts Association of Universal Restorationists, 1839

The Massachusetts Restorationist Association held its annual meeting for this year on the seventeenth and eighteenth of September, with Brother Lyman Maynard's parish at South Hingham. Rev. Paul Dean was chosen moderator, and Rev. Edwin M. Stone, clerk. Sermons were preached by Brothers Daniel S. Whitney, Edwin M. Stone, William Morse, and myself, with a closing address by Rev. Paul Dean. Discussions in council were pleasant, notwithstanding honest differences between the two wings.[44] I remained at South Hingham over Sunday by exchange with Brother Maynard and preached morning, afternoon, and evening.

Quarterly Conferences

Quarterly conferences, as they were termed, had been started under the auspices of our association, and were kept up with a considerable degree of regularity during the period covered by this chapter, and thenceforth in subsequent years. They were welcomed wherever we had a foothold, were occasions of exceeding interest, and accomplished much good. I took care to attend them all and to render them as profitable as was in my power. To increase their efficiency as a means of awakening and deepening the religious life, I made a compilation of about a hundred of the most reverential and inspiring hymns I could find, interspersed with a few original ones, which I had printed and put in a form convenient for use at these gatherings and at other times, and they proved most serviceable. Several of the brethren were men of deep and vital religious experience and of fervent piety, and their ministrations in that regard were highly appreciated and beneficial. These conferences, under the circumstances, were replete with salutary preaching, counsel, and devotional exercises, and gave our cause a decidedly spiritual as well as intellectual character. They helped to nourish the divine life in us all.

The New England Non-Resistance Society

My first appearance before the general public in my new role as a Christian Non-Resistant was at the annual meeting of the New England Non-Resistance Society, which was held in Boston on Thursday and Friday, the twenty-fourth and twenty-fifth of September, 1839. It was a most remarkable occasion – remarkable for its numbers, considering the unpopularity of the cause it represented, for the variety of its personal elements, for the free, unfettered utterance of diversified opinions, and for its uncompromising testimonies. Though not a member of the association, I was permitted to participate in its discussions, making an address on "Non-Resistance in its relation to human governments," which received high commendation. It was published in the organ of the society and in tract form, and had a wide circulation among reformers and in the general community. I deem it one of my best expositions of the subject upon which it treats and will try to have it preserved for the benefit of posterity. Of the society itself, its work, and ultimate extinction, I shall speak more fully hereafter.

End of the Independent Messenger and Beginning of the Practical Christian

The *Independent Messenger*, which was started under my superintendence in 1831 as the organ of the Restorationists, was suspended at the close of the year 1839, with the promise of an early resumption, which, however, was never fulfilled. It had passed into the hands of parties alien in no small degree to the spirit and purpose of its founders and incompetent to give it much vitality on any basis or in any behalf.[45] It had no sympathy and no encouragement for a progressive Christianity, on which account the reformatory wing of our body lost all interest in and withdrew all support from it. This, with other considerations, resulted in its speedy demise.

But those composing this wing, and especially the subscribers to the "Standard," were unsatisfied with the idea of having no organ through which to make known their principles, purposes, and doings to the world. They also felt the necessity of some bond of union among themselves – of some organization on their own ground, and accordingly formed an incipient one in the early months of 1840. This being accomplished, they then, though weak in numbers and in pecuniary resources, proceeded to lay plans and provide means for the publication of a small semi-monthly periodical, to be called the *Practical Christian*, the chief responsibility of its editorship and general management being assigned to me. The first number appeared April 1, 1840, just before the thirty-seventh anniversary of my birth, and thenceforth it was regularly issued for twenty years.

CHAPTER 17

1840-1842

For several years I had been comparatively free from editorial and other journalistic cares and responsibilities, but resumed them again, as before indicated, about the time of the opening of the period which the present chapter passes in review. The *Practical Christian*, our new periodical, of which I was given charge by my sympathizing associates, was but a small folio of four pages and could contain only a moderate amount of reading matter. Though it named "Mendon, Massachusetts" as the place of publication, yet for the first two years of its existence it had to be put to press at the nearest printing-office, either in Worcester, [Massachusetts] or Woonsocket, Rhode Island. It was devoted chiefly to the various reforms to which our section of the Independent Restorationists had professed adhesion, as set forth in the "Standard"; but it did not ignore our common Restorationist theology, inasmuch as all connected with its management believed and felt that that theology was the only basis upon which all reform, all true practical Christianity, logically rested. Both were therefore expounded and defended as inseparable counterparts and complements of each other. According to this view, which implies the vital relation existing in the nature of things between faith and works, theory and practice, fundamental principles and right action, belief and life, the *Practical Christian* was conducted during its entire existence.

Christian Union
An interesting religious movement bearing this designation originated in central New York a few years previous to the date of the occurrences just narrated. Its rallying cry was "Union of all Christians: Away with Sectarianism."[1] Among its progenitors and leading promoters was a no-less-distinguished personage than Gerrit Smith,[2] a world-renowned philanthropist, who, a few years before, had distributed a hundred thousand acres or more of his vast landed possessions among free negroes and other poor people, whereon to build homes for themselves and earn a livelihood. It had come to have so much of a foothold in central and eastern Massachusetts that in the summer of 1840 a general convention of its friends and those sympathizing with its declared sentiments and objects was called to meet in the town of Groton on the twelfth day of August. One Rev. Silas Hawley[3] seemed to be its chief representative in this part of the country and a prominent mover in getting up the Groton

convocation. The call for it was addressed "To all the friends of the Redeemer and of Reform." Our little group of progressives, though doubtful of a cordial welcome on account of what might be regarded as their theological heresies, were in a mood to hope something from such an ostensibly well-meant and philanthropic enterprise, and resolved to lend it, in a general way, their sanction. The meeting was accordingly announced with favorable comments in the *Practical Christian*,[4] and immediately after a pleasant conference of our own in Southborough, most of us repaired to Groton – myself and wife among the number. We were kindly received, respectfully treated, and so far had no cause of complaint.

But such a heterogeneous gathering assembled as can hardly be imagined, made up, as it was, of Christian Unionists proper, Perfectionists, Transcendentalists, Come-outers, and nondescript eccentrics of widely varying types and peculiarities. The whole number of enrolled members of the convention was about 275. Dr. Amos Farnsworth (residence unknown) was chosen president, and Edmund Quincy of Dedham, Oliver Johnson of Boston, and Lucius M. Burleigh of Plainfield, Connecticut, secretaries.[5] The parties interested in calling and providing for the meeting found themselves so involved with erratic and chaotic opinionists that they had hard work to control the proceedings or utilize the occasion to the advantage of their special cause. Many unacceptable subjects were introduced and warmly discussed; generally, however, in good temper. There was a large number of earnest talkers who dispensed profitable thoughts and suggestions as well as unprofitable ones, but few satisfactory conclusions were reached. Finally, as I recollect, the Christian Unionists succeeded in making their favorite and distinctive affirmations.[6] These in condensed form were that sectarianism is abhorrently anti-Christian and that the divided branches of the professed Christian church ought to come at once into harmonious fellowship. How this was to be done was not stated, nor was it found practically possible to realize it, even among those present. Could it have been accomplished there and extended thence throughout Christendom, it would have produced little improvement in the popular theology or ethics, or in the characters and lives of men. Names and externals might have been changed, but not *evil things*. I tried to be just and generous to these self-styled reformers, but was obliged to conclude that their aims and claims were comparatively superficial, and that, whatever their merits, we of the Practical Christian household of faith could derive no special edification from them.

Communities

Soon after the publication of our "Standard of Practical Christianity," my mind began to be exercised with the question of how it could be actualized. How could the principles and sentiments it contained be made the basis of individual and social life? I could not suppress this inquiry on my own part and my brethren were burdened with the same problem. To treat our declaration of principles and duties as a mere speculation or rhetorical flourish would be alike false to our highest convictions and "disobedient to the heavenly vision"[7] – it would be both inconsistent and wicked. We must not only preach but live by what we had received as truth, or else renounce it honestly as impracticable.

Conscience and a proper self-respect forbade its renunciation. There was no honorable retreat for us; we must go forward. But if we went forward, to whom could we look for cooperation and support? With whom could we affiliate in carrying our declared theories into effect? We had broken with the existing social system in three fundamental respects – in respect to (1) the non-resistance of evil with evil, (2) the serviceship of superiors, and (3) the fraternization of property. And we could not suppose for a moment that those who believed in and were a part of the existing order of society would encourage and aid us in preaching what was in its very nature opposed to and subversive of that order, or in any attempts we might make to establish and build up one that was radically different from it and designed in due time to supersede it in the administration of human affairs. We had nothing whatever to hope for from that quarter, either in the way of maintaining our ministry in the promulgation of the principles we had avowed, or in any effort we might put forth to apply and carry out those principles to their logical and moral results in life's varied interests and concerns. We must therefore depend on ourselves, under divine providence, and on the converts we could make to our cause in both its theoretical and practical aspects.

Here, then, we took our stand. For us there was no other alternative. Upon the Practical Christian platform which we had adopted and given to the world, we must try to build a new civilization radically higher than the old, which should hold inviolate the distinctive principles of truth and duty just enumerated and declared by us to be essential to the realization of a divine order of human society founded on the great ideas of the fatherhood of God and brotherhood of man. Could we hope to succeed in such an enterprise as this? We were credulous enough to believe that with the favor of heaven we might. At least we must try, however we might fail. In the light of a bitter experience our presumption now seems almost insane. But we were honest and conscientious, and perhaps our endeavors were necessary and useful, all things considered, as contributing to the final solution of the great social problem which still confronts the Christian philosopher and philanthropist.

As to the course we were to pursue in order to realize our purpose, we were for some time much in doubt. We were new converts to our own principles and ideas – novices even in our theoretical positions, and wholly inexperienced in everything like the practical workings of what we vaguely contemplated as the ultimate outcome of our movement. Moreover, we had nothing to guide us or help us in the experience of others. Nothing like what we were to undertake had been attempted before since the world was made. We were pioneers in the field of social reconstruction and must work our way along with such wisdom as we possessed;

slowly, cautiously, as best we could, until the end we sought was gained or failure obliged us to relinquish our efforts in that direction.

For a few months, my coadjutors and myself as their leader entertained and discussed somewhat indefinitely the plan of purchasing a common farm, settling upon and running it as a means of mutual physical self-support – making it a sort of missionary post whence our preachers might go forth to localities where an opportunity was offered us, like the apostles of old, and proclaim an untrammeled gospel as we understood it in its application to all the affairs of life. This plan, after much consideration, grew into the more ample one of a community, which should be composed of a considerable number of persons sympathizing with us and representing a variety of interests pertaining to the welfare and prosperity of society. Having deliberated sufficiently, as I thought, upon the subject, I issued in the *Practical Christian*, on the fifteenth of September, 1840, an article entitled "Communities," in which I announced and explained our private discussions and the result to which they brought us: *the desirability of establishing a colony of persons pledged to the principles of our standard, for mutual encouragement and support in proclaiming and exemplifying those principles before the world.*[8] In that communication I endeavored to answer many questions which would naturally be asked by persons of a practical turn of mind concerning such an undertaking, even going so far as to present a *suggestive constitution* for its general management. I also, in closing, set forth what I thought would be the advantages of the proposed scheme, as follows:

> Such a community would furnish a happy home to many pure-hearted Christians now scattered abroad, insulated from each other, ignored or maligned by a corrupt church, and oppressed by the unregenerate world. It would enable them to secure, with less severe toil and more certainty, a comfortable subsistence for themselves and their dependents. It would render it much easier for them to reform many pernicious habits of living and to promote the true physical health and comfort of themselves and families. It would remove them from the dominion of many corrupt and demoralizing influences to which they are now exposed. It would enable them to set up and maintain a purer religious worship, a holier ministry, a more salutary moral discipline, and altogether a better spiritual state of things than they now enjoy. It would enable them to send forth true-hearted religious, moral, and philanthropic missionaries into the surrounding world for its conversion; men and women who would not be bribed or frightened into subserviency to popular iniquities, and who, when weary, might return, like Noah's dove, to the window of a peaceful ark and find repose. It would enable them more effectually to prosecute every branch of moral reform and human improvement by means of the press, of well-ordered schools, and of teachers qualified to go out and inculcate our holy principles wherever people might welcome them. It would enable them to bring up their children "in the nurture and admonition of the Lord,"[9] free from those loose and corrupting influences so prevalent elsewhere. It would enable them to establish asylums for the orphan, the widow, and the outcast, in which they might

be duly cared for and directed into the paths of life. In fine, it would be a powerful concentration of moral light and heat, which would make "Practical Christianity" known and felt by the world.

Blessed dream, aspiration, and hope! but whose realization was too liable to be frustrated and indefinitely postponed by the frailty, inconsistency, and backsliding of its professed devotees!

Nevertheless, the undertaking was urged ardently and carried forward to very promising attainments. Its development was the theme of my profoundest study and my most constant efforts. All ordinary duties were performed with my accustomed fidelity, but more or less subordinately to the actualization of this darling project, which commanded the best energies of my primal manhood, and which, if we had possessed sufficient pecuniary means, I flatter myself would have risen to a triumphant success. But we were continually dependent on the will of those who could not love the cause as I and some of my early fellow-laborers did – albeit the former wrought well for it while their devotion lasted. It may have been, however, on the other hand, that had I chanced to have been wealthy by some fortuitous combination of causes, I should not have possessed the mind and heart to enlist in such a philanthropic, disinterested, and noble enterprise.

The Fraternal Communion

Little more was published concerning our proposed movement until, by patient elaboration, I had matured what I deemed a suitable constitution and submitted it to the careful consideration of those most interested, in a series or meetings held for that purpose. Meantime, my wife, who at first demurred at embarking in such a responsible and uncertain experiment, gave her adhesion to it, and several others pledged it their encouragement. In fact, matters progressed so rapidly that at a quarterly conference held at Mendon in January, 1841, a definite organization with a general constitution was effected, under the name of "The Fraternal Communion." This provided for the establishment of local communities wherever feasible, and one was immediately formed by those present who were ready to unite for practical operations. This body was first called "Fraternal Community No. 1," afterwards "The Hopedale Community."

It consisted of about thirty persons at the outset, and its affairs were placed in charge of a provisional committee consisting of Adin Ballou, E. D. Draper, Nathan Harris,[10] William H. Fish, Henry Lillie,[11] David R. Lamson, Daniel S. Whitney, and George W. Stacy, who received such instructions as seemed needful to insure the practical realization of their aims at the earliest possible date. Among the duties with which these persons were charged was that of collecting "such information as they may be able, respecting the location of the proposed community, the form and construction of buildings, the internal economies of communal and boarding establishments, hospitals, etc.; respecting agriculture, manufactures, and education; and any other matters likely to promote the prosperity of our enterprise." One hundred dollars were appropriated for the use of the committee, as they were expected to go to work at an early day. This imposed heavy responsibilities upon me as chairman of the same. What came of all this will be recounted in due time.

Other Socialistic Experiments

A remarkable wave of social inspiration, aspiration, and experimentation swept through our country during the year 1840, resulting in numerous attempts similar to our own not long afterward. One of these was made at Northampton, Massachusetts, under the leadership of George W. Benson, previously of Brooklyn, Connecticut, which had a character and form of organization peculiarly its own.[12] Another, called the North American Phalanx, located in Monmouth County, New Jersey, was based upon principles first promulgated by a French philosopher and philanthropist, Charles Fourier, and introduced into this country by Albert Brisbane, Parke Godwin, Horace Greeley, and others.[13] Several were started under various auspices in the Western States, most of which were of a temporary duration.[14] Rev. George Ripley, a Unitarian clergyman of the transcendental school, whose name appears in a preceding chapter, and a few sympathizing coadjutors projected the Brook Farm experiment in [West] Roxbury upon a plan of their own devising, though, in some of its later phases, it possessed many characteristics of the Fourier System.[15]

It is a somewhat singular fact that our "Fraternal Communion" originated altogether independently of the general agitation referred to, and of the movements mentioned, as it did in utter unconsciousness of the existence of any published expositions of the general subject of social reconstruction. It grew primarily out of New Testament Christianity as we understood it, as a practical issue of its essential spirit, principles, and precepts; though our general reading and acquaintance with what was going on in the world soon advised us of the broader field of discussion and experiment which others, in this and foreign lands, were occupying. When this occurred, we availed ourselves of the opportunity of examining their theories and suggestions, hoping to get some light not before obtained upon the problem we were earnestly trying to solve. But to little profit. For after comparing the various schemes accessible to us with our own, we preferred the latter with the peculiarities which distinguished it from each and every other brought to our notice.[16]

A very kindly feeling sprang up between us and our Brook Farm neighbors, and there was much friendly conference and correspondence between us, looking to a union of the two movements. Mr. Ripley and his associates were very cordial and earnestly urged us to join them at West Roxbury. The temptation was strong for us to do so. We were few, poor, and comparatively unlearned. They were more numerous, rich, and scholarly. In these respects they could be of great service to us and our children. On the other hand, we could be a help to them in more ordinary ways. But there were serious, insuperable objections to anything of the kind proposed. Their transcendentalism and individualistic independence made them quite averse to our views upon historic and authoritative Christianity, to our positive ethical position on several important points of doctrine and duty, and to our uncompromising religious and reform pledge. On our own ground, which we had carefully and conscientiously chosen, we were equally averse to their extreme views of personal liberty and their noncommittalism. Such being our incompatibilities, neither party being able to yield to the other without giving up some things it regarded as most sacred in principle and most vital to success, we wisely decided to close all negotiations in peace and mutual good will, and go our own respective ways.

Hopedale

In proceeding to get ourselves into proper working order, it seemed desirable to abridge and modify somewhat the fundamental basis of our association as expressed in the constitution of our "Fraternal Communion." Our prolix "Standard of Practical Christianity" was consequently condensed into the following "Declaration," to be openly made by each individual entering our membership:

> I believe in the religion of Jesus Christ as he taught and exemplified it according to the scriptures of the New Testament. I acknowledge myself a bounden subject of all its moral obligations. Especially do I hold myself bound by its holy requirements never, under any pretext whatsoever, to kill, assault, beat, torture, rob, oppress, persecute, defraud, corrupt, slander, revile, injure, envy, or hate any human being – *even my worst enemy*; never in any manner to violate the dictates of pure chastity; never to take or administer an oath; never to manufacture, buy, sell, deal out, or use any intoxicating liquor *as a beverage*; never to serve in the army, navy, or militia of any nation, state, or chieftain; never to bring an action at law, hold office, vote, join a legal posse, petition a legislature, or ask governmental interposition *in any case involving a final authorized resort to physical violence*; never to indulge self-will, bigotry, love of preeminence, covetousness, deceit, profanity, idleness, or an unruly tongue; never to participate in lotteries, games of chance, betting, or pernicious amusements; never to resent reproof or justify myself in a known wrong; never to aid, abet, or approve others in anything sinful; but, through divine assistance, always to recommend and promote with my entire influence the holiness and happiness of all mankind.

As chairman of the provisional committee of Fraternal Community No. 1, I proceeded, as soon as practicable, to the discharge of the duties assigned us, with such assistance as my colleagues could conveniently render.[17] I wrote a full exposition of our constitution, which need not be inserted here, but which was published and will appear in full in my proposed *History of the Hopedale Community*.[18]

The second meeting of our newly-formed association was held in Boylston, then the parochial home of Brother George W. Stacy, April 28 and 29, in connection with our regular quarterly conference.[19] Interesting friendly letters which I had received from Rev. Dr. William Ellery Channing,[20] Edmund Quincy, Gerrit Smith, and other notable philanthropists were read; the provisional committee made a report of their doings which was accepted as satisfactory, and the members were discharged from further service. No selection of a location for a Community home had been made, but much needful preliminary information had been obtained, and our prospects were full of promise. Several new members were admitted to our fellowship and fraternal enthusiasm waxed ardent. The respective officers required by the constitution, composing an executive council, were chosen, I being president, and were to serve till the first Wednesday in January, 1842, the day and month designated for the holding of the regular annual meeting of the body.[21] The Community was now properly organized and made ready to start out on its chosen mission.

The third meeting took place in connection with the quarterly conference at Millville, Brother William H. Fish's parish, August 26 and 27 following.[22] The executive council made a cheering report of progress in the march of affairs. Localities for the Community had been examined and one selected as decidedly preferable to all others. This was a farm in Milford containing 258 acres, which had a considerable stream of water called Mill River running through it, with a good fall for mill sites, and other natural advantages suited to our prospective needs. The land, however, was much run down in culture and the buildings were correspondingly dilapidated. It had long been known in the vicinity as the "Jones Farm," deriving that name from an early proprietor, and was sometimes called "The Dale," by reason of its situation. It had been offered for sale on moderate terms and was likely to find a ready purchaser. It seemed so well suited to our purposes that I, on my own responsibility, fearing the chance of obtaining it might be lost, had closed a bargain for it on the thirtieth of June, two months before. The council had examined the estate critically, approved of my action, and concurred with me in recommending its purchase by the Community. The recommendation was accepted, and our whole proceeding was unanimously and joyously ratified by our constituency. This included the christening I had given the domain, "Hopedale" – a name which united the high expectations we cherished for the future of our movement with the previous appropriate designation of the pleasant valley in which those expectations were to be realized. All our members hailed the name with delight as most happily chosen and befittingly applied.

At this meeting, important resolves were passed, bylaws, rules, and regulations were adopted, and all necessary preparations authorized for taking possession of our new home at the earliest possible date. Groups of friends soon after made pleasant excursions to Hopedale, and all were enthusiastically impatient to inaugurate the contemplated undertaking there. In the opening autumn I decided upon the general outlines of a village site and had it surveyed and laid out by my ever kind friend, Newell Nelson, Esq., who had previously taken the measurement of the fall in the river with a view to its subsequent utilization for mechanical purposes, his services being rendered gratuitously as a token of his good will towards me and the cause. In October, Brother Henry Lillie, one of our council, settled himself and family in a part of the ancient Jones domicile accorded to him by the resident tenant, Cyrus

Ballou,[23] a nephew of mine, through whom, as agent, I had purchased the premises. About the first of December, Mr. Ballou, by mutual arrangement, moved out of the house altogether, and Brother Nathan Harris with his wife and four children took possession of the rooms thus vacated.

The fourth meeting of the Community – its prescribed annual meeting – convened in Mendon, January 5 and 6, 1842, the quarterly conference being held under the same auspices.[24] The occasion was one of great religious interest and edification. While the exercises pertaining more directly to the conference were unusually earnest, impressive, and refreshing, the proceedings of the Community were eminently cheering and satisfactory. Not a jar of discord or distrust broke the happy unanimity of spirit, action, purpose, and hope that prevailed. The report of the executive council was encouraging, and called forth many expressions of gratification and delight. Eight new members were received into our fellowship and three persons became probationers for future consideration and approval, if deemed worthy. Official servants for the ensuing year were elected as follows:

ADIN BALLOU, *President*
WILLIAM W. COOK, *Secretary*
DAVID R. LAMSON, *Auditor*
LEMUEL MUNYAN,[25] *Intendant of Finance and Exchange*
EBENEZER D. DRAPER, *Intendant of Agriculture and Animals*
HENRY LILLIE, *Intendant of Manufactures and Mechanical Industry*
DR. BUTLER WILMARTH,[26] *Intendant of Health and Domestic Economy*
DANIEL S. WHITNEY, *Intendant of Education, Arts, and Sciences*
WILLIAM H. FISH, *Intendant of Religion, Morals, and Missions*.

For other particulars, see *History of the Hopedale Community*. Provision was made at this meeting for the settlement of at least ten families on or near the Hopedale territory the following spring and early summer.

The new social experiment was now fully organized and put in the way of speedy actualization. Thenceforth there was a steady rush of activities till we took full possession of our Community home about the first of April, 1842, and, of course, no cessation thereof occurred afterward. The number of persons anxious to commence residence and occupation with us at Hopedale was quite in excess of our domiciliary accommodations, as it was also of our means of profitable employment. Important expectations were sometimes disappointed as a consequence, and even honest pledges, it was found, could not always be fulfilled. Our pecuniary obligations, which were heavy considering our circumstances, had to be provided for and reputably met, as they were then and forever afterward.

Before the close of March, seven families and one unmarried member, aggregating twenty-eight persons, occupied the "old house," forming a unitary household, over which myself and wife presided by unanimous consent. We boarded at common tables and lodged in small but distinct apartments, too small and cluttered for comfort, yet passably endurable. Our faith, hope, and zeal enabled us to bear many privations, inconveniences, trials, vexations, disgusts, with reasonable patience and composure. Under ordinary circumstances, they would have seemed simply intolerable. We gradually settled into our respective places, took up our several lines of duty, and the wheels of our unique social mechanism revolved with something of their intended regularity, quietness, and efficiency.

End of the Massachusetts Association of Universal Restorationists

From the details of our new life at Hopedale, I now turn to other items of personal experience.

The Massachusetts Restorationist Association gradually declined in interest and usefulness from the time when our reform wing began to push their convictions of duty beyond the approval of their more conservative brethren. These, however, tolerated and endured us until we promulgated our "Standard of Practical Christianity," when they honestly gave us up as impracticable fanatics, with whom they could go no further. I knew that I was largely responsible for what so disaffected and disappointed them. It was strange almost to myself that it was so – that I, who had devoted myself so ardently to the cause represented by that association, as if it were a finality, should have come to be so transcendentally interested in moral reform, even to the extreme of social reorganization, that I was ready to give that body up or let it cease to be.

How did all this come about? I had not repented of my protest against ultra Universalism; I had no regrets for helping to form the Restorationist Association; I had not renounced or come to undervalue my Restorationist theology. On the contrary, I regarded that theology as dearer than ever before, and felt that every one of my reformatory advances was in strict logical consistency with its fundamental truths. Nor was I in any way disposed to fall out with any of my brethren of the Restorationist faith and play the eccentric, but the opposite was true, and nothing troubled me so much as to alienate myself from their fellowship and approbation. The fact is, I felt impelled from step to step in my course, often reluctantly on my part, by a power within and above me which I could not resist and which then seemed and still seems divine. The truth involved in the great philanthropic movements I had engaged in had been revealed to me and I could not but act in accordance with it. My own avowed religious principles and ideas – the universal fatherhood of God, the universal brotherhood of men, the all-redeeming grace of Christ, the final redemption of all men – these all, in their practical application, tendencies, and results, not only suggested, but required, *necessitated* the course I felt myself sacredly bound to pursue. Logical and moral consistency, supplemented by an agency higher, mightier than my own, determined my action, even to the extent of Non-Resistance and Practical Christian socialism, and I could do no otherwise than I did. "Woe was me if I did not preach that gospel"[27] and order my life accordingly.

The Restorationist Association held a meeting with Brother Charles Hudson's parish in Westminster, October 14 and 15, 1840.[28] This was not long after the more advanced of us had taken our stand in favor of a new social order, and this fact may have had something to do in giving tone and character to our proceedings, though no direct reference was made to our action in that respect. Brother Lyman Maynard was moderator and I was scribe of the ministerial council. Public exercises took place in the church, at which sermons were preached by Brothers William H. Fish, Norwood Damon,[29] Lyman Maynard, and myself, and were accompanied by customary singing, prayers, and exhortations. In council, an interesting discussion took place upon the general question whether or not combinations of persons have any moral authority or right to do what their members as individuals cannot rightfully do. Brother Hudson read a carefully prepared dissertation on "Expediency," which was also fully discussed. These discussions naturally called out the ethical differences between conservative and reformatory brethren, but they were all conducted in an amicable manner.

Indeed, the entire meeting was a remarkably pleasant, edifying, and satisfactory one, both to the ministers and laity present. I was appointed a committee to select a place for the next annual gathering and notify the brethren accordingly, and was also requested to write a dissertation for the occasion. But this convention at Westminster proved to be the last one ever held. I notified another, as provided for, to convene at Millville, August 26 and 27, 1841, when our Practical Christian quarterly conference was to meet. But only one or two of the conservative members were there, and no organization of the association was deemed advisable. No arrangements were made for another gathering of that body, and so, at ten years of age, it fell quietly asleep to wake no more.

The quarterly conferences, so frequently spoken of, occurred regularly during this period of 1840-42, under the auspices of our Fraternal Communion, and were characterized by great fervency of spirit and unabated interest. They took place mostly in central and eastern Massachusetts, and were the most soul-stirring and religiously profitable gatherings it has been my privilege to attend during my long life of four score years and more.

Reform Labors

At the time of which I am now writing, I was much engaged in connection with my regular ministerial duties in Mendon and their collateral activities; in giving lectures upon humanitary subjects about the country, sometimes far from home; and in attending reform anniversaries in Boston, and conventions held in the same interest at various points elsewhere. On these occasions, especially when I had the exercises in charge, it was my custom to extend to any persons present differing from me an opportunity to state their views, and to invite questions and objections that I might answer them. This often gave much additional interest and effect to the proceedings.

A memorable instance of this kind occurred at Concord, Massachusetts, in February, 1841. I had been engaged to lecture there before the town lyceum on the subject of Non-Resistance. A large audience, including many of the literary and professional elite of that community, honored me with their presence and with a respectful hearing. At the close of my regular address, the usual privilege being granted, I was plied with a goodly number of the hardest questions their sharpest critics could devise. I was favored with a good measure of spiritual inspiration, answered their inquiries as successfully as I could, kept all in good humor, and at the close was cordially congratulated by the venerable and Honorable Samuel Hoar, father of the present Senator George F. Hoar,[30] who, though not a Non-Resistant, was an advanced International Peace man, and gave me his best wishes for the conversion of the people at large from their idolization of brute force to a more kindly and humane attitude of mind and heart.

This visit to Concord was memorable to me as furnishing the only opportunity I ever had of a personal interview with the distinguished Ralph Waldo Emerson.[31] It was a pleasant one, being devoted chiefly to a free conversation between us upon questions of reform, but fruitful of no important results.

Bereavements

Two severe bereavements threw their shadow across the pathway of my mortal pilgrimage in the early part of 1841. The first was the death, at Milford, January 7, of Rev. John Dale.[32] He was an Englishman by birth, and for a time a devoted Methodist clergyman, who, emigrating to this country, was brought into contact with our little band of Practical Christian Restorationists, finally adopting our views and dying in the full hope of a blissful immortality, not only for himself but ultimately for all mankind. Besides being a most excellent man, he was a valued personal friend, and his demise was a great loss to me, as it was to the cause of pure and undefiled religion.

The second afflictive visitation referred to was the decease, on February 27, of the mother of my first wife and grandmother of my now only surviving child – Mrs. Abigail (Scott) Sayles, wife of Smith Sayles of Smithfield, Rhode Island. She was one of the best of women and all my recollections of her are precious.[33]

Two Notable Letters

Before closing this chapter, it seems fitting that I should refer somewhat particularly to two remarkable letters relating to the movement of which I was the reputed leader, that came to me during the year 1841.

One of these, already referred to, was from Rev. William Ellery Channing, D.D., of Boston, then at the height of his fame as an able and eloquent divine and as the foremost champion of the great revolt which sprung up a few years before against Calvinism and all allied forms of theological belief. It is not necessary to insert it here, but I desire to say that it was an admirable communication – worthy of its illustrious author! Friendly, kind, candid, breathing noble aspirations, sentiments, and benedictions, and replete with wise suggestions. I appreciated it highly at the time of receiving it, and more highly after serious experiences in Community life. It may be found in full in *Channing's Memoirs*, prepared by his nephew, William Henry Channing, vol. 3, pp. 119-122, and will appear in my history of the Community.[34]

A few months later there came to hand an elaborate letter on the same subject, though of a very different character, from Rev. Paul Dean, formerly of Boston, but at the time preaching at Westminster as successor of Rev. Charles Hudson. Preceding pages have shown the close and sacred relationship in which I long stood to Brother Dean in the Restorationist movement, and how we drifted apart by reason of my espousal of the great reforms. The Community enterprise completed the estrangement between us. He was fatally grieved and perhaps disgusted that I should go to such extremes, and I suppose gave me up as hopelessly bewildered if not fatally demented.

Brother Dean, unlike Dr. Channing, never dreamed of an ideal Christian community in which the members, "instead of preying upon one another and seeking to rise above one another after the fashion of this world, should live together as brothers seeking each other's elevation and spiritual growth,"[35] to be established by human thought, effort, and cooperation, in the spirit of Jesus Christ. He looked for the kingdom of God to come on the earth in the old miraculous way and traditional millennial form. Until it should so come, society must go on with some gradual improvement perhaps, but substantially in the future as in the past. He was entirely sincere in this view, and had not one particle of faith in the so-called "Fraternal Communion" I had devised and was about to inaugurate. He *knew* all such schemes were but *bursting bubbles*, people universally being too selfish, weak, capricious, untrustworthy, to do right and live together voluntarily in any such way as that proposed. With such views and feelings, he wrote his letter as a warning to me and a final protest against my absurd undertaking. Two or three brief letters respecting the publication of this lengthy missive and an open reply to it from me, to which he seemed to object, closed all correspondence between us.[36] We never met but once afterward – at the funeral of a mutual friend in Roxbury, in 1857. He died three years later at Framingham, aged 77 years, 6 months, and 21 days.

Close Of Mendon Pastorate

From the time when it was decided that an attempt should be made to put our new social theories into practical operation at Hopedale, the general expectation and understanding among our members were that I and my family would be among the earliest to locate there. As I had led off in avowing and promulgating the principles of a reconstructed order of human society and in formulating plans and methods of action in accordance with those principles, so must I lead off in the work of carrying the plans and methods devised into effect. Hence, as the date when we were to come into complete possession of the purchased property drew near, and when actual operations under Community auspices were to begin, which was the date of the termination of my pastoral engagement at Mendon, I made all necessary arrangements for removal thither. I preached my valedictory discourse to an overflowing house on the afternoon of March 27, 1842, from 2 Corinthians 13:11: "Finally, brethren, farewell. Be perfect, be of good comfort, be of one mind, live in peace; and the God of love and peace shall be with you." It was published in the *Practical Christian* of June 25, 1842. The occasion was a profoundly interesting, impressive, and affecting one – one long remembered by those participating in it. Thus closed my ministry of eleven years and two months as pastor of the First church and society in Mendon. Thenceforth my story hails from Hopedale, where I at once located.

First Religious Meetings at Hopedale

The first public religious meeting on our new domain was held the Sunday following that just spoken of, April 3, in our ancient domicile, about 120 years old. It was a day of sacred meaning and solemnity, inasmuch as on that day we dedicated ourselves anew and our domain to the service of God and humanity. There were twenty-eight of us residents on the premises, who, with a considerable number of friends from the neighborhood, made a very respectable congregation. Our enthusiasm ran high, notwithstanding our temporal poverty, limited circumstances, and uncertain outlook for the future. In the morning I preached an earnest discourse from Psalm 133:1: "Behold how good and how pleasant it is for brethren to dwell together in unity." In the afternoon Brother Daniel S. Whitney, as chief speaker, resumed the joyful strain while I added my exhortation. We were all happy, little dreaming that we were ever to be otherwise, although even then disappointment and sadness awaited us at no great distance ahead.

Thursday, April 7, was the annual State Fast Day. A public meeting convened, agreeably to custom in general society outside. No sermon was delivered, but we had several excellent addresses. The great pleasure was given us of entertaining for the first time Frederick Douglass, the famous fugitive slave, and of being more than entertained by his stirring words.[37] He remained with us some days and did much during his stay to break into floating fragments much of the pro-slavery ice of Milford and vicinity. Memorable times those!

I have no memorandum of what transpired at Hopedale on Sunday, April 10, but a week later I preached in the morning, ministered at a funeral in Mendon early in the afternoon, and at 4 o'clock attended a temperance lecture there delivered by the celebrated John H. W. Hawkins of Washingtonian reform movement distinction.[38] An ample delegation from Hopedale swelled the large concourse of people present, and a lecturer could never have been more triumphantly eloquent. Our Community, having undertaken with its infant hands to encourage and help all efforts to uplift humanity, was called upon to appear at the front on many similar occasions in our general neighborhood.

CHAPTER 18

1842-1845

Man is naturally a religious being and also a responsible moral agent. As a religious being, he instinctively looks up to, reverences, adores, worships some kind of deity, power, or authority, which to him is supreme, absolute, and irresistible, and which he must submit to and obey or suffer loss. As a moral agent, he is conscious of an essential difference between right and wrong, good and evil, and of an inherent ability, to an indefinite extent, to choose, follow after, and act the right and good as against the wrong and evil, thereby fulfilling his duty in the varied relationships of life, and finding satisfaction and happiness. Man may be ignorant or enlightened, ill-disciplined or well-disciplined, of lower or higher attainments in every conceivable degree, but there is one irrevocable necessity laid upon him – he must be faithful to his duty in order to secure the benefits and blessings which duty brings. He must do this for himself under the divine law of personal responsibility. What is right and good is always best, regardless of circumstances or consequences, both to him who acts and to all beside. This was my doctrine and that of my associates when we adopted our "Standard of Practical Christianity" and inaugurated the Fraternal Community movement. It is mine still.

Again. Man as a religious being and moral agent acts more or less in three general spheres or departments of effort and responsibility: the individual, the social, and the civil or governmental spheres. All we think, say, and do, which relates to our own personality without regard to others, belongs to the individual sphere. All we think, say, and do, in concurrence with any number of our fellow human beings in the ordinary course of life, belongs to the social sphere. And all that we think, say, or do, as subjects, citizens, or officers of any kingdom, state, or nation, belongs to the governmental sphere. It follows, therefore, that there are individual duties, virtues, sins; social duties, virtues, sins; and governmental duties, virtues, sins. In each sphere our religious and moral obligations are the same. Right and wrong confront human beings at every step. To be perfect, one must think, say, and do what is right in each and all the spheres of responsibility named. In human life, strange inconsistencies, in these particulars, are exemplified. One may be very saintly in his personal character and in his ordinary social relations with his fellow-men, but a barbarous sinner in his governmental capacity – perpetrating the most abhorrent acts of tyranny and cruelty. Or he may be above reproach in his social life, but individually immoral and untrustworthy. So we have a very mottled righteousness, often among would-be saints. In our Fraternal Community No. 1 we sought to be all-sided saints – bound to obey the law of divine righteousness as individuals, in social life, and in all governmental concerns. This was right, even though it should serve on trial to expose our frailties and imperfections.

Community Affairs

As was stated in the last chapter, twenty-eight persons were located upon the Hopedale territory before the first of April, 1842 – myself, wife, and two children among the number – all residing as a unitary household in the one dwelling house there and adjusting themselves to each other as far as they could, and to the unique circumstances in which they were placed. At the expiration of three weeks, when I entered upon the fortieth year of my life, domestic affairs had assumed a good degree of regularity, order, and efficiency, considering the crowded condition in which we found ourselves and the limited culinary appliances and utensils with which we had to do. My wife had been seasonably appointed director of housekeeping by the executive council, and she had for chosen assistant, our good sister, Anna T.,[1] wife of Ebenezer D. Draper. Two most excellent and capable women they were, admirably fitted for the positions they occupied, and they executed the trust reposed in them most quietly, promptly, and successfully.

Before the month closed, great progress had been made in outside matters. A practical division of industrial operations had been arranged, and each one assigned to a position of responsibility, entered upon his or her duties with commendable fidelity and earnestness. A small building, thirty-two feet long by fourteen and one-half wide, a story and a half high above the basement, was nearly completed – the first building erected by the Community. It contained six rooms: two on the main floor for a printing office and school, with two dormitories above and two apartments for whatever use they might be needed in the basement. A larger two-story dwelling house had been voted, but it was found that a mechanics' shop, in which a portion of our water power could be utilized, was indispensable, and that, therefore, first received attention. It was the second structure we put up and served a most important purpose in our earlier years. Our agricultural interests were judiciously provided for, the months of April and May being spent in preparing the soil and putting in the seed for an autumn harvest. When June opened we had on the farm 13 cows, 4 yokes of oxen, 2 horses, and 6 swine. We had also 17 acres of land under cultivation, and everything in this department of activity promised well for the future.

At the same time, as the weeks passed by and as our industrial and general business affairs developed, we were learning some very suggestive and valuable lessons by experience. Novelty wore off and enthusiasm cooled down. We began to see that we had undertaken more than we were aware of, and had not fully estimated our difficulties. We were greatly overcrowded by numbers, newcomers frequently appearing and almost forcing themselves upon us; and as greatly pushed for want of money and means to do with. All meant well in the main, but none of us had any wisdom, strength, or patience to spare, and some of us too little of these requisite qualities for our common use. We had been led to hope for funds which did not come, and some which we had received were unexpectedly withdrawn.

We had made a fine show of our plans for a new social state on paper, and had published them far and wide through the land. The rich and well-to-do derided our scheme and clutched their treasures the closer; the poor, needy, and homeless eagerly applied for a share in our privileges. Moreover, less than a third of our reliable associates had sufficient money at command to meet their own family expenses – much less to help in housing and furnishing subsisting employment to others. I, as the leader in this undertaking, ought to have been wise enough to postpone practical operations till there had been accumulated a common fund sufficient to give a comfortable home and fairly remunerative employment to those who might be enlisted under the banner of our new social state. But I was in too much haste to see the realization of my theories and plans. My hope was too large and my economic judgment too small. Two fundamental duties required by the Gospel of Christ, which I had not then discovered, would have simplified and benefited the whole movement: the limitation of property expenditure to the demands of personal and domestic well-being, and the devotion of surplus means (riches) to the welfare of humanity. These two duties will be taught, insisted upon, and sacredly guaranteed in the regenerate Christian church and in the order of society which such a church shall evolve on earth.

In addition to the evils and hindrances adverted to – insufficient household accommodations and the virtual abandonment of family life, the lack of needful funds and the continual pressure of applicants for residence and membership with us, the enforced denial of whom caused disappointment and sometimes embittered feeling – in addition to these, we were troubled with too much hard work and wearisome anxiety on the part of those burdened with official responsibility, and with a growing preponderance of material interests over those of a moral and religious nature, which subverted the cardinal principle, process, and object that our movement was designed to embody and represent. Moreover, as we went on, we found increasing in our ranks the number of those who were evidently more anxious to secure "loaves and fishes" for themselves than to build up that "kingdom of heaven" on the earth which alone insures the highest rectitude and good of all classes and conditions of people.

Not that anything transpired among our early Hopedale settlers grossly aggravating or flagrantly improper and wrong. But the conditions and circumstances of the situation were such as to give my weak heart some serious aches and discouragements. I was loaded down, overborne almost, by unavoidable cares and responsibilities. I had the general management of our social organization on my hands, its extensive correspondence, much of its incidental writing and considerable physical labor connected therewith, besides attending to the editorial and publication departments of the *Practical Christian*, preaching, lecturing, ministering at funerals, etc., as I was often called to do. Moreover, there were specialties devolving upon me still more difficult and wearisome: to preside over frequent, long-drawn-out discussions, reconcile incompatibilities, settle disputes and misunderstandings, regulate the children and youth, maintain order in the dwelling house and on the outside premises, preserve harmony and good feeling among all classes, and keep up the general courage and hope. I was so favored as to enjoy the confidence of old and young, and was held in such general respect as to give me authority and render me a successful counselor and mediator amid my associates of every condition in life.

The younger inmates of our domicile I found to be deferential and obedient, tractable, pleased to improve themselves, and willing pupils in the school of good manners, and the ordinary moralities of life. I was told beforehand that in this unitary household of ours and other close relations, the greatest trouble would be with the women; that they could not or would not work together without contention and quarreling. But I am happy to record that these evil predictions proved false. Their leaders were eminently discreet, unassuming and judicious, and the rank and file were peaceable and uncomplaining. If there were frictions among them, they were successful in oiling the machinery among themselves, and no whisper of discontent or murmur ever reached the president's ear.

I wish I could say the same of our men. But this would be contrary to the facts in the case. We had not been together two months before an instance of incompatibility between two of our mechanics had, by fostering indulgence, become so unpleasant and offensive that my kind interference was required to restore good feeling and reconcile the parties involved. I but partially succeeded, as the two, of widely different constitution and temperament, could never perfectly harmonize. One of them, inveterately disposed to sarcasm and cutting remarks, soon after left us and that trouble ended. It was the first difficulty of the kind we had encountered, and being so trifling and so unnecessary, mortified me exceedingly. It was, however, followed by others, equally causeless and equally trying. They were all small matters to begin with, but rose to importance by dwelling upon and magnifying them. For the most part they arose, not from any evil intention or purpose of wrong, but from some peculiarity of judgment, idiosyncratic opinion, or question of expediency exalted into the place of a supposed ethical principle, made more aggravating by protracted discussions at mealtime or in Community meetings. One of them grew to such proportions and had such a bearing upon our constitutional polity as to require special attention and finally a change in our fundamental laws and the methods of their administration. It deserves a brief notice.

Defects in the System

A small minority of our members, under the leadership of Brother David R. Lamson, conceived the notion that our joint-stock proprietorship, which constituted the basis of our industrial and financial operations, tended to produce an aristocratic spirit among us to the degradation of the poorer members, and that this tendency ought to be counteracted and overcome by a closer approximation to a system of common property. From this view I and a large majority of my associates strongly but kindly dissented. This called forth argument on the part of its friends, which was met by counter argument. The discussion *pro* and *con* waxed warmer and warmer until it became apparent to me and my friends that there were some serious defects in the system under which we had started out, though not of the nature charged. It was not working as smoothly and to such harmonious, beneficent, and happy results as we had anticipated, but on the contrary, was producing irritation, division, alienation, and dissatisfaction to a serious extent.

It was not, however, closer affiliation that was needed to remedy the existing difficulties as the dissentients claimed, nor the merging of all personal interests in the common welfare, nor the absorption of the individual in the community, but a more practical recognition of every one's inborn rights and obligations; more opportunity for personal seclusion, activity, and development; more individual freedom, enterprise, and responsibility. Above all, there should be in our organic social scheme a true and clear distinction made between rights and privileges, between benefactions and debts, between the dictates of charity and those of strict justice. Beneficiaries should not be allowed the claims of exacting creditors, much less usurp preeminence over their helpers. Nor must the weak, incompetent, and irresponsible be permitted to hamper or overburden those who were straining every nerve of their superior ability for the common welfare. Probably no one of our fraternity was conscious of practicing or engendering any of these evils. Nevertheless, I knew they were actually doing so, however good their motives, however unconscious they were of harm. I knew also that thereby they were imperiling the cause we all professed to hold dear, and I determined to rescue it if possible – to save it from impending destruction.

This I saw could be done only by amending the constitution, by making some radical changes in the organized policy of the undertaking, by striking out such portions of our plan of administration as were calculated to produce the disabilities and unfortunate conditions under which we were laboring, and substituting those of an opposite character, tendency, and legitimate result. To the task thus set before me I then addressed myself, and in due time prepared and brought before my constituency the amended charter of our enterprise. There were seven distinct changes proposed by me as necessary in my judgment to meet the exigencies of the case and put the Community on a sure foundation for the years ahead.[2] And I urged the adoption of the amendments under which those changes could be made substantially for the following reasons:[3]

1. They restore a large amount of individuality to the members of the Community, leaving everyone at liberty to form with others a unitary household and invest his capital and labor in the joint stock operations, or to dwell in his own house and transact business by himself, as may please him; in either case acknowledging his obligations to the great principles and objects which the body represents.

2. They make the Community to combine all the advantages of a well-ordered village of free-minded, conscientious individuals, and of a close cooperation of capital and labor without the disadvantages of either. They adapt the Community organization to the wants of all classes of Practical Christians without imposing excessive burdens or restraints upon any, and thus give the idea of associative life the vantage ground of a fair experiment on its own merits.

3. They prevent all unreasonable dependence of any upon the more provident in the Community, quicken industry, induce economy, promote self-reliance, and make the just distinction between alms and wages, gifts and debts.

4. They place all the members of the Community, whether they have much or little in the joint-stock, on a common level as regards reciprocal obligations and responsibilities. Justice is the same to all and charity is to be exercised by all. None can hide within the mass nor screen themselves behind constitutional prescriptions from voluntary contributions to support schools and relieve the needy. Everyone will appear in his own true light.

5. They will disencumber capital of its present great risks and dangerous liabilities, give it moderate but sure profit, and at the same time secure to labor its just compensation.

6. Finally, they simplify the whole social machinery of the community, make the experiment perfectly safe on a large or small scale, and render the mutual relationship at once more pleasant, more just, and more practicable to all free, honest, unselfish minds.

It required all the ability and influence I could command to obtain the adoption of the proposed amendments; but I succeeded in my endeavors, though so much to the disappointment and grief of the minority that six persons gave up their membership in the organization, while several candidates for membership, who had leanings towards a common property financial policy, lost all interest in the movement. I lamented this, but saw no way to prevent it and save our undertaking. Most of those who sent in their resignations on the impulse of the moment, afterwards relented and became reconciled to the new order of things. But their chieftain and oracle, Brother Lamson, was permanently alienated. He soon after consorted with the Shakers, but finding himself after a little time no more at home with them than with us, returned to general society, giving up the ministry and locating at West Boylston, where he died, July 2, 1886, aged 80 years. His wife, an estimable woman, shared his varied fortunes sympathetically while she lived, preceding him but a few years to the world of spirits.

The lessons taught us by the experiences just narrated were more or less depressing to us all. I felt them deeply as did those of my associates who stood by and preserved the imperiled ship. The charm of our early enthusiasm had vanished, but our principles and objects remained sacred in the shrine of our devotion. We therefore girded up the weakened loins of our minds and resolved to push forward our renewed undertaking. We had done as well as could have been expected in our more material affairs – the harvest from garden, orchard, and field was fairly good, our little school was well started, several kinds of mechanical activities were in operation and others prospectively near, the mill-dam and attached shop were almost completed before winter set in, and the inmates of the "Old House," reduced somewhat in numbers, had been reorganized into six distinct families and made reasonably comfortable.

The annual Community meeting occurred January 4, 1843.[4] In my address as President, I reviewed the operations of the year, noting especially the changes that had been made, and prophesying a happy future. Several new members united with us, among whom was my worthy third cousin, Amos J. Ballou,[5] an experienced and successful farmer, who was at once chosen intendant of agriculture and animals. The other requisite officers of the body were elected, business matters were discussed, suggestions made, and plans for the coming season considered, and we entered upon our respective duties and labors with fresh zeal and determination.

Missionary Labors

Although largely engrossed with cares and activities relating to the internal order and welfare of the young Community, I yet performed much external service. I not only continued my general efforts in behalf of religion and reform, but I made special lecturing excursions for the purpose of promulgating our own distinctive Practical Christianity. In the early autumn of 1842, I gave four evening addresses in the Unitarian church, Grafton, upon "The Fraternal Communion, its principles and objects," to fairly sized and interested audiences. Soon afterwards I lectured twice in the Baptist church at New England Village, two miles north of the center of the same town upon "Christian Non-Resistance," and "The Inviolability of Human Life." I had a few choice friends in these places, and it was through their active influence and generosity that my labors were introduced and provided for. Respectable audiences, including ministers of different denominations, listened attentively to my testimonies, and many strong prejudices were no doubt meliorated though few full converts were made.[6]

I next visited Providence, Rhode Island, on a similar mission. This, my little native state, had been for some time in a ferment with the famous Dorr agitation.[7] The mass of the people were in a belligerent mood, but there was a remnant ready to welcome the principles of peace. My ever firm and faithful friend, Samuel W. Wheeler, stood in the van and effectively favored my ministrations.[8] I was happy to meet Elders Benjamin and James Taylor, McKenzie, and Cheney,[9] on terms of general accord. The two first named were ministers of the Christian Connexion whom I knew in my youth but had not seen for many years. They were men of great hearts. Elder Benjamin was the one who, at the time of my excommunication from the Christian church in Cumberland, protested against the act as contrary to the avowed principles and policy of the denomination. I was also greeted cordially by a goodly number of friends of various persuasions, callings, and stations, who received my word gladly. I delivered three discourses in Elder [John] Taylor's new chapel, Pawtuxet Street,[10] to appreciative audiences: the first on Christian Non-Resistance; the second on the relation those accepting that doctrine should sustain towards existing human governments; and the third on slavery, intemperance, licentiousness, and other social evils. Later, I lectured upon the same themes in Hampton, Connecticut and West Wrentham, Upton, Medway, Wrentham Center, Northbridge, and Leominster, Massachusetts.[11]

These efforts of mine evinced my zeal and industry in promoting what I sincerely deemed the cause of truth and righteousness. I trust they did some good in enlightening the minds, rectifying the hearts, and elevating the conduct of men; though very little compared with what they would have done if the Hopedale Community had been loyally sustained by those who earlier and later rallied around its standard, but who subsequently forsook it. For the seed of truth must not only be sown and nurtured, but harvested into preservative granaries. In our case it was all important to demonstrate *practically* that our divine principles could be permanently lived out in a higher order of social life. And this must be done *voluntarily* – not by mere human law or compulsion, but by human agreement, fellowship, and cooperation. Those who would not or could not support our movement from honest choice and of their own free will, were sure to fall out by the way and go to their own place in compulsory society. Unfortunately, these predominated at last, and failure was the final issue.

Second Advent Discussion

In the winter of 1842-43, during the widely prevailing excitement concerning the speedy coming of Christ and the accompanying end of the world,[12] I was drawn into a discussion of the subject with some of its leading advocates. They had invaded Millville and set up their proselyting machinery with a bold flourish of trumpets, challenging anybody and everybody to meet them in public debate. Brother William H. Fish, our minister there at the time, asked Mr. Mayers, their leader, if he was willing to publicly discuss the matter with me, to which he replied in the affirmative with great self-assurance. I was at once communicated with and consented to the proposed meeting. Upon going to Millville to make needful arrangements with the challenger for the conflict, I found his bravery giving way somewhat to discretion, cunning, and strategy. He was not quite ready to champion his cause against me but must send off for an expert debater in his stead, which necessitated a delay of some days, my actual competitor appearing at length in the person of a Mr. Follett of Worcester. Rev. M. W. Burlingame, a

Free Will Baptist, and Mr. Holbrook, Orthodox Congregationalist,[13] were made moderators of the meeting at which the discussion was carried on. A full report of what was said and done was inserted in the *Practical Christian*,[14] of which only a brief comment can be given here.

In the first place, Mr. Follett and his friends were over-cautions, timid, and non-committal, even in regard to points upon which they had been making the most positive statements and concerning dates which were blazoned on their grand pictorial chart hanging in full view of the crowded audience. They had demanded beforehand a statement of my several positions and line of argument, which I willingly furnished them, desiring to treat them fairly and candidly in all respects. In the discussion they dodged some of the main points at issue, prevaricated, and flatly refused to defend several of their fundamental assumptions. It was soon apparent that they were sick of their own bargain. I gave them but one cause of complaint: just and unanswerable criticism of their fallacious assertions and specious argumentation. In the second place, they became so tired of the contest that they caused it to be brought to a close without allowing me half the time virtually pledged me for the presentation of my side of the case. But I good-naturedly excused them on the ground that their weakness compelled a retreat on their part. The result was that their efforts in Millville, begun with such bombastic pretensions, came to a premature and inglorious close. The comment made by one of their local sympathizers upon the affair was, "If the Lord begins any good work in these parts, the devil presently sends Adin Ballou to kick it all over." Truly, "If they have called the master of the house Beelzebub, how much more those of his household" (Matt. 10:25).

A kindred discussion grew out of the preceding one. Before leaving the pulpit where the speaking occurred, Rev. Mr. Burlingame, one of the moderators, signified a desire to meet me the next week at the same place to debate the question whether or not the second advent predicted in the scriptures is a yet future event, himself taking the affirmative, in opposition to views presented by me in my argument with Mr. Follett. He had no ambition to defend the damaged cause of the Millerites, but was sure that Christ was to appear again upon the earth, substantially as set forth by my opponents, though at an indefinite date, and he lamented that the public mind should be turned against that theory by any exposure of the assumptions of those who fixed that consummation in the autumn of 1843. I cheerfully accepted the challenge and it was arranged that we should meet Thursday, February 23, at 2 o'clock P.M., each party to have half an hour alternately till 5 o'clock and then fifteen minutes in which to conclude his argument. The affair came off accordingly in the presence of a crowded assembly. The question was phrased thus: "Did the second coming of Christ, predicted in the scriptures, take place about the time of the destruction of Jerusalem, or is it yet in the future?" This form of it gave me the affirmative and, of course, the opening speech. Mr. Burlingame and his assistant, a Mr. Snow, had the negative. Messrs. Amos W. Pitts and Francis Kelly[15] acted as moderators. My leading opponent requested me to furnish him some days in advance a definite statement in writing of my doctrine, the principal positions I should attempt to maintain, and reference to the more important proof-texts of scripture I proposed to use. I did so, but neither asked nor received anything of the kind from him.

My views upon the subject in question I stated and explained plainly and fully in my opening speech. The audience, composed of persons of various opinions and prejudices, listened eagerly to what I had to say, and I could see that my doctrine was new to most of them and that the general feeling was against the possibility of my maintaining it by any fair show of proof and argument. But my convictions were the result of a thorough study of the New Testament, and I knew them to be more accordant with the teaching of that book than any that had ever been brought to my notice. As the discussion proceeded, I had the satisfaction of seeing the tide of feeling turn in my favor, especially when the weakness of my opponents in trying to refute my positions became apparent. The debate went through and closed according to program. Finding it impossible to say all I desired in the time allotted me, I proposed another session, but was overruled by the opposing party, who was evidently glad to end the discussion as soon as possible. I, however, notified the congregation that I should conclude my argument on the following Sunday in Brother Fish's church, and did so. The challenger and those sympathizing with him gained nothing by their venture, but they made the best of their discomfiture, virtually confessing the weakness of their cause by warning their adherents to keep away from me and my dangerous teachings. I soon after published an ample pamphlet on the subject, entitled, *The True Scriptural Doctrine of the Second Advent: An Effectual Antidote to Millerism and All Other Kindred Errors*, which may be found among my numerous publications.[16] To the general positions and explications contained therein, I have ever since adhered, although on critical revision I might make some modifications and qualifications, but none of vital importance.

Life at Hopedale

The details of progress in Community affairs being given in full in my history of the undertaking still, at this writing, in manuscript, I will offer in these pages only an outline of what transpired from time to time with the passing years. The new order of things, already sufficiently portrayed, contributed at once to our prosperity. During the year 1843, nine half-acre house lots were sold to members for $100 each, whereby our treasury was to that extent replenished, and on three of these were dwelling houses erected – one two-story double tenement structure by Amos J. Ballou and Edmund Price,[17] one story-and-a-half cottage by George W. Stacy, and a similar one by myself, in which I and my family have ever since resided. Our mechanic shop was completed and supplied with labor-saving machinery so far as the main floor and basement were concerned, while the second story was divided in such a way as to accommodate our printing office in the southerly part and our school and Sunday meetings in the northerly. Desirable improvements were made in respect to our barns, of which there were three, standing separate from each other. They were brought together, placed over good basements, put in proper condition within and without, and made neat and convenient for use in the agricultural department. The principal streets of the village site were opened, partially graded, and designated by appropriate names. Late in the autumn, ground was broken and a beginning made for a schoolhouse, to be used also temporarily as a chapel, with a basement designed to accommodate a Community store. It was to be surmounted by a cupola or belfry, so constructed as to furnish the needful conveniences for a public clock. It was completed in the spring of 1844 and immediately occupied. Originally twenty-six feet square, it was some years afterward doubled in length to serve the growing needs of the place in those respects for which it was first designed.

Meantime the major portion of our industries was organized and carried on under general joint-stock arrangements in distinct branches, and the minor portion by individual members on their own responsibility. We had common farming, gardening, carpentering, printing, hat making, tin and sheet-iron working, boot and shoe manufacture, transportation, etc., all, of course, on a small scale, giving manual employment to our men, while our women were engaged in household and kindred duties. All our residents were busy people, idlers and dawdlers not being encouraged or even tolerated. New members took the places of seceders, a considerable number of probationers were received among us, and a few families, not of our way of thinking, were allowed to reside in our midst as temporary inhabitants of the place, enjoying its educational, social, moral, and religious advantages, and engaging in its industrial activities to a greater or less extent. Every vacant tenement on the premises was filled and a few in the vicinity were hired for the accommodation of persons more or less closely connected with us.

In the spring of the year now in review, the Community received a valuable donation from a sympathizing and generous friend in Cincinnati, Ohio, Andrew H. Ernst, Esq., who, with his excellent wife, née Sarah H. Otis of Boston, had long stood in cordial Christian fellowship with me as Restorationists and well-wishers to our social reform enterprise.[18] He was a practical horticulturist, having extensive nurseries at Spring Garden, on the outskirts of the then queen city of the West, and his gift consisted of more than three hundred young apple trees of several choice varieties, carefully selected and packed, and forwarded to us by the most available and rapid means of transportation. They were received in good condition and gave us great joy, but it was our misfortune not to have in proper state of preparation sufficient ground upon which to set them, so that a considerable portion of them were virtually lost. Those that we had a suitable place for were planted with due care and judiciously trained, thriving well and becoming fruitful bearers at an early day. Some of them still remain, large, flourishing, and productive, on my own homestead.

Regular religious meetings, two always on Sunday and sometimes three, with a social conference on Thursday evening, were established early in our Community life, and creditably sustained from week to week for many years. These were generally led by one of our approved public speakers or preachers, who usually gave a formal discourse, although in the absence of such, some layman or laywoman, of whom there were several among us competent for the task, conducted the service. At the same time those of us who had formally entered the Christian ministry preached either statedly or occasionally at various places within a convenient distance of home, some of which we regarded as distinctive missionary stations for the inculcation and dissemination of the spirit and principles of Practical Christianity. Vigorous quarterly conferences of two or three days' continuance were held at these stations or wherever we had friends to invite us. Besides devoted attention to these religious gatherings by our ministers and people at large, we took active part in mass meetings, conventions, and celebrations held for the purpose of promoting the cause of temperance, antislavery, non-resistance, social reform, or whatever promised the improvement of our kind. A more industrious propaganda of regenerative religious and moral principles than this little cluster of Hopedalians existed nowhere else probably on the face of the earth.

But we labored all the while under great disadvantages, having to provide for our own material subsistence as well as for our distinctive social reform enterprise, besides helping along those other activities which have just been named. I stood in the forefront of those industries upon which we relied for means wherewith to live and lend aid to every good word and work, and though weighed down with home duties and cares, yet found time for considerable active effort abroad in behalf of truth and humanity.

In October 1843, I was chosen president of the New England Non-Resistance Society, which imposed a new tax upon my time and energy. The Washingtonian Movement, which led to a conflict between the friends of moral suasion and those of legal coercion as methods of promoting the temperance reformation,[19] and the division arising in the Abolitionist ranks upon the question of political action,[20] both appealed to me through the issues raised, in a form and with a force which I could not wholly ignore, my feeling and conviction from the beginning being unequivocally in favor of moral and religious effort rather than legal and political, in carrying forward the work of individual and social regeneration upon the earth. I also took a decided stand and wrote against the ultra anti-Sabbatarians[21] of those days, setting forth and promulgating what I deemed true and rational views upon the observance of the first day of the week under the Christian dispensation. The consideration of these great practical questions filled, in my thought and action, the place previously occupied by more strictly theological discussions.

The growth and general prosperity of the Community during the year 1844 was all that its friends could have reasonably expected. But it was not exempt from more or less internal friction. The great difficulty against which Dr. Channing warned us – that "of reconciling so many wills, of bringing so many individuals to such a unity of judgment and feeling as is necessary to the management" of Community affairs, was always present with us, and was aggravated in our case by the preponderance of minds more or less deficient in mental and moral discipline. All meant well, and had sincere reverence for our "great principles," as we termed them, but all had not a nice sense of order, justice, and fitness of action in little things, nor patience and forbearance with what crossed their feelings, habits, and tastes. On this account our membership was occasionally reduced by voluntary withdrawal, our doors always swinging outward as well as inward to those who at any time cast in their lot with us.

Another difficulty encountered by us was that of steering the vessel of our social system safely between the Scylla of organic arrangements and the Charybdis of individual license.[22] If we adopted rules and regulations seemingly necessary to good order and permanent success, we were in danger of overriding personal rights or at least of making somebody unhappy. And if we relaxed in favor of greater individual liberty, there were some to jeopardize our enterprise by unjust usurpation or uncomfortable eccentricity. In seeking to find the happy and safe middle passage, we veered first one way and then the other a little too far, like unskilled craftsmen in that kind of seamanship. Nevertheless we came to our annual meeting in January, 1845, with a good showing for the preceding year, and started out anew with unfaltering courage, hope, and zeal, believing and feeling that better days than we had yet seen were before us. Detailed information concerning Community affairs other than what pertained more particularly to myself, I remand to the pages of my history of the movement.

Death of Wife's Father

A heavy bereavement befell our family in the sudden decease of my wife's honored father, Pearley Hunt, Esq. of Milford, March 29, 1844, in the seventy-third year of his age. He was an estimable man in public as in private life, dear to his own family and a great loss to the town and general community. His memory is very precious to both my wife and myself on account of his tender affection and innumerable kindnesses, from infancy in her case and from first acquaintance in mine. His paternal interest in our temporal welfare and comfort culminated in liberally assisting us to establish the home wherein we have dwelt since September, 1843. We therefore hallow his memory. From a brief obituary in the *Practical Christian* of April 13, I make the following extracts:

> The deceased has been long and extensively known in this general vicinity as an enterprising merchant, an influential public-spirited citizen, and a civil magistrate,

in which several positions he has sustained his responsibilities with more credit to himself and less censure, with more favor and less hostility, with more friends and fewer enemies, than ordinarily falls to the lot of men passing through such varied scenes and manifold duties of public activity. In the more private relations of life, he was a man in whom the best domestic and social affections predominated – kind, provident, indulgent, generous, and faithful as a husband, father, brother, friend, and neighbor. His funeral was attended by a large concourse of people with every becoming demonstration of respect.

CHAPTER 19

1845-1852

In the present chapter I propose to include as many of the experiences and events of my life during the period covered by it as space and convenience will allow. Much of my time, strength, and active effort was given to the affairs of the Community, of which I continued president until January 1852, eleven years from the date of my first election to that position. I shall only glance in the briefest possible manner at what transpired in this sphere of activity, inasmuch as it is presented in full elsewhere, as I have before stated, with all the needful accompanying circumstances.

As the projector and practical head of the social experiment at Hopedale, I had from the outset an intense ambition to have it succeed, to actualize my ideal of a civilization based upon and fashioned after the true practical Christianity of the New Testament. In this ambition I was unconscious of a single selfish motive. I desired no good for myself which I did not believe would be equally good for all my associates, and indirectly for the whole human race. I sought no salary and no emolument whatever, and never received pecuniary support beyond the cost of a workingman's board – probably less than that. I never coveted a particle of authority or power which did not clearly seem to me to be respectful of every other person's rights and promotive of the general welfare. To domineer and dictate was abhorrent to my nature, habits, and moral principles. I loved to see every one do his or her duty willingly – from choice and not from compulsion, from inward conviction and not merely to please me. And I was always as happy to follow another's nominal leadership as to be followed, if I was sure that I was being led right. For these characteristics I claim no credit. They were born in me and cost me no effort or self-crucifixion. My errability and besetting sins were always enough in other directions to need the cross of humility and self-denial, and to make me a contrite suppliant and penitent before the divine mercy seat.

My companion in the household was, by my position, largely burdened with domestic labors imposed upon her by a constant influx of what might be called Community company; that is, visiting inquirers of all varieties, who for years made our humble home their hotel *gratis*, no public place being provided for the hospitable entertainment of such till 1847, and then not entirely to our relief. But she bore her toils with womanly fortitude and patience, receiving no other reward than the consciousness of duty well performed and of faithfully sustaining her husband in meeting his dubiously chosen responsibilities. I sometimes reproached myself for having drawn her into such hardships, for she had ordinary family cares enough for her health and strength, and servants other than ourselves were seldom at command had we desired them. But all this seemed inevitably involved in what I had undertaken, and if its exactions were seriously regrettable we were consoled with the thought that they were less severe and wearisome than is often the case in families of "high life" under the domination of style and fashion. Be this as it may, such were the personal and domestic circumstances amid which I performed the duties of my official position in the Community.

Nevertheless, I kept up a courageous and cheerful heart. The cause I had espoused was dear to me and worthy of all the trials I endured in its behalf. I rejoiced in all its prosperities and sorrowed in all its adversities. I watched for its welfare in all directions, and vindicated it against all its assailants. I deprecated its imperfections and aberrations, and to the utmost of my influence quieted its internal disharmonies. I devised, drafted, and revised most of its constitutions, bylaws, rules, and regulations, and prepared for the press nearly all its published documents. In fine, I served the Community to the best of my ability – not as infallible and sinless, but with upright intentions and without hope of earthly reward. And it is with great pleasure that I record the treatment I received in return from a large majority of its members and dependents. It was emphatically kind, courteous, and deferential throughout – one of confidence and loyalty. There were occasional crises of dissatisfaction, unrest, and threatening commotion when mine seemed to be the only voice that could calm the disturbed elements and restore the desired harmony. Seldom in times of confusion and distrust did my earnest appeal to the heart, conscience, and reason of those involved fail to win a gratifying response. For this, I devoutly thanked my Heavenly Father, from whom descendeth "every good and perfect gift."[1]

Withdrawal of Rev. George W. Stacy

The year 1845 was one of marked prosperity with us in nearly all respects. Unbroken health prevailed on our domain, and general success crowned our various industrial and other activities. Our numbers and village homes increased on the whole, though we lost a few members by withdrawal. Notable among these was Rev. Brother George W. Stacy, one of the original subscribers to our constitution – an ordained preacher with whom I had been in very close and confidential relations and from whom I had counted much in carrying forward the work of social reconstruction on the principles of Practical Christianity. The reasons for his abandonment of this work were given in full in the columns of our Community paper.[2] They seemed to me specious and unsatisfactory, as I endeavored to show in the same issue of the publication as that in which they appeared. There is no occasion for reproducing the *pro* and *con* of the case here, or to comment on it farther than to say that in closing his public pronunciamento, the departing brother declared that he still cherished a deep and unwavering faith in the heavenly principles which drew him to Hopedale, and at the same time professed for me personally the most sincere and unabated respect and love. Much as I differed from him and deeply as I regretted the step he felt impelled to take, I certainly could cherish only the kindest feelings towards him and the best wishes for his future prosperity, welfare, and happiness. He located in the neighboring village of Milford, soon became interested in town affairs, was honored by his fellow citizens with various public offices, including that of representative to the General Court, and maintained a reputable standing in general society. He was successful in business and real estate transactions, acquiring a handsome property, most of which he left to his heirs. He continued faithful to the antislavery cause to the end, and also to temperance, being for several of the last years of his life a devoted political Prohibitionist. But for Christian Non-Resistance and social reform he had no further testimony. He is still living at an advanced age, but without serious decline of that physical, mental, or moral energy which characterized his earlier life.

Visit from Robert Owen

In the late autumn of 1845 our Community was honored with a visit from the celebrated English Communist, Robert Owen,[3] widely known among social reformers for his practical efforts in his native land to realize his ideal of a reconstructed civilization upon principles which seemed true and sacred to him. Though his views differed radically from ours in many particulars, yet he was no less welcome to our domain and hospitality on that account, and the interview with him was cordial, agreeable, and gratifying.

The System Simplified

As already indicated, the annual report in our Community affairs in January 1846,[4] was highly favorable and encouraging, and I, in my official address, indulged in glowing representations of our condition and prospects. My rose-colored prophecies for the future were not destined to fulfillment. The very year upon which we then entered reversed our good fortune with sickness, several deaths, and general decline of business prosperity, causing much regret and discouragement. In 1847 matters went from bad to worse till, amid the increasing confusion and dissatisfaction, I myself well nigh lost heart and hope. At length we reached a crisis which obliged us to drop the existing industrial arrangements, again alter our constitution, and swing back still further toward individualism. In doing this, we did not change our declaration of principles, our cardinal objects, or our integrality of joint stock property. But we greatly simplified our organic system of operations, and seeing little prospect of a Fraternal Community No. 2, concluded to call our association thenceforth "The Hopedale Community."[5]

About this time the lot of land across the river, which had been designated for burial purposes, was properly surveyed and laid out under my general direction by my friend David Davenport[6] of Mendon, a gentleman every way competent for the task, who rendered his valuable services without compensation. Thus were made the beginnings of the present beautiful Hopedale Cemetery.

Our village, with territory adjoining and the inhabitants thereof, was also, after protracted importunity, set off by the town of Milford as an independent school district; the final vote being large and cordial in behalf of the project, a result with which I was much pleased.

Immediately after the modification of our system just mentioned, we sold or rented most branches of our secular business to individuals or to small partnerships of our members. This worked well enough in cases where the party in control had a scrupulous conscience and good practical judgment. In other cases, risks were incurred, foreign help,[7] which proved unsatisfactory, was hired, and poor work was turned out. This injured our credit in the business world and involved us in manifold troubles which necessitated an early resumption of management on the part of the Community.

While this experiment was going on, we made a very important rectification and consolidation of all our land titles under the professional guidance of our kind friend, Ellis Gray Loring, Esq.,[8] an eminent conveyancer of Boston, who also generously made us welcome to his services. This was deemed desirable and necessary even, to render us and those coming after us absolutely secure in our real estate possessions to the latest generation.[9]

Withdrawal of Rev. Daniel S. Whitney

Admissions to and withdrawals from our membership were comparatively numerous during these years, but the former greatly exceeded the latter, causing a steady increase of adherents and a growing expansion of all our varied activities. I regretted the departure of any of our number whose character and standing among us were above reproach, and especially of any who had embarked with us full of hope and zeal at the outset, and upon whom I had confidently relied as co-workers in making our movement a success. It was so in the case of Brother George W. Stacy, mentioned a few pages back. It was so with Rev. Brother Daniel S. Whitney, who resigned his membership with us in a letter dated March 29, 1850. The missive, which was a lengthy one, giving his reasons in full for his act, appeared in the *Practical Christian* of the next issue with a rejoinder from my pen.[10] Like Brother Stacy, he made no charges against his associates for "dereliction from principle or duty," but rather against "the industrial organization," which he deemed productive of many evils too grievous to be borne, and which, to use his own words, "cost more than it was worth."

As regards the principles underlying the movement, he said, "I most thankfully accept them as the truth of God. They are alike needful in their spirit and power to redeem mankind individually and socially." Nevertheless he could go back into the prevailing order of society in which these principles are systematically and persistently set at defiance and openly violated, and, without any scruples apparently, engage in the support and management of a government whose fundamental law in various particulars he had often declared to be hostile to and subversive of the government of God – "a covenant with death and an agreement with hell."[11] I was never able to see the consistency or wisdom of all this, but somehow, he, like Brother Stacy before him, did, and acted accordingly. He became much interested in local and general politics, was for a long time an active member of the Republican party, but for some years past has been in close affiliation as ally and adviser with the political Prohibitionists or Third Party men.[12] He had the distinction of representing the town of Boylston, where he located after leaving Hopedale, in the state constitutional convention of 1853.[13] Subsequently taking up his abode in Southborough, he for many years held the office of postmaster in that town, where he still resides. His interest in temperance, peace, woman's rights, and other specific reforms on the basis of the existing social order, remains unabated.

A New President

The affairs of the Community went on prosperously, though without any noteworthy event or occurrence, through the year 1851, and my heart rejoiced again in the hope that all serious troubles were over and that the future of our cause and movement was secure against all hindrances and adversaries. Under this inspiration I wrote and presented an address at the annual meeting in January 1852, in which I magnified our good condition and prospects as the result of our many and varied studies, experiences, and labors, and declined being considered a candidate for re-election to the office of president, which I had held from the beginning. I was so fully assured that the Community was well and permanently established that I thought I had better retire and let it be put in charge of a new executive head[14] who might not only safely direct its activities but perhaps impart new energy to them, though I soon doubted the wisdom of my course. In view of my contemplated action, I made my address essentially a valedictory.[15] It was so regarded by my associates, who, after its delivery, "*Voted*, that a copy of it be requested for record, for publication in the *Practical Christian*, and for separate distribution; also that a committee be appointed to prepare a response thereto," to be presented at an adjourned meeting. All was done as provided for, the response, which was unanimously adopted, being as follows:

> DEAR BROTHER BALLOU: Though your resignation of the presidency of the Hopedale Community, tendered at the late annual meeting, was not unexpected by any of our fraternity, it was nevertheless received with much general reluctance and a most sincere wish that you might change your purpose and still continue in the position which you have so long filled with great ability, fidelity, and usefulness. But we know that the duties of the office have been many and arduous, absorbing

so much of your time and energy that there was left to you little leisure for study and other pursuits in which you have a deep interest; and we did not feel, therefore, that we could justly insist upon your longer acting in a capacity imposing such demands upon you. Whilst, then, we have submitted to your desire and decision, we have deemed it a duty and a pleasure to express the deep sense of obligation and of gratitude which we cherish towards you for your important services in our common cause. This, we, the undersigned, most cordially now do as a committee of the Community and in accordance with a vote unanimously passed immediately after hearing your able, interesting, and excellent farewell address. Of that address, we deem it unnecessary to say anything at length, as it will go forth into the world to speak for itself. You know that it was appreciated and heartily responded to by all who heard it, and that they were prompted by its impressiveness and its intrinsic worth to call for its publication. To you such a response from your co-laborers must be of far greater value than any eulogy our feeble words could pronounce, and those outside our fellowship yet in sympathy with us, will judge of it by its own character and therefore pass upon it a sentence of approbation.

We will only add that though you are succeeded in the presidency by one competent and worthy to occupy that position, being a pioneer and a constantly devoted and generous laborer in the cause of Christian Socialism, we shall still regard you, as you will naturally be regarded by the world, as really the leader in our enterprise, to whom we shall constantly look with fraternal sympathy, confidence, and hope, certain of all the aid you can render us whenever needed and called for. We therefore take an affectionate leave of you as our *nominal* head, wishing you continued health and prosperity, both temporal and spiritual, and what will be still better to you, success in all your philanthropic and Christian labors; and after this earthly life, a still higher and broader mission of love and usefulness, in association under the Infinite Father with the good and faithful who have gone before us and whose rest is unwearied activity.

WM. H. FISH, EDMUND SOWARD,[16] *Committee.*

Great Sorrow

These days of exultation, hope, and mutual congratulation were followed by a season of profound bereavement and lamentation. On the twenty-first of January [1852] Miss Susan Fish,[17] one of our worthy and highly esteemed members, was taken from us by death, to the deep regret and sorrow of all who knew her; and on the eighth of February ensuing, our beloved son, Adin Augustus Ballou, followed her to the world of spirits. This was a vast, irreparable loss to us all. He was the star of love, hope, and trust to his family, to the Community, and to a large circle of admiring friends. I shall recur to this sad affliction further on.

Interested But Not Converted

What I have thus far recorded in this chapter pertained almost exclusively to what transpired in connection with my relation to the Community. Its remaining pages will be devoted to matters of a more strictly personal and domestic nature. As to myself, I not only performed a large amount of mental, moral, and physical service for the cause in which I was engaged within our own borders, but no small amount in a general way for the public at large in the capacity of religious teacher, moral reform lecturer, writer, and controversialist. By definite arrangement with my associates, I preached at home, as a rule, two Sundays in a month at a morning service, and also elsewhere at convenient localities in the vicinity in the afternoon or evening. On the remaining Sundays I was employed in ministerial duties farther away, at distances so great usually as to necessitate my leaving home on Saturday and returning on Monday. These outside labors were with rare exceptions among friends personally interested in the principles of Practical Christianity and in movements for the bettering of the condition of their fellow men. I, of course, had no access to wealthy and fashionable parishes, and but rarely to those of humbler rank in so-called "liberal denominations." But many of the common people, some of whom, for one reason or another, were outside of all ecclesiastical organizations, heard me gladly. Wherever I thought it practicable, I attempted to form some sort of association on the basis of our "fraternal communion," but with little success. I procured, when I could, subscribers to the *Practical Christian*, sold books, and circulated freely tracts which had been prepared as expositional and illustrative of our distinctive principles and objects. Of full and devoted converts to our "Standard of Practical Christianity," I made but a small number. There were good and sufficient reasons for this. Many who acknowledged the absolute truth of that "Standard" shrank from espousing it on the ground that it was too high, too good for them to think of attaining it or of ordering their lives by it. Others had, for various reasons, left old religious bodies and were determined not to jeopardize their much prized liberty by entering new ones. They were not only "Come-outers," but "Stay-outers." Still others were wool-dyed indifferentists to all positive religion and clear-cut principles of righteousness. I could transiently interest such as these while exposing the errors and sins of existing society, but they cared little for definite constructive methods of personal or social regeneration. Nevertheless, I sowed the divine seed diligently, taking no thought as to whether it fell "by the wayside" or "on stony places" or "among thorns" or "into good ground"; but being willing to accept such results as the "Lord of the harvest" might find in his reckoning.[18]

My labors in behalf of specific reforms continued abundant throughout the whole sphere of my personal acquaintance and public activity. Generally, I spent but a day or two in response to any given call for service of this sort, but at two different times I went out under the auspices of the Anti-Slavery Society as lecturing agent for a term of several weeks; once to eastern Pennsylvania, where I had a very pleasant campaign in 1846, and again to central New York in 1848.

Christian Non-Resistance
In the former of these years [1846] I prepared a small volume of 240 pages, entitled *Christian Non-Resistance in all its Important Bearings, Illustrated and Defended*. It was published by my good friend, James Miller McKim,[19] of Philadelphia, and

re-published some years later by friends of the cause in England. It was critically reviewed, with some pretty sharp animadversions, in the *Christian Examiner*, a Unitarian quarterly, in its issue of January, 1848. The reviewer was my former ecclesiastical brother, Rev. Charles Hudson, then a representative in Congress from the Fifth Massachusetts District. He caused his article to be struck off in a pamphlet form and sent me a copy. I honored it with a thorough examination and reply in the columns of the *Practical Christian*, which may sometime be given a wider circulation.[20]

Public Debates

Respecting oral debates, I held several of interest and importance during the period now in review. One of these was with Mr. Origen Bacheler, an able Calvinistic layman fond of controversy, a zealous but fair opponent whom I had encountered before, as may be remembered, and whom I afterward met in verbal conflict on different occasions.[21] On the twenty-first and twenty-second of October, 1845, by mutual pre-arrangement, we discussed at Norton, Massachusetts, the following question: "Ought Christians to participate in any government whose constitution authorizes the destruction of human life under any pretext whatsoever?" The disputation was well conducted before attentive and deeply interested audiences.

During the same year I had two rather curious rencontres with Rev. Thomas Williams,[22] a venerable Hopkinsian clergyman, sometime of Providence, Rhode Island, who was also addicted to polemic controversy, though not in forensic form. He was encouraged to lecture in Uxbridge by Rev. Mr. Orcutt,[23] pastor of the Trinitarian church there, upon "The divine ordinance of civil government and the punishment of crime." I had many friends in the place who were specially invited to be present. They accepted the invitation on condition that the lecturer allow questioning and criticism by some competent person after he had closed his formal discourse. This was promised and I was sent for to be present and avail myself of the proffered opportunity. I responded favorably and was an attentive auditor with many others on the occasion. The address of Mr. Williams was very long, continuing till 10 o'clock (it being given in the evening), which left me little time for any suitable rejoinder. I used what I had, however, faithfully, spite of discreditable artifices to prevent me, and my questions and criticisms did good execution in behalf of the truth. Not long afterward, I had another contest with the same reverend lecturer in Upton, upon the same general subject. He seemed dissatisfied with the result of the Uxbridge interview and desired an opportunity to retrieve himself before the public. The subterfuges employed to get me to Upton and then to deprive me of a fair chance to defend my beleaguered views at the meeting were worthy of the cause which inspired them.

Besides these and other oral discussions upon some phase of the subject of Non-Resistance, I was drawn into many similar or kindred written ones in the *Practical Christian*, as will be found by consulting its files. Indeed, I was very unfortunate in respect to my differences from both the extreme conservatives and the extreme radicals around me. I was either too fast or too slow for nearly all with whom I had to deal. Very few, even of my professed friends, could keep exact step with me. Nevertheless, I managed, as I stated in our little periodical, "to respect myself and maintain a cheerful countenance." I was entirely confident that "my leading objects, principles, and positions, however unpopular now," were "approved of God and will be approved by future generations." "Pursuing the tenor of this humble but ever blessed path of wisdom and peace," I said, "I shall not be ashamed of my testimony, nor terrified by popular opposition, nor discouraged by seeing only 'here and there a traveler.'"[24]

Spirit Manifestations Examined

For a considerable time I received the newspaper reports of the mysterious phenomena which first appeared at Hydesville, New York, and thence spread into Rochester and elsewhere in 1848-49,[25] with great incredulity. I made no haste to investigate the alleged occurrences, though I was soon impressed from what I could learn that there was some unaccountable reality about them. Previous to 1840, I had become so infected with modern Sadduceeism[26] as to presume that I had outgrown the traditions of my childhood and even a part of my own profound spiritual experience. Demons, ghosts, haunted houses, etc., I supposed had been remanded by liberal learning and philosophy to the limbo of exploded superstitions. I had no doubt, however, that the soul or spirit was the essential entity of every human being, radically distinguishable from the material body; that it survived physical dissolution in a conscious state of existence; and that every individual commenced the super-mundane life at the same intellectual and moral point of development attained in the earthly life. But in respect to the power of departed spirits to manifest themselves to those still in this mortal state, I was exceedingly skeptical – groping in mental darkness. The Bible in its literal form plainly taught that doctrine, but I had been persuaded that all passages of such a nature could and should be otherwise explained. There was a long catalogue of books published at different dates during past centuries testifying to the reality of inter-communication between this and the unseen world, but I was ignorant of them and their contents. Animal magnetism, clairvoyance, and other psychological phenomena had arrested my attention and excited my wondering consideration, without suggesting the possibility of departed spirits having anything to do with them or being capable of acting upon principles which those realities illustrated.

In 1841 I had an opportunity of testing the alleged claims of the so-called "divining rod" as an indicator, in the hands of certain persons, of subterranean springs and water courses. I entered upon the investigation of those claims thoroughly unbelieving; I pursued it with great patience, care and thoroughness; I came out of it an unqualified believer. By my experience in that matter, I was led to conclude that "there are more things in heaven and earth than are dreamed of" in our common mundane philosophy,[27] and was admonished never again to allow my self-conceited wisdom to flatter me that I had outgrown all the knowledge of the ancients.

This experience, supplementing my general faith in the superiority of mind over matter, predisposed me to the courteous and hospitable treatment of the purporting spirit manifestations when they appeared in our village and at my own doors in 1849 or 1850. I then determined to satisfy myself what the credible facts of the phenomena which challenged my conscientious consideration were. I ardently desired to know the truth and the whole truth in this matter, and to avoid all delusion. I felt that I had enough common sense, intellectual discernment, and honesty of purpose, to do justice to the proposed investigation and to accept the issue. Great prudence, caution, candor, and acumen were demanded, in order to reach a result that could be relied upon as final and unquestionable. Whatever of these capabilities I possessed, I exercised through a long series of séances held under circumstances that precluded all possibility of deception, trickery, or mistake. By such means, I arrived at the following conclusions: (1) that inter-communication between the spirits of those gone before to the unseen world and those still in the flesh was a reality; (2) that many cases of communications from the departed were clear and reliable, though the personal identity of those producing them was often uncertain; (3) that both *high* and *low* spirits, morally considered, were capable of producing manifestations; (4) that there were frequently equivocal and unreliable communications, due sometimes to the untrustworthiness of those making them and sometimes to the imperfection of the medium or the mesmeric influence of others consciously or unconsciously exerted; (5) that some professed mediums were deceivers and not to be trusted; (6) that all purporting spirit communications must be subjected to rational and moral criticism, like those made by persons in the flesh. To this extent and with these qualifications I became at that time and have ever since remained a Spiritualist. I avowed myself such and defended my position unequivocally, both in speech and through the public press.[28]

Growth and Education of Children

Domestic labors and responsibilities of a general nature underwent little change with us from year to year. But during the period traversed by this chapter our two children were coming rapidly on towards maturity, and their training for the duties of the not far off future and for honorable usefulness in the world was a matter of increasing interest and solicitude on our part. We desired to educate them physically, industrially, mentally, morally, religiously, and socially, in such a way as to enable them to answer the great ends of existence, and they were good subjects for such an education. It was no part of our ambition to secure for them classical and professional distinction on the basis of our common civilization, but to qualify them for solid service in the better order of society we were endeavoring to institute. This included the scholastic acquirements of real value taught in the public schools of Massachusetts. Beyond these we did not care to push them, leaving what more of erudite knowledge might be desirable to their own genius and self-exertion as opportunity should offer or occasion require.

Our eldest surviving child, Abbie, was early qualified to teach primary rudimental classes at Hopedale. But to enlarge her scholarship, make her acquainted with the best methods of imparting knowledge, and prepare her for efficient service in the higher grades of instruction, we sent her to the State Normal school, then located at West Newton under the very competent preceptorship of Rev. Cyrus Peirce.[29] Thence, after a regular course of tuition, she graduated reputably near the close of 1847. Early the next year she entered upon a long series of valuable labors at the head of our public district school, and later as co-principal of a private seminary known as the "Hopedale Home School." Her success was eminent and surpassed only by her usefulness. She became an influential member of the Hopedale Community, having been admitted to our ranks August 24, 1850, and has never swerved from the principles then professed.

May 11, 1851, she was married to Rev. William S. Heywood,[30] the event being solemnized at the close of the regular Sunday service in our chapel with my paternal benediction and amid the congratulations of a friendly congregation. The groom had studied with me for the Practical Christian ministry and been approved and ordained to his chosen work May 25, 1849. He was received to Community membership October 17 of the same year, and for fourteen years was one of our regularly appointed preachers. Subsequent changes at Hopedale, hereinafter to be detailed, necessitated his leaving the place with his family in 1863, soon after which he entered the Unitarian fellowship, under whose auspices himself and wife have been serving God and humanity in different localities unto this day, September 2, 1889.

Our son, Adin Augustus, the inestimable treasure of our hearts and golden staff of our earthly hopes, was destined to an early translation from mortal conditions of existence to the abodes and societies of the angelic realm. We gave him the best common school privileges at our command till he was over seventeen years of age, and then much better ones in the State Normal school at Bridgewater, whereof that excellent scholar and disciplinarian, Nicholas Tillinghast,[31] was principal. Meanwhile the influences of home and of the Community had been happily of a nature to develop his intellectual and moral capabilities in the right direction, and to these, as to all positive endeavors to call forth the best that was in him, he responded heartily and nobly. Though not physically strong, he yet enjoyed tolerable health which seemed to improve as he grew in years. He had an active, elastic mind, and a genial, cheerful temperament, which combined to render him a universal favorite among his associates, young and old. At ten years of age he entered the Hopedale printing office, becoming expert enough at fourteen to assume charge of it as foreman. At the same time he planned, edited, and published on his own account a miniature semi-monthly paper for young people, which he facetiously entitled *The Mammoth*. It had quite a run among his friends as long as he chose to continue it.[32]

On August 8, 1850, he entered the Bridgewater school, as stated, where he prosecuted his studies through the regular year's course and an additional supplementary term. He then stood so high in the estimation of the principal and his associates that he was cordially invited by the proper authorities to take the position of junior assistant teacher in the institution. He accepted the invitation and entered upon the duties of the position full of enthusiasm and hope, December 5, 1851. Here I turn aside for a moment from what was soon to transpire at Bridgewater to affairs relating to our son at Hopedale.

He had become so thoroughly inducted into the principles and life-work to which his parents were devoted that he was ready to consecrate himself to the same before entering upon his new responsibilities in the Normal School. He was accordingly proposed and admitted to membership in the Community, November 22. This consummation was an inexpressible satisfaction to me and scarcely less so to many others. I had watched the indications of his maturing ambition with anxious solicitude lest the temptations of the prevailing civilization should allure him from the struggling cause of Christian Socialism so dear to my heart. Nothing was more natural to one with his abilities and opportunities than to yield to such temptations, but whether he should do so or not depended on his own free choice. If he could not espouse the cause to which I had devoted my life of his own accord and with a full heart, he would be worth nothing to it, even though its nominal adherent. But he did so espouse it, to my great joy, and I could implicitly trust his fidelity. I had been deserted by coadjutors whose defection sadly disappointed me, and I longed to have their places filled with others whose congeniality, mental breadth, moral stability, and judicial competency should not be swerved from our holy standard by petty inconveniences and vexations. He was, I felt confident, by nature, by culture, and by divine grace, one of this reliable type.

Plans for Hopedale Educational Home

Moreover, at the time when he took his stand for what I deemed right and good, I was maturing a favorite educational scheme to be put in operation in connection with our Community, and had organized an association for its actualization. It had been publicly announced and had awakened much enthusiasm among our friends at home and abroad, and all eyes were turned to him as the leading teacher and manager of the institution, soon, it was hoped, to be established. He himself entered most earnestly into the project and was looking forward with intense interest, as his letters testify, to the time when everything should be in readiness for him to assume a position which was full of attractions to him as opening a career of great service to truth and to humanity. A prospectus of the contemplated establishment, which was to be called "The Hopedale Educational Home," setting forth with considerable minuteness of detail its leading characteristic features, its special advantages, its claims upon the rationally religious and reformatory public, and making an urgent appeal for funds, was issued and widely circulated among our friends scattered abroad.[33] To it was appended the constitution of the body organized to prosecute the undertaking and carry it forward to a successful issue, the first section of Article I, indicating its character, reading as follows:

> The grand aim and work of this association shall be to educate the young who may be intrusted to its charge for that purpose; to develop properly, thoroughly, and harmoniously all their natural faculties, moral, intellectual, and physical; to give them, if possible, a high-toned character based on scrupulous conscientiousness and radical Christian principles, a sound mind, well cultivated, stored with useful knowledge and capable of inquiring, reasoning, and judging for itself; a healthful, vigorous body, suitably fed, exercised, clothed, lodged, and recreated; good domestic habits, including personal cleanliness, order, propriety, agreeableness, and generous social qualities; industrial executiveness and skill in one or more of the avocations necessary to a comfortable subsistence; and withal practical economy in money matters. In fine, to qualify them, so far as a comprehensive and thorough education can do it, for solid usefulness and happiness in all the rightful pursuits and relations of life.

Death of Adin Augustus Ballou

This circular, which was issued while Adin Augustus was with us just before taking up his duties as teacher at Bridgewater, was the last work done by him in the printing office – the last manual labor indeed that he ever performed. Little did any of us dream at the time he was thus engaged what an overwhelming storm-blast was gathering its ruthless forces to paralyze our affections and blight our fondly cherished hopes. Yet so it was. Two months later, February 8, 1852, the shadow of death settled down in thick darkness upon our beloved one, and all the brilliant prospects which clustered around his mortal personality vanished forever. After a few days of suffering from an insidious attack of typhoid fever, which his overtaxed energies were unable to repel, he expired at Bridgewater in the arms of his agonized parents, and his pure spirit was translated to its immortal mansion. Only his lifeless body and hallowed memories of him remained to the saddest of mourning circles. None doubted his blessedness in the heavenly realm; but oh, how desolate the places he had beautified and cheered on earth! The void was great and dreary and could never again be filled. Down into his grave went all the cherished plans whose fruition depended so largely on his earthly life, genius, and ministry. Alas, so willed our Heavenly Father, in all-wise love, no doubt, but to the shrouding of our brightest and fondest anticipations for this world. I need not here repeat the story of his life, character, sickness, death, and funeral. For lo, it is written in full in the truthful volume of 192 pages which I published a year afterward, entitled *Memoir of Adin Augustus Ballou. By his Father*. Read that, all ye who have sympathizing hearts, and bless his precious memory.

The shock of our bereavement almost crushed the fondly doting mother, and was all that my own stronger energies could endure. Neither of us ever entirely recovered from its desolating effect. We have been comforted and sustained down to a favored old age, but our consolation and strength have descended from the invisible world. To that fountain of all good we looked for help and received it. Having become convinced of the reality of communications from departed loved ones, we availed ourselves of favoring opportunities of hearing from our beloved son. He came to us presently with messages of soothing assurance, intelligence, and counsel, and our broken hearts were anointed, alleviated, and made glad.

Spirit Manifestations

This tragic experience and the resulting circumstances just narrated hastened the preparation for the press of a work which I had for some time contemplated upon the general subject of spiritualism, as my investigations and studies had caused me to understand and believe it. The volume was published during the ensuing summer with the following title: *An Exposition of Views Respecting the Principal Facts, Causes, and Peculiarities Involved in Spirit Manifestations*, etc. It had a wide circulation among believers and students of psychical phenomena, and a second edition considerably enlarged was issued a few years later. It was also re-published in England, where it commanded the attention not only of professed Spiritualists but of scientists and savants who were not too wise in their own conceit to candidly examine the subject of which it treated. So far as I am personally concerned, I abide confidently by the views and statements presented in that work, though not by all the expectations then entertained of early good results from the movement it aimed to interpret, explain, and set before the public in its true light.

The Non-Resistant

I have now come down in the order of time to the date at which I propose to bring this chapter to a close, but there are a few additional incidents and events of a personal significance and interest deserving of record which I have thus far omitted to mention, and which I will briefly notice in the order of their occurrence.

The New England Non-Resistance Society, of which I was many years president, took measures in 1845 to resuscitate its suspended organ, the *Non-Resistant*, in order to impart new vigor and efficiency to the cause it represented. An arrangement was made whereby the periodical in pamphlet form was to be printed at Hopedale under my editorial charge. The experiment was attempted in good faith, but failed for lack of adequate support, and subscribers who had paid for the publication were supplied to the extent of such payment with our own *Practical Christian*. This paper three years later was adopted by the society mentioned as its organ, at least in part, and to indicate the change made it was given the title *The Non-Resistant and Practical Christian*. Very naturally, I was the responsible managing editor, although most of the matter for the new department was furnished by Henry C. Wright,[34] lecturing agent for the society concerned. He had just returned from Europe, and entered upon the duties of his office with vigorous enthusiasm. Hopedale was his nominal center of operations, though he was there but little. He traversed the country on his mission in all directions, and his correspondence, presenting an account of his labors, with comments and reflections thereon, filled the columns assigned him and gave variety and interest to the paper's contents. His zeal and activity were preeminent, his devotion to the cause unquestionable, his pen prolific, but his discrimination and soundness of exposition did not always command my admiration or satisfy my judgment.

Oliver Johnson and the Practical Christian Ministry

It is proper to mention in these pages a brief connection which my friend, Oliver Johnson, at one time sustained to myself and our Community. An organization called "The Practical Christian Ministry," composed of our properly constituted preachers and lecturers, had been formed, to the membership of which this brother was admitted September 23, 1848. He was a devoted Abolitionist, a teetotaler, peace man, and general moral reformer on Christian principles, and also an able and acceptable public speaker and writer. While in our fellowship he occupied pulpits that were open to us, filled lecturing appointments as one of our approved ministers, and assisted me in editing the *Practical Christian*, making himself in these and other ways very useful to us and our cause. But our field was too narrow for his talents and aspirations, and after a few months he left for a broader one in which he felt that his time and endowments could better serve his Maker and his fellow men. Originally an Orthodox Congregationalist layman, a printer by trade, and sometime publisher of the *Christian Soldier*, he became an early convert to antislavery through William Lloyd Garrison, and subsequently to the whole reformatory gospel, of which he was a staunch apostle and defender, as editor or sub-editor of various progressive publications, to the end of his days. Most of his later life was spent in New York City, where he died December 10, 1889.

Death of Wife's Mother

The decease of my wife's mother, Mrs. Chloe (Albee) Hunt, widow of Pearley Hunt, Esq., occurred September 14, 1849, at the house of her daughter, Mrs. Diana (Hunt) Cook of Milford, inflicting a heavy bereavement upon our household, as did the decease of her husband five years before. Her many estimable qualities justly commanded the veneration and love of her children, grandchildren, other relatives, and friends. Her prayer that she might be spared a long and distressing sickness was graciously answered. She experienced but a few hours of pain and sank gently and without a murmur into that sleep which knows no waking here below.[35] She had passed the allotted time of the psalmist, being in the seventy-sixth year of her age.[36]

Preaching to Theodore Parker's Congregation

On April 11, 1852, just before entering the fiftieth year of my life, I preached by particular request of a few friends to Theodore Parker's congregation at the Melodeon in Boston,[37] upon the subject of Christian Non-Resistance. I always felt that it was a mistake for me to have undertaken this service. The circumstances were unfavorable in many respects, and thwarted my best expectations concerning it. I was still suffering from the shock of our great sorrow. I was mentally and physically enervated and depressed, and had but indifferent command of my thoughts and energies. My voice was sensibly impaired and incapable of filling the vast auditorium in which I spoke. Moreover, the large audience present, with a few exceptions, not only had no sympathy for or interest in my doctrine, but was evidently disappointed, if not disgruntled, at not being privileged to hear the silvery tones and eloquent sentences of their favorite preacher, nor did it fail to manifest a general uneasiness and discontent thereat. To make the matter worse, the introductory exercises, including one of Mr. Parker's long prayers, were so protracted that I did not begin my discourse till half past eleven o'clock. I was therefore in the midst of my argument when the hour of twelve struck, causing considerable numbers of those present, eager perhaps for their dinner, to leave the house, creating thereby much confusion. Mr. Parker, who was very kind and courteous, entreated all to wait patiently and hear me through, but to little purpose. Seeing and comprehending the situation, I cut short what I had intended to say and hurried on to the end that I might as soon as possible relieve those to whom I was proving myself a burden and a bore. I felt at the time, as I have felt ever since, that I brought my wares to an unappreciative market, and that I gained no credit for myself or my cause.

I cannot refrain from mentioning a peculiarly interesting incident that occurred in connection with this service. I read for a scripture lesson the twelfth chapter of Romans in full. Upon taking my seat by the side of Mr. Parker, he smilingly whispered in my ear, "I never read publicly the words 'If thine enemy hunger, feed him; if he thirst, give him drink; for in so doing thou shalt heap coals of fire on his head.' They seem vindictive to me." I marveled greatly at his sensitiveness on this point, especially in view of his known hostility to the doctrine of Christian Non-Resistance which I was there to advocate.

In the afternoon, at Mr. Parker's social conference, the previously announced theme for consideration was set aside and the subject of my crippled morning's sermon was offered for consideration. About 150 persons were present, among whom were William Lloyd Garrison[38] and other able Non-Resistants. Mr. Parker and one or two others freely stated their objections to the doctrine, whilst Mr. Garrison and the rest of us defended it and answered the objections to the best of our ability. It was a free and fair discussion, a respectful and courteous spirit characterizing the disputants and the entire meeting.[39] Taken as a whole, this effort on my part was one of the most disappointing and unsatisfactory of my life.

CHAPTER 20

1852-1858

I entered upon the fiftieth year of my life enfeebled somewhat in body and mind, as I was sadly depressed in spirit by the heavy bereavement that had befallen our household. That visitation came so unexpectedly, seemed so untimely, and prostrated so many cherished hopes, that though divine support and consolation were all we could reasonably pray for, it enveloped us in a very dark cloud of disquietude and grief. I could not wholly throw off the burden that weighed so heavily upon me and hence performed the tasks incumbent upon me with depleted vigor and zeal. The enterprise contemplated by the Educational Home Association, upon which I had lavished so much thought and labor, and in which centered so many and such glowing anticipations on my part and on the part of our ascended son, was paralyzed by what had transpired and ere long was abandoned altogether. The "staff of accomplishment,"[1] so far as its practical realization was concerned, was gone, and though advised by devoted friends to push the project forward, I had no heart to struggle further in its behalf. My Sabbaths were all occupied at home or abroad in the exposition, defense, and diffusion of my long-entertained moral and religious convictions of truth and duty, which were as dear and sacred to me as ever, if not more so, but it was a long time before I could discharge the obligations under which they placed me with that elasticity, fervor, and enthusiasm which formerly inspired me and fitted me for the work I felt called upon to do.

My friends, of whom I had many scattered far and wide over a large territory, were kind and sympathetic towards me, giving me ample opportunity to visit them and to preach my Practical Christian gospel in their respective neighborhoods. I have many pleasant memories of these missionary excursions enjoyed during the period of which I am writing, one of which gave me unusual satisfaction at the time, as it gives me much delight to recall it, now that so many years have passed away since it transpired.

Visit to Troy, New York
The last Sabbath in September, 1852, and the two ensuing days, I spent in Troy, New York, where there was quite a circle of persons sympathizing with me in my general theological and reformatory views as I had published them to the world. Conspicuous among these was Thatcher Clark, formerly of Medway, in which town

I had known him many years before. He had for a long time been a sort of disciple of mine, a liberal patron and gratuitous distributor of my writings. He had often in correspondence urged me to visit his adopted city and address such free-minded seekers after truth as he might induce to hear me. When I finally yielded to his wishes, I was cordially welcomed and hospitably provided for by him and his family, and, during my stay in the city of his adoption, made many new acquaintances, who manifested a genuine interest in my mission, entertained me genially, heard my messages gladly, and purchased my writings with a liberal hand.

In a commodious hall belonging to Brother Clark, I addressed every way respectable audiences three times on Sunday, and also on Monday and Tuesday evenings. My themes of discourse in their order were (1) "The theology, piety, and morality of the Sermon on the Mount"; (2) "The Infinitarian Philosophy," as I termed it, or the doctrine of the absolute illimitableness of God in all his attributes of space, duration, worlds, beings, and variety of conditions; (3) "The kingdom of God *on earth*"; (4) "Spirit Manifestations"; (5) "The Christianization of human society." I was heard with uniformly profound attention, encouraging me to hope for a reasonable amount of good fruit from the seed sown.

Relations to Spiritualism

As already stated, I had at this time become so firmly convinced of the truth of spirit communication, that I had not only been prompted to publish a volume devoted to its defense and elucidation,[2] but to preach and lecture upon it as I found opportunity, and to cooperate in various ways with its accredited advocates and promoters for its promulgation in the community and world. I attended and took part in conventions held in its behalf, wrote for papers devoted to its extension, and consented for a time to be accounted an agent of the Spiritualist Association. I continued this open and active support of the cause for several years, or until I came to feel that my unwavering loyalty to Jesus Christ and his religion, which I never gave up or kept in abeyance even before a spiritualistic assembly, made me an unwelcome coadjutor. I then quietly withdrew from the ranks. But I have never repudiated my deep-seated convictions on the subject, nor declined to express them at proper times and on proper occasions. Nor have I ever cherished any sympathy with the skepticism and contempt shown in high places towards spiritualistic phenomena, but deem most of such contempt and skepticism unreasonable, absurd, and pitiable. There are falsities, errors, and follies connected with nominal Spiritualism with which I have no sympathy, but I am well assured that there is in it a considerable percentage of phenomenal reality and philosophical instruction which no wise mind can reject or despise. Such a mind will select the gold and cast the dross away.

An Encouraging Year

No remarkable developments in Community affairs occurred during the year 1852. There was a small deficit in our industrial operations, which was satisfactorily adjusted. In all other respects, our experiment was eminently encouraging. Our numbers increased, our business interests multiplied, our intellectual, moral, and religious instrumentalities were healthfully vigorous, and our organic arrangements seemed ripening into well-assured solidity and permanence. There were still frictions and difficulties to be overcome, but no dangers to be feared, save from our own frailties and imperfections. We owed more money than was wise through unavoidable necessity, but our pecuniary credit was above suspicion and bound to remain so. We had only to keep the faith, abide steadfastly by our principles, and persevere to the end, and all would be well.

The year 1853 opened auspiciously and all hearts were gladdened by the outlook. But another great and lamentable bereavement befell us ere we had gone far on our way. Br. Butler Wilmarth, M.D., a prominent member of our fraternity, on his way home from a Hydropathic Medical Convention in New York City, was one of the victims of the memorable railroad disaster which occurred at Norwalk bridge, Connecticut, the sixth day of May.[3] As soon as his body was identified and his place of residence ascertained, the former was transmitted to Westborough where he had an institution for invalids, and thence to Hopedale where he received well-deserved funeral honors. He was a pillar in our social edifice, honored and beloved by us all and by a multitude throughout the general community in which he had practiced his profession. The depth and extent of mourning for him can be but faintly imagined. His grave is a marked one in our little cemetery among others of our sainted dead. During the ensuing year, Rev. Brother William H. Fish prepared an excellent memoir of him, which was published with a good steel engraved likeness in a duodecimo volume of 256 pages.[4]

Aside from this afflictive visitation the year was eminently a successful and gratifying one. So hopeful were we for the cause of social reconstruction that schemes were devised and projects contemplated for founding offspring communities in the distant west, several states offering apparently favorable opportunity and inducements in the way of men and means for enterprises of that sort. Some of these seemed near ripening to a practical consummation a year or two later, but proved to have too little vitality to grow into permanent and self-sustaining movements.

In addition to my ordinary routine of labors which continued essentially the same from year to year, I had caused to be instituted not long before the time of which I am now speaking what was called "The Inductive Communion," which was designed to indoctrinate our young people in the principles and methods of social reform, and prepare them for the assumption in maturer life of the responsibilities and duties which they involved and required. This was under my immediate charge for many years, and, meeting as it did every Monday evening, required no little study and effort on my part to make it subservient to the general good of all connected with it.

Inquiries Answered and Errors Withstood

As editor of the *Practical Christian*, I was much occupied in replying to querists and opponents on various points of theology, ethics, and social economy. Standing also, as I did, between extreme radicals and equally extreme conservatives, I was obliged to contend right and left against what seemed to be pernicious errors in both directions. This was especially true on the radical side. All sorts of reformers were abroad, with whom we were in much sympathy as to their main object, but whose notions and declarations on collateral questions of truth and duty often tended, in my judgment, to nothingarianism and social anarchy. Of the pernicious errors from this source that I had to withstand were an incoherent Transcendentalism, which made every individual his own prophet, priest, king, and God;[5] a rabid anti-Bibleism, which treated the scriptures of the two Testaments indiscriminately as a jargonic mass of pseudo-sacred rubbish, of no divine authority whatever;[6] and a gross anti-Sabbatarianism, which left no use for any sort of Sabbath, even for the moral and religious improvement or physical comfort of needy humanity.[7] All such views, in my opinion, were false in principle, prejudicial to human welfare and destructive of the growth of Practical Christian Socialism, and I therefore opposed them with all the vigor at my command.

A truly hallowed production of my pen in 1853 was the *Memoir of Adin Augustus Ballou*, our departed son, already mentioned, which came from the press in September. It was eagerly sought for and read with deep and tender interest by all who had known him and by many beside, both old and young. It had the charm of a novel, the impressive force of a truthful biography, and the moral influence which excites aspiration for a type of life far above the popular level.

The Practical Christian Republic

My health and strength, mental and physical, after a few months were so far restored that I felt ready to undertake the elaboration and completion of a project for a confederacy of communities, which I had long contemplated. I was prompted to do this by the unprecedented prosperity of our Hopedale enterprise, the consequent probability of an early colonization of some of its members in some western state, and the general increase of interest in Social Reform movements throughout the length and breadth of the land.

I therefore spent much time in the autumn and winter following in devising and putting in proper form a general plan for the formation and government of such a confederacy, which I entitled "Constitution of the Practical Christian Republic." This I submitted to my brethren of the community for their examination, criticism, emendation, and perfecting, before giving it to the public. After long and patient consideration of it, article by article and section by section, resulting in sundry alterations and amendments, it was finally approved and adopted, each part by itself, and as a whole, May 7, 1854. By this action a definite public policy and the line of confidently expected progress for the future were clearly sketched and authoritatively prescribed.

The accepted constitution was framed on the most inclusive and comprehensive plan and sought to make provision for a wide diversity of methods and operations in the direction of social reorganization. It granted the privilege of forming, as conviction, inclination, or circumstances might suggest, four different kinds of Fraternal Communities, under the same general head and as co-equal parts of the same general system, to be denominated respectively Parochial, Rural, Joint Stock, and Common Stock Communities. All the details of organization and administration usually embodied in documents of a similar nature, were set forth according to the light I then had, and to the best of my ability.

This being accomplished, I felt the importance, as the new constitution was sent out into the world, of having it accompanied with some explanation or elucidation of its distinctive characteristics and methods of operation; and this feeling grew upon me until I resolved upon preparing and having published a complete exposition of what I deemed the true system of human society, comparing it carefully with the prevailing system and with certain proposed new ones that were claiming the attention of philanthropists and reformers in both our own and foreign lands. I then addressed myself to the assigned task, devoting my time and strength, so far as they were not demanded by more urgent duties, for several months to the preparation of such a work. As a result, there issued from our Community press near the end of 1854 an octavo volume of 655 pages, entitled *Practical Christian Socialism: A Conversational Exposition of the True System of Human Society*, in three parts: I. Fundamental Principles; II. Constitutional Polity; III. Superiority to Other Systems.[8]

The book was written and put in print in very great haste and under many embarrassing circumstances, occasioning numerous defects and errors when considered from a literary point of view, which more time and care would have prevented and which I afterwards had reason to regret. Moreover, I have come to see, by profounder study of the subject, that I could amend what I have written on certain points of theory and practice, as I have amended them in some of the later fruits of my pen. But I still adhere to the grand essentials of the work and am sure that in coming time social reformers will find it rich in suggestions and a helpful guide in any proposed organization of society on a sure and enduring basis.

Journey to the West

Meanwhile there occurred an interesting and noteworthy episode in the story of my career – an exceptional ripple in the usually quiet current of my life. It comprised the experiences of a five weeks' tour with my wife through several of our American States and Canada, taken by the invitation and at the expense of our generous brother, E. D. Draper, who, with his wife, Anna T. Draper, accompanied us. Little time or inclination have I ever had for traveling farther than duty called me for missionary or reformatory purposes, and this was the only extended excursion ever made by me as a release from ordinary cares and labors, or from readily accessible means of recreation. It afforded me, however, great pleasure and satisfaction, and brought me into contact with phases of human life and character I had never met before, and with personages whose acquaintance I was happy to make – some of them being distinguished as friends and champions of truth and righteousness in some one or other field of progressive, philanthropic, humanitarian effort. A few of the salient points of this expedition I am prompted to record.[9]

We bade adieu to our relatives and friends in Hopedale, with tender emotions and amid a shower of good wishes, on the morning of the eighth of May, 1854, proceeding via Springfield, where we spent the night, to New York City. We were kindly and courteously welcomed to the great metropolis by our friend, Morgan L. Bloom,[10] to whom and his accomplished wife we were indebted for many attentions during our four days' stay there. We filled up the time pleasantly and profitably by visiting places of instructive interest, attending public convocations of various character, holding interviews with old or new-made friends, and seeing many of the sights of this modern Babylon. A very unusual experience with us was the going to the theater, where we witnessed and heard the admirable play of *Uncle Tom's Cabin* which had been repeated from the same stage more than three hundred times. We also attended the annual meeting of the American Anti-Slavery Society, went to an exhibition of the Five Points Reformatory Mission[11] and to the then far-famed Crystal Palace,[12] finding at each of these places something attractive and morally profitable.

We availed ourselves of the opportunity of taking a brief trip to "The North American Phalanx,"[13] the Fourierite community in Monmouth County, New Jersey, where we were courteously received and hospitably entertained by President [Charles] Sears[14] and his associates – gentlemen and ladies all. We were shown the premises generally, with the buildings and appurtenances thereto belonging, and the different departments of domestic, industrial, social, and educational activity. We were greatly pleased and edified, leaving the place well stored with topics for salutary reflection and practical use.

May 13 we extended our journey to Philadelphia, spending the Sabbath in quietude there and devoting Monday to the famous Fairmount Water Works, Laurel Hill Cemetery, and other celebrated localities in and about the city.[15]

On the sixteenth we proceeded through Baltimore to Washington, taking rooms at Beers' well-known Temperance Hotel. There we remained four days, dividing our time between the various imposing public buildings, congressional proceedings, and personal interviews with the great champions of freedom then in vigorous conflict with the slave power over the infamous Kansas-Nebraska bill,[16] which was on its final passage in the House – American tyranny thereby driving its triumphal chariot furiously over the forms of its temporarily vanquished opponents. I had brief conversations with Charles Sumner, Joshua R. Giddings, and Gerrit Smith, neither of whom had I met before, and with Thomas Davis of Providence, Rhode Island, a former acquaintance – all unsuppressible Anti-Slavery members of the National Legislature and worthy of their great reputation.[17]

On Saturday, May 20, we left Washington on our way westward by the Baltimore and Ohio Railroad, whose mighty and amazing constructions awaken wonder and admiration in the minds of all beholders.[18] We stopped over Sunday at Cumberland, Maryland, resuming our journey early Monday morning and proceeding to Wheeling, Virginia, where we took a steamer to Cincinnati, Ohio. Arriving there early on Wednesday we were soon conveyed to Spring Garden, a semi-suburban part of the city, and to the residence there of our long-tried, faithful, and estimable friends, Andrew H. Ernst and his wife, Sarah H. (Otis) Ernst, formerly of Boston. This was our objective point and the western limit of our pilgrimage. Mr. and Mrs. Ernst welcomed us with the warmest cordiality to the unstinted hospitality of a home abounding with every convenience and comfort that ample wealth could furnish or appreciative visitors enjoy. Our sojourn lasted eight days, during which we received all the attention that could possibly render it pleasant and memorable. We were taken to numerous places of interest and instruction in and about the city, and introduced to many distinguished and excellent people; in fine, were filled to the brim with experiences and recollections calculated to gladden and enrich a lifetime.

During our stay in Cincinnati, I was exceedingly happy to renew a former slight acquaintance with Rev. Abial Abbot Livermore,[19] pastor of the Unitarian church of the city, and to expand it by two or three delightful interviews. I met him at a Sabbath-school picnic on Saturday, May 27, when he informed me that an arrangement had been made for me to occupy his pulpit the following day. This I accordingly did, gratified as I was at the fraternal courtesy of my clerical brother and with the opportunity of preaching to his people the gospel of a pure and practical Christianity. Such a gospel in essential respects they have from Brother Livermore. For his is an enlightened, liberal, reformatory, Christian soul. He bears faithful testimony against all manner of wickedness in high places and in low places, and in favor of truth, righteousness, and human improvement in all things. He is the author of a valuable commentary on the gospels and the two following books of the New Testament, of an excellent Prize Essay on the Mexican War, and of other meritorious works. He was formerly pastor of the Unitarian church in Keene, New Hampshire, and for some twenty years now past has been the able, revered, and beloved president of the Theological School at Meadville, Pennsylvania.

We spent a delightful afternoon on Wednesday, May 31, at Rev. Mr. Livermore's with our fellow-travelers, Brother and Sister Ernst, and Rev. Daniel Parker,[20] an old Restorationist and Practical Christian friend from New Richmond, Ohio; and also enjoyed the services and festivities connected with the marriage of one of Brother Ernst's daughters the day following. On Friday morning, June 2, we took leave of our kind and beloved host and hostess, and turned our faces homeward. The former we never met again and the latter only two or three times in her subsequent widowhood. They both with Brother and Sister Draper are at home in the world of spirits, while wife and I survive them until now (December 1889), but must soon rejoin them in the better land.

From Cincinnati we journeyed via Cleveland to Buffalo, New York, and took lodgings there. The next day, Saturday, we proceeded to Niagara Falls, engaging rooms at the Clifton House on the Canada side,[21] where we were quartered till Monday. Meanwhile we traversed the enchanted country thereabouts and filled our souls with the majestic wonders and glories displayed on every hand, making our stay one ever to be remembered and enjoyed. Thence we went to Queenston, lingering *en route* for an hour or two at the awful whirlpool, and from Queenston crossed the then longest suspension bridge in the world to Lewiston, New York.[22] Boarding a steamer, we sailed across Lake Ontario to Ogdensburg and thence to the semi-antique city of Montreal, passing, as we entered St. Lawrence river, through the midst of the far-famed Thousand Isles and all the loveliness of scenery they enshrine, and, farther on, the fearful rapids, which seemed ready at any moment to engulf our floating palace and all it contained in one common doom. But brave hearts and skilled hands had our fortunes in their keeping, and we all came into quiet waters at length without injury or harm.[23]

At Montreal everything was novel and strange to us – had a decidedly foreign aspect. The style of architecture, the appearance of the streets, the manners and speech of the people, soldiers taking their rounds, Catholic priests in long black robes, Sisters of Charity gliding about, the great cathedral with its ponderous bell, penitential confessions, and spectacular performances before its altars, all told us how unlike ourselves these northern neighbors are and how little we had yet known of the peculiarities and diversities of human life and its manifestations.

Leaving Montreal by the Grand Trunk railway, we whirled rapidly through the wild and picturesque landscapes of northern New Hampshire and western Maine, arriving at Portland in the evening of June 9. Thence the next day we journeyed to Boston, spending the night there, and going to our Hopedale home on the eleventh, where we received most cordial greetings from all our relatives and friends.[24] We had been gone thirty-three days and had been greatly favored and blessed in all our wanderings and visitations. We returned glad and grateful that we had been preserved from all harmful casualties and had found refreshing and new life to both body and spirit. All were well and prosperous in our beloved dale, and we at once resumed the places and duties to which we were accustomed and from which we took leave of absence more than a month before.

New Communities Contemplated

The year upon which this pilgrimage was made, 1854, was the palmiest in the history of the Hopedale Community. It throve in all its departments, operations, and interests. Materially, socially, and religiously, its progress was most satisfactory. It was much the same through the succeeding year, 1855; no serious reverses or drawbacks occurring to diminish the fruit of our labors in any field of effort, to awaken distrust of the success of our undertaking, or chill the ardor of our fondest hopes. So well assured were we of the soundness of our position as Christian Socialists and of the not far distant triumph of our cause that a reawakened interest was generated in the subject of founding new communities in the virgin territory of some of the western states, and steps were taken looking to the practical realization of the involved idea and purpose. Offers of a domain of considerable size were made us by a gentleman in Wisconsin who had been converted to the doctrine of social reconstruction by my writings (though not fully to Christian Non-Resistance), and who was desirous of having that doctrine put to the test of practical experiment in his vicinity with himself as a coadjutor. Numerous articles appeared in the *Practical Christian*, mostly over the signature of Brother William H. Fish, urging a movement in the same behalf on general principles, without indicating any particular locality, and calling for the names of persons ready to enlist in it.[25] As a result of this renewed agitation of the matter, several of our own Hopedale brethren left home in the autumn of 1855 for the definite purpose of securing lands and taking the initiatory steps towards the realization of the object which commended itself to so many minds and which now seemed near achievement. Their objective point was the state of Minnesota, then rapidly filling up with new settlers, as offering the most advantages for the proposed undertaking. A series of unavoidable misfortunes prevented them from doing anything towards the accomplishment of their purpose until the following spring, when lands were secured and a settlement was made. This was done by individuals of the party on their own personal responsibility and in their separate behalf, though with a view of future consolidation and communitization, under one of the forms prescribed in the constitution of the Practical Christian Republic. This, however, never came to pass.[26] Events that were even then ripening to a disastrous culmination at Hopedale, as will soon be narrated, not only put an end to all efforts in that direction, but postponed the whole great question of social regeneration and the work of building up on earth a new and divine order of human society according to the New Testament ideal, to an indefinite future.

Lecture Tours

While these things were transpiring, I was devoting my time and energy to the advancement of the principles and cause I held dear, at home and abroad, wherever I could get a hearing. Rarely, if ever, did a Sunday pass by when I was not engaged in two or three religious services, and rarely a week in which I did not lecture upon some theme pertaining to some one of the great reforms with which I had become identified and to the bettering of the condition of my fellow-men. Many were the localities I visited in Massachusetts, Rhode Island, and Connecticut, as fields of missionary labor, for one or several days at a time; some of them regularly and others as mutual convenience would permit.

In June 1855 I spent ten days at Mystic, Connecticut, by invitation of Rev. S. S. Griswold, a Seventh-day Baptist minister[27] of catholic spirit, preaching and lecturing there and in the vicinity with scarcely an intermitting day. In October I journeyed as far away as Pennsylvania and New York on a distinctively missionary tour which was made memorable by interviews with two or three distinguished personages of that period of American history. I first went to Philadelphia where I visited Passmore Williamson,[28] a devoted Abolitionist, arbitrarily incarcerated in Moyamensing prison for alleged contempt of court in refusing to testify against certain fugitive slaves, of whose experiences he was accused of being conversant. He was in good spirits and in no wise humiliated or intimidated by his pro-slavery assailants and persecutors. I also by invitation dined one day with the celebrated Professor Robert Hare,[29] a recent convert from stiff, scientific skepticism to modern Spiritualism and faith in immortality. He was kind, polite, affable, and we naturally fell into a friendly conversation upon the subject to which both of us had given considerable attention. It was only good manners for me to allow him to lead off in the talk, to assent to his views when I could, and to dissent, when I must, with all the deference my conscience would allow. He was honestly blunt in contemning Moses and the prominent Old Testament characters generally, as unprincipled and cruel, Christ and his apostles as foolish and impracticable enthusiasts, and all the alleged spirit manifestations of the past as unreliable and of little or no account. But those of the present day, he claimed, are scientifically demonstrated to be true and so worthy of hearty acceptance. The reader can judge how his assertions and animadversions struck me. He was a Spiritualist, as I was, but of a very different type from myself. I puzzled him with some Socratic questions which he failed to answer to my satisfaction. All passed off pleasantly and we parted courteously.

After a four days' sojourn in Philadelphia, where I addressed public audiences some half a dozen times, I went via New York City and Albany to central New York, visiting my old, honored, and beloved friend and brother, Rev. Samuel J. May, at Syracuse. I remained with him over the Sabbath, preaching to his people in the morning and giving them a lecture on Christian Non-Resistance in the evening.

Appeal to Gerrit Smith

The day following I made a detour to Peterborough for the purpose of calling upon the distinguished reformer and philanthropist, Gerrit Smith, who kindly welcomed me to his commodious and hospitable mansion. I found him, true to his reputation, a man of dignified personal presence, thoroughly educated and devoutly religious, a devoted moral and political reformer, the heir to a princely estate, eminently charitable to the poor, a generous donor to public institutions, an outspoken friend of the suffering classes, a liberal entertainer of thousands, with wife and children to match. The special object of my visit was to solicit a loan or donation in aid of our Practical Christian Republic, having then in prospect the purchase of new Community domains.

He listened to the presentation of my case and appeal respectfully and kindly, but all his disposable funds were at that time pledged to other important objects of a humanitarian character, chief among which was the endowment of a university wherein should be taught his own peculiar views of "Righteous Civil Government," one of his leading hobbies.[30] Hence all he could give to my movement was five dollars. I thanked him and left somewhat disappointed, though I had undertaken this suit rather on other people's judgment and faith than my own. Experience, not in this case only but generally, has taught me that rich people must not be expected, much less depended upon, to contribute largely to the building up of such a kingdom of God on the earth as is proposed in my Practical Christian Socialism. I soon after returned to my Hopedale home to prosecute the labors devolving upon me nearer at hand, and to share at an early day the bitter disappointment and grief resulting from the utter wreck of the most sacred hopes of my life, all the more bitter and crushing because so sudden and undreamed of when it occurred.

The Fatal Crisis

As I have already stated, the affairs of the Community were apparently in a highly prosperous and encouraging condition through the years 1854 and 1855, and I flattered myself with the idea that all was well for the future beyond doubt or peradventure. So I felt when we convened in annual meeting, January 9, 1856.[31] The financial statement of the treasurer was not ready in all its details, but the general declaration was made by him that the joint stock operations had suffered no detriment and that the industrial and financial outlook was bright and encouraging. I was greatly pleased with this assurance and my gratification was enhanced by the concluding sentences of the address of our president, Brother Ebenezer D. Draper, as follows:

> We may rejoice together in considering the degree of harmony that exists at the present time in our Community; greater, I think, than ever before. And I hope and believe that with our past experience and present advantages, we shall continue to increase in love and wisdom and so become more and more a light to those around us, proving to the world that Christian Socialism opens a more excellent way in which men may live together as brethren, and that it gives us, as it will all who yield to its saving power, peace and goodwill to one another and to the whole human race. May the good God prosper and bless us all.

After such an assuring benediction, which set the bells of gladness ringing in all our hearts, what but a thunderclap from a clear sky could fill us with greater consternation than the announcement of the same president, only six weeks later, that the financial condition of the Community was so desperate and hopeless that he and his brother, George Draper,[32] had decided to withdraw their investments from the joint stock capital. What had happened to cause such a reversal of the representation made at the annual meeting? We were then told that the deficit in the entire operations of the previous year was only $146.15 – an insignificant sum. But a more critical examination of monetary affairs disclosed the fact that the four-percent dividends due to the joint stock had not been reckoned, and that the natural depreciation in the value of buildings, machinery, etc., had also been overlooked; which, with sundry other omissions, made our actual loss some ten or twelve thousand dollars – an ominous and, as was thought, insurmountable burden!

As soon as this state of things became known, a Community meeting was called and continued by adjournment through several sessions. Earnest and pungent discussions were carried on, and the feelings of many members were greatly disturbed. If there were blame anywhere in the management, it was found difficult to locate it. Evidently there had been lack of business ability or gross neglect somewhere, and, failing to discover where it was, it was natural and easy to attribute it to the system, and this was the culminating accusation. In making it, the lead was taken by George Draper, who had been with us but two years, and who, from the beginning, had only dubious faith in Community life. He was a natural born man of the world, given to money-making, impatient of high ideals, but thoroughly honest in his opinions, upright in his dealings, and of unquestioned integrity and honor. He was moreover inflexible of will and purpose, and when once determined upon an object, he pursued it without hesitation or prevarication. So thoroughly persuaded was he in his own mind that our socialistic scheme was impracticable and the cause of all our troubles, and so persistent was he in attempting to bring his brother, our president, with whom he was closely associated in business, over to the same conclusion, that he at length, though with much difficulty, succeeded. This accomplished, the doom of the Community was irrevocably sealed.

Our fate was in the hands of these two men. They were in possession of three-fourths of the joint stock, and the withdrawal of their share would so cripple our movement financially, that it would be absolutely impossible for it to go on. The rest of us were poor, having no means to purchase their interest in the property, and though our credit was good and might have been used to meet the emergency, to have so used it would have been foolhardy and perilous – would have been to load ourselves with a burden which all could see would not only crush us to the earth but defraud those who might befriend and help us. This therefore was not to be thought of for a moment. The only alternative was to yield to the inevitable and make the best of it.

As soon as this was settled in my mind, my first care was to see to it that in the final adjustment of affairs with the Draper brothers, provision should be made for the full payment, principal and interest, of all just demands against the Community. This was accordingly done, to the satisfaction of all parties, and no creditor of ours ever lost a dollar by his confidence in us. Then there came, under my general direction and by my hand, a radical change in our Community constitution, whereby our industrial arrangements were all abolished, our real and movable property was made over to the proper claimants or otherwise disposed of, and the organization itself reduced to the form of a religious society – a mere shadow of its former self.[33] This being accomplished, many members withdrew and went to localities more favorable to self-support or to the realization of their best purposes in life for themselves, their families, and their fellow-men, while newcomers multiplied as convenience, business interests, or general worldly considerations influenced them. But never afterward did a single person settle in Hopedale from any regard to its original moral, social, and religious principles, spirit, purpose, and aim.

My distress and mortification at this issue of our Community enterprise – at this overthrow of my most cherished hopes and plans for the regeneration and progress of individual and social humanity, were inexpressible – almost unendurable. I felt like one prematurely consigned to a tomb. My darling expectations were blasted, my noblest ambition was crushed. I had been disappointed and deserted before, yet I could fall back on remaining resources sufficient to sustain me and urge me forward in my work. But now my calamity was greater than ever – overwhelming and irreparable. Nothing remained but to submit with the best grace possible to a deplorable failure, and in after years to search out the errors and mistakes which had caused it, and, having found them, to make such record of them as should render them serviceable as admonitions and warnings to philanthropists and social reformers in coming generations. This I resolved to do, and by the preserving and helping mercy of God, have lived to accomplish it, as witnesseth my *History of the Hopedale Community* and my third volume of *Primitive Christianity*; both of which works I leave in manuscript for my successors to publish and give to the world.[34]

Commune No. 1

While the occurrences just narrated were taking place, but before any serious results were apprehended, I became involved, much to my subsequent discomfort, in an undertaking of a more secular nature, though not disconnected with our Community system. Hoping to strengthen our common bond of union and aid the common cause, as well as to secure better employment for a portion of our members not adequately provided for in that particular, I devised a plan for the formation of what was called a *Commune* within the pale of our general jurisdiction.[35] This new body was to have certain specified franchises and privileges of its own for the associate use of those disposed to join it in the management of such kinds of industry as might by common consent be established. The plan received the sanction of the parent body, signatures to its compact or constitution were obtained, and *Commune No. 1* was organized and equipped for its designed work. It embraced some half dozen members and their families, mine included. In order that the venture might be well inaugurated, I accepted its presidency and fathered its financial obligations. Two or three kinds of business were begun, chiefest of which was the manufacture of a patent tackle block for the lifting of heavy bodies in warehouses and on board vessels. Our required financial output exceeded our calculations and available resources, and we found ourselves at the start heavily burdened with debt. Just as we were getting under tolerable headway, though our principal article of production did not find the market we anticipated, the Community crisis burst upon us, producing confusion in our ranks and in our arrangements; and our infant Commune was strangled in its cradle. The upshot of the whole matter was that I had to shoulder a large percentage of the incurred liabilities, which in due time were honorably met and canceled; though it was many years before I outgrew all the losses sustained by this fruitless effort to help some of my less fortunate associates. So it was that another of my favorite projects vanished before my eyes.

The New Dispensation

The Hopedale Community, though it had been transformed into a mere religious body, still bore its old name, retained a few nominal guaranties against ignorance, poverty, and vice, and struggled on in its dismantled state as best it could. It kept up its public and social meetings with a good degree of regularity and zeal, and even its quarterly convocations for a time. Its declaration of principles remained unchanged, and some flickering hopes that possibly it might be resurrected lingered in the breasts of its more devoted friends. Its educational activities were not permitted to languish, but its membership diminished, residents uncommitted to anything it had formerly stood for were peopling its surrendered domain, and it had no recognized part or lot in promoting the growing industrial prosperity of the village whose foundations it had laid in toil and tears. If its missionaries went abroad to proclaim the gospel hitherto represented by it, their words were shorn of much of their power by reporting the failure of their efforts to actualize that gospel in the manifold relations of life at home.

Personally, I was hedged in on every side by circumstances that I could neither destroy, overcome, nor escape. I could not go back on my record so long as I was unconvinced that I had been in the wrong, nor could I cease from my ministrations in behalf of what, notwithstanding all disappointments and failures, I still believed with all my heart was true and right. I must go forward in the same course as before, not utterly cast down but upheld by an invisible guardianship which has never forsaken me.

Arrangements were made whereby I came into entire control of the *Practical Christian*, assuming all the pecuniary responsibility of its publication, and conducting its editorial department essentially on the lines previously followed and in such a manner as, in my judgment, would most effectually serve my Maker and my kind. Funerals and weddings, distributed over a wide extent of territory and occurring with unabated frequency, still commanded considerable of my time and attention, while calls and opportunities for preaching and lecturing on Sunday and during the week came from far and near, leaving me no time for idleness or ennui. I was still devoted to all the great reforms of the age and stood ready to champion them on moral and religious grounds, although the Hopedale apostasy had cut the nerve of my missionary zeal in behalf of Christian Socialism – the one great comprehensive reform which included all the rest. I found ample field for the expenditure of whatever ability I could command in expounding the distinctive characteristics of pure and undefiled religion, in showing their applicability to all human affairs in individual and social life, and in urging them upon the attention and acceptance of those who would listen to my appeals – thus broadcasting the seed which should in some coming day yield a harvest of good, both in an improved personal character and in a higher order of society. If I could not attain to all I had calculated upon and striven after for so many years, I trusted that somehow or other in the economy of God I could be a sort of modern John the Baptist, preparing the way for a better future and making ready for the coming of the divine kingdom, perhaps after my earthly labors were over.

Moreover, in those days my views upon Spiritualism were in good demand and I was always ready to give a reason for the faith and hope that were in me upon that subject, endeavoring to set it forth and defend it on rational and scriptural grounds and so to save it, if possible, from over-credulity, which encouraged fraud and humbuggery on the one hand, and from anti-Christian and super-Christian radicalism on the other, which was equally hostile to what I deemed the truth and equally offensive to me. The readiness with which some people swallowed without discrimination whatever assumed to be a revelation from the spirit world was hardly less unreasonable and deplorable than the flippancy and irreverence with which others ignored the claims of pure Christianity and scorned to recognize the beauty, power, and glory of the principles and precepts of the religion of the New Testament.

Vision of Thomas Lake Harris

It may not be out of place to note in this connection an interview I had in the autumn of 1856 with Rev. T. L. Harris,[36] a sometime Universalist minister, but for many years a Spiritualistic seer and lecturer of wide repute, and the founder of a

Community of Spiritualists at Mountain Cove, Virginia. It occurred during a six days' preaching and lecturing visit I made with my wife to the town of Southold, Long Island,[37] upon invitation of friend Joseph H. Goldsmith, whose acquaintance I formed during my brief pastorate in New York City twenty-eight years before. His father, Zaccheus Goldsmith, was an intelligent, upright, noble-minded man, a Christian philanthropist, and an earnest Abolitionist as early as 1795.[38] The son had imbibed most of the same spirit and was ready to welcome my views upon religious, moral, and social theories and to aid me in promulgating them in his general neighborhood. At the time of the visit spoken of, Mr. Harris was boarding with a Mr. Richmond a few miles away, who asked us to spend an afternoon at his house that we might see the widely-known prophet of the new dispensation. It was a deeply interesting and enjoyable occasion. The most memorable incident of it was the description of a vision seen by Brother Harris, which, aside from its poetic beauty, was sublimely grand and holy, and agreed so closely with my highest aspirations, convictions, and inspirations, that I could but accept it as substantially true. The interview gave me unqualified satisfaction, and I returned to my Hopedale home greatly strengthened, encouraged, and blessed.

Events from 1858 onward will constitute the subject matter of another chapter.

CHAPTER 21

1858-1862

There is little to be said concerning Community affairs during the four years whose transactions and experiences the present chapter purports to put on record. The sanguine hearts of its disappointed devotees still clung to the dubious hope that it might be made a rudimental seminary for preparing men and women to be founders and co-operators of more permanent movements elsewhere, the character and purpose of which should be similar to what its own originally were. Its regular weekly, monthly, quarterly, and yearly meetings were continued in vigorous activity, and its semi-monthly organ, the *Practical Christian*, went its regular round as in former days. Its promulgatory publications and other instrumentalities for reaching and enlightening the public mind upon the great moral and religious truths and duties which it still represented were not suffered to decline, while its common and higher grade schools were reputably sustained under teachers of its own rearing.

The Hopedale Home School, though a private enterprise, reflected honor upon its proprietary principals, patrons, and the Community under whose approving auspices it was originally started. It was established and first opened to pupils in the spring of 1855 by Morgan L. Bloom and wife from the city of New York, but a year later passed into the hands of my son-in-law, Rev. William S. Heywood, and his wife, Abbie B. Heywood, whose management rendered it eminently serviceable in its proper educational field to many youthful aspirants of Hopedale and vicinity, and to the children of progressive and reformatory families in other and sometimes far distant localities. It was in operation some seven or eight years, acquiring an enviable reputation for scholarship and moral standing and leaving behind it, when it came to be closed, a fragrant and enduring memory.[1]

My labors during the year 1858 were expended mostly near home. On twenty Sundays I ministered in Hopedale; on twenty-three in Milford by special arrangement with a society of Spiritualists there; the other nine in places more or less distant where I had friends desirous of hearing me. My themes of discourse were generally drawn from my favorite field of Practical Christianity, though a considerable number of them pertained to some phase of the subject of Spiritualism, there being then a large demand for utterances of that sort. But my kind of Spiritualism in no wise conflicted with my theological and ethical system, long well known to those familiar with my preaching and writings. I never allowed my views upon any one great topic belonging to the realm of truth and duty to contradict or undermine those I entertained upon any other. And there was a corresponding harmony and consistency in all my testimonies. Christ, as the great teacher of truth, righteousness, and love – the Prince of Peace, never resisting evil with evil but overcoming it with good[2] – was always the central figure on my banner, and I always abjured all carnal weapons as instruments or agencies for building up the kingdom of heaven on the earth, many distinguished personages to the contrary notwithstanding.

Views on the Bible

About this time an unusual interest was awakened in our populous town of Milford and vicinity upon the subject of the inspiration and authority of the Hebrew and Christian scriptures. It was the result of certain bold discussions and criticisms which were started and continued for some time in a series of meetings instituted by an association formed for the purpose of examining the claims of those writings and matters akin thereto. Several Spiritualistic lectures, treating more or less freely and iconoclastically the sacred volume, increased the popular feeling. The Milford Bible Society, to counteract what its members thought to be the harmful tendency of these public utterances, inaugurated a course of Sunday evening lectures to be given at the town hall by able clergymen in defense of the so-called doctrine of Plenary Inspiration. In the midst of the prevailing excitement, *pro* and *con*, I was called upon for a presentation of my views upon the book in question, which were understood to differ somewhat from any of those that had been advocated and urged upon the attention of the public.

In answer to this call I prepared with much care and comprehensiveness an address which I delivered to a very large and deeply attentive audience in the town hall on the evening of Sunday, January 16, 1859. It was entitled "The Inspiration of the Bible." It was received with more favor than I could reasonably have expected under the circumstances, and seemed to meet a general want in the community. Its publication was earnestly solicited, in response to which a large edition was issued and a wide circulation secured. In order to give my present readers some definite idea of the ground I took, defended, and illustrated in that discourse, I present herewith a liberal extract from the pages of the published pamphlet.[3] After distributing the general mass of the professed friends and admirers of the book into five different groups under a system of classification distinctively my own, I proceeded as follows:

> I must differ more or less from all these specified classes and offer you views not in entire accord with any of them. For many years I have believed that the fundamental principles of the Bible are absolutely divine, but that its explicative ideas and language are properly human. To explain, justify, and illustrate this view is the principal design of the present lecture.

What do I mean by the phrase "fundamental principles of the Bible"? To answer this question I must state definitely my general estimate and appreciation of the Bible. I hold its essential excellence is solely of a spiritual and religious nature. It sets forth, commends, and insists on certain great spiritual and religious truths and certain great spiritual and religious duties which are indispensable to human well-being and happiness in both the present and future states of existence. These great truths man must receive into his understanding, either by knowledge or faith, and cherish them in his soul with a profound love and loyalty, or he cannot be eminently and permanently blest. Also, on the basis of these same truths, he must perform and habitually practice the corresponding spiritual and religious duties, or he can never be eminently and permanently blest. These truths and duties are the fundamental principles of the Bible.

The Bible is not to be regarded as an encyclopedia of universal knowledge. It is not of authority in the physical sciences. We are not to consult its pages to learn astronomy, geology, chemistry, anatomy, natural history, physiology, agriculture, etc. These we can study better elsewhere. Nor are we to go to the Bible to acquire a knowledge of mathematics, logic, grammar, music, statuary, painting, etc. It settles no questions of such a nature. Casually, incidentally, and fragmentarily, it affords us somewhat that may be of service to us in those departments of inquiry, but nothing authoritatively important. Its grand object, use, and excellence are purely of a spiritual and religious character. We are to go to it as spiritual and religious beings to obtain help in the knowledge and practical application of the fundamental principles of true religion. In respect to these, it is of inestimable value, because all the physical and merely intellectual knowledges in the universe, if we were masters of them, would be insufficient to render us eminently and permanently holy and happy; whereas, these essentials of true religion would do so with or without much proficiency in the things of the physical and intellectual life.

Next, what do I mean when I assert that "the explicative ideas and language of the Bible are properly human"? I mean that there is a radical difference between its fundamental principles and the forms of speech in which they are expressed and made intelligible to the human mind. Every essential principle of religious truth and duty existed before the Bible was written; yes, before it was revealed to the understanding of man. It existed intrinsically from eternity and will exist to eternity, independently of all human knowledges, ideas, and writings. God himself is from and to eternity the same, whether known or unknown by His creatures; so are the great principles of true religion. The Bible did not originate them. They do not depend on the Bible, but the Bible depends on them. They emanated from and are co-eternal with God. If the Bible had never existed, they would exist; if every copy of the Bible were annihilated, not a particle of those divine essentials would cease to be. By some means they became known to the writers of the Bible and were therein recorded. Thus they became known to millions more. I hold that those who first had knowledge of them obtained it by divine revelations and inspirations. How did God give them these revelations and inspirations? This is purported to have been done in several ways:

(1) Through angels and spirits; by sensible manifestations and communications, oracular voices, signs, and tokens.

(2) Through the opened spiritual senses of persons in visions, dreams, and trances.

(3) Through strong impressions, suggestions, and convictions, divinely produced upon the soul.

(4) Through special divine quickenings and intensified activities of the intuitive, rational, and religious faculties.

(5) Through that common and universal influx from the unseen world which operates more or less on all moral agents according to their various degrees of susceptibility.

Now let us consider certain facts necessarily attendant upon all divine revelations and inspirations.

(1) They were not mentioned in any book of the Bible till after they had taken place. They came to pass and were recorded some time, sooner or later, afterwards.

(2) They were given to *human beings* and had to be adapted to their finite capacity and comprehension. It was impossible in the nature of things to make mankind fully understand and comprehend them at once, in all their bearings, whether receiving them at first or second hand.

(3) They were given at particular times, and not equally at all times. Angels and spirits did not come frequently and regularly. Oracles, signs, tokens, visions, dreams, trances, strong impressions, and high inspirations, occurred only on special occasions, and at divinely-appointed seasons. Prophets, sages, and apostles were wonderfully illumined for a while and then left to themselves. Some who were heavenly-minded and wise under certain circumstances, were, under others, carnally-minded, sensual and foolish. For instance, Solomon.

(4) After receiving divine revelations and inspirations, so as to see and partially comprehend central facts and fundamental principles, the patriarchs, prophets, and inspirees exercised their own powers of thought and judgment as to details, and clothed essentials more or less with explicative ideas which were after the manner of men. Thus the absolutely divine became clothed with human habiliments and sometimes obscured by error.

(5) When the Bible inspirees came to express and record their experiences, it could be done only in human speech. God never invented a peculiar language to be exclusively used in the Bible. The Hebrew, Chaldaic, and Greek, used to record the divine revelations and inspirations of the Old and New Testaments, were substantially the same inside and outside the sacred volume. They had to be such as the people, whose instruction was designed, could understand.

(6) Many ideas, opinions, sentiments, and particulars, which appear in connection with the fundamentals of the Bible, were obviously written by prophets, legislators, kings, priests, apostles, and evangelists, simply from their own minds – not from absolutely divine inspiration.

Such are my general views of the subject and I am confident I can fully sustain them by adequate proofs and illustrations.

These extracts will indicate where I then stood and where I still stand in my reverence for the Hebrew and Christian scriptures; between the Plenary Inspirationists on the one hand and the sweeping deniers of its divine authority on the other. Of the latter there were in those days several varieties, some of whom stood in the high places of religious, moral, and philanthropic reform. I did not question the sincerity of such, but I did question their knowledge, judgment, and inevitable influence. Of one thing I was certain: that the leaven of their doctrines was a fatal poison to the Practical Christianity and to the new social order I desired to build up, inasmuch as whoever received these doctrines became straightway his own lord and master – an individual sovereign and hence incapable of cooperating harmoniously with others in the reconstruction of society and the establishment of the kingdom of God on the earth. I therefore withstood and protested against all such denials of Bible authority, as the files of the *Practical Christian* abundantly show.

Pleasant Memories

Among the pleasant memories of those days is that of a visit from our highly esteemed friend and sympathizer in every good word and work, John Child of Philadelphia.[4] I became acquainted with him and his estimable wife, Rachel, in 1846, when I first shared the hospitality of their delightful home. They were Hicksite Friends[5] in religious conviction and association, largely philanthropic and eminently intelligent, upright, and noble-hearted. Rachel had departed to her heavenly mansion and her venerable survivor cheered and gladdened us, as stated, in the summer of 1858.

Another happy event, the flavor of which still lingers in our hearts, was a reception given us by our Milford friends to whom I was then ministering regularly twice a month, with the concurrence of a few Hopedalians, in our home chapel early the following spring. It was a simple, unpretentious occasion, but rich and fragrant in all that renders such gatherings valuable. Its material, moral, and social components were excellent and were accompanied by substantial and abiding tokens of respect, affection, and gratitude, of which both myself and wife were appreciative recipients.

The Practical Christian Church in Hopedale

The Hopedale Community, with its environing population, fell away from the high moral level formerly maintained and slowly descended the plane which inclined towards the old social state – a retrogression to which it was doomed by the revolution of 1856. The village it had founded amid toil and trial prospered externally under the control of its temporal lords, with many demonstrations of successful business enterprise. But the personally religious life of the people as manifestly declined, notwithstanding the maintenance of the usual appointments of public instruction and worship, and this decline prompted a few of the more spiritually minded and zealous of our number to propose the formation of a church, distinctively so called. The proposition met with considerable favor, and an organization with appropriate covenant, declaration of principles, and rules of discipline was effected, January 29, 1860; impressive ceremonies giving importance and sanctity to the event.

The new movement started out favorably and promised success, but predominating influences were against it. Many prominent reformers and progressives, disgusted by the hostility of the church *as it was* to all philanthropic activities, had come to distrust and condemn all religious bodies as such, and hold them in great disesteem. This leaven had pervaded Hopedale to a considerable extent, and was a potent though silent obstacle to the growth and prosperity of the new association. Moreover, the animating spirit of the place was more ambitious to obtain wealth and worldly distinction than it was to gain "the kingdom of God and his righteousness."[6] Under these circumstances "The Practical Christian Church in Hopedale" died an early death. Other instrumentalities for the special promotion of personal religion languished and finally ceased to be, the weekly Sunday school and service of public worship only remaining as permanent institutions of faith and piety.

Death of Friends

On the thirteenth of February, 1860, my devoted friend mentioned in a former chapter in connection with our visit to Cincinnati in 1854, Mr. Andrew H. Ernst, departed this life at his beautiful home at Spring Garden in that city, in the sixty-fifth year of his age. He was born in Korningen,[7] Germany, came to this country when a young man, and distinguished himself by remarkable intelligence, enterprise, and noble-minded characteristics. He was in religious faith an ardent Restorationist and made himself known to me soon after I started the *Independent Messenger* in 1831 as a cordial sympathizer and patron, remaining my steadfast and generous Christian friend as long as he lived. His second wife, whom he left a heart-stricken widow, stood in the same kindly relation to me for many years.

Rev. Samuel Henry[8] of Thorndike, Massachusetts, died March 17 of the same year. Not rich in earthly goods, he yet was rich in the wealth of Practical Christianity and fruitful in all good works. Originally a Methodist, he became finally an independent Practical Christian – a reformer on all the lines of human regeneration. He was widely known, truly revered, and bore the name of "Father Henry." I had met him on several occasions, carried on frequent correspondence with him, and held him in profound esteem.

The John Brown Raid

The year of my life on which the events just narrated occurred is memorable for the culmination of the career of the famous John Brown. It is not needful for me to tell who John Brown was, what were his distinguishing characteristics, how he undertook to overthrow the system of American slavery, or what the end to which he came at last. All these things are written in the history of those times and everyone is more or less familiar with them. It *is* needful, however, and important as a part of my personal record, that I make note of my own attitude in respect to the foolhardy undertaking by which he fell under condemnation of the judicial authority of the state of Virginia as a capital malefactor and was made to expiate his offense upon the gallows. For the same reason, it is needful and important that I shall speak at some length of the controversy that sprung up between me and certain of my antislavery coadjutors on account of their abandonment of their former professed Non-Resistant principles in the approval they gave of the course which John Brown pursued and in the eulogies they lavished upon his name and memory.

I was not surprised that the *pro*-war Abolitionists of the country should, many of them, be roused to vehement laudations of the hero of Harper's Ferry, to fierce denunciation of his captors, and threats of vengeance against all pro-slavery tyrants. But it was hard for me to understand how professing *anti*-war Abolitionists of long standing should so forget or ignore their former protestations against the use of violent means for carrying forward their work and freeing the bondsmen, as to be swept into the same foaming vortex of blood and death. As for me, I remained unmoved, except by sorrow for such a deplorable exhibition of mistaken ambition to promote a good end by evil means, and pity for the sufferer who had rashly plunged into a lion's den.

My brethren exclaimed, "Behold his religious sincerity, his noble motives, his self-sacrificing devotion to the cause of the oppressed, his matchless heroism in behalf of human rights and liberty! How can you restrain your sympathy and admiration, even if you cannot approve his methods and means! Above all, how can you deprecate and censure his courageous and disinterested acts!"

I replied, "Because the great points at issue are not his religious sincerity, his worthy motives, his self-sacrificing devotion to the cause of the slave, or his heroism in behalf of human liberty. These might all be excellent in the abstract, and doubtless were, to his own consciousness. But what were his methods, measures, deeds? Were *they* Christian or anti-Christian, right or wrong, good or evil, praiseworthy or reprehensible?" These were the questions I had to settle according to my own judgment when viewed from my own Non-Resistant standpoint, and, having settled them, then I had to speak out my honest convictions without fear, favor, or compromise. This I did adversely to the truly great emancipator, and to the disgust of the whole school of red revolutionary Abolitionists, as well as to the declared regret of most of my old associates on the antislavery platform. But how could I do otherwise without recreancy to my own publicly avowed fundamental principles – principles dearer to me than mortal praise, earthly advantage, or life itself?

I was solemnly committed and pledged, as were all my fellow members of the American Anti-Slavery Society, to certain distinctive methods for advancing the cause it was founded to promote, as follows:

> Our principles forbid the doing of evil that good may come and lead us to reject and to entreat the oppressed to reject the use of all carnal weapons for deliverance from bondage; relying solely upon those which are spiritual, and mighty through God to the pulling down of strongholds. – *Declaration of Sentiments.*
>
> But the society will never in any way, countenance the oppressed in vindicating their rights by resorting to physical force. – *Article 3, Constitution.*

This is Christian antislavery – the kind to which I had subscribed and considered myself bound by solemn pledges. John Brown publicly repudiated and denounced this kind of antislavery – setting it at defiance by resorting to rifles, pikes, and bowie knives – a course of procedure which I abominated, and I spoke, argued, and acted accordingly.

For a long time before the attack upon Harper's Ferry took place, the war spirit had been entering more and more into the discussions of the great question of the country, inflaming the public mind and preparing for bloody things to come. Against this aspect of the case I had protested with voice and pen as I had opportunity, though without abating one jot or tittle of my deep-seated and ineradicable hostility to the gigantic system of American oppression. My testimonies had called forth numerous criticisms and expostulations from some of my highly esteemed friends, to which I in turn replied. In the midst of the discussion thus inaugurated and carried on, came the startling intelligence of the event referred to and of the discomfiture of the chief actors in it, which increased the prevailing excitement to an intensity unknown before.

The raid of Brown occurred on the seventeenth of October, 1859, and on the next Sunday, October 23, a special meeting of the Worcester County South Division Anti-Slavery Society was held at Worcester for the purpose of considering and taking action upon the matter. By reason of the recent decease of its president, Effingham L. Capron,[9] I, as first vice president, was called upon to act as moderator of the proceedings. I had no doubt it was intended on the part of its projectors that the meeting should conduce not alone to more active hostility to the slave power, but to the diversion of the society from its hitherto peaceful channels of operation into those of violence and blood, by eulogizing and glorifying John Brown and his daring exploit. I determined to meet this aspect of the case at the outset and put myself on record against the scheme, though I had little hope of preventing its consummation. I did so by introducing a series of resolutions reaffirming the peace principles announced in the original organization of the society and insisting on a faithful adherence thereto. These resolutions I defended and illustrated, in several speeches during the day, against a considerable array of opponents, among whom several of my old Non-Resistant brethren stood conspicuous. Though my arguments could not be answered, I was overborne by numbers, my resolutions being laid upon the table and others passed in their stead almost unanimously. The gist of the adopted ones was contained in the last, to wit:

> *Resolved*, that as Abolitionists we have no disclaimers, no apologies to offer for the recent attempt of certain anti-slavery men at Harper's Ferry to break the rod of the oppressor by the same means by which our revolutionary fathers secured our national independence. On the contrary, while in the absence of all reliable information we are unable to judge of the wisdom of their measures, we are prompt to avow our cordial sympathy with the spirit and our devout admiration of the heroism of that valiant little band who preferred to die struggling for their

country's freedom to living in a land where education is a crime, where marriage and the family relation are trampled in the dust, and where a million women are daily offered in the market for purposes of prostitution.

I contrasted this resolution, when it came to be discussed, with the antislavery declaration and constitutional pledge of 1833, and chose to abide by the old platform, leaving the new heroes of the cause to glory in the sword on their own responsibility. But where were my high-professing Non-Resistant brethren? Alas, they were shouting with the rest for John Brown and his insurrectionary methods. He had captured them, though himself a captive, wounded and helpless at the feet of the slave power. Brother Stephen S. Foster[10] at the Worcester meeting and elsewhere could stand shoulder to shoulder with Andrew T. Foss, Charles L. Remond, Thomas W. Higginson, and others,[11] whose voice was still for war, exclaiming, "I am a Non-Resistant, but not a fool," and so incite men on to deeds of blood and death. And – must I write it! – even Brother William Lloyd Garrison, the man who penned the declaration and constitution referred to – who penned the "declaration of sentiments" adopted by the Peace Convention of 1838, whence sprang the New England Non-Resistance Society – this man became more than an apologist, he became a eulogist of the blood-shedding hero of the Harper's Ferry tragedy.

At a great meeting held in honor of John Brown in Boston on the evening of the day of his execution, Mr. Garrison spoke, as reported without subsequent contradiction, thus:

> Mr. Garrison then paid a tribute to the courage and character of Captain Brown. His mission, the speaker alleged, at Harper's Ferry was peaceful. He did not mean to shed blood. And if he had weapons of war, they were only to be put into the hands of slaves that they might defend themselves in retreating to Canada. "The men," he said, "who decry Brown are dangerous men, the old tories of the revolution." He would that we had the spirit of the Revolution that it might make the Commonwealth too hot to hold them. The speaker was a peace man and therefore disarmed John Brown. He was also a Non-Resistant, but he was emboldened to say, "Success to every insurrection against slavery, here and everywhere." His heart was always with the oppressed, therefore "Success to revolution." It was the way to get up to the doctrine of Non-Resistance.[12]

Such language did not sound much like what he uttered in September 1838:

> The history of mankind is crowded with evidences that physical coercion is not adapted to moral regeneration; that the sinful disposition of man can be subdued only by love; that evil can be exterminated from the earth only by good; that it is not safe to rely on an arm of flesh – upon man, whose breath is in his nostrils – to preserve us from harm; that there is great security in being gentle, harmless, long-suffering, and abundant in mercy; that it is only the meek who inherit the earth.
>
> We advocate no jacobinical doctrines. The spirit of jacobinism is the spirit of retaliation, violence, and murder. It neither fears God nor regards man. We would be filled with the spirit of Christ. If we abide by our principles, it is impossible

for us to be disorderly, or plot treason, or participate in any evil work; we shall submit to every ordinance of man for the Lord's sake; obey all the requirements of government, except such as we deem contrary to the commands of the gospel; and in no wise resist the operation of law, except by meekly submitting to the penalty of disobedience.[13]

In these paragraphs we have the pure doctrine and spirit of Christian Non-Resistance. I love it with all my heart. But what concord is there between the sentiments they embody and those of the previously quoted speech? I see none at all. I was therefore grieved and disturbed by the speech, dissenting from it and remonstrating against it in the columns of my paper. My old friend's response was brief and decisive. He had "spoken deliberately" and "had nothing to take back." My "animadversion was uncalled for" and I had "no occasion being disturbed." Of course I had nothing more to say, but I was in no wise satisfied with his curt rejoinder, having no sympathy whatever with those professed Non-Resistants who vied with avowed pro-war men in paying homage to one whom I could regard only as a well-meaning, misguided, unfortunate zealot. So much for the John Brown episode and my position in reference to and controversy with the Abolitionist leaders concerning it. Further details may be found in the columns of the *Practical Christian*, Vol. 20.

But what became of the bellicose John Brown Non-Resistants? They gradually declined in numbers from that time on and in a few years essentially disappeared. There was no further use for their kind of peace doctrine, and they did nothing to propagate or preserve it. The slaveholders took the insurrection business into their own hands, leaped into the vortex of civil war, and gave these professed peace men the opportunity which many of them seemed to covet of helping on the compulsory abolition of the system of American oppression. Some of them went into the Federal army, others encouraged their sons to enlist, while the more masterly by pen, oratory, and various expedients, urged the war-chariot on its bloody way to victory. And when the victory at length came, they had been converted to the doctrine of the rightfulness of forcible resistance of evil, or to some indefinite conservative peace policy, or to silent indifference upon the whole subject. Scarcely a survivor of the antislavery insurrectionary Non-Resistants was to be found. Had Jesus Christ and his apostles undertaken to abolish slavery and other evils in the Roman Empire by similar means, we should probably never have heard of their doctrine of universal love and good will, nor of them either. Their religion and reformatory methods were of a higher order – "not of this world."[14]

Scripture Commentary

As my peculiar views upon the character and authority of the Bible and of Christ, when compared with other religious teachers, ancient and modern, became more widely known through the tract before spoken of and otherwise, I was importuned by some of my warm friends to prepare a commentary on the New Testament scriptures, insisting that such a work would be a valuable contribution to the sacred literature of the world and of great use to multitudes who in all directions were breaking away from the old bibliolatry and seeking some satisfactory interpretation of the early records of the Christian faith. Upon careful deliberation I concluded to assume the task to which they urged me, making due announcement of my determination in the columns of my paper. Pursuant thereto, I commenced the undertaking in the spring of 1858, my "General Introduction" and "Preface to Matthew's Gospel" being published in No. 1, vol. 19 of the *Practical Christian*, issued May 1 of that year. I continued the work through that volume and far into Vol. 20, when adverse circumstances led me to abandon it, having gone as far with my exposition as the twelfth chapter of Matthew, where it came to an abrupt and final termination.

End of the Practical Christian

The same circumstances and the generally discouraging aspect of the cause of Practical Christian Socialism occasioned by the growing unrest of the country as it went hurrying on to the great rebellion, led me early in 1860 to advise the discontinuance of the *Practical Christian* at the close of Vol. 20, which would occur the following April. The paper had never been self-supporting pecuniarily, and although it was in that respect in as good condition as ever before, its future prosperity and usefulness were unpromising. The changed condition of things at home in regard to the paramount object for which it was started, and the changing condition of things abroad in regard to its distinguishing reformatory principles, seemed to justify the proposed step in the judgment of its more responsible patrons and supporters, and the career of our little semi-monthly sheet came to an honorable close with No. 26, Vol. 20, April 14, 1860. This was a cause of regret to a large number of subscribers, who, whether they could practically accept and live up to all the high moral and social requirements of the publication or not, nevertheless felt that they were founded in the truth and ought to be promulgated as far and wide as possible, as they also felt that they and their families had been greatly benefited by the little visitant and needed its stimulating influence to keep them from falling utterly away from their high ideals of personal and social excellence. A considerable number of letters from different parts of the country expressed a grateful appreciation of the high character and wholesome influence of the *Practical Christian* upon themselves and the community and a sense of loss in the thought that they were to see it no more, together with sentiments of kindly regard for its editor. The press, also, especially the progressive journals, philanthropic and religious, added testimonials of the same general character.

Among these was one so unexpected and remarkable in certain ways that I cannot deny myself the satisfaction of giving it in full to my present readers. It was from the pen of Rev. Thomas Whittemore, D.D., editor of the *Trumpet and Universalist Magazine* – the same redoubtable dialectician and antagonist with whom in earlier days I had so often measured swords in the conflict between the Restorationists and ultra Universalists. We had years before buried the last remnants of strife on honorable terms of his own proposing and sealed the same in a friendly and cordial personal interview, and the green grass had already covered the grave. His parting salutation was as follows:

> We deeply regret to learn that the *Practical Christian*, hitherto published by the Hopedale Community and edited by Rev. Adin Ballou, is about to be discontinued.
>
> We have always felt a love for this publication. We did not agree with every word it uttered, but we found little in it to disapprove. It has done us good and had we obeyed all its precepts we should have been a better man. We still hope the publication may be continued, but if it must be closed, here is a farewell hand to Brother Ballou. By his practical Christianity he has won us over to himself. In the days of the Restorationist controversy, thirty years ago, we were bitter to each other, but the bitterness has all gone from his heart and ours. He believes as he did and we believe as we did; but both have learned the law of love. We both believe the great fact of the restoration of all things, a point on which Brother Ballou has never wavered for a moment.
>
> One word as to the Hopedale Community. So far as we know, they are a band of brothers and sisters who seek to honor God by good lives. They are good citizens; they live quietly and peaceably, and the Lord blesses them. Often when we have been in Milford, we have desired to visit their houses, but we felt (perhaps more than we ought) that in their sight we were a heretic, and they would not receive us. Never have we had an unkind word from them, however. Perhaps it was a mere suspicion on our part. We will yet go to Hopedale. We should love to live where practical Christianity reigns. – *The Trumpet, January 28, 1860*

This generous, whole-souled tribute was copied into the last number of the *Practical Christian* with the subjoined response:

> Thank you, Brother Whittemore. You speak good words. They reach our heart. We reciprocate them. Welcome to Hopedale and our humble home always. – *Editor, Practical Christian*

Although this little unpretending sheet – the *Practical Christian* – was suspended at my suggestion and with my hearty consent and approval, yet the consummation of the act gave me not a little pain. It was a child of my own begetting, born out of a profound, overmastering love for the truth and for humanity. For twenty years it had been an instrumentality by which I had been able to serve the truth and humanity according to the dictates of my conscience and judgment. It had for that period been a medium through which I could hold communication with my friends scattered abroad and the public at large upon the most important questions that can enlist the attention of the wise and good, and disseminate far and wide those ideas and principles of morals and religion, those views of Christ and Christianity, which I believed and felt to be founded in the nature of things and the will of God, and to be indispensable to the progress, elevation, regeneration, and happiness of mankind. And I had experienced unspeakable comfort and delight in employing it to the ends indicated and in seeing it made serviceable to their accomplishment. How could I give it up without a pang! How could I be denied the satisfaction I had for so long time derived from it, and not feel a sense of loss and heaviness of heart!

I tried, however, to keep up good spirits and to hope it was all for the best, to be proved so in due time. To supply the place of the little messenger and keep open communication with the world, as well as to mitigate what I was obliged to confess was a misfortune if not a calamity, I recommended the formation of a society whose office and mission it should be to publish and circulate leaflets, tracts, and other printed matter, in exposition and illustration of the distinctive principles which constituted the basis of our former social experiment, and which, notwithstanding our failure to carry them out to their final practical results in personal life and a new order of society, we still professed to believe in and hold dear. My recommendation was favorably received by a goodly number of my Hopedale friends who were ready to cooperate with me in the proposed plan. A society was accordingly formed and an organization effected, February 6, 1860, which bore the name of *The Practical Christian Promulgation Society*. The Hopedale Community made over to it the assets of the *Practical Christian* with certain bequeathed funds, to which special contributions were from time to time added. It went on prosperously for a few years, was instrumental in distributing a considerable amount of wholesome literature, most of which was the production of my pen, for I could not give up the idea of keeping the doctrines and ideas for which I had done so much before the world, but it at length lapsed into a moribund state and finally died out and was numbered with its predecessors.

New House of Worship

An event of much importance in the history of Hopedale during the year 1860 was the erection of a new house of public worship, of respectable dimensions and many conveniences, on an eligible lot which in early Community days had been set apart for the purpose. The structure was completed in the autumn and dedicated with appropriate exercises on the fifteenth of November. Two sessions were held with a crowded auditorium during the day, Brother William S. Heywood preaching from the first great command in the morning, emphasizing the value and importance of piety, and I from the second in the afternoon, urging the value and claims of morality and philanthropy as essentials of a true personal character and of a perfect order of society. A third service was held in the evening at which there was a good attendance with exercises of an informal and miscellaneous character. There was no lowering of the standard of a true Practical Christianity in the utterances of the occasion and no discordant notes marred the harmony of its proceedings. Besides our own home speakers, clerical and lay, who participated in the exercises during the day or evening, were Revs. John Boyden of Woonsocket, Rhode Island, Samuel May of Leicester, Robert Hassall of Haverhill, and George Hill of Milford, our near neighbor.[15] Our beloved Joshua Hutchinson of Milford, New Hampshire, the sweet singer of the notable "Hutchinson family,"[16] had charge of the music and took part in it, charming his auditors with his delightful strains. It was a day long to be remembered.

A Remarkable Séance

A remarkable spiritual séance at which I was present was held about this time at the house of my old friend, George W. Burnham[17] of Willimantic, Connecticut, whither I had gone on one of my incidental preaching excursions. There were some twenty or twenty-five reliable witnesses to the singular phenomena, the most striking of which occurred in connection with a little girl medium only nine years of age. She was seated in front of a heavy cooking stove, upon which she rested the tips of her fingers. Questions both audible and mental were put to what purported to be disembodied spirits, all of which were answered promptly and intelligently and to the astonishment and satisfaction of the entire company by the raising and lowering of a portion of the stove nearest to her, which came down with a thud sometimes that jarred the house. A skeptical friend, an educated professional gentleman to whom I related this experience, said that while he did not doubt my conscientious veracity, he was sure I must have been deceived, for such alleged phenomena were flatly contrary to the laws of nature and therefore impossible. Yet I knew them to be genuine realities beyond all doubt or peradventure. Nature has many grades of expression, and all her laws are not in schoolbooks nor in libraries of the literati. Whatever may be true of spiritualistic credulity, materialistic assumption and incredulity often outmatch it. I know how to estimate and eschew both.

Election of Abraham Lincoln

In the autumn of 1860, after unprecedented excitement that convulsed the nation from center to circumference, Abraham Lincoln was elected president of the United States on a platform that pledged him and his party to a firm, unfaltering resistance to the aggressions of the slave power hitherto unchecked and defiant of justice and the fundamental principles of a republican form of government. The public mind continued to be greatly agitated even after the election was over, and greatly confused in regard to the nature and extent of those aggressions and what was to be done by the victors now that they had gained the ascendancy. In order to throw some light upon the vexed problem and clear the airs of the fogs and vapors that bedimmed them, I prepared a lecture entitled "Violations of the Federal Constitution in the Irrepressible Conflict between the Pro-Slavery and Anti-Slavery Portions of the American People," which I delivered many times to large and deeply interested audiences and which was afterwards printed and circulated very generally throughout the community.

Debate on Immortality

I also during the same autumn held two public discussions with the celebrated Second Adventist, Miles Grant:[18] one at Holden, which continued through five sessions of three hours each, and one at Worcester, where there were four sessions of three hours each. The question debated at the first was "Has man an immortal entity?" I taking the affirmative and my opponent the negative sides respectively. At the second, the question in dispute took the following form: "*Resolved*, that immortality is a gift from God dependent on character," the order of discussion being reversed. Proper decorum prevailed on both occasions, large audiences were present, and a lively interest was manifested in the arguments presented. The doctrine advocated by Elder Grant was that man has no undying element in his native constitution, all human beings becoming utterly unconscious at death; that all will be restored to consciousness at the general resurrection, when God will render the righteous immortal by special gift and annihilate the wicked by what is termed "the second death." The doctrine I maintained was that the human soul is by nature immortal; that at physical death all human beings enter a state of moral discipline suited to their different characters; and that all will be raised through successive stages of regeneration to final holiness and happiness. The debate was conducted throughout in a mutually amicable temper and my antagonist complimented me as the fairest and most agreeable opponent he had ever met. As usual, both parties claimed the victory in the argument and retired self-satisfied.

The Civil War

Time went on. The mutterings of coming war were heard in the distant Southland, and near at hand were there declarations and pledges of resistance to the uttermost, should violent measures be inaugurated. The shattered ark of the covenant of our fathers was approaching new perils which would try it as never before. At length the outbreak came. Rebellion raised a bloody hand against the Republic and must be met. Political and martial patriotism was ringing ardent appeals in all directions, and Christian Non-Resistance seemed to some minds akin to passive treason. Still the majority of our members were loyal to our original standard and clung to the hull of their half-wrecked social ship. They tried to stop its leaks and keep it afloat for some possible future use. But no expedient could avail to prevent downward tendencies and open withdrawals from our ranks. On the ninth of June, 1861, Brother George Draper, one of our most influential associates, sent to the recorder of the Community a letter resigning his membership, "having become satisfied," as he says, "that I am not in spirit or feeling or practice or purpose a Non-Resistant." Yet he expressed a desire to do all he could to perpetuate what he believed Hopedale to have been and to be, "the most desirable village to live in on earth." He did not denounce the principles on which Hopedale was founded and by which it had been made what it was as wrong, but as "impracticable under existing circumstances." A great crisis had arisen in the country and it could be successfully met only by resorting to the sword. Several other members shared his sentiments and followed his example. Others left us for other reasons, reducing our numbers to less than fifty persons, who remained faithful to their ideals and determined to die an honest death when their hour should come.

Rational Spiritualists

In the spring of the year upon which the civil war broke out, a society of what were termed Rational Spiritualists was organized in Milford for the purpose of establishing regular Sunday services, a Sabbath school, and other activities conducive to the moral and religious edification and improvement of the people. I was engaged to preach under its auspices at least once a month and oftener if I could, and to procure supplies for the rest of the time. For a while the experiment went on prosperously, but before a year expired it came to an end, either because my Spiritualism was too rational and Christian to suit the prevalent taste, or because modern Spiritualism lacks the genius of organization and cohesive unity. Probably both these considerations operated to bring about the issue designated, causing me to betake myself to other fields of service.

Birth of Granddaughter

An event of special interest to me and mine this year was the birth of a granddaughter, Lucy Florence Heywood,[19] in the Home School mansion on the twenty-eighth of July. She proved to be the only child of our only surviving child, Abbie Ballou Heywood, wife of Rev. William S. Heywood, who was at the time joint occupant with me of the Hopedale pulpit. She was well born in respect to all native endowments and capabilities, has been liberally educated, being a graduate of Smith College, Northampton, Massachusetts, in the class of 1884, and has served as assistant teacher in the High School at Sandwich in this state. She is still living at this writing, April 5, 1890, a cherished blessing to all her relatives and a large circle of devoted friends.

The Monitorial Guide

During this year I prepared and caused to be issued from the Hopedale Press, owned and operated by Brother Bryan J. Butts,[20] a small liturgical volume of 336 pages, entitled *The Monitorial Guide*. It was designed to aid in the intellectual, moral, and spiritual quickening and culture of both youth and adults in the principles and objects of the Practical Christian Republic by using it in inductive conferences and other socially religious gatherings subordinate to that more comprehensive and definitely organized body. Its value was satisfactorily tested in the Hopedale Inductive Communion for several years before its dissolution, with which event it dropped out of sight. It has merits which some future generation may recognize and render serviceable in the great work of making the world better.

Interview with Departed Friends

About this time occurred some of the most wonderful and convincing phenomena purporting to be produced by the denizens of the spiritual world in which I was ever privileged to participate. I had heard much through the public press and otherwise, especially through the personal experience of Brother E. D. Draper and wife, of the unique mediumship of the celebrated Charles H. Foster,[21] then holding séances and astonishing multitudes of witnesses in Boston. Myself and wife had become so much interested in the reports received that we decided to visit Mr. Foster and see and judge for ourselves in regard to what transpired. We accordingly appeared at his boarding place, No. 75 Beach Street, one autumn morning and there awaited developments. We were ushered into a plainly furnished room, where we found the medium, to whom we were absolute strangers, and were asked to sit by the side of a common table, on which there were slips of writing paper, several pencils, and a card with the letters of the alphabet in distinct type upon it. Being previously advised, we had written the names of quite a number of our departed relatives and numerous questions in fine script before leaving home, and rolled the paper on which they were inscribed into compact wads or balls, bringing them with us as means of testing whatever might be subjected to us for consideration and judgment. These were all placed before us, by the side of the other articles mentioned.

A few minutes elapsed when distinct raps were heard as if under the table, and the medium, after a few convulsive motions of the countenance, said, "There is a band of bright spirits present, intelligent, affectionate, and unusually desirous of communicating with you. I perceive near *you*" (pointing to my wife) "a noble spirit, deeply interested in you, as if closely related." Then this spirit purported to say through the medium, "We rejoice to meet you in the presence of one through whom we can make most unmistakable manifestations of ourselves. And to convince you beyond a doubt who *I* am, I will cause my name to appear on the medium's arm at full length." Whereupon Mr. Foster bared his arm and then the name PEARLEY HUNT was distinctly seen, as if written with red ink in a hand which we at once recognized as that of the father of my wife when he was in mortal form. She at once, deeply affected, exclaimed, "O! that is my father." Further communications were received from him, partly in response to questions and partly of his own motion, but all strikingly characteristic of him, when he shook hands with us through the medium and departed.

Then came a wholly unexpected but scarcely less impressive and satisfactory interview with my wife's spirit mother, who spelled out her name CHLOE HUNT, at her own suggestion, by my pointing to the letters of the alphabet in their order, the right ones being designated by distinct rappings when they were reached. In the course of the interview this communicator said, "It was I who spoke to you in the garden." This was an explanatory answer to a question wife had addressed to our son, Adin Augustus, in one of the small wads lying on the table before us. It related to an incident that occurred more than a year before when she thought she heard the word "mother" one day when she was among her vegetables and flowers. This utterance she had always attributed to Augustus and had directed an inquiry to him on this occasion accordingly – an inquiry which her mother had now voluntarily answered. Here was strong presumptive proof that we were dealing with real invisible entities, as convincing as it was unanticipated and unsolicited.

Then occurred a manifestation which professed to be from our dear son himself. He was announced by the medium as a very bright and beautiful spirit, around whom everything was pleasant and cheerful, as indicating great affection and joy – "the one," it was said, "you are most anxious to communicate with." He then extended to us through his interpreter most hearty congratulations accompanied by enthusiastic shaking of hands and expressions of intense pleasure that he had an opportunity of making us certain of his presence and identity. After referring to certain matters spoken of in the little balls before us and treating them satisfactorily, he continued: "Now I will sensibly assure you that your son is indeed personally present with you by displaying my initials on the medium's arm." This was instantly done, the letters A. A. B. appearing in the exact shape familiar to us in his earthly lifetime – the final curve of the *B* descending considerably below the line on which the other letters rested, as was his wont to make it. He then wrote with the medium's hand a somewhat lengthy message, subscribing what he had written with his well-known signature, "Adin Augustus Ballou," the same characteristic distinguishing the initial of the last name as before. Numerous questions were put to him which he answered intelligently and satisfactorily. This feature of the séance was profoundly impressive and convincing.

Similar interviews, though not all of them so directly personal and affecting, were held with my venerable sainted mother, whose hands I was told were raised as if invoking a blessing upon me; with our beloved Brother Butler Wilmarth, M.D., one of the victims of the Norwalk bridge disaster of ten years before; with my much esteemed friend E. N. Paine,[22] formerly of East Blackstone; and with David Stearns Godfrey,[23] a resident of Milford in his earth-life, from whom I had received many tokens of appreciative regard and to whom I was bound by very tender ties of confidence and affection. Referring to one of my last interviews with him in the flesh, when we had conversed freely upon the subject of spirit communion and when he pledged me that he would report himself to me in due time and give me a certain test-word as a sure token of his identity, I asked him if he was ready to name that word, according to our agreement, of which I had never spoken to a living human being. He said that he was, and asked me to call over the letters of the alphabet. I did so and he by loud raps indicated the letters that spelled the word *Portrait*, which was correct. He then dashed off through the agency of the medium, "True! True! True. I have tried since I left earth to give you the test agreed upon. It is now done. Take courage for all is well, PORTRAIT."

To conclude this remarkable demonstration or series of demonstrations, I requested the spirit relatives and friends present to give us their farewell benediction by a united succession of raps. This elicited a memorable response that seemed to carry inspiration with it, thrilling all our hearts. So closed the most remarkable and satisfying spirit séance at which I was ever a personal witness and participant, the descriptive account of which, as above given, is strictly and reliably true.

There will be plenty of skeptics with whom what I have recorded will have no weight. For such I do not write. They are resolutely determined not to be convinced of the truth of these things. They discard all the testimonies of sacred and profane history concerning the manifestations of angels, spirits, and demons from the unseen world made to mortal human beings, ancient and modern alike. I am a believer in such manifestations on rational and moral grounds, not holding a traditionary faith in the marvels of the Bible while contemning those of other records and especially those coming in later days, nor on the other hand magnifying the latter as wonderful outgrowths or indications of human progress, to the disparagement of all the sacred writings of times long since past and gone. Nor do I exalt any modern spiritualistic revelation or philosophy above those principles of truth and righteousness declared to be essential to human welfare and happiness in the gospel of Jesus Christ.

The Lord's Freeman

An interesting and happy achievement in my life career was attained about the time when this chapter closes: my deliverance from the bondage of pecuniary indebtedness. As a result of my ambition to possess and enjoy a comfortable home, to encourage and relieve the needy, to accommodate and help real or supposed friends, and above all to further enterprises calculated to improve the condition of my fellow men, I had been more or less financially involved from my first starting out in life. I was a borrower and therefore often a sorrower. But I was never a beggar, a defaulter, or a dependent on alms. My obligations were always faithfully kept, my word was sacred, and my credit beyond suspicion from first to last. And now, after all my struggles, disappointments, losses, I became "the Lord's freeman," owing "no man anything but to love one another."[24] Thanks be to God, whose I am and all I have forevermore.

CHAPTER 22

1862-1872

The Hopedale Community, at the time of the opening of the present chapter, was little more than an ordinary religious society, though still maintaining nominally its originally adopted principles of Practical Christian truth as founded in the will of God and in the constitution of the moral world, and as applicable to all human affairs in all the relations of life. It continued to hold fast its primary guaranties against the evils of ignorance, poverty, vice, and crime, but the chief instrumentalities or means organically provided for in its distinctive industrial and social system, by which those guaranties were to be made good, had been essentially abandoned. Practically, we were no longer the vanguard and illustration of a new order of society, but only a quiet, peaceful, well-governed neighborhood of the old order, to the habits, practices, customs, and prevailing spirit of which our village was becoming year by year more fully and more complacently conformed.

The institutional routine of religious observances along the former lines and much in accord with the former spirit of the place was pursued with commendable regularity and to general satisfaction. Rev. William S. Heywood and myself were the accredited ministers of the church, each rendering about an equal amount of service, only now and then a Sunday being assigned by definite arrangement to special invitees. Neither of us had abandoned the theological, ethical, and social theories adopted intelligently and conscientiously many years before, and our testimonies in no wise belied or undervalued our still cherished convictions. But the trend of things was manifestly against us and our teachings – to other issues than those we deemed of supreme moment and sought diligently to promote and secure.

The business interests of the village prospered exceedingly, its population increased, and wealth rolled in upon its leading citizens. Money-making, political engineering and advancement, and martial patriotism absorbed the thought and energy of the populace, while Practical Christianity, as a motive power in the individual community, state, and nation, fell proportionately into abeyance. Newcomers to the place cared little or nothing for the distinctive Christian principles of the men and women who founded it, while a goodly number of those who still cherished them and sought to honor them were obliged, under the newly-established regime, to seek employment and a home elsewhere. So it was that the Community, as an organic body, grew weaker and weaker in membership and in moral power from year to year, while the influence of the pulpit, Sunday school, and conference room became more and more neutralized by prevailing indifference or hostile influences outside.

With the opening and progress of the civil war, causing in all directions great financial embarrassment and uncertainty, the patronage of the Hopedale Home School, which for several years enjoyed much well-deserved popularity, declined to such an extent, especially in respect to its boarding department whence its chief support was derived, that it was deemed advisable to close it permanently. This was accordingly done, much to the regret of its many friends in the vicinity and elsewhere, in the year [1863].[1] The following spring its proprietors and principals [William S. and Abbie Ballou Heywood] disposed of the property and a few months later removed to West Newton. They have since resided in Scituate, Hudson, Holyoke, Boston, and Sterling, their present home (1890), in all of which places Mr. Heywood has labored as a settled minister in the fellowship of the Unitarian denomination.

Discourses of William Lloyd Garrison

A somewhat serious occurrence took place among us in July, 1862, the main features of which, as they concerned me personally, I cannot permit to sink into oblivion. By invitation of the committee of the Community on pulpit supply, my old-time friend and co-laborer in the antislavery cause, William Lloyd Garrison, delivered two discourses on the first Sunday of the month named in our Hopedale house of worship. He made use of the occasion to express and defend opinions on several important points of a religious nature which he must have known to be radically opposed to the faith and practice on which I had tried to build the Hopedale Community and was still trying to found the Practical Christian Republic. I and my friends had always held him in high regard as a distinguished philanthropist and treated him with fraternal deference, and I did not see why, under existing circumstances, he should raise controversial issues between me and him. I was present and listened with close and thoughtful attention to his disquisitions, but received no hint that he desired or expected me to say anything in defense of those views of mine which he vigorously assailed, though, of course, without reference to me. His utterances pleased all present who disliked my teaching upon the topics treated but naturally grieved me, and those who revered the principles I maintained, exceedingly. By reason of the seriousness of the case when considered in all its bearings, I deemed it my duty, without in any way impugning my friend's motives, to procure if possible a public discussion of the particulars upon which I took issue with him, in presence of our congregation, that they might better understand the merits of the whole case. How I succeeded will be learned from the following correspondence:

Hopedale, July 9, 1862.

To Ebenezer D. Draper, Jerome Wilmarth, and Nancy W. Lewers, *Committee:*[2]

DEAR FRIENDS: Our respected friend, Wm. Lloyd Garrison, who occupied the Hopedale pulpit last Sunday under your auspices, in the frank expression of his honest convictions, felt it his duty to teach the people, as I understood him, substantially as follows, to wit:

1. That there is no divine authority whatever for setting apart the first day of the week as a sabbath or as time to be sacredly devoted to religious uses of any kind.

2. That to thus set it apart and to teach people to respect it as in any sense holy, is unwarrantable, superstitious, and pernicious.

3. That all such sabbatizing sprang from and is sustained by priestcraft for the mere advantage of a clerical or priestly class.

4. That all such sabbatizing, with its usual public religious exercises of prayer and other demonstrations of so-called worship, is essentially pharisaical.

5. That it is untruthful, improper, superstitious, and pernicious to call the Bible a holy book, because it was written nobody knows when, by nobody knows whom; because it settles nothing in theology or ethics, proves all sorts of conflicting tenets, and carries with it no divine authority whatever – though nevertheless, it is worth more than all other books in the world.

6. That all authority to determine what is true or right in religion is vested absolutely in each human individual for himself – never to be overruled by the claims of any other person or persons as divinely inspired, commissioned, or authorized.

7. That Jesus Christ Himself is not to be regarded as an infallible and perfect religious teacher.

8. That it is wholly by or from human nature that we must finally settle all ethical questions.

9. That Non-Resistance is in no way necessarily connected with or dependent on the teaching, example, or official authority of Jesus Christ.

10. That although Non-Resistance holds human life in all cases inviolable, yet it is perfectly consistent for those professing it to petition, advise, and strenuously urge a pro-war government to abolish slavery solely by the war-power.

Now it is well known to the people of Hopedale that my preaching and practice have always been to a greater or less degree contrary to these positions. It is also well known that a considerable number of persons in the village are opposed to my faith and practice on these points, and were delighted with friend Garrison's exposition of the subjects they involve. In view of all this, I deem it not only due to my self-respect but an imperative religious obligation to put myself in a way to be converted by fair argument to Mr. Garrison's views or by such argument to defend and sustain my own. I therefore respectfully request you to engage the service of our friend for some forthcoming Sunday or other day as soon as may be convenient, with the full understanding that he and I shall hold a free public discussion of the aforesaid and other collateral topics, to be continued through not less than two nor more than three sessions of two hours each, the parties to occupy uninterrupted equal portions of time. Your prompt attention and reply to this request will greatly oblige your brother and servant,

ADIN BALLOU.

The committee at once forwarded my letter to Mr. Garrison and in due time received the following response:

Boston, July 11, 1862.

To Ebenezer D. Draper, Jerome Wilmarth, and Nancy W. Lewers, Committee:

DEAR FRIENDS: The letter addressed to you by my friend, Adin Ballou, which you have kindly sent to me for my consideration, gives me very great surprise. It seems that he found several things in my discourses last Sunday at Hopedale from which he so strongly dissents and which he deems so heretical that he feels constrained to invite me (through you as a committee) to a public discussion of these controverted points at the same place as soon as may be convenient!

In reply I beg leave very respectfully to say that I decline the invitation thus given:

1. Because there seemed to be no reason why my friend Ballou should not have interrogated me, as did others in the audience, in order to a clearer elucidation of my views – as he was present at both meetings and expressed no dissent from anything I advanced.

2. Because I shall be too busily occupied for a month to come to attend to a discussion of this kind, even if I had (as certainly I have not) the inclination to do so.

3, Because my worthy friend gives me altogether too much credit and underrates his own efforts as a religious and ethical teacher for so long a period in his chosen Community, in declaring that he deems it not only important to his self-respect, (?) usefulness, and happiness, but "an imperative religious duty" (!) to put himself in a way "to be converted by fair argument to friend Garrison's views or by such argument to defend and sustain his own"! This magnifying the influence of my two impromptu discourses on his part is the more remarkable inasmuch as he says in his letter, "It is well known to the people of Hopedale that my preaching and practice have always been in greater or less degree contrary to these (recited) positions." Does he not discredit both his preaching and his practice by virtually admitting that my two poor discourses may measurably nullify their efficacy if not soon controversially replied to? I cannot permit such unnecessary depreciation of himself on the one hand, nor such absurd exaggeration of myself on the other. Besides, my friend Ballou has the field at Hopedale all to himself in the future as he has long had it in the past, and I am well content to leave in his hands the "considerable number of persons" in your village, who, he says, "were delighted with my sentiments."

4. I have never yet consented to an appointed public discussion with any person on any subject and am too much of a non-resistant to accept any such challenge. Indeed, I have an unconquerable aversion to any set disputation after the manner of belligerent theologians, and believe little or no good ever resulted from it. It tends to beget partisanship rather than conviction, and it is something quite different from a general free discussion meeting.

Finally, allow me to express my regret, and I will add my surprise, that my friend Ballou did not seek to have a frank interchange of views with me, socially, before I left Hopedale. Perhaps he could not possibly command the time on Sunday evening for that purpose. If so, I shall have no cause for surprise – only for regret that I was deprived of the pleasure and edification of such an interview.

Thanking the committee for their kind overture, I remain,

with warm regards, yours truly,

WM. LLOYD GARRISON.

Under the circumstances in which I was placed by this letter, what could I do? If I remained silent, it must be inferred that I acquiesced in friend Garrison's doctrines or that I felt unable to refute them. If either of these inferences were true, I ought to renounce many of my fundamental positions as a religious teacher, social reorganizationist, and Christian Non-Resistant; or, at least, to modify radically much of my theory and practice. Inasmuch as I was not converted to Mr. Garrison's views, but had good and sufficient grounds for rejecting them, I saw no other alternative but to *review* and *expose* both his objectionable affirmations and his reasons for declining to meet me in a fraternal public discussion. This I decided to do, and gave ample notice that my discourses of Sunday, July 27, would be devoted to that service. I therefore addressed myself to the task set before me. In order to do justice to my subject in all its phases and bearings I had to go over considerable ground, only a brief abstract of which can be transferred to these pages.

TEXTS.

"I also will show mine opinion." Job 32:10.

"Come now, let us reason together." Isa. 1:18.

"He that is first in his own cause seemeth just, but his neighbor cometh and searcheth him." Prov. 18:17.

"How can two walk together except they be agreed?" Amos 3:3.

I. FRIEND GARRISON'S REASONS FOR DECLINING A PUBLIC DISCUSSION.

I will not consume space by repeating them in full but refer to them by numbers as they appear seriatim in Mr. Garrison's letter, giving my several responses in their proper order.

1. I clearly understood every affirmation made by friend Garrison and needed no information as to his meaning on any point. But I wanted the reasons and proofs of what he assumed and an opportunity to test their validity and conclusiveness. To have asked for these and had my request granted would have turned the occasion into a critical debate and prevented the speaker from presenting his views fully, distinctly, and fairly. As to dissent, there was neither freedom nor opportunity to express any intelligibly and effectively. Our committee had said that Mr. Garrison wished me to be present and participate with him in the exercises of the meeting; but he offered no space of time for me to do this, nor so much as hinted that he would be pleased to have me express my opinions counter to his own, though he well knew from what I had publicly said and written that I differed essentially from him in many of his declarations. He apparently desired to occupy all the time at his command, and I therefore felt at no liberty to claim any hearing that would have abridged his opportunity. A full and fair discussion

at some other time was the desideratum needed. This I respectfully asked for, but it was refused; whether reasonably or otherwise, I leave others to judge.

2. The discussion would have been willingly deferred on my part to any more distant day mutually convenient. But if there was no "inclination" on his part, of course no convenient later day could be fixed upon between us.

3. The fallacy of this special pleading will be made obvious by considering the following facts: (1) Mr. Garrison was a talented, eloquent, and effective public speaker. He had a wide reputation not only for his ability but as a reformer and philanthropist. He was held in high esteem by our Community, myself included. He was invited to our pulpit as an honored friend and left free to choose his own theme of discourse. He delivered his two "impromptu discourses," consisting largely in broad, sweeping assertions and not in critical and discriminating reasonings, in his own offhand but earnest, emphatic, impressive way. Much that he said was subversive of the fundamental principles and organic policy of our Practical Christian Socialism, and of such a nature as to produce doubt, distrust, and alienation respecting those principles in all susceptible minds, especially of the young, unstable, and inexperienced. The positive declarations of such a man, though impromptu, would naturally do more to undermine the social structure I was endeavoring to build up than years of constructive effort could replace. I therefore deemed it important that he who had been instrumental in creating doubt and uncertainty among those whom I had been trying to train to a high ideal of moral and social excellence, should be held answerable for his utterances in a fair discussion before the people whom he had previously addressed. (2) I was a religious teacher and social reformer. I had left the general prevailing order of civilization because in many of its distinguishing features it was largely wrong and anti-Christian. My new order was based upon and illustrated higher and diviner principles of truth and righteousness. In the construction of such an order of social life, all the natural factors of human society must be included and harmonized, and all that is necessary to both private and public welfare must be provided for. The individual, the family, and the community must conform to such regulations, customs, and courses of life as the highest wisdom shows to be morally right and practically advantageous to all conditions and classes of people. The Hopedale Community, while aiming to realize this Christ-like ideal, had never attained thereunto even in its best estate, and at the time of these "impromptu" discourses had sadly fallen away from what it had at one time achieved. Moreover, the village was rapidly filling up with a population who preferred the old order to the new, thus helping to hasten the utter overthrow of all my cherished plans and aspirations for the enlightenment, moral renovation, and social regeneration of mankind. Nevertheless, in the midst of all this discouragement, I was still trying to hold up the true standard of personal and social righteousness in hope of a better future. Now friend Garrison was troubled with none of my scruples concerning organic society and with none of my constructive responsibilities. He was pre-eminently an Individualist rather than a Socialist of any kind. His mission was to destroy evil customs, institutions, and isms, and let good ones grow up as best they could. Mine was not only to overthrow what was wrong and prejudicial to human well-being and happiness, but to build up what was right and helpful of mankind. He magnified personal liberty as the right of all men,

seeming to think if this were secured all other blessings would follow as a matter of course. I always insisted that personal liberty must be inseparably conjoined with personal obligation, duty, and responsibility, on the basis of the divine moral law. In religion, he discarded creeds, covenants, churches, and all external observances as useless and pernicious. On the contrary, I always insisted upon a coordinate unity of the human reason and emotional sentiments as expressed in religious beliefs, observances, confessions, and institutions founded in the essential truth of things and calculated to foster and promote high types of individual and social life, confident that without such, mankind will have false, absurd, and mischievous ones, or else sink into debasing irreligion or lawless, irresponsible nothingarianism. The differences between Mr. Garrison and myself thus indicated I earnestly desired to have considered in an orderly, candid, friendly discussion, testing them by the standard of reason and the moral law in the presence of the people; leaving nothing to anyone's *ipse dixit* or personal assumption. This was what I asked for, but I asked in vain.

4. Considering the friendly relations in which Mr. Garrison and myself had for many years stood before the public and the uncalled-for assault he had made upon some of my cherished opinions, I could hardly be ranked, I think, among "belligerent theologians" in seeking the proposed discussion. The abuses of appointed set disputations afford no just ground for the alleged "unconquerable aversion" to them, since they have the great advantage over casual and random debates that ample time is allowed for the presentation of conflicting views and that the parties concerned are given a co-equally fair opportunity to be heard. They are indeed "quite different from a general free discussion meeting," for in such a meeting the lions of the occasion and the expressed impatience of their partisan admirers leave little chance for modest and over-awed dissenters to give a full and fair presentation of their views. I have listened to many discussions of this character which yielded little profit to candid, truth-seeking hearers.

Finally, I invited Mr. Garrison to call on me the Sunday evening after the objectionable discourses were delivered and he promised to do so, but failed to keep the promise. He left for Boston early Monday morning, sending in to me the apology that he was detained by pressure of company at the house of his host. There was therefore no opportunity for an interview at that time. For if, instead of waiting for him at my own home, as courtesy required, I had gone to the place where he was stopping, he could not, without manifest incivility, have turned away from his numerous other visitors for any protracted and satisfactory interchange of views with me.

II. Objectionable Doctrines of Friend Garrison Reviewed.

1. Concerning the Sabbath.[3] If what he states is true, then the Hopedale Community, in assuming that the first day of the week is a divinely-sanctioned day of rest and in some proper sense holy time, has acted without the warrant of reason, morality, or religion. The observance of that day by its members has been superstitious and pernicious, and their religious exercises and formalities, under the name of worship, have been pharisaic and hypocritical. Its ministers have been conducting these exercises and formalities for the advantage of their own priestly class.

To this serious charge, I, for myself and associates, plead "Not guilty." We believed, as Christ taught, that the Sabbath as an institution coming down from the earliest ages of human history "was made for man and not man for the Sabbath"[4]; that it was established, not because one day is in itself holier than another, but for the benefit of mankind; that it is sacred only in the sense of being devoted to good uses; and that the right keeping of it includes not only attention to distinctively religious offices and ceremonials but also to the doing of all necessary, healthful, humane, and beneficent work. Needless secular business and ordinary amusements on that day were discountenanced by us, and general attendance upon the services of the house of worship was expected and provided for. In all this there was not one particle of priestcraft, superstition, or unreasonable strictness. By it the highest good and happiness of individuals, of families, and of the Community, were conserved and promoted. Such observance of the day was productive of salutary and desirable results and found in such results its complete justification. That the day may be abused, perverted, and made to serve selfish, partisan, and reprehensible ends is conceded, but it is no more just to denounce it on that account than to arraign and condemn anything else essentially right and good because human ignorance, folly, hypocrisy, and selfishness have sometimes falsified and dishonored it.

2. Concerning the Bible. Friend Garrison says "that it is untruthful, improper, superstitious, and pernicious to call the Bible a holy book, because it was written nobody knows when by nobody knows whom, settles nothing in theology or ethics, proves all sorts of conflicting tenets, and carries with it no divine authority whatever. Nevertheless, it is worth more than all the other books in the world."[5] What consistency is there in these statements? How can the Bible be worth more than all other books if so destitute of all authenticity, homogeneity, and authority? The truth really is that no books of equal antiquity are so well authenticated as those comprised in the volume under notice. From the nature of the case more or less obscurity hangs over their date and authorship, yet this does not invalidate their claims to our confidence and regard, as it does not disprove or depreciate the essential truth they contain, the great principles of righteousness they declare and magnify. That truth – those principles – culminate in the New Testament, and the New Testament centers in the person of Jesus Christ, whose authority as teacher and exemplar determines the absolute religion of the Bible. The Bible, as Jesus interpreted, applied, and left it, does, as I understand it, determine what is fundamental in theology and ethics, affirms no conflicting tenets, and carries with it all the divine authority needful for the practical uses of life – authority which he claimed to have derived from the Father.

Friend Garrison asserted that "Jesus Christ himself is not to be regarded as an infallible and perfect religious teacher." Then he was a false witness concerning himself and a pretender, for he said, "I do nothing of myself, but as my Father hath taught me I speak ... he that sent me is with me; the Father hath not left me alone, for I do always the things that please him." –John 8:28-29. This was His uniform claim through all his ministry – a claim I feel bound in reason and conscience to admit. I do not believe he was a mere visionary or an arrogant pretender but an infallible and perfect religious teacher. And among all those who have asserted the contrary I have never found one who could fortify and maintain their assertions with good and sufficient reasons.

3. Concerning Human Nature as Authority in Religion. But while friend Garrison denied that the Bible carried with it any divine authority and regarded Christ as an imperfect religious teacher, he could set human nature on an infallible throne. See Nos. 6 and 8 of my letter [to the committee]. Then no human being needs any inspired teacher, prophet, Christ, or God even, outside of himself. Then it logically follows that there is no absolute, universal, eternal, religious truth and righteousness which all men are in duty bound to seek out and obey, but each one's intuitions, opinions, conclusions are equally true to those possessing them; and all religious and ethical theories are equally authoritative to those professing them. The Bible settles nothing; Christ is no reliable teacher; human nature settles everything! And what a mighty, endless babel of theories, doctrines, ideas we have in the world, all equally right, good, and true to those who entertain and cherish them! I prefer the theology and ethics of Jesus Christ – one universal fatherhood over all, one universal brotherhood uniting all, one universal law of duty for all, love to God and man – these I prefer to the theology and ethics of human nature as illustrated in all ages of the world's history. I cannot believe in the self-sufficient divinity of human nature as it ever has been and now is; my faith centers in universal divine principles, revealed from heaven through many media, but most clearly and perfectly through Jesus Christ.

4. Concerning Non-Resistance. Under this head I will first notice the declaration that "Non-Resistance is in no way necessarily connected with or dependent on the teachings, example, or official authority of Jesus Christ." Then according to the theory just noticed, it must be connected with and dependent on the teachings, example, and inherent authority of human nature; that is, of such individual human beings as fancy it to be the outgrowth of their own personal intuitions, the number of which is not one in ten thousand of the race of man. To the masses of our kind – the uncounted multitude – Non-Resistance is simply *nonsense*, as has been repeatedly affirmed by men standing high in public esteem and in the annals of reform. That is the manner in which human nature *as a whole* settles the ethics of Non-Resistance. It pronounces against it in terms most emphatic and with a verdict overwhelming so far as majorities are concerned. Yet the testimony of Christ by both precept and example is equally emphatic and overwhelming. Which of these – human nature or Christ – speaks in this case with the greater authority? Which is most worthy of homage and reverence? Let professed Non-Resistants answer.

And now let us see how the elect few who derive their faith in Non-Resistance from human nature – that is, from their own human nature – settle the question with themselves and determine their duty in reference to it. Mr. Garrison is a competent representative of all such and it is but just that he be heard in their behalf. He says, "Although Non-Resistance holds human life in all cases absolutely inviolable by professed Non-Resistants yet it is perfectly consistent for them to petition, advise, and strenuously urge a pro-war government to abolish slavery by the war power."[6] Now the war power assumes that it is right to wound, mutilate, slaughter, any number of human beings who resist the authority of any state or nation, or who seek by violent means to prevent the execution of its will. And to ask a government to use the war power for the accomplishment of an object confessedly good, is to ask it to do what Non-Resistance teaches is essentially wrong. Can such a course be justified upon sound ethical principles? What one does by another he does by himself. This is true both in morals and in jurisprudence. And what one requests, advises, urges another to do, he is personally responsible for, if the thing be done. And to petition the government to abolish slavery by the exercise of the war power, is to become morally involved in the bloodshed and death resulting from such action. It is to adopt the Jesuitical maxim, "The end sanctifies the means,"[7] which is false in morals and suicidal in policy. Any worthy cause which is carried forward on that principle cannot long survive; will soon die by its own hand or the hand of its own advocates, as did that phase of Non-Resistance. It has been silent in its grave ever since it thus lent itself to the work of human destruction for the promotion of human liberty.

True Non-Resistance – Christian Non-Resistance – is of another type, of a higher genus. It came down from heaven. It was born, not of *human* nature but of the *divine* nature – of the pure wisdom and love of God. Human nature was constituted with a capacity for understanding, reverencing, cherishing, and exemplifying it, but not without more or less of self-crucifixion and help from on high. Jesus Christ did not originate this sublime doctrine, but he taught it and clearly illustrated it, enabling his disciples to comprehend and proclaim it to their fellow men. As he taught and illustrated it, there was in it no inconsistency or self-contradiction. He did not preach one thing and practice another. He did not theorize beautifully about love and good will to all men, even to the worst of offenders, and then when a storm of wrath and war, engendered by human folly and transgression arose, straightway advocate the resistance of evil with evil, or ask and urge others to wield the battle axe and "let slip the dogs of war"[8] in order to gain some greatly-to-be-desired good and help bring his righteous kingdom in. His kingdom was not of this world[9] and could not be advanced after the fashion of this world's red revolutionary reformers,[10] but rather by the regeneration of individual men through repentance for sin unto good works, and the love of righteousness whereby they would be brought into true relations with each other – into that state of unity, harmony, and brotherhood in which all should strive together for the universal good and happiness, blessing and cursing not.[11]

The banner of love, beneficence, forgiveness that he as "Prince of Peace" flung to the breeze and called his followers to rally under and maintain as they went forth to the conquest of the world, has long been dishonored by his nominal church, which prostituted it to the service of the war power and of sword-sustained human governments. But the end is not yet. There will surely be some day a new and regenerate Christian church which will re-affirm, exemplify, and triumphantly glorify the original righteousness of the divine kingdom in this regard, and so truly honor him whom it professes to believe in and serve. Here I rest my faith and close my defense of the truth as it has been made known to me against the detraction and false assumptions of my honored friend, William Lloyd Garrison.

A Case of Conscription

At this point I must put on record one special exploit of the high-pretending war-power of the United States government which we were counseled to summon to our aid in seeking the overthrow of slavery. In August, 1863, under a law authorizing the conscription of soldiers for replenishing the depleted ranks of the army,[12] one of the loyal members of our Community, John Lowell Heywood,[13] was drawn for the required service. As he could not conscientiously respond in person to the demand made upon him nor employ a substitute to fill his place, it was deemed advisable, after considerable hesitancy and discussion, that the prescribed commutation equivalent of three hundred dollars should be paid by him and such of his friends as might be moved to assist him in the crisis, rather than that he should be made to suffer the penal infliction provided for those who, under such circumstances, refused to join the forces then in the field. This was accordingly done. I have since feared that we acted wrongfully in the matter, feeling that it would have been more consistent with our principles and a more effective testimony against the wicked exactions of the government to have allowed the law to have taken its proper course and dealt with our unresisting brother to the full extent of its despotic and inexorable requirements.[14] I do not recommend a repetition of our course in future cases of a similar sort, although in the unprecedented pressure of events I advised the payment of the money. It was done, however, under public protest formally presented to the military authorities at the time, a copy of which, prepared by myself and approved by the Community, I take the liberty to submit to my readers and to coming generations as follows:

> To the governmental authorities of the United States and their constituents, the undersigned, John Lowell Heywood of Hopedale, in the town of Milford, in the eighth congressional district of Massachusetts, respectfully maketh solemn declaration, remonstrance, and protest, to wit:
>
> That he has been enrolled, drafted, and notified to appear as a soldier of the United States, pursuant to an Act of Congress approved March 3, 1863, commonly called the Conscription Law.
>
> That he holds in utter abhorrence the rebellion which the said law was designed to aid in suppressing and would devotedly fight unto death against it if he could conscientiously resort to deadly weapons in any case whatsoever.
>
> But that he has been for nearly nine years a member in good and regular standing of a Christian Community whose religious confession of faith and practice pledges its members "never to kill, injure, or harm any human being, even their worst enemy."
>
> That in accordance with his highest convictions of duty and his sacred pledge as a member of said Community, he has scrupulously and uniformly abstained from participating in the state and national governments under which he has lived – not only foregoing the franchises, preferments, emoluments, and advantages of a constituent co-governing citizen, but also the privilege of righting his wrongs

by commencing suits at law, and of calling on government for protection against threatened violence – in order thereby to avoid making himself morally responsible for their constitutional *dernier resorts* to war, capital punishment, and other kindred acts, and also to commend to mankind by a consistent example those divine principles which prepare the way for a higher order of society and government on earth.

That, nevertheless, it is one of the cardinal Christian principles to respect existing human government, however imperfect, as a natural outgrowth and necessity of society for the time being, subordinate to the providential overrulings of the supreme divine government, and therefore to be an orderly, submissive, peaceable, tribute-paying subject thereof; to be no detriment or hindrance to any good thereby subserved; to countenance no rebellion, sedition, riot, or other disorderly demonstration against its authorities; to oppose its greatest abuses and wrongs only by truthful testimony and firm, moral remonstrance; and in the last resort, when obliged for conscience' sake to non-comply with its requirements, to submit meekly to whatever penalties it may impose.

That with such principles, scruples, and views of duty, he cannot conscientiously comply with the demands of this Conscription Law, either by serving as a soldier or by procuring a substitute. Nor can he pay the three hundred dollars of commutation money which the law declaratively appropriates to the hiring of a substitute, except under explicit remonstrance and protest that the same is virtually taken from him by compulsion for a purpose and use to which he could never voluntarily contribute it, and for which he holds himself in no wise morally responsible.

And he hereby earnestly protests, not only for himself but also in behalf of his Christian associates and all other orderly, peaceable, tax-paying, non-juring subjects of the government of whatever denomination or class, that their conscientious scruples against war and human life-taking, ought, in justice and honor, to be respected by the legislators and administrators of a professedly republican government; and that, aside from general taxation for the support thereof, no person of harmless and exemplary life who is conscientiously opposed to war and deadly force between human beings, and especially no person who for conscience' sake foregoes the franchises, preferments, privileges, and advantages of a constituent citizen, ought ever to be conscripted as a soldier, either in person or property.

Now, therefore, I, the said John Lowell Heywood, do pay the three hundred dollars commutation money to the government of the United States, under military constraint in respectful submission to the powers that be,[15] but solemnly protesting against the exaction as an infraction of my natural and indefeasible rights as a conscientious, peaceable subject. And for the final vindication of my cause, motives, and intentions, I appeal to the moral sense of all just men, and above all to the inerrable judgment of the Supreme Father and Ruler of the universe.

Subscribed with my hand at Hopedale, Milford, Mass., this 18th day of August, A.D., 1863.

JOHN LOWELL HEYWOOD.

Excursions to Long Island and Philadelphia

The arrangement by which I was to supply the pulpit at Hopedale one-half the time continued till the close of the year 1865, my other Sundays being occupied elsewhere, usually in neighboring towns or localities not very far from home. The month of September of the year mentioned, I spent in part at Southold, Long Island, with my esteemed friends, Joseph H. Goldsmith and wife, and in part with the family of my equally esteemed friends, Dr. Henry T. Child[16] and wife, in Philadelphia, preaching and lecturing upon my favorite themes several times during each week as opportunity offered. The kindness and hospitality of these friends at this and other times are among the most cherished memories of my life.

While on this visit to Philadelphia, I was privileged to attend a most wonderful musical exhibition given at Concert Hall by the then celebrated "Blind Tom,"[17] as he was called – a rustic negro, formerly a slave but recently set free by the famous Emancipation Proclamation of President Lincoln. There was nothing in the performer's external appearance to indicate unusual powers of any sort, but that he was a prodigy in his art no one who saw and heard him could question. He was but a youth, less than twenty years of age, and had received nothing that could be termed a musical education. But as a pianist his accomplishments were marvelous, while his vocal renderings were scarcely less than that. He surprised and delighted his auditors by his execution of popular airs as well as pieces of his own composition. Two of the latter – one entitled "The Thunder-storm," and the other, "When This Cruel War is Over" – were of surpassing excellence. Some of his feats with voice and instrument were as unique as they were astonishing. He imitated the common music box with unaccountable precision; produced "Yankee Doodle" in a reversed position, his hands being behind him; and, to crown all, played one tune with his right hand, another with the left, while a third was sung by him – all going on simultaneously. Here were modern miracles indeed! I could but think that "Blind Tom" was a medium for some musical genius of the unseen world.

A year later, in September 1866, I repeated the visits to both Southold and Philadelphia, accompanied by my wife, to the great satisfaction and enjoyment of both of us. A peculiarly interesting incident occurred at the former place. By special invitation I attended a temperance meeting in the Presbyterian church one evening, and made a brief address in connection with other speakers. During a little pause in the proceedings, a stranger came forward unannounced and delivered a most charming speech. The audience was greatly pleased and, when he closed called for the unknown man's name. With modest reluctance he at length said, "Andrew Leighton of Liverpool, England."[18] I was surprised beyond measure, for I had corresponded for some years with Andrew Leighton and had longed to see him but never expected to enjoy that privilege. And now, without any forewarning or intimation that he was within three thousand miles of me, he was standing in my very presence. The reader can judge of the fervor of the greeting we gave each other at the close of the exercises, which took place immediately, and of the mutually gratifying interview we had afterward at the house of friend Goldsmith. It seemed Mr. Leighton had been called suddenly to America for business purposes. Determining to see me, he went to Hopedale to learn of my absence and whereabouts. Hurrying on to Southold, he traced me to the temperance meeting, heard me speak, and finally made himself known in the way indicated. He proved to be a very intelligent, large-minded, companionable gentleman, well informed upon subjects in which I was interested, and ready in conversation, which he enlivened with choice anecdote, poetry, and song. He remained with us only about twenty-four hours, which he rendered memorable by the richness and variety of his communications and the warmth, generosity, and nobleness of his spirit. He left Southold for Boston and I never saw him more.

The Hopedale Parish and its Pastor

During the then current year [1866] I was occupying the pulpit at Hopedale three-fourths of the time, being the only regularly employed minister of the Community, which still had a name to live and still continued to make provision for the moral and religious activities of the place. My son-in-law, with whom I had been so long associated in the work of the ministry there, had withdrawn entirely from the field, having been settled as pastor of the First Church and Society of Scituate, Massachusetts. At the opening of the year 1867, I was invited to preach at home all the time, my salary, which had been five dollars per Sunday in 1864, eight dollars in 1865, and twelve dollars in 1866, being fixed at fifteen dollars, or seven hundred and eighty dollars for the year – no provision being made for a vacation.

On May 26 and June 9, 1867, respectively, I delivered two carefully prepared discourses in the Hopedale church which were deemed worthy of publication. They were entitled "Human Progress in Respect to Religion." The first was upon "The Tendency of the Age to Dispense with the Specialties and Personal Responsibilities of Religion"; the second on "The Ultimate Convincement of Progressive Minds in Favor of the Pure Christian Religion and Church." These discourses were put into tract form and distributed far and wide in the general community. There was urgent need of the lessons and admonitions which this tract contained in 1867; there is no less need in 1890, and I apprehend this will be the case far on in the indefinite future.

As time advanced, the disproportion between the number of members of the Community resident in Hopedale and the number of persons who were not members was continually increasing, until it came to pass that the latter were greatly in the majority. And yet these had no voice in the management of the general affairs of the place, and especially of those pertaining to moral and religious culture and to the institutions and activities by which the moral and religious interests of the people at large – non-members as well as members – were to be fostered and perpetuated. There was seen to be an inequality – a wrong in this state of things which ought to be remedied. Those outside of the Community, technically speaking, were practically as much concerned in the moral and spiritual interests of the village – in public and private virtue and piety – as those inside, and should, as a matter of right, be privileged to act in reference to them – should be allowed to cooperate with their fellow residents in guarding and promoting them. This was recognized and conceded on all hands, and it was generally felt that some change was needed to meet the requirements of the case – some new method of administration so far as related to the things mentioned.

Hence, after due deliberation and conference, and with the consent of all interested parties, there was organized in the month of October, 1867, what was called the Hopedale Parish, whose membership was composed of persons outside as well as inside the pale of the Community – of all in the place who desired to unite and work together, as set forth in the constitution, for the moral and religious education and improvement of all classes of the population and for the public welfare and happiness. This being done, the Community, in its distinctive capacity, transferred its powers and responsibilities in the matters indicated to the Hopedale Parish, which at once assumed them and entered upon the discharge of the involved trust. Everything was settled to the satisfaction of those concerned, and the regime then established has continued to the present day, as it is likely to continue indefinitely in days and years to come.[19]

This being accomplished, largely through my agency and by my advice, the next question of importance to me was, "What am I now to do?" – a question which pressed heavily upon my mind and heart. I pondered it seriously and prayerfully before answering it and deciding upon my future course. My high convictions of truth and duty and my manner of life for many years had unfitted me to resume the pastoral office under the auspices of any denomination involved in the maintenance of the existing order of society; and I saw no opportunity of renewing the Community experiment elsewhere with the least hope of success. Moreover, my surviving friends in the village, and what remained there as the result of my long-continued struggles, seemed to deserve my sacred regard; so that when the unanimous desire of the parish, including the new as well as the old settlers, was expressed that I should be their sole preacher for the immediate future, accompanied by an urgent invitation to that effect, I deemed it wise and right to accept and occupy the field of service thus opened to me. This was done with a full and fair understanding that I was to be as independent, outspoken, and free under the new system as I always had been under the old – as true to my own convictions and to the Master in whom I believed and whom I professed to follow. Not the slightest intimation was given me then or ever after that I would be expected to change or suppress any of my long-cherished ideas, principles, or peculiarities. And though the wind and tide were so obviously against me – so decidedly favorable to the established order of civilization that I had little to hope for a truer, a more Christian one – yet I felt that I could do something to preserve the fruit of my labors from utter extinction in the locality where they had been chiefly expended, or at least be able to transmit the memorials of them to coming generations. I thought that in addition to my covenanted pulpit work, which I was bound to perform faithfully, I might command the time and means of writing a truthful history of a frustrated experiment in behalf of a regenerated form of human society, set forth the causes of failure and show how they might be avoided, for the benefit of social reformers in some age yet to be. And I furthermore thought that I might find time and opportunity to prepare a series of carefully studied expositions of my highest and best ideas concerning some of the great questions of morals and religion relating to the progress, welfare, and happiness of mankind, for future examination and use. This I finally resolved to do, hoping thereby to be of substantial service to the world after I had passed to other spheres of being – leaving behind me some of the fruits of my inspiration and endeavor which would prove my life-work less a failure than otherwise it might appear to be.

United with the Unitarians

Three months after the inauguration of the new ecclesiastical regime, in January, 1868, the Hopedale Parish, with myself as pastor, was formally admitted to the Worcester Conference of Congregational (Unitarian) and other Christian Societies, at a meeting convened in the neighboring town of Westboro. Our application had been fraternally received at a previous session and we were cordially welcomed to the fellowship of the body. As the Unitarian polity imposes no creed, covenant, or stringent conditions of affiliation upon either its individual members or associated co-laborers, recognizing only a general loyalty to Christ and his religion on the common basis of the fatherhood of God and brotherhood of man, we entered this new alliance on easy and satisfactory terms – neither giving nor exacting specific pledges of any kind. I was personally in no wise embarrassed thereby. I was not required or expected to renounce or modify any of my favorite beliefs, nor did I expect or require others to renounce or modify any of theirs on my account. There was mutual freedom, tolerance, friendliness. On many points of theology and morality there was entire harmony, theoretically, between me and my new allies. Among both clergy and laity of the conference I had many old acquaintances – some of them temperance, antislavery, and peace reformers – between whom and myself there existed sincere respect and confidence. So the dominant condition and aspect of things was pleasant to me and promised a chance for me to infuse wholesome leaven into the general body to which I became attached, without compromising myself or my sacredly cherished principles. At any rate, we could work harmoniously together for the common good and aid each other in promulgating among our fellow men the distinctive doctrines and ideas of a rational, liberal, practical Christian faith. Such were the reasons for the step thus taken as they lay in my own mind, and if the good resulting from it did not realize all I desired, probably I could not have done better. I have always been treated with the utmost kindness and hospitality by my Unitarian brethren and sisters, and they have listened to my testimonies with attentive and gratifying interest, even when they could not accept them in all their bearings and applications.

I had been invited by the proper conference authorities to deliver an address at the opening session of the meeting referred to, which was held on the evening before our parish was admitted to membership. I accepted the invitation, presenting my views of the objects, principles, and methods which I believed all followers of Christ ought to cooperate in maintaining, prosecuting, and carrying out to their legitimate practical results. My effort was appreciated beyond my highest anticipations. Not only was the usual vote of thanks accorded me, but a copy of my discourse was requested for publication in the *Christian Register*. I cheerfully granted the request, furnishing the desired copy for the editor, who accepted it and gave it a place in his issue of February 22, 1868. It was entitled, "The World's Need of the Church," and was designed to be, as I believe it was, a systematic, comprehensive, and incontrovertible vindication of the church of Christ as a redemptive force in human society; as an institution established in the nature of things and ordained of God for the enlightenment and regeneration of mankind.

Work for Coming Generations

I was now in full charge of the Hopedale pulpit and of the general moral and religious activities connected therewith, to the duties of which I addressed myself with diligence and zeal. I labored assiduously both at the sacred desk and in the Sunday school to impart a high order of instruction to old and young – sound, uncompromising Practical Christianity, amply illustrated and judiciously applied. I could not have striven harder if I had served a very large, sympathetic, enthusiastic congregation in one of our prosperous cities. Instead of this, I had but a small audience, respectful indeed, yet only partially sympathetic and responsive to my utterances, with little manifestation of interest and zeal in the work I was trying to do. I preached and taught the gospel of the new life, individual and social, for I could preach and teach no other. But more than half my people were committed to the old milito-political dispensation of the unregenerate world, and the minority, holding still to their former faith in something better and more Christlike, were powerless against the receding tide. The currents of the home, the school, the market, the shop, the street, were against me for the most part, and were augmented by the dominant forces of the great world outside, neutralizing nearly everything I had to say or do. I was often made to feel that I was trying with all my heart to promote what most of those before me deemed impracticable and were invincibly pre-committed to disregard. But I did not see what I could do different or better. So I kept on, often with a sick and fainting heart.

In this condition of things, I was more and more impelled to contemplate the future, and to live and labor for coming generations. I gave up expecting to accomplish much for the reformation of my fellow men in my natural lifetime and was led to devote more and more of my energies and pecuniary means to the benefit of my successors. Omitting no known duty arising from day to day and from year to year, I yet worked steadily as much as I could for the days and years ahead. To this end I busied myself in collating for preservation such of my published writings as I deemed worthy, adding thereto from time to time such new matter upon important subjects as I was able to prepare.

In 1868, by special request of Mr. C. C. Drew, publisher of the Milford directory,[20] I wrote for his work a rudimentary sketch of the town's history, including an appropriate notice of the Hopedale Community. This was the crude beginning of my voluminous *History of Milford*, given to the public some years afterward.

During the years 1869-70, I prepared with great care and put in manuscript a series of twenty discourses, which I first delivered from my pulpit, and, two years later, pursuant to my original design, caused to be published in a duodecimo volume of 331 pages. The work bore the following title: *Primitive Christianity and its Corruptions: Department of Theological Doctrines, etc.* It was intended to be the first of three volumes on the same general subject – the other two to be made ready for the press subsequently as opportunity offered – the second to treat of *Personal Righteousness*, and the third of *Ecclesiastical Polity*. These were written in due time, as will be noted hereafter, and are still in manuscript. I have provided for their publication after my decease.[21]

The Restorationist Secession

In 1871 I had occasion to correct a long series of misrepresentations which had appeared from time to time in the periodicals of the Universalist denomination concerning the Restorationist secession of 1831. The last appeared in *The Universalist*, the Boston organ of the sect, January 21. The entire list had been characterized by a disregard of facts and by gross disparagement and contempt of the seceding brethren. I had read many of these offensive diatribes with disgust and indignation, but kept silent, hoping they would die without special contradiction. But this fresh outburst of perversion and abuse led me to think that my hopes were vain, and to fear that these manifestos were likely to become chronic falsifications of history and go down to the unsuspecting future as trustworthy recitals of what had transpired. I determined, therefore, if possible, to correct them, especially as I was one of the few survivors of the maligned party, and master of all the facts of the case. I accordingly solicited the privilege of making the correction in the columns of the paper in which the offense was last committed. The favor was granted and I furnished two articles reviewing the whole matter and giving a brief but effective statement of it which seemed to be accepted as satisfactory – which, at any rate, silenced our detractors forever. The articles appeared in the issues of *The Universalist* for February 11 and 25 of the year mentioned [1871].[22]

Relations with Unitarians, Spiritualists, Reformers

In connection with the various labors thus noted, I kept up my usual round of weddings, funerals, and friendly visitations in my larger parish of the neighboring towns, and rendered many miscellaneous services as speaker at home and abroad on occasions of a religious, reformatory, secular, and commemorative character, to which I can only incidentally refer. My correspondence was still large, and I was still beset by visitors from near and far for conversation and counsel upon matters of religion, philanthropy, and reform, including inquirers after the way of a better social life.

I generally attended the three sessions per year of the Worcester Conference with my six parish delegates, and frequently took part in the exercises. As a religious body, the Unitarians in some respects were quite below my ideal of Practical Christianity. I had no affinity with the extreme radicals among them[23] and disliked their general indifference to questions of personal, moral, and social regeneration, as I did their invincible attachment, in common with all the sects, to the institutions and customs of governmental civilization as it now is. But they were an intelligent, tolerant, and courteous people, having among them truly elect souls, with whom I could heartily sympathize and cooperate for good and noble ends. I was furthermore in full accord with them in their great central idea of love to God and man as the sum and substance of the religion of Christ. For this reason I could not coalesce with the so-called Evangelical sects, whose dogmas of limited probation and endless punishment are virtual denials of the universal divine fatherhood – self-evident theological barbarisms which logically destroy the moral character of God and poison religion at its fountainhead. Such dogmas I hold in inconceivable abhorrence.

In respect to the Spiritualists as a body, I had become weaned from my former attractions to them and ceased to attend their general public convocations. Not because I had discarded one particle of the Spiritualism I had ever believed in and advocated, but because I adhered inflexibly to Jesus Christ as my religious Lord and Master, superior to all spirits or spirit mediums of ancient or modern times, and maintained that his expositions of truth and righteousness were divinely authoritative. The leaders and zealots of the spiritualistic gospel gave me to understand that they wanted nothing of this Christly supremacy. I therefore declined to urge it upon their devotees, and having no relish for *their* supremacy, quietly withdrew from their active fellowship and went about my Father's business.[24]

As to special reformers, they had mostly fallen away from my high ideals of Practical Christianity. The Non-Resistants, with few exceptions, had failed in the hour of trial and yielded allegiance to the war-god when with his battle-axe he cleft asunder the fetters of the slave. The American Peace Society protested that it stood only for international disarmament and arbitration, not for extreme disuse of injurious force. A more radical movement, the Universal Peace Union, was started, but with some objectionable complications; yet I took an interest in it, lent it moderate support, and rejoiced in whatever of good it was able to do.[25] Antislavery had become apotheosized by its war-power triumph and rested from its labors. All that could be done in its behalf was to carry relief to the freedmen, to which I contributed by words and deeds.[26] The temperance cause called for devotees, and I gave it the support I could without involving myself in its reliance upon penal laws, arbitrary exactions, and final resort to violence.[27] The same was true with the cause of women's rights. When it became chiefly absorbed in the question of suffrage and the use of the ballot box, I shrank back somewhat from it, yet never abandoned the fundamental principles of justice and equity upon which it was based, nor withdrew my admiration from its more essential and distinguishing characteristics.[28] Finally, the working people's movement flung its standard to the breeze and called for recruits to its heterogeneous ranks. I was interested in its objects and professed claims, as I had been in similar movements in America and England for many years, and I studied and watched it with sympathetic desire and hope. But I found in it little of the spirit of fraternity, of cooperation between the strong and the weak; little of the spirit of Christian brotherhood. It sought to level down, but not up. Its trust was in legislation and governmental coercion. The sword was its *dernier resort*. It belonged to a moral and social sphere and to a field of reform from which I had withdrawn forever.[29] So with nothing but the best of wishes for this and all other efforts to do good in the world, though by ways and methods which neither my judgment nor my conscience could approve, I addressed myself all the more devotedly to my own proper mission, that of preparing the way for future generations to dwell together as co-equal brethren and sisters of a common family – the loving children of the one heavenly Father. Thus I reached my birthday in the year 1872.

CHAPTER 23

1872-1882

Near the close of the last chapter I spoke of the preparation in 1870 of the first volume of my comprehensive work on *Primitive Christianity and its Corruptions*, to be completed in two additional volumes at some convenient subsequent date. In that initial number of the series, which was entitled *Theological Doctrines*, I undertook to show how, from a very early period in its history, the Christian church, through ignorance, bigotry, and other agencies incident to an undeveloped, barbarous age of the world, had been diverted from the simplicity that is in Christ and led to adopt doctrines and beliefs which were not only an offense to enlightened reason and a quickened moral sense, but a travesty on the gospel as Jesus taught and exemplified it. I also endeavored to show that many of these early perversions of Christianity had come down to our own times and were still exerting a pernicious influence upon the faith and life of mankind – dishonoring the character of the heavenly Father and vitiating the primary conditions of human welfare and happiness.

The only formal literary notice worthy of consideration which this book received appeared in the *Universalist Quarterly* for April, 1872. It was from the pen of Rev. A. St. John Chambré,[1] a courteous, scholarly, conservative clergyman of ritualistic tendencies, then in the ministry of the denomination indicated, but since gone over to the Episcopalians. He saw little in my performance to approve, but much to condemn.[2] He animadverted somewhat severely upon my spiritualistic interpretations, my rejection of the dogma of the Immaculate Conception,[3] and other points definitely taken by me. I could not regard his strictures as just, discriminating, or valid, and they therefore brought conviction neither to my understanding nor my moral sense. I prepared, not long after, a critical rejoinder to his article, but as there was no good opportunity to give it to the public, I stored it away for future use.

Most of the topics deemed objectionable by my reviewer are treated in some other connection in this narrative and I need not advert to them here. One of them, however, not mentioned elsewhere, I will briefly notice – the doctrine of the Immaculate Conception. I had been led to set aside the accounts in the gospels of Matthew and Luke on which that doctrine assumes to be based, with extreme reluctance – not at all from a general sweeping disbelief in miracles, as they are termed, but solely on the ground of irreconcilable contradictions in the accounts themselves, which render them of doubtful origin, and of the utter silence of all the other New Testament scriptures concerning the matter. If it were true that Jesus was born as the popular creedists claim, not in the regular order of nature, but by supernatural intervention, and if this view is of the importance in the Christian economy of redemption attributed to it, then the fact that it is not once mentioned nor even alluded to by the other evangelists or by St. Paul is most surprising and utterly inexplicable. It is much more satisfactory to my reason and moral judgment to regard the passages relating to it as interpolations, agreeably to the conclusions of some eminent Biblical scholars, or as erroneous interpretations of the actual facts in the case, than to accept the prevailing views of the nominal Christian church. And this I say while fully persuaded that the main body of the New Testament is entirely trustworthy as to the essential truth of the statements therein made. My only exceptions are a very few passages obviously self-contradictory or uncorroborated by collateral testimony in the record. Most of what ultra-modern critics discard as untrustworthy in these scriptures I adhere to with unwavering confidence. I am particularly desirous of being understood correctly in this matter of faith in the reliability of the New Testament records.

At the regular meeting of the Worcester (Unitarian) Conference held at Brookfield in May 1872, I, by invitation, read an essay upon "The Relation of the Intellect and Emotions Respectively to the Development of the Religious Life." The wording of the subject enabled me to present to the assembled representatives of the thirty or more societies of which the conference was composed, my favorite idea that true religion requires the coordinate and harmonious exercise of the various faculties of the human understanding and those of the emotional nature usually termed the sentiments. The purport of what I said may be deduced from my opening sentences:

> If we should find a person intelligent and rational, honest and conscientious, benevolent, considerate, and kind unto others; reverential toward God and divine things, devout, spiritually minded, exemplary in all the duties of true morality and piety, we should say the religious life was well developed in such a person. If we could find a whole society or denomination exhibiting generally these characteristics, we should pronounce the same verdict upon those composing it, collectively considered. On the other hand, if we should find individuals, societies, and denominations intelligent and rational, with a decent morality and ordinary philanthropy, but lax and indifferent in respect to religious duties and especially to devotional exercises, we should say there was an imperfect development of the religious life. Or if we should meet another class, very devout and zealous according to the fashion of their sect, yet unintelligent, contemners of human reason, bigoted and superstitious, not over moral in their common life, denouncing homely good works as of little worth in the sight of God, we could justly affirm the same concerning them. They, with the others, would exhibit a very one-sided and defective religious development.

These thoughts were elaborated, illustrated, and applied along the lines indicated, giving the reader a general conception of my effort on the occasion, concerning which I need not enlarge.

Parochial Christian Union

In my endeavors to discharge the duties devolving upon me as pastor of the Hopedale parish and as in some sense the guardian of the moral and religious interests of the people of the village, I was led to see the need of some more definite, positive, direct methods of culture and inspiration than the ordinary exercises of public worship and the Sunday school afforded, and of a closer personal relation between me and the objects of my charge than as yet, under the new dispensation, had been enjoyed. With a view of supplying that need, I made a serious attempt early in 1873 to establish a "Parochial Christian Union," which I hoped might grow into an institution of permanent value, mentally, morally, religiously, and socially considered, to our entire population. I flattered myself with the idea that something of the kind would bring different classes together for purposes of self-improvement, developing in them the spirit of mutual helpfulness and aspirations after a higher and a better life. I therefore drew up a well-devised constitution as a basis of cooperative action, and calling those together who felt as if they could be interested in and profited by such a movement, went so far as to organize a small body of volunteers under its provisions. A few meetings were held and some steps were taken to put its proposed methods of study and discipline into practical operation. But it did not strike the popular mind favorably, it received no encouragement from influential quarters, and it had too small a number of competent adherents to work its machinery with satisfactory results. After a brief trial the effort was given up. There was no doubt of the intrinsic importance of the objects contemplated and no defect appeared in the plan or proposed methods of operation, but like many of my previous devices for doing good, it looked well on paper but failed when an attempt was made to put it to practical use, for want of appreciative, capable, and faithful devotees. Disappointed once more, I turned from special activities calculated to benefit and bless those living in the present time, to work with renewed diligence and zeal for what I believed might benefit and bless unborn generations.

Resignation Tendered and Withdrawn

Soon after my discomfiture in this every way laudable and praiseworthy undertaking, I, in the month of April, 1873, resigned my position as pastor of the Hopedale parish and congregation. I did this partly because of that discomfiture, which made me feel that the dominant influences of the place were against me, neutralizing my labors and thwarting my plans for carrying forward the work to which I was called, and partly because I had reached the age of seventy years and might be expected to give way to a younger man, whose matter, manner, and method would be more acceptable to the people generally than mine. Much to my surprise, not only was my resignation not accepted, but was met with a remonstrance so unanimous, positive, and urgent that I immediately recalled it and settled down for another term of service in my accustomed place – a term which, as the issue proved, was to continue for seven full years more. But I never afterward ventured far out of my conventional routine of prescribed pulpit and Sunday school labors – never renewed my endeavors to institute any new methods of moral and spiritual instruction and quickening, or any special social machinery for advancing the cause of virtue and piety, but going my own narrow round of official duties, left my parishioners and their dependents to their already established usages and to such other training and discipline as might please them.

I was now at greater liberty than ever before to go on with the work upon which my heart was so much set – that of putting my thoughts and ideas upon matters pertaining to human progress and redemption into proper form for preservation and transmission to those who might appreciate and use them after I should have passed beyond the scenes and cares of earth and time. I had already begun to elaborate and prepare for the press a second series of discourses upon *Primitive Christianity and its Corruptions*, which was to be published as Volume II of my comprehensive work upon that general subject and to bear the specific title of *Personal Righteousness*. This series, the several parts of which were preached as sermons to my Sunday congregation, was carried through to completion during the year, the more important events and occurrences of which, so far as concerned me personally, I am now recapitulating. It was composed of twenty-eight discourses, each declaring and elucidating some important point of Christian duty as related to the individual man, woman, or child, the whole making a manual or study of the special topic of which it treats, symmetrical in statement and exhaustive in argument and illustration. In it I was careful to set forth, defend, and apply to human character and life the distinctive morality of the New Testament scriptures, and to show the corruption of the same in the theory and practice of the nominal Christian church. I was especially careful to emphasize and magnify those sublime duties of piety and morality which have been most perverted and disregarded by professing Christians, and which really constitute the transcendent excellence of Primitive Christianity, as compared with all other moral and religious philosophies and systems of the world.

Last Scene in the Drama of the Hopedale Community

It has been already stated that in 1868 the Hopedale Community, by its proper officers, transferred all its parochial prerogatives and responsibilities – the care of the moral and religious interests of the village – to the newly-formed parish, which at once entered upon the discharge of the trust thereby imposed upon it. Five years later, in December, 1873, the trustees of the Community, as the custodians of its remaining possessions, conveyed to the same authorities all their right, title, interest, and control in, unto, and over Community Square and its appurtenances, the meetinghouse standing thereon, and the Hopedale Cemetery, to be held, cared for, and used by them and their heirs and successors after them forever. There was still in the trustees' hands the "Soward fund," so called, amounting to eight hundred dollars, the income of which was to be expended for the mental and moral improvement of the young through the agency of the Sunday school. This fund was made over to the parish in December, 1875, which was the final transaction pertaining to Community affairs – the closing act of the drama of our new social state. Thus was the Hopedale Community laid in its tomb and consigned to the keeping of history. A few devoted survivors still live to hallow its name and memory, but the multitudes who once knew it heed not its ashes nor the memorials of its checkered career.

Primitive Christianity Continued

The third and closing volume of my work on *Primitive Christianity and its Corruptions* was chiefly prepared during the year 1874. It was entitled *Department of Ecclesiastical Polity*, and consisted of twenty-five chapters devoted to organic church life and its bearings upon sociological problems. Its grand aim was to show what the primitive church, as instituted by its great Founder, really was; when and how it became deteriorated and despoiled of its original character; and by what means it can be regenerated, reconstructed, and perfected. The general drift and purpose of its contents may be gleaned from a few considerations derived from well known facts of Christian history.

The New Testament scriptures nowhere assert or assume that Christ came into the world in order to prosecute his saving mission to mankind by raising up and establishing a church on the low moral level of carnal respectability, which merely educates and ornaments the intellect, animal propensities and powers, without transcending their instinctive selfishness and brutality. Refined, cultivated, polished, genteel selfishness and brutality are selfish and brutish still – often intolerably so, in utter hostility to the principles and spirit of the gospel. Jesus sought to lay the foundations of a church which should be "the light of the world" and "the salt of the earth," composed of those who were "wise as serpents and harmless as doves," who were "not of the world," but "chosen out of the world" to redeem the world. But if the light "be hid under a bushel" and the "salt have lost its savor"[4] – if the members of the church bearing his name illustrate in their individual and social life no higher virtue and piety than prevail elsewhere, must not moral darkness, corruption, and iniquity still reign?

What, then, are we to think of the nominal church of Christ as it is and has been ever since its union with and practical surrender to the organized civilization of the world under Constantine the Great in the fourth century? Giving it all the credit which truth and justice demand, yet, as a whole, has it been essentially "of the world," with the same general admixture of good and evil, of righteousness and unrighteousness, which have characterized the unregenerated governing classes of society from generation to generation down the stream of time? Its worthiest and most Christlike representatives in all ages have been individuals, groups, and small sects – mostly persecuted heretics or schismatics – who went to the fountainhead of Christian knowledge to learn what truth and duty are and taught and lived what was there revealed to them. It is these who have kept Christianity in its primitive purity alive in the world, preserving it from utter perversion or absolute extinction.

It is, however, claimed by some that the church is greatly improved in these later days, having put away many of the follies, absurdities, barbarities, iniquities, which it tolerated and fostered a few centuries ago. Perhaps so. But tried by the standard presented us in the precepts and injunctions of Jesus, what is it now? Do its leading denominations and their adherents scrupulously exemplify almsgiving, prayer, religious duties and observances in a way "not to be seen of men?"[5] Do they render no idolatrous worship to the god Mammon, covet no property advantage over their fellows, and bestow their superfluous wealth on needy, suffering humanity for its relief and moral elevation? Do they heed scrupulously the Savior's counsel, "Be ye not called Rabbi, for one is your Master, even Christ,"[6] and not only refrain from all efforts to obtain self-exaltation and positions of superiority over their fellows, but use whatever gifts or opportunities they may have that others do not possess, not for their own emolument but for the good of those less fortunate than themselves? How much regard do they pay to the command, "Swear not at all, but let your communication be Yea, Yea, and Nay, Nay"?[7] Do they renounce all resort to injurious and deadly force in their treatment of offenders, love their enemies, bless those that curse them, and continually endeavor to overcome evil with good? It is true that many members of the church at large are personally meek, generous, upright, charitable, and faithful to most of the sacred trusts of life, as is the case with some of the unchurched and irreligious; yet vast multitudes of them – making up its average constituency and determining its predominating character and polity – are grossly recreant to their acknowledged Lord's most sacred, important, and vital principles, precepts, and commands, making solemnly pertinent His condemnatory words, "Why call ye me Lord, Lord, and do not the things that I say?"[8]

To meet the exigencies of the case thus indicated and the needs of the world, I, with much painstaking and deliberate thought, made ready for publication the volume mentioned, believing and feeling that I was thereby rendering some effectual service to the cause of truth and righteousness and storing up for future use counsel and admonition calculated to aid in the ultimate enfranchisement of humanity and in the building up of God's kingdom on the earth.

History of the Hopedale Community

This being accomplished, I set myself about writing a detailed and authoritative *History of the Hopedale Community* from the first inception of it in 1840 to its final extinction in 1875, through all its multiform phases and vicissitudes. I felt that although the undertaking, begun in all sincerity and faith, had met with disappointing and, in some respects, humiliating failure, it would be a great misfortune to have its experiences lost to the annals of human progress and reform. I felt, furthermore, that no one was so familiar with its doings and endeavors, its records and relics – with all its affairs from first to last, as myself; and that if I did not prepare a memoir of it and provide for having it put in permanent form no one else would do it, and the whole nobly conceived undertaking with all the aspirations, hopes, struggles, achievements it represented, would fall into oblivion and be irretrievably gone from the knowledge of men, or remembered only as another token of human conceit, folly, and fanaticism. Unwilling that such a fate should swallow up a movement characterized by so much that was unselfish, exalted, and Christlike; by so much that promised only good and happiness to mankind; by so much worthy of grateful commemoration, I devoted what time I could command aside from that necessarily taken up with other duties during the year 1875, to the preparation of this work, bringing it to completion in the January following. What I then wrote and regarded as final has been supplemented by a brief addenda, compiled from data not then in my possession, the whole going to make a volume of considerable size, and one which I trust will prove suggestive and helpful to social students and reconstructionists in coming time.

History of Milford

At the urgent solicitation of the authorities and leading citizens of the town of Milford, I entered into an engagement in the spring of the just-named year to write a comprehensive history of that municipality, and soon after took such preliminary action as seemed necessary to the successful prosecution of the undertaking. It proved to be a tedious and withal somewhat irksome task – a long-drawn-out performance of literary plodding and drudgery. I spent all the time and labor upon it which I could spare from other imperative activities during the next six years, receiving, as I proceeded, much valuable assistance from my wife. My cares and responsibilities in regard to it were much increased toward the last by my consenting to act as chairman of the town's publishing committee, making it incumbent upon me to look after many of the details incident to the passage of the work through the press. It was finally completed in all its parts in 1882 and given to the public, with whom it won well-earned credit as well as encomiums from those competent to judge concerning that kind of production. It made a royal octavo volume of 1154 pages, crowded with historical, genealogical, and biographical matter, the collection, arrangement and writing of which required immense toil, carefulness, and patience. This achievement was not in the line of religious and moral reform, and so not altogether to my taste and pleasure. It was rather a business affair, entered upon mainly from the motive of a moderate moneyed compensation to be added to other small earnings and savings with which to provide for the printing and distributing of more important but less remunerative works directly promotive of human regeneration, elevation, and happiness. It served this purpose to a reasonable extent, was useful and gratifying to the general public, compromised none of my conscientious scruples, and, on the whole, added to my personal influence in fulfilling my recognized mission on the earth.

Termination of Hopedale Pastorate

I continued to discharge the duties of my position as pastor of the Hopedale parish and allied congregation down to April 23, 1880 – my seventy-seventh birthday – when I finally resigned and closed my labors in that capacity, though still remaining in service as minister-at-large in the general community. This I did, not because I was made to feel that I was no longer wanted as religious teacher and guide, for I was always listened to with respectful attention, even by those who professedly and practically could not accept or conform their lives to my most pronounced testimonies, and treated with the utmost kindness and cordiality in all my relations to and intercourse with my employers and the people at large. Nor was I ever, even by intimation, restricted in my freedom of preaching, illustrating, or applying the gospel as I had received and understood it. But I felt that at the age I had attained it were better for all concerned that I should be released from the routine of ministerial service which I had been following under then existing auspices for thirteen years and under varying conditions for nearly sixty years; and also that my hold on the faith and conscience of my parishioners was too weak to bring them into working harmony with my highest convictions of Christian duty or to do them much good on the worldly plane of individual and social life which they occupied and to which they were determinedly committed for the rest of their mortal days – my preaching and the plain requirements of the Sermon on the Mount to the contrary notwithstanding.

I was honorably discharged from the pastoral office, agreeably to my expressed desire and purpose, and through the influence of my ever kind friend, George Draper, was made the recipient of an annuity of four hundred dollars, to continue in quarter-yearly payments to the end of my natural life. This annuity, though coming nominally from the parish by a formal vote, was nevertheless contributed by Mr. Draper until his decease, and by the executors of his will afterward, agreeably to a provision specifically made in that instrument. This regularly received stipend, together with my small incidental earnings, funeral and marriage fees, and the savings of more recent years, augmented by the cooperation of a remarkably prudent wife, gradually overcame the pecuniary losses which still followed me, enabled me to meet all my financial obligations, placed me beyond beggarly dependence on others, and insured me a competence for more unproductive years. It also furnished me with means to answer the calls of incidental charity, to contribute to worthy causes, and to reciprocate some of the manifold expressions of respect and love shown me, without fear of coming to want or subjecting myself to special acts of self-denial as in former times. And what was to me best of all, it gave me an assurance of having something beyond the supply of my earthly needs for the promulgation of those divine principles which I had labored so disappointedly to make subservient to the uplifting and happiness of mankind, after I should have passed away. This was to me a token of the good providence of my Heavenly Father which awakened in my soul sentiments of profound gratitude and joy. It fulfilled not only the assurance of Christ that they who seek first the kingdom of God shall have all needful temporal things added to them, but the promise repeatedly made to me in moments of deep despondency and gloom by the voice of the Spirit speaking to my inner consciousness and saying, "I will never leave thee nor forsake thee"; "My grace is sufficient for thee." Blessed be the name of the Lord and His faithfulness forever and ever. Surely my soul shall love and trust Him even in the valley and shadow of death.⁹

At this point of the narrative recorded in these pages, reached on the twelfth of July, 1890, the strength of the writer, which had been perceptibly failing for some months, so far gave way as to oblige him to lay aside his pen for needed rest. He did this reluctantly and with the earnest hope that a few days' respite from labor would revive his energies sufficiently to enable him to resume his work and carry it through to completion – a consummation he ardently desired to accomplish with his own hand. That hope, alas! was vain. Instead of the anticipated restoration, he sank slowly into that confirmed but painless illness which three weeks later terminated in death. This event left the story of his long, busy life to be finished by another, who, while he assumes the task with a sincere desire to discharge the trust imposed on him faithfully, yet feels his inability to fill the place of the autobiographer or do justice to that part of his career, small though it be, which remains to be delineated.

  Happily, however, he himself, although too weak to wield the pen, was for some days so far in possession of his mental powers as to be able to specify the more important things he wished to have mentioned in what was still to be written, which, with the aid of an elaborate diary, will enable his representative not only to carry out the general purpose of the work and so preserve its essential unity, but do it largely in the original author's way and even in his own language. For much of what follows is quoted from his exact words and what is not is dictated by a careful study of what he has left on record of himself. Such being the case, the autobiographical character of the book is preserved, although it will necessarily lack many observations and reflections which the one of whom it treats would have introduced; much to the regret of his surviving friends and to the loss of the reading public. With this note of explanation and an appeal for the kindly indulgence of all concerned, the narrative proceeds to the end. — W. S. H.

Centennial Celebrations

As no reference has thus far been made to a memorable occasion in the annals of the town in which the autobiographer had been a resident for nearly sixty years and to the prominent part he took therein, it seems to be the first duty of his deputy to take appropriate notice of the same and make record accordingly. On the fourth of July, 1876, the one hundredth anniversary of the signing of the Declaration of Independence was patriotically observed in all the larger municipalities of the land. The citizens of Milford made arrangements for contributing to the general demonstration of festal joy, resulting in what the *Journal* characterized as "the most imposing and successful celebration ever witnessed in the vicinity." Mr. Ballou, who had already begun to collect material for his history of the town, was very properly honored with an invitation to deliver the principal address of the day. The invitation was accepted and the involved duty faithfully performed. The orator, in what he had to say, reviewed briefly the circumstances attending the early occupancy of the territory then known as the "Easterly Precinct" of Mendon; the privations, struggles, and sacrifices of the pioneer settlers; the incidents connected with its incorporation; the inception and growth of its various industrial, educational, social, moral, and religious interests and institutions; as he also portrayed its general position and importance in the community at large and in the state and nation. Giving due credit to all who had in any way aided in promoting the common prosperity, and bringing to notice many things in the endeavors and achievements of its population worthy of grateful commendation, he, with characteristic regard for great principles of moral and social order, pointed out existing evils and defects, declared what in the body politic ought to be outgrown or overcome, and closed with a few eloquent and incisive sentences setting forth the only adequate remedy for whatever was working or threatened peril and disaster to the public or private well-being and happiness. In his peroration he referred a second time to the courage, integrity, and faith of the founders of the town, proceeding thence to say:

> Let us emulate their real virtues, their fidelity to their light and privileges, and their indomitable energy in overcoming the difficulties of their lot. They exterminated the wolves and rattlesnakes that infested this territory and turned its rugged forests into fruitful fields. Be it ours to subdue our own wild animal natures – the ravenous lusts and venomous propensities and crude passions of the carnal man. Let us dwell less in the basement and more in the upper story of our natures. If we cannot wholly shun or remove the temptations which are incident to material,

intellectual, political, or social progress, let us manfully resolve to overcome them by the cross of rational and Christian self-denial. Herein lies the remedy for the present threatening distempers of our whole nation.

After indicating in a few terse passages the lofty and splendid attainments of personal and social excellence to which men are summoned "as children of the All-Father and sympathizing fellow members of the great human family," he concluded as follows:

This is the sublime march of moral progress that opens before us. It comes next in order to the splendid material, intellectual, and political progress we this day celebrate. Say not it is impossible, unattainable. I tell you it is the will of God – our duty, our privilege, our destiny. Therefore, let us gird up the loins of our solemn resolve, of reason, faith, hope, charity. Our fathers were the heroes of the past; let us be the moral heroes of the coming age. Let gratitude and a sense of responsibility inflame our ambition to achieve a glorious and God-approved future.

The oration was listened to with rapt attention and received from various quarters appreciative commendation "both for the matter embodied in it and its eloquent delivery." It was published in full the following morning in the Milford *Journal* and subsequently given a place in the voluminous history of the town.

At the time of the centennial celebration of the incorporation of Milford, June 10, 1880, Mr. Ballou excused himself from participation in the public exercises of the occasion, save as a silent and deeply interested listener and observer. He, however, contributed to its success so far as to loan his manuscript history, then nearly ready for the press, to the accomplished and patriotic orator of the day, Gen. Adin Ballou Underwood,[10] from which to obtain data for his able, eloquent, and highly acceptable address.

Letter from Mr. Garrison

As has been repeatedly intimated in other chapters of this work, Mr. Ballou, through his espousal of and labors for the antislavery cause, became early acquainted with the great champion of universal liberty, William Lloyd Garrison, between whom and himself a friendship was formed as lasting as life. Not that he was in any sense a blind follower or partisan adherent of that distinguished agitator, for he differed very radically from him in some important particulars, as has been before shown; but that he believed in the man – in the purity of his motives, in the disinterestedness of his purpose, in the intrinsic excellence of his character, and in the grandeur of the work he was commissioned to do for God and humanity. Frequent correspondence was carried on between the two while the conflict with the slave system was going on, and occasional missives passed to and fro ever afterward. Some time in 1878, the year before Mr. Garrison's decease, Mr. Ballou seems to have sent him congratulations and kind wishes on some noteworthy occurrence in his life, possibly a birthday, to which in due time came a response, accompanied by a picture of the eminent civilian and philanthropist of Great Britain, George Thompson, M.P.,[11] whom Mr. Ballou had met personally on some of his visits to this country. The letter was greatly prized by the recipient and will be read by the friends of both him and its author with interest.

Roxbury, Mass., Nov. 23, 1878.

DEAR FRIEND BALLOU: Receiving your postal card with its good wishes is next to seeing you face to face, which it would give me very great pleasure to do, including your estimable wife. The days of "auld lang syne" can never be forgotten by me, when we were working actively together for the promotion of temperance, justice, and freedom to the southern bondmen, non-resistance, and practical righteousness in all its bearings. Your labors and testimonies were of invaluable service in enlightening the understanding, quickening the conscience, melting the heart, animating the spirit, and giving a powerful impulse to the various philanthropic and reformatory movements against which all "the powers of darkness"[12] were fiercely arrayed. Yours was the standard of immutable truth and absolute right, unflinchingly maintained by you through trials and privations of no ordinary kind. I contemplate your whole life admiringly. It has been unreservedly consecrated to the service of God and your fellow men, with patience, fortitude, courage, exemplary self-abnegation, and in the spirit of all-embracing love. You have labored "in season and out of season"[13] for the good of others, for the reconstruction of society on the basis of mutual rights, interests, responsibilities, and duties after the exact pattern of the golden rule; for noble conceptions of the fatherhood of God and the brotherhood of man; for the largest freedom of thought, inquiry, and speech in matters of religious faith and worship; and for the arrival of that blessed period when all wars shall cease throughout the earth and the kingdom of peace be established thereon.

Nor have you labored in vain. On all these subjects great advances have been made in public sentiment since you began to bear those testimonies which can never return void, and which, from your life and pen, have exerted a widespread influence, multiplying converts and shaping human destiny. Let this be comforting to you, even though your aspirations and efforts have failed to accomplish much that you had hoped to realize before seeing the "last of earth"[14] and entering into rest. You will pardon me for this expression of my feelings.

I was sure you would feel gratified in receiving the very striking heliotype of dear George Thompson, representing him, as it does, almost in his prime. His was a most desirable translation. With kind regards to your wife, I remain

yours in warmest fellowship,
WILLIAM LLOYD GARRISON

Memorial Day Address

It is a noteworthy fact in the experience of Mr. Ballou that by his high personal character, his kind and courteous bearing, and recognized purpose to be impartially just and honorable in his treatment of all classes and conditions of men, he was able to gain and retain the confidence and regard, not only of those who were in hearty accord with him in his distinctive principles and views, but of those opposed to him in those respects – of those who were sometimes brought into emphatic condemnation by the practical application of his principles and views to human conduct in the various interests and relations of life. This was strikingly illustrated in the incident now to be narrated.

In the spring of 1879 he was invited, agreeably to the prevailing custom in town, to take his turn with other resident clergymen in addressing the Maj. E. F. Fletcher Post, G. A. R.,[15] of Milford, on the Sunday preceding the approaching Memorial Day, when the members as a body would attend the church in Hopedale, where he was at that time the regular minister. The invitation was accepted and a sermon was delivered as proposed on May 25, a large congregation besides the soldiery being present. To show how he acquitted himself on that occasion – how he could be true to his own avowed principles as a radical peace man and at the same time address a company of men whose organic existence not only implied the rightfulness of armed resistance to enemies of the public order and welfare, but was based upon the fact that those men had been personally engaged in the work of human slaughter – to show how he could do this without compromising himself and yet secure the approbation and continued regard of his military hearers, liberal extracts from his discourse are subjoined:

> Render, therefore, to all their dues; tribute, to whom tribute is due; custom, to whom custom; fear, to whom fear; honor, to whom honor.
> — Romans 13:7.

> Christ, his apostles, and the primitive Christians took no part in civil government, in war, in military affairs, or in politics, claiming to stand on a higher moral plane and to lead mankind, by precept, example, and voluntary association, into a state of universal brotherhood and peace. But it was one of their settled principles to pay due respect to civil and military rulers in their sphere, to be no detriment to civil society, as it necessarily existed for the world's general good under divine providence, and scrupulously to fulfill their own grand mission by peaceably showing a more excellent way of social order. I have been endeavoring to stand faithfully and consistently on this primitive Christian platform for over forty years, and today I most firmly and sincerely believe it to be the highest which any human being can occupy. Now you, military gentlemen, have honored me with an invitation to preach you a sermon appropriate to the Sunday next preceding your annual decoration of the graves of your comrades who died in defending the national union in the late gigantic civil war. You do not expect me to be disloyal to my own long-declared standard of Christian righteousness, but you have a right to expect me, in accordance with a sacred principle of that standard, to render to yourselves and those you represent due honor. I intend to do so; how, then, shall I do it?

> In the first place, how am I to determine what honor I owe you? By what moral standard must I measure your deserts? There are three moral standards by which all men may be justly tried: first, the highest conceivable absolute standard of righteousness, which I hold to be that taught and exemplified by Jesus Christ;

second, the commonly acknowledged civil and moral standard of one's age and country; third, the moral standard which an individual himself professes to be governed by.

This third standard may agree with the first or with the second, or, on peculiar points, may differ from both. It is strictly the standard of the individual whose highest convictions of duty it declaratively expresses. No moral standard measures any one's strict moral deserts in a particular case, because personal circumstances always affect each individual's merit or demerit. But any moral standard determines what shall be considered right or wrong in human conduct under that standard, and generally, to some extent, the merit or demerit of actions. Now, for myself, I accept what I have called the absolute standard of Christian righteousness as my own. You must therefore, measure my conduct by that standard, giving me the benefit of palliating circumstances whereinsoever I fall short of my own acknowledged duty. But I cannot justly measure your conduct by this standard unless you acknowledge it to be yours, which I take for granted you have not done. I presume your standard is the second one stated, viz: "the commonly acknowledged civil and moral standard of your age and country." Therefore, I must measure your conduct by that standard, and give you the benefit of all mitigating circumstances whereinsoever you may have fallen short of your acknowledged duty. Thus I shall obey the precept of my text, rendering to you your dues, and so honor to whom honor.

Under your standard, patriotism is an indispensable duty. If not the highest, it is one of the highest civil and moral duties. Such you doubtless regard it. Patriotism requires you to stand by and maintain by force of arms and sacrifice of life, if need be, the existence, integrity, independence, laws, government, and honor of your country. The army, navy, militia, and warlike resources of every country are pledged to all this. All war rests for its justification on the rightfulness of self-defense by deadly force whenever endangered by enemies. It is deemed not only rightful, but an absolute necessity in the last extreme. The principle is the same for individuals, families, communities, and nations. And whoever holds this principle at all, as a part of his moral standard, is logically bound to hold it equally sacred in respect to individuals, families, communities, and nations.

Granting this civil and moral standard of your age and country, which makes patriotism by deadly force in the last extreme an indispensable duty, to be the one by which I must measure your conduct, gentlemen, my duty is clear. You have, under that standard, done great and noble service. So did your comrades, whose graves you annually decorate with flowers, and whose deeds you are in various ways endeavoring to commend to posterity as worthy of patriotic imitation. There are three classes to whom honor is due for services rendered and burdens borne for their country, to make it triumphant in the last memorable conflict. First, the soldiers who fought its battles amid such peril of life, limb, health, and home comforts – many myriads of whom went down to an untimely grave. Second, those who sympathetically contributed so much of personal attention in the hospitals and on the sanitary commission for the alleviation of soldiers' sufferings – in which the women of the country exhibited such patriotic devotion. And third, the mass of citizens and people who furnished warlike supplies and have borne the inevitable burdens of consequent taxation. Foremost of these classes, by common consent, the post of honor belongs to the soldiers – and foremost among these to their dead and crippled living. Your fellow patriots have appreciated the services of their warriors none too highly, but far better than such services were ever appreciated before, since war on earth began. They have relieved, honored, and compensated them incomparably more justly than in any past generation a nation ever did those of its fighting defenders. Still, there remains, as results of the war, a vast amount of privation, loss, and suffering, which can only be compensated in some general way by national good. Go, then, as you have done for many a year in the vernal season, and commemorate the fame of your fallen associates with your wonted floral tokens. Go and teach posterity to serve and die for their country in like manner so long as they profess to be governed by the same civil and moral standard. And I, too, will accord to the dead and living the tributes and honors which fidelity to their own highest acknowledged standard of duty merits.

But while I am bound to render these dues to others, I am no less solemnly bound to be true to my own highest convictions, under that absolute standard of righteousness which enjoins pure good will to all mankind, friend and foe, and which requires me to lay down my life rather than intentionally kill, injure, or harm any human being.

The preacher then went on to reaffirm his own long-maintained views upon the subject of war and peace, declaring his unfaltering conviction that the principles involved in the Christian doctrine of perfect love to all human beings are true and invulnerable and will sometime prevail throughout the world, and that his own well-known course of theoretical and practical fidelity to them will at length be vindicated in the entire deliverance of mankind from bloodshed and slaughter, and the universal reign of amity and brotherhood. He concluded as follows:

> I have respect enough for you, military gentlemen and sympathizers, to believe that you understand my position, my ideas, my sentiments, and my exposition of the subject discussed. I trust, therefore, that our respect for each other is mutual and will remain forever steadfast. I have always found those who had most distinguished themselves on the field of battle and won laurels in war most ready to deprecate its horrors. For they have seen and felt them. No great military chieftain loves war for its own sake. Such define it only as a necessity, and as the least evil in extreme cases, because the world is not yet wise and good enough to do right without martial compulsion. Well, then, if this is your best thought and highest conviction, my friends, fight when you must, as you have done, on the side of justice, freedom, and human rights; and I will be one to render you due honor – judging you by your own acknowledged standard of civil and moral rectitude. In turn I trust you will reciprocate these sentiments and bid me do my duty as I understand it; bid me be true to my highest convictions; bid me be faithful to my acknowledged standard; bid me serve my country and humanity in the most excellent way I can, conscientiously; bid me do what little I may in my generation to fraternize our race, what little I can to render war morally avertable, to spare you and the soldiers of the future the sad necessity of sacrificing life in suppressing the violence of public enemies, and of weeping with widows and orphans over the graves of fallen comrades. And thus if our paths of duty diverge in some important respects,

may we all unite in the one holy prayer of faith, hope, and charity: "Thy kingdom come; Thy will be done on earth as in heaven"; singing with the poet:

> Let love and truth alone
> Hold human hearts in thrall;
> That heaven its work at length may own
> And men be brothers all.[16]

Serious Illness of Wife

Early in the year 1881 the subject of this life-history passed through one of the most notable and trying experiences of his whole mortal career – one which his own graphic pen, and that only, could adequately describe. It was occasioned by the serious and well-nigh fatal illness of his devoted wife, from which she recovered in a marvelous manner as if by some special healing agency or power from on high. As far as possible, he will be permitted to tell the story of the occurrence himself, liberal notes concerning it being taken from his diary.

The first indications of the existence of the insidious disease (pneumonia) he speaks of in his record of Thursday, January 6, as follows:

> Wife very busy upon a letter to Abbie. Four o'clock finished it and I carried it to the P.O. at once. She had written it seated by the north side of the sitting-room, complaining of feeling cold. She ate but little supper and soon began to be sick at stomach, vomiting and shivering with increasing chills. I was much alarmed and gave undivided attention to her.

He assisted her in retiring early and administered such palliatives or remedies from the household stock as seemed advisable. "But she passed a miserable night, and I an anxious one ... praying for relief but fearing the worst."

"The next day, Friday, she seemed in the way of recovery," and so continued until towards noon on Saturday, when unfavorable symptoms appeared and the family physician, Dr. Jerome Wilmarth[17] of Upton, was immediately sent for. He "came promptly, examined the sick woman, pronounced one lung partially congested," and prescribed accordingly. The night following "she rested better than I feared." Nevertheless, in spite of the acknowledged skill and tireless attentions of the doctor, the best of nursing, and the utmost solicitude and tender watching of relatives and friends, the invalid gradually lost strength and vitality for the week following, when she seemed past all power of recovery. On Thursday, January 13, the anxious husband writes: "Dr. comes; gives no hope of dear sick wife. Oh, my sad heart!"

On the next morning the diary reads thus: "Wife is much flushed with fever. Dr. pronounces her no better." And in the evening, after a second call, "He left, saying she was worse and sinking." The husband and all the household felt that she could not survive till morning. He retired to his chamber to get what rest he could, having been promised that he should be notified upon the slightest indication of the apprehended change. "But before this," he says,

> I had free though brief interchange with wife in which she spoke beautifully of her faith in the future, her resignation and confidence, and also about what I should do when she had gone, etc. She said she should be as near me and as much with me as permitted. All this was a great satisfaction to me, for I could not bear to have her leave me under a mental cloud. At the same time she expressed an intuitive hope that she might be spared a little longer.

About this time the night-watcher, Mrs. Dutcher, brought in a beautiful bouquet of flowers.

> She was delighted with it. She brightened up instantly and seemed almost transfigured. At length I retired. I kissed her good night and went to my bedchamber groaning in spiritual prayer and dreading a summons to see her expire before morning.

Happily this was not to be. The diary contains an account of what transpired.

> In the morning daughter Abbie, who had been summoned to the parental home some days before, came to surprise me with the news that her mother had passed a remarkably comfortable night and that her symptoms were better. What trembling, hopeful thanksgiving went up from my soul to heaven! ... Up a little past 7. Everything indicates that wife is really better. But I must wait and see if Dr. confirms it ... At length he comes, expresses a happy surprise to hear so good reports of the patient's comfortable night, examines her, and declares her to be decidedly better. Blessed be the Most High God whose holy angels have done what unaided man could not do. I will hope reverently, with unspeakable thanksgiving, for brightening prospects.

Nor did he hope in vain. The crisis had indeed passed and the course of the stricken one was thenceforth onward and upward to health and strength again. Her recovery was necessarily slow, but sure, with few, if any, reactionary and discouraging indications. Not many weeks elapsed before she resumed the general charge of domestic affairs, finally regaining in large measure her accustomed health and strength, though not her former power of endurance, and these were continued to her until near the end of her mortal pilgrimage, which occurred somewhat suddenly at last, after two or three premonitory attacks, on the seventh day of August, 1891.

About a fortnight after the crisis just mentioned took place, the convalescent, remembering that the anniversary of the birth of her devoted daughter, who had been with her during most of her illness, was drawing near, conceived the idea of having the event celebrated in some appropriate way, and, quite contrary to the judgment and advice of both her nurse and husband, formed plans for carrying that idea into effect. The result can be best learned from the diarist's own words, penned January 30, 1881, to wit:

> This is daughter Abbie's 52d birthday, and wife insists on giving her a surprise by inviting in her kind watchers, making a parental present, etc. I had doubted the

propriety of this proceeding, fearing wife could not stand the excitement. But she was not to be overruled and I consented. It was a most extraordinary occasion. She had ordered preparations made for a collation ... I had written a congratulatory note ... and enclosed a present, half from her purse and half from my own, to be given her, the daughter, during the exercises. The convalescent, chief of the occasion, was bolstered up in bed and all of us (thirteen in number) either seated or standing near. She opened the proceedings with a very affecting speech, considerably and pathetically broken by uncontrollable emotion. The whole company was affected to tears and sacred impressions were made. I followed with an address and the final presentation of my note and its contents. Daughter Abbie was deeply moved and made suitably appreciative response. Then came reciprocal congratulations, etc., succeeded by a repast, wife partaking with the rest. It was a solemn, loving, sacramental communion, at once tender, joyous, never-to-be-forgotten.

This little episode, instead of overtaxing the sick woman and hindering her progress healthward, as was feared, seemed to inspire her with new courage and to contribute substantially to her ultimate recovery. She improved rapidly thereafter, and at an earlier day than seemed possible was able to take her accustomed place again in the domestic and social circle. Gladder or more grateful heart never beat in human breast than that of Mr. Ballou at the denouement of this semi-tragedy – at the providential averting of this threatened disaster to his home and happiness. He ever afterward felt that on the memorable night of the fourteenth of January, 1881, when mortal help and hope failed, help from the unseen world was granted to save the dearest one on earth alive to him, that she might still share with him the cares and burdens of his lot, shed light and cheer upon his onward way, aid him in the prosecution of the work he had in hand, and by her kind and gentle ministry comfort and gladden his last hours in the flesh, and finally smooth his passage to the tomb. He was never able to speak of this trying experience afterward without deep feeling and some expression of the gratitude which the memory of it kept ever alive in his soul.

Miscellaneous Writings

Little more occurred during the decade covered by the present chapter that requires extended notice. Most of the time, as it drew toward its close, Mr. Ballou gave to the completion of his *History of Milford*, which was published early in 1882. To gratify his prevailing tastes, however, and further the supreme object of his life, he would snatch a few hours now and then from the swiftly passing days to prepare some paper or article upon some of the great themes he deemed important to mankind – "salting down" his views, as he was accustomed to say, for coming generations.

In addition to the more elaborate volumes mentioned in preceding pages, he prepared in 1880 a review of an "Exposition of Matthew 16:26 by Rev. Hosea Ballou, 2d, D.D.," a theological dissertation, and also a critique upon the same author's interpretation of the text, "Resist not evil," the true meaning of which he felt had been perverted or misapprehended by his esteemed kinsman. He also about the same time reviewed a pretentious pamphlet entitled "Be Thyself," by William Denton,[18] a popular lecturer upon scientific, reformatory, and religious subjects, and prepared an essay upon "The Importance of Definiteness in Religion," a favorite theme with him.

It may be stated in this connection that all through the daily chronicles of Mr. Ballou, especially during the later years of his life, there are to be found comments and criticisms of greater or less length called forth by current events, topics of the times, utterances of the pulpit and press, which may some day be gathered in a volume and given to the public. The nature of such a work can be determined by referring to some of the more important themes discussed, to wit: "The Relation of Science and Religion"; "The Assassination of President Garfield"[19]; "Anti-Christian Spiritualism"; "Judge Waite's *Christian Religion*"[20]; "Proceedings of Unitarian Conferences"; "Tendencies of Unitarianism"; "The Office of Conscience and Reason"; etc.

On the twenty-second of April, 1882, the day before he entered upon the eightieth year of his age, Mr. Ballou made an arrangement with his brother, Ariel Ballou, M.D., and Hon. Latimer W. Ballou,[21] a distant kinsman, both of Woonsocket, Rhode Island, whereby he engaged to compile and edit an elaborate *History of the Ballou Family in America*, on the one part, while they, on the other, became jointly responsible for the cost of publishing the same, and for the payment to him of a moderate compensation for his services. Of the details of this contract and other matters pertaining to its fulfillment, due notice will be taken in the next chapter.

CHAPTER 24

1882-1890

The history of Milford was completed early in the year 1882, and at the date of the opening of this chapter had been widely distributed throughout the town and vicinity. Mr. Ballou was therefore relieved of all responsibility relating to the preparation and printing of the volume, although, as a member of the publication committee, he was not wholly free from the obligations he had assumed in regard to it for several years afterward. He hoped and fully intended, when it was off his hands, to devote himself to his autobiography and to such other writings as he ardently desired to execute before his decease, and while in the full strength and exercise of his powers of both body and mind. He did not care to enter again upon any line of work outside of his own chosen pursuits or engage in any undertakings which should divert his time and energy from carrying his determined purpose into effect. It was not of his own motion or choice, therefore, that he entered upon the task of compiling and editing an extended genealogy of the Ballou family already spoken of, but by the most urgent solicitation of his highly esteemed kinsmen, Dr. Ariel and Hon. Latimer Ballou, who were deeply interested in the matter and quite willing to meet all needful expenses that might be incurred, and who felt that he, of all the men they knew, was the one to have the matter in charge.

The contemplated work had been begun many years before by Ira Ballou Peck[1] of Woonsocket, Rhode Island, a member of a collateral branch of the family, long and meritoriously engaged in historical and genealogical labors in other fields of inquiry. He had collected a considerable amount of information pertaining to the immigrant Maturin Ballou and his descendants, but advancing years and lack of encouragement on the part of those more immediately concerned induced him at length to desist from further efforts in that behalf. What he had done having been brought to the notice of the gentlemen mentioned, they negotiated with him for the transfer of all the materials in his possession to them, with the understanding that it should be used and disposed of in such a way as to best secure the end which both he and they desired to have accomplished.[2] This being done, they made the contract with the subject of this biography, referred to near the close of the last chapter. The terms of that contract were that they should deliver up to him all the data – letters, family registries, copied records, transcriptions, and papers of every kind – received from Mr. Peck, and assist in obtaining further information of the same sort; and also assume all pecuniary obligations incident to its preparation and publication, including the payment to the compiler, once in three months, of a salary equal to thirty cents an hour for time actually expended; excepting such sums, not exceeding ten percent of the aggregate amount, as he, of his own free will, might be pleased to contribute to the undertaking. (In the several settlements, it may be said, he voluntarily made a reduction of fifteen percent instead of ten, the limit formally agreed upon.) On his part, he was to collect, collate, arrange, and put in proper form whatever material, within reasonable bounds, could be obtained in order to make the work comprehensive, thorough, and symmetrical; prepare it for the press; superintend the printing, proofreading, binding, and, in fact, everything necessary to its completion, making of it a volume well-proportioned and attractive in appearance, acceptable to his employers and to its patrons, and every way worthy of an honorable place in the historical and genealogical literature of the age.

Certain preliminaries being attended to, such as issuing circulars asking for information, looking over the medley of material furnished him for the purpose of ascertaining to what extent it could be made to serve the end in view, formulating plans for systematic labor, etc., he entered upon his task with great earnestness and zeal, and pushed it forward towards accomplishment with all possible dispatch. Yet, as for many years before, the time he was called upon to attend funerals, entertain visiting friends, and answer demands of various kinds at home and abroad, greatly interfered with regular consecutive work and desired progress. But he toiled on amid a multitude of delays, annoyances, and discouragements for six long years, when he had the satisfaction of seeing the end of his labors in that direction, and of feeling that his efforts were crowned with success. He had produced a volume of huge size, "much larger than any of us anticipated," the preface states, "containing more than twelve hundred octavo pages, over nine thousand names, and numerous artistic illustrations, printed and bound in creditable style." It was a monument of painstaking research, of unwearied toil, of scrupulous attention to details, reflecting great credit upon its author and upon all who aided him in bringing it to a successful issue.

It is eminently fitting and proper, as it is an act of simple justice, to state in this connection that Mr. Ballou was greatly assisted in the arduous task of producing this volume by his devoted, faithful, efficient wife, Lucy Hunt Ballou, whose services in looking over the manuscript copy and preparing it for the press, in helping to correct the proof, in working upon the index, and otherwise, were of indispensable value. Without her aid, it would have been far more difficult, if not impossible, for him to have done the work with that thoroughness and accuracy which now characterize it, and which have evoked from many quarters appreciative commendation. To her effective cooperation, he himself bears willing and grateful witness on the pages of the book itself.

The Family Burial Lot

In the early days of the Hopedale Community, the founder, in concurrence with his wife, whose judgment and wishes he was accustomed to consult upon all matters of common interest, had selected in the public cemetery a family burial lot, to which was transferred, soon after, all that remained of the mortal bodies of his first wedded companion and two sons, previously interred elsewhere; in which was deposited, some years later, the manly form of his beloved Adin Augustus, and where he and the still living partner of his household expected in their turn to sleep the last sleep of earth and time.[3] The exact localities of the remains of the departed had been marked by appropriate headstones suitably inscribed, that of Adin Augustus being the most elaborate and artistic, as it was the most modern of them all. It had, however, been for some time the desire of both Mr. and Mrs. Ballou to have erected in the center of the lot a more substantial and imposing monument, representing the unity of the family and displaying more dignity, strength, and durability than those already standing within the confines of the hallowed place. Pursuant to that desire, a contract was entered into on the seventh of June, 1882, with Evans & Co. of Worcester, mortuary sculptors, by the terms of which they were to construct and put in position a memorial column of a specified design and finish, the whole to be completed early the following autumn. The provisions of the contract were fulfilled, and on the twentieth of October the structure was set up in its designated place. It consists of a neat, pyramidal shaft, eighteen inches square at its lower extremity and fourteen feet high, having a base of suitable proportions, with appropriate plinth and die, resting on a massive pedestal, the whole being supported by a solid substructure, making it substantial, firm, and sure. On the front or easterly face of the pedestal is the family designation, BALLOU, in large letters, while above on different sides of the base are inscribed the names of those buried around and beneath, with the proper dates of birth and death affixed. The headstones formerly standing remain, and places of interment more recently occupied are similarly marked. The central structure presents a majestic, commanding appearance, due regard being paid to good taste and artistic requirements, and is eminently typical of him who was the head of the household group sleeping around – erect, calm, dignified, unmoved alike in sun and storm, and ever pointing to the skies.

Essays, Dissertations, and Reviews

In whatever work Mr. Ballou was engaged, his thought, when not otherwise definitely occupied, turned instinctively to his first and most constant love – to the contemplation of great principles of truth and righteousness, and to the devising of ways and means by which those principles could be carried out to practical issues and applied to the various relations and concerns of individual and social life; that so mankind might be benefited and blessed and God be glorified. This was manifest not only in his private conversation and public addresses, but in the casual products of his pen. His ever-active mind was making continual sallies into the realm of the infinite wisdom, gaining fresh acquisitions of knowledge or formulating some new plans for doing good in the world, the results of which he was wont to commit to paper and file away for future reference or use. The number of such productions would astonish one not familiar with his life habit in this particular. Without dwelling upon these, either separately or in the aggregate to any great extent, it yet seems proper that the titles of some of the more important of those prepared during the few last years of his life should be chronicled, and in certain instances the circumstances which called them into being or attended their appearance.

Early in 1883 he wrote an essay upon "The Relation of the Christian Church to Civil Society." This was a concise exposition of his views upon the true mission of the church of Christ in the world, which, in his judgment, was not to conform itself to and sanctify the self-seeking, mammon-serving, war-engendering habits, customs, and institutions of existing civilization, striving to direct, purify, elevate, and regenerate them as an inside factor, pledged from the start to a support of the very things needing reform and supersedence; but to organize and establish an ideal social system on an independent basis, and so illustrate the better way by a consistent example, without demoralizing alliances or crippling entanglements of any sort. Nothing, he believed, was more irrational and futile than to attempt to rectify abuses, remove evils, transcend a low form of moral and social life while consenting to and participating in what was to be rectified, put away, and transcended. And this theory he applied remorselessly to the position of those who, while professing a desire to build up a divine kingdom on the earth, are committed by organic relationship and practical cooperation to the support of institutions and activities in which the spirit and principles of such a kingdom are either ignored or virtually set at naught.

Later in the same year he wrote a review of a work brought out under Spiritualistic auspices and bearing the mystical title of *Oahspe*,[4] which its friends claimed was "a new Bible," destined to take the place of the Hebrew and Christian scriptures among all enlightened and progressive people. The absurdity of such claims he vigorously exposed, while setting in their true light the real merits of the book.

The following year he examined, in a paper of considerable length and in searching and depreciative terms, Rev. Hosea Ballou's *Treatise on Atonement*,[5] published many years before, with the conclusions of which, calculated to defend the "death and glory" theory of a certain class of Universalists, he had no sympathy, deeming them unscriptural, irrational, and morally illusive and mischievous.

He also, about the same time, prepared a tract upon "The Knighthood of Peace," designed to elucidate the truth of the saying of Milton, "Peace hath her victories no less renowned than war,"[6] or, in other words, to show that true courage, heroism, chivalry, can be cultivated and find opportunity to display itself in the innocent, bloodless pursuits and ambitions of life as well as upon the battlefield amid scenes of violence, carnage, and death.

Another of these incidental productions of his pen was entitled "The Mistakes of Christ as Discovered by the Wisdom of this World," the object of which was to rescue the name of the Great Teacher from the undeserved reproach of certain classes of so-called advanced thinkers in modern times.[7]

In the latter part of 1885, Mr. Charles K. Whipple,[8] an old-time Abolitionist and Non-Resistant, wrote an article for the Boston *Commonwealth*, giving therein his reasons for renouncing his radical peace principles and re-adopting the barbarous maxim, "Peaceably, if we can; forcibly, if we must"[9] – the shibboleth of all the defenders of violence and bloodshed since the world began. A review of the article, setting forth the fallacy and inconclusiveness of the argument therein, was written by Mr. Ballou and sent to the author, who made a reply that called forth a lengthy and exhaustive rejoinder from the reviewer. The original article with subsequent correspondence and supplementary comments, forming a document of considerable size, has been carefully preserved.

An essay upon "What is Religion?" another upon "The Union of Church and State in America," and a third upon "Three Spheres of Man's Action and Responsibility in Life," prepared at a later date, have a place in the archives of the household.

It was about the same time that the busy student and author planned a new volume, to be called *The Laconic Expositor*. It was evidently designed to be a comprehensive disquisition or statement of views upon "Systematic Theology" and topics germane thereto. The first chapter, or article, as he terms it, "Concerning God," seems to have been the only one ever written – the others having been left for that convenient season which never came. Nor was this the only instance in which similar plans and purposes of Mr. Ballou failed of realization. Among the multitude of miscellaneous papers, memoranda, etc., left by him have been found lists of subjects, more or less definitely expressed, upon which he wished to write – a lengthy catalogue involving the labor of his brain and pen for years ahead. Had he been permitted to round out a full century here upon the earth with a good measure of health and strength, he would not have been able to realize all his wishes in this respect – to finish the work he felt himself impelled to do.

In the year 1888 Mr. Ballou prepared a historical sketch of the town of Hopedale for a voluminous *History of Worcester County*, published in March 1889, by J. W. Lewis & Co., Philadelphia.[10] This necessarily included a brief account of the inception, founding, growth, temporary prosperity, and final abandonment of the Hopedale Community, the lineal ancestor of the now incorporated township of Hopedale, and without which the township would never have existed. It is probable that no truer presentation of the spirit, purposes, and aims of the more active participants in that undertaking, of their hopes and disappointments, their trials and triumphs, their transitory success and final failure, with the causes of the latter, was ever given to the public than can there be found. To that authoritative repository of information upon the matter, the interested inquirer may refer while awaiting the publication of the more complete history of the movement by the same author at no very distant day.

Diary Notes

The daily record of current events, personal experiences, incidents from private and public life, etc., kept with much minuteness of detail during Mr. Ballou's later years, is thickly studded with off-hand comments upon what arrested his attention and awakened a train of consecutive thought in his mind. In order to give the reader some idea of the nature and character of these spontaneous effusions, a few specimen quotations are introduced, with the occasions of them, as they came from his pen.

After listening to a sermon suggested by the death of Ralph Waldo Emerson, in which the preacher indulged in what was deemed a somewhat fulsome panegyric of the illustrious author and philosopher, Mr. Ballou gives his own less adulatory but not unappreciative estimate of him as follows:

> I never read his wonderful writings with much pleasure or spiritual profit. His orphic truisms, when interpretable to common sense, are far better expressed in the language of scripture or by plain old poets; other sayings of his are not to me truths at all, or only in some vague, metaphorical sense ... As to Emerson's moral character, it was amiable, harmless, blameless. But I never understood that his practical ethics lifted him much above the surrounding civilistic, social, and scholastic level. He quietly cogitated and elaborated his own transcendental abstractions, many of which, if carried into individual and social practice, would regenerate the world. But the fatal hitch with such moralists is that neither they nor their admirers can sail out of the old ship of society as it is. They are so serene and softly that they live and die content to magnify their own cherished reveries and speculations. I once said to him, "Mr. Emerson, why cannot you, with your handsome estate and the cooperation of congenial friends, start a community that shall illustrate a true fraternal order of society from which the world may take a pattern?" We had been accordantly deprecating the selfishness and antagonism of the world about us. His reply was: "Mr. Ballou, I am no builder; if I can only set myself and my own family imperfectly right in these respects, it will be my utmost." After some further conversation, the topic subsided. He was a very kind-hearted, well-disposed, and thoroughly honest man on his own plane, but powerless to rise above it.

Upon a sermon from Matthew 11:4-5, in which Jesus, in proof of his divine mission, says: "The blind receive their sight, the lame walk, etc.," Mr. Ballou observes:

> He [the preacher] inserted the word *moral* before blind, lame, etc., and literalized the word *gospel* into mere good tidings, as if Christ wrought no physical miracles and preached no great religious doctrines or ideas. He went full tilt against creeds,

beliefs, and right heart motives, in glorification of good works, external morality, leaving it to be inferred that outward righteousness has no necessary connection with true religious belief or positive right-heartedness of conviction or principles. I go for a union of the understanding and the outward conduct – no divorce of the one from the other.

The following train of thought was awakened by an article in a Spiritualistic journal, "glorifying modern Spiritualism in contrast with the Bible and Christianity."

> The chief priests of Spiritualism and the large majority of its adherents are now [1884] undisguisedly anti-Christian. Their genius is radically infidel in every respect excepting that of the fact of human existence after death. This they boast is a matter, not of faith, but of knowledge – with them scientific knowledge. As to scorn and hatred of a religious faith and life, properly so-called, they are hand in hand with Thomas Paine and his adherents. A small minority only grieve and protest, mostly in private. The result of all this will be to break down false traditional religion and prepare the way for the regenerate Practical Christian church. Like all other anti-supernaturalists, anti-religious creedists, these people can pull down but never build up much. They are unconscious axes in God's overruling hand to hew away what must be gotten rid of in order to the incoming of the kingdom of heaven.

At a later date he writes upon the same general subject thus:

> I am more than ever convinced that neither Swedenborg nor modern Spiritualistic mediums can be accepted as wholly reliable in their teachings. Between them and their spirits there is such a mixture of reality and unreality, of truth and error, that the elective sieve must be used freely.

These utterances may be regarded as indicative of his final conclusions concerning the matter to which they refer. Holding to the last a rational belief in the possibility of spirit intercourse, and of its occasional realization under favoring conditions, he yet would accept nothing claiming to come from the unseen world except upon the most trustworthy and incontestable evidence. With him every voice professing to speak of things within the veil must prove itself worthy of credence before hospitable reception could be given to its testimonies.

Concerning a discourse to which he listened, upon the subject of "Patience," the general doctrine of which was, "Do not struggle and worry to reform the world and make martyrs of yourselves by running ahead of the multitude; there is a natural growth of truth and righteousness; be patient and wait for nature's law of progress, etc.; things always come round in their season," he remarks:

> But when did any great reform ripen without its anxious, self-sacrificing pioneers – its martyrs? What if Jesus and His apostles had taken things easy and waited for nature to establish Christianity in the world, thus avoiding persecution and martyrdom! If nature has anything to do with radical reform and progress,

I am pretty certain she always begins by raising up a humble few who dare to outrun the wise and prudent leaders of the multitude and act the part of disliked pioneers and martyrs. But I prefer to think that the Divine Father Spirit manages this business of human progress – not Dame Nature!

The Town of Hopedale

In the spring of 1885 a movement was started by some of the leading residents of Hopedale village, which had been growing rapidly in population, wealth, and in social and political importance for many years, contemplating its separation from municipal alliance with Milford and the incorporation of it, with considerable contiguous territory and the inhabitants dwelling thereon, as an independent township clothed with all the rights, immunities, and privileges belonging to other townships of the Commonwealth of Massachusetts. The first rumor of this action was received with much incredulity by the people round about and especially by the leading citizens of Milford, who affected to regard the project as too preposterous to be either worthy of serious consideration or within the possibility of successful achievement. But when it was subsequently learned that the persons interested were in earnest and determined to leave no stone unturned that was needful to gain the end in view, a powerful opposition was raised in the mother town, equally earnest and determined to prevent the proposed division of its municipal territory and population. A vigorous warfare between the two parties thus formed was inaugurated and waged with tireless activity on both sides during the ensuing autumn in anticipation of the action of the incoming legislature, before which the question at issue was to be presented for final settlement. When the matter came up in that body for consideration and was referred to the committee on towns, who called for a hearing of the case, each party was represented by able counsel and many witnesses, to whose testimony and arguments protracted and respectful attention was given. After due deliberation the committee reported in favor of the petitioners and submitted a bill of incorporation to that effect. The bill was discussed at length in both branches of the General Court, passing through the different stages in each by a decisive majority, and received the approving signature of the governor, George D. Robinson,[11] April 7, 1886. The event was duly celebrated by the people of Hopedale a few days afterward.

With the incipient steps leading to this consummation, Mr. Ballou had nothing whatever to do. He first heard of what was going on by incidental report, but interested himself in it very little until asked to sign the petition praying the legislature to establish a township as proposed. His judgment approving the measure, he decided to give it the benefit of his name and personal influence. Some effort was made on the part of opponents of the measure to induce him to reverse his decision, but he had acted advisedly and was not disposed to yield to solicitations of that sort. He had resolved, however, to maintain an independent position in the matter, and take no active part in the conflict respecting it, even to secure the object which he deemed wise and right. And it was with great reluctance and after much urging that he consented to appear before the legislative committee in behalf of the petitioners for a new town, which he did on the morning of Wednesday, January 27, 1886, in the "green room" of the State House at Boston. He was permitted to present his views upon the matter for the most part in his own way, though subject to considerable questioning by opposing counsel, and the usual cross-examination. So intelligible, full, and exhaustive was his statement, made in such a spirit of candor, conscientiousness, and impartiality, that it without doubt carried great weight with it to unprejudiced minds, and contributed considerably to the final result in the petitioners' favor. For the position assumed in this affair and his general course regarding it, Mr. Ballou had no occasion for subsequent sorrow or regret. His action may, for the time being, have grieved some of his warm personal friends in Milford, but it probably never caused the loss of one of them, and if there was in any direction some transitory feeling of dislike aroused, it soon passed away and the happy relations of former years were restored, never more to be broken or disturbed.

Dedication of the Town Hall

While the agitation of the question of incorporation was going on, Mr. George Draper, who was then at the head of the manufacturing interests of the village, and the virtual father of the town that was to be, caused to be laid the foundations of a substantial, commodious, imposing structure, which he designed to present to the proposed municipality for public use, in case it should become an established fact. The building was to contain a spacious hall with convenient anterooms on the second floor, and a store, library-room, post office, and apartments for other public uses, underneath. The erection of the superstructure went slowly on after the town was incorporated and was approaching completion at the time of the owner's unexpected decease in June 1887. But this greatly deplored occurrence did not prevent the execution of his original purpose concerning the building, the provisions of his will making everything sure in that particular. It was finished in the succeeding autumn, and appropriate dedicatory services were held in it on the twenty-fifth of October. Beautiful floral and other decorations graced the occasion, vocal and instrumental music gave it added interest, prayer was offered, formal addresses were made, a bountiful collation was served, followed by miscellaneous exercises of a more spontaneous character.

The oration, or dedicatory address proper, was delivered by Hon. ex-Governor John D. Long,[12] and was a production of unquestioned merit, replete with eloquent passages and words of wisdom. There were in it, however, one or two paragraphs, relating to the Hopedale Community, which reflected somewhat disparagingly and reprehensibly upon the experiment and those engaged in it, contrasting it and them in no favorable light with the existing state of things and the more recent actors upon the stage – the latter of whom the orator eulogized in that graceful, exuberant rhetoric, of which he is an accredited master. Mr. Ballou sat near the eloquent speaker, and listened with attentive interest and becoming patience to the depreciatory and pleasantly sarcastic criticism of the men and women who had toiled and suffered in the former days for truth, humanity, and God, and who, by their labors, as arduous and unremitting as any of later date, had made possible the Hopedale which was now the subject of ornate, unqualified panegyric. When he arose to address the assembled company, which filled every part of the spacious hall, immediately after the distinguished gentleman had taken his seat, every eye was fixed upon him and every ear was eager to hear what he had to say. He began by duly complimenting his predecessor's brilliant and able oration, and proceeded thence, as he felt bound to do in justice to himself, to his co-laborers in the endeavor to illustrate a Christian form of social life forty years before, and to the truth of history, to make a brief reply to the strictures, animadversions, and implications which had fallen from his excellency's lips. The scene has been delineated in part by Mr. Ballou himself in his sketch of Hopedale prepared for the Worcester County History spoken of a few pages back, an extract from which is here given verbatim, as found in that work.

> The writer was the only speaker of the occasion who represented the primary Hopedale of Community days, and he deemed it both a privilege and a duty to revive its memory and show that it had something more to do with preparing the way for subsequent success than appeared on the present surface of things. The honorable and eloquent orator of the day had indeed made one brief reference to it, but in terms of disparaging commiseration rather than commendation. He said:
>> On this spot some forty years ago one of those communities which spring up from time to time and from which so much is anticipated by the enthusiasm of their members, had undertaken, under the sweet guidance of the venerable and beloved pastor who is here today, to solve the problem of a happy, peaceful, industrious Christian brotherhood. It was a joint stock association, sharing capital and profits and run on common account. The result was a practical bankruptcy, avoided only by a change which followed no longer any transcendental lines, but turned to the line of hard, practical, American business; for George Draper took the plant into his vigorous hands, and enlightened and liberal selfishness became, as it usually does, a beneficence to which a weak communism was as the dull and cheerless gleam of decaying punk to the inspiring blaze of the morning sun. The man of affairs was, in temporal things, a better leader than the priest, as he usually is, and as nobody will so emphatically assure you as the priest himself. A meager manufacturing enterprise that made a few boxes and cotton-spinning temples and employed a dozen hands began that marvelous expansion which in these few years, under George Draper's direction, has come to employ five hundred men, has grown from an annual product of twenty thousand dollars to one of more than twelve hundred thousand,

has built and incorporated a Massachusetts town, has erected these trim, convenient homes of skilled and prosperous labor, has enlarged the original industry into four great business houses, constituting one of the largest cotton machinery manufacturing centers in the world.

Well, how was the "venerable and beloved pastor" – the priest – likely to appreciate this rhetorical picture of "weak communism," etc.? Did he wish to detract from the merits and fame of his lamented friend, the deceased George Draper? By no means. But he did not feel that the honorable reputation of that departed friend needed to be magnified by the unjust disparagement of the Hopedale Community or any member thereof. He was possessed of all the facts in the case and knew that the orator, through some mistake, had radically misrepresented the most important of them. He knew that Ebenezer D. Draper, the elder brother of George, was president of the Community when its joint stock and unitary interests were dissolved; that he was then a much larger capitalist than his brother and wielded much greater power; that he pronounced the condition of the Community eminently harmonious and prosperous less than two months before they decided to withdraw their capital; that there was really no bankruptcy nor any necessitating cause for a dissolution of unitary interests, except their withdrawal of three-fourths of the joint stock; and that "the plant" was taken into the vigorous hands of the two brothers only to be changed into a successful manufacturing establishment managed on the principles of "enlightened and liberal selfishness." Therefore, knowing perfectly the entire history of the Community without whose devoted labors and sacrifices this new town of Hopedale would probably never have attained the importance now being glorified, and knowing that the rising generation was in danger of remaining uninformed on the subject, the aged "priest" improved the few moments allotted to him in stating the salient facts of the case.

His speech was listened to with respectful attention and he was cordially thanked by many auditors for his exposition. He believes it made a salutary and lasting impression on the assembly.

It is to be regretted that the address of Mr. Ballou on that occasion had not been reported in full as it was delivered, so as to have given it a place here. For the transcriber of the above paragraph, who was present, cannot but feel that while it gives a generally correct idea of what was said, it at the same time but partially and feebly represents the pertinency, vigor, eloquence, and effectiveness which characterized it from beginning to end. It was a severe but merited rebuke of one who had spoken from gross misinformation, or who counted the godliness of gain better than the gain of godliness.

Dr. Richard Eddy and the Restorationist Schism

A circumstance growing out of Mr. Ballou's former connection with the Universalist denomination occurred about this time, giving him great pleasure and satisfaction. Rev. Richard Eddy[13] of Melrose, an able and eminently worthy clergyman of that body, had been for some years engaged in writing a history of the form of faith it represented, to take the place of previously prepared ones nearly if not entirely out of print. The work was to consist of two volumes, the first of which had been already published. The second was mostly written and would soon go to press. It was devoted chiefly to modern Universalism and covered the period of Mr. Ballou's affiliation with its advocates and of the separation of the Restorationist wing from their ultra associates. The editor, an honorable and high-minded man, in treating of the schism referred to, determined to be just to all parties concerned in the controversy which caused it, and to give the whole matter a candid and impartial presentation in his work. In seeking to do this, he applied to Mr. Ballou, the only living person on the Restorationist side who had participated in it, for such information as he was pleased to communicate. The request was cheerfully granted. After the chapter treating of the subject was written, the author visited Mr. Ballou for the purpose of reading it to him in order that he might correct any errors that should have inadvertently been made, or suggest any emendations necessary to render it true to the facts in the case. Of what Mr. Eddy had prepared, Mr. Ballou says: "It was very full, clear, able, well-stated, truthful. I suggested one or two slight additions, which he cheerfully promised to insert in the proper place. The interview was exceedingly pleasant and gratifying." Mr. Ballou, as one of the leaders in the controversy noticed, had always felt that he and his sympathizing brethren had never had their position fairly stated by their opponents and the managers of the Universalist press, nor their motives and aims truly set forth, and it gave him great satisfaction to know that at length in a work that was to go down to posterity as an authentic history of the whole affair, even-handed justice was to be done them, and that they and their cause were to be placed upon their own merits before an enlightened public and the discriminating judgment of coming generations. This was all he had ever desired and, this gained, he was content and happy.

Correspondence with Tolstoy
Upon the appearance in this country of the first of the translated writings of this Russian author and the consequent heralding of him as a new interpreter of the gospel of Christ and as a restorer of primitive Christianity as Jesus taught and exemplified it, Mr. Ballou availed himself of an early opportunity of becoming acquainted with the views and principles upon which such unusual representations were based. From what he learned incidentally through the public press, he hoped to find in this previously unknown author[14] a man after his own heart – a consistent and radical advocate of peace, a friend of all true reform, and a wise counselor in the work of inaugurating a new order of society from which all injurious force should be excluded and in which all things should be subordinated to and animated by the spirit of pure love to God and man. That his hopes in this direction were not realized – that he was seriously disappointed indeed in both the man and his teachings, the sequel clearly shows.

The first mention of the new luminary in the religious firmament made by Mr. Ballou was in his journal of February 16, 1886, as follows:

> Commenced reading a lately purchased book, Count Tolstoy's *My Religion*. Found many good things in it on ethics, with here and there an indiscriminating extremism in the application of Christ's precepts against resisting evil with evil, and in his views of penal judgment and covetousness, or mammonism. But on theology found him wild, crude, and mystically absurd. His ideas concerning the divine nature, human nature, eternal life, Christ's resurrection, humanity's immortality, and the immortality of individuals, etc., are untrue, visionary, chaotic, and pitiably puerile. So it seems to me in this first perusal. But I will read further and think him out more thoroughly.

Further reading and more thorough thinking, however, did not bring him to a more favorable conclusion.

> The saying of Christ, "Resist not evil," Tolstoy interpreted in its most literal sense, making it inculcate complete passivity not only toward wrong-doers but toward persons rendered insane and dangerous by bad habits, inflamed passions, or unbalanced minds, to the exclusion of non-injurious and beneficent force under any and every circumstance of life.

To Mr. Ballou's apprehension this was carrying the doctrine of non-resistance to an illogical and extravagant extreme, warranted neither by the teachings of Jesus nor by a true regard for the welfare of the evil-doer, the irresponsible maniac, or society at large, which often required wholesome restraint and physical force exercised without accompanying harm or injury to anyone. Moreover, the distinctively religious expositions and indoctrinations of Tolstoy, as expressed in the book specified and in subsequent works, met with little favor from Mr. Ballou, whose ideas of God, man, immortality, etc., were as definite and pronounced as his ethical principles, and in his estimate as essential to a high type of personal character or a true order of social life.

Some three years after Mr. Ballou began to acquaint himself with the writings of Tolstoy, Rev. Lewis G. Wilson,[15] then pastor of the Hopedale parish and an interested reader of the latter, sent him some of the former's published works, with his photograph and an explanatory letter. On July 5, 1889, he received a responsive communication in which the Count highly commended, in their principal features, the views contained in the publications forwarded to him, though subjecting some of their applications, especially the one relating to the rightful use of uninjurious force as mentioned above, to emphatic protest and denial. This communication Mr. Wilson handed to Mr. Ballou for perusal and a reply if he chose to make one. This he did in due time, taking up the more important points of Tolstoy's dissent – those pertaining to the practical application of Non-Resistant principles, the right to hold property, and no-governmentism particularly, and answering them by extended argument and illustration. Thereto were added also some comments upon certain theological and spiritual positions assumed in *My Religion*.

On the twenty-sixth of March, 1890, the mail brought a rejoinder to this missive, of which the recipient writes:

> It relates to some points of difference between us as expressed in a letter sent him some months ago. He declines to argue and refers me to one of his published works, yielding nothing of his extreme Non-resistance even against madmen, but saying, "I exposed all I think on those subjects ... I cannot now change my views without verifying them anew." The dictum with which the letter opened, "I will not argue with your objections," characterized its entire contents and put an end to all discussion. It closed, however, with the statement that "Two of your tracts are translated into Russian and propagated among believers and richly appreciated by them."

Tolstoy's communication was answered about two months afterward, but no acknowledgement ever came back, by reason, no doubt, of the writer's death a few weeks later – an account of which was sent by Mr. Wilson to the distinguished author, whose daughter responded, "Your tidings are very sad, and my father is deeply grieved."[16]

Of the relation between Mr. Ballou and Count Tolstoy, nothing further need be said save that Mr. Wilson embodied the correspondence between them with collateral letters of his own in a sermon read to his congregation on Sunday, April 20, 1890, of which the diary says: "We were all deeply interested, pleased, and enlightened. I never was so much gratified with Brother Wilson's performance. His scripture-reading, prayer, hymns, etc., were all in harmony with Christian Non-resistance, and he dropped not a word or hint that implied reserved dissent from my views." It may be added that the substance of this discourse was subsequently rearranged by the author and published in *The Arena* for December 1890 – a portion of the last letter of Mr. Ballou to Tolstoy being omitted.[17]

Not Lost But Gone Before

The inroad that death was continually making both upon the circle of Mr. Ballou's general acquaintance and that of his more intimate, tried, and trusted relatives and friends, imparted a pathetic and sacred interest to the last years of his earthly pilgrimage. At the obsequies of many of these he had been called upon to minister with words of comfort and consolation, often under a deep sense of personal bereavement and sorrow. Numerous instances of this kind have been already mentioned, with such tokens of esteem and affection as his heart prompted. Others occurred at a date subsequent to that of which his pen bore record for the pages of this work, a few of which may be noted here.

In 1883, Mr. William H. Humphrey, an old member of the Community and a near neighbor for thirty-five years – a man exemplifying in a marked degree the entire circle of Christian qualities and powers, and one of Mr. Ballou's most steadfast, appreciative, and highly-prized friends – went to join the companion, equally true, faithful, and worthy, who some years before had been translated to the spirit home.[18] Few persons sympathized more fully with him in his peculiar views of truth and duty and in his hopes and struggles for humanity than Mr. and Mrs. Humphrey, and few remained more true to their early professions of loyalty to him and the causes of which he was the trusted champion and promoter. The departure of each of them in turn sent a new pang of loneliness and grief through his breast.

Another death which affected him most sensibly was that of Mr. George Draper, a sometime member of the Community, who, though abandoning it and renouncing its essential principles, yet always held its founder in high regard and veneration, as attested by abundant proofs from time to time. "This lamentable event," to quote from Mr. Ballou's sketch of Hopedale alluded to,

> took place in Boston whither he had gone for a temporary sojourn to obtain medical relief from kidney and other ailments, which, though not seemingly dangerous, he was anxious to overcome. Unexpectedly to all, he presently became alarmingly sick under treatment and in a few days expired. His remains were brought home and on the 11th of June his funeral was solemnized with every demonstration that bereaved family affection and public grief could bestow. Thousands appreciated his merits, sympathized in a great public loss, and united in reverential tributes of respect to his memory.

On the occasion an appropriate address was made by Rev. Mr. Wilson, but the eulogy proper was pronounced by the old pastor of the departed, who had lived side by side with him for more than thirty years, and who could portray the strong points and many excellencies of his character better than any other living person. A sense of justice and the remembrance of unnumbered expressions of kindly consideration and personal esteem received through so long a period, served to render the testimonial paid the deceased, tender, loving, faithful, and true.

It was only about four and a half months after the demise of George Draper, that his elder brother, Ebenezer D., followed him to the world of spirits. The latter for years had been an intermittent sufferer from the same troubles that caused the former's death, which, in the early summer, had assumed an unusually serious and threatening form. As time advanced they increased in severity and painfulness until they reached a fatal issue on the nineteenth of October, at the house of his brother-in-law, Mr. Green, in Boston, where he had a short time before taken up his residence.

It was while [Adin Ballou was] engaged in the ministry at Mendon that this Mr. Draper and his then newly married wife, Anna (Thwing) Draper, a most excellent woman, became religiously interested in Mr. Ballou's preaching, and, though living in Uxbridge, united with his church. They embraced his teachings with a full heart in all their applications, and followed him devotedly through the several stages of practical reform, even to the extent of Non-Resistance and Social Reconstruction. They were among the first to subscribe to the Hopedale "Declaration of Principles," as they were among the first to locate upon the territory where those principles were to be brought to the test of actual experiment and made the basis of a new order of society. In fact, Mr. Draper may be regarded as the most important factor, next to Mr. Ballou, in that enterprise, through the entire period of its existence. He was the only one of its original members who had any money to speak of to invest in it, or any recognized standing in the financial world. He had a taste and training for business, and was the most responsible person in the Community's industrial and pecuniary affairs, as Mr. Ballou was in its moral and spiritual concerns. The two were complements of each other, and stood by each other through good and evil report, through prosperous and adverse fortunes, through joy and sorrow, till the great crisis of 1856, when Mr. Draper, yielding to the assumed financial exigencies of the situation and to his brother's pertinacity, united with him in withdrawing their mutual support from the undertaking, thus bringing about its speedy dissolution. The friendship formed under the circumstances named, and continuing steadfast through so many years, could not be wholly disrupted by the calamitous issue which separated them in many of the particulars in which they had worked so long together, but was continued, though in a modified form, through life. Mr. Draper remained at Hopedale some years after the Community was given up, was prospered in business as senior member of the firm of "E. D. & G. Draper," acquiring a satisfactory competency with which he separated from the partnership in 1868. Two years later his most Christian wife passed on, soon after which he removed to Boston, where, having married again, he spent the remainder of his earthly days.

And now the end had come, and what was mortal of the right-hand man and trusted counselor of Community times was brought back to Hopedale, to receive funeral honors in the house of worship which he, more than any other person, had helped to build, and to be carried thence to its final resting place in the rural cemetery beside the sleeping dust of his first betrothed, who for a generation had filled his home with music and sunshine, and rendered it attractive and delightful to hosts of appreciative friends by her blessed presence there. At the obsequies, fitting addresses were made by his long-time friend and pastor, and by his adopted son, Rev. Charles H. Eaton, D.D.,[19] of New York, interspersed with music and prayer, in the presence of a goodly company of relatives, friends, and acquaintances of other days, assembled to lay upon his bier a wreath of respect and affection sacred to his memory.

Another death that came very near to the subject of this biography and gave him a peculiar sense of loneliness and grief was that of his junior brother, Ariel Ballou, M.D., of Woonsocket, Rhode Island. Though the so closely akin had differed widely from each other in many things, they yet ever held each other in mutual confidence, esteem, and love. In his Ballou history, the elder of the two pays merited honor to the natural ability, high character, and social standing of the younger, testifying to his personal worth "as an intellectual, judicial, self-poised, upright, courageous, high-toned man"; to his professional acquirements, imparting to him "increasing usefulness and fame for more than fifty years"; to his interest in education as "a strong and devoted friend of the public schools"; and to his religious fidelity as "a conscientious, devout, exemplary member of the Episcopal church." It was with a profound feeling of personal loss that the author of these justly commendatory phrases was called to look for the last time upon the face of him to whom they applied, and with unqualified regret that he who was so much interested in, and had done so much for, the compilation and publication of the *History of the Ballous in America* could not have lived to see the consummation of that great undertaking. But in the order of nature and Providence, it was not so to be. He died while the work was passing through the press, July 15, 1887, aged 81 years.

Last Public Efforts

With the advance of age, Mr. Ballou's labors abroad became less frequent, being naturally less called for, as they were less desired on his part. Yet he had numerous invitations to preach, lecture, or speak on public occasions, but felt impelled to decline the greater part of them. Under existing circumstances, he thought he might be excused from all such efforts save those he could easily perform or that made some special appeal to him. He purposed at one time to refuse all further calls to funerals, but the importunities of surviving relatives and friends, and the sympathy of his own heart for the stricken and bereaved, made it difficult for him to carry that purpose into effect. So that, as a matter of fact, the number of such occasions upon which he actually served in some of his later years was as great as at any equal period of his life. His weddings, as a matter of course, diminished toward the last, those at which he officiated occurring in the quietude of his own home. Occasionally he supplied a pulpit at Milford or Upton, or elsewhere not far away, but more frequently at Hopedale, in aid of and as a favor to the regular minister there. At gradually lengthening intervals he attended the meetings of the Worcester Conference, where he frequently had a message to deliver, and where he was always listened to with respect, interest, and acknowledged profit. He was, however, little from home during the last eight years of his life, rarely, if at all, to remain over night; his own work and the uncertain state of his wife's health combining to forbid prolonged absence on his part. He was a regular attendant at church on Sunday unless called elsewhere by a funeral or otherwise, or detained at home by the inclemency of the weather.

Mr. Ballou carried on an extensive correspondence throughout his entire public career. The nature of it changed with the changed conditions of his personal experience. At the outset and far on beyond mid-life, it was of a religious, moral, and reformatory character, but after engaging in historical and genealogical work it took on more of that peculiarity, though never losing the former altogether. He was a free and familiar off-hand writer, the sentences flowing readily from his pen, much of his own genial, affable, courteous, kindly spirit characterizing his letters, of whatever sort they might be – expositional, instructive, advisory, sympathetic, or consolatory – making him a pleasant, much prized, and much enjoyed correspondent.

Some two or three years before Mr. Ballou's decease, a few of his Hopedale friends, under the leadership of Rev. Mr. Wilson, who seemed ever ready to show his veneration and love for his honored predecessor, interested themselves in a project to secure a life-size portrait of him to be presented to the town as a perpetual memorial of his character and career. The object in view was finally gained by calling into requisition the superior skill and exquisite taste of Otto Grundmann, an artist of genius and of excellent standing in Boston and vicinity.[20] By using several of the later photographs of his subject, with the aid of two or three personal sittings, he succeeded in producing a likeness worthy of his reputation and acceptable and gratifying to those employing him. The picture was paid for by private contribution and presented to the town of Hopedale at a regular meeting held November 6, 1888. It was put in charge of the trustees of the public library, the walls of which institution it now adorns and honors.[21]

Work on Autobiography

During the two years and more that intervened between the conclusion of Mr. Ballou's labors upon the family history and his last illness, all the time and energy he could command were devoted with conscientious fidelity to his autobiography. Still, the former was so much broken in upon by calls to funerals, by visitation of friends from near and far, by domestic claims, or otherwise, that he found it impossible to accomplish what he desired in furthering his appointed task. He greatly regretted this, nay, was at times impatient at the delay which he seemed powerless to prevent. He realized that the infirmities of age were creeping upon him, that his days on earth at most could not be very many, and that the night was not far away "in which no man can work."[22] He was anxious to complete with his own hand what he had begun and carried so far towards the end, feeling, no doubt, that no one else could do it so well as he – could make it so much what he earnestly desired it to be, a faithful portraiture of himself in all his inner and outer life. In this anxiety his family and friends fully sympathized, sharing with him the regret occasioned by hindrances it seemed impossible to foresee and prevent, or in any way escape. To add to the trying circumstances of the case and increase the delay, his eyesight, which had been remarkably good till he was past eighty years of age, enabling him to read and write without the aid of glasses, had, by reason of over-taxation in deciphering illegible manuscripts while engaged in historical and genealogical researches, become considerably impaired, causing more or less pain and threatening total blindness at no distant day. To such an extent had this trouble increased at length that he was obliged to give up using artificial light and even to cease from labor on dark and stormy days. Nevertheless, he kept up a good heart, was grateful for blessings still enjoyed, patient under the limitations that hemmed him in, and wrought on as best he could, cheerful and brave, till his weary brain and enfeebled hand could no longer respond to the mandates of his strong and earnest will.

Birthday Reflections

On the twenty-third of April, 1890, the eighty-seventh anniversary of his birth, Mr. Ballou put on record the following outflow of devout and heartfelt meditation, worthy of a St. Francis of Assisi or of his own favorite, Thomas à Kempis:

> My 87th birthday! "Bless the Lord, O my soul, and forget not all His benefits." Surely "His goodness and mercy have followed me all the days of my life." When I obeyed His voice, He sustained me; when I sinned, He rebuked me in love and forgave me; He encouraged all my repentances and still accepted my services. When I was crushed by disappointment, He revived my despondent spirit. In all my troubles and sorrows, He accepted me. When I lost friends and feared desolation, He bade me trust Him, saying, "I will never leave thee nor forsake thee." And He never has. With temporal and spiritual blessings, manifold and innumerable, has He crowned my life. In prosperity and adversity, in judgment and mercy, He has been to me the same "Father of lights, with whom there is no variableness or shadow of turning." All my sins have been against His faultless and salutary laws, the ways whereof were death. All my righteousness has been imperfect and profitless to Him, but to me and my fellow men a granary of unmerited and inestimable good. Therefore will I glorify Him evermore as the Holy Paternal One truly revealed by His son, Jesus Christ, "of whom, through whom, and to whom are all things." And now, Father, keep me in Thy bosom and in the guardianship of Thy holy angels during the few remaining days of my mortal pilgrimage, till I finish the work Thou hast given me to do. Then take me to the home Thou deemest suitable for me in the higher life.[23]

End of Ministry

There is little more to add to this narrative. Few acts or incidents worthy of note occurred during that portion of the eighty-eighth year of his age the subject of it was permitted to spend on the earth. His last sermon had been preached in his old pulpit at Hopedale November 3, 1889; his last funeral was attended June 1, 1890; his last marriage was solemnized on the twenty-sixth of the same month; and his last public service was rendered on the twenty-ninth – a prayer at a Masonic gathering held in Music Hall, Milford, as a testimonial to St. John [the Baptist],[24] instinct with fervor, impressiveness, and spiritual power.

Thus ended a ministry of sixty-eight years and eleven months, remarkable for its length, its activity, and its usefulness – for its eminent service of God and man. During the eight years, three months, and twelve days represented in this chapter, Mr. Ballou participated in 499 funerals, a larger number than ever before in the same length of time, making the aggregate of his life 2606; and presided at the marriage altar of 16 couples, filling out an aggregate of 1199, or of 2398 persons in all. So ends the category of his ministrations in these respects.

Last Illness and Death

The health of Mr. Ballou, which, with rare exceptions, was unusually good from early youth through middle life, continued so till near the end of his earthly pilgrimage. The familiar apothegm, "A sound mind in a sound body,"[25] had in him a striking illustration, due, no doubt, to his well-controlled appetites, his regular habits, his even and cheerful temperament, and the simplicity of his whole manner of life. The infirmities of age came upon him with a lingering tread. Until past fourscore years his frame was wonderfully erect, and his step correspondingly firm and sure. The glow of his countenance and the vigor of his bodily powers were plainly discernible and subjects of remark far on toward the final hour. Such an example of well-preserved physical endowments, able to discharge their respective functions and free from the ills and pains often accompanying such length of days, is rarely seen.

Nor did his mind seem less vigorous and sound than was his physical system. Its faculties remained singularly acute and active almost to the last. People who met him in private or listened to him in public commented upon the clearness and energy of his thought and utterance. Happily for him and for his family and friends, no weakening of his intellectual powers manifested itself and no lack of command or balance of the attributes of the understanding, until stricken with the painless illness which brought his earthly labors to an end, and which, not many days afterward, terminated his mortal career.

Nevertheless, his bodily powers had for some time previous to that final attack been slowly giving way, and his hold on the things of earth and time had been growing less and less secure. His neighbors and friends, kindly solicitous for his health and general welfare, and watchful of changes in his personal appearance, had noticed through the spring and early summer of 1890 what they thought and feared were indications of increasing debility on his part. He had himself indeed become aware of loss of strength and vitality, making note of the same, though deeming it nothing more than a little dullness or weariness which by rest would soon pass away. Yet his resolute spirit would not allow him to give up work altogether until absolutely compelled to do so by sheer inability to prosecute it further. His diary shows that during the first days of July he spent a portion of his mornings in the garden, going thence to his writing, which he followed up, only as interrupted by his customary siesta after dinner and incidental intrusions, as long as he could see.

On Saturday, the twelfth of the month named, he refers for the last time to his work on his life-history. After noting numerous items which had claimed his attention, he adds: "Resumed autobiography at 10:15. On till dinner. Our siestas. Up at 3 P.M. More autobiography and sundries till supper."

The next day, Sunday, he attended church as was his custom, taking a walking stick to support his faltering steps, "the first time," he pleasantly said to a fellow worshiper, "you ever saw the old gentleman at church with a cane." In the afternoon he wrote his daughter, Mrs. Heywood – the last letter he ever penned – detailing interesting incidents of family and neighborhood life with characteristic comments, and closing with a few sentences of a personal nature, in which pathos, prophecy, and grateful piety are significantly blended, as shown by a brief extract:

> Autobiography crawls slowly along. Another chapter coming down to 1882 is almost finished. But dimness of vision greatly hinders progress. There is no improvement. The smoke grows gradually more dense, with little hope of betterment. But we must be patient and thankful for the good that remains. Dissolution must come to us both ere long and all will be right. The Heavenly Father doeth all things well. With ever-abiding love to you all, we remain, affectionately yours,
>
> ADIN AND LUCY H. BALLOU.

Alas, dissolution came to *him* sooner than he thought, no doubt – sooner than any of his friends dared to anticipate. On Monday he was in the garden again, but only for a short season, doing little else through the day except to assist in some trifling domestic matters, most of the time being spent upon the lounge. Tuesday he helped the carpet cleaners and his wife put the house to rights for the summer. At night was "tired." The next day his final entry in his journal was made. Brief extracts reveal his condition at that date:

> I, shiftless and languid, helped [wife] what I could. My blindness worse than any time yet. Lounged and lazied away most of the forenoon, feeling rather cheaply in body and mind. Dinner; siestas until three. Brought up diary until six P.M. Sundries. Eyesight sadly dim.

The remainder of the week he kept quiet, getting all the rest he could, hoping thereby to regain his lost strength and revive his exhausted energies; but all in vain.

The Sunday following, July 20, he rose early and at the proper hour began to prepare for church, but his caretaking wife, who knew how weak he was better than he knew himself, dissuaded him from attempting to go. As the day wore on, his power of vision failed rapidly, and before evening it was lost to him forever. When he realized that he could no longer see, his heart for the time being sank within him and he bewailed the sadness of his lot. But sustained and encouraged by the cheerful words of his wife and by voices from the invisible world, which had comforted him in many a trying hour before, he became calm and resigned, saying, "Light comes to me. The heavens are once more opened; all is right and well," and no expression of murmuring or disquietude afterward escaped his lips.

The next day he spoke of his autobiography, regretting that it was not finished and asking his wife if he could not dictate to her what she could write out for him. Upon being told that he was too ill to do anything of that kind and must be quiet in order to promote recovery, he readily acquiesced, but soon after proceeded to mention certain things he wanted to have noted by whomsoever might complete the work, provided he should not be able to do it himself. He was told that all should be done as he desired and it would be right, which seemed to satisfy him, putting his mind at rest, and he never mentioned the matter again. That night he went to the bed from which he never rose.

The following morning it was deemed advisable to call a physician, and Dr. Jerome Wilmarth, mentioned before, who was then residing in Milford, was summoned. He found the patient suffering from a slight pulmonary trouble and prescribed remedies which brought apparent relief.

On Wednesday the daughter, Mrs. Heywood, and her husband, who had been informed of her father's illness, arrived by an afternoon train, finding him seriously but they hoped not dangerously sick, free from pain, and able to converse intelligently and with little difficulty. He greeted them cordially and affectionately and had a somewhat lengthy interview with them, giving directions much in detail in anticipation of his possible approaching departure, with accompanying assurances of love, gratitude, and pious trust.

On Thursday he asked his daughter to read to him favorite passages in the Bible and also his own account of a highly gratifying séance with Rev. T. L. Harris, an eminent Spiritualistic impressionist and seer, enjoyed many years before.[26] Her doing so gave him evident satisfaction, comfort, and peace. His physician, at his evening visit, said he was "holding his own" and saw grounds for hope that he would rally from the attack and be about again in a few days. But a slight paralytic shock before morning, affecting his entire left side, foreclosed all further expectation of such a devoutly-to-be-wished-for issue.

After this new feature of the case appeared, his difficulty of speaking, declining strength, and waning consciousness precluded all continued conversation, and foreshadowed, beyond all peradventure, the not-far-distant fatal result. He, however, continued able to recognize those about him, answer questions in brief terms, and respond to expressions of interest and affection by intelligent signs and tokens, almost to his last expiring breath. Gradually, with no show of suffering, peacefully he sank away, the thread of life becoming manifestly attenuated day by day as time went on. He was tenderly and lovingly watched over by the members of his household, conscientiously and effectively cared for by his physician and a skillfully trained nurse, Mrs. Belle A. Varney of Worcester, until the morning of the fifth of August, when, in the presence of his family and of a neighbor watcher,

Mrs. Sarah Jane Hatch,[27] at 4:45 o'clock, just as the rising sun began to fleck with golden hues the surrounding hills, he passed without a struggle to the more immediate companionship of the dear ones gone before, and to the rest and reward "of the people of God."[28]

Funeral Services

On the afternoon of Friday, August 8, appropriate burial rites in honor of the departed were duly solemnized in the Hopedale church. A large concourse of people was present, coming from near and far to pay their tribute of respect, veneration, and love to the relative and friend whose earthly labors had now come to an end, and to mingle their sorrow and tears sympathizingly with each other under a sense of one common bereavement – of one profound, heartfelt grief. The exercises of the occasion had been arranged for the most part by the deceased and were carried out in accordance with his wishes. The pallbearers were of his own selection and the several speakers had been named by him as among the truest and best of his much prized friends. It was his request that his Masonic brethren should have his body in charge and render the beautiful and impressive burial service of the Order at the grave, and this was done. In the unavoidable absence of Gen. William F. Draper,[29] whom he had personally asked to act as conductor at his obsequies whenever they should take place, Mr. Eben D. Bancroft[30] was invited to the position, the duties of which were discharged with gratifying quietude, system, and efficiency. A Masonic quartet interspersed the exercises with most appropriate and admirably executed selections of vocal music.

Everything pertaining to the sacred occasion was as simple and unostentatious as, in the nature of the case, it well could be. The usual emblems of distress and gloom were dispensed with, and a hopeful, cheerful, but subdued and reverent spirit prevailed. The body was encased in a massive broadcloth-covered casket, heavily but not gorgeously mounted, and flowers in abundance, wrought into chaste and expressive forms, testified to the thoughtful love of earthly friends, as well as to the fatherly kindness of the great Giver of All Good.

At 12:45 o'clock, prayer was offered at the house, where the family and other near relatives were convened, by an almost lifelong friend, Rev. William H. Fish of Dedham, preliminary to the more public services at the church. These were introduced by an organ voluntary, effectively given by Prof. Origen B. Young[31] while the funeral cortege was passing in. A brief invocation was followed by singing and readings from the scriptures and from Whittier's "Eternal Goodness."[32]

Rev. George S. Ball[33] of Upton spoke most feelingly and impressively of Mr. Ballou as one called by God to a great and noble work, which he had most conscientiously and faithfully performed, in a spirit of self-consecration, animated by a living faith in the eternal realities and an all-prevailing love of God and man. Rev. Samuel May of Leicester[34] said that the lesson of the hour was "the worth of a life, and how much can be accomplished in a single life," as illustrated in the career of the departed, who had exemplified the highest type of faith, hope and charity, and whose translation to the company of the great cloud of witnesses by which we are compassed about,[35] made heaven seem nearer and the spiritual life more real and abiding. Rev. Carlton A. Staples[36] of Lexington paid an earnest and tender tribute to his early pastor and always revered friend, reviewing briefly his Mendon ministry and the wonderful success he achieved therein as a preacher of a large and noble Christian faith, as a champion of all good causes, and as a winner of human hearts to himself and to a better life. Rev. Mr. Fish, referring to his early acquaintance with the deceased, expressed profound gratitude that at the outset of his professional experience he came under the influence of so enlightened and noble a mind, and so able a preacher of pure Christianity, breathing "peace on earth and good will to men." He also alluded to the calm and happy close of his earthly pilgrimage and of the undoubted joy with which he had already been greeted by his beloved Adin Augustus and other dear ones gone before in the spirit home, whence had descended blessed ministrations in days gone by, and where he would welcome all the loved ones left behind in days to come.

At the conclusion of the address of Mr. Fish, the present writer, by special request of his father-in-law, read portions of the sermon [Adin Ballou] had himself prepared some years before for his own funeral, the full text of which may be found in the appendix. Of this part of the service, the Milford *Journal* said:

> It was most affecting. Through it [the discourse] pulsed the old-time fervor of devotion to others, of lofty ideals, of generous self-effacement, so significant of the writer. The power and beauty of the periods – of a voice literally "from out of the grave" – was indescribably touching. The tall, kindly form, the saintly, benevolent face, the modestly courageous but eloquent speech, all stood out visibly as the beautiful sentences fell from the reader's lips. At the tender farewell close, the mourning in the hearts of those present well nigh broke restraint, and grief was uncontrollably visible.

Rev. Mr. Staples followed this reading with a prayer full of fervor and tender feeling, overflowing with Christian hope and trust, thanking the Giver of All Good for the noble life now closed and for all the benefits resulting from it, and invoking upon the immediately bereaved and all sorrowing with them, the blessing of the Heavenly Father and all needed heavenly comfort, encouragement, consolation, and peace. After the singing of another sacred hymn, Rev. Mr. Ball pronounced the benediction, bringing this part of the service to a close.

Then came the leave-taking, when the assembled multitude, filling not only the auditorium of the church but the stairway and vestibule with much of the vestry below, passing by the coffined form, looked for the last time upon the familiar face – benignant, kindly, expressive, saintly, in death as in life – the relatives and family following all the rest. When the last lingering look of bereaved affection was given, the casket was reverently closed and borne forth from the place where the voiceless sleeper had so long and devotedly ministered in holy things to the burial carriage awaiting it outside, in which, followed by a long procession in vehicles of various kinds and on foot, it was conveyed to the rural cemetery across the river clothed in all the loveliness and glory of nature's midsummer garniture, as if to welcome a royal inhabitant to its peaceful abodes. And there in the family lot, already consecrated by the dust of loved ones sleeping beneath its turf of living green, the wearied frame was laid to rest. The impressive burial service of the Masonic brotherhood was feelingly rendered by Master Frank E. Mathewson of Montgomery Lodge, Milford, and Chaplain [Elbert W.] Whitney,[37] accompanied by further singing on the part of the quartet, whose deep, rich voices, blending in perfect harmony and floating aloft and away on the gentle air, seemed like echoes or preludes of the anthems of heaven. A sprig of green dropped from the hands of brethren of the mystic tie upon the casket already deposited in its lowly bed, a tender, tear-dimmed glance into the place of sepulture by each one of the passing throng, and all was over.

> And now he rests; his greatness and his sweetness
> Blend without jar or strife;
> And death has molded into calm completeness
> The story of his life.
>
> Where the dews glisten and the song-birds warble
> His dust to dust is laid;
> In nature's keeping, with no pomp of marble
> To shame his modest shade.
>
> Around his grave are quietness and beauty
> And the sweet heaven above;
> The fitting symbols of a life of duty
> Transfigured into love.[38]

APPENDIX A

Tributes and Testimonials

The foregoing pages present in distinct outline and with sufficiency of detail a portraiture of the man whose life history they rehearse, drawn from the standpoint of his own personal consciousness and considerate judgment of himself and of his work in the world. It seems most desirable that this delineation should be accompanied by an additional one representing him as he was seen by others – by those who knew him well and whose mental and moral discernment and sense of justice fitted them to render a trustworthy verdict concerning the distinguishing and meritorious features of his character and career. Hence it is that a few tributes and testimonials derived from various sources are introduced as an appropriate supplement to what has gone before.

I. Funeral Voices

Rev. George S. Ball
Upton, Massachusetts

Our brother, our father in Israel, has been long spared to us. He has "come down to the grave in full age, like as a shock of corn cometh in its season."[1] Far back in his youth a great vision opened to him, changing the whole tenor of his life. Like Paul, he was not disobedient thereto. Though he went forth bearing his seed weeping, he has gathered great sheaves into God's garner,[2] and could repeat in retrospect the apostle's words, "I am ready to be offered; the time of my departure is at hand. I have fought a good fight, I have finished my course, I have kept the faith. Henceforth there is laid up for me a crown of righteousness."[3]

... But let us not forget that even the grave bears not away all. There is a life of soul above its reach. Let memory hold its living power still.[4] Let souls commune and even the dead shall speak.[5]

And first there rises, at the recall, a beautiful simplicity that marked his life. How great was the impulse that sent forth this character on its mission! How luminous the vision that consecrated that long life of love in his chosen profession! Simplicity marks God's work. We can believe all that Paul portrays as the result of faith. The call came. The vision opened such a view of the character of God, such ineffable beauty, that he was ever afterward drawn to Him as the All-Father. Not far away but present, for "in Him we live and move and have our being."[6] The Father of all, hence one family tie binds all spirits together. It was this Christian idea of the mutual relation between God and man that entranced and inspired his soul; from this came his consecration. How from this central thought he reasoned, argued, and led men! Christ became real to him – the elder brother and master, "the way, the truth, the life."[7] His ideal, so grand, was taken into life, became a power for the uplifting of humanity, for the salvation of the world here and now. His philosophy took in all men, high and low, rich and poor. How he sought to inaugurate this life of God among men as practical Christianity, that they might make it real here and now, and be prepared for the living, loving work of eternal growth! He saw through the Great Master's eyes that which ever drew him on, called him to advocate every reform, and to labor for every class and condition of mankind.

How was he thus consecrated to the antislavery work! What blows he struck at all those evils and sins that degrade men and lead them into bondage, that imbrute them and take away that peace and happiness which come only from obedience to the higher law of their being! His broad soul could welcome all working to the same great ends. How faithful in all these relations! How various his calls! What tasks he performed! And through all, his soul has grown and the love that inspired him has illumined his face, given sweetness to his smile, fervor to his voice, and warmth to the grasp of his hand, that we shall bear on the tablet of our hearts[8] as long as affections remain.

Perhaps more marked than all has been the practical outcome of his great mind and faith. Ever active, he never outran his conscience and so has shown an example we all may welcome as a height of greatness rarely attained. He held fast the good[9] while aspiring for the better, showing to us the sources of that power whose loss we now mourn. All this culminated in a spiritual habit that made his later life a walk with God – a commerce with the sky. Often thwarted and apparently failing as he worked with men, he has felt a divine presence upholding him if for a moment cast down.

His own experience prepared him to speak directly to hearts overwhelmed in affliction. To him the veil of death had been pierced, the light of God shone through, the voice of Him who had brought life and immortality to light was heard proclaiming the mansions of the Father's house[10] open to our feet. Night was changed to morning, and the eternal day for all souls dawned.

REV. SAMUEL MAY
Leicester, Massachusetts

The lesson of this hour is of the worth of life and how much may be accomplished in a single life. I am almost awestruck in the presence of this long-protracted, now finished life – a life devoted with such singleness of purpose, such unintermitting industry, such uniform gentleness, yet such manifest force, to the highest and noblest human ends. Compare it with lives we daily look upon, spent aimlessly and weakly – still more with those spent viciously and injuriously. Compare its wise and generous activities with the self-seeking and frivolous course of many; its wealth of thought and purpose with their emptiness; its precious product with their waste. Can these so different lives all come into one category and be classed as *human* lives – one so full, the others so barren; one so positive and high, the others so negative and low? We understand why it is asked of the latter, "Is life worth living?" We cannot imagine its being asked of the well-ordered, high-principled, consecrated life which has just come to its close.

... A life well spent! Can there be any truer, better eulogy? Could human life have a more perfect crown than to be thus sealed? An honorable life too and a happy life – and both because it was well spent, because it was filled with the service of truth, of man, and of God. What cause of human good did he ever refuse? What service to humanity has he turned from? What divine truth has he ever feared to accept and to proclaim both by word and deed? Is a deep, living faith in those high ideas and principles which take hold of the very throne of God, in itself a rich possession, a pearl of great price?[11] Such faith he had. Is a hopeful trust in men, in their power of progress and attainment, and in their larger and nobler future – a hope stronger than all doubts and fears – to be desired? Such hope was his. Is a generous sympathy, taking in all sorts and conditions of men, ministering gladly to all sorrows and needs, encouraging all hearts – which has patience for weakness, pity for failure, which refuses to despair of those whom God cares for, which brings its own human love to work with God's to turn the sinful from the error of their ways – is such wide charity to be revered and sought? We can truly say, it lived in his bosom. Yes, he had all these graces – this faith, this hope, this charity; and which of them were greatest in him it were hard to tell.[12]

I do not know the precise time when Mr. Ballou first declared himself to be of the grand army of antislavery workers – grand not in numbers, but in its principles, in its aims, in the spirit of moral courage and self-sacrifice, which inspired it and held it together. I *do* know that it was in the very early years that he took his place in that warfare, standing strong and firm as a good soldier of God, in line with its most outspoken advocates, its most earnest friends, giving to that cause, though then "everywhere spoken against,"[13] his unqualified adherence, the influence of his pulpit, the force of his mental training and of his earnest, searching speech, and, better than all beside, of his high personal character, his generous sympathy, his clear and true conscience ... Had the American pulpit, with a proper loyalty to the gospel it professed to teach, with a general accord, and with a courage and Christlike mind such as Mr. Ballou manifested, lifted up its voice against slavery, we should have been saved a thousand evils, and, in all human probability, the long and destructive war, with its costly sacrifice of life and substance, would have been averted.

The departure of this dear friend enlarges that "cloud of witnesses" by which "we are compassed about." As he passes out of sight and joins that "innumerable company"[14] of which the sacred writers tell us in so many a glowing figure, with so many a lofty and inspiring phrase, we feel sensibly that it becomes of greater personal interest to ourselves; that heaven is nearer; that this brief earthly life is really far less substantial and sure than we have regarded it, the spirit's life more vivid and infinitely more worthy. New motives come to us. Our purpose to lay aside every weight which holds us down is quickened. Oh, how greatly should it be quickened, till we wholly understand what manner of men we ought to be, seeing that we have had such companionship as his, seeing that we may hope for it again, seeing that we are ever surrounded by this "so great a cloud of witnesses!"

May a portion of his spirit fall on us who remain. His witness for God and truth does not cease with his mortal breath. He lives to God, who will not forget his promises, and who will visit the bereaved, the lonely, the stricken, with his comforting spirit. So may his kingdom come, and his will be done "on earth as it is in heaven."[15]

REV. CARLTON A. STAPLES
Lexington, Massachusetts

Mr. Staples was a native of Mendon, belonging to one of the families connected with the parish of which the deceased was for eleven years pastor, and grew up to manhood largely under his guidance and influence. He ever held him in sincere esteem and reverence, and his tribute on the occasion under notice was most earnest, tender, and affectionate. The substance of it, much amplified and illustrated, was embodied in a "Memorial Sermon," preached in the old Mendon church shortly afterward, extracts from which appear on a subsequent page.

Rev. William H. Fish
Dedham, Massachusetts

I have probably known him [the departed] intimately and associatively longer than almost any other person present, which is nearly sixty years. For fifty-three years I have been in ministerial fellowship with him, he introducing me to my first society in Millville, and taking an important part there in my ordination, which was effected by a friendly union of Restorationists and Unitarians. And today I certainly have good reasons for gratitude that I early came under the helpful influence of so enlightened and noble a mind, and so able and efficient a teacher of that pure gospel of Christ which breathes only "peace on earth and good will to all mankind."[16] It is fifty-six years since I first visited him in his hospitable home in Mendon, and our parishes were so near to each other for several years that he was of great assistance to me by frequent pulpit exchanges and in various other fraternal ways. And very pleasant to me is the memory of those opening days of my public ministry – among the happiest of my life.

... And that was a blessed close of a consecrated life – a life consecrated to God and humanity in the Christ faith and spirit. The messenger which we call Death seemed to approach him in the best possible way for both himself and his beloved and elevated companion of sixty years. The first shock that came to him, rendering him helpless, and turning the light of day into darkness, was sudden, indeed, but after this prostration his life ebbed so slowly, so peacefully away, and the heavens opened so clearly and brightly to him, that the two weeks interim thoroughly fortified his afflicted and anxious wife for the change, and comforted and sustained by the divine presence and, as she believed, by the ministry of angels, she was able to say in her trusting heart, "Even so, Father, for so it seemeth good in thy sight,"[17] and now she only patiently and hopefully waits, "till the shadows are a little longer grown,"[18] to rejoin him in the heavenly home, which has for so many years been their mutual anticipation and their constant consolation and encouragement. As they have lived so long together in the spiritual as well as in the material world, confident that their dear, long-ago departed Adin Augustus was with them as a ministering presence, there must now seem to her to be but a thin veil between her and them, and that soon they will be brought together to realize their highest dearest hopes, and the fulfillment of all the promises made to them by the various revelations of the universal Father received in filial faith and trust. So this great light, which has just ceased to shine upon us through that noble form that is presently to be laid away in the beautiful cemetery planned originally by him, will shine henceforth in some more glorious form, wherein the pure spirit will enjoy a happiness that "eye hath not seen, nor ear heard, nor the heart of mortal man conceived."[19] May we, dear friends, make this our hope, by living the faith which our elder and departed brother so long preached in your midst and so tenderly and impressively brought home to you in your hours of bereavement and sorrow, and may that hope be fully realized by us all, when we also shall be summoned hence.

II. Tributes of Friends

Rev. Charles A. Eaton, D.D.
New York

I can sincerely say that in my moral and spiritual nature I owe more to Mr. Ballou than to all the ministers and men with whom I have ever come in contact. His superior allegiance to the truth, his boldness and humility, his wisdom and love, excited my admiration as a boy and have been my constant inspiration in later life. We may say of him what Tyndall said of Faraday, "Surely, here was a strong man; but let me not forget the union of strength with sweetness in his character."[20] We cannot regret the going home after so long, rich, holy, and helpful a life. For *him*, certainly, "to die is gain."[21] May God help us to love him so much that we may grow to be like him, and if we may not realize his power we may attain something of his spirit.

Hon. Latimer W. Ballou
Woonsocket, Rhode Island

Brother Ballou was one of my earliest school-teachers, a near neighbor of my father, and though afterward separated by our varied callings, we have been warm friends more than seventy years. I am grateful for the noble life, the warm friendship and the blessings the dear departed has conferred, and the bright hope and faith he proclaimed to so many sorrowing hearts.

Gen. William F. Draper
Hopedale

It is with the most profound regret that I read in the papers here [in Europe] of the death of Mr. Ballou. Notwithstanding his extreme age, the news came like a shock to me. I admired and respected – nay, revered him more than any other man I ever met. To me he combined a perfectly blameless life with most extraordinary reasoning powers. I feel that he has done much to develop the best that there is in me.

Rev. Lewis G. Wilson
Hopedale

Closing paragraphs of a sermon from the text, "The strength of the hills is his also,"[22] delivered September 14, 1890.

What a great good fortune it has been to us all, that we have so long dwelt near him whose vacant place fills us with grief, even in the midst of our gratitude! How like some great mountain of spiritual strength he has been these many years! Like a white-crowned hill, he towered above us, and to be near him was to feel safe, and in our trouble to gain courage to go on our way cheerfully, trusting in the Father in whom he trusted.

The strength of the hills was his, but it was his because he went up to their summits, as his Master did. There he prayed; there he labored with the hard and knotted problems of life; there he received and brought down to hundreds of waiting and expectant hearts the consolation of a changeless love.

If such a life, filled with such a power, does not have its weight with us and linger in our memory as a constant inspiration of faith and reminder of duty, then are we pitifully weak and thoughtless. But such will not be the case. We shall go forth and labor to realize his ideal of brotherly love and peace – the fundamental principles of Christianity.

Those bright summits which he saw in his prayers, those angels with whom he communed across the silent sea, those star-fretted heavens[23] into whose realm his spirit has been welcomed – we will think on these things[24] and tell them to our children while we do good service in the name of God, in the name of Christ, and in the name of a glorified humanity.

Rev. Carlton A. Staples
Lexington, Massachusetts

Extracts from a discourse given in the Unitarian Church, Mendon, August 24, 1890, and afterwards printed at the request of his hearers.

In Memoriam.

> When the ear heard me, then it blessed me; and when the eye saw me, it gave witness to me ... The blessing of him that was ready to perish came upon me.
> –Job 29:11, 13.

It is now nearly sixty years since Adin Ballou, then a young man less than thirty years of age, was installed in this house as the minister of the society worshipping here. He had been preaching then for ten years, having entered his profession when barely eighteen, and had already attained popularity as an interesting and eloquent preacher.

... Into the town life he entered heartily; he was in sympathy with its people in their struggles, sufferings, and sorrows, and their friend and counselor in all the experiences of life. He soon won their confidence and their love. He delighted to talk with them upon their affairs, their opinions, and their hopes. He made himself one with them in their homes, at their work, in their afflictions and their joys. A kindly, genial, courteous man who never held himself above anybody – black or white, saint or sinner, poor or rich – who had a cordial greeting for everyone whom he met on the street, and who was as ready to stop and talk with a bronzed, rugged farmer or his son and daughter, as with the finest gentleman and lady of the town; it is no wonder that the whole population was drawn to him and gave him their sincere respect and affection. His beaming face, his pleasing manner, his soft, musical voice, his interest in the humblest people, and his readiness to help and encourage all who were in want and trouble, opened the way to everybody's heart. The children and the young men and women were his sincere friends, drawn to him and held fast by his friendly spirit toward them and his devotion to their good. He impressed their minds with moral and religious truths. He awakened an ambition in them to do and to be something worthy of their opportunities, an honor and a blessing to their fellowmen and their country. The influence of his teaching and of his spirit did much to mould their characters and cheer and elevate their lives. To many of them he has been a power for good in all the subsequent journey of life, and to their dying day they will remember him as the gentle, persuasive teacher and faithful friend who first turned their thoughts toward God as our loving Father, Jesus as our faithful Guide, and Heaven as our eternal home.

Mr. Ballou soon became popular with the society and influential in the town. As a preacher, he was interesting, forcible, practical, and often eloquent. Of a logical mind, strong reasoning powers, tender feelings, and a devout spirit, he moved, convinced, and uplifted his congregation. This meeting house was usually filled with interested worshipers, who came from all parts of the town and from neighboring towns, attracted by the fervor and power of his pulpit services ... He was a preacher who brought home to his hearers the great truths of religion and the duties of life in a way that people understood, illustrated them with facts and stories often homely but pungent and moving, appealed to the reason, the conscience, and the heart with convincing power. His themes were not far removed from the common experience; they touched the great issues of life and questions of individual and social well-being. He had an impressive manner, a fine, commanding presence, a voice of singular pathos and sweetness. It was a pleasure to look at the man and follow his discourse. I suppose the first five years of his ministry here were the period of his greatest popularity as a preacher. The congregation was large, united, proud of its minister; and he was winning new admirers and friends in the adjoining towns. Through his paper, his lecturing and preaching, he gained a wide influence in this portion of the State, and made a reputation as a controversialist, writer, and preacher, which might well have satisfied his ambition. Thus the prospect of a long, prosperous, and peaceful pastorate seemed open before him. Few ministers at his age had achieved so enviable a reputation.

... Forty-eight years of life remained to him after his connection with this society as pastor came to an end. Of this long period of work and care, of heavy responsibilities, of bitter disappointments, yet of useful labors and of large achievements, I can speak only very briefly ... What good cause, however unpopular, what cause founded on justice, on purity, on Christian truth and love, did he not engage in and help forward by word and deed and influence? None such ever appealed to him in vain. He was a brave, fearless soldier in the battle for truth and righteousness; and he never shrank from any sacrifice of personal advantage to do his duty toward God and man. Of untiring industry, he accomplished an amount of difficult and disagreeable literary work such as few ever attempt and fewer ever finish; and he ceased not until almost fourscore and ten years had been reached. Nothing could turn him aside from his purpose and the task before him. Of firm Christian faith, he sought to embody its principles and its spirit in the institutions of society, and make them the guide of human conduct and the basis of character. The gospel of Christ and above all the spirit of Christ were to him the final court of appeal, before which all institutions, all enterprises, all lives, must be brought for judgment, and approved or condemned as they harmonized or antagonized them. He rested in the faith that the immutable right and good were brought to men in the Christian revelation, and before it man should bow in obedience and love.

But one word more needs to be spoken. He was a man of large and tender sympathies, of a kind and generous heart, and that brought him near to other hearts. Few men ever won the love of so many people, in all classes and in all conditions. They knew him to be their friend, they found him to be their helper and comforter. He spake to the heart, because he spake from the heart, of God, and heaven, and eternal life. Invisible things were real to him; he lived much with them and in them, and when he spoke of them it strengthened human faith and comforted human sorrow. There are few homes in this town and in many adjoining towns where he was not known, and where his voice and presence are not associated with the most solemn and the most joyous occasions of life, and where he is not remembered gratefully and lovingly; and many there are, scattered far and wide in our country, who remember words of his that touched their hearts and kindled some higher purpose, some nobler ambition, or some kinder feeling. And many there are who have forgotten his words, but are conscious, nevertheless, that his influence has given their lives a worthier aim, and made their characters brighter and better. "Let me die the death of the righteous, and let my last end be like his,"[25] was the prayer of an ancient man, as recorded in the Bible. It is a beautiful prayer. So we would all meet death at last. But to die in the peace and assurance of the righteous, man must live in his faith, in his devotion to what is right and good, loving and serving God, walking in the sweet ways of charity and holiness. Thus I believe Adin Ballou lived – a righteous man, a Christian man, the faithful servant of God, the friend and helper of his fellow beings. He died in peace, honored and loved; and his name and influence will long remain to bless the world.

GEORGE L. CARY[26]
President of Meadville Theological School

More than any other individual, [he] was instrumental, without being aware of it, of arousing and strengthening in me that interest in a rational and practical Christianity, which, as I grew older, deepened into an earnest desire to devote my life to some form of helpful human service. He was such a warm friend of my father and his name was such a household word in our family, that when a boy I used to think of him as a sort of thirteenth apostle, and from the beginning of the publication of the *Practical Christian* to the end I doubt if there was a column of it I did not read. This and his *Christian Non-Resistance* exerted such a powerful influence over me that, until I was twenty years old, I was most thoroughly and completely his disciple.

In two directions I can most clearly trace Mr. Ballou's influence upon my mind and character. How wonderfully strong he was on the ethical side of his nature! Whether it was his moral enthusiasm which first kindled the same flame in my own life, or whether it was only his breath which fanned the spark that nature had placed there, my indebtedness to him in this direction was beyond price. Later years and wider experience naturally modified to some extent the opinions formed in those early years concerning the various relations of man to man, but the spirit I imbibed from his teachings has never ceased to be my inspiration.

Mr. Ballou's New Testament expositions in the *Practical Christian* laid the foundation of whatever success I have since had as an interpreter of the scriptures. It was only the planting of the germs, and yet I can distinctly trace, even in some of my present opinions, the development of ideas which first came to me as I read that series of articles.

III. TESTIMONIES OF RELIGIOUS AND PHILANTHROPIC BODIES

THE HOPEDALE PARISH

Whereas, In the Providence of God, the Hopedale Parish has, in the decease of the Rev. Adin Ballou, lost the founder of this community, a valued friend, a wise counselor, a comforter in bereavement, and in all things a spiritual father, therefore be it

Resolved, That his life has always been, and the memory of it must continue to be, to ourselves and to our children, an example of noble allegiance to the truth, of unequivocal integrity, and of the faith which knows neither fear nor doubt; that his presence for many years has been an inspiration to the highest life and thought; that in his decease we have lost one who merited the love which thousands were glad to accord him; and that while we are deeply grieved at his departure into that realm where all who loved and knew him shall seek his presence again, we can never cease to be grateful that such a life has been spent in our midst.

THE UNIVERSALIST CHURCH, WOONSOCKET, RHODE ISLAND
By its Pastor, Rev. Charles J. White[27]

At a meeting of our church held Monday evening, July 28, the severe and possibly final illness of Rev. Adin Ballou was reported. At the mention of the fact, all our hearts were touched with deep sorrow, for his name has been a household word[28] in our homes for three-quarters of a century, and none knew him but to respect and love him. Many were the kind words spoken and many the sacred memories of the past rehearsed.

It was voted to spread upon our records the expression of our loving esteem for and our deep sympathy with the faithful servant of God and our dear friend lying so very ill at his home in Hopedale, with the prayer that, if it were possible, he might yet longer be spared to us and to the world; but, if not possible, then God's will be done;[29] commending him to the Father whom he loved and to the great company in the immortal life whom he had blessed. The pastor was requested, if he could make it convenient, to carry this expression and message of love in person to Mr. Ballou.

We have inscribed in our records a brief biography with an account of his funeral. We feel that we owed it to him and that the whole community owes it to him to recognize the great service to a reasonable religion and a righteous life he rendered in his long years of residence in the vicinity. We congratulate the widow and all your family that you have such precious memories of your departed one. Surely, if ever the words of the psalmist were appropriate, they are in his case: "Precious in the sight of the Lord is the death of his saints." "They go down to the grave in a full age, like as a shock of corn cometh in its season."[30] He had made royal all of this life and was ripe for the better world beyond. My field of labor for these twenty years has been especially fragrant with the names of Rev. John Boyden and his beloved neighbor and lifelong friend, Rev. Adin Ballou. I shall never cease to be grateful to them. "They labored and we are entered into their labors."[31]

> Only the actions of the just
> Smell sweet and blossom in the dust.[32]

The Worcester Conference

At a meeting of this body held in Templeton, Oct. 2, 1890, the opening session was devoted to an appropriate service in appreciative and grateful memory of Rev. Adin Ballou. Tender and impressive tributes to the disinterested spirit, eminent virtues, and noble work of him whose recent decease touched with a sacred grief so many hearts, were rendered by Revs. Alvin F. Bailey[33] of Barre, George W. Stacy of Milford, Austin S. Garver[34] of Worcester, and Grindall Reynolds[35] of Boston, secretary of the American Unitarian Association; after which the following declaration, with an accompanying resolution of sympathy for the afflicted and bereaved, was unanimously adopted:

> The recent departure of our revered brother, Rev. Adin Ballou of Hopedale, to mansions of glorious rest, is indeed remembered with widespread grief. His was a well-spent life – a life devoted to the cause of practical Christianity, based on the enthusiasm of humanity; a life ever helpful in advancing righteousness as required by the precepts and illustrated by the example of Jesus Christ, our Lord and Master.

Worcester Co. Commandery, K. T.[36]

He was widely known and, where best known, was loved and respected. His life was long, peaceful, busy, and useful – kind in action, gentle in speech, and agreeable in manner, never making enemies, but always gaining friends. He was a man of commanding presence and his pleasant smile and kindly words greeted everyone and won all to a mutual friendship. This is but a faint picture of a noble man and a Christian gentleman and Knight Templar, who was honored and respected in life and now sincerely lamented in death.

The Universal Peace Union, Philadelphia

His long life of nearly eighty-eight years has been devoted to the purest principles of true peace, and he has left us a legacy of more worth than can be computed in silver or gold. As one of the founders of the Universal Peace Union, having been present at the preliminary meeting in 1865 and at the organization of the society in 1866, and continuing with us in spirit ever since, sending us occasional letters of encouragement and always living the very incarnation of peace – we testify to his high worth and feel we have cause of thankfulness that we had so faithful an officer to labor with us.

IV. Eulogies of the Press

Milford Journal

His life was gentle, and the elements so mixed in him that nature might stand up and say to all the world, This is a man.[37]

It is doubtful if in all New England there is another clergyman who has entered so many homes as a comforter, to whom it was given to personate so becomingly the loveliness of eternal truths. About his ministrations clustered the spiritual lives of thousands; under his tender offices grew the solemn links of life – the hours of birth, the hours of christening, of marriage, and of mourning, until his mild presence breathed a perpetual benediction and his steps brought peace. Few in all this section there are but have known his tender offices, whether the hour was of nuptial joy, of tremulous rejoicing for nativity, of life dedication in uprightness, or binding up the hearts of bereaved mourners in the hour of desolation.

A gentle minister to all grief, a partaker of all homely joy, he is a part of the innermost life of thousands like a sacred experience, something to remember and revere.

Milford Gazette

Early Tuesday morning, Rev. Adin Ballou, widely known for his many virtues, died at his home in Hopedale, after an illness of only two weeks' duration ... His was a busy life. Aside from his ministerial duties, he devoted considerable attention to literature, was the author of several books, including a history of the town of Milford and a genealogy of the Ballou family in America, besides various pamphlets and tracts.

He was a man of simple habits and quiet tastes, large-hearted and full of sympathy, rejoicing with the happy, comforting the sorrow-stricken. His friends are legion, and to those in whose joys and griefs he has shared, his departure is a heavy loss.

Boston Herald

The late Adin Ballou ... grew up with such scanty advantages as could be secured in a plain New England home and at the district school ... From the first he was a person of mark. He was large for his age, uncommonly advanced in thoughtfulness, and reached at a bound the mature decisions which belong to people of ripe years. His tendency from the first was toward religious thinking and living...

He had in him the self-confidence, the burning enthusiasm, the fearless self-assertion, the irresistible impulse, which constitute a natural leader of society, and though he exercised his gifts without the aid of a distinguished position, he was early known as one of the strongest agitators in a community that was as full of reform ideas as an egg is full of meat.[38]

... Mr. Ballou was one of the interested believers in the new form of associationism, and he had seen too little of the practical development of Christian communism in the Christian church to feel that, within its existing limits, the higher forms of social life could be developed and maintained. He wished to try the experiment for himself, and in the spring of 1842, he secured an extensive domain in the town of Milford in this state, and there, with the aid of others, organized what has since been known as the Hopedale Community ... He had matured his plan after long and constant study of the different systems for renewing civil society which were in vogue at that time, and he had such an original mind, and had gone so far into the foundation of things, that his own social scheme took shape from his own liberal and devising brain ... What he contemplated was nothing less than a new incarnation of the spirit of Jesus Christ in community life. What he aimed at was to institute and consolidate a true order of human society, in which all individual interests should be harmonized for the common good, and be controlled by divine principles as their supreme law ... In the statement of these principles, Mr. Ballou was a happy optimist. He inculcated the existence of one Infinite God, his mediatorial manifestation through Jesus Christ, the doctrine of a perfect divine retribution, the necessity of spiritual regeneration, and the final universal triumph of good over evil.[39]

What is remarkable in Mr. Ballou's work is that he gave it a distinctive religious purpose and character. He did not expect to reform people unless he controlled their spiritual life and the religious direction of the community was the principle to which everything else was subordinated. He also insisted that the family life should be maintained in its purest and best possible forms.

... Adin Ballou was one of the most remarkable self-made men that New England has ever produced. He belonged to the century ... He was the product of the spirit of associationism or community life, permeated and guided by Christian principles, which was in its day an attempt to realize the larger mission of the Christian church through a social unity.

He was a man of charming simplicity of manner, of firm yet childlike faith, of keen and natural intellectual force, and of unusual contentment of mind and spirit ... He was a Christian Socialist more than a decade before Maurice and Kingsley and Hughes began that movement in England,[40] and one of a high and pure type which men are attempting to realize today ... It was his misfortune to live and think at a time when the world was not yet ready for his services in the form in which he desired to render them, but as one of the strong personal forces in our practical yet speculative New England life, he was as distinct an incarnation of the spirit of the forefathers as Cotton Mather, or Sam. Adams, or Ralph Waldo Emerson.

Boston Journal

Rev. Adin Ballou, who died at his home in Hopedale, Mass., Tuesday morning, was widely known and where best known was loved and respected. His life was long, peaceful, busy, and useful, and he probably leaves not an enemy behind, as he had not one in life. He was kind in action, gentle in speech, agreeable in manner ... His kindly words of wisdom and advice have truly gained for him the title of Father Ballou. Entering so many families in time of trouble and in time of joy, he has gained the hearts of many people who in his death will feel a personal loss.

He was a strong anti-slavery man, a firm advocate of temperance, and a man of peace in all the walks of life ... He was of commanding presence, benignant countenance, and his kindly smile greeted everyone and won all hearts.

Banner of Light[41]

Rev. Adin Ballou, whose pilgrimage of eighty-seven years on earth terminated on the fifth of this month, commenced when quite young to work out the mission of his life, which was evidently to enlighten his fellowmen on spiritual things.

... When seventeen he preached a sermon to his young companions and at eighteen formally adopted the ministry as his profession.

From 1831 to 1842 he was pastor of a church in Mendon, where his literary and controversial labors may be spoken of as incessant, for aside from his theological warfare he assailed every species of society evil – intemperance, war, slavery, business dishonesty, etc. – with all the vigorous ability of voice and pen.

As might be expected of a man of his liberal views and honesty of purpose in his profession, Mr. Ballou availed himself of the earliest opportunities that presented themselves to investigate the claims of Modern Spiritualism. The result was that he soon received indubitable evidence that those claims rested on a sure foundation and that the veil which had long been suspended between this and the life beyond, had indeed been rent asunder, and immortality had become to mankind an assured fact.

The Christian Leader[42]

The death of Adin Ballou, at venerable years, takes from earth as white a soul as ever animated a human form ... In various ways he sought to make immediately practical the unselfish life enjoined by the Divine Master; and in pursuing this end, no personal sacrifice could be large enough to dull his ardor or shake his endeavor. His memory will ever be sacred to all who knew him or shall know of him. Every righteous cause found a champion in Adin Ballou.

He was a man of great intellectual gifts, and no theory or rule satisfied his heart that did not accord with his reason.

Mr. Ballou sought by original devices to give practicality to the doctrine of doing as we would be done by. He originated the "Christian Socialism" that was embodied in the Hopedale Community. It did not succeed, but only a man of great force and originality could have even started such a movement. It certainly had a moral success; it witnessed to the power of the doctrine of Christian brotherhood when that doctrine was lodged in an earnest and consecrated soul.

Mr. Ballou was by instinct a believer in universal salvation. His faith in the power of Divine Goodness was implicit. His logical mind could see no possibility of failure in the plan of God – in the outcome of His saving grace.

... Mr. Ballou reached venerable years. He passed from earth loved and honored by all who knew him, and literally reverenced by the few who knew him intimately. Peace be to the ashes of the sainted dead.

The Christian Register[43]

Rev. Adin Ballou was a marked figure among the men of the present generation. Though he did not hold so conspicuous a place in the church as the Rev. Hosea Ballou, still he must be regarded as a force in the religious and social life of New England. His bent, even in early years, was toward religious thinking. He worked his way out of the popular religious creed and became a devoted minister of the Universalist church. Here he soon engaged in theological discussions, taking ground against the view then taught by Thomas Whittemore and others – known as "death and glory" – and advocated the doctrine of restoration. This controversy resulted in an ecclesiastical break and he afterwards became identified, for a time, with the Unitarians. He was an earnest Abolitionist and was associated with Garrison and other pioneers of this great struggle. He was deeply impressed with the evils of intemperance and entered with his wonted vigor and enthusiasm into the efforts to remove this curse from the land and also to plead for the cause of universal peace. But the chief point of interest in his life was his organization of the Hopedale Community on the basis of Christian Socialism. Kingsley, Thomas Hughes, and Maurice were at work in London, in their efforts to apply this theory, but as Mr. Ballou was an independent thinker, he wrought out his own plan. He was fully steeped in the spirit of Christian philanthropy, and he designed to make his society a practical Christian republic on the basis of the teachings of Jesus... The leading idea of his life was to make of the community a true Christian Church – the kingdom of God on earth.

Mr. Ballou was a man of striking personal features. He had a kindly eye and a genial face... His old age was serene and beautiful. He had consecrated his life to noble ends. So when the angel voice of death[44] came, to few would the words of Jesus, whom he loved and whose spirit was the guide of his life, more fitly apply: "Inasmuch as ye have done it unto the least of these my disciples, ye have done it unto me. Enter thou into the joy of thy Lord."[45]

APPENDIX B

Funeral Sermon

BY ADIN BALLOU

Prepared as a part of the service at his own funeral

Moreover, I will endeavor that ye may be able, after my decease, to have these things always in remembrance.
2 Peter 1:15

Peter clearly anticipated his decease – the time when he must put off his mortal tabernacle and be clothed upon by his immortal one.[1] So have I, these many years. He was not so much concerned to be personally remembered after he had passed away as to have the things remembered which he had taught; for he was deeply sensible of his personal frailties and shortcomings, but knew that the doctrines, truths, and duties he had made known to men were divine. Hence the endeavor expressed in the text. And as with the Apostle in this respect, so has it been with me. With a similar endeavor I prepared this discourse while I was yet in the flesh and in the full possession of my mental powers, in order that it might be read at my funeral. It may seem strange to my relatives, friends, and former hearers that I should have done so. But I felt moved to it by influences from the spiritual world as more likely to do justice to the proper demands of the occasion than might otherwise be done. Attend then to the words I have left you.

1. I thank my Heavenly Father for the hosts of kind friends he raised up to me through a long life, besides those of my loving and precious family. He knoweth their innumerable ministrations to my comfort and welfare under all the changing vicissitudes through which I have passed – ministrations of the near and dear within the home circle – ministrations of personal associates and friends more or less intimately connected with me in social relations – and ministrations of a more casual and general nature from thousands who knew me as a public teacher. I always desired to appreciate gratefully every favor, token of affection, and expression of respect thus conferred on me. Doubtless I fell short in many instances of doing so. But I regarded them all as flowing out, through whatever channels, from the Giver of every good and perfect gift.[2] I know they are all in the book of His remembrance and that whoever bestowed them at His prompting will not go unrequited. Therefore, I need not enter into specifications.

2. Notwithstanding general good intentions toward God and my fellow-creatures, I have often sinned against both in ways of commission and omission. It has pleased God to make me very sensible of all these sins, to give me a humble, penitent, and contrite heart, and to assure me a thousand times of his forgiving grace. So of my fellow-creatures, one and all, whom in any manner I have harmed or neglected, I this day entreat their forgiveness, as they themselves implore human and divine forgiveness. And I tenderly conjure my friends

who think I have done any good in the world, not to eulogize me as a sinless man or as one inherently excellent in any respect, or as being anything at best but an instrument in the Divine Hand, acted upon and through by a measure of wisdom and goodness above my own. For this is the absolute truth to my highest and inmost consciousness. If I had done my whole duty and come up to my best ideal of Christlike excellence, I should have had no self-sufficiency to boast of, and only reason for profound thankfulness to the one infinite Fountain of All Good. But instead of such complete dutifulness, I take to myself shame for my many sins, faults, and follies. I credit all good to God and charge all evil to the frailty of the creature. This is the light in which I stand, and thus I wish to be represented by the friends who may remember me. Here I end what is strictly personal to myself.

3. I come now to the doctrines, principles, and duties which I have been privileged to preach and teach. These are "not mine, but His that sent me."[3] They are distinct from and incomparably above my mere personality. It is these that, now I am gone, I would have you keep always in remembrance. You may forget me, but do not forget them. For though I failed to work them out and illustrate them in social institutions or in the individual character of many receivers, I am sure they are from Heaven and will finally prevail. What are they? They are all both theoretical and practical. I have endeavored to preach no theological doctrine as essential to religious faith, but what legitimately required of its believers great duties of essential righteousness in strict accordance with it. And on the other hand, I have preached no duty as essential to absolute righteousness which was not dictated by some great theoretical principle plain to the understanding as a sufficient ground for it. Thus I have been careful never to divorce reason and religion, the understanding and moral sentiment, faith and practice, the head and heart.

I have preached the existence of one infinite, all-perfect God – the supreme Divine Mind – a self-existent, omnipresent Spirit and the Father of all intelligent finite spirits, whose love, wisdom, and power are illimitable, faultless, and unchangeable from and to eternity. I have not confounded this God with mindless nature, fate, or law, but held him up to the awe, confidence, and adoration of rational moral agents as perfect in all the attributes of mental personality – governing all worlds, beings, and things by intelligent will-power as the infallible, supreme, free, moral agent. And I have carefully avoided ever representing Him as willing, purposing, or treating any one of his intelligent offspring – friend or foe, good, bad, or indifferent – otherwise than as a just, benevolent, merciful, and wise Father, in time or eternity. I have, therefore, steadfastly rejected and protested against all forms of the doctrine of endless punishment, and also of every kind of vindictive or unbenevolent punishment whatsoever as morally impossible under the Divine Government – uncompromisingly affirming that all God-given law and God-administered retribution must be in perfect accordance with His supreme and inerrable Fatherhood. On this basis I have built the whole superstructure of my ethics, accepting as unquestionable the duties of piety toward God and fraternal treatment of all fellow moral agents in the universe, according to the two great commandments – love to God and the neighbor.[4] I have, therefore, always faithfully insisted on supreme love toward the All-Father with the whole heart, mind, and strength, as a duty and privilege absolutely indispensable to the highest good of each individual soul, of human society, and the universal whole of moral intelligences. And in harmony therewith, I have preached the duties and privileges of worshiping that Father "in spirit and in truth,"[5] praying to Him, thanking Him as the source of all good, trusting implicitly in His providence, reverencing His laws of order, opening the soul to His inspirations, accepting His spiritual revelations, exercising repentance toward Him for all sin, relying on His pardoning grace, being led by His spirit, ever striving to put on His moral character, and by His help to be holy as He is holy, just as He is just, merciful as He is merciful, and perfect as He is perfect. Then, under the second comprehensive commandment, I have urgently insisted on the brotherhood of man and the vast neighborhood of all moral natures, and taught that each should love every other as himself and do unto every other as he would be done unto; that love to God can be proven only by love to one another; that this love must not only be exercised toward those who love us, but toward them that hate us – toward the unthankful and evil,[6] as God's love is – toward our enemies and injurers to the extent that refrains totally from rendering evil for evil,[7] resisting evil with evil,[8] and that consummates itself by overcoming evil with good;[9] and also that whatsoever in us it be that hates, or seeks to harm, or knowingly does harm, even the worst fellow moral agent, is contrary to pure love toward either God or man. I have preached and insisted on this perfect righteousness toward God and fellow moral agents, not only as an indispensable duty but as the grandest privilege and crowning glory of the holiest souls.

I have steadfastly preached Jesus Christ and His gospel as set forth in the scriptures of the New Testament – not according to the scholastic theology of the degenerate Church – as the highest and most authoritative revelation of the All-Father's nature, will, law of order, grace, truth, regenerating dispensation, and purposed destiny of the human race. In so doing, I have placed Jesus of Nazareth where He Himself claimed to have been placed by the Father, neither below nor above, ordained before the foundation of the human world,[10] predictively promised, through the best of ancient prophets, as the Christ-man, born in the fullness of time,[11] plenarily anointed with the Father's holy communicable spirit for the accomplishment of His mission, and rendered preeminently the Son of God and Savior of the world. I have held Him up as the model man, the moral and spiritual head of the human race, saying and doing nothing of His mere selfhood, in virtue of His own inherent human attributes, but all officially as the chosen organ of God, in virtue of the indwelling Spirit of the Father, constantly inspiring and directing Him. Therefore I have insisted that He has shown us the Father's moral perfections, His true character, will, law, and purposes; so that "God was in Him reconciling the world to Himself";[12] to which end he said, did, and suffered all that distinguished Him as the Christ, and entered into the heavenly existence where He will reign in glory until "God shall be all in all."[13]

Thus placing Jesus Christ where he claimed that the Father placed Him, I ascribe to Him a name and authority above every other name, unto which every creature in heaven, earth and the spirit world must bow and "every tongue confess that He is Lord to the glory of God the Father."[14] I have not held him up as an ordinary man. Nor as one among many other Christly men, speaking and acting from His own partially developed intuitions and aspirations, and so, at best, a fallible religious teacher, sometimes right and sometimes wrong; but as invested by the Father with infallible spiritual and moral authority over human souls in this world and the next, during his mediatorial reign. I have not ranked Him with Plato, Pythagoras, Socrates, Confucius, or any of the ancient sages, or with any of the famous philosophers, poets, scientists, and literati of later times, firmly believing that by divine endowment, He outranks all other human beings. With me His thoughts were God's thoughts, His will God's will, His wisdom God's wisdom, His controlling spirit God's spirit, His word God's word, His righteousness God's righteousness, His example

God's example, and His authority God's authority, to be reverenced and conformed to accordingly.

In preaching concerning the veneration due to the scriptures of the Old and New Testaments, I have placed them above all other human writings as intrinsically more divinely inspired and religiously excellent than any others, but I have not claimed for them anything diviner than they purport to claim for themselves on a fair interpretation. I have not put them on a level of superhuman perfection, nor confounded their higher testimonies with their evidently lower and ordinary ones, nor made the Old Testament co-equal with the New, nor construed their mere letter and verbalism to be the word of God, but have insisted that they ought to be interpreted and understood in strict accordance with their essential spirit and highest fundamental principles – never otherwise. No mere literalism of sound or sense, no mere figurative words, phrases, or texts, have been held up by me as divine truth against declared fundamental objects, principles, and spiritual essentials, clearly ascertainable. On this ground I have, for myself, studied, understood, and expounded the scriptures of both Testaments in respect to faith and practice, never sacrificing the spirit to the letter, nor a great principle of truth and duty to the mere literal phraseology of a text. Consequently, I have carefully avoided placing Moses above Christ, or the patriarchs and prophets above His chosen apostles, or the law above the gospel, or a threatening against a promise, or a lower form of righteousness against a higher, or retribution against a destined end, or temporarily permitted evil against its final overrulement for good, or a dispensation of pain against an eternity of blessedness. After this method, I have searched, understood, and explained the scriptures. After this method I have ascertained to my satisfaction who and what Jesus Christ claimed to be, what His mission and authority really were, what He taught as the highest truth and righteousness, how He exemplified that truth and righteousness in the flesh, and how He still more gloriously exemplifies them in the heavens. My theology, piety, and ethics – my entire religion – have thus been determined, defined, preached, and established harmoniously.

I have not belonged to the indefinite, creedless school of religionists, always seeking and never finding the truth, groping my way through a maze of uncertainties and doubtful speculations, with unsettled convictions about this world and the future world. I have indeed been a free inquirer, but not a schooled doubter, on the gravest questions of religious concern. I have tried not to be a self-sufficient, traditional Pharisee on the one hand, nor on the other, a self-sufficient Sadducee, too learned and proud to feel the force of evidence in support of immortality or the existence of angels and manifestable spirits. I was and am a rational Christian Spiritualist, accepting all the reliably proven spiritual phenomena of ancient and modern times as belonging to one continuous succession of manifestations. But I have never embraced any form of spiritualism that ignored or belittled Christ or reduced Him to the grade of a mere medium for the communication of departed spirits, nor allowed myself to trust to spirit-mediums beyond good evidence of their reliability, nor to accept the teachings of the departed as infallible, nor to receive any so-called spiritual philosophy which conflicted with or set at nought the teachings, example, and spirit of Christ. On the contrary, I held it my duty, and also my privilege, to "try the spirits"[15] out of the flesh as well as those still in it, whether they were of God or mere self-deifiers. For I had no doubt that the spirit spheres are peopled with good and evil angels, with good, bad, and indifferent departed human beings corresponding to those that inhabit the realm of flesh and blood.

You know, too, that I have not been any more of an indefinitist in ethics than in theology. Non-organizationism and non-committallism were never agreeable to my reason, conscience, or taste. Having satisfied myself as to the great truths of religious faith and the great duties of practical righteousness, I declared them and bound myself to them by unmistakable pledges. I could not preach the Fatherhood of God and go on just as if He might sometime, somewhere, treat His creatures like a cruel despot; nor as if mankind might excusably treat Him with habitual filial contempt, as millions do. I could not preach the brotherhood of man and all moral agents, and then teach them to kill, oppress, wrong, and trample one another under foot, as if only beasts. I could not apologize for chattel slavery, war, and the various customs of general society whereby the strong, cunning, and favored classes flourish at the expense of their underlings. I could not preach that mankind were immortal spirits, all governed by their Heavenly Father by law, justly and graciously, as destined to immortal blessedness; and then look on their cruelty to each other, their intemperance, licentiousness, and all manner of debasing practices with indifference, with tacit fellowship, and no confrontment of reproof and counter-example. I could but point out their sins, call them to repentance, and above all show them by my own practice the right way – yea, the most excellent way.[16] And this I must do whether they would bear or forbear,[17] whether they would heed my counsel and example, or rush like the war-horse into the battle.

And I call you to record this day, as you look for the last time on my earthly tabernacle[18] from which I have ascended, that these things have been my chief concern during the major portion of my long life. The trumpet of my testimony has given no uncertain sound, either in precept or example. When the cause of total abstinence from intoxicating beverages came up for serious consideration, did I hide myself from responsibility or burrow among the sophistries of apology, non-action, and noncommittalism? Or was I in the front of the battle? And ever since, where have I stood but on the safe ground of unswerving fidelity to my pledge? If I have withheld my hand from attempting to drive others into temperance by penal laws, nevertheless no one mistook which way my precept and example besought him to go. So in the anti-tobacco reform, have the old or the young mistaken my position? Have they seen me waver in my theoretical or practical testimony? If I refrained from words, did anyone ever suspect my course?

When the antislavery agitation summoned every inhabitant of the land to protest against that horrible abomination, I could do no otherwise than respond. Yea; though all but one in a thousand were so drugged with pro-slavery as to be utterly indifferent to the wails of the downtrodden, or so maddened against the Abolitionists as to jeopardize their very lives by mobocratic outrages. The millions in bondage were no less my brethren and sisters than their oppressors. Truth was truth, justice was justice, and I could not refrain from uncompromising denunciation of such utter wrong inflicted by the strong against the weak. So I took my stand with the few against the many in those dark days.

The bloody theme of war loomed up for consideration, and I was summoned by the voice of God to decide whether I would stand for or against it. I saw that it was a vast system of manslaughter, even in its most excusable form – unfraternal, savage, and barbarous; anti-Christian, irrational, and full of monstrous evils. I saw that it was based on the assumed rightfulness of resisting evil with evil and overcoming deadly force with deadly force, which Christ both by precept and example unqualifiedly forbade His disciples to do, even toward their worst enemies. He had laid His great regenerative axe at the root of this upas-tree,[19] and it must be destroyed, trunk and branches. I was fully convinced of this and took my stand accordingly. Beginning where the Son of God did, I left no room for compromise with the least of its rootlets or sprigs. Starting from the divine fundamental principle of pure, universal good will, absolute love, I felt bound to go with that principle wherever it carried me, for all that it dictated, against all that it condemned. I did not allow myself to be sophisticated into any excuses for defensive war or resorts to so-called justifiable deadly force in extreme cases, but committed myself to total abstinence from all war, preparations for war, glorifications of war, commemorations of war, and organic action involving any resorts whatsoever to deadly force against my fellow-men. I would neither be an officer nor private in any warlike organization, nor in any social, political, religious, or governmental organization by which I made myself responsible for the infliction of death or injurious force on any human being. I would neither fight, vote, pray for, nor give any approval of any custom, practice, or act which contravened the law of perfect love toward God, toward my fellow moral agents, or the universal highest good. I would have no deadly weapon on my person or in my habitation, and held all resorts to their use (except for the destruction of animal life in proper cases) to be a hateful abomination. Thus I was an unmistakable peace man from the crown of my head to the soles of my feet. And I died without a doubt of my Christlikeness in these respects, yea, without a doubt that all men must come up to this plane of righteousness, in order to perfect safety and blessedness.

In respect to worldly property, power, and distinction, I long ago learned of Christ and became fully convinced that they ought to be entirely subordinate to the law of pure fraternal good will, perfect love toward God and fellow moral agents; that property should neither be acquired, used, nor expended contrary to the Golden Rule, nor to the degradation, neglect, or unhappiness of any human being; that no one should consume for personal or family gratification, more than would be his equitable share in well-ordered human society, whilst his surplus beyond this should be devoted in some rational way to the relief, elevation, and welfare of his needy fellow-creatures; that riches and poverty are both great evils which ought to be done away with by the voluntary concurrence of all right minds, and that until this shall be accomplished property will be grossly abused, to the misery of the human race. I learned also that all power and preeminence of one human being over another, however rightful or justifiable, ought to be exercised and manifested in conscientious conformity to Christ's unequivocal injunction, "He that is greatest among you, let him be as the younger, and he that is chief as He that doth serve"[20] – which exactly reverses the carnal ambition of superiors in the world, who aggrandize themselves more and more at the expense of their inferiors and exalt themselves to their degradation. Not so Christ himself; not so His true followers; and not so ought it ever to be among human beings. The law of perfect love imperatively requires that the more talented, or wise, or rich, or gifted in any respect one is, so much the greater is his obligation to serve and help the less favored. And until this law is voluntarily and conscientiously obeyed, the strong will continue to take advantage of the weak, and superiors to prey on their inferiors to an abhorrent extent.

I have faithfully preached the ethics of this doctrine and no less faithfully exemplified it in my practice. I have never acquired, used, or consumed property contrary to the Golden Rule. I have never exacted a high price for my services. I have never made merchandise of the gospel, nor received anything for my ministrations but what was voluntarily contributed by those who enjoyed them. I have sued no man at the law to obtain my dues. I have occupied no finer house, kept no better equipage, eaten no costlier food, worn no richer clothing, nor consumed any more for the gratification of myself and family than would be my equitable share with all others in a well-ordered state of society. Nor in any respect wherein I was superior to others or moved as a leader, have I ever exacted deference, or assumed airs of importance, or taxed others to support my dignity, or shirked hard labors of body or mind for the common good; but have willingly served rather than be served. What I did to found and establish a fraternal order of society in Hopedale, in which these sublime virtues might be illustrated, but in which I succeeded so poorly, I need not remind you. My aspirations, convictions, and principles never changed in respect to the fraternalization of the social conditions of men. I girdled them firmly about my heart even unto death, and they live in my bosom as a spirit forevermore. They will yet be realized in their highest excellence on earth by devoted disciples who will rejoice in the sacrifices necessary to insure their blessings to suffering millions. The last, best labors of my head and pen have done all in my power to prepare the way for this grand Social Reform, and my small pecuniary savings have been consecrated to its promotion. I have left the world under a very strong assurance from Heaven that a regenerate Christlike form of the Church will ere long be developed to prosecute this work, and now leave you a solemn prophecy that the coming century will witness a glorious practical consummation of the cardinal principles in behalf of which God made it my high privilege to bear testimony.

Having thus indicated the principal things which I desire you to have in remembrance, and for which I wish to be personally remembered by all my survivors, I now draw to a close. In doing so, I sincerely repeat that I claim no merit or credit for any of the truth and good illustrated through my instrumentality. God has inspired and wrought it through me. I have at best done merely my indispensable duty, and am but an unprofitable servant[21] with no reasons for boasting, though unspeakable ones for gratitude to the Most High Father. On the other hand, I take shame and humiliation to myself for all my shortcomings. I am profoundly sensible of my unworthiness. Though my sins have mainly sprung from passional frailty, aberration of temper, misdirected appetites, and weak judgment, they have filled me with pungent sorrow and prostrated me in the dust of contrition before the throne of my Heavenly Father. I have never confirmed or excused myself in evil in His presence, but constantly confessed that His law was holy and just and good, and thanked Him for all His faithful rebukes. And he has graciously responded to all my penitent confessions, "Whom I love I correct"; "Go, and sin no more."[22]

I wish it also to be remembered and understood that while I have strictly and uncompromisingly claimed that the Christ-plane of truth and righteousness on which I planted myself was absolutely the highest in the moral universe, I have never denied that there was more or less truth and righteousness on lower moral planes, nor taught that those who occupied those lower planes were void of conscientiousness and worth in acting up to their light. I have tried to judge all by their own acknowledged moral standard, or left them to the infallible judgment of the All-perfect God. Nor have I ever allowed myself to withhold due credit for right feelings, intentions, or conduct in any human being, whatever his general moral character, knowing that on every moral level there are good, better, and best; or contrariwise, bad, worse, and worst. Thus I have humbly endeavored, without sacrifice of truth, to be just and charitable to all mankind, always considering the force of circumstances and making the best I could even of the worst. My prayer, in the language of the great practical poet, has been

> Teach me to feel another's woe,
> To hide the faults I see;
> The mercy I to others show.
> That mercy show to me.[23]

And now farewell to you all; to the nearest and dearest of kin that sit as mourners today; to my religious and sympathizing friends; and to all of every relationship and class who have known me during my long earthly life. I have "finished my course" and "the ministry which I received of the Lord Jesus, to testify the gospel of the grace of God."[24] I have commended my spirit[25] to the disposal of infinite love and wisdom, and am at rest in my appropriate mansion of the All-Father's vast house.[26] I shall meet you again in due time on the immortal shore.[27] Until then, I invoke on you all the richest benedictions of Heaven, and thenceforth will invoke them on you forevermore.

APPENDIX C

The Adin Ballou Lectureship of Practical Christian Sociology

It was the long-cherished desire of Mr. Ballou that whatever property he might be in possession of at the time of his decease should be used to promote the same philanthropic and noble objects to the attainment of which the crowning aspirations and efforts of his life had been directed. That desire was embodied in the several clauses of his *Last Will and Testament,* and with it detailed requisitions in regard to the ways and means of accomplishing the end it had in view. After providing for the payment of funeral expenses and all just claims against his estate, and making a few private bequests of inconsiderable amount, the testator ordered that there be set apart, as a Publication Fund, a sum sufficient for printing certain specified volumes already prepared or to be prepared by him and to be left in manuscript, together with one or more others composed of selections from his miscellaneous writings, if his executors deemed it expedient, and for distributing the same, free of expense, to theological schools, libraries, and educational institutions, where they would be accessible to those of coming generations desirous of learning how to make the world better; and that the residue be held in trust until a church should be organized upon the ethical and religious basis set forth in his treatises on Primitive Christianity, and should have entered practically upon the work of reconstructing the existing social system along the lines presented in the same series of volumes – a consummation which he was confident would be reached within fifty years – when it should be paid, with all its accumulations, in full and without restriction, to such church, to be used at its discretion in carrying its purposes and plans into effect.

The legally appointed administrators of the estate, deeming the contemplated achievement exceedingly problematical, especially within the period stated, and fearing that the money appropriated to its aid would be frittered away and lost, so far as the ends proposed were concerned, petitioned the court in authority to set aside the clause of the will relating to this particular matter and issue a decree assigning the amount of property involved to the only surviving heir thereto, Mrs. Abbie B. Heywood, wife of Rev. William S. Heywood of Sterling, Massachusetts, to be used or expended as her best judgment might dictate. The petition received favorable consideration and an order was issued accordingly. Whereupon Mrs. Heywood, conjointly with her husband, neither of whom wished to gain any personal advantage or profit from the decision of the court, but rather to employ the means thus put at their disposal for purposes in harmony with the general spirit and design of the Will, began to institute inquiries in respect to some method or agency by which that result could be accomplished. Numerous schemes were suggested and considered with conscientious deliberation, but the one which commended itself most unqualifiedly to the judgment and moral sense of those immediately concerned, and which secured their final acceptance, was that indicated in the following copy of a communication, the meaning and purpose of which are expressed with so much clearness and precision that they require no comment or elucidation.

To the President and Trustees of the Meadville Theological School

GENTLEMEN: Having come into possession of what may remain of the estate of my revered father, Rev. Adin Ballou, late of Hopedale, Massachusetts, deceased, when the several obligations specifically mentioned in his Last Will and Testament have been fully met and cancelled, I desire in grateful honor of his name and memory to devote the same, amounting to about sixteen thousand dollars ($16,000) now in hand, to the promotion of those great objects of Christian beneficence and philanthropy in which he was deeply interested when upon the earth, and to the advancement and realization of which he consecrated the best energies and efforts of his long and active life. After careful and mature deliberation upon various means and methods of accomplishing the end in view, I have at length decided upon the plan embodied in the following proposition, which I am pleased to submit to you for consideration and for such action on your part as your best judgment may dictate, to wit:

I propose to give to the Institution of which you have charge or to its properly authorized representatives, the aforesaid sum of sixteen thousand dollars ($16,000), to be held in trust as a permanent fund for the establishment and maintenance of a department of instruction therein to be called *The Adin Ballou Lectureship of Practical Christian Sociology*. The purpose of this offer is to secure the annual delivery of a course of lectures, by the most satisfactory talent that can be obtained, upon the social aspects of the religion of Christ and the consequent duty and importance of applying the principles and spirit of that religion to the intercourse of man with man, in all the actions and relations of life. In these lectures special attention shall be paid to such subjects, for example, as "The Barbarism of War" and the consequent "Claims of the Cause of Peace"; "The Extinction of the Evils of Intemperance"; "The Proper Relation of the Sexes," including "The True Doctrine of Marriage and Divorce"; "The Higher Education and Complete Enfranchisement of Woman"; "The Adjustment and Harmonization of the Relation between Capital and Labor"; "The Prevention of and Remedy for Poverty"; "The Care and Reformation of Criminals"; "The Amelioration and Improvement of the Condition of the Unfortunate and Perishing Classes"; including in their full range all topics calculated to enhance the well-being and happiness of mankind and to fashion human society after the Christian ideal of the kingdom of heaven on earth. These lectures, or such of them as shall be deemed most valuable by the president and board of instruction, shall be published from time to time and sent, free of expense, to other theological schools and to leading educational institutions, libraries, etc., throughout the land, to the end that their usefulness may be extended as far and wide as possible.

It is furthermore my express wish and desire that the contemplated lectureship shall be based upon the distinct and positive recognition of the eternal excellency of the religion of Christ in its fundamental truth and essential spirit, as taught and exemplified in the scriptures of the New Testament and as interpreted by the advancing intelligence of mankind, and that its administration shall be absolutely impartial and free, regardless alike of denominational peculiarities and limitations, and of all artificial distinctions of race, sex, or nationality.

This offer is made with the full expectation and assurance that, if accepted, the endowment involved will be held sacred to the purposes for which it is designed, and in the earnest hope that the work of human improvement and social regeneration, so dear to the heart of my beloved father, will be advanced by the instrumentality it provides for and ordains, and that his name and influence for good in the world may be conserved and perpetuated unto many generations.

Sincerely and respectfully yours,
ABBIE B. HEYWOOD

Heartily concurring in the above proposition,
I indicate the same over my own proper signature.

WILLIAM S. HEYWOOD

This proposition was formally accepted by the Trustees of the Meadville school at a meeting held soon after it was received, January 31, 1891, when a resolution was passed, thanking the donor for her generous gift and assuring her "that the objects which the said donation is intended to promote meet with the cordial approval of the Board as being in harmony with the work of the school." Three months later the money was paid into the treasury of the institution and steps were immediately taken to provide means of improving the opportunity thus opened to its students during the then coming academic year. Those steps proved effectual, and the lectureship was inaugurated and started out on its mission of usefulness the following winter. Its work to this date (1896) has been highly satisfactory and gratifying to its founder, so far as she has been made acquainted with it, as it seems to be with others interested in the principles and purposes it was designed to foster and carry forward in the world. Numerous testimonials from students, alumni, and members of the faculty of the school have been received, assuring her of the great good already done through its instrumentality and of the rich promise of good it gives for the days and years to come; leading her to believe and feel that her action in regard to the money assigned her was timely and judicious; that the cause of Practical Christian truth and righteousness is to be permanently subserved thereby; and that the name and memory of her father are to be correspondingly preserved and honored with the advancing years of time.

The first course of lectures upon the foundation thus established was given during the winter of 1892-93 by Rev. Washington Gladden, D.D.[1] of Columbus, Ohio, a most profound, conscientious, and reverent student of the problems that enter into the organization and improvement of human society. His addresses were subsequently published by Houghton, Mifflin & Co., Boston, under the somewhat enigmatical title, "Tools and the Man," which had a wide circulation, five hundred copies of it having been distributed by the authorities at Meadville, agreeably to the specifications of the communication quoted above.

The principal course for the year 1893-94, consisting of seven lectures, was delivered by Rev. Francis G. Peabody, D.D.[2] Plummer professor of Christian morals in the Harvard Divinity School, which was supplemented by two lectures from Rev. Edward E. Hale, D.D.[3] of Boston. The course for 1894-95 was by Rev. E. B. Andrews, D.D.[4] President of Brown University, and consisted of ten lectures, of which five were given in the autumn of the first-named year and five the following spring.

Rev. Lyman Abbot, D.D.[5] the widely known pastor of Plymouth Church, Brooklyn, New York, and editor of the *Outlook,* gave the fourth course, during the scholastic year 1895-96. His lectures, which were delivered extemporaneously, have been written out in an amplified form, and, with some correlative matter, have been embodied in a volume of 370 pages entitled, "Christianity and Social Problems," just issued from the press of

Houghton, Mifflin & Co. This also will be in part circulated, as was the work of Dr. Gladden, in accordance with the conditions upon which the lectureship was established.

The lectures for the current year, 1896-97, it is expected, will be by Rev. Samuel W. Dike, LL.D.[6] upon "The Family"; by Rev. John Graham Brooks[7] on "The Organization of Charity"; and by Benjamin Trueblood, LL.D,[8] secretary of the American Peace Society, upon "International Arbitration."

APPENDIX D

Lucy Hunt Ballou

This estimable woman, the second wife of the subject of the narrative contained in this volume and for more than sixty years his household companion and helper in manifold ways, belonged to one of the oldest and most substantial of New England families, and possessed in large measure those sterling qualities of mind, heart, and character which have distinguished the New England name from the beginning and clothed it with luster and renown throughout the civilized world. Her paternal immigrant ancestor was William Hunt, a native of the mother country, born about 1605, who, under the leadership of the celebrated Rev. Peter Bulkeley, came to these shores in 1637 with Capt. Simon Willard, the Wheelers, and other notable men,[1] and assisted in founding the historic town of Concord, Massachusetts. He was made freeman in 1641, and is represented as an upright, God-fearing man, a good citizen, earnestly devoted to the principles of the Puritan faith, exemplary in the discharge of his domestic duties, training up his children "in the nurture and admonition of the Lord."[2] From him, in the line of Isaac of Concord, Isaac of Sudbury, Abidah of Holliston, and Daniel of Holliston and Milford, descended Pearley of Milford, the father of the subject of this sketch. He was an enterprising merchant and leading citizen of the town, "a man of superior natural abilities, aptitudes, and qualifications to make a respectable mark in society." He was a Democrat in politics, and in religious faith a Universalist. For twenty-one years he held the office of postmaster, and that of justice of the peace during all the later part of his life. Much interested in public education, he was repeatedly chosen a member of the school committee, serving with skill and efficiency. "He lived beloved and esteemed in domestic and social circles for his kindness, urbanity, generosity, hospitality, and kindred virtues, and died in honor and peace."[3]

Lucy Hunt was the daughter of Pearley Hunt, Esq., and his wife, Chloe (Albee) Hunt, and was born October 31, 1810. She inherited from her parents good intellectual capabilities and a personality marked by unusual independence of opinion and action, great power of will, and resolute perseverance in whatever she undertook to execute. In her childhood and youth she manifested a gentle nature and a disposition characterized by thoughtfulness, cheerfulness, kindness, and amiability. These qualities not only made her an agreeable associate and companion, gaining for her a large circle of devoted friends as she grew up to womanhood, but rendered her susceptible to those moral and spiritual influences and tuitions which afterward brought into prominence the best that was in her and nurtured those attributes and graces of character which crowned and glorified her maturer life. An apt and diligent scholar, she profited exceedingly by the educational opportunities accessible to her in her native town, meager and poor indeed compared with what are now offered there, and by a brief term of instruction at a higher institution of learning in Providence, Rhode Island, from which, however, she was unexpectedly summoned home to minister at the bedside of Mr. Ballou, her future husband, who had been stricken down with a well-nigh fatal illness, and to whom she was already affianced, as narrated in its proper place in the body of this work. A few months after his recovery, on the third of March, 1830, they were married, she being not far advanced in the twentieth year of her age. But though so young, she was yet unusually mature, both in womanly qualities and executive ability which, brought, it would seem, prematurely into requisition, vindicated themselves most fully by the wisdom, tact, and efficiency with which she met the responsibilities and discharged the duties of wife and mother at the very outset, as she did thenceforward to the end of her mortal pilgrimage. By her conscientious, painstaking fidelity in the performance of the tasks imposed upon her in the home, which were increased in number and in burdensomeness for some years by reason of the circumstances and exactions incident to her husband's calling and career, she so overtaxed her energies that they at length gave way in part, seriously impairing her health and power of endurance and causing her to suffer a sort of semi-invalidism during the remainder of her earthly days. Yet by a constant, watchful care of herself and the prudent use of the resources left to her, she was able in her quiet, leisurely way to bring more to pass than many with much greater strength and vitality than she, attending to the cares and labors of the household and performing other duties of a various nature, with such occasional help as could easily be called in and only a single interruption of a few weeks, through a life lengthened out far beyond the Psalmist's allotted period of three score years and ten.

Nor was she competent and efficient in the strictly domestic concerns of the household alone. Her clear-seeing intellect, practical good sense, and literary accomplishments enabled her to render substantial aid in many ways to her husband in the varied phases of the work to which he devoted his life. She assisted him greatly in his labors as editor and author, especially in his later years, and by her suggestion, counsel, and criticism contributed largely to the success of those labors. Moreover, she did much to cheer and strengthen him in the midst of the trials and disappointments which at times, as he repeatedly confessed, almost overwhelmed him, and to encourage him to continued efforts for the enlightenment, uplifting, and redemption of mankind. Her faith in the eternal verities – in God and immortality – was unwaveringly sure and steadfast and served to reinvigorate and stimulate his when, for any cause, it grew faint within him. For many of the last years of her life, it was her great care, as it was her joy also, to do for him and make him comfortable and happy, and her prayer was that she might live to minister to him to the very last – to smooth his dying pillow, to close his eyes in the sleep that knows no waking here below, and to see his physical frame properly prepared for its sepulture and laid away tenderly in the family burial lot which they had planned together and fitted up as the final resting-place of all that was mortal of themselves and of those they held most dear.

That prayer was graciously answered; and when it was answered she was ready to follow on and be forever with him and all the loved ones gone before, in some higher mansion of the Father's house towards which for many years their united thought and heart had been turned with unfailing, triumphant hope and trust. The two were not long separated. She survived him a year and two days only, passing peacefully away after a two weeks' illness on the seventh of August, 1891, at the age of 80 years, 9 months, and 8 days.

Mrs. Ballou was a most hearty and earnest sympathizer with her husband in all his religious convictions, principles, and ideas, as she was in his manifold labors of philanthropy and reform. Her conceptions of duty toward God included love and good will to men, which she exemplified in a disposition to help and bless them in all possible ways, according to her ability. Many were they in her immediate neighborhood who shared her kindness and her benefactions, and her ear and hand were ever open to the appeals of the poor, needy, suffering sons and daughters of men. All good causes enlisted her interest and received her cordial encouragement and support – the cause of peace being especially near to her heart, as attested by repeated contributions to its treasury while she lived, and by a bequest of two thousand dollars to the Universal Peace Union of Philadelphia, of which that eminent philanthropist, Alfred H. Love,[4] is president, provided for in her Last Will and Testament. She was most emphatically.

> One who, calm and true,
> Life's highest purpose understood;
> And like the Blessed Master, knew
> The joy of doing good.[5]

To the high character, marked ability, effective service, and genuine worth of his household companion and helpmeet for so many years, Mr. Ballou himself pays appreciative and grateful tribute in his *History and Genealogy of the Ballous in America*, as follows:

> In my marriage to my present wife, who has grown old in my companionship, I have been greatly blessed. Solomon well said, "A prudent wife is from the Lord."[6] Mine is such – a model of discretion, domestic order, executive industry; a constant minister of good under all circumstances in her family and neighborhood; an intelligent counselor in all emergencies, and a sympathetic companion in all high principles and endeavors. Though not robust in health and physical strength, she excels in actual accomplishment through mental judgment and persistent will-power ... We have shared our joys, sorrows, labors, and trials together for more than fifty-seven years. We are now nearing their completion and preparing for our summons to the higher life.

The *Milford Journal*, in noticing the death of Mrs. Ballou, bore the following testimony concerning her:

> Mrs. Ballou, throughout her entire life, admirably cooperated with her husband in all his work, ardently supplementing his efforts to promote the social and religious growth of his fellow beings. It is not too much to say that she was a great help to him; she was most loyal and unwavering. Her life was always kindly and by those to whom she was best known she was most highly esteemed. Many will regret her departure as the cessation of a gentle, lovable, charitable influence from their visible midst.

Rev. Lewis G. Wilson, the pastor of the Hopedale parish, who knew her well in her later years, prepared a brief obituary of her for the *Christian Register*, in which he most appropriately and expressively says:

> Her life was beautiful and saintly. Her nature was an earnest of the pure devotion and perfect faith of an exalted humanity. As the needle to the star, so was her spirit to the Father. In her ways as simple and unpretentious as a child, in her belief as sure and steadfast as an apostle, and in her practical piety an example for all who knew her. For more than sixty years she entered deeply into all the great spiritual aspirations and achievements of her husband, and by a well-nigh infallible intuition, sympathized and counseled with him in the perplexing emergencies of his remarkable life. Almost unconsciously to herself, she became an influence to inspire love and peace, to engender the sense of spiritual serenity,

and to yield an inestimable blessing to the community in which she lived. Her mission, so well accomplished, cannot fail to be the source of pure motives, noble efforts, and blessed memories for many years to come.

> The blessing of thy presence
> And all thy tender care
> Was like the peaceful sunlight
> That enters everywhere.
>
> It cheered us in our sorrow,
> And strength of soul it gave;
> It lifted high the spirit
> Above life's troubled wave.
>
> O, blessed spirit, visit
> And teach us as of yore –
> A presence be to guide us
> Where thou has gone before.

APPENDIX E

Works of Adin Ballou

Items marked with an asterisk (*) are available on Google Books, Internet Archive, or other online sources. The Friends of Adin Ballou web site (www.adinballou.org) includes a bibliography with links to online versions of many of Ballou's works.

BOOKS

* *Christian Non-Resistance, in all its important bearings: illustrated and defended.* Philadelphia: J. M. M'Kim, 1846.

    Reprint of 1846 edition. London: Charles Gilpin, 1848.

    Christian Non-Resistance illustrated and defended. London: Peace Society, 1878.

    Christian Non-Resistance, in all its important bearings. Philadelphia: Universal Peace Union, 1910.

    Reprint of 1910 edition, with an introduction by Larry Gara. New York: Da Capo Press, 1970. Includes "A discourse on Christian non-resistance in extreme cases" (1860) and "Christian non-resistance defended against Rev. Henry Ward Beecher" (1862).

    Christian Non-Resistance. With a foreword by Michael D. True and introduction by Lynn Gordon Hughes. Providence: Blackstone Editions, 2003. Includes "Christian non-resistance in extreme cases" (1860).

* *The Hopedale collection of hymns and songs: for the use of Practical Christians.* Hopedale: Hopedale Press, 1849.

* *An exposition of views respecting the principal facts, causes, and peculiarities involved in Spirit Manifestations.* Boston: Bela Marsh, 1852.

    Reprint of 1852 edition, with an introduction by G. W. Stone. London: H. Baillière, 1852.

    [2nd edition] *An exposition of views respecting the principal facts, causes, and peculiarities involved in spirit manifestations: together with interesting phenomenal statements and communications.* Boston: Bela Marsh, 1853.

    Reprint of 1853 edition. Liverpool: Edward Howell, 1853.

    Reprint of 1853 edition, with an introduction by R. A. Gilbert. London: Routledge, 2000.

* *Memoir of Adin Augustus Ballou.* Hopedale: Hopedale Press, 1853.

APPENDIX E

* *Practical Christian Socialism: a conversational exposition of the true system of human society; in three parts: I. Fundamental principles. II. Constitutional polity. III. Superiority to other systems.* Hopedale, A. Ballou; New York, Fowler & Wells, 1854.

    Reprint. New York: AMS Press, 1974.

    [Abridged edition] *Practical Christianity: An epitome of Practical Christian Socialism.* Edited and arranged by Lynn Gordon Hughes. Providence: Blackstone Editions, 2002.

* *Monitorial Guide: for the use of inductive conferences, communities, etc. etc., in the practical Christian republic; recommending suggestively various forms of proceeding, service and exercise, promotive of religious and mental culture.* Hopedale: Spiritual Reformer Office, 1862.

* *Primitive Christianity and its corruptions ... discourses delivered in Hopedale, Mass. Vol. 1: Department of theological doctrines.* Boston: Universalist Publishing House, 1870.

* *History of the town of Milford, Worcester County, Massachusetts, from its first settlement to 1881; in two parts: Part I. Strictly historical. Part II. Biographico-genealogical register.* Boston: Rand, Avery, & Co., 1882.

    Reprint. Salem, MA: Higginson Book Co., 1988.

* *An elaborate history and genealogy of the Ballous in America.* Providence: A. Ballou, L. W. Ballou, 1888.

    History and genealogy of the Ballous in America. Reprint. Evansville, IN: Unigraphic Inc., 1981.

    Reprint. Boston: New England Historic Genealogical Society, 1998.

* *Autobiography of Adin Ballou, 1803-1890: Containing an elaborate record and narrative of his life from infancy to old age.* Completed and edited by William S. Heywood. Lowell, MA: Vox Populi Press, 1896.

    Reprint. Philadelphia: Porcupine Press, 1975.

    Autobiography of Adin Ballou: annotated edition. Introduction and notes by Lynn Gordon Hughes and Peter Hughes. Providence: Blackstone Editions, 2016.

* *History of the Hopedale Community, from its inception to its virtual submergence in the Hopedale Parish.* Edited by William S. Heywood. Lowell, MA: Vox Populi Press, 1897.

    Reprint. Philadelphia: Porcupine Press, 1972.

    Reprint. New York: AMS Press, 1974.

    History of the Hopedale Community: annotated edition. Foreword and notes by Lynn Gordon Hughes. Providence: Blackstone Editions, 2010.

* *Primitive Christianity and its corruptions ... discourses delivered in Hopedale, Mass. Vol. 2: Department of personal righteousness.* Edited by William S. Heywood. Lowell, MA: Vox Populi Press, 1899.

* *Primitive Christianity and its corruptions ... discourses delivered in Hopedale, Mass. Vol. 3: Department of ecclesiastical polity.* Edited by William S. Heywood. Lowell, MA: Vox Populi Press, 1900.

SERMONS, TRACTS, AND OTHER SHORT WORKS

* *Review of a lecture sermon, delivered in the Second Universalist Meeting-House, in Boston: on the evening of the third sabbath in January, 1820, by Hosea Ballou.* Providence: Miller and Hutchens, 1821. 39 pp.

* *The furious priest reproved: a letter to the Reverend Abial Fisher, of Bellingham, Mass.: relative to his conduct, at the meetinghouse, in said town, on the afternoon of the third sabbath in May, A.D. 1823.* Providence: John Miller, 1823. 12 pp.

* *An oration, delivered July 4th, A.D. 1827, before the Republican citizens of Milford, and the neighbouring towns, at the Universalist Meeting House, in said Milford.* Boston: True & Greene, 1827. 35 pp.

* *The inestimable value of souls: a sermon, delivered before the Universalist Society in Medway, (Mass.) May, 1830.* Boston: The Trumpet Office, 1830. 23 pp.

An oration delivered before the citizens of Blackstone village and its vicinity, Mendon, Mass. July 5, A.D. 1830. Providence: Cranston & Knowles, 1830. 18 pp.

An argument on punishment and forgiveness and the doctrines of penalty and pardon [argument between Revs. Adin Ballou and Barton Ballou]. Providence: H. H. Brown, 1832. 32 pp.

* *Report of a public discussion between the Revs. Adin Ballou, and Daniel D. Smith: on the question, "Do the Holy Scriptures teach the doctrine, that men will be punished and rewarded subsequently to this life, or after death, for the deeds done in this life?"* Mendon: Press of the Independent Messenger, 1834.

* *A discourse on the subject of American slavery: delivered in the First Congregational meeting house, in Mendon, Mass., July 4, 1837.* Boston: I. Knapp, 1837. 88 pp.

The touchstone, exhibiting Universalism and Restorationism as they are, moral contraries. Providence, 1837. 16 pp.

* *Non-resistance in relation to human governments* [Remarks of Adin Ballou at the first annual meeting of the Non-resistance Society, held in Boston, Sept. 25, 1839]. Boston: Non-resistance Society, 1839. 24 pp.

Constitution of the Fraternal communion, with an exposition of the same, including the first proceedings of Fraternal community no. 1. Milford, 1841. 16 pp.

The true scriptural doctrine of the Second Advent: an effectual antidote to Millerism, and all other kindred errors. Hopedale: Community Press, 1843. 32 pp.

* *The voice of duty: an address delivered at the anti-slavery picnic at Westminster, Mass., July 4, 1843.* Hopedale: Community Press, 1843. 12 pp.

* "Non-Resistant Catechism," from the *Practical Christian*, August 3, 1844.
>Probably existed as a pamphlet, since Lewis G. Wilson sent a copy to Tolstoy in 1889; but no copies are known to exist. Tolstoy included an adaptation of the "Catechism" in *The Kingdom of God Is Within You* (1894).

Constitution, by-laws and regulations of Fraternal Community number one: located at Hopedale, Milford, Worcester Co. Mass.; as recently revised and approved. Hopedale: Community Press, 1845. 16 pp.

* *The superiority of moral over political power* [Anti-Slavery tracts, No. 5]. Philadelphia: Anti-Slavery Office, 1845. 4 pp.

* *Non-resistance tract, No. 2* [Includes: "Learn to Discriminate"; "Losing Influence"; "Consistency with a Vengeance"; "How Many Does It Take"; "Might and Right"]. Hopedale: Community Press, n.d. [c.1846.] 16 pp.

Constitution of the Practical Christian Ministry. Hopedale: Hopedale Press, 1848. 12 pp.

Address delivered before the Thwing family annual gathering, at Ebenezer D. and Anna T. Draper's in Hopedale, Thanksgiving Day, Nov. 29, 1849. Hopedale: Hopedale Press, 1849. 16 pp.

What entitles a person to the name Christian [Practical Christian tracts, No. 1]. Hopedale: Hopedale Press, 1849. 16 pp.

Christian non-resistance: questions answered [Practical Christian tracts, No. 2]. Hopedale: Hopedale Press, 1849. 8 pp.

The Bible: in its fundamental principles absolutely divine. In its explicative ideas and language properly human ... (Conversation between a traditionalist and a principalian) [Practical Christian tracts, No. 3]. Hopedale: Hopedale Press, 1849. 16 pp.

Endless punishment rejected: conversation between inquirer and expositor. Hopedale: Hopedale Press, 1849. 16 pp.

Constitution, by-laws, rules and regulations [of the Hopedale Community]. Hopedale, 1850. 28 pp.

* *Capital punishment: reasons for its immediate abolition.* Hopedale: Hopedale Press, 1851. 8 pp.

A concise exposition of the Hopedale Community: descriptive, statistical, historical and constitutional. Hopedale: Hopedale Press, 1851. 8 pp.

An inquirer answered. Hopedale, n.d. [c.1853]. 15 pp.

* *Constitution of the Practical Christian Republic.* Hopedale: Hopedale Press, 1854.

The Practical Christian Republic. Hopedale: Hopedale Press, 1854. 39 pp.

Fundamental principles, the only final and absolute authority, in religion. Hopedale: Hopedale Press, n.d. [c.1854]. 16 pp.

Lecture on the inspiration of the Bible: delivered in the town hall, Milford, Mass., Sunday evening, January 16, 1859. Hopedale, 1859. 8 pp.

* *A discourse on Christian non-resistance in extreme cases.* Hopedale: Spiritual Reformer Office, 1860. 32 pp.

Practical Christianity and its non-resistance in relation to human governments. Hopedale: Spiritual Reformer Office, 1860. 20 pp.

Practical Christianity in relation to different Christs and Christianities. Hopedale: Spiritual Reformer Office, 1860. 8 pp.

Practical Christianity in relation to education and amusements [Unbound sheets remaining from the 1854 ed. of Ballou's *Practical Christian Socialism*, pp. 278-385]. Hopedale: Spiritual Reformer Office, 1860.

Practical Christianity in relation to marriage and divorce in a right order of society [Unbound sheets remaining from the 1854 ed. of Ballou's *Practical Christian Socialism*; pages not numbered consecutively]. Hopedale: Spiritual Reformer Office, 1860.

Practical Christianity in relation to the dogma of endless punishment; presenting three grand reasons for its rejection. Hopedale: Spiritual Reformer Office, 1860. 47 pp.

Practical Christianity in relation to the superiority of moral over political power. Hopedale: Spiritual Reformer Office, 1860. 15 pp.

Practical Christianity in relation to voting at the polls. Hopedale: Spiritual Reformer Office, 1860. 8 pp.

Violations of the Federal Constitution, in the "irrepressible conflict" between the pro-slavery and anti-slavery sentiments of the American people: a lecture, delivered in sundry places during January and February, 1861. Hopedale: Spiritual Reformer Office, 1861. 48 pp.

Christian non-resistance defended against Rev. Henry Ward Beecher, and his discourse on Ephes. 4:13, published in "The Independent" of March 14, 1861. Being a review, in part, of said discourse. Hopedale: Spiritual Reformer Office, 1862. 20 pp.

The golden wedding, or fiftieth marriage anniversary of Arnold Taft, Esq. and wife, celebrated at their residence in Mendon, Mass., September 4, 1865. Hopedale: The Age Office, 1865. 16 pp.

Human progress in respect to religion: two discourses, delivered in the Chapel at Hopedale, Mass., May 26th and June 9th, 1867 [I. On the tendency of the age to dispense with the specialties and personal responsibilities of religion; II. On the ultimate convincement of progressive minds in favor of the pure Christian religion and church] Hopedale, 1867. 40 pp.

An address, delivered in the chapel at Hopedale, Mass., Feb. 2, 1870; at the funeral of Mrs. Anna T. Draper, wife of Mr. Ebenezer D. Draper; who passed to the higher life, Sunday, Jan. 30, preceding, after a long and distressing sickness, in the full assurance of a blissful immortality. Hopedale, 1870. 15 pp.

"History of Milford," in *History of Worcester County, Massachusetts*, 2:64-99. Boston: C. F. Jewett, 1879.

* *Reply to Parson Hor on War* [Four essays in verse: "Reply to Parson Hor on War: Perversions of Scripture corrected"; "The Ballot-Box: a suggestive Ballad for those who think"; "Practical Christian Gospel: Who will hear it?"; "Our Communal Declaration: Rhymed and Versified"]. Undated pamphlet. 16 pp.

WORKS NOT IDENTIFIED

The following works are included in the list of "Published Works of Adin Ballou" (Appendix E in the 1896 edition of the *Autobiography*). No surviving copies have been found.

Sunday School Manual. 1836.

Conference Hymn-Book: A Compilation. 1839.

The Hopedale Community: Historical Sketch. 1853.

APPENDIX F

An Epistle General to Restorationists

From the Independent Messenger, *1 January 1831*

To all sincere believers in the doctrine of universal restoration whithersoever dispersed. Wisdom and grace be with you from God our Father and his Son Jesus Christ.

BELOVED BRETHREN – Having been called by the God of our fathers to the defense of that ancient truth, whereof he hath spoken "by the mouth of all his holy prophets since the world began,"[1] I deem it my solemn duty to submit to your consideration an undisguised exposition of the motives and feelings with which I enter upon so responsible an undertaking. In order to render this exposition more clear and forcible, I have chosen to present a brief historical sketch of my life and experience during the last eight years.

In the year 1822, after much anxious inquiry, and many trying exercises of mind, I at length found repose in the full persuasion that God through Jesus Christ will finally restore the whole human family to holiness and happiness. An honest avowal of this persuasion involved me in the censure of my former religious friends, and resulted in my exclusion from their fellowship. Soon after, having received intimations that the denomination of Universalists would give me a friendly admission into their connexion, I made application and met a cordial welcome. I entered into this new connexion with the confident expectation of enjoying fraternal countenance and protection, without sacrificing my religious liberty. I verily believed, from the professions held out, that I was associating myself with an order of people whose glory it was to befriend all its members in the faith and practice of what might be most conformable to the dictates of their own understandings and consciences. I did not even suspect, that in numbering myself with the preachers of this order, I was supposed to lay myself under obligation to think, speak and act in subserviency to the sectarian policy of its leaders. Consequently, I promised myself greater mental and conscientious freedom than I was destined to enjoy.

The commencement of my acquaintance with Universalists was with several of the most conspicuous advocates of the doctrine of no future punishment. Against these men, and their distinguishing tenets, my prejudices had formerly been very strong; nor, as yet, had I entirely divested myself of their influence. I was, however, received and treated by them with so much courtesy, kindness and apparent friendship, that my unfavorable impressions were soon exchanged for those of confidence and respect. I *seemed* to find them persons of sounder heads and better hearts than I had anticipated, and before I was well aware, passed from suspicious dread to an extravagant credulity. I presently arrived at that easy, unsuspecting frame of mind, in which all distrust subsides, and every thing is allowed to pass at its *nominal value*.

My new associates took care to improve their opportunity for gradually doctrinating me into their views. They solemnly assured me, that although they believed the doctrine of no future punishment to be more sound and consistent than that of limited future retribution, as held by Restorationists, yet they had not the least inclination on this account to treat their brethren of that faith with unkindness or disrespect. That all were Universalists, who believed in universal salvation, whether holding to *limited* future or *no* future punishment, and as such bound to consider themselves under mutual obligations to preserve the rights of each from violation. Hence that Restorationism subjected no member of the order to any disadvantage whatever; and might be as freely enjoyed as any other doctrine. This assurance, being perfectly satisfactory to my mind, went far towards preparing it for an entire surrender to their direction.

Knowing, however, that there had recently arisen a somewhat serious disturbance between certain eminent Restorationists, and the leading members of the no future punishment class, I desired some explanation of its cause and object. It was replied, with some circumlocution but much apparent candor, that very unhappy difficulties had indeed taken place; but that they originated, not in a conscientious regard to particular doctrinal views, so much as in personal rivalry, envy, and hatred. It was gravely represented that the Rev. Edward Turner, Paul Dean, and Jacob Wood,[2] principal men of the disaffected party, had been aspiring to the most influential rank in the order – but that upon finding the Rev. Hosea Ballou perpetually in advance of them, both with respect to talents and the good opinion of the laity, they had conceived an envious ill will towards that gentleman, and conspired his overthrow. That in pursuance of their design they had availed themselves (for the sake of a convenient pretext) of the difference which existed in the faith of Universalists on the question of punishment, intending to excite an evil prejudice, in relation to *his* well known doctrine, which should prostrate his reputation among the societies. That in reality the disaffected cared not whether *their* doctrine or the *other* were uppermost; provided they themselves could stand at the head of the order. And finally, that the whole scheme of operations was a contrivance of hypocritical wickedness, from which every well-disposed man in the denomination could but recoil with abhorrence.

This representation went down into my soul cold and bitter as the dregs of death;[3] yet there was so much semblance of truth in the numerous circumstantial criminations which were made against the accused, and all was delivered with so many appearances of *injured innocence*, that I could not allow myself to doubt its correctness. I was too far carried away to think of inquiring, as I ought to have done, what the accused could offer in justification of themselves – and from that time forward, deemed it not only a dictate of prudence but of duty, to stand aloof from such dangerous men. I abstained purposely from all intimacy, and only interchanged such civilities with them as seemed unavoidable. Forthwith espousing the cause of the *pretended injured party*, I employed my little influence in strengthening the tide of opinion among the laity, that the disturbance of Messrs. Turner, Dean and Wood, was the offspring of inordinate ambition, personal rivalry and splenetic envy. And that as its design was to break down so great and good a man as the Rev. Hosea Ballou – one who had been so long in the field, had borne the burden of the day,[4] and was growing venerable with age – it deserved the reprehension of all good brethren. Still I was a believer in future retribution, rather than ultra Universalism; though the changes which had been going on in my mind in consequence of the evil bias given it against the leading Restorationists, had rendered me nearly neutral. All these things were experienced in the course of six months after the first acquaintance with my new friends.

I was now considered on good ground by the no future punishment class, and in a fair way to obtain the whole truth in due time. With all around me the grand watchword was, "research and improvement." Many were becoming enamored with the discovery of new truths, and I began to fear that without better efforts I should discover myself a dull scholar. I therefore read with solicitude a multitude of different publications in favor of the doctrine of no future punishment. In most of these I found it a leading business of their authors, not to prove from scripture and reason by direct testimony that all mankind would certainly be happy upon their entrance into the future state, but to show that there was no proof that *any part* would be miserable or suffer punishment in that state. Numerous passages of scripture, generally understood to teach future retribution, were examined, explained, and elaborately shown to have no reference to the future state. Indeed I know of no important text relating to future judgment, or punishment, which had not undergone such an explanation.

The writings of Rev. Hosea Ballou, whom I had learned to look upon with extraordinary reverence, contained many of those expositions of scripture, several of which for a time I regarded as extremely plausible. And if I rightly recollect, that gentleman himself expressed privately and publicly his settled conviction, that not a single passage of scripture, fairly interpreted, either *declared* or *intimated* the doctrine of retribution in the future state. To hear a man for whom I entertained so elevated a respect, deliberately declare such a conviction, with so much confidence in its truth, was well calculated to impress me with the idea that possibly he might be right. In a few instances, I endeavored, in private conversation with him, to obtain more perfect explanations of his views concerning universal salvation; but was never so happy as to receive any thing more explicit or satisfactory than I had read in his works. This was a circumstance that rather perplexed me, and the more so, as I did not find all that freedom which I needed, in order to propose my doubts and difficulties. Yet I suffered it not to diminish my deference for the man; and applied with double diligence to his writings for more thorough information.

Rev. Walter Balfour's[5] first *Inquiry*[6] came out with an imposing importance, as a learned and valuable work; and I read it with high raised expectations of deriving satisfaction on many points, concerning which I had been perplexed. I had been informed that he was a thorough scholar, particularly in the original languages of the Bible, a man of sterling sense, a strong reasoner, and withal remarkably candid. I consequently read his work with interest, and with a prejudice in his favor. Indeed I had grown so respectful to the no future punishment scheme, and was so intimate with its influential friends, that I greatly desired to be convinced of its soundness, and was if possible too willing to find sufficient evidence in its support. Yet even in this frame of mind, all I had read came short of affording me the desired proof. Mr. Balfour's work just noticed, though the most able and candid of all his Universalist productions, and though embracing much on the subjects discussed which deserved respectful consideration, did by no means settle the queries which chiefly agitated my mind. I however thought tolerably well of it, as I endeavored to do of all the works I had examined on that side of the question.

But as my Restorationism had now become silent, my neutrality was little better than partiality to ultra Universalism. And while in my preaching I said nothing directly in support of future retribution, I went as far as I could with those who were its opposers. I never preached the no future punishment scheme at full length, for I never believed it true. Yet I went so far sometimes, as to use arguments founded on those expositions of scripture, which refer most of the divine threatenings and promises to the destruction of

Jerusalem.[7] I did this also in some instances of private argument; and therefore became regarded by many friends and opponents as a thoroughgoing Universalist. In fact I was not much less; for I had arrived at a state of doubt concerning future punishment, which led me frequently to acknowledge that I could not well understand how there should be any suffering after the resurrection from the dead. On that point I had been more affected by ultra Universalist writings, than any others. I had partly assented to their explanations of those scriptures, which speak of the resurrection of *"just and unjust,"*[8] of some coming "forth to the resurrection of life," and some to the "resurrection of damnation"[9] – and was therefore scarcely able to deny the inferences they had drawn from the 15th chapter of 1 Corinthians in favor of their well-known position that the resurrection state must be inaccessible to sin, guilt and pain.[10] Still, however, I was far from being convinced of the truth of this position, in such a sense as to admit the argument generally employed upon it to be conclusive.

As to the style of my preaching, it had insensibly become remotely imitative of that which distinguished the leading Universalists. Although irony, satire and witticism was never pleasing to me, and therefore not indulged in my discourses, yet in other respects I went too far. In following the example of those who use their texts by way of accommodation to smite at the prevailing sects, I have since thought I sometimes erred. Those preachers, who had become most acceptable to the laity, distinguished themselves by often selecting texts, which with an ingenious treatment would enable them to cast the severest reflections upon their opponents with the best grace. If I fell into this practice it was only to a brief extent, for which I can plead no other excuse, than it was the fashion of my associates and therefore difficult wholly to avoid. Otherwise I retained so much of my early religious feeling, that my discourses were in a good degree characterized by seriousness, moral sentiment, and moderation – so that not unfrequently, strangers and opposers would retire from the meeting with the remark, that I did not preach like a Universalist. Thus I spent three years or more of my life, in addition to the first six months before mentioned.

During this period I professed to be neutral concerning the doctrines of *no future*, and *limited future* retribution – believed in the latter, if I might be said to believe in either – inclined to the former so far as to desire, and even harbor the expectation, that I might one day be convinced of its truth; but strictly speaking preached neither. As to my influence, however, if I exerted any, it went into the no future punishment scale; and I presume I was generally viewed as a promoter of that interest. In devotion to the denomination, I was not a whit behind the foremost – an enemy to what was denominated faction, alarmed at any thing which portended disunion, and proud to deserve the credit of a peaceable brother. I deprecated that "bad spirit," which tended to "make difficulty in the order," and thought of nothing but success and prosperity to the common cause. In the meantime the disaffected Restorationists were considered as defeated, silenced, humbled and rendered harmless. They were indeed treated externally as brethren, on the ground that the difficulties they had excited were settled, yet both they and their doctrine had evidently fallen into discredit with a majority of the societies; which majority evinced their determination, not only to befriend the *no future punishment* clergy, but to discountenance any thing that deviated from their distinguishing tenets. This influence seemed to be fatal against *Restorationism*, and necessitated its preachers to keep their doctrine chiefly to themselves, or seek a new field for its dissemination.

I had now arrived at the twenty-fourth year of my age, and was passing the perihelium of my proximity to *ultra Universalism*. Up to this time I had persuaded myself that my preaching, and that of my brethren, exerted or tended to exert, a salutary influence upon the moral condition of society, and believed that when fully proved in its effect it would vindicate itself against all reproach. I knew well that some, who pretended to propagate Universalism, were too rough and vulgar to do any great good either for their own cause or any other (and such I could have wished might remain silent) but as the clergy generally promised better things, for such I accordingly hoped. Henceforth, however, I perceived so much bitterness indulged, so much labor bestowed to show that the Bible teaches no future judgment or retribution, so much ridicule of the religion of professing Christians, and so much *smart witticism*, even in the preaching of those who were thought most eminent, that I began seriously to doubt whereunto things would grow. Close moral, practical and evangelical preaching seemed to be going out of date, and when occasionally I struck into a vein of it, I found that it was evidently unwelcome to those ears, which were so much delighted with a different style and subject. This troubled me exceedingly, and was an evil which I knew not how to remedy. I learned that to declaim against the superstition, bigotry, hypocrisy and fanaticism of the various religious sects entertained a certain class of people very agreeably, yet without ever producing the effect to reform them of a single vice. In contemplating the faults and follies of their neighbors, as described by an ingenious speaker, those people would evince the highest gratification; but the certain result, I observed always to be, a growing disrelish of all serious religion, and a forgetfulness of their own sinfulness in denouncing that of others. I looked to my elders in the ministry, those who had it in their power to give tone to the taste and feelings of the laity, but I soon ascertained that they were as far from the mark at which I was aiming, as any of the people. Gradually entering into their secrets, I began to discover some doctrines, practices and feelings not altogether consistent with the good opinion I had formed of their moral and intellectual worth. I found them disposed to think lightly of that kind of preaching called *moral*. They would speak of it as a sort of weakly, insipid, tiresome repetition, calculated to reflect no great honor upon the preacher, and to do no essential good to the hearer. *It* would do well enough for those whose gifts fitted them for nothing higher – but *doctrine*, and exposure of the errors of the Church should be mainly attended to, by all who wished to attain celebrity.

Family devotion – asking blessings and returning thanks at table, etc. etc. they considered well enough for those who thought proper to observe them, but on the whole, as idle ceremonies which could be beneficial neither to God nor man. With regard to a future state of existence, many of them disbelieved that mankind will in *that* state possess any consciousness of having previously existed in the *present*.[11] Some of them also privately confessed their disbelief in the existence of *angelic beings* of a higher nature than human. These and other similar skepticisms, which from time to time leaked out, occasioned me much bitter anxiety for the issue. Then in relation to the Restorationist doctrine of limited future retribution, I found the whole ultra party, both clergy and laity, to hold it in abhorrence and contempt. As I was supposed to have got over that childish notion, its opposers laid aside their reserve, and gave me an opportunity to discover their real feelings. I found the doctrine regarded as a relic of heathenish superstition – a weak and silly whim – an indication, wherever held, of a shallow mind – and finally, as a serious detriment to the reputation of young preachers among the societies. It would do well enough for people who had just been released from the dungeon of *error*, whose mental vision could not at once endure the full light of day.

It was, perhaps, a necessary evil, which as a convenient stepping stone into the knowledge of the truth, must be tolerated. But as a permanent ground of faith, no man of intelligence could long rest upon it – for if any misery were admitted to exist in the future state, it was far more consistent to believe it would be endless. Hence the man who should presume to urge it upon public attention, in distinction from their Universalism, could expect no less than to be denounced by them as an emissary of discord, and a promoter of "difficulty in the order." Such indeed, they appeared to esteem everyone, who had independence enough to say any thing in its vindication.

All these things I carefully observed, without appearing to do so, and along with many a painful pang locked them up in my own bosom. Feeling that I was inextricably involved in the net which enclosed me, I resolved to make the best of my case, and to wait in silence for better times. Yet even in this situation of mind I was a *doubtful neutral*, and thought it an almost impossible task to disprove the reasoning employed by Messrs. Ballou and Balfour to show that the scriptures do not teach the doctrine of future judgment and punishment. But I no longer felt any anxiety to be persuaded of the soundness of their peculiar opinions; having become quite disposed to be content with whatever might finally appear most conformable to divine truth and reason.

About this time Rev. Charles Hudson's *Letters* made their appearance.[12] I read them with interest, and was constrained to acknowledge that the author had done more for his cause than I had had any idea was possible. The many strong and seemingly irresistible arguments with which he had met the opposite scheme, produced a powerful impression on my mind, and prompted me, afterwards, to a critical examination of all the works of ultra Universalists within my reach. I *commenced* reading Mr. Hudson's *Letters* with some prejudice against the *man*, on account of his having been, as I conceived, a disturber of the peace of our denomination – but I *concluded* the perusal with a determination to honor him as an able advocate of his doctrine, and moreover, to be satisfied with nothing short of a thorough answer from his opponents. Such an answer I believed would soon appear; and as I had no doubt, the whole strength of the no future punishment scheme would be brought out, I anticipated a final settlement of the question.

But to my astonishment and mortification the Rev. Hosea Ballou at length announced through the columns of the *Universalist Magazine*, that he had not even read Mr. Hudson's work – but having been credibly informed by those who *had* that it contained nothing *new* on the subject, he should not reply. How to interpret this mystery I knew not. The elevated opinion I had entertained of Mr. Ballou's moral and intellectual worth forbade my imputing his conduct to any thing wrong in feeling, or deficient in mental ability. Yet I could not defend his conduct, nor be satisfied with his rejecting so good an opportunity to establish his doctrine, if true, upon a permanent basis. But when I learned that Mr. Balfour had engaged to meet Mr. Hudson, I recovered my spirits, and looked forward in anticipation of a production which should concentrate the whole force of evidence and argument, belonging to that side of the great question at issue.

The promised work at length made its appearance,[13] but it came far short of my expectations. It discovered ability, reading and ingenuity in its author, and in a few points seemed to gain advantages over Mr. Hudson's arguments. But the bitterness of spirit, the smart repartees, the sarcastic thrusts, and above all the formal imputation cast upon Mr. H. of having written his *Letters* to gratify an "old grudge" against Mr. Ballou did not to me betoken a great and candid mind – such as should have stood forth to discuss so momentous a question. Then the fundamental points, on which I conceived Mr. Hudson had showed his doctrine to the best advantage, were not treated of in the reply to an extent answerable to their importance. And more than all this, entirely new ground had been assumed by Mr. Balfour in relation to the soul and other things. The system of Mr. Ballou, which laid so much stress upon the immaculate purity of the immortal soul, and which seemed to make salvation chiefly consist in separating this immortal soul from the sinful flesh at death, was silently discarded by Mr. Balfour, and his new system introduced in its stead. This of course materially changed the bearing of many prominent arguments – so that Mr. Hudson's *Letters to Mr. Ballou* were left in several respects wholly unanswered.

During this period, I was invited to the pastoral charge of the Universalist Society in Prince Street, New York. This I accepted, but remained with the society only about nine months. The Rev. Abner Kneeland was then flourishing at the head of a society in that city, part of whom had followed him from Prince Street, which he had left a short time before my arrival. He was on the highway from ultra Universalism to Atheism, and had reduced things to such a state of confusion that I soon became convinced of my incompetency to restore them to wholesome order. Party feuds, personal animosities, jealousy, envy and strife, with obvious symptoms of skepticism, even in some of the most respectable individuals, reigned on all sides among those who called themselves Universalists. I endured this state of things till I could neither hope for better times, nor successfully withstand existing evils – then asked dismission and returned to Milford, whither I had been earnestly invited by my former friends.

While in New York I became acquainted with Rev. E. Mitchell, Pastor of the Society of United Christian Friends, a Restorationist who had long stood aloof from the denomination of Universalists. I found him a man of sound moral principle, devoted piety and sincere Christian feeling. He had stood, amid the swelling surges of skepticism and infidelity, firm as a rock of the ocean, and notwithstanding ultra Universalism had somewhat diminished the number of his society, he still retained a respectable congregation. I have since fully appreciated his motives in declining the fellowship of Universalists as a denomination, and do not in the least wonder at the course he has pursued. He has proved himself a genuine friend of the Christian religion, of moral order, and practical godliness. And as a faithful minister of Christ, an independent minded man, and an uncompromising opponent of all sorts of licentiousness, he will receive the approbation of every good man.

I returned from New York deeply disgusted with Atheism, libertinism, Kneelandism, and, I may add, ultra Universalism. I had seen so much in the management of those who were distinguishing themselves as the friends of these *isms*, which did not meet the approbation of either my conscience or understanding, that I resolved henceforth to think and act wholly for myself. I immediately examined all my opinions, reviewed the whole pathway of my mind since I first became a neutral, searched the scriptures with renewed diligence, analyzed the doctrines and arguments of the *ultras*, and in the course of a few months settled down into a firm belief of Restorationism, as I first received it in the year 1822. My mind has since remained undisturbedly satisfied of the soundness and truth of that doctrine.

Having always determined, that if I should become sufficiently assured of the truth of Restorationism, I would openly preach it, at the risk of all I held dear, I had now to undergo the trial of carrying my determination into practice. To do my duty was placing myself in an attitude of manifest opposition to my interest and reputation, as a member of the Universalist order – not to do it was exposing myself to the reprehension of the Judge of quick and dead at the last day, as an unfaithful servant. I was with a society tutored up under the influence of ultra Universalism, and some individuals of which I was sure would never compromise with my doctrine, if plainly preached. I *might* be dismissed, or if not, an unhappy commotion, at least, would certainly be excited. Then in the estimation of the no future punishment clergy and laity, I must sadly sink the moment I was known to dissent from their doctrines and practices. As to Restorationism, it had become a byword and reproach among the reigning powers of the order. To espouse and defend it would procure me the *dislike* of *some*, and the sovereign contempt of *many*. Yet with me it was the truth, and such truth as I felt able to defend against all fair opposition. To believe it and not preach it, was pitiful and cowardly, dishonest and unpardonable – above all it was exposing myself to the insupportable rebuke of God. I decided that I would do my duty, that I would proclaim what I regarded as truth, whether people would hear or whether they would forbear, whether I met the *smiles* or the *frowns* of the world, and whether I had the countenance of few or many. The moral welfare of mankind, the testimony of a good conscience, and the final approbation of Christ I have resolved to respect as objects of paramount importance.

It was not however, without a severe struggle and some delay, that I obtained the entire mastery of my timidity – shook off the fetters which chained me to the pillar of neutrality, and became properly independent in the avowal of my opinions. My strong natural and habitual aversion to contention, especially with those whom I had so long held as brethren – and the remains of those prejudices into which I had formerly been misled against the "*factious Restorationists*," for some time rendered me almost unjustifiably cautious in defending my own distinct ground. Dread of the dark tempests which I foresaw would howl around me the moment I took a decided stand, with now and then a glimmering hope that the condition of things might be meliorated without a convulsion, prevented my immediate advance.

In the meantime I applied myself studiously to criticism on all the writings of modern Universalists within my reach, and to close observation of the effects of the doctrine on its warmest advocates. I discerned daily in these writings what appeared to me to be irreconcilable inconsistencies and contradictions. Absurdities, which I had before no apprehension of finding, stood forth in bold relief; and I felt an indescribable mortification in reflecting that the ancient doctrine of Restorationism must be suffocated by such errors. Yet nothing could be done without making "*difficulty in the order*;" because there was no medium of fair public investigation through which to act successfully against false doctrine. I once addressed a few queries to the editor of the *Trumpet*, concerning his exposition of the sin against the Holy Ghost, which though he published, his reply was such as to satisfy me, that he meant to evade the leading difficulties, and stand aloof from discussion.[14] I made no further attempt towards public investigation till within the last year.

But I have kept a watchful eye upon the periodicals, as well as other publications of the denomination. The *Trumpet*, in particular, I have scrutinized as the most immediate outlet of ultra Universalism, and the most influential organ of its defense. Proceeding from the pure source of that doctrine, conducted by one of its most sanguine advocates, and continually favored by the united counsels of the most distinguished preachers, I knew that there, if anywhere, the spirit, genius and tendency of the *new scheme* would develop itself. I also knew that the whole order would receive tone and character from the influence of such a paper. The editor in his editorial character has always pretended to act impartially with respect to the controversy between Restorationists and his own class; but instead of doing so in the case of Messrs. Balfour and Hudson, he has lauded the writings of the former, and decried those of the latter.[15] When Mr. Hudson's reply to Mr. Balfour's essays first appeared, I felt exceedingly aggrieved to perceive in the *Trumpet* a notice of the work, containing some dozen or more picked extracts, so selected as to prejudice the laity against reading it. Those extracts were set forth as a specimen of the tone, spirit and merits of the *Reply*, and accompanied with expressions of regret, that the author should write in such an exceptionable style. They comprised most of the sharp and severe sentences of the whole book, and were nothing like a fair sample of its contents. Yet they answered their intended purpose.

I waited for Mr. Balfour's *Letters* in rejoinder, meaning to observe whether Mr. Whittemore would prove his impartiality by treating them after the same method. But he had by that time quite changed – and though there is not an impartial man in America, who, after reading the works of both, would not decide that Mr. Balfour's style, spirit and language are more bitter and invidious than Mr. Hudson's; yet *he* pronounced those of Mr. Balfour to have been "written in the spirit of candor, and to be replete with sound argument." Moreover he used his influence, editorially, as well as privately, to give them sale and circulation; all of which was the reverse of his conduct in Mr. Hudson's case. With such "impartiality" I was not satisfied.

Another injustice that aggrieved me was the frequent statements which appeared in the *Trumpet* and elsewhere, of the faith of our order. Universalists were set down in the aggregate as believing all the tenets of the *ultras*, and the impression thereby sent abroad among the uninformed, that no man could be a Universalist, without holding those tenets. I had preserved the original idea, given me upon my first acquaintance with the denomination, and always inculcated it; i.e. that all men were Universalists who believed in universal salvation – as much those who held the doctrine of future retribution, as those who rejected it. But I found by the statements alluded to, that I was a believer in universal salvation, and yet not a Universalist. These statements made no more allowance for Restorationism, or for the different opinions maintained by its advocates, than for *Mahometanism*. Indeed the design in this management evidently was, to give modern Universalism full currency as the true and only faith of the order. Thus amid darkness and silence, in violation of many solemn professions of fellowship and protection, would Restorationism have been smothered out of existence, and not even an audible groan alarmed the world of its departure. Many of the laity, to my knowledge, received the impression, that Restorationists were not, and ought not to be called Universalists. In this they were right, according to the *Trumpet* and the writings of several eminent no future punishment preachers. Finding that the distinction was unavoidable, I henceforth ceased to call myself a Universalist – and acknowledged the name of Restorationist only. But the statements under notice were, in my humble opinion, after all, extremely unfair – as implying that the whole sect held doctrines to which a respectable minority were decidedly opposed. It was virtually saying that there *were* no Restorationists – or that they deserved no respect as an integral part of the denomination.

Added to all this was the occasional discovery of a deep disgust at every thing said in our general meetings not conformable to all their *improved notions*. I have known an ultra Universalist preacher, upon hearing a Restorationist speak in the pulpit of *"appearing in the presence of God,"* of *"standing at the judgment seat of Christ,"* or of *"suffering the retributions of a future state"* – signify his contempt and dislike by sneers and whisperings. Such things added fuel to the fire shut up in my bones, and urged me on to independence. I have attended but few Associations, and only one General Convention of Universalist ministers.

The General Convention of 1829, at Winchester, N.H., was the only session of that body, and the last general meeting of clergymen at which I have been present. I there saw a spirit in the *ultras*, which made me resolve it should be the last time I would meet with them on any such occasion. There Brother Paul Dean was prohibited by a vote of the Convention from inviting Brother David Pickering to pray with him in the desk. When I found such a vote about to pass, I left the meeting with grief and astonishment.

But still I remained chiefly silent, waiting in dubious indecision, whether to speak out or forbear. I said very little concerning these troubles except to a few intimate friends, who were as unable to devise a remedy as myself. Time rolled on only to increase my dissatisfaction. Weary with the repetition of doctrines, opinions, and practices, which I could not approbate, and of which, therefore, I regretted to be considered by the Christian public a supporter – I resolved to make one more attempt to redeem the truth by plain, friendly discussion. Accordingly, about the first of May last, I sent to the editor of the *Trumpet* an *article* containing a review of Rev. W. I. Reese's[16] sermon on *"punishment and forgiveness"* – and desired that, if consistent with his feelings, he would publish it in his paper. In that article I proposed a friendly public discussion with the advocates of ultra Universalism, on any or all the points of difference between them and myself. Mr. Reese I had never seen, and in animadverting on his arguments, considered myself as opposing a doctrine common to all the brethren of the no future punishment class. This was my last hope of bringing about a better era for Restorationism without a general commotion. If there should be a friendly controversy in which both classes might speak plainly, I had no doubt a favorable issue would be the result. The *Review* was received by Mr. Whittemore, and a partial encouragement given that it should ere long be published. Its publication was deferred for a few weeks, as being immediately inconvenient. But during those few weeks important events transpired, which hastened on an inevitable revolution.

In June the Southern Association of Universalists held a session at Berlin, Connecticut. At that Association, Rev. Hosea Ballou, Thomas Whittemore and others, procured the passage of resolutions denouncing the Providence Association – and virtually prohibiting those brethren, who had of late met with it, from giving it their further countenance, on pain of excommunication from the General Convention. Although I was not then a member of the Providence Association, and had never happened to be present at one of its sessions, yet I considered the passage of these resolutions an unwarrantable assumption of ecclesiastical authority – and an aggression upon all the Restorationists in the Convention, which if passively endured, must involve the ultimate surrender of their most sacred rights.

Soon after this, early in July, the editor of the *Trumpet* came out in his paper against a sermon of mine just published at his office entitled "The Inestimable Value of Souls." This sermon had been delivered before my friends in Medway, and by their particular request a copy furnished for the press. They carried the copy directly to the *Trumpet* office, and contracted to have it printed. Its great design was to illustrate and establish the doctrine of Universal Restoration in opposition to that of endless misery. But as I did not construe scripture according to the light of modern Universalism, and distinctly inculcated the faith of future limited retribution, Mr. Whittemore and his brethren could not silently brook my independence. He therefore, in accordance with the advice of his counselors, lost no time in testifying his disapprobation of the sermon and the presumption of its author. Ere the sermon reached me in print, the number of the *Trumpet* containing Mr. W.'s strictures was laid before me. Those strictures breathed a spirit of censorious intolerance and hostility, warm from the fountain of ultra Universalism, which left no room to doubt the feelings and designs with which they were given to the world. They *virtually* denounced me and my production as unworthy the respect and confidence of the denomination of Universalists. The public were cautioned against receiving the sentiments of the sermon as those of American Universalists. I was accused of having shown great irreverence towards my elders in the ministry; of having construed my text and other passages of scripture in contempt of better light; and finally as being, in Mr. W.'s opinion, "*certainly far behind the orthodox in rescuing the sacred writings from perversion.*" My sentiments, motives, and conduct were so misrepresented, misjudged and censured, that I considered the article no less than a *ban of outlawry*.

When I wrote and consented to the publication of the Medway sermon, I did not dream that it would receive the least public attention from the *ultras*, or indeed, from any others, except the circle of friends and opponents in my immediate neighborhood. And though I took decided ground in favor of Restorationism, in distinction from the *modern scheme*, yet I had no intention of making the sermon a provocation to hostilities. But it appears to have given great offense, and therefore the determination was taken to rebuke me before, not only the whole denomination, but as it were the whole world. Mr. W. knew well that his strictures would tend essentially to my prejudice, throughout the whole order, and above all, with a portion of the society to whom I was ministering. He well knew that I should not only be assailed with murmurs at home, but distrusted among all Universalists over whom his paper excited any influence. So that whether at home or abroad, every devotee to his doctrine would upon hearing me preach, say to himself, or whisper to his friend, "We shall hear strange things today – that man is not a Universalist – he is far behind even the *orthodox*!" He also well knew that the consequence would be – either that I should be so alarmed with the apprehension of a dismissal from my society as humbly to submit, apologize and promise future silence; or else, if I presumed to persist in my course, that I should be swept away by the irresistible current of opposition. But if I should be *silenced*, it appears to have been quite indifferent to him by what means it might be effected!

I read those strictures with great grief and mental agitation, took into consideration their character and tendency, the authority whence they emanated, the spirit which dictated them, the motives of the author, the undoubted support which he would receive from his clerical and lay friends – and beheld that there was no alternative left me, but to make peace by a sacrifice of that independence, honesty, and liberty, which constitutes the richest treasure of human nature – *or* to jeopardize every thing else in this world, by an uncompromising persistence in the path of my conscientious duty.

Although I had previously become ripe for a separation from the *ultras*, yet such was my weakness in this season of trial, that at first my courage quailed in view of the consequences. But after ruminating on the relative magnitude of the evils between which I had to choose, for three unhappy days and nights, I at length came to the determination, that "*sink or swim, live or die,*"[17] I would be free, honest, and independent – that I would do my duty, and leave the issue with God.

I now prepared and forwarded to the editor of the *Trumpet*, a vindication of myself against his attack, and requested that he would give it immediate publicity in his paper, or if he decided not to publish it at all, to return it to me within four days. About a week afterwards he returned it, without note or comment. He refused to publish it, gave no notice that he had received any reply from me, and deigned not even so much as to signify his reasons for returning it. But I soon learned that he and his coadjutors were industriously circulating a report in private circles, that my article was so fiery, bitter, and abusive, as to be unfit to appear in print. To others it was pretended to be an act of friendship towards me, to suppress an article, which, if laid before the public, would certainly reflect deep disgrace upon my name. But among the uninformed *ultras* abroad, the conclusion seemed to be readily drawn, that Mr. Whittemore's rod had taught me silence. They presumed I should in future take care to respect my betters. Thus was I accused, denounced and condemned without a hearing.

This sealed the protest of my utter separation. I immediately announced to my society from the pulpit, my views, feelings, and determination, in the most undisguised terms – offering to receive dismission from their pastoral charge, at any moment, declaring that I considered others as free to withhold their fellowship and support from me, as I was to enjoy and propagate my own honest opinion. I assured them that compromise with my ultra Universalist persecutors could never take place, consistently with my sense of *duty* to myself, to God and my fellow men – and that if I should stand entirely alone in the religious world, I would be an independent Restorationist. Several of the most valuable of my friends assured me, they thought none the worse of me for my frankness, and should not be in haste to dismiss me from their service. The *disaffected* probably meditated *other* things, without choosing to express them. But whatever might be meditated gave me no concern, as I had made up my mind to count all things dross for the sake of duty and truth. After this I came out without reserve in defense of my doctrine, and of course in opposition to modern Universalism. The excitement was everywhere great, and I had full opportunity to know how much abhorrence and contempt the real *ultras* felt towards Restorationists and their faith. The more coarse and immoral poured out their profanity upon and denounced me most heartily, together with what they were pleased to denominate my "hell junior," "tophet" and "purgatory." In these vituperations they have been encouraged by at least some of their preachers. Some contented themselves with saying that they had as lief hear *orthodox* preaching as mine, and that there was no true Universalism about me. But others, who are distinguished for their greater candor and moderation, though inclined to the side of modern Universalism, have treated me with respect, and say that they are ready to hear, read and consider whatever Restorationists have to offer in support of their views. With such men I have no contention. As to decided Restorationists, and those who are friendly to the upbuilding of their cause, I have found for my encouragement many more than at first I had any anticipation – and I now feel fully persuaded that God will not suffer me to travel in solitude to the grave.

With respect to an entire separation from the no future punishment Universalists, I had only to join the Providence Association, and share the impending fate of its members – viz., be cut off from the General Convention, by the probable vote of our opposers in that body. I accordingly became a member with the brethren of that Association, and at the session of the General Convention holden in Lebanon, N.H. during September last – we were *virtually* excluded from the Universalist *order*. The separation has thus been consummated, and I shall henceforth govern myself accordingly.

When this separation was foreseen to be inevitable, it became an object of the highest importance to have a periodical publication, through which to speak to the world in our defense. As no one came forward to undertake such a publication, I engaged in it myself; and now after much care and expense have at length commenced the work under more favorable auspices than I at first expected.

Since the Prospectus went out, every effort has been made by my opposers to hedge up my way.[18] Not one of their papers, to my knowledge, has given my prospectus a favorable notice – several of them none at all – and one or two have appeared in opposition. The old cry has been raised, in which I once ignorantly joined, "he is making difficulty in the order," exciting "disunion, discord and strife among brethren," etc. Slander is everywhere privately whispered against me by those who have not courage to utter it publicly; I am represented as acting under the influence of delusion, envy and revenge – and it seems to have become with some a righteous thing to prejudice as many as possible against me, that they may thereby hinder the circulation of my paper. Those people dread nothing so much as that Restorationism and its friends should have a full hearing.

The Editor of the *Trumpet*, finding that *this* publication would inevitably issue, has latterly proclaimed himself a man of *peace*, a friend of union, concord and good fellowship; and with grave professions of devoting his paper to the interests of the "whole order," calls upon all to sustain him. He deprecates disunion among Universalists, and warns them against the emissaries of discord. It were well if men like him and others, who are such friends of *union* and *good feeling*, had always exercised that justice and moderation towards their brethren, which is the only basis and security of uninterrupted peace. But with the spoils of honest independence and injured innocence about them, with the reproach of having attacked the defenseless and given them no chance for redress – let them not flatter themselves with the vain hope that the *despoiled* will listen to their delusive professions of friendship and love of peace. Restorationism will in future occupy its own ground, and rise or fall upon its own merits. It will not continue to knock at the unyielding doors of ultra Universalism for shelter, nor with unpitied tears beg to be heard in its own defense through the columns of papers unfriendly to its existence. But through the *Independent Messenger* it will speak its own pure native language, and command a hearing even from those who have hitherto shut their ears upon its voice.

With the help of God these columns will be devoted to an unfettered discussion of the doctrines which divide *ancient* and *modern* Universalists. Through them I shall assign to the world the reasons which have led me to reject the interpretations of Scripture, doctrines, opinions etc. of the *ultras*; and whosoever reads it will in due time know whether Restorationism is susceptible of self defense or not. But never as its editor will I treat my opponents with the injustice of prohibiting them an opportunity to defend themselves on any point wherein I assail them. And if I lay unsparing hands in the way of *review* upon all influential modern Universalist writings – if I oppose them ever so strenuously, they shall find me as honorable, open and fair an opponent as I am severe and uncompromising.

And with regard to my feelings and motives in this business, I desire to be distinctly understood, when once for all I solemnly declare, that though I cannot fellowship or make common cause with them, yet I have no personal hostility to gratify, nor a single wish to hinder their free enjoyment of all the social, civil and religious rights, which I claim for myself and brethren. I ask justice, and will render it – I ask a patient hearing, and will give the same – I ask nothing which I am not willing to reciprocate. I will consider no man my personal enemy because he controverts my doctrine or animadverts on my writing, and I wish no man to consider me so to him for any such reasons. Whatever is good and praiseworthy in my opponents, I mean to acknowledge as such, however much I may condemn. And I require only a reciprocation.

And now, beloved brethren, having thus long detained your attention upon the history of events which have so deeply affected the experience of my life, since I became a believer in universal restoration – having laid open to you an honest statement of facts, and thereby developed the feelings, motives and reasons which have rendered me what I am, I submit the whole to your serious consideration. It is for you to judge whether I am deserving of your fellowship, approbation and support – whether I have espoused a *good* cause, for good reasons, with good intentions, and a good resolution – and whether you will cooperate with me in the great work upon which I have entered – *or not*. I offer you my heart and hand – I invite you in the name of Christ, of truth and religion to rally around the banner of the "*ancient doctrine*" – to come up every man of you into the mountain of the Lord with living stones,[19] that we may erect a temple to our God, in which we and our children may worship him in holiness and peace, without fear and without oppression.

Think of the great and good men, who in different ages have stood forth to inculcate and defend the faith of Universal Restoration. Think of *Clemens, Origen, Gregory*, and many other illustrious Christian Fathers[20] – of *Tillotson, Newton, Law, Hartley, Ramsay, Petitpierre*,[21] *Chauncy* and *Winchester*. Remember that those eminent Christians were true Restorationists – not *ultra Universalists* – that they were men of deep religious feeling, devoted piety, refined benevolence and Christian godliness. Would you not choose to follow in the path of such men? Would you not choose like them to set examples of piety and virtue before the world, which should compel reverence even from enemies? They believed in the infinite goodness of God – in his purpose to save the whole human family through Jesus Christ, and looked forward with rapturous vision through the divine promises to the complete regeneration of the Universe – to the perfect endless glory of that era, when God shall be all in all.[22] But they had not learned to limit divine rewards and punishments to the shores of time – they never discovered that the *destruction of Jerusalem* was the day in which Christ should appear, and reward every man according to his works – nor that *then* the *new heaven and earth* superseded the *old*.[23] Neither did they cherish that unholy spirit, which disposes its possessors to look upon their fellow men of a different religious faith and practice, as objects of ridicule and reproach. They exemplified religion without superstition, liberality without licentiousness, and free inquiry without skepticism.

Will you, dear brethren, follow them as they followed Christ?[24] Will you rise in the strength of your God and unite to build up an order of Christians, which may be to every persecuted *Lazarus*, an Abrahamic bosom[25] of faith, hope and charity?[26] Will you resolve to act in such a manner as to insure the approbation of the Great Judge of quick and dead? The eyes of many liberal Christians in every denomination are upon you, and if once they become convinced that you mean to be a truly liberal, and at the same time Christian people, you will receive at least their friendship, if not their immediate social support.

Finally, brethren, having discharged the duty which I conceived to devolve upon me in the present crisis, I now leave you to consult the dictates of your own consciences, and the direction of the divine spirit. Reflect patiently, seriously, and prayerfully on these things – and may the All-wise God give you wisdom and strength to perform your duty. But however you may decide to act, or whoever you may choose to serve, be assured that "as for me and my house, we will serve the Lord."[27]

Your humble fellow servant and brother,

ADIN BALLOU

APPENDIX G

The Restorationist Secession

Part 1: From The Universalist, *11 February 1871*

It is with satisfaction and gratitude that I find myself welcomed to the columns of *The Universalist* to attempt the correction of historico-traditional errors which for a whole generation have disparaged and impugned an ecclesiastical movement really deserving respectful consideration. I will endeavor not to abuse my privilege, but, in substance and spirit, improve it to the best of my ability. Having at my command what I regard as the essential facts necessary to a just appreciation of that whole movement, I will state them comprehensively, in their natural order, under three divisional captions.

I. Preliminary Facts

1. The Universalist denomination, as an organized ecclesiastical body, was originally Restorationist in faith, and so remained in doctrinal exposition, without innovation, till after the year 1815. (Exceptions have been alleged, but none of public importance.)

2. The doctrine of universal salvation without any disciplinary punishment after death, was advocated by certain persons in England and America, before and after the formation of the Universalist General Convention in 1785, but was strongly denounced by Winchester and Murray, the leading founders of that Convention. (Proof if required.)

3. Hosea Ballou was the first preacher (at least of any note) inside the Universalist denomination, who advocated universal salvation without any disciplinary punishment after death, some time between 1815 and 1820.[1] (See Whittemore's *Modern History of Universalism*, ed. 1830, p. 437.)

4. The Universalist denomination, during its first half century, was bitterly opposed, denounced and aspersed, almost universally by other denominations of professed Christians, as damnably heretical, if not absolutely infidel. This rendered it largely a polemical people, rather than a personally religious one, made up in the main of persons who delighted in bold, telling, controversial argumentation, rather than pietistic appeals to conscience and pungent exhortations to a consecrated life. This also rendered those preachers and writers who could give the common enemy the most staggering polemical blows decidedly the most popular and influential in the order. It multiplied theoretical adherents, but gave little encouragement to Church membership. Probably there were not a thousand church communicants in the whole denomination in 1830. I doubt if there were five hundred. The same causes rendered a large portion of the denomination indifferent to the question of future limited disciplinary punishment, and disposed the majority to embrace enthusiastically any ingenious theory which discarded Restorationism; if only it stoutly defended universal salvation, and seemed to confound "the orthodox" – a term which meant all who held that any human souls would finally fail of heaven.

5. Hosea Ballou, Thomas Whittemore, Walter Balfour, and other talented advocates of universal salvation without any disciplinary punishment after death, in the fore-described polemical stage of the denomination, very naturally became its popular favorites and leaders. They were eminently so in 1830, as some of them had been growing to be for the dozen preceding years. They were men of uncommon ability; and like most able men of controversial genius, with numerous applauding and supporting adherents, they felt their importance and did not suspect themselves of any impropriety in manifesting it on numerous occasions.

6. But there were still Restorationists in the denomination; and some of these had the vanity to imagine that they were entitled to respectful consideration. Why they should presume to imagine any such thing may seem strange to many now, as it certainly did then to their progressive brethren. Yet so it was. For a time some of them were rather "rusty," hazy and lukewarm concerning their doctrine of future disciplinary retribution, having been quite absorbingly occupied in the general conflict with the common foe. But when the no future retributionists began boldly to assert that there was not a passage in the Scriptures which taught the notion of rewards and punishments after death for the deeds of this life, and to multiply their peculiar explanations of texts always before generally admitted to teach that doctrine, a few grew restive, and were stimulated to examine the subject critically. The more they did so, the stronger became their conviction that the doctrine of a salutary retributive discipline after death was true, was a plain doctrine of the Bible, was rational, and viewed in all its bearings was indispensable to sound faith and practice among a people professing to believe in universal salvation. It was not to them a doctrine of mere times and measures of divine retribution, but involved the truth that the soul of man is a responsible moral agent, forever under the divine government, that itself, and not the mere body, is the really accountable being, and that neither physical death, nor a physical resurrection, nor *any* process without its own moral volition, can perfect its own salvation. Moreover, many of the no-future-retribution interpretations of Scripture seemed to them unwarrantable, overstrained, puerile and indefensible; yes, some of them absurd. How they could or dared think so, I will not presume now to say. I only know that they did. Such were Paul Dean, Edward Turner, Jacob Wood, Charles Hudson and others, between 1818 and 1830.

7. These outspoken Restorationists were as much devoted to the common cause of universal salvation as their ultra brethren. They felt that they had just as good a right, without fear or favor,[2] to defend the original Restorationism of the denomination, as the innovators had theirs. This, too, may seem strange, but somehow they took it for granted. They were just as sincere in their doctrinal convictions as their differing brethren, and could not conceive why any body should be offended at the frank expressions of one party more than the other. Yet scarcely had they earnestly begun to preach and publish their distinctive sentiments, when their opponents, at first privately and afterwards publicly, charged them with insincerity, with not caring at heart for their peculiar doctrine, with being actuated by an ambition to be greatest, with envy of their superiors, with a spirit of rivalry, personal pique, &c. &c. – in fine with a mischievous propensity to make "difficulty in the order." The accused, however, were so ignorant of their own evil hearts, that they were utterly unconscious of the base motives alleged; nay more, they were conscious only of worthy motives, and "verily thought they ought"[3] to stand up manfully for their faith. But this availed them little, outside of their own bosoms and a small circle of adherents.

Their accusers seemed just as honestly certain of their guilt in the premises, as of the mathematical fact that two and two make four. They claimed to have indubitable proof of it. They convinced all their particular friends and partisans that it was certainly so. They made nine-tenths of the quiescent Restorationists believe it. They made me, who entered the denomination in 1823, believe it. And possibly I might have continued like many others, in the same belief to this day, had not I myself been charged with substantially the same ignoble motives. *Then* I did not merely think, guess, or suppose; but absolutely *knew* there was not a particle of foundation for the charge in my own breast, which soon enabled me to satisfy myself that all the rest were equally innocent.

8. Finding themselves thus accused, thus adjudged by nine tenths of their clerical and lay associates in the denomination, thus condemned without an impartial trial, suspected even by some who really preferred to be their friends, and crippled of their rightful influence in almost every ecclesiastical direction, it is not wholly unaccountable that they grew somewhat *sore* and *sour*. For they fell considerably short of saintly perfection, and seemed to have got into the fix akin to that of a man presumed to be insane; who, if he says nothing must go to the *hospital*, and if he blusters, is sure to be sent, perhaps in a strait waistcoat. Certainly, speaking out inside the order in those days was pretty sure only to make their case worse. But it was impossible for such turbulent spirits to remain entirely still, so a part of them kept on making "difficulty"; for which they received a great many "more kicks than coppers"[4] or thanks. Some, nearly starved out of the ministry, betook themselves to secular pursuits, and troubled Israel no more.[5] The noble and venerable Edward Turner sacrificed his popularity in the parish at Charlestown, attempted to establish another with a nucleus of seceding friends, but did not succeed, and finally found shelter with a liberal Congregational parish in Charlestown, where he ended his ministerial life.[6] He was intellectually and morally the peer of the first men in the Universalist denomination of his time. Poor man! was the charitable exclamation of his triumphant opponents; what a pity that he took the wrong side, yielded to bad influences, kept bad company, and thus blighted all his fair prospects! If, however, his own cherished doctrine of a future just and salutary retribution is, as I firmly believe, true, his case may have had a different hearing, and he be less an object of pity, in the other world than here. "Shall not the Judge of all the earth do right?"[7] But let me not further diverge. I will only add under this head, that several others of the outspoken Restorationists were gradually prepared and finally determined on ecclesiastical independence, as the only self-respectful alternative left them. Of that movement, and its results, I will treat in my remaining communication, under the captions, *Central Facts* and *Terminal Facts*.

Meanwhile I remain respectfully and gratefully,

ADIN BALLOU

Part 2: From The Universalist, *25 February 1871*

II. CENTRAL FACTS

1. A series of earnest and uncompromising discussions between Restorationists and Universalists of the no-future-retribution school, marked the period from 1826 to 1835 – say eight to nine years. These discussions were chiefly carried on through the press in the form of solid books, or in pamphlets, or in articles of the religious periodicals then published. In 1827 Charles Hudson published his nine letters to Hosea Ballou, a duodecimo volume of 308 pages. It received no other notice from H. Ballou than the

remark, that he had not read it at all, but had been told it contained nothing new. It was, however, a very able production, and could not be quite ignored. So Walter Balfour, who had come into the denomination about the year 1824, with his new phase of the no-future-retribution doctrine, gave Hudson a severe handling. This he did in his subsequently published volume, entitled *Three Essays* &c, in which he denied the immortality of the soul, contended that man remains unconscious between death and the resurrection, and affirmed the resurrection to be a state of absolute moral perfection at the instant of its commencement.[8] This materialistic theory was radically different from that which had previously prevailed among the deniers of future retribution; which assumed that all human souls are immortal – that they are immaculate emanations from God himself – that as such they enter this state of flesh and blood, continue in it from birth till death uncontaminated, and then return to God as pure as they came from him; hence that all sin and misery begin and end in the flesh. This is the theory which Hudson vs. Ballou assailed. But Balfour left that theory undefended and pushed his own. Yet he charged Hudson with "willfully misrepresenting" Ballou, and writing his book to gratify an "old grudge." Hudson replied in 1829, disdaining to deny so absurd a charge, as having written a book to gratify a *grudge,* but incisively answering all the points he deemed worthy of serious consideration. Balfour rejoined with great sharpness in his *Letters* &c. published the same year. The following brief extracts will show that Hudson got little courtesy.

> If no such grudge [against Hosea Ballou] ever existed ... why not repel my charge? Why not say – *I can take my oath that no such grudge against him ever existed, or influenced me in writing my Letters, and that this charge is utterly false.* (p. 15)
>
> Your hell is not to be compared to the Catholic purgatory; for a speedy reformation of souls. Nor are your means of reforming them one-half so rational as theirs. (p. 45)
>
> By your own account hell is a bad missionary ground. (p. 210)
>
> Catholic priests, if well paid, can pray your souls out of purgatory speedily. But you neither pray them out, nor reform them there. (p. 188)
>
> I have shown that your doctrine of an immortal soul and its punishment after death is but heathen chaff. (p. 342)

Yet the *Trumpet* extolled Balfour's works as "written in the spirit of candor!" Not one of the immaculate immortal soul theorists objected to his materialism, or publicly owned that they had changed ground, but indorsed him by the same mysterious semi-silence, which since his death seems to have discarded his theory. That theory came and went very strangely, but it was one of the bitter ingredients that intensified the growing discord.

2. In May 1830, I delivered a discourse to my friends in Medway, Massachusetts, on the text, "What is a man profited, if he gain the whole world and lose his own soul," &c.[9] It was directed solely against the doctrine of endless punishment, and to establish that of universal restoration. But in applying and explaining the Scriptures, I ignored the ultra Universalist interpretations, and followed my own highest light. Among the other instances of this, I quoted 1 Peter 3:18-20 and 4:6, in proof of my doctrines.[10] My friends requested a copy of this sermon for publication and got it printed at the *Trumpet* office, Boston. It came out about the first of July, but was deemed by the editor of the *Trumpet* so heretical and mischievous, that he felt it his duty to denounce it in his paper of that date, as unsound in doctrine, contrary to the prevailing views of "American Universalists," disrespectful to the fathers of the order, and "far behind the orthodox in rescuing the sacred writings from

perversion." (See the first July No. of the *Trumpet*, 1830.) He had often before assumed for his school the title of "American Universalists" *par excellence*, notified opponents that it was of no use for them to argue down the earlier or later Restorationists, but they must refute modern American Universalists, if they could. See *Trumpet*, Vol. 3 No. 4. And again later: "Universalists now know of no condition for man beyond the grave but that in which he is as the angels of God in heaven." Vol. 3 No. 40. Also: "We avoid the heathen notion of recompensing men in one state of being for the conduct they do in another. Of all reveries this is the wildest." (*Notes on Parables*, p. 110)[11]

If this was really so, of course I was a heretic, and ought to be decried accordingly. But I regarded all such assumptions as usurpations, and was determined to stand by my rights. This was the first application of the lash to my back, and it smarted. I immediately wrote an article in self-defense, addressed to the whole denomination, protesting against such treatment, and requested its insertion in the *Trumpet*. It was refused, without even a public hint given of its receipt, and returned to me within ten days unaccompanied by a word of explanation. That article I preserved among my manuscripts, and should not be ashamed to have it read by the whole world. Suffice it to say, I was now thrown into complete sympathy with what was scandalized as "the faction."

3. The Providence Association of Universalists had been formed in 1829, with a constitution which made it independent of the General Convention but held it to be in fellowship with all Universalists and Universalist bodies *on equal terms*. The Maine and New York Conventions then stood on the same ground. But this Providence Association was made up of the recusant Restorationists, and no good was boded from it to "American Universalists." It was censured as disorderly by a resolve of the Southern Association in June 1830, and by the General Convention in the autumn of that year, on the ground that the same persons could not properly act in two independent ecclesiastical bodies having conflicting regulations. After the affair of the Medway sermon, I at once joined the Providence Association, which was "the beginning of the end." It was now proposed and arranged among us to start a weekly religious newspaper, which should be the fearless organ of our cause. Against all discouragements the *Independent Messenger* was commenced, and the first number issued under date of January 1, 1831. I undertook the responsibilities of editor and publisher. Of course no favors were expected, and certainly none received, from the ruling powers of the Universalist denomination. At first our organ was carefully ignored by them. But as I editorially made a full, frank, square exposition of our whole movement, without fear or favor, the religious press of the country, outside of "the order," recognized us at once in a very respectful manner. The first notice we got from the *Trumpet* was a sidewise one, under color of a reply to the *Boston Recorder*, as having republished our slanders, and by thus endorsing them rendered them worthy of public attention. Henceforth there was hot work for a few years. On my part, I made it my business not to let a single hostile charge, imputation or innuendo, whether personal, doctrinal, or polemical, go unrefuted during this period of active warfare. What I did in that line, and how I succeeded, can be known only by searching the files of the *Independent Messenger*. Also the creditable assistance therein of my coadjutors.

4. On the 16th of August, 1831, the Providence Association met in Mendon, Massachusetts, then my pastoral residence. On the 17th and 18th the plan of our separation from the Universalist denomination was matured, and we formed "The Massachusetts Association of Universal Restorationists." The original ministers of the new order were

Paul Dean, David Pickering, Charles Hudson, Adin Ballou, Lyman Maynard, Nathaniel Wright, Philemon R. Russell, and Seth Chandler – eight. Many of the ensuing events, otherwise desirable to record, my limits oblige me to pass over. Our association greatly prospered in its most important interests for ten years. It met regularly every one of those years, and more than trebled its original number of ministers. Among those added were Edmund Capron; William H. Fish, now of South Scituate, Massachusetts; Edwin M. Stone, minister at large in Providence, Rhode Island; William Morse; George W. Stacy; Daniel S. Whitney; David R. Lamson; James H. Sayward,[12] &c., &c. – nearly all of whom had been either ministers or laymen in the Universalist denomination. At the time of our final meeting in 1841 we had a larger ministerial membership than the whole General Convention of Universalists had forty years before. (See *Modern History* &c.) And this was that ill-born, sickly faction, which could not grow, "and died a natural death in a year or two"! Who now will believe my statement? And if any believe, how will they account for the disparaging representations so many times reiterated?

III. Terminal Facts

It will now be asked how this Secession Association came to its death? and why? I will give the facts and reasons.

1. The Unitarian denomination, which previously to our secession had kept itself almost silent (not entirely so) concerning the final destiny of mankind, began at an early moment to sympathize with, encourage, befriend and fellowship us. Never did a little body of people more need such treatment, and never was one more grateful. Many of the Unitarian clergy, hitherto cautiously silent, avowed themselves Restorationist in sentiment. We were allowed perfect freedom to preach and publish our Restorationism. We were welcomed to Unitarian pulpits and parishes. We became to a considerable extent fused into their denomination. Can any body guess what effect all this was likely to have on our judgment as to the propriety of maintaining a separate denomination?

2. The battle was over with the Universalist denomination. It was virtually over in 1835, by the cessation of all offensive language towards Restorationists as such. It was found not *to pay*. The very last demonstration of contempt, that I can now recollect, was made in the spring of 1834, by the editors of the *New Haven Examiner* and, I think, *The Gospel Anchor*, respectively. Samuel C. Loveland,[13] a learned Restorationist in Vermont, who, though cordially sympathizing with us, still remained a member of the General Convention, publicly offered to write a Commentary on the New Testament for the denomination. Thereupon the said editors came out with such remarks as the following:

> S. C. Loveland, of Reading, Vermont, who for some years past has been endeavoring to make himself notorious... very modestly offers to write a Commentary on the New Testament for the Universalists – since Mr. Ballou has declined. We consider him unqualified in every respect for the undertaking. His peculiar views of doctrine are at variance with the great body of Universalists. He possesses little in common with the denomination to which he nominally belongs. – *Examiner*

> Whatever our author might furnish in reference to the interesting subject of *punishment*, would be written in full view of his *fabled gulf of purgatorial sufferings in the future immortal state* – a sentiment which we regard as a relic of heathenism, &c. &c. – *Anchor*

Such fraternal compliments roused Dolphus Skinner,[14] editor of the *Evangelical Magazine*, Utica, New York, hitherto a quiescent Restorationist, who came out in a powerful article, of which the following is an extract:

We have all along blamed our Restorationist brethren at the East for seceding from the connexion, and supposed that they would never have done it had they possessed a proper spirit of forbearance and charity. But if they experienced many manifestations, from the brethren of opposing views, of a similar spirit and treatment to that we are now called to notice, we shall cease to wonder at, or blame them for such secession. Nay, we shall not only approve their course, but can assure these editors and the Universalist public, that a perseverance in, and the general prevalence (among Universalists) of the spirit these two editors have manifested, will be followed, not merely by the secession of a dozen clergymen in one State, but by the secession of many scores, if not hundreds, throughout the Union.[15]

I should like to note the whole article, but of course cannot. This closed forever the ultra Universalist policy of making its peculiar *ism* the orthodoxy of the sect. From that day to this, Restorationism within the denomination has breathed freely, until at length nine-tenths of it are Restorationists.[16] And I venture to say that, in respect to the doctrine of future discipline, and also the care for personal religion zealously promoted throughout the body, the Universalist denomination is much nearer what we set out to make our association, than like its former self when we seceded. That the tide had turned in this direction began to be indicated in 1841. What room was there likely to be for working the machinery of a Restorationist sect between the Unitarians and Universalists, under these changed circumstances? Is it probable such a change could have been brought about without the intervention of our secession? Why then not accept the result? We did.

3. The great moral reforms, temperance, anti-slavery, &c., &c., were sweeping across all the religious denominations, throwing theological and ecclesiastical interests into the background for the time, forming new associational ties, and weakening old ones. The Unitarians and Universalists felt this new influence powerfully. (Remember the *Christian Freeman*, etc.)[17] Our association felt its full force. A part of us became radical (and perhaps even zealous) reformers, even to Christian non-resistance and social reorganizationism. The other part remained (perhaps wisely) conservatives on many points. We had no bitter differences, but honest ones, concerning these upheaving agitations. So it was with several of the older and larger sects. We met in 1841, on our tenth anniversary, and in view of all these changed circumstances, decided to suspend our denominational organization for the then present. It has remained suspended ever since, and there is no good reason why it should be revived. Its mission was a moral necessity, and well fulfilled – to the lasting good of all sects and parties affected by it.

It remains for me to say, in closing, that the memory of its principal and most influential members, departed and surviving, is to me precious and blessed. I stood in the center and forefront of them. I had intimate personal, religious, and pecuniary dealings with them. They were conciliatory, just, honorable, and generous men. I know nothing mean in one of them – nothing that made them uncomfortable to counsel and act with. Paul Dean was often represented as an ambitious, plotting, intriguing man, making tools of his weaker brethren – even of me. I never saw the first particle of such qualities in him. So far as I know or believe, he was always delicate, gentlemanly and considerate towards his juniors. I had sometimes to urge and hurry him to the front, but never he me. He was, in fact, conservative, cautious and uncombative. In doctrine he was nearly a Sabellian, semi-orthodox on the atonement, and constitutionally averse to every thing radical in faith or practice. He was one of the dignified sort of men who prefer to let alone, and be let alone. But he was a sincere Restorationist, a self-sacrificing man, free from all sordidness, stinginess, or disposition to make a cat's paw of dupes. In fine, he was a Christian according to his highest light. He and I honestly differed on various points, but always in kindness. I wanted to bear this testimony in his particular case, because I fear injustice may be done to his memory, as I know it was done in respect to the part he acted in our secession. And of all concerned therein, if any one was foolish, faulty, or guilty, none was more so than myself, either in organizing, supporting, or suspending the Massachusetts Association.

I have tried, in these communications, to testify to essential facts, without sitting in judgment on the hidden motives of opposers. If they wronged me at all, I freely forgive them. If in any way, formerly or latterly, I have wronged them, I pray that I may see it, repent of it, and be forgiven of God and men. If any one can point out any mistake or error I have made in this *synoptical history*, I shall be glad to have it done, and to acknowledge it publicly.

And now reiterating my thanks for the privilege granted me in these columns, and wishing nothing but blessings to the Universalist denomination, and the whole human race, both in time and eternity, I subscribe myself the friend of truth, righteousness and all good.

ADIN BALLOU

APPENDIX H

The Ballou-Tolstoy Correspondence

The correspondence consists of four letters, two by Tolstoy and two by Ballou. There are two published sources for these letters:
   1. *"The Christian Doctrine of Non-Resistance: By Count Leo Tolstoï and the Rev. Adin Ballou. Unpublished correspondence compiled by Rev. Lewis G. Wilson," The Arena (December 1890), 1-12.*
   2. *Frederic I. Carpenter, "A Letter from Tolstoy," New England Quarterly (1931), 777-782.*

Lewis Wilson's part in initiating and publishing the correspondence is described in chapter 24 of the Autobiography. The other source was Frederic Ives Carpenter Jr. (1903-1991), a professor of English and a prolific writer on American literature and cultural history. In his 1931 article he explained that the last two letters in the Ballou–Tolstoy correspondence had come into his hands (he did not say how) and that they differed significantly from the version printed in The Arena. He wrote, "Wilson, who edited the letters, deleted several passages from them, and corrected (without notice) Tolstoy's use of the English language. The originals ... seem of such interest as to justify republication in their original form."

The letters here generally follow the version in Wilson's article. Where possible, text omitted by Wilson has been restored based on Carpenter's article; this added text is shown in square brackets. In a few cases (in Ballou's letter as well as in Tolstoy's), Carpenter's reading of a word has been used in preference to Wilson's. These changes are shown in square brackets and discussed in footnotes.

LEO TOLSTOY TO LEWIS G. WILSON
July 5, 1889

Dear Sir:—
I have seldom experienced so much gratification as I had in reading Mr. Ballou's treatise and tracts. I cannot agree with those who say that Mr. Ballou "will not go down to posterity among the immortals." I think that because he has been one of the first true apostles of the "New Time" – he will be in the future acknowledged as one of the chief benefactors of humanity. If, in his long and seemingly unsuccessful career, Mr. Ballou has experienced moments of depression in thinking that his efforts have been vain, he has only partaken of the fate of his and our Master.

Tell him, please, that his efforts have not been vain. They give great strength to people, as I can judge from myself. In those tracts I found all the objections that are generally made against "non-resistance" victoriously answered, and also the true basis of the doctrine. I will endeavor to translate and propagate as much as I can, the works of Mr. Ballou, and I not only hope, but am convinced, that the time is come, "when the dead shall hear the voice of the Son of God; and they that hear shall live."[1]

The only comments that I wish to make on Mr. Ballou's explanation of the doctrine, are, firstly, that I cannot agree with the concession that he makes for employing violence against drunkards and insane people. The Master made no concessions, and we can make none. We must try, as Mr. Ballou puts it, to make impossible the existence of such persons, but if they are – we must use all possible means, sacrifice ourselves, but not employ violence. A true Christian will always prefer to be killed by a madman, rather than to deprive him of his liberty. Secondly, that Mr. Ballou does not decide more categorically the question of *property*, for a true Christian not only cannot claim any rights of property, but the term "property" cannot have any signification for him. All that he uses, a Christian only uses till somebody takes it from him. He cannot defend his property, so he cannot have any. Property has been Achilles' heel for the Quakers, and also for the Hopedale Community. Thirdly, I think that for a true Christian, the term "government" (very properly defined by Mr. Ballou) cannot have any signification and reality. Government is for a Christian only regulated violence; governments, states, nations, property, churches – all these for a true Christian are only words without meaning; he can understand the meaning other people attach to those words, but for him they have none, just as for a business man if he were to come in the middle of a cricket party, all the divisions of the ground, and regulations of the game, could have no importance or influence upon his activity. No compromise! Christian principles must be pursued to the bottom, to be able to support practical life. The saying of Christ that, "*If any man will come after me, let him deny himself and take up his cross daily and follow me,*"[2] was true in His time, and is true in ours; a follower of Christ must be ready to be poor and suffer; if not he cannot be his disciple, and "non-resistance" implies it all. Moreover, the *necessity* of suffering for a Christian is a great good, because otherwise, we could never know, if what we are doing we are doing for God, or for ourselves.

The application of every doctrine is always a compromise, but the doctrine in theory cannot allow compromises; although we know we never can draw a mathematically straight line, we will never make another definition of a straight line than "the shortest distance between two points."

* * * * *

"*I am come to send fire on the earth, and what will I, if it be already kindled!*"[3] I think that this time is coming, and that the world is on fire, and our business is only to keep ourselves burning; and if we can communicate with other burning points, that is the work which I intend to do for the rest of my life. Many thanks for your letter, and for Mr. Ballou's portrait and books. Please tell him that I deeply respect and love him, and that his work did great good to my soul, and I pray and hope that I may do the same to others.

Your brother in Christ,
Leo Tolstoy.

Adin Ballou to Leo Tolstoy
January 14, 1890

Dear Sir and Brother:—

I gratefully appreciate your approval of my work on Christian Non-Resistance and your fraternal sympathy with me therein, as expressed in your letter of July 5, 1889, to Rev. Lewis G. Wilson, of this place. I am an old man of little distinction or fame in this world, and must soon pass into the realm of the Invisible where the ambitions of this world are of small account. It gives me little concern to know that a mere handful of mankind concur with me in this sublime doctrine and that the vast multitude, even in the so-called Christian church and state, hold it in contempt; for I am none the less certain it is divinely true and excellent, and will finally prevail.

I have candidly considered your exceptions to some of my definitions and qualifications of Christian Non-Resistance, and do not complain of your frank dissent from them. Such differences are to be expected among free and independent minds. But I am obliged to say with the same fraternal frankness, that I am confirmed in my persuasion that on the minor points of difference between us I am in the right. I desire therefore, briefly, to defend my positions as against yours. In this I am sure you will indulge me.

1. You say, "I cannot agree with the concession that he makes for employing violence against drunkards and insane people: the Master made no concessions and we must make none." I made no concessions for employing *violence* in any case; but for employing uninjurious, benevolent physical force, in the cases alluded to, where the absolute welfare of all the parties concerned should be scrupulously regarded. I make no concession to killing, injuring, or harming any human being. What I approved, is not only sanctioned but dictated by the law of pure good will. This class of cases includes all cases of delirium, partial delirium, and passional outrage wherein the assailant, as well as the victim, will have reason for thankfulness that beneficent restraint and prevention was imposed. There are multitudes of such cases in human experience; and the employment of beneficent physical restraint in such cases must not be confounded with the popular doctrine that it is right to employ deadly physical force against human offenders and enemies. *This* is the resistance of evil which Christ forbade.

2. You say, "The Master made no concessions and we must make none." True, he made no concessions allowing us to employ vindictive, or deadly, or harmful force against our human offenders and enemies, and we must make none. The use and employment of such forces had been sanctioned by law and custom from time immemorial as necessary and right for the resistance of evil doers. It is still the fundamental assumption of all legislators, governments and worldly-minded individuals. But Christ uncompromisingly prohibited it. What then? Did he ever prohibit the resistance of evil by uninjurious and beneficent forces of any kind, physical or moral? Never! And to construe his precept, "Resist not evil," as meaning absolute passivity to all manner of evil, because he made no specific qualifications, is to ignore the context and make him the author of self-evident absurdity. The context clearly shows what kind of resistance of evil had been sanctioned by law and custom, and what he meant to abrogate. And it shows exactly the application and limitations of his precepts. It means neither less nor more than the context plainly indicates. And enlightened reason goes the same length.

3. You say, "The application of every doctrine is always a compromise, but the doctrine or theory cannot allow compromise, etc." I am not sure that I understand this statement. If I do, it means that no doctrine, theory, or precept can be carried out in practice without compromise. If this be your meaning, I must dissent. In ethics, I think no doctrine, theory, or prescribed duty is sound that cannot be put in practice uncompromisingly. And it seems to me to be a dangerous concession to make to human tergiversation, that a moral precept strictly right is expected to be compromised in application to actual practice. Religionists and moralists the world over, have ever been professing to hold sacred many great precepts – such as the Second Commandment and Golden Rule – yet wholly violating them on this very ground that, as the world is, they cannot be applied and lived out without compromise. Should we – non-resistants – go and do likewise? – be rigid in statement of our doctrine, yet lax and inconsistent in practice?

4. You say, "True Christians will always prefer to be killed by a madman rather than to deprive him of his liberty." And by parity of reason from the same principle, I suppose you must say, a true Christian, if watching with a delirious sick man, would prefer to see him kill his wife, children, and best friends, rather than restrain or help restrain him by uninjurious physical force of his insane liberty. What precept of Christ makes insane liberty thus sacred? Or what dictate of enlightened reason, humanity, or fraternal love demands such conduct towards the insane?

5. You say, "A true Christian not only cannot claim any rights of property, but the term 'property' cannot have any signification for him; all that he uses, a Christian only uses until somebody takes it from him." But food, raiment, and shelter are necessaries of mortal existence to Christians as to all human beings. They are indispensable material goods to this extent at least. Jesus said, "Your heavenly Father knoweth that ye have need of all these things."[4] If they are necessaries of mortal life, they certainly have a very important "signification." Jesus said, "Seek ye first the kingdom of God and his righteousness, and all these things shall be added unto you."[5] When they have been "added" to true Christians according to the will of the Father, whose are they? Are they not the rightful property of those who possess them? – to whom God has "added" them? as truly theirs as their bodily faculties – for the just use of which they are morally responsible – and which no human beings have any right to deprive them of by fraud or force?

Yet, you say, "A true Christian cannot claim any rights of property... All that he uses, a Christian only uses till somebody takes it from him." But has anybody a right to take it from him at will? Is there no such thing as theft, robbery, extortion, or crime against property, against which a true Christian may protest? On the other hand, is there no such thing as a true Christian having any property to give away in alms or charity, according to Christ's injunction? I do not so understand Christ or the dictates of reason, or the law of love.

6. You say, "Government is, for a Christian, only regulated violence ... governments, states, nations, property, churches – all these for a true Christian are only words without meaning, etc." But these are realities, we cannot ignore them as nonentities. They are outgrowths from nature, however crude and defective. Man is a social being by natural constitution, he is not and never can be a solitary, independent, individual being. He must, and will be inevitably more or less a socialist. Families, governments, states, nations, churches, and communities, always have existed, and always will. Christ came to establish the highest order of governmental association, a purely fraternal social order – a church "against which the gates of hell should not prevail."[6] For this he lived and died. No-governmentism, non-organizationism, sheer individualism, is no part of true Christianity. It is impossible, unnatural, irrational – a chaos. We should aim with our Master, to transform by the moral forces of divine, fundamental principles uncompromisingly lived out, all barbaric, semi-barbaric, and unchristian social organizations into his ideal one, the true church, wherein the greatest are least and all in unity of spirit with him, as he with the universal Father. If in this holy aim we must dissent from the selfish and warlike multitude, let us follow him even unto death, till the final triumph arrives. These are my highest convictions of truth and righteousness.

Permit me to add a few queries on some positions assumed in your work entitled "My Religion."

1. Concerning the Son of Man you say, "The son of man is homogeneous (of the same race) with God." (p. 125) "The son of man is the light in every man that ought to illuminate his life." " This light is reason, which alone should be the object of our worship,

since it alone can show us the way to true wellbeing." (p. 126) "The son of man, endowed with true kingly authority will call upon the faithful to inherit the true life; they have fed the hungry, given drink to the thirsty, clothed and consoled the wretched, and in so doing they have ministered to the son of man who is the same in all men. They have not lived the personal life, but the life of the son of man, and they are given the life eternal." (pp. 142-3)

Query. If the son of man is "homogeneous with God," is the light from heaven given to illuminate – is *reason,* which alone should be worshipped – how is it in any sense of man? Is it not of God, or rather the very God himself? But if it is God how can it need or receive ministrations from men, for which it should return compensation? Are not these ministrations said to be rendered, by human beings personally, to human persons? Are not givers and receivers said to be personally blest? Again, did not Christ uniformly represent himself as personally the son of man? Once more – Is reason really and absolutely God, alone to be worshipped? Is it not rather a faculty of God, and also finitely of the human soul? Pardon these queries of an unmystical mind.

2. Concerning individual conscious existence after death, etc., you say, "Strange as it may seem, Jesus, who is supposed to have been raised in person, and to have promised a general resurrection – Jesus not only said nothing in affirmation of individual resurrection and individual immortality beyond the grave, but on the contrary, every time he met with this superstition, he did not fail to deny its truth." (p. 143) "Jesus affirmed only this, that whoever lives in God will be united with God; and he admitted no other idea of the resurrection. As to personal resurrection, strange as it may appear to those who have never studied the Gospels for themselves, Jesus said nothing about it whatever." (p. 144) I have diligently studied the Gospels for myself more than seventy-five years, and these assertions are so utterly contrary to the sense in which I have understood many passages in those Gospels, that had I familiar opportunity to question you, I fear I should be troublesome. But as I have no such opportunity, I will content myself with the following inquiries: Will the most righteous derive any conscious good from their faithfulness, except here in this present mortal existence? If united to God, as you express it, will they have any consciousness of it after physical death? And as the vast majority of mankind abide in spiritual death, disunited from God, and have no opportunity for improvement after death, of what value is their personal existence at all? And what credit does such an abortive existence reflect on their Creator?

Trusting that your Christian consideration will make generous allowance for the freedom with which I have addressed you and for even any seeming impertinences, I remain, with high esteem and Christian affection,

Your friend and brother,
ADIN BALLOU.

LEO TOLSTOY TO ADIN BALLOU
Undated; received March 26, 1890

Dear Friend and Brother:—
I will not argue with your objections. It would not bring us to anything. Only one point which I did not put clearly enough in my last letter I must explain, to avoid misunderstanding. It is about compromise. I said that compromise, inevitable in practice, cannot be admitted in theory. What I mean is this: Man never attains perfection, but only approaches it. As it is impossible to trace in reality a mathematically straight line, and as

every such line is only an approach to the latter, so is every degree of perfection attainable by man only an approach to the perfection of the Father, which Christ showed us the way to emulate. Therefore, in reality, every deed of the best man and his whole life will be always only a practical compromise – a resultant between his feebleness and his striving to attain perfection. And such a compromise in practice is not a sin, but a necessary condition of every Christian life. The great sin is the compromise in theory, is the plan to lower the ideal of Christ in view to make it attainable. And I consider the admission of force (be it even benevolent) over a madman (the great difficulty is to give a strict definition of a madman) to be such a theoretical compromise. In not admitting this compromise I run the risk only of my death, or the death of other men who can be killed by the madman; but death will come sooner or later, and death in fulfilling the will of God is a blessing (as you put it yourself in your book); but in admitting this compromise I run the risk of acting quite contrary to the law of Christ – which is worse than death. As soon as I admit in principle my right to property, I necessarily will try to keep it from others, and to increase it, and therefore will deviate very far from the ideal of Christ. Only if I profess daringly that a Christian can not have any property will I in practice come near to the ideal of Christ in this instance.[a] There is a striking example of such a deviation in theory about anger (Matt. 5:22) where the added word "without any cause" has justified and justifies still, every intolerance, punishment, and evil, which have been and are so often done by nominal Christians. The more we keep in mind the idea of a straight line, viz., the shortest distance between two points – the nearer we will come to trace in reality a straight line. The purer we will keep the ideal of Christ's perfection in its unattainableness, the nearer we will in reality come to it.

Allow me not to argue upon several dogmatical differences of opinion about the meaning of the words "son of God," about personal life after death and about resurrection. I have written a large work on the translation, [encordance][b] and explanation of the Gospels in which I exposed all I think on those subjects.[7] Having at the time – ten years ago – given all the strength of my soul for the conception of those questions, I cannot now change my views without verifying [everything] anew.[c] But the differences of opinion on these subjects seem to me of little consequence. I firmly believe that if I [consecrate][d] all my powers to the fulfillment of the Master's will which is so clearly expressed in his words and in my conscience, and nevertheless, should not guess quite rightly the aims and plans of the Master whom I serve, he would still not abandon me – and do the best for me.

I would be very grateful to you should you send me a line [from yourself. Please give my love to Mr. Wilson.] Two of your tracts are very well translated into Russian and propagated among believers, and [highly][e] appreciated by them. With deep veneration and tender love, I remain,

Your brother and friend,
LEO TOLSTOY.

---

[a] Wilson interpreted this sentence as a question: "Only when I profess daringly that a Christian cannot have any property, will I not in practice come near to the ideal of Christ in this instance?"

[b] Wilson omitted the unusual word "encordance," or harmonization.

[c] Wilson changed this to "verifying them anew."

[d] Wilson read this as "... if I concentrated all my powers ..." However, it is clear from Ballou's next letter that "consecrate" is correct.

[e] Wilson read this as "... richly appreciated by them."

ADIN BALLOU TO LEO TOLSTOY
May 30, 1890

[*Very Dear Sir and Brother:*—
Your fraternal and kind letter, undated, was duly received on the 26th of March last. I have delayed my acknowledgment of its receipt much beyond my original intention. Old age slackens my activity, and you must excuse my tardiness. I fear that the bluntness with which I stated some points of dissent from your views may have seemed hardly courteous to you; though they were in no wise so meant. I thank you for the kindness of your reply, and for the explanation of your statement respecting the compromise in practice of an uncompromisable theory. I am far from desiring controversy or argumentation concerning our wordy differences. Let them sleep. And I assure you I heartily concur in the conclusion expressed in one of your closing sentences, "I firmly believe that if I consecrated all my powers to the fulfillment of the Master's will, which is so clearly expressed in his words and in my conscience, nevertheless should I not guess quite rightly the aims and plans of the Master whom I serve, he would still aid and do the best for me." So we will trustfully govern ourselves accordingly.

Our mutual brother L. G. Wilson, appreciates your loving remembrance, and cordially reciprocates it. I herewith send you a few more of my publications of various date, which I do not expect you to endorse in the gross, and from which I give you perfect liberty to dissent, according to your own highest convictions. But if you can find time and patience to read them, they will make you more acquainted with my peculiar trains of thought. I hope they will safely reach you, in spite of the stringent censorship which prevails in your country. I am highly gratified to know that I have a goodly few Non-Resistant brethren in Russia, and I remember them in my daily prayers, thanking our heavenly Father that he has begotten them into this supernal faith, and that my writings minister in any degree to their edification. I wish I could report more growth of this heavenly doctrine in my own country.] It is [gradually] leavening many minds, but the bewitching influence of [worldly] politics, and the temporal [advantages]^f which the old system, founded on deadly compulsion, affords to multitudes of professional aspirants, are almost omnipotent. The one and almost only argument I encounter is, Your doctrine is heavenly, grand, and Christ-like, but it is [impracticable]^g as society *is*. We must have government, hold office, and make money. So church, state, and the political multitude are anchored securely in compulsory civilization until the millennium!

But none of these seductions swerve me a hair's breadth from Him who is "The Way, the Truth, and the Life."[8] And I am confident of two conclusions. First, that Christianity will never enter its promised land till the nominal church re-embraces non-resistance as its capstone; and second, that this doctrine will finally be thus re-embraced. It is now accounted foolishness, but will prove to be the "Wisdom of God."[9] It is now set at naught by the builders, but will yet become "the headstone of the corner."[10]

Wishing you benedictions, divine and innumerable, I remain your friend and brother in Christ Jesus, evermore,

ADIN BALLOU.

---

f   Wilson: "advantage."
g   Wilson: "impractical."

Notes

References and Abbreviations

The following works are referenced in the Notes:

Ancient History of Universalism — Hosea Ballou 2d, *Ancient History of Universalism: from the time of the Apostles, to its condemnation in the Fifth General Council A.D. 553* (Boston, 1829).

Genealogy — Adin Ballou, *An Elaborate History and Genealogy of the Ballous in America* (Providence, 1888).

History of the Hopedale Community — Adin Ballou, *History of the Hopedale Community, from its inception to its virtual submergence in the Hopedale Parish* (Lowell, MA, 1897; reprinted, Providence: Blackstone Editions, 2010).

History of the Town of Milford — Adin Ballou, *History of the Town of Milford, Worcester County, Massachusetts, from its First Settlement to 1881* (Boston, 1882).

Hopedale Reminiscences — *Hopedale Reminiscences: Papers Read before the Hopedale Ladies' Sewing Society and Branch Alliance* (Hopedale, 1910). Reprinted in *Hopedale Reminiscences: Childhood Memories of the Hopedale Community and the Hopedale Home School* (Providence, Blackstone Editions, 2006).

Modern History of Universalism — Thomas Whittemore, *Modern History of Universalism: from the era of the reformation to the present time* (Boston, 1830).

Practical Christian Socialism — Adin Ballou, *Practical Christian Socialism: A Conversational Exposition of the True System of Human Society* (Hopedale, 1854; reprinted, New York: AMS Press, 1974).

The following abbreviations are used in the Notes:

MAUR	Massachusetts Association of Universal Restorationists
UGC	Universalist General Convention
UPU	Universal Peace Union

Notes

Chapter 1

[1] The town of Providence was founded in 1636, when Roger Williams donated the land he had earlier purchased from the Narragansetts in order to establish "a shelter for persons distressed of conscience." The new community was established upon a shareholding basis. Those who could afford to buy a share were granted a hundred acres of land and a house lot. These were the "co-proprietors with Roger Williams in the first settlement of Providence Plantations." Many of the people who came later could not afford the price of a share. These settlers were granted "freedom of inhabitation," but did not own land and could not vote. Maturin Ballou was one of these. In 1646, he and thirty-five others were allowed to purchase land by quarter shares. They did not receive voting rights until 1658. It was in this extended sense that Maturin Ballou could be called a co-proprietor.

[2] Adin Ballou's maternal grandparents were Levi Tower (1742-1826) and Mary Whipple Tower (1745-c.1815). In 1817 Levi married Mary's sister, Hannah Whipple Emerson.

Levi Tower was a captain in the militia and served in the Revolutionary War, 1775-81. His experiments in mining and metalworking may have been an attempt to exploit the region's unusual form of iron ore, called "cumberlandite." There was a Levi Tower who owned a sawmill in Cumberland in the 1780s, but it is not clear whether this was Ballou's grandfather or another member of the family.

[3] Later, when he was researching the Ballou genealogy, Ballou was able to determine that his grandmother Jerusha Slack Ballou, at least, was a member of the Baptist church.

[4] Adin Ballou's siblings from his father's first marriage ranged in age from Rosina, who was a married woman of twenty when he was born, to Alfred, who was just four years his senior.

In his *History and Genealogy of the Ballous in America* (1888), Ballou wrote in respectful and affectionate terms of his four oldest siblings. Rosina was "an excellent woman – generous hearted, intelligent, conscientious." Abigail was "upright in moral character, indomitably industrious, and richly endowed with the qualities of a good wife, mother, and neighbor." Cyrus and Arnold, who both died when Adin was in his teens, were remembered for "vigorous intellect, high moral integrity, and a predisposition to religious affections" and "amiable disposition, intelligent mental capacities, and exemplary moral character." Adin never knew his sister Sarah, who died at the age of eight the same year he was born. His brother Alfred, however, seems to have been one of the few people that he really disliked. In the *Genealogy* he wrote about Alfred – then recently deceased – with uncharacteristic bitterness:

He was not much tinctured with the heretical hope of divine mercy to the wicked after death, nor with *"rose-water philanthropy"* towards rebels against law and order under human government. He retained some of the good old faith in the wholesomeness of the sword and gibbet in this world, and of an unsparing hell in the next for all incorrigible evil doers. We mention these traits in our brother's character for the edification of those readers who may think the Ballous prone to be a little too lenient toward sinners ... They are not all Universalists, much less Restorationist Non-Resistants like the erratic compiler of these family records.

Adin and Alfred were clearly separated by differences of temperament, beliefs, and values, but the tone of this passage suggests a deeper hostility dating back to childhood.

⁵ Ariel Ballou Jr. (1805-1887) received his diploma from the Maine Medical School in 1830 and set up practice in Woonsocket, Rhode Island. He was responsible for the introduction of the bill in the Rhode Island state legislature that abolished capital punishment. He was an Episcopalian and a longtime Freemason, serving as Grand Master of the Rhode Island Grand Lodge from 1861 to 1865.

⁶ Ballou's son-in-law, William S. Heywood, who completed and edited the *Autobiography* after Ballou's death, inserted the following note at the end of this paragraph:

Later investigation convinced the author that his family was not of Huguenot descent, but sprang from one Guinebond Balou, who probably passed over from Normandy with William the Conqueror in 1066 and served as one of his marshals at the battle of Hastings. See introduction to *The Ballous in America*.

Although the *Genealogy* was published before the *Autobiography*, the early genealogical portion of the autobiography was written before the *Genealogy*, and reflects family tradition as handed down to Adin Ballou. As a result of information provided by Frederick M. Ballou, who traveled to England and France in 1884 to collect information for the genealogy, Adin Ballou changed his mind and, despite the family tradition that Maturin Ballou was a Huguenot, decided that the New England Ballous were related to the Bellew family in England, and were descendants of a Norman nobleman. This conclusion has been incorporated into many genealogical and biographical reference works for which the *Genealogy* is the source.

None of the ancestors of Maturin Ballou has ever been traced. The seemingly authoritative pronouncement of the English genealogist whom the Ballous consulted is based entirely upon similarity of pronunciation. Adin Ballou argued in the *Genealogy* that Maturin Ballou was unlikely to have been a Huguenot refugee, since he arrived in America prior to the revocation of the Edict of Nantes in 1685. The revocation, however, did not mark the beginning, but the culmination of a century and a half of persecution of French Protestants.

A more thorough examination of the problem, taking into account the distinctively French spelling and pronunciation of Maturin Ballou's name, would have rendered the hypothesis that the Ballous were descended through countless generations of English Bellews quite unlikely. Furthermore, the name *Ballou*, spelled in just that form, is found among other, better-documented, Huguenot settlers in America.

Based upon the fragments of family tradition recorded in the *Autobiography*, it seems most likely that Maturin Ballou's parents (or, possibly, grandparents) were Huguenot refugees who settled in England. From England, Maturin Ballou, perhaps already assimilated into an English Independent church, emigrated again, along with the Massachusetts Puritans, in the wave that fled the pressure put on them in the 1630s to worship in conformity with the Book of Common Prayer and the established English Church.

For a more detailed discussion see Lynn Gordon Hughes, "The European Origin of the Ballou Family: A Review of the Evidence" (http://www.ballewassn.org/ballou_origins.htm).

[7] Hosea Ballou (1771-1852) was the leading theologian and the most prominent preacher among American Universalists in the early nineteenth century. He persuaded most of his fellow Universalists to reject doctrines generally considered fundamental to the Christian faith, such as the Trinity and vicarious atonement.

Hosea Ballou was raised in a Baptist family, but his study of the Scriptures led him to embrace the doctrine of universal salvation before he was twenty years old. He began to preach universal salvation in Rhode Island and central Massachusetts while supporting himself by teaching school. When he was twenty-four he gave up teaching to become a full-time itinerant preacher, based in Dana, Massachusetts.

From 1801 to 1809, while serving five churches in rural Vermont, Ballou wrote his first and perhaps most important theological works, *Notes on the Parables* (1804) and *Treatise on Atonement* (1805). He argued that human beings do wrong, not because of a fallen nature, but because they are mortal and therefore fallible. Suffering is not divine punishment, but the natural consequence of human imperfection. The task of the Mediator (his preferred term for Christ) was not to reconcile God to humanity, but to reconcile human beings to God – to free them from the blindness of sin, and allow them to see the divine love and goodness hidden beneath the appearance of evil and suffering.

From 1809 to 1817 Ballou served Universalist churches in Portsmouth, New Hampshire, 1809-15, and Salem, Massachusetts, 1815-17. During these years Universalists began to debate the question of "future punishment" – that is, whether all souls would be restored to "holiness and happiness" immediately after death, or whether a finite period of discipline or punishment would be needed to make them fit for salvation. Ballou's understanding of human nature inclined him to the no-future-punishment side, but he did not come out strongly on the issue until 1817, when he debated the question with his friend Edward Turner in the pages of a Universalist periodical called the *Gospel Visitant*. Sadly, the debate grew so acrimonious that it irreparably damaged the friendship between Ballou and Turner. This was one of the seeds of the "Restorationist controversy" that shook the denomination during the 1820s (see chapter 5, note 13).

In 1817 Ballou settled in Boston as minister of the newly-formed Second Universalist Society, a position he held for the last thirty-five years of his life. In addition to being a prominent preacher and theologian, Ballou was a pioneer of Universalist journalism. In 1819 he founded a weekly newspaper, the *Universalist Magazine*, in partnership with the printer Henry Bowen. Ballou's disciple, Thomas Whittemore, and his great-nephew, Hosea Ballou 2d, became co-editors in 1822. Whittemore became sole editor and proprietor in 1828 (see chapter 8, note 4).

[8] For a discussion of the effectiveness of this light as a summons to battle, see Raymond Palin, "Revolutionary Cumberland: A Note on a Historical Controversy," *Rhode Island History* 51 (November 1993), 129.

[9] The meetinghouse, a two-story, shingled structure, measuring 25 by 30 feet, was erected in 1745 on land deeded to the First Baptist Society in Cumberland by James Ballou (1684-1764), the great-grandfather of Adin Ballou. In its early days, during the pastorates of Josiah and Nathaniel Cook, the building was called the Elder Cook Meetinghouse. After the Cooks were succeeded by Elder Abner Ballou, the popular name for the meetinghouse changed. The building stood in Iron Rock Meadow until 1962, when it fell victim to arson.

[10] The cemetery, and the Ballou family graves, are still to be found on the south side of Elder Ballou Meetinghouse Road in Cumberland, Rhode Island, still obscured by "wild grass and brush."

[11] The five principles generally accepted by Baptists were repentance, faith, baptism, resurrection of the dead, and eternal judgment. Six Principle Baptists added another principle: the laying on of hands, which was administered after baptism. They practiced two other unusual rites: foot-washing and anointing the sick with oil. Unlike Calvinist Baptists, they believed in general redemption; that is, that any person, not only the elect, might be saved. Ballou wrote in the *Genealogy* that they "leaned more towards Arminianism, were Trinitarians rather indefinitely, and otherwise quite evangelical" (p. 92).

The Six Principle congregations maintained a tight internal discipline. They practiced rigidly closed communion, avoided people who belonged to other churches, and excommunicated those who married out of their sect. They rejected any tendency that might produce a separate clergy class or an ecclesiastical hierarchy; ministers, who were referred to as elders, were not specially educated, nor were they paid for their services.

The Six Principle Baptists gained control of the Baptist church in Providence in 1652. By the mid-eighteenth century, however, their simple worship, communal discipline, and unlearned ministry no longer suited the needs of the emerging urban commercial class. In 1770 the more traditional members of the church seceded and formed a new Six Principle congregation in Johnston, west of Providence. They remained the dominant religious sect in the rural north and west of Rhode Island during the eighteenth century.

[12] Abner Ballou (1725-1806) lived his entire life in the "Ballou neighborhood" of Cumberland, Rhode Island. In 1755 he joined the Baptist church led by Elders Josiah and Nathaniel Cook. Around 1770 he became its minister, a position he held for the last 35 years of his life. Like many Baptists of his era, Abner Ballou was opposed to "school-made" and "hireling" ministers. He accepted freewill offerings for preaching, but depended on farming for his livelihood.

[13] Stephen Place (c.1750-c.1830) was a Six Principle Baptist preacher from Scituate, Rhode Island. In 1780 he gathered a Baptist church in Foster-Gloucester, Rhode Island. He gained a reputation as an eloquent preacher and spent much of his time on preaching tours throughout the area. In 1792 he moved to a Baptist church in Springfield, Massachusetts. After a brief return to Foster-Gloucester in 1801, he moved on to Vermont, where he organized churches in Wethersfield, Springfield, and Windsor. In 1804 he returned to Rhode Island as minister of the Elder Ballou Meetinghouse, where he remained until he retired around 1820.

[14] Adin Ballou's great-uncle James Ballou (1723-1812), originally a member of the Cumberland Six Principle Baptist Church, became interested in "New Light" revivalism in the 1760s. His unauthorized prayer meetings led to his expulsion from the Elder Cook Meetinghouse. When he moved to Richmond, New Hampshire, James Ballou joined a Baptist church, but resigned in disgust when a number of the members cast aside their "old flood wives" to take new "spiritual" wives. After this he considered himself an independent Christian until, after further investigation, he became a Universalist.

[15] Several distinct branches of the Ballou family helped to colonize Richmond, New Hampshire. Rev. Maturin Ballou, father of Hosea Ballou, moved from Scituate, Rhode Island, to Richmond in 1767. James Ballou arrived with his family from Cumberland in 1775. Jesse Ballou, from Burrillville, Rhode Island, settled in Richmond in 1779.

[16] James Ballou (1761-1808) was known as far away as Boston as a clairvoyant and astrologer. Adin Ballou's article on him in the *Genealogy* does not discount the possibility of his having genuine psychic powers, but notes that he supplemented his natural gifts by being "a quick reader of human nature," as well as a showman with his "conjuror's robe, wand and hieroglyphics, masks and hocus-pocus." Adin Ballou was careful to point out that James used his fortune-telling to entertain and to give helpful advice to his clients, and was "careful to wrong no one."

[17] Silas Ballou (1753-1837) was the resident poet of Richmond, New Hampshire, providing hymns, patriotic ballads, elegies, epitaphs, and songs for all occasions. He wrote the earliest New England Universalist hymnal (1785). Adin Ballou thought his hymns "often homely and commonplace, with poor rhythm and accent, yet nearly all containing more or less poetic flashes of genius."

[18] Eli Ballou (1808-1883) was ordained a Universalist minister in 1832. In the early years of his ministry he preached a circuit that encompassed parts of northern New York, Vermont, and southern Québec. After settling in Vermont, he published and edited the *Christian Repository* for thirty years, 1840-70. He preached for a year in Kansas and Iowa before returning to Vermont in 1872.

[19] Until the early 20th century, young children of both genders wore dresses, called "frocks." A "frockling" was a boy who had not yet graduated to distinctively masculine attire.

[20] In evangelical Christianity, a "professor of religion" is one who has given credible evidence of a conversion or "born again" experience.

[21] The Puritans of the seventeenth century identified strongly with people of Israel as described in the Hebrew Scriptures. In England they saw themselves as struggling against the oppression of modern incarnations of Egypt and Babylon. Emigration to America was their Exodus and New England was the Promised Land where they would live in covenant relationship with God. Accordingly it became commonplace to refer to respected elders or forebears as "fathers and mothers in Israel." One early example is found in Cotton Mather's *Magnalia Christi Americana; or the Ecclesiastical History of New England* (1702):
> Of all Historical Narratives, those which give a faithful Account of the *Lives* of eminent Saints, must needs be the most edifying... It must needs therefore be in itself, a thing pleasing to God, and a special Act of *Obedience* to the *Fifth Commandment*, to endeavour the preservation of the Names, and Honour of them, who have been *Fathers in Israel*.

[22] 1 Corinthians 13:11.

[23] This description of Major William Ballou and his family is more forthright than that found in the *Genealogy*. The article on William Ballou in the *Genealogy* focuses on his military career and does not even mention his occupation as a tavern-keeper. The only one of his children who is given a full article is the eldest daughter, Pearley Ballou Bates, who married a farmer and raised a family of "temperate, industrious, economical farmers." The other four children are combined in a single article. There, indeed, the tavern is mentioned, but only in a general description of taverns and inns in the area.

[24] Captain Amos Cook was the proprietor of Cook's Hotel in Cumberland. In the *Genealogy*, Ballou described Cook's establishment in glowing terms as "the *last* of the old country taverns," a popular venue for sleighing parties, dancing parties, and turkey suppers (p. 565).

[25] At this period, before the first phase of the temperance movement, the average American consumed over seven gallons of alcohol a year, nearly three times the modern rate.

²⁶ The early population of Rhode Island, fleeing from the domains of the established Congregational Church, rejected all of the appurtenances of the Puritan system, including public education. When the government of Rhode Island first attempted to create a system of public schools in 1800, towns in the north and west parts of the state organized to have the act repealed. Until the passage of the Free School Law of 1828, Rhode Islanders had to rely on a patchwork of private, independent, and locally-organized institutions.

²⁷ After children of this period had memorized the alphabet, they were given exercises on all the two-letter vowel and consonant combinations. This process was known as learning the "a, b, abs."

²⁸ *Hamlet* 1.2.

²⁹ An anonymous poem from the anthology *Beauties of British Poetry* (1801), edited by Sidney Melmoth.

³⁰ Caleb Alexander, *An introduction to the speaking and writing of the English language: according to grammatical rules intended to assist learners in acquiring a thorough knowledge of syntax* (Boston, 1794).

³¹ Barton Ballou (1791-1844) received the Bachelor of Arts and Master of Arts from Brown University. After a few years as a teacher, in 1820 he began to study for the ministry under Hosea Ballou. His weak pulpit presence and poor health, however, frustrated his attempts to secure a church. He spent the rest of his life in various obscure teaching positions not far from the Ballou neighborhood in Cumberland, Rhode Island.

³² Samuel Slater (1768-1835), "the father of the American industrial revolution," emigrated to America from Derbyshire, England, in 1789. Defying a law prohibiting the export of British manufacturing technology, he brought with him the knowledge he had gained as an apprentice to pioneer textile manufacturer Jedidiah Strutt. In partnership with Moses Brown and William Almy of Providence, Slater built the first successful water-powered textile mill in America on the Blackstone River in Pawtucket, Rhode Island, in 1791.

³³ This was a period of explosive growth in the textile industry. In 1808 there were fifteen cotton spinning mills in the United States. By the end of the War of 1812 there were about 250.

³⁴ This is a rather misleading description of the state of the textile industry in 1811. Slater's original mill had been in operation for twenty years by the time of the Ballou family's venture. To say that Slater's mill "had already begun operations with a most promising outlook" hardly does justice to this long history, or to the existence, by that time, of a hundred or so other mills, many larger and more modern than Slater's.

³⁵ The first mill building was so small that it was called the "Pistareen," after a small silver Spanish coin worth about twenty-five cents. Although U.S. currency had been in existence since 1793, until mid-century there was not enough in circulation to displace the foreign coins that were used in most everyday transactions. Thus the pistareen would have been a familiar coin in 1811.

³⁶ The Social Manufacturing Company was typical of the "Rhode Island system" mills that flourished during the first generation of textile manufacturing in America, from about 1800 to 1830. The chief characteristic of the Rhode Island system was the employment of families.

In England most textile factory workers were children. Having seen the disruption and misery that resulted when children worked while the adults were unemployed, Samuel Slater was determined to avoid reproducing this pattern in his own factories. As in England, most of the actual factory work in the Slater mills was done by children. The children, however, were not hired or paid directly by the mill owners. Instead, the family was hired as a unit, with the head of the household handling the negotiations over wages and positions. Children and unmarried women might spin yarn in the factory, while men and married women wove it into cloth on hand looms at home. The company also provided employment for construction workers, teamsters, artisans, and farmers, for the Slater-style mill town was designed to be a complete, traditional New England village. In this way Slater hoped to support, rather than to undermine, the integrity of the family.

Slater-style mills tended to be small, ideally suited for utilizing the limited water power available from small streams like the Mill River. They were usually owned by family partnerships or groups of friends, like the partnership that formed the Social Manufacturing Company. The owners and their families worked in the mills alongside their employees. After 1830 Slater-style mills were increasingly supplanted by Lowell-style mills. These were larger factories, employing mostly young women, and incorporating mechanized weaving as well as spinning. (Slater had resisted the introduction of the power loom, which would have disrupted the balance of the community and the family system of labor.) They were owned by stockholders rather than owner-managers. This completed the transition to a market economy in which labor and capital alike were treated as commodities.

[37] This job, hand-picking debris out of the raw cotton, was typically the first job entrusted to a child mill worker, usually around age seven.

[38] *Roping*, or sliver, is the soft, thick rope of aligned fiber produced by the carding machine. It is then processed by intermediate machines, the drawing and roving frames, to transform it into *roving*: a lightly twisted yarn that is processed by the spinning frame into finished thread. The *throstle frame* was a kind of spinning frame that produced strong, coarse thread. After becoming acclimated to work as a "cotton bug," a child advanced to the carding machines, the drawing and roving machines, and the throstle frames. The job of the operator of a roving or spinning frame was to reconnect broken threads and replace full spools with empty ones.

Chapter 2

[1] The "leading Republican paper of the state" was the *Columbian Phenix: or Providence Patriot*. It represented the interests of the rising middle class of prosperous farmers and small-scale manufacturers, who stood to gain by anything that would favor the growth of American industry. They favored westward expansion, high tariffs on imported goods, and war with Britain, which they saw as completing the work of the American Revolution.

[2] Zephaniah S. Crossman (c.1780-after 1830) was originally from Shelburne, Massachusetts. In 1805-06 he was a Baptist minister in Norton and Taunton, Massachusetts. By 1811 he had joined the Christian Connexion. His ministry at the Christian church in Cumberland, 1813-18, was probably the most successful of his career.

After leaving the Cumberland church, Crossman became a Universalist and was received into fellowship at a meeting of the Southern Association in December 1820. At the New England Universalist General Convention in 1821, he was listed as a minister from Shelburne. For about a year, 1824-25, he served Universalist societies in Norwich, Preston, and Groton, Connecticut. In 1830 he was living in Providence, Rhode Island. Of his later life nothing is known except what Adin Ballou tells us (see chapter 3): that he renounced Universalism, "vacillated for awhile between different forms of faith," fell into "irregularities," and left the ministry.

3 The Christian Connexion in New England was one of several similar, though independent, religious movements that arose in different regions of the United States during the early nineteenth century. Their rallying cry was "No master but Christ, no creed but the Bible, no other name than that of 'Christian.'" Rejecting the "man-made" creeds and doctrines that characterized the various denominations, they insisted on the right and obligation of ordinary people to read and interpret the Bible for themselves.

The ideals of Christian unity and religious liberty gave the "Christians" a more open and inclusive worship style than many contemporary churches. They championed the rights of African Americans and women, and had notable female preachers and evangelists. Their commitment to religious liberty did not, however, extend to the acceptance of diversity of religious belief, since they believed that all who read the Bible with an open mind would come to the same conclusions. Though they had no formal creed, they did have a theology, expressed in articles of faith and practice adopted in 1802. They rejected both predestination and universal salvation as denying human freedom. "Christians" believed that the experience of spiritual rebirth or regeneration was necessary for salvation, and that the fate of the unregenerate would be total destruction rather than endless punishment. They held an Arian view of Christ similar to that of many early Unitarians.

The first "Christian" congregation in New England was founded in 1801. By 1815 there were 43 congregations in the Christian Connexion, mostly in Vermont, New Hampshire, southeastern Massachusetts, and Rhode Island. Toward mid-century the Christian Connexion began associating informally with two similar movements, one founded by James O'Kelly in Virginia and the other by Barton Stone in Kentucky. Disagreements about slavery and reluctance to become a "denomination" prevented formal union until 1890. The resulting General Convention of Christian Churches was involved in several mergers during the twentieth century and is now part of the United Church of Christ.

4 Ballou's reference to "sixteen hundred years" of entanglement between church and state is puzzling. Sixteen hundred years before the time of writing would go back to the 280s, when the Christian church was still a persecuted sect in the Roman Empire. Christianity became a tolerated religion in 313 but did not become the official religion of the empire until 380. Thus, a figure of fifteen hundred years would seem more accurate.

5 The "Great Gale" of 1815 was the most devastating storm to hit southern New England until the hurricane of 1938. See Robert P. Emlen, "The Great Gale of 1815: Artifactual Evidence of Rhode Island's First Hurricane," *Rhode Island History* 48 (May 1990), 51-61.

6 Abner Jones (1772-1841) is known as the founder of the "Christian" movement in New England. As a young man he experienced the call to preach, but was unwilling to join any existing denomination, because he rejected as unscriptural not only doctrines such as the Trinity, predestination, and eternal punishment, but also church creeds, covenants, ecclesiastical hierarchies, and the division of Christians into denominations. His solution was to organize, in 1801, the first "Christian" church in New England, "rejecting all party and sectional names, and leaving each other free to cherish such speculative views of theology as the Scriptures might plainly seem to them to teach."

In 1802 Jones met Elias Smith (1769-1846), who had independently developed similar ideas. Together Smith and Jones led a revival in Portsmouth, New Hampshire, which led to the foundation of the First Christian Church of Portsmouth. They also cooperated in founding a "Christian" church in Boston in 1804. During his career Jones served several other churches in Massachusetts and New Hampshire, but had trouble finding one whose members shared his determination "not to bind their consciences and limit their investigations."

In contrast to Jones's emphasis on personal freedom of interpretation, Smith insisted on a rigid Biblical literalism. In his *New Testament Dictionary* (1812), he attempted to free New Testament terms and concepts from centuries of theological corruption by explaining them in their simplest, most literal sense. His *Herald of Gospel Liberty*, founded in 1801, was one of the first weekly religious newspapers published in the United States. It served as an important medium for allowing like-minded people in different parts of the country to become aware of each other's activities.

[7] Frederick Plummer, a disciple of Elias Smith, served a Christian Connexion church in Woodstock, Vermont, before moving to Philadelphia in 1811. He introduced Elias Smith to Thomsonian medicine and facilitated the partnership between Smith and Samuel Thomson (see chapter 3, note 4). After the break between Thomson and Smith, Plummer became one of Thomson's closest collaborators.

[8] Daniel Hix (1755-1838) served a church in Dartmouth, Massachusetts, for more than fifty years, 1780-1834. The church, originally affiliated with the Baptists, adopted the principles of the "Christian" movement in 1807.

[9] Benjamin Taylor (1786-1848) was born in the port town of Beverly, Massachusetts, and went to sea for three years as a young man. In 1809 his family joined Abner Jones's church in Salem. After being ordained in 1811, Taylor served a number of Christian Connexion churches in southeastern Massachusetts. He spent some years in Michigan before returning to the East Coast in 1840. His last years were spent as minister and administrator of the Seamen's Bethel in Providence. He was known for his tolerance, and exchanged pulpits with Baptists, Methodists, Congregationalists, and Universalists.

[10] Asa Messer (1769-1836) was president of Brown University from 1802 to 1826. He was ordained a Baptist minister, but spent his whole career at Brown, as student, tutor, professor, librarian, and finally president. Although he remained a member of the Baptist church until his death, from about 1816 he held Unitarian views and attended a Unitarian church. Opposition to his religious views among the students and trustees of the university was one of the factors leading to his resignation from the presidency.

Chapter 3

[1] Restorationists were Universalists who believed in a limited period of disciplinary "future punishment" between death and reconciliation with God.

[2] In 1818 the nearest Universalist societies were the recently incorporated First Universalist Society in Attleboro, Massachusetts, and the preaching station at Bellingham, Massachusetts. Bellingham and Attleboro, and the area between them that included the Ballou neighborhood, had since the late eighteenth century been visited by circuit preachers operating out of the Universalist societies in Oxford and Milford, Massachusetts.

[3] Elias Smith became a Universalist in 1817. He received ministerial fellowship in 1818, served a church in Boston, and edited a Universalist newspaper, the *Herald of Life and Immortality*, 1819-20. In 1823 he renounced Universalism and asked to be accepted back into the Christian Connexion. He was received into their fellowship, with reservations, four years later. He retained this affiliation for the rest of his life, but was always suspected of universalist tendencies. He seems never to have resolved his theological doubts.

⁴ Thomsonian medicine was the invention of Samuel Thomson (1769-1843). Observing the effects of various medical treatments on himself and members of his family, Thomson developed a system of herbal medicines and steam baths designed to restore health by restoring the body's heat and insuring its unimpeded flow.

After recovering from a serious illness with the aid of Thomsonian medicine, Elias Smith studied medicine under Thomson's personal supervision. He became Thomson's agent and publicist, helping him to package his system and writing the instruction manual. In the early 1820s Smith developed his own version of herbal medicine. Thomson unsuccessfully sued him for patent infringement in 1822. Smith continued to practice various forms of medicine and dentistry for the rest of his life. In 1830 he established a private sanitarium and in 1832 published a medical handbook, *The American Physician and Family Assistant*.

⁵ Reuben Potter (1796-1842) was a promising preacher of the Christian Connexion, but his career was cut short by alcoholism. At one time he was expelled from the ministry because of his drinking, but was reinstated when he showed signs of improvement.

Potter spent his entire life in his native Rhode Island, except for a preaching tour to Virginia in 1825. In 1823-24 he edited and published a semi-monthly newspaper, the *Gospel Palladium*, in Warren, Rhode Island. A Universalist reviewer noted approvingly, "Although the editor's principles and ours do not agree, it is due him to say, that he has thus far evinced a liberality highly becoming an independent editor, and showed to the world, that he is not governed by those narrow and limited feelings that characterize the whole fraternity of the professedly orthodox editors." (G. B. Lisher, *Gospel Inquirer*, 13 March 1824)

⁶ Dexter Bullard (1799-1865) was ordained as joint pastor with Reuben Potter over the Christian Connexion congregation in Cumberland Hill, Rhode Island, at the age of 19. In 1833, while serving a church in eastern Connecticut, he and his wife were among the few to support Prudence Crandall, a Quaker schoolteacher who was persecuted for accepting African American students at her school in Canterbury, Connecticut. After retiring from the ministry due to ill health, he lived for a time in Virginia, but was unhappy living in a slave state. The Bullards moved to Wisconsin in 1852.

⁷ Mark Fernald (1784-1851) began his long career as an itinerant preacher in 1809. He traveled widely in New England, New York, and Canada. Like many Christian Connexion ministers, he practiced medicine, purveying his own form of herbal medicine, "unknown to others, which I learned from study, practice, a revelation, or all."

⁸ Lorenzo Dow (1777-1834) became an itinerant Methodist minister in 1796. From the early days of his ministry he was often in trouble with his Methodist superiors. He freely criticized his political and religious opponents, including the Methodists, whom he accused of being "tainted with popery." He preached the presence of the divine in everyday life and the duty of individuals to think and experience religion for themselves. He opposed class distinctions, especially the privileges of the professional clergy. He coined the famous definition of Calvinism: "You shall and you shan't, you will and you won't; you'll be damned if you do, and be damned if you don't."

Dow was said to have been the most widely traveled American of his time. He journeyed frequently to the South, where, among other things, he was a pioneer preacher to the Indians in Alabama. He made voyages to Ireland, 1799-1801, and to England, 1805-07 and 1818-20, where he introduced the idea of camp meetings.

⁹ Lorenzo Dow, *Perambulations of Cosmopolite; or Travels and Labors of Lorenzo Dow in Europe and America* (1814).

¹⁰ The Missouri Compromise of 1820 was the first of several attempts to settle the question of whether slavery would be allowed in new states as they entered the United States. Under the provisions of the compromise, Missouri was admitted as a slave state, Maine as a free state, and slavery farther west was prohibited north of Missouri's southern border.

¹¹ Otis Mason was Adin Ballou's first cousin on his mother's side: Otis's mother, Chloe Tower Mason, was the sister of Adin's mother.

¹² Caleb Ward Wilson (1795-1826) married Adin Ballou's second cousin, Lucy Thompson, in 1821. The world of Ballou's childhood and youth was an intricate network of kinship ties.

¹³ 1 Samuel 17:28-29.

Chapter 4

¹ 1 Corinthians 9:16-17.

² Ebenezer Robinson (1801-1861) started out as a minister of the Christian Connexion but later became a Unitarian minister, serving Unitarian churches in Beverly, 1830-33, and Hubbardston, Massachusetts, 1833-36. He served a Universalist church in Lebanon, Connecticut, 1839-48, though he never formally entered Universalist fellowship. He seems to have been informally associated with the Restorationist denomination led by Adin Ballou (see chapter 11). An 1839 letter to the *Universalist Union* noted, "At present, Rev. Ebenezer Robinson (Restorationist) is preaching to us" in Lebanon.

³ The majority of the earliest generation of Universalists were content to believe that all people would eventually be saved, and did not inquire into the details of what might transpire in the afterlife. Some theologians, including John Murray and Elhanan Winchester, thought that there would be a finite period of probation or suffering after death and prior to the final reconciliation. Caleb Rich (1750-1821) preached that there need be no punishment in the world to come, but it was Hosea Ballou's advocacy of this doctrine that led to its adoption by an influential group of ministers in the denomination.

Adin Ballou frequently used the expression "ultra Universalism" to describe Hosea Ballou's theology. The "ultra" editor Thomas Whittemore credited Adin Ballou with inventing the term (*Trumpet and Universalist Magazine*, 27 April 1833). Ballou, however, denied it: "The words ultra-Universalist and ultra-Universalism were used in your Trumpet, with your approbation, in their present sense, eighteen months previous to my adoption and use of them" (*Independent Messenger*, 16 May 1833). He cited a letter in the February 7, 1829, issue of the *Trumpet*, which used the term "ultra-Universalist" as if it were already in common use.

⁴ Hosea Ballou, *The New Birth. A Lecture Semron [sic] delivered in the Second Universalist Meeting House, in Boston* (Boston, 1821); reprinted in Hosea Ballou, *Select Sermons, delivered on various occasions, from important passages of Scripture* (Boston, 1832).

Hosea Ballou began a year-long series of evening lectures, or "lecture-sermons," at the Second Universalist Church in Boston in August 1818. In these lectures Ballou gave his own interpretation of Biblical texts usually cited as proof-texts against the doctrine of universal salvation. The next year he offered four lecture-sermons between January and March 1820. The earliest of this second set was "The New Birth."

In "The New Birth" Hosea Ballou rejected the view that to be born again is to be transformed from a state of nature to a state of grace, noting that those who claimed to have been born again did not seem to behave better than other people. He described new birth instead as an experience of illumination leading to an improved understanding of the gospel. Several such experiences might be required, but he thought they would ultimately lead to belief in universal salvation.

Perhaps the most controversial point in Hosea Ballou's interpretation of John 3:3, "Except a man be born again, he cannot see the kingdom of God," was his understanding of the term "kingdom of God." To "see the kingdom of God" was not, in his view, to be saved; nor was it to understand that one is saved, or even to understand that all are saved. Instead, it referred to the establishment of institutions that embody the true meaning of the gospel. This sort of regeneration could not happen to an individual, but would happen to society when enough individuals had experienced the new birth.

5 Adin Ballou, *Review of a lecture sermon, delivered in the Second Universalist Meeting-House, in Boston ... by Hosea Ballou, Pastor* (Providence, 1821).

Adin Ballou ventured into print because he considered Hosea Ballou's reinterpretation of "new birth" to be not merely mistaken, but provocative: a deliberate trivialization and perversion of the language used by born-again Christians to describe their most profound spiritual experiences. In retaliation, he reduced to absurdity Hosea Ballou's definitions of the doctrines of new birth and the kingdom of God, by substituting them into the lecture-sermon's scripture text to produce, "except a man believe the doctrine of Universalism, he cannot see Universalism." He exclaimed sarcastically, "A most wonderful kingdom indeed! A most wonderful birth, surely this!"

The greatest measure of venom was reserved for Hosea Ballou's argument that ordinary new birth did not result in moral improvement and his implication that Universalist new birth did:

> We are acquainted with many of these new-born sons, the inhabitants of the kingdom of heaven. Some of them we know to be respectable citizens, good neighbors, affectionate companions and parents, dutiful children, and loving brethren and sisters ... Does this arise from a pure principle of love to God or from a belief in this doctrine? I doubt of its coming from either; for by careful examination, we shall see that not only Universalists, but Deists and Atheists, will bear this character, some of them at least ... there may be some who profess to be Universalists that are actuated by the pure principle of love; but it is, in my opinion, very rare; and if there should be such a character, it is not from a belief of Universalism that he is induced thus to act ...
>
> Will it do to trust many of these heaven-born subjects, with all their pretensions to a new birth and so much love, with property, or any thing valuable, without having the arm of the civil law open against them? I think I am not afraid to answer, No!

6 Actually, Adin Ballou's *Review of a Lecture Sermon* did receive some notice from his opponents. Shortly after it was published, the review generated a brief controversy in the pages of the *Universalist Magazine*. Zephaniah Lathe (1754-c.1827), a disciple of Elhanan Winchester, accused Adin Ballou of un-Christian hostility toward his elder kinsman and Universalists in general:

> He has poured a volley of abusive language, upon a beloved and respected minister of the gospel; whose age, experience, usefulness and moral conduct, entitle him to the esteem of

the world. He has endeavored to degrade the character of a respectable class of christians, by representing them as "quarrelsome, tyrannical, unnatural, disobedient, unkind, dishonest, unjust, immoral, intemperate, angry, resentful, desperately proud, and blasphemous." ("Ballou versus Ballou," *Universalist Magazine*, 25 August 1821)

The same string of adjectives, ostensibly a quotation from Adin Ballou's *Review*, appeared ten years later in an article by Thomas Whittemore ("Reply to the Boston Recorder," *Trumpet and Universalist Magazine*, 5 February 1831). At that time, Ballou responded:

> Mr. W. pretends to have given our own words ... But is it strictly true, that he has used our own words? Is this detaching of adjectives from their substantives properly giving our own words? If so, would it not be justifiable to cull from an author's whole work such words as one pleased, so as by arranging them into a sentence and applying them ever so perversely, to pretend (as Mr. W. has) that they were "his own words"? And what by such a rule might not an author be made to say? Anything that his enemies desired. ("Reply to the Trumpet," *Independent Messenger*, 11 February 1831)

This was a far abler defense than Ballou was able to mount in 1821. In his reply to Lathe (*Universalist Magazine*, 6 October 1821), instead of arguing the unfairness of having his words rearranged out of context, Ballou resorted to facetious mock self-deprecation – "as you are possessed of Universal Benevolence, this unworthy worm feels that he has a claim upon your attention" – a stylistic device that caused Lathe to wonder if the author of the *Review* and the writer of the letter were the same person (*Universalist Magazine*, 20 October 1821).

[7] Acts 17:5.

[8] The official name of the state of Rhode Island comes from the names of two separate colonies that united in 1644. Rhode Island (probably from the Dutch *Roodt Eylant*, "red island") is an old name for Aquidneck Island, where the settlements of Portsmouth and Newport were located. Providence Plantations was the colony on the mainland, founded by Roger Williams. In the early 2000s there was a movement to change the name of the state, on the grounds that the word "plantations" conjures up images of slavery, but a 2010 referendum overwhelmingly endorsed the original name.

[9] Thomas Mann (1769-1852) was a farmer, manufacturer, and chief justice of the Court of Common Pleas for Providence County.

[10] Reference to *Measure for Measure* 2.2: "But man, proud man, dress'd in a little brief authority ... plays such fantastic tricks before high heaven as make the angels weep."

[11] *Hamlet* 5.2.

Chapter 5

[1] Elhanan Winchester (1751-1797), along with John Murray, Caleb Rich, and others, was one of the founders of American Universalism. Winchester was originally a New England Baptist evangelist. During a spectacularly successful revival in South Carolina in 1779, he began to doubt that the number of the elect could be as small as it was said to be. In 1780 he was called as the minister of a Baptist church in Philadelphia. The following year he was expelled for heresy and led a portion of the congregation to found a Universalist church. On preaching tours in New England in 1785-86 and 1794-95, he attracted many converts to his faith in universal salvation. He was in England, 1787-94, where he helped to shape British Universalism.

Winchester's most important work is *The Universal Restoration, Exhibited in Four Dialogues between a Minister and His Friend* (1788), commonly called *Dialogues on the Universal Restoration*. Along with Charles Chauncy's *The Mystery Hid from Ages and Generations* (1784) and Hosea Ballou's *Treatise on Atonement* (1805), it was one of three great American Universalist theological works available to the young Adin Ballou. Winchester presented the doctrine of restoration as more reasonable and more godly than that of endless punishment, and also as more apt to move a willing heart to repentance. He offered alternative understandings of Hebrew words often translated as "everlasting," and argued that, logically, no finite human creature can commit a sin meriting infinite punishment.

2   Lewis Metcalf, Luke Jenckes, and Levi Ballou were all in their forties in 1822, "elderly" in the eyes of the 19-year-old Adin Ballou. Lewis Metcalf (1773-1859), who was related by marriage to the Ballou family, was an active Universalist layman who occasionally hosted Southern Association meetings at his house. Luke Jenckes (1774-1848) was an investor, along with Adin Ballou's father, in the Social Manufacturing Company (see chapter 1). Levi Ballou (1782-1836) and his family were neighbors of Adin's family in Cumberland. Some of Levi Ballou's children, including Latimer W. Ballou (see chapter 23, note 21), were Adin's students at the district school.

3   One source of ultra Universalist influence in Wrentham and Cumberland was the ministry of Hosea Ballou's zealous disciple Thomas Whittemore, who had a training ministry in nearby Milford, Massachusetts, in 1821-22. Whittemore visited Wrentham in February 1821 and stayed at the home of Luke Jenckes. In his autobiography he mentioned Luke Jenckes, Lewis Metcalf, and Darius Ballou as pillars of the Universalist faith in that area.

4   The Southern Association was founded in 1815 as a regional conference for Universalists in southern New England (Massachusetts, Rhode Island, and Connecticut). During the years 1816-23 the Southern Association met twice a year, in June and December.

The preachers at the West Wrentham meeting were Barzillai Streeter, Hosea Ballou, and Fayette Mace. Barzillai Streeter was a Restorationist whose ministerial career would be short. Fayette Mace was an inexperienced preacher who had become the first pastor of the new church in Providence in April of that year; he would resign in December. The other ministers present were Hosea Ballou 2d, Jacob Frieze, Seth Stetson, Thomas Whittemore, Benjamin Whittemore, Barton Ballou, and Zephaniah Crossman (Ballou's former "Christian" pastor, then in his brief Universalist period). The dominating presence of the Ballou-Whittemore contingent would have insured that Hosea Ballou's no-future-punishment doctrine was presented as the Universalist norm.

5   Hosea Ballou 2d (1796-1861) was the grandson of Hosea Ballou's older brother Benjamin. So great was the age disparity between the brothers that Benjamin's oldest son, the father of Hosea 2d, was actually a few months older than his uncle Hosea. Hosea Ballou 2d studied under Hosea Ballou and adopted many of his theological ideas. Although he did not agree with his mentor in rejecting the doctrine of future punishment, he was intensely protective of the reputation and standing of the elder Ballou and supported him in the party struggles within Universalism.

Hosea Ballou 2d served Universalist churches in Stafford, Connecticut, 1817-21, Roxbury, Massachusetts, 1821-38, and Medford, Massachusetts, 1838-54. From 1822 to 1826 he was a co-editor of the *Universalist Magazine* with Hosea Ballou and Thomas Whittemore. Later he established himself as a scholar. His most important work was *Ancient*

History of Universalism (1829). He was the first president of the Universalist Historical Society and of Tufts College, a Universalist foundation. In 1845 he received an honorary D.D. from Harvard University, the first awarded to a Universalist. When Adin Ballou referred to him as "Rev. Hosea Ballou 2d, as he was then called," he was calling attention to the fact that he had not yet been awarded his doctorate.

6   1 Corinthians 15:28.

7   William S. Heywood inserted the following editorial note at the end of this paragraph: "As he was also of the fact that of the six great schools first founded to promote the interests of Christian philosophy, four taught absolutely that distinctive doctrine."

Universalists were frequently reminded that their doctrine was contrary to centuries of Christian tradition. As the orthodox interlocutor says in Winchester's *Dialogues*, "If this doctrine of the final Restoration of all things had been true, surely our wise, good and learned ministers would have discovered it, and proclaimed it long ago." It was therefore a common apologetic strategy among nineteenth-century Universalists to look for evidence of universalist belief in Christian history. The most thorough examination of the subject was Hosea Ballou 2d's *Ancient History of Universalism*, which argues that belief in universal salvation was tolerated, and held by many theologians who were considered orthodox, during the first four centuries of the Christian era. *Ancient History* identifies Clement of Alexandria as the first to express recognizably universalistic views, and Origen as the most influential. It describes in detail the power struggle that led to the adoption of the ideas of Augustine and the rejection of those of Origen. The implication is that universalism was condemned merely because it was taught by Origen, and not for any sound theological reasons.

8 The autobiographical preface to Winchester's *Dialogues* contains a passage that may have influenced the way that Ballou experienced and interpreted the crisis of his conversion to Universalism, as well as the pattern of his subsequent adoption of Restorationism, abolitionism, pacifism, and Christian socialism. Winchester wrote:

> I now foresaw the storm, and I determined to prepare for it, not by denying what I had said, but by examining and determining for myself, whether the sentiment was according to scripture or not. If I found that it was not, I was determined to retract, but if it was, to hold it fast, let the consequences be what they might ... I shut myself up chiefly in my chamber, read the scriptures, and prayed to God to lead me into all truth, and not suffer me to embrace any error; and I think that with an upright mind, I laid myself open to believe whatever the Lord had revealed ... I became so well persuaded of the truth of the Universal Restoration, that I was determined never to deny it, let it cost me ever so much, though all my numerous friends should forsake me, as I expected they would, and though I should be driven from men, and obliged to dwell in caves or dens of the earth, and feed on wild roots and vegetables, and suffer the loss of all things, friends, wealth, fame, health, character, and even life itself. The truth appeared to me more valuable than all things, and as I found it, I was determined never to part with it, let what would be offered in exchange.

9   Matthew 18:17. "Publican" in this context is derived from the Latin *publicanus*, a collector of public revenues. In New Testament times tax collectors were doubly despised, for not only did they exact taxes and tolls for the benefit of the hated Roman regime, but it was well known that many took far more than they turned over to the government.

Matthew 18:17 is the culmination of a passage that has frequently been used to define the method and pattern of Christian discipline. There are three stages of correction: first private remonstrance, then discussion with a small group to act as witnesses, and finally public confrontation in the church. Only if all these processes fail is the sinner to be cast out of religious society. Although the account given in the *Autobiography* omits the second stage, a letter that Ballou wrote just after this event, referring to "the chief men of the church" and "some of the Elders," makes it clear that the exclusion process was followed in its full, proper form when Ballou was disowned by the Christian Connexion.

[10] Hebrews 13:5.

[11] Adin Ballou's letter, "Another Conversion in the Ministry," was printed in the *Universalist Magazine*, 24 August 1822.

[12] Hosea Ballou's oldest son, Hosea Faxon Ballou (1799-1881), was indeed a Universalist minister in Vermont: he served the Universalist church in Whitingham, Vermont, for twenty-five years, and that in Wilmington, Vermont, for fifteen years. However, Adin Ballou was mistaken in saying that he was already a minister in 1822. He was a farmer and schoolteacher before entering the ministry in 1832.

The second son, Massena Berthier Ballou (1800-1890), studied for the ministry under his father. His principal settlement was at Stoughton, Massachusetts, 1831-53. He retired due to ill health in 1853, but lived on in Stoughton for an additional thirty-seven years.

Cassandana Ballou Wing (1803-1866) was the only one of Hosea Ballou's six daughters who was married at the time of Adin Ballou's visit. She and her husband, Joseph Wing, lived with and took care of her parents in their later years.

The daughters living at home were Mandana (1804-c.1890), Elmina (1810-1856), Clementina (1812-1899), and Fiducia (1814-1885). All four eventually married, the oldest two to Universalist ministers. Mandana married Benjamin Whittemore, the brother of Thomas Whittemore.

The youngest of the Ballous' eleven children was Maturin Murray Ballou (1820-1895), only two years old at the time of Adin Ballou's visit. He became a journalist and a prolific writer of travel books and sensational novels and novelettes. He was the founder and first editor of the Boston *Globe*. He is best known in Universalist circles as the author of the *Biography of Rev. Hosea Ballou* (1852).

[13] Adin Ballou is alluding here to the so-called "Restorationist controversy," which embroiled New England Universalists from about 1815 to 1835.

The controversy began when Hosea Ballou began to preach that all souls would be fully reconciled with God immediately after death, a position known as "death and glory." Hosea Ballou had been successful in earlier years in leading Universalists into new theological territory: around 1795 he began to lead them away from Trinitarianism, and beginning in 1805 he persuaded most Universalists to reject the doctrine of vicarious atonement. But he was not as successful with his new view of the afterlife. No more than half of the Universalists were convinced by "death and glory." During the controversy, however, Hosea Ballou and his disciples preached the new doctrine energetically and often mocked, or pressured into silence, those who did not accept it. After Ballou founded the *Universalist Magazine* in 1819, the debate entered its editorial columns. The harmony of several sessions of the New England Universalist General Convention was marred by ill-feeling and political maneuvering on both sides.

The first phase of the controversy climaxed in the winter of 1822-23. Six avowedly Restorationist ministers – Paul Dean, Edward Turner, Charles Hudson, Jacob Wood,

Barzillai Streeter, and Levi Briggs – published a two-part manifesto in the *Christian Repository*. The first part, "A Declaration to the World," proclaimed that Restorationism and immediate universal salvation "are distinct and different doctrines, and are incapable of being reconciled together," and that the doctrine of immediate universal salvation was subversive of morality. The second, "An Appeal to the Public," complained of the conduct of the no-future-punishment ministers, especially those who controlled the *Universalist Magazine*. Both articles were signed by Jacob Wood alone, though the Declaration, at least, had been approved by all six of the Restorationist ministers.

The "Appeal and Declaration," as it became known, enraged the majority of New England Universalists, regardless of their beliefs about the afterlife. By staking out a narrow theological position, and by threatening schism if their demands were not met, the Restorationists had violated a long-standing Universalist principle: that no one who professed belief in universal salvation was to be excluded from membership on theological grounds. The Restorationist six were immediately isolated and threatened with discipline. During 1823-24 negotiations were held to restore peace and to impose a penalty upon the Restorationists. All six were officially welcomed back into the fold by 1824. However, the old resentments and divisions, which had merely been papered over, emerged again in the years leading up to 1830.

The second phase of the controversy, beginning in the late 1820s, resulted in the defection of a minority of Universalist ministers, who in 1831 set up their own denomination, the Massachusetts Association of Universal Restorationists (MAUR). Adin Ballou was an important participant in this phase of the conflict. Hostilities were maintained until around 1835, when polemicists on both sides began to lose interest in this kind of theological controversy. After the period of polarization caused by the controversy, Hosea Ballou's "ultra Universalism" became far less popular and was eventually dropped.

The story of the controversy is told in detail in two articles by Peter Hughes: "The Origin and First Stage of the Restorationist Controversy," *Journal of Unitarian Universalist History* 27 (2000), and "The Second Phase of the Restorationist Controversy: Disciplinary Crisis and Schism, 1824-1831," *Journal of Unitarian Universalist History* 28 (2001).

[14] Paul Dean (1783-1860), a rival of Hosea Ballou for Universalist leadership, was a leading Restorationist and one of the few Universalist ministers to remain a Trinitarian. After short ministries in his native Vermont and in central New York State, in 1813 he was called to be the associate and successor to John Murray at the First Universalist Society in Boston. After Murray's death in 1815, his hopes for achieving eminence by virtue of his position in the only Universalist pulpit in New England's greatest city were dashed when a second Boston society was created and Hosea Ballou was called to be its minister.

In 1822 Dean was compelled to move to another newly created church in Boston, on Bulfinch Street. Sebastian Streeter, a friend and partisan of Hosea Ballou, replaced him at First Universalist. By this time Hosea Ballou's great-nephew, Hosea Ballou 2d, was established as the Universalist minister in Roxbury; Ballou's disciple, Thomas Whittemore, was installed in Cambridge; and in 1823 Dean's ally, Edward Turner, was dismissed from his pulpit in Charlestown, leaving Dean isolated in the Boston area. Following the 1823 crisis that climaxed the first phase of the Restorationist Controversy, during which he was accused of acting out of envy and ambition, Dean resigned from Universalist fellowship. He was readmitted the following year, but not quite reconciled.

After his proposals for the organization of a national Universalist convention were rejected in 1828, Dean became further disenchanted with organized Universalism and helped Providence minister David Pickering found the Restorationist-dominated Providence Association. The existence of this association, seen by many Universalists as subversive, precipitated a new Restorationist crisis that resulted in the creation in 1831 of a new denomination, the Massachusetts Association of Universal Restorationists. Dean was a leading voice within this small sect during its decade of existence.

Unlike his colleague Adin Ballou, Dean was a social conservative. After the more progressive Restorationists abandoned the MAUR to found the Hopedale Community, Dean and the other conservatives fell back upon their Unitarian connections. Some already served Unitarian churches. Dean's Bulfinch Street church became Unitarian in 1839, the year that he retired.

[15] Edward Turner (1776-1853) was at first a friend and close ministerial partner of Hosea Ballou. He served Universalist churches in Salem, 1807-14, and Charlestown, Massachusetts, 1814-23. Circumstances surrounding his move to the Charlestown pulpit, which Hosea Ballou also coveted, may have damaged his relationship with his old friend. Within a few years Ballou and Turner were at odds over theology: in 1817 they represented opposite sides in a published debate over future punishment, Turner maintaining that some finite period of discipline would be necessary in the afterlife, while Ballou held that there would be immediate salvation. This debate hardened Ballou's position, which he had previously held only provisionally.

In 1823, with Paul Dean and others, Turner was a signatory of the Restorationist manifesto, the "Appeal and Declaration" (see chapter 5, note 13). Perceived as having unjustly attacked Hosea Ballou and other Universalist ministers, Turner was hounded out of the Charlestown pulpit. Although he retracted the manifesto and signed a document of reconciliation, he remained bitter, convinced that Hosea Ballou had played a role in his expulsion from Charlestown. After a pastorate in Portsmouth, New Hampshire, 1824-28, Turner shocked his fellow Universalists by relinquishing his fellowship and accepting a call from the Unitarian church in Charlton, Massachusetts. Unsuccessful there, he shortly afterwards moved to Fishkill, New York, whose Unitarian church he served until his retirement in 1840.

[16] Charles Hudson (1795-1881) was one of the most learned of the Restorationist ministers (although reportedly a dull preacher). During the interval between the two phases of the Restorationist controversy he engaged in a written debate with the ultra Universalists, publishing *A Series of Letters Addressed to Rev. Hosea Ballou* (1827) and, when Walter Balfour answered on behalf of Ballou, *A Reply to Mr. Balfour's Essays* (1829). His principal ministry was in Westminster, Massachusetts, 1824-42. While in Westminster he was a Massachusetts legislator and later a Whig member of the U.S. House of Representatives, 1841-49. He held other government offices, was a political journalist, and was a writer of local history.

[17] Olney Ballou (1784-1849) was a brother of Levi Ballou (see chapter 5, note 2) and Barton Ballou (see chapter 1, note 31). Like them, he was a Universalist. He served for many years in the Rhode Island state legislature and ran unsuccessfully for governor in 1847. In the *Genealogy* Adin Ballou took special note of the kindness of Olney Ballou and his wife: "The writer will never forget their sympathy and generous friendship towards him at a trying period of his early married life ... They were friends in *need* and friends *indeed*."

[18] It has been implied by a number of writers, from Thomas Whittemore on, that Paul Dean was a less than effective minister to the First Universalist Society of Boston, and that the church was in a decline during his pastorate. There is no evidence that this was the case. Dean had a difficult task: to follow in the footsteps of the revered John Murray, while at the same time holding his congregation together in the face of severe competition from the new Second Universalist Society and its charismatic preacher, Hosea Ballou. Lemuel Willis, in his short biography of Paul Dean (*The Universalist*, 10 April 1875), described the situation as follows:

> The withdrawal of those families and individuals that went from the first Universalist church and society to the second, affected the first considerably for a time. But Mr. Dean's popularity as a preacher at that time in Boston, was so great that he drew large congregations to his church and the places left vacant were soon taken by others who became permanent worshipers at the altar where he ministered. Mr. Ballou coming to Boston with the prestige and great ability as a preacher of Universalism, it must have been a severe test of the ability and preaching talents of Mr. Dean. I do not know any other minister in our order that could have met it as he did. But he succeeded in keeping the first church and society large, united, and prosperous several years after this.

Chapter 6

[1] When Bellingham was founded in 1719, it was, in typical New England fashion, both a town and a Congregational parish; the meetinghouse served for both religious and civic assemblies. But the established church was never strong in Bellingham. In 1745 the Baptists were exempted from taxes for the support of the church. Two years later the town petitioned the Massachusetts legislature to "free the town from the obligations of a parish." Preaching at the Congregational church became irregular and finally stopped altogether. The meetinghouse was demolished in 1774.

During the 1780s and 1790s various schemes were put forward for building a town hall. A proposal for the town to build a hall jointly with the Baptist society, which was then the only organized church in Bellingham, was rejected due to concern about public support for a religious institution. Finally a compromise was reached, involving an elaborate system of bonds and guarantees to ensure that no public funds would be used for religious purposes. Although financed by the Baptists, the meetinghouse was explicitly non-denominational. The dedication sermon, preached by a prominent Baptist minister from Boston, included the pledge, "These doors shall be cheerfully opened to the faithful ministers of the gospel of different denominations." The key of the building, and the final authority over its use, rested with the town selectmen. Indeed, by the time the meetinghouse was completed in 1802, there were no organized churches in Bellingham; the Baptist church had dissolved in 1799. It was reorganized in 1812. In the interim, various ministers (all Baptist) supplied the pulpit at the invitation of the town.

Abial Fisher (1787-1862), who served the revived Baptist church from 1816 to 1829, led a campaign to obtain exclusive use of the meetinghouse for the Baptists. The incident described by Ballou was just one episode in that long struggle.

[2] Joseph Ray, Henry Thayer, and Aaron Burdon were all substantial citizens of Mendon. Ray and Burdon were frequently chosen for town offices, including selectman, school committee, and militia officer.

In 1823 Joseph Ray (1791-1847) was an up-and-coming entrepreneur who had recently moved from constructing textile mills to manufacturing machinery for them, and would soon become a mill owner himself. (His prosperity was short-lived. He became entangled in lawsuits with his business partners and was bankrupt by 1839. At this time, however, he was on the upward trajectory of his rags-to-riches-to-rags story.)

Henry Thayer (1777-1824) owned a hotel and store in the Five Corners section of Mendon. It served as an important gathering place for the people of Mendon. In 1821 the town meeting voted that notices of meetings were to be posted in three places: the North Parish and South Parish churches, and Henry Thayer's store.

Aaron Burdon (1788-1878) was active in local politics, and went on to serve in the Massachusetts House of Representatives, 1828-31. He was coroner of Mendon, and then of Blackstone, for nearly two decades, 1835-53.

3   In 1821, after the Baptists broke down the door of the meetinghouse, they were sued by the town for trespass. The case was decided in the town's favor in 1824.

4   Adin Ballou, *The Furious Priest Reproved: A Letter to the Reverend Abial Fisher of Bellingham* (Providence, 1823).

5   In 1825 the Universalists and the Congregationalists offered to unite with the Baptists and to accept a Baptist minister, as long as someone other than Abial Fisher was chosen. Rather than dismiss their minister, the Baptists built a new church.

6   John Murray (1741-1815) has often been referred to as the "Father of American Universalism." Although he was but one of several founders, he played a unique role in gathering the founders together, uniting the various groups, and establishing Universalism as a denomination with legal recognition.

Murray came to America in 1770 from England, where he had been a Methodist evangelist, and then a disciple of the British Universalist, James Relly. Although he had no plans for a religious career in the New World, when his ship landed to take on supplies at Good Luck Point, New Jersey, he was called upon to preach by Thomas Potter, a local farmer who believed in universal salvation and who had built his own chapel. Murray's success was such that he ended up evangelizing in and around that area for the next few years. Although a Universalist, he preached to a wide audience, most of whom were not at first aware of his belief in universal salvation.

In 1774 Murray became acquainted with a group of people in Gloucester, Massachusetts, who had been studying Relly's major work, *Union*. He then settled there, serving as minister to these Universalists. In 1779 they founded the Independent Christian Church, the first Universalist church in America. Their legal battles to be recognized as a separate denomination lasted until 1787. Before that final resolution, in 1785 Murray helped organize a convention of Universalists in Oxford, Massachusetts. He also helped found the Philadelphia Convention of Universalists in 1790 and the New England Universalist General Convention in 1793. In the same year he settled with the First Universalist Society of Boston.

After suffering a stroke in 1809, Murray was forced to take on associates to perform his pastoral labors. There were few candidates for the position because they had to conform to Murray's Trinitarian theology, by then considered out-of-date. His second associate, Paul Dean, inherited the First Universalist pulpit on his death.

Murray believed that all souls were immediately saved at the time of death, but that they would nevertheless continue to suffer through delusion until they accepted God as fully as God accepted them. Because of the ambiguity inherent in this form of Universalist eschatology, both the Restorationists and the ultra Universalists claimed to be his true heirs.

The claims of John Murray and others to be called the founder of Universalism in America are discussed in Peter Hughes, "The Origins of New England Universalism: Religion without a Founder," *Journal of Unitarian Universalist History* 24 (1997).

[7] This is about as explicit a reference as can be found to the reasons for Dean's departure from the First Universalist pulpit. The preserved records of the church are reticent on this account. There was, evidently, a rift within the church, which was settled by the emigration of a substantial minority. This gave Dean a way of departing gracefully – appearing to be not leaving at all, but remaining a Universalist minister in Boston.

The new Universalist churches that were founded to accommodate Hosea Ballou and Paul Dean in 1817 and 1823 were made possible by a substantial increase in the size of the city of Boston. The churches on School Street and on Bulfinch Street were located to follow the movement of population, serving new neighborhoods as the city expanded.

[8] Sebastian Streeter (1783-1867) was the eldest of three brothers who were all Universalist ministers. After pastorates in Weare, New Hampshire, 1807-11, and Haverhill, Massachusetts, 1812-16, he followed Hosea Ballou as minister in Portsmouth, New Hampshire. His next settlement, at First Universalist Society in Boston, was his last, from which he retired after nearly forty years. He was celebrated for eloquence, spirituality, and pastoral ability.

[9] There is no mention in the minutes of Adin Ballou being admitted to fellowship at this meeting of the Southern Association. The report of the Fellowship Committee contained only two names: Lucius Paige and William Morse.

[10] When held at a denominational meeting, the ceremony of ordination was part of the service that formed the climax of the gathering. At Adin Ballou's ordination, Hosea Ballou preached, Richard Carrique gave the charge to the minister, and Hosea Ballou 2d offered the right hand of fellowship.

[11] The Milford church, organized in 1785, was one of the first three Universalist churches organized in America (the other two are Gloucester and Oxford, Massachusetts). Milford was at first one of the preaching stations in the circuit of the pioneer Universalist evangelist Adams Streeter. Streeter made Milford his residence from 1781 until 1785. In response to a recommendation made by the first Universalist convention held in New England, in Oxford, Massachusetts, 1785, the "Independent Christian Society in Milford, commonly called Universalists" was formally organized. The Milford Universalists arranged for services to be held regularly and to give Streeter a stipend. After Streeter's death in 1786 there was no regular preaching for several years.

The second Universalist minister at Milford, Zephaniah Lathe, served from 1790 to 1804. In 1791 the Universalists were granted occasional weekday use of the Milford town hall, a provision that allowed them to host the New England Universalist General Convention in 1797. After Lathe's departure, the Milford society was unable for nearly twenty years to raise the funds necessary to attract a minister. Among the supply preachers who visited during this period were Joshua Flagg, Richard Carrique, and Caleb Rich.

The Milford Universalist society grew in membership and prosperity as the result of a controversy within the established church that began in 1819. The wealthy Pearley Hunt was among the leaders of the disaffected Congregationalists who chose to join the Universalists. With Hunt paying a quarter of the cost, the Universalists were able to build a church in 1820. Hosea Ballou preached the dedication sermon. Soon afterwards, his student Thomas Whittemore was invited to settle.

[12] Thomas Whittemore (1800-1861), a disciple of Hosea Ballou and the most influential Universalist journalist of his time, co-edited the *Universalist Magazine* and, from 1828, edited its successor, the *Trumpet and Universalist Magazine*. As a young minister he served the Milford church in 1821-22. He then settled in Cambridge, Massachusetts, 1822-31. He was also a politician serving in the Massachusetts legislature and a historian who helped to found the Universalist Historical Society. His major works were *Modern History of Universalism* (1830) and a four-volume *Life of Rev. Hosea Ballou* (1854-55).

Whittemore was an ardent ultra Universalist and an enthusiastic controversialist. During the first Restorationist crisis of 1822-23 he was the most resistant to re-establishing fellowship with the signatories of the "Appeal and Declaration" (see chapter 5, note 13).

[13] Jacob Frieze (1789-1880) was ordained by the Southern Association in 1822. After settlements in Milford, 1822-24, and Marlborough, Massachusetts, 1824-26, he became a special evangelist in North Carolina. He organized the Southern Convention of Universalists and founded a Universalist newspaper, the *Liberalist*, neither of which lasted long after he left the area. In 1828 he returned to his native Rhode Island, where he succeeded Stephen Cutler as minister to the new church in Pawtucket. After two years the society was disbanded, largely because of financial problems in the community. There does not seem to be any substance to later allegations that Frieze destroyed the church by "turning infidel."

Although his 1831 tract, *A Dissertation on the Subjects of Death, the General Judgment, and Future Interminable Punishment,* shows his continued interest in Universalism, Frieze retired from the ministry after the loss of the Pawtucket church, becoming a political journalist and pamphleteer. From 1863 to 1875 he was private secretary to William Sprague, United States Senator from Rhode Island.

[14] David Long (1772-1850) was the Congregational minister in Milford for his entire career, 1801-44. He belonged to the Hopkinsian, or evangelical, wing of the Congregational denomination. Though considered an unexciting preacher, he was respected as a faithful pastor to a struggling church. In *History of the Town of Milford*, Adin Ballou wrote of him, "He was a man of good commonsense, respectable learning, much prudence, great fidelity to his religious convictions, and eminently exemplary in all the walks of life."

[15] The "North Purchase" was an area of some three square miles that was added to the town of Mendon in 1691, supplementing the territory originally purchased from the Nipmuck Indians in 1662. The North Purchase was included in the "easterly precinct" of Mendon, which became the town of Milford in 1780.

[16] Zebediah Flagg (1785-1848) was a Milford farmer, and one of the twelve "proprietors" who financed the construction of the Universalist church.

[17] Pearley Hunt, Arial Bragg, and Sullivan Sumner were prominent citizens of Milford and leaders in the Universalist church. Hunt and Bragg were among the twelve proprietors responsible for building the church. Sumner, who was nearly a generation younger than the others, was not a proprietor, but his father and uncles were.

Pearley Hunt (1771-1844), who would later become Adin Ballou's father-in-law, started as the proprietor of a modest variety store. As his means increased he invested in real estate. His real-estate business was so prosperous that in 1818 he was able to sell the store to his assistant and retire from trade. He was the largest investor in the Universalist church, putting up a quarter of the funds needed to build it. He served many terms as selectman and assessor, was a justice of the peace from 1811, and was postmaster of Milford from 1829 until his death.

Arial Bragg (1772-1855) was one of the first wholesale shoe manufacturers in the United States. At a time when shoes were generally made individually by itinerant shoemakers (as described by Adin Ballou in chapter 1), Bragg pioneered the mass production of ready-made shoes using the "putting-out system." Beginning life as a destitute orphan, he became one of the richest men in Worcester County, proprietor of the village of Braggville at the intersection of Milford, Mendon, and Holliston. He was a colonel of militia, served many terms as selectman and assessor, and represented Milford in the state legislature in 1838 and 1843.

Sullivan Sumner (1789-1867) and his wife owned the principal hotel in Milford from about 1820. During the 1830s he served as town assessor, treasurer, and representative to the state legislature.

[18] A doctor's office had stood on this spot since at least 1810, but Dr. Allen Fay (1803-1880) did not arrive in Milford until 1836. Dr. Gustavus Peck, who practiced in Milford from 1810 to 1836, possessed the office at the time in question.

[19] The word *hospital* (along with the words *hospice*, *hostel*, and *hotel*) derives from a Latin root, *hospes*, referring both to strangers and to the people who entertain them. In early America a hospital was an institution of general charity, a combination of poorhouse, hostel, asylum, and infirmary. (It was not until 1821, when the Massachusetts General Hospital opened, that there existed in New England a hospital whose sole purpose was to treat the sick.)

Much of this public charity was dispensed not in institutional settings, but in private homes, by individuals or families paid by the community. This system was liable to abuses, as towns contracted out these services to the lowest bidder and did not always provide much supervision. During the first half of the nineteenth century, home-based poverty relief was gradually replaced by direct government aid provided in almshouses. Adin Ballou's friend Arial Bragg, who served as Milford's Overseer of the Poor in 1842, wrote proudly in his autobiography that he ended the practice of "letting out the poor at auction to the lowest bidder…[with] but little regard to the bidders' means or disposition to provide for their actual wants. This attention to the poor he thinks the best act of his life."

[20] It is interesting that Ballou was exchanging with Paul Dean as early as 1824. In that year Dean was only just being accepted back into Universalist fellowship. In both "An Epistle General to Restorationists" (see Appendix F) and the *Autobiography*, Ballou implied that he was prejudiced against Dean and the other Restorationists until a much later date. But "ministerial intercourse" usually implies a certain level of mutual compatibility, or at least toleration.

[21] David Pickering (1788-1859) became minister of the First Universalist Society in Providence in 1823. There he edited a Universalist newspaper, the *Christian Telescope*, 1825-29, and engaged in controversy with an ardent anti-Universalist, Origen Bacheler (see chapter 8, note 12). Pickering felt that ultra Universalists such as Hosea Ballou and Walter Balfour damaged the reputation of Universalism and made it harder to defend. He also believed that Universalist ministerial discipline was used selectively against Restorationists, while "infidels" such as Abner Kneeland (see chapter 7, note 12) were treated more leniently.

Pickering founded a local conference, the Providence Association, and attracted to its meetings Restorationists from Massachusetts. In 1829 he resigned from fellowship with the Universalist General Convention. Other Universalists then closed ranks against the Providence Association, forcing its members to reorganize themselves as a separate denomination, the Massachusetts Association of Universal Restorationists. Pickering was unsuccessful in bringing his church into the Restorationist fold and, as a consequence, in 1835 was forced to resign. After trying unsuccessfully to succeed Edward Mitchell, a Trinitarian Universalist, in New York City, Pickering lived and preached in western New York State and in Michigan. These moves took him away from participation in Restorationist affairs. He was accepted back into Universalist fellowship in 1841.

[22] Pearley Hunt was an active member and a past master of Charity Lodge. It is likely that he introduced Adin Ballou to Freemasonry and sponsored him for membership. Ballou became Worshipful Master of the Charity Lodge in 1826. After the closing of this lodge, Ballou maintained an active connection with the Montgomery Lodge in Milford from 1829 until his death, speaking at funerals and on Masonic festival days.

Many Universalist ministers, including John Murray, were affiliated with the Masons. Hosea Ballou joined the Masons in the 1790s and was Master of Warren Lodge No. 23 in Woodstock, Vermont, in 1807. Other Universalist ministers who were Masons include Sebastian Streeter, Edward Turner, Paul Dean, Jacob Frieze, David Pickering, Jacob Wood, and Nathaniel Stacy. Among these Paul Dean had the most distinguished Masonic career, rising to become Grand Master of the Massachusetts Grand Lodge, 1837-40.

[23] The "anti-Masonic excitement" began in western New York State in 1826 with the disappearance of Captain William Morgan, who had published a book revealing Masonic secrets. It was alleged that he had been kidnapped, and perhaps murdered, by Masons. When justice moved slowly, it was revealed that most of the local officials in charge of law enforcement and the judicial system were lodge brothers. Opponents of Freemasonry accused it of being a secret government whose purpose was to subvert democracy. So great was the hysteria on this subject that a national political party was created whose major issue was the suppression of Freemasonry. In the 1830s the anti-Masonic movement was absorbed into the Whig Party.

Many Masons were forced to resign or conceal their memberships during this time of trouble. Churches put pressure on their ministers to repudiate Freemasonry. A large number submitted, but others remained firm in their Masonic loyalty. Nathaniel Stacy, the great pioneer preacher of Universalism in central New York, resigned his pulpit rather than renounce the fraternal connection that he had held for twenty-five years. Paul Dean and Sebastian Streeter were among the Universalist signatories to the "Boston Declaration," an expression of support for Freemasonry, published in the *Boston Masonic Mirror* in 1831. In Rhode Island a defense of Freemasonry was undertaken by Jacob Frieze.

[24] The method of discipline described here is indeed remarkably similar to one used by the Transcendentalist educator A. Bronson Alcott (1799-1888) at the Temple School in Boston. Assistant teacher Elizabeth Palmer Peabody described Alcott's approach to discipline: "When he first began to teach school, he thought no punishment was desirable, and spent an immense amount of time in reasoning. But . . . he was convinced in the course of his observations, that the passions of the soul could not in all cases be met by an address to the understanding." Accordingly, with the consent of the children, misbehavior was punished by exclusion from the class, or by "one blow with the ferule upon the palm of the hand."

> Having brought the whole school to this state of feeling, Mr. Alcott introduced a new mode. He talked with them, and having . . . brought them to acknowledge the uses of this hurting of the body, (as he always phrased it,) in concentrating attention, &c., he said, that

he intended to have it administered upon his own hand for a time, instead of theirs; but that the guilty person must do it... They said they preferred being punished themselves. But he determined that they should not escape the pain and the shame of administering the stroke upon him, except by being themselves blameless.

Chapter 7

[1] Nathanael Emmons (1745-1840) was the minister of the Congregational church in Franklin, Massachusetts, for fifty-four years, 1773-1827. Emmons represented the "New Light" strain in Congregational theology, which emphasized the absolute sovereignty of God and the inherent depravity of human nature. He was influential in interpreting Jonathan Edwards's theology for his own generation. Eighty-seven students trained for ministry under his direction.

Long before the abolitionist movement was organized, Emmons was preaching against racial prejudice and slavery. He taught that all humans were members of one family, equal in intellectual and moral capacity ("equally involved in the same corruption and depravity of heart"). On similar grounds, he opposed war, condemning as "false, selfish, and sinful" the sort of patriotism that causes a nation to pursue its own interests at the expense of other branches of the human family.

[2] Matthew 3:8.

[3] Matthew 5:26.

[4] In ancient Roman religion, the *manes* were the spirits of the dead. The main concern of Roman religious practice regarding the dead was to ensure that their spirits would not remain near the earthly sphere to plague their relatives, but would be expeditiously conveyed to permanent homes in the underworld.

[5] The 1896 edition of the *Autobiography* has 1827, but the context makes it clear that 1826 is meant.

[6] Prior to the semicentennial of the United States in 1826, the Fourth of July had been celebrated primarily in a partisan political fashion. The pattern set in Washington, DC, on July 4, 1826 – military exercises, processions, a reading of the Declaration of Independence, an oration, dinners, and toasts – was copied for years to come in cities and towns all over the country as a civic ritual intended to bind the community together.

[7] The description of the 1827 Fourth of July celebration marks the first appearance of Lucy Hunt, who would later become Ballou's second wife.

It is notable how many of the people mentioned in connection with the Fourth of July celebration were associated with the Universalist Church – probably a reflection of the large part played by Pearley Hunt in organizing the festivities. Of the people named, all were Universalists except Isaac Davenport.

Clark Sumner (1794-1868) and John Corbett Jr. (1799-1873) were both well-respected farmers who held various local offices in Milford. John Corbett represented Milford in the Massachusetts House of Representatives, 1837-38. He was the brother-in-law of Adin Ballou's predecessor at Milford, Thomas Whittemore.

Newell Nelson (1784-1869) and Isaac Davenport (1786-1852) were both land surveyors. Both served as selectmen and held other municipal offices in Milford, and both were later appointed Justice of the Peace. Newell Nelson made the first maps of Milford, Mendon, and Bellingham, Massachusetts, and Cumberland, Rhode Island.

The three girls who presented the standard were all part of Pearley Hunt's family circle: his daughter, his niece, and his future daughter-in-law. Harriet Hunt (1811-1887) was the daughter of Pearley Hunt's brother Ebenezer. Laura Ann Adams (1808-1871) married Pearley Hunt's son Hiram in 1829.

[8] Ballou's speech was printed as *An Oration delivered July 4, 1827, before the Republican Citizens of Milford* (Boston, 1827). This speech is notable for containing Ballou's first recorded use of the expression "non-resistance." It was used in quite a different sense from what it later meant to him. The British, he said scornfully, believed that the colonists owed "passive obedience and non-resistance" to the crown.

[9] Timothy Walker's letters remained part of local lore for a surprisingly long time. They were reprinted in the *Hopkinton Observer* in 1874, nearly fifty years after their first publication. Walker's grandson sent a copy of the *Observer* article to Ballou while he was working on the *History of the Town of Milford*, thereby refreshing Ballou's memory of Walker, his letters, and his Fourth of July toast.

[10] *Bohon* (or *pohon*) and *upas* are rough renditions of the Malay words for "tree" and "poison." The upas tree probably entered popular culture in the English-speaking world via Erasmus Darwin's botanical poem *Loves of the Plants* (1789). It was reputed to have the power to lay waste to the soil for miles around. A poison tree, *Antiaris toxicaria*, does exist in India and Southeast Asia, but its blighting effect has been much exaggerated. As a metaphor, the upas tree gained a wide currency in the nineteenth century, notably in the vocabulary of temperance advocates.

[11] The First Universalist Society of New York was founded by Henry Fitz, a lay preacher, in 1822 (see chapter 8, note 1). By 1823 the society was offering Sunday services, often led by Edward Mitchell, minister of another universalist church in New York. A building was begun that same year, at the corner of Prince and Orange Streets, and completed in July 1824.

The first minister of the Prince Street church was Nehemiah Dodge, a recent convert from the Baptist ranks. He served for just over a year. During the summer of 1825 Abner Kneeland arranged with Dodge to exchange pulpits for three months. At the end of this period the New York congregation called Kneeland as the settled minister, a move that some Universalist ministers found inappropriate. William Balch wrote that Kneeland had "by peculiar management, contrived to turn Jacob and supplant his brother, stealing away his bishopric." By early 1827 Kneeland's ministry had become so controversial as to precipitate a schism in the church. Kneeland left the church and began preaching to his supporters in a rented hall. This breakaway group was organized as the Second Universalist Society.

The last minister of the Prince Street church, whose pastorate followed that of Ballou after an interregnum of a year, was John F. Myers. He served for only a few months, leaving in the summer of 1829. Shortly thereafter the society disbanded.

[12] Abner Kneeland (1774-1844), a longtime friend of Hosea Ballou, was an admired proponent of Universalism between 1803 and 1829, despite periods of doubt about Christian revelation. During one of these periods, in 1814, he resigned his fellowship. Hosea Ballou engaged him in a correspondence (later published) that brought him back into the denominational fold.

By the time he came to New York City, Kneeland was under the influence of the skeptical British communitarian Robert Owen (see chapter 19, note 3), and his religious doubts were again in the ascendant. In 1827 he revealed his opinions to his congregation at Prince Street, causing a crisis that split the church. Kneeland left and founded a new congregation. As his ideas became more radical, the new church rejected him as well. In 1829 Hosea Ballou at last gave up on his friend and negotiated his resignation from the Universalist convention.

Moving to Boston in 1831, Kneeland began lecturing to the First Society of Free Enquirers. When, in 1833, he wrote in his newspaper, the *Boston Investigator*, that "Universalists believe in a god which I do not," he was prosecuted, and, after several trials, convicted of blasphemy. He eventually spent sixty days in jail, the last person to be incarcerated on this charge in the United States. In 1839 he moved to Iowa and founded a utopian community, Salubria, which did not long survive his death.

[13] In 1827 steamboats left Providence for New York on Tuesdays, Thursdays, and Saturdays (hence Ballou's disappointment at finding that there was no boat on Friday). The fare was $8.00 – a substantial sum at a time when Ballou's salary was $330.00 per year. The single-engine steamboats in use in 1827 normally took between 24 and 30 hours to make the trip, departing Providence at 11 A.M. or noon in order to allow time for passengers from Boston to make the six-hour stagecoach trip to Providence. He must, therefore, have had "good wind, weather, and luck" in order to arrive in New York in time for the morning service.

[14] The New York City that Ballou encountered in 1827 occupied only the tip of Manhattan Island, extending north as far as Houston Street. With a population of about 200,000, it was the largest city in the United States, although the enormous influx of immigration that would transform the city was still in the future.

New York's position as "the nation's metropolis" was based on its importance as a seaport. The Erie Canal, which opened in 1825, consolidated New York's position as the principal port serving the interior of the country: in 1825 the port of New York handled about half the imports and a third of the exports for the entire country. The commerce of the port led to the development of auxiliary financial services. By the time of Ballou's visit, New York was the undisputed center of insurance, banking, and brokerage, "the London of America." Culturally, Boston was still considered "the Athens of America," though by 1820 New York had become the center of the printing and publishing industry.

Ballou's first impressions of the streets and the water were rather more favorable than those of most contemporary observers. In fact, the streets were notorious for their filth, crowding, and the pigs that roamed freely, feeding on the city's garbage. The stagecoaches used for public transportation contributed to New York's first traffic jams. The water supply was considered particularly poor. The first adequate reservoir was completed in 1842; sewer construction did not begin until 1849.

Ballou's observation that New Yorkers seemed "less stiff and starched" than New Englanders may have reflected the fact that the 1820s and 30s were an interval of unusual equality and class mobility in New York. Property requirements for voting were reduced in 1821 and again in 1826, so that virtually all white men (and some black men) could vote and take part in politics. The city's prosperity created widespread economic opportunity, without the extremes of wealth and poverty that would accompany the increased immigration that came later in the century.

[15] The main idea behind the two-week exchange was to allow Hosea Ballou to attend the meeting of the Hudson River Association at the Prince Street church and the New England Universalist General Convention in Saratoga Springs, New York, without missing a Sunday

in the pulpit. Adin Ballou would ensure continuity of ministerial services at School Street, while Hosea Ballou would preach in New York on the way to and from Saratoga Springs.

[16] John S. Thompson (b. 1787) was an immigrant from Ireland (or Scotland – accounts differ on this point) who converted from Methodism to Universalism after his arrival in America. He was the minister of the Universalist church in Rochester, New York, 1823-25, where he edited a Universalist newspaper, the *Rochester Magazine*. In 1828 the Southern Association noted that he "has voluntarily and publicly withdrawn himself from the Universalist Connexion, without giving any reason for such procedure."

[17] Adin Ballou took the first steamer of the week, departing Providence on Tuesday morning. Depending upon the weather, it could have arrived in New York at any time on Wednesday afternoon. Hosea Ballou had to leave New York on Thursday morning in order to be back in Boston in time for the following Sunday's services. Hard as it may seem to expect Adin Ballou to proceed directly from the steamboat landing to his own installation, scheduling the service on Wednesday was the only way to allow both Adin and Hosea Ballou to take part in it and still keep all of their preaching commitments. Given the uncertainties of travel, the installation should, perhaps, have been scheduled for a later hour. The time may have been chosen for the convenience of other participants; that the evening service "came off with much less than the customary display of parts" suggests that some of the participants had not been able to stay.

[18] This address is just south of the corner of Thompson and Prince Streets, not far from the church. This part of New York was far uptown in 1827. Just to the north, about to be engulfed by the expanding city, lay the still-suburban villages of Bowery and Greenwich.

[19] In a front-page editorial in the first issue of the *Dialogical Instructor*, Ballou described the new paper as "a Miscellany of religion, morality, reason, and common sense; consisting chiefly of original matter, arranged in the form of dialogues, allegories, fables, and short pieces of various composition, designed to illustrate and defend the Bible, the Christian Religion, the doctrine of Universal Salvation, plain Morality, religious Liberty, and the truths of reason, nature, and experience generally." The lead item of an issue was usually a dialogue in which a character espousing Universalism argues with and defeats an opponent.

Chapter 8

[1] Henry Fitz (1785-1848), a native of Newburyport, Massachusetts, was converted to Universalism by reading James Relly's book *Union* and hearing the preaching of John Murray. When he moved to New York City in 1819 he joined Edward Mitchell's universalist Society of United Christian Friends. Fitz began a weekly religious newspaper, the *Gospel Herald* (1820-27), which at first reflected Murray's and Mitchell's trinitarian teaching, but soon shifted to a unitarian Universalist point of view. In 1822 Fitz founded the Society for the Investigation and Establishment of Gospel Truth, precursor to the First Universalist Society (Prince Street).

[2] This trip by Hosea Ballou is passed over in Thomas Whittemore's usually detailed *Life of Hosea Ballou*: "In the month of May [1828] Mr. B. made his second visit to Philadelphia, the first having been made in the year 1820. No particular account of the second journey has been preserved." However, it is clear from an article he wrote in 1831 ("Reply to the Boston Recorder," *Trumpet and Universalist Magazine*, 5 February 1831) that Whittemore was aware of Hosea Ballou's having been approached by the New York church in 1828.

³ Russell Streeter (1791-1880) studied for the Universalist ministry while living with his older brother Sebastian in Swanzey, New Hampshire. While Sebastian became an urban preacher, Russell remained a rural evangelist all his life. Everywhere he lived he founded churches, which he used as bases from which to travel widely. His principal settlements were Springfield and Rockingham, Vermont, 1813-20; Portland, Maine, 1821-27; Woodstock and South Woodstock, Vermont, 1834-47; and Portland again, 1847-53. During his first pastorate in Portland, Streeter founded the *Christian Intelligencer,* which he edited for six years.

⁴ In April 1828, Thomas Whittemore and Russell Streeter issued a prospectus for a new Universalist periodical, the *Trumpet.* This proposal was met with hostility by many Boston Universalists, including Hosea Ballou, the senior editor of the *Universalist Magazine.* They considered the idea disloyal and unfair to Henry Bowen, the publisher of the *Universalist Magazine* since its inception nine years previously. While Hosea Ballou was on his trip to New York and Philadelphia, Whittemore and Streeter bought out Bowen's interest in the *Universalist Magazine.* Three months later, Whittemore bought out Streeter's interest and became the sole editor and proprietor. The first issue of the combined *Trumpet and Universalist Magazine* was published on July 5, 1828. Although Hosea Ballou was induced to write a moderate commendation of the new magazine, he did not contribute to the *Trumpet and Universalist Magazine* for several years.

⁵ The transfer of the subscription list of the *Dialogical Instructer* to the *Trumpet and Universalist Magazine* became a point of contention at the time of the controversy between Adin Ballou and Thomas Whittemore over the "Epistle General to Restorationists" in 1831. Whittemore cited the transfer to cast doubt on Ballou's claim, in the "Epistle General," that when he left New York he was deeply disgusted and disillusioned with ultra Universalism. In his reply Ballou explained that the transfer was originally requested by Whittemore, and that he agreed to it "partly because we then believed its proprietors would give [the *Trumpet*] a much more elevated character, than afterward proved to be the case."

⁶ The complete title of Charles Hudson's book is *A Series of Letters Addressed to Rev. Hosea Ballou of Boston: Being a Vindication of the Doctrine of Future Retribution Against the Principal Arguments Used by Him, Mr. Balfour and Others.* Although Hosea Ballou did not respond to Hudson's book, Walter Balfour did, publishing in 1828 *Three Essays on the Intermediate State of the Dead, the Resurrection from the Dead, and on the Greek Terms rendered Judge, Judgment, Condemned, Condemnation, Damned, Damnation, &c. in the New Testament: With Remarks on Mr. Hudson's Letters in Vindication of a Future Retribution, addressed to Mr. Hosea Ballou of Boston.* Hudson and Balfour each pursued the controversy in another book in 1829. Adin Ballou gave a detailed account of his reaction to the controversy between Hudson and Balfour in his "Epistle General to Restorationists" (see Appendix F).

⁷ Hosea Ballou's response to Hudson's *Letters* is in the *Universalist Magazine,* 22 December 1827.

⁸ Edward Mitchell (1768-1834) was a New York City bookseller who, with several other believers in universal salvation, left the John Street Methodist Society in 1796 to found the Society of United Christian Friends. This small group evolved into an independent church, universalist in theology, but not affiliated with the Universalist denomination. Mitchell served as minister to this congregation from 1803 to 1810, when he was called to be the associate to John Murray in Boston. Since his trinitarian theology was similar to Murray's, Mitchell was a logical choice to succeed Murray. However, within a year the members of the Society of

United Christian Friends decided to recall their old pastor. Mitchell got permission to leave Boston for three weeks, and did not return. He mailed in his resignation several months later.

For another decade the United Christian Friends prospered. Mitchell was a popular and influential preacher. However, his intolerance began to alienate New York universalists during the 1820s. Mitchell was so upset by the controversial ministry of Abner Kneeland at the Prince Street Church that he devoted much of his preaching in the last decade of his life to denouncing unitarian Universalists, most of whom he regarded as no better than infidels.

[9] Slightly misquoted from the final lines of Samuel Taylor Coleridge's *Rime of the Ancient Mariner*.

[10] Sophocles, *Oedipus Rex* 1450.

[11] See Micah 4:4.

[12] Origen Bacheler (1800-1848) was founder, editor, publisher, and chief contributor to the *Anti-Universalist* (1826-30). Later he edited the *New-York Evangelist* (1830-33) and the *Family Magazine: or, Monthly Abstract of General Knowledge* (1833-41). In addition to his newspaper and magazine work, Bacheler produced a series of books and pamphlets attacking religious viewpoints with which he disagreed. His first was *The Universalist Bible* (1829), a collection of parody Bible passages originally published in the *Anti-Universalist*. His later works were *Mormonism Exposed* (1838), *The Restoration and Conversion of the Jews* (1843), and *Episcopacy* (1845).

[13] The *Anti-Universalist* was published in Providence from August 1826 through December 1828 and in Boston from January 1829 to December 1830. It seems to have been founded largely in response to the Universalist *Christian Telescope*, published in Providence by David Pickering. One of the main features of each issue of the *Anti-Universalist* was a review of the latest issue of the *Telescope*. Much of the criticism of the Universalists took the form of mockery and satire, a strategy that left Bacheler open to charges of being abusive, contemptible, trivial and so on. He was clearly sensitive to the criticism and felt compelled to defend his methods, saying, "We deny that our paper is scurrilous; it merely answers scurrilous writers according to their scurrility, in a sense altogether allowable."

In spite of its name, the *Anti-Universalist* did not restrict its attacks to Universalism. Bacheler also opposed rationalistic and deistic philosophy, liberal tendencies within all Christian denominations, and the secular communitarianism being promoted by Robert Owen. With considerable prescience, he predicted the formation of something like the Unitarian Universalist Association. The advocates of "open Deism, Atheism, &c." were, he said, "seeking shelter under Universalism; and as to Unitarianism, its natural tendency is, to Universalism. Heretics and infidels may therefrom soon be expected to form one body – and that body, the Unitarian Restoration Universalists" (6 August 1828).

[14] The series, entitled "Hear Both Sides," ran to seventeen articles, spanning a period of nine months, November 1828 through July 1829. Ballou prepared an article for each issue of the *Anti-Universalist* throughout this period, except for one that he missed due to the illness and death of his wife. By the end of the series, some of Ballou's articles were so long as to take virtually the entire issue.

This debate was a long-sought prize for Bacheler, who was eager to engage in debate with a Universalist. In the early days of the *Anti-Universalist*, he had tried to enter into a correspondence with David Pickering, but Pickering dismissed the *Anti-Universalist* as "too scurrilous to be noticed." The debate with Ballou served both to legitimize the paper and to revive the interest of readers growing bored with same arguments against Universalism. It is less easy to see what Ballou gained from the debate. Yet it was clearly important to him at the time, since he wrote faithfully and at length during a difficult period in his life.

Ballou and Bacheler appeared together on the lecture circuit almost two decades after the "Hear Both Sides" debate. In January 1847 Bacheler gave a lecture in Woonsocket, Rhode Island, which was followed by a reply by Ballou. The following month the two men debated capital punishment. John Boyden, minister of the Universalist church in Woonsocket, recorded in his diary that he thought Ballou "too strong for his antagonist altogether."

[15] Gustavus Darling Peck (1787-1875) studied medicine with Dr. Daniel Thurber (see chapter 8, note 16). He practiced medicine in Milford from about 1810 to 1836. After leaving Milford he practiced in various other Massachusetts towns until he retired in 1867.

[16] Daniel Thurber (1766-1836) was a prominent physician in South Milford. In *History of the Town of Milford*, Ballou described him as "one of the most popular, trusted, and beloved physicians that ever gladdened our sick-chambers." Though his only training consisted of an apprenticeship to a physician in his native town of Rehoboth, Massachusetts, Thurber was awarded honorary M.D. degrees from both Harvard and Brown University. He represented the town of Mendon in the state legislature for twenty-five years and held many municipal offices.

[17] Lamentations 3:19.

[18] Hosea 2:22.

[19] The earliest known use of the expression "not lost but gone before" is in Seneca, *Epistola* 63.16. It has since appeared in countless poems, hymns, songs both serious and parodic, gravestone inscriptions, memorial books, sermons, and letters. It lives on in the Internet age in memorial web sites and online books of condolences.

Chapter 9

[1] Seth Chandler (1806-1889) served the Universalist church in Oxford, Massachusetts, 1833-34, then became minister of First Parish Church in Shirley. He held this position for forty-five years, 1834-79. After he retired he wrote the *History of the Town of Shirley, Massachusetts* (1883). Though most of his career was spent as a Unitarian minister, he retained a lifelong interest in the Universalist denomination and its history. In his later years he was a close friend of the Universalist historian Richard Eddy. In his will he bequeathed "to the Universalist Historical Society about six hundred valuable books, embracing the periodical literature of the Restorationists."

[2] Ballou is clearly paraphrasing, rather than quoting from his 1829 diary. Two dates, September 3 and September 20, are given in the text; the dates in brackets are deduced from these.

[3] The motion denying Pickering the opportunity to pray at the convention passed by a margin of 15 to 10. The text of the motion was as follows:

> Voted, that, considering his recent withdrawal of fellowship from this body, together with the circumstances under which the withdrawal took place, and the manner of his accounting for it to the public, the Rev. Mr. Pickering be not invited to take any part with us in the services of this session of the Convention.

In his editorial response to Adin Ballou's description of the incident in his "Epistle General to Restorationists," Thomas Whittemore blamed Paul Dean for offering a part in the service to Pickering, who had resigned his membership in the Universalist General Convention, passing over others who were members in good standing. He also accused Pickering of grave, though unspecified, offenses and claimed that Pickering had resigned from the UGC in order to avoid the consequences of his misdeeds ("Reply to the Boston Recorder," *Trumpet and Universalist Magazine*, 5 February 1831). Pickering accused Whittemore of spreading "tales of slander and falsehood." He said that he had resigned his membership "because I did not approve of the laws of the Convention [but] I had neither renounced my faith nor the fellowship of the order" and that it was customary to invite Universalist ministers who were not members of the UGC to take part in the services (*Independent Messenger*, 25 March 1831).

4   This sermon extract illustrates the extent to which Ballou's preaching was steeped in Biblical language. This short passage quotes or refers to Psalms 16:15, 21:7, 55:14, 69:30, 116:9, 121:8, and 125:2, as well as 1 Kings 8:28; 2 Kings 8:1; Proverbs 16:15; 2 Peter 1:4; Revelation 4:9-10.

5   Three parables from Luke 15: the lost piece of silver (Luke 15:8-10), the lost sheep (Luke 15:4-7), and the prodigal son (Luke 15:11-32).

6   John 3:16; Matthew 5:44-45; Luke 6:36, 6:35.

7   Romans 5:8; Ephesians 2:4-5.

8   1 John 4:10, 19.

9   This is not a quotation from Calvin, but from the first "point" of a formulation of the "Five Points of Calvinism" that was widely known in the nineteenth century by both proponents and opponents of Calvinism. The five theological points were taken from the Canons of the Synod of Dort (1618). The wording was adapted from the Westminster Confession of 1646. Universalists knew this point well; many Universalist preachers, including John Murray and Hosea Ballou, quoted it in their attacks on Calvinism.

10 Ballou never worked full time at Milford. In order to support himself and his family, he, like many ministers of the time, had a circuit of preaching stations in addition to his settled pulpit and, much of the time, taught school as well.

In 1831, during the newspaper debate following the Restorationist secession, Thomas Whittemore implied that Ballou had to struggle to fill his "vacant Sabbaths" by preaching at "different societies, as opportunities offered." Ballou responded, "What he calls our 'vacant sabbaths' were spent with our brethren in Medway – with whom we were as regularly employed one half the time, as at Milford the other ... As to 'vacant sabbaths,' we have had none; and are not likely to have – all the efforts of Rev. Thomas Whittemore to the contrary notwithstanding" ("Reply to the Trumpet," *Independent Messenger*, 11 February, 1831).

Chapter 10

1   The first regularly-scheduled Universalist conventions were held in Philadelphia beginning in 1790. Though John Murray was the only New England delegate ever to attend, the early sessions were conducted as if they had authority over the entire denomination. In 1792 the Boston church applied to Philadelphia for permission to hold a regional convention in New England. The balance of authority began to shift to New England over the next decade. In the early 1800s, while the New England General Convention was growing rapidly, the Philadelphia Convention was having difficulty holding meetings and attracting delegates. Its last session was held in 1809.

² In 1791, in response to an inquiry into the Philadelphia Convention's position on the question of future punishment, a letter was drafted and approved by the Convention that let it be known that its delegates believed "that all that die without the knowledge of their salvation in Christ Jesus... will not be purged from their sins or unbelief by death, but necessarily must appear in the next state under all that darkness, fear, and torment, and conscious guilt which is the natural consequence of the unbelief of the truth."

³ Thomas Whittemore's *Modern History of Universalism* included responses to a survey that Whittemore had addressed to "the principal Universalist clergy," concerning their opinion of the proportion of Universalists who believed in future punishment. Eleven preachers responded, only one of whom thought that a majority of the Universalists in his locality believed in future punishment. Although this was not a representative or unprejudiced sample, the results of this survey must have made discouraging reading for Restorationists. Adin Ballou may have developed his nine-tenths figure partly from this source. His estimate of his theological opponents' numerical strength was also confirmed by his experiences with the Prince Street and Milford congregations.

The actual proportion of Universalists who believed in some form of future punishment was much greater than Whittemore's unscientific survey indicates. According to Hosea Ballou 2d, the outspoken Restorationists in the denomination were outnumbered by those such as himself, who held restorationist theological views but did not join the Restorationist party. Many of these kept silent or sided with the ultras, out of respect and loyalty to Hosea Ballou or because they believed this was the best way to preserve unity and harmony in the denomination. Among the ministers who attended the New England Universalist General Convention between 1827 and 1830, about fifty percent believed in future punishment. For more detail on this calculation see Peter Hughes, "The Second Phase of the Restorationist Controversy: Disciplinary Crisis and Schism, 1824-1831," *Journal of Unitarian Universalist History* 28 (2001).

⁴ This is an accurate depiction of the views of Hosea Ballou. For example, in "A Short Essay on Universalism," reprinted in *A Voice to Universalists* (1849), he contended that "we know of no passages of Scripture, which teach the doctrine of a future state, which imply the existence of either sin or punishment in that state." Thomas Whittemore, in his biography of Hosea Ballou, quoted him as saying, "It appears very evident that all those passages which have been generally applied to a state of retribution, in a future world, are capable, to say the least, of an application which finds their accomplishment in the present mode of existence." A summary of the ultra Universalist interpretations of Restorationist proof texts can be found in Thomas Whittemore, *Modern History of Universalism*, pp. 437-441.

⁵ Thomas Whittemore, "Controversy with Universalists," *Trumpet and Universalist Magazine*, 2 April 1831.

⁶ In his *Inquiry into the Scriptural Import of the Words ... Translated Hell* (1824), Walter Balfour wrote, "Intelligent heathen had no more faith in infernal punishments, than people now have in the Salem witchcraft." In his controversy with Charles Hudson, Balfour frequently referred to future punishment as a heathen idea.

⁷ Though originally delivered in April, the Medway sermon was eventually printed as *The Inestimable Value of Souls: A sermon delivered before the Universalist society in Medway (Mass.), May, 1830* (Boston, 1830).

⁸ The most controversial portion of "The Inestimable Value of Souls" is a paragraph near the end of the sermon dealing with the so-called "spirits in prison" passage (1 Peter 3:18-20):

> The apostle Peter, so far from making this life the only probationary state, plainly declares that the gospel has been preached to the dead, to the *spirits in prison*. He says, "For Christ also hath once suffered for sins, the just for the unjust, that he might bring us to God, being put to death in the flesh, but quickened by the spirit; by which also he went and preached to the spirits in prison; which sometime were disobedient, when once the long suffering of God waited in the days of Noah while the ark was preparing," etc. (1 Peter 3:18-20). "For this cause was the gospel preached also to them that are dead, that they might be judged according to men in the flesh, but live according to God in the spirit" (1 Peter 4:6). What was the use of this preaching to the spirits of the dead in prison, if there can be no change after death? If souls cannot be converted and saved after, as well as before death? *No man can tell.* I am aware of the pains at which many divines, both *orthodox* and *heterodox*, have put themselves to make it appear that these texts have no reference to a future state; but they have tortured language to no other purpose than to show their ingenuity. They have not gained their point. While this epistle of Peter remains in the New Testament collection, its meaning must be plain to every unbiased and candid reader.

Adin Ballou was here challenging a deeply personal and historically important interpretation of this passage by Hosea Ballou. In the early 1810s Hosea Ballou had been leaning towards a no-future-punishment theology but was restrained by 1 Peter 3:18-20, which appeared to show souls being reformed after death. In 1812 he published his first interpretation of the passage, which seemed to settle the question in favor of future punishment, but he remained unhappy with the result. Then, in 1818, in the midst of his published controversy with Edward Turner in the *Gospel Visitant*, he hit upon a new way of understanding the words of the epistle: that it represented, not Christ speaking to souls in the underworld, but rather Christ's preaching being extended, after his death, to the Gentile nations. This reinterpretation was an important event in Universalist history, for it allowed Hosea Ballou fully to embrace no-future-punishment theology, and further alienated him from his former friend Edward Turner and others. This exegesis, and the response to it, was an immediate cause of the Restorationist controversy in the early 1820s and the seed of the denominational disunity that lingered afterward.

It was therefore inevitable that Hosea Ballou and his circle would read this passage as a provocative and unkind attempt to attack Hosea Ballou in a sensitive place. Adin Ballou, however, was probably not aware of the full significance of the passage to the elder Ballou. The *Gospel Visitant* debate and the breach between Hosea Ballou and Edward Turner took place several years before Adin Ballou became a Universalist.

⁹ In his review of the Medway sermon (*Trumpet and Universalist Magazine*, 3 July 1830), Thomas Whittemore let it be known how much Hosea Ballou had been hurt and offended by Adin Ballou's treatment of this subject. "We are sensible," he wrote, "if he [Adin Ballou] is not, of the deep attention, the studious and prayerful hours, the diligent comparing of scripture with scripture, which these brethren who are included in his remarks have given to the passages in question; and it is a poor reward, and gives them not a little grief, to be told by a Universalist clergyman, 'that they have tortured language to no other purpose than to show their ingenuity.'"

¹⁰ Charles Chauncy (1705-1787) was a leader of the Arminian, or liberal, wing of the Congregational ministry in eighteenth-century Massachusetts. Over the course of his career he gradually moved toward both unitarian and universalist beliefs. His universalist

work, *The Mystery Hid from Ages and Generations* (subtitled *The Salvation of All Men*), was published anonymously in 1784.

[11] Restorationists claimed Murray, Winchester, and Chauncy as forerunners, since all of these early universalists believed in a time of suffering (or reward) after death. On the other hand, they held other beliefs that link them to ultra Universalists. For example, Murray and Winchester, like Hosea Ballou, were determinists.

[12] *Hamlet* 3.2.

[13] The expressions "heathen notions" and "wild reveries" were often used by Thomas Whittemore in reference to future punishment. For example, in his *Notes and Illustrations of the Parables of the New Testament* (1832) he called beliefs concerning punishment after death "the wild reveries of the heathen."

[14] See 2 Kings 9:16-20.

[15] The reference to Transcendentalism, as a feature of Unitarianism in 1830, is an anachronism. The "New School" of Unitarian thinking did not make its appearance until 1836.

[16] See Ecclesiastes 8:8.

[17] Topheth was a high place in the Valley of Hinnom (Gehenna) associated with ritual immolation of children. The grisly reputation of this valley led to these names being used, in late biblical times, to indicate a place where the wicked suffer after death.

[18] By 1816 a simple associational structure had developed within the New England Universalist General Convention, divided along geographical lines: the Northern Association (Vermont and New Hampshire), Southern Association (Massachusetts, Connecticut, and Rhode Island), Eastern Association (Maine), and Western Association (New York). The associational pattern became more complicated as local Universalist organizations emerged within the territory of the Northern and Southern Associations, with no clear definition of their relationship to the UGC: the Franklin Association (1823), Rockingham Association (1824), Old Colony Association (1827), Green Mountain Association (1829), and Boston Association (1829). Hosea Ballou was present at the foundation of most of these new local Universalist associations, and was typically chosen as moderator of the organizational meeting.

In the midst of this flurry of organization-building, the Providence Association was formed in 1827. Though at first it was simply another local association, it became a center of the Restorationist movement when Paul Dean, seeking a more congenial group with whom to share his brand of Universalist fellowship, began to attend the Quarterly Conferences in the Providence area, where he could see his old friend David Pickering. Both Dean and Pickering had grievances against the UGC: Dean because his plan for establishing a national Universalist convention was rejected without discussion in 1828, and Pickering because he felt that the UCG misused its disciplinary procedures to discriminate against Restorationists. When the Providence Association was formally chartered in 1829, Pickering resigned his membership in the UGC and "all the Associations under its jurisdiction" but retained his membership in the Providence Association. It was the implication that the Providence Association was independent of any other Universalist authority, rather than its Restorationist sympathies as such, which led to the Providence Association being placed under a "ban of outlawry" by the Universalist General Convention.

[19] Neither the idea of a Restorationist newspaper nor the proposed name was new in the summer of 1830. Charles Hudson had issued a prospectus in 1825 for a periodical to be called the *Independent Messenger* (Charles Hudson to Edward Turner, 29 July 1825).

[20] George W. Stacy (1809-1892) was apprenticed at age 14 to a printer in Boston, where he was a member of Paul Dean's congregation. He began his journalistic career as printer and co-owner of a short-lived weekly newspaper, the *Groton Herald*, 1829-30. In 1830 he went into partnership with Adin Ballou to print the *Independent Messenger*. After studying for the Restorationist ministry with Paul Dean, he served Unitarian churches in Carlisle, Massachusetts, 1836-41, and Boylston and Gardner, Massachusetts, 1839-41.

Stacy was one of the original members of the Hopedale Community, where he had charge of the print shop. In 1845 the Community, in one of its periodic reorganizations, adopted a complicated system, inspired by the works of Charles Fourier, which organized the members into "bands" and "sections" with monitors to ensure that each person contributed the requisite 48 to 60 hours of work each week. Stacy then resigned his membership, calling the new system an "artificial and burdensome machinery" and an "infringement upon parental and social rights." His departure was a bitter disappointment to Ballou.

After leaving Hopedale, Stacy settled in Milford, where he owned a printing and stationery shop. Later in life he became fairly wealthy through real estate transactions and was active in local politics. He held three part-time Unitarian pastorates in Massachusetts: Hopkinton, 1848-51; Hudson, 1854-62; and Sharon, 1868-70.

[21] See Hosea 2:6.

[22] The full text of "Epistle General," as printed in the *Independent Messenger* (1 January 1831), is given in Appendix F.

[23] Isaiah 30:7.

[24] "Universalism," *Boston Recorder*, January 1831. The *Recorder* column was reproduced in its entirety under the heading "Boston Recorder" in the *Trumpet and Universalist Magazine*, 29 January 1831.

[25] Ballou's second Fourth of July oration was shorter and more pointed than the first. While the 1827 speech concluded with a brief and vague injunction to be vigilant against internal enemies, the 1830 address warned against two specific hazards to democracy: selfish office-seekers who did not care what means they used to discourage well-meaning, competent citizens from engaging in the political process, and undisciplined partisan newspapers that valued truth less than factional ends. A sample of his rhetoric indicates that he might have had his own difficulties with the ultra Universalists in mind when he prepared his remarks:

> With some honorable exceptions, the newspaper presses throughout this Union have become mere trumpets of faction. To promote the cause of some party or individual by every means, whether laudable or contemptible, honorable or unprincipled, seems to have become the summit of their ambition ... they foam out torrents of falsehood and misrepresentation to strangle and intoxicate the public mind, and thus, silence the voice of both reason and common sense.

[26] Whittemore's "Reply to the Boston Recorder," *Trumpet and Universalist Magazine*, 5 February 1831, contained the following hostile biographical sketch of Adin Ballou:

> It will be proper for us, in the first place, to answer a question which will be asked by many of our readers, viz.: who is this Mr. Adin Ballou? They will not recollect to have heard of him before, and it is necessary therefore that we make them a little acquainted with his life. He

was brought up, we believe, in the town of Cumberland, R. I., and at an early age became a preacher among the Free Will Baptists, or Christians. Not far from this time he published a review of a sermon by Rev. Hosea Ballou on the New Birth, in which he represented the Universalists as being (we use his own words) "quarrelsome, tyrannical, unnatural, disobedient, unkind, dishonest, unjust, immoral, intemperate, angry, resentful, desperately proud, and blasphemous." Shortly after this he professed to be converted to Universalism, and was invited to Boston to preach as a candidate to the First Society of Universalists, over which Mr. Streeter is now settled. No Universalist minister in the neighborhood of Boston was more vehement than he in declaiming against the doctrine of future punishment. After preaching awhile as a candidate, his services were required no longer by the society, and he went again into the country. On the removal of Rev. Jacob Frieze from Milford, Mass., Mr. Ballou took the pastoral care of the Universalist Society in said town, where he remained until he was invited to New York to become the minister of the congregation of Universalists worshiping in Prince Street. Here he tarried but a short time. The affairs of the society did not prosper, and in a few months we find him returned to Milford, which has since been the place of his residence. The society in Milford, which from 1821 has enjoyed steady preaching with little intermission, has, for the last year, spared his services a part of the time, and his vacant Sabbaths he has spent with different societies, as opportunity offered.

See chapter 4, note 6 ("quarrelsome, tyrannical," etc.) and chapter 9, note 10 ("vacant Sabbaths").

[27] In his "Reply to the Boston Recorder," *Trumpet and Universalist Magazine*, 5 February 1831, Whittemore referred to certain "certificates" that, if published, would discredit one of the Restorationists – presumably Paul Dean, though his name was not mentioned. The alleged wrongdoing turned out, rather anticlimactically, to be "unprovoked and deliberate malice" toward Hosea Ballou.

[28] The correspondent in question was probably Edward Turner. Emotionally drained by his quarrel with Hosea Ballou, Turner was serving a Unitarian church in Charlton, Massachusetts, and watching this second phase of the Restorationist controversy from the sidelines. Had he wished to reenter the fray, the movement of the other Restorationists out of fellowship with the Universalists and the attachment of a number of them to Unitarian congregations would have given him the perfect opportunity. Turner, however, made no move to align himself with the Restorationists.

Adin Ballou's reply to Turner is notable for the intensity of the animosity he expressed toward Hosea Ballou and his associates:

> I thank you for the favorable light in which you speak of my Epistle to Restorationists, in the first No. of my paper, as also of my cause generally. I am still more thankful for the freedom with which you suggest a few hints, in relation to the blemishes interwoven with my memoirs of conducting the controversy against the ultra Universalists. There is danger of overstepping the bounds of prudence in the warmth of such a contest – and especially where one has come to look with such utter loathing and abhorrence, which I feel obliged to, upon the men, and doctrines and practices I stand forth to oppose. Having been myself wretchedly deceived in the moral character of their leaders – and knowing the wicked hypocrisies every day practiced by them upon the unsuspecting, in order to promote their own selfish ends, I cannot sit down contented without protesting against their evil doctrine, and still more evil deeds. Restorationism cannot live in such a pestilential atmosphere as that created by the writings, preachings and management of such men as Hosea Ballou, Walter Balfour & Thos. Whittemore. The true friends of the true doctrine of universal salvation (the only doctrine of universal salvation that will bear the test) have been left with no other alternative than to separate by force from a corrupt mass, or sink, doctrine and all, into the dark and unfathom-

able gulf of skepticism and irreligion. As things were going on, a very few years would have placed the whole Universalist body on a level with the disciples of Tom Paine etc. O that the Restorationists had long ago, even from the beginning stood on their own ground. Had they done so, they would by this time have become a light and glory in the earth – a great, and happy, and honored people. Now we are obliged to bear the reproach and answer for the sins of men, whose feelings, hopes, fears, and sentiments are the very antipodes of our own. But I verily believe God will yet redeem us in triumph from the power of the adversary in which we have been holden captives. (Adin Ballou to Edward Turner, 20 May 1831)

[29] Matthew 10:16.

Chapter 11

[1] Simeon Doggett (1765-1852) was a schoolmaster before entering the Congregational ministry in 1813. As a candidate for the Mendon pastorate, he candidly revealed his liberal views and asked the church to modify its creed and covenant to accommodate his beliefs. The parish agreed to these alterations and Doggett settled with them. His theology only became an issue after 1815, when the controversy surrounding publication of Jedidiah Morse's pamphlet *American Unitarianism* revealed the gulf between the two wings of the Congregational church in Massachusetts. In 1817 Doggett survived an attempt to dismiss him from the church. The triumph was a costly one, however. While the parish retained the church building and its liberal minister, the withdrawal of the orthodox left insufficient money to honor Doggett's contract.

Late in the 1820s, faced with a decline in active membership, First Parish entered into merger negotiations with the orthodox. The evangelical church, however, refused to consider any union while Doggett was settled in Mendon, and insisted on the form of church covenant that had been used prior to Doggett's alterations. The negotiations ended after the parish passed resolutions affirming their Unitarian theology and their support for Doggett's ministry. Despite their loyalty and affection for their elderly pastor, the people of First Parish felt themselves in need of a more dynamic minister whose preaching and leadership would enable them to compete with the local evangelicals for membership.

[2] The North Congregational Church in Mendon was formed in 1828 by a group of people who withdrew from First Parish during the pastorate of Simeon Doggett, preferring a more evangelical style of preaching and a strict Calvinist theology. They built a meetinghouse in 1830.

[3] In his letter to Edward Turner, written less than four months after his arrival in Mendon, Ballou described his position thus:

> I am happy to inform you that in my situation at Mendon with the Congregationalist Society my lot is pleasant – my friends many – my congregation respectable for numbers, talents, character, and zeal – my enemies few – my support competent though not large, and my prospects encouraging. (Adin Ballou to Edward Turner, 20 May 1831)

[4] Lyman Maynard (1801-1862) began his ministry at the Universalist church in Medway, Massachusetts. In 1828 he moved to Oxford, Massachusetts, where he reorganized the failing church and gave the congregation its first regular preaching in many years. He so impressed his parishioners that, after he left, they voted to call only Restorationists in the future. In 1832 Maynard succeeded Philemon Russell in Winchester, New Hampshire. Two years afterwards he moved to Amherst, New Hampshire, where he worked to revive a declining church. Later he served Unitarian churches in Hingham and Needham, Massachusetts. Around 1850 he retired from ministry to settle in Milford as a grocer.

5   Nathaniel Wright (c.1805-1859) was one of the few trinitarian Universalists at this time. (Others were Paul Dean and Edward Mitchell.) After studying with Paul Dean, 1827-28, he served Universalist churches in Madison, New York, in 1828, and Attleboro, Massachusetts, 1829-34. He was the standing clerk for the MAUR until he moved to Illinois in 1834.

6   Philemon R. Russell served Universalist societies in Winchester and Chesterfield, New Hampshire, in 1831; Watertown, Massachusetts, in 1832; and West Boylston, Massachusetts, in 1833. He was an early and ardent abolitionist. Many of his contributions to the *Independent Messenger* promoted either abolition or the American Peace Society.

Russell became a corresponding editor of the *Independent Messenger* in early 1835. By the middle of 1835, however, he had decided that he could not support a movement with a sectarian name or any articles of faith. After writing an editorial in favor of the organization and principles of the Christian Connexion (3 July 1835), he became a Christian Connexion minister. In 1842 he published an anti-Universalist tract, *A Series of Letters to a Universalist*, principally aimed at the ultra Universalists. In the preface he admitted that he had once been "deluded with a species of Universalism."

7   Minutes of the meeting of the Providence Association and the text of the circular letter are in the *Independent Messenger*, 27 May 1831.

8   In addition to the two explicit quotations (Matthew 5:16 and Titus 2:11-12), the circular letter uses language from Exodus 36:1; Judges 2:16; Isaiah 32:17; Daniel 6:11; Matthew 6:6; Acts 20:32; Ephesians 4:14, 6:16; 2 Thessalonians 3:1; 1 Timothy 6:4; 2 Timothy 2:15; Titus 2:10; 1 Peter 1:13.

9   Minutes of the meeting of the Providence Association are in the *Independent Messenger*, 26 August 1831.

10   The eight Restorationist ministers who signed the statement were Paul Dean, David Pickering, Charles Hudson, Adin Ballou, Lyman Maynard, Nathaniel Wright, Philemon Russell, and Seth Chandler. The only minister who is recorded as having been present, but who did not sign the document, was William S. Balch (1806-1887).

Balch had begun his career as an itinerant preacher in the area around Newfane, Vermont, and nearby Winchester, New Hampshire. In 1831, when Philemon Russell was ordained and installed in Winchester, Balch delivered the sermon and attended, with some curiosity, the meeting of the Providence Association held the next day. A few months later he was a dissenting participant at the meeting at which the Massachusetts Association of Universal Restorationists was founded. Balch attempted to remain friendly with the Restorationists until they began to suspect that he was a spy. Adin Ballou complained, "We have seen enough of his disposition to accommodate himself to all parties, and carry intelligence from camp to camp." Paul Dean called him a "non-commital man." Balch expressed his philosophy more positively in the title of the newspaper, the *Impartialist*, which he established in 1832.

In 1836 Balch succeeded David Pickering in Providence, where he led the church away from its Restorationist affiliation. Balch's preaching fostered so much growth in the congregation that an additional Providence church was founded.

11   George Bradburn (1806-1880) studied for the Universalist ministry under Thomas Farnsworth King. He also attended Harvard Divinity School and received preaching credentials from the American Unitarian Association. His first pastorate was at the Restorationist church in Nantucket, 1831-34. After the church dissolved, Bradburn remained in Nantucket, which he represented in the Massachusetts state legislature, 1839-41.

In 1839 Bradburn became an agent of the American Anti-Slavery Society. He is best remembered for an incident at the World's Anti-Slavery Convention in London in 1840. When the credentialling of women abolitionists was opposed by clergy who based their arguments upon scripture, Bradburn was reported to have risen and said, "Prove to me, gentlemen, that your Bible sanctions the slavery of women – the complete subjugation of one half of the race to the other – and I should feel that the best work I could do for humanity would be to make a grand bonfire of every Bible in the universe."

[12] Seth Chandler's ordination is described in the *Independent Messenger*, 28 October 1831.

[13] "The New Sect," *Trumpet and Universalist Magazine*, 17 September 1831. Adin Ballou's quotations from this article, and from his own reply to it in the *Independent Messenger*, are somewhat condensed, and differ in many small ways from the text as printed in the newspapers.

[14] Thomas Whittemore, *Modern History of Universalism*, p. 432.

[15] Psalms 9:16.

[16] Walter Balfour, *Letters on the Immortality of the Soul, the Intermediate State of the Dead, and a Future Retribution, in Reply to Mr. Charles Hudson* (Charlestown, MA, 1829), pp. 32, 181-182.

[17] The New England Universalist General Convention was actually founded in 1793 at a meeting in Oxford, Massachusetts. The 1785 meeting to which Ballou refers also took place in Oxford, and was the first meeting of American Universalists held with the intention of forming a denomination. Although there may have been one or more annual meetings following the one in 1785, it did not create any lasting organization.

[18] Winchester believed that a loving God, whose purpose could not be thwarted, would eventually succeed in bringing all creatures, even the most obstinate, to repentance and grace. Winchester's eschatology was elaborate and largely orthodox, with three changes: the duration of suffering was finite (though it might be agonizingly long); the purpose of the punishment was reformation; and the result would be the salvation of all of God's moral creatures. Winchester considered himself neither predestinarian nor Arminian, but one who held a middle ground, incorporating the best of both contending theologies.

[19] Whittemore wrote, "The doctrine of a limited future punishment, as a distinct question, has never excited a very general interest. For twenty years a difference of opinion has existed on this point; but the difference itself has not been the cause of alienation of feeling, or disruption of fellowship." *Modern History of Universalism*, pp. 434-435.

Hosea Ballou gave his account of the 1817 debate with Edward Turner, and the development of his beliefs on the subject of future punishment, in a letter to Whittemore, which was printed as a footnote in *Modern History of Universalism*, pp. 437-438.

[20] Minutes of the meeting of the Southern Association are in the *Trumpet and Universalist Magazine*, 26 June 1830.

[21] Minutes of the 1830 annual meeting of the UGC are in the *Trumpet and Universalist Magazine*, 25 September 1830.

[22] Minutes of the 1831 annual meeting of the UGC are in the *Trumpet and Universalist Magazine*, 15 October 1831. The official response to the proclamation of the MAUR took the form of resolutions stating that (1) the Universalist General Convention has not

departed from the Winchester Profession and is willing to admit into fellowship anyone who would be willing to adopt these articles of faith; (2) all people who believe in universal restoration are Universalists; (3) the General Convention has never discriminated against the authors of the proclamation and has not taken any part in the theological debate on future punishment; (4) none of the Restorationists have been expelled from the General Convention, except insofar as they have excluded themselves; and (5) by becoming members of a totally separate ecclesiastical body, the members of the MAUR have formally resigned from the General Convention.

[23] The "Inquirer" discussion had its origin in a short note, published in the *Independent Messenger* on 10 June 1831, asking which doctrine of atonement formed the theological basis of Restorationism. Adin Ballou answered that human suffering did not, in itself, satisfy any divine demand, but that "the only ground upon which God now restores sinners, or on which we believe he will in the future state restore them, is, their sincere acknowledgment of his divine authority, their perfect contrition for sin, and their entire submission to his will."

The numbered articles, each consisting of a letter by "Inquirer" and a reply by Ballou, appeared on 12 August; 2, 9, 16, 23, and 30 September; 7 and 14 October; 4, 11, and 18 November; and 2, 16, and 23 December, 1831. By the time the debate reached its thirteenth installment, Ballou's patience had begun to wear thin: "Dear Sir, The empty assertions with which you have seen fit to fill out the foregoing No. are only repetitions of what you have offered our readers in previous Nos." At the end of the fourteenth reply he brought all discussion to an end, taking the editor's privilege of having the last word: "If I have deserved your thanks for giving you a patient hearing, you have deserved mine for condescending to afford so fair a demonstration of the indefensibility of your sentiments."

[24] Nathaniel W. Taylor (1786-1858), professor of theology at Yale College from 1822 to 1858, was one of the leaders of the liberal wing of the Congregational church in New England. In successive controversies with Deists, Episcopalians, Unitarians, and the more conservative branch of his own denomination, Taylor preached his version of Calvinist theology, which emphasized free will and personal accountability, the use of reason in religion, and the importance of the conversion experience. He insisted that there was no contradiction between the traditional Calvinist belief in the absolute sovereignty of God's will and belief in genuine human freedom – a paradox that he summed up in the formula "certainty with power to the contrary."

In their insistence that "God demands only a rational faith of rational beings," and in the emergence of Yale as a theological school to challenge both the Unitarians of Harvard and the orthodox of Andover, Taylor and his colleagues vigorously resisted their rivals' attempts to portray "the orthodox" in terms of the most unattractive features of strict Calvinism. Their efforts are credited with containing the spread of Unitarianism, and with preparing the way for the transformation of the Congregational Church from a relic of Puritan orthodoxy to a major voice in liberal Christianity.

[25] This is an allusion to a famous sermon, "The Faith Once Delivered to the Saints," preached by Lyman Beecher in 1823, and considered a classic statement of the beliefs of the "New Haven school" of theology.

[26] Amos A. Phelps (1804-1847) studied theology at Yale under Nathaniel W. Taylor and served Congregational churches in Hopkinton, Massachusetts, and in Boston. He was a founding member of the American Anti-Slavery Society, served on the committee that

drafted its constitution, and was elected to the Board of Managers. In 1834 he resigned his ministerial settlement to devote full time to antislavery work. He wrote and lectured extensively and served for a time as editor of the society's journal, the *Emancipator*. In the late 1830s he came into conflict with William Lloyd Garrison, especially over the role of women in the antislavery movement. At the various state and national antislavery conventions, Phelps introduced resolution after resolution, first to bar women from membership, later to keep them out of leadership positions. In 1840 he was among the conservatives who resigned and formed the American and Foreign Anti-Slavery Society (see chapter 18, note 20).

[27] Edwin M. Stone (1805-1883), a printer and journalist in Boston, was inspired by the preaching of Paul Dean to study for the Restorationist ministry. He was ordained by the MAUR in 1833. His first ministerial position was at Second Congregational Church in Beverly, Massachusetts, a small society divided over the Unitarian question. There may have been hopes that a Restorationist minister would be acceptable to both parties. However, the more conservative members withdrew and formed a new church in 1834, leaving Second Church for the time being in the Unitarian camp. The two churches were reunited and rejoined the Congregationalist denomination in 1866. Stone remained at Beverly until 1847, when he became minister-at-large in Providence, Rhode Island, under the auspices of the Unitarians.

Though serving a Unitarian church, Stone retained his ties to the Restorationist denomination. When he resigned as proprietor of the *Messenger* in October 1833, he announced that he was doing so in order to have more time to devote to the advance of the Restorationist cause. In 1834 he became corresponding secretary of the new Society for Restorationist Itineracy.

[28] Ballou's congregation in Mendon included some of the town's leading citizens. William S. Hastings (1798-1842), an attorney and Mendon's first postmaster, was a member of the Massachusetts House of Representatives, 1828, and the Massachusetts State Senate, 1829-33. He was elected to the U.S. House of Representatives as a Whig in 1836. Twice re-elected, he served until his death in 1842.

Amariah Taft (1785-1862) was one of Mendon's wealthiest citizens, a director of the Mendon Bank and a large dealer in real estate.

Jabez Aldrich (1778-1838) was the proprietor of the Aldrich General Store, an important center of commercial, social, and political life in Mendon. In addition to selling agricultural and household items, it served meals and was the town's stagecoach stop and post office. Aldrich frequently served on town committees, and served a term in the Massachusetts House of Representatives, 1833-34.

[29] Bernard Whitman (1796-1834) entered Harvard at the age of twenty-one following several years of work in textile mills. After a year of study, he was suspended for participating in a student rebellion. He was readmitted the next year, but left again when it became clear that he would not be permitted to graduate with his old classmates. Afterwards he pursued private theological studies under orthodox Congregationalist ministers.

Before he began his ministerial education, Whitman had been opposed to Unitarianism. As he examined the Bible closely, his religious views moderated to the point that he decided to stand apart from the Unitarian controversy. It was only after he had begun his first, and only, pastorate at the Second Congregational Society in Waltham, Massachusetts, 1825-34, that he declared himself a Unitarian. Thereafter he was active in the promotion of

Unitarianism, traveling extensively in New England, the west, and the south, evangelizing for liberal Christianity. He wrote works defending William Ellery Channing and Freemasonry, produced critiques of revivalism and ultra Universalism, and started the monthly magazine *The Unitarian* (1834), to which Adin Ballou contributed. Though he maintained collegial relations with the Restorationists, Whitman was not a universalist. He hoped that all sinners would be saved, but he did not feel certain enough to preach universal salvation.

Because of his own irregular education, Whitman made a special effort to reach out to people whose circumstances did not permit them to pursue formal education. In Waltham he organized classes for mill workers. He became a mentor to ministerial aspirants who could not afford college. In keeping with his belief that Unitarianism should be accessible to people of all social and intellectual classes, Whitman cultivated a plain and direct style of preaching, using examples drawn from everyday life in order to help his hearers become "practical Christians." In the last year of his life Whitman became an abolitionist and a lecturer for temperance. His interest in reform issues and Christian unity was an important influence on Adin Ballou.

[30] Samuel J. May (1797-1871) was a Unitarian minister and a prominent abolitionist. His first settlement, 1822-35, was in Brooklyn, Connecticut, the only Unitarian society in the state. There he befriended and assisted Prudence Crandall, a Quaker schoolteacher who was persecuted for opening her school to African American students. He also worked to desegregate the Brooklyn church. These efforts eventually cost him the support of his congregation. In 1835 he left Brooklyn to become General Agent of the Massachusetts Anti-Slavery Society. Although many other abolitionists tried to avoid the potentially divisive issue of women's rights, May, like William Lloyd Garrison, insisted that the two issues could not be separated.

May was an early convert to the peace principles taught by Noah Worcester, the founder of the Massachusetts Peace Society, and Jonathan Dymond, an English Quaker. When the alliance between pacifism and abolitionism began to unravel in the late 1830s, May was one of the few abolitionists who remained faithful to his pacifist ideals.

During his final pastorate in Syracuse, New York, 1845-57, May became a labor reformer, helping to unionize women in the textile industry. This experience made him an outspoken critic of the capitalist system. He called for reforms such as a minimum wage, equal pay for women and men, graduated income tax, and an end to property-based voting rights. His interest in Christian socialism was sparked by the experience of several relatives who participated in experiments in utopian communitarianism. His sister Abigail May Alcott and her husband A. Bronson Alcott were leaders at Fruitlands, a short-lived experiment in communal living. His brother Charles lived for a time in the Hopedale Community.

[31] Daniel Austin (1793-1881) was the minister of First Parish in Brighton, Massachusetts, 1828-37. He then served as assistant at Kings Chapel, Boston, for two years before retiring from the ministry.

[32] Charles Chauncy Sewall (1802-1886) was the Unitarian minister in Danvers, Massachusetts, 1827-41. Like his cousins Samuel E. Sewall and Samuel J. May, he was an outspoken abolitionist, active in the American Anti-Slavery Society. After retiring from the ministry for health reasons, Sewall lived the rest of his life on an inherited estate in Medfield, Massachusetts, where he held various positions in local government, represented the town in the state legislature, and did occasional pulpit supply at Unitarian churches.

Chapter 12

[1] Samuel Barrett (1795-1866) was the minister from 1825 to 1860 of the Twelfth Congregational Society in Boston, the first Boston church founded by Unitarians. (The other Unitarian churches of that time had originated as parishes of the established church prior to the Unitarian controversy.) Barrett was one of the principal founders of the American Unitarian Association, associate editor of the *Christian Register,* and founder of the Unitarian Book and Pamphlet Society. He developed one of the first Unitarian Sunday Schools. He was an organizer of many charitable efforts in his own church and in the city of Boston. Though he was not a frequent controversialist, Barrett did take an occasional stand, unpopular in his church, promoting temperance and abolition.

[2] Psalms 55:14.

[3] Matthew 17:4; Mark 9:5; Luke 9:33.

[4] Isaiah 11:1.

[5] Psalms 133:1.

[6] Ephesians 4:3.

[7] Bernard Whitman, *A Discourse on Christian Union: Delivered at the Installation of Adin Ballou... May 3, 1832* was printed at the press of the *Independent Messenger* in 1833. The *Independent Messenger* carried brief excerpts from the sermon on 25 April 1833. Dean's charge, Pickering's address to the congregation, and May's Right Hand of Fellowship were printed in the *Messenger* on 2 May, 9 May, and 27 June 1833, respectively.

[8] A variant form of 1 Corinthians 4:6, dating back at least to the sixteenth century. It is frequently used in preference to the wording found in the King James Version, "to think of men above that which is written."

[9] Acts 4:13.

[10] *Othello* 1.3.

[11] Efforts to control the use of alcohol began in New England in the 1810s. The earliest reformers preached "moderation" and sought stricter enforcement of existing regulations governing the use and sale of alcohol. This campaign, led by Congregational clergy, was opposed by dissenting denominations such as Baptists, Methodists, and Universalists, and was neither popular nor effective.

A more successful effort was organized in the 1820s under the leadership of the American Temperance Society. This new generation of temperance reformers embraced a spirit of self-improvement and perfectionism, seeing temperance as a prerequisite for other social reforms. This campaign grew into a broad-based movement that included women and young people.

In the 1830s the base of support expanded to include people interested in more secular ideas of progress. The growing manufacturing economy required a sober work force. Physicians warned of the medical consequences of intemperance. Instead of "moderation," these reformers advocated "total abstinence," that is, a complete ban on the use of distilled spirits (but permitting beer, wine, and cider). Their goal was not just to reform the small population of problem drinkers, but to bring about real change in community standards of acceptable behavior. By 1833 one million people had "taken the pledge" to abstain from the use of spirits. Between 1830 and 1840, consumption of alcohol dropped from over 7 gallons per capita to approximately 3 gallons (for comparison, in 2010 the figure was 2.25 gallons).

[12] John M. S. Perry (c.1800-c.1836) was ordained as minister of North Congregational Church in Mendon in 1831. He was a strong supporter of the temperance movement: in 1834 his church voted to make "signing the pledge" a prerequisite for church membership. Perry was also active in the abolitionist cause. He championed not only emancipation, but full integration of freed slaves into American society, and denounced the racial prejudice of those who would abolish slavery but compel the former slaves to resettle in Africa.

[13] As in chapter 9, Ballou is paraphrasing rather than quoting from his diary.

[14] Fisher Ames Tyler (1812-1902) was hardly more than a youth when Adin Ballou knew him, but he was about to embark on a career that would take him far from Mendon. Upon receiving his law degree in 1835 he moved to the south, where he practiced law and journalism in various places in Mississippi and Tennessee. He later became a Presbyterian minister and the editor of a religious newspaper. During the Civil War he was a colonel in the Confederate army. After the war he returned to journalism in Mississippi and Tennessee.

[15] Lucius R. Paige (1802-1896) studied for the ministry in the household of Hosea Ballou in 1823. After serving Universalist congregations in Springfield and Rockport, Massachusetts, in 1832 he was called to the church in Cambridge, which had just been vacated by Thomas Whittemore. Two years later he married Whittemore's sister, Abby. After seven years of ministry in Cambridge, Paige retired to concentrate on biblical scholarship and a career as a bank executive. He represented Cambridge in the state legislature, 1878-79. He was an eminent Mason, becoming deputy grand master of the Grand Lodge of Massachusetts, 1851-54.

[16] In 1832 Bernard Whitman published *Village Sermons Doctrinal and Practical,* a collection of twenty-two sermons. Between 21 July and 11 August 1832, the *Trumpet and Universalist Magazine* printed four letters by Lucius Paige that took issue with the way Whitman described future punishment in *Village Sermons*. Paige thought that the sentiments expressed by Whitman were self-contradictory and hard to reconcile with either the scriptures or the statements Whitman had made in *Two Letters to Moses Stuart; on the subject of religious liberty* (1830). When Whitman wrote to the *Trumpet* (25 August 1832) asking Paige to clarify his own position on future punishment, Paige responded (1 September 1832) that his own doctrines were irrelevant to the issue and would not be helpful in clearing up the difficulties in Whitman's book. Whitman's answer to Paige was not published until 1833. In the meantime Adin Ballou took it upon himself to provide a response ("Paige's Letters to Whitman," *Independent Messenger,* 6 September, 11 and 18 October, and 1 November 1832).

[17] Mary Hastings Hayward (1802-1861) was the sister of William S. Hastings (see chapter 11, note 28). Her husband, attorney Caleb Hayward, had died in March 1832. It might seem surprising that three-year-old Abbie Ballou was included in the party, but Mary Hayward was only thirty years old and had five children under age ten.

[18] Warren Rawson (1777-1848) was a Mendon lawyer and justice of the peace. He was a director of the Mendon Bank and had held various town offices, such as selectman and town clerk. He was elected to the Massachusetts state legislature in 1833.

[19] James 4:8.

[20] Josiah Snow (1809-1886) began his journalistic career by establishing the *Southbridge Register* in Southbridge, Massachusetts, when he was just twenty years old. He continued as editor and proprietor until 1832. He then moved to Geneva, New York, where he edited and published the *Geneva Gazette,* 1833-39. In 1849 he founded his most important

newspaper, the *Detroit Tribune*, which he edited until 1862. Throughout his career Snow used his newspapers to advocate for social reform, including the abolition of slavery.

[21] Cholera, a disease endemic in India, spread into Europe for the first time in 1831. Immigration brought it into many North American port cities in the summer of 1832. Montreal, New York, and New Orleans were hit particularly hard. In order to avoid the epidemic, Boston and Providence spent large sums on sanitation and established boards of public health. Religious energy was mobilized as well: August 9 was declared a day for "fasting, humiliation, and prayer" in the state of Massachusetts. As it turned out, Boston did escape being ravaged by the disease. Providence, while not avoiding the epidemic entirely, suffered relatively few casualties. Cholera remained, at a lower level, in the countryside for two years following the initial outbreak, then disappeared until 1849.

[22] James Whittier Hoskins (1799-1833) had a ten-year career as a Universalist preacher, scholar, and writer before his death at the age of 34. He served a small church in Hampden, a few miles from Bangor, Maine, before being called to a larger congregation in Bangor just prior to his final illness.

In 1832 Hoskins withdrew from the Maine Convention of Universalists because he did not think the organization sufficiently disciplined and evangelical. His decision was influenced by a disagreement with some of his colleagues on the subject of future punishment. The ultra Universalist obituary minimized the importance of this separation, saying that "he did not withdraw his fellowship. He still considered himself a Universalist, belonging to the Penobscot Conference. He had not joined, nor probably would he ever join, any other ecclesiastical body" (*Trumpet and Universalist Magazine*, 22 June 1833). Edwin Stone, editor of the *Independent Messenger*, thought otherwise. "Had he lived, he would probably soon have united with the Massachusetts Association" (*Independent Messenger*, 20 June 1833).

[23] Arnold Buffum (1782-1859) was a member of a prominent Quaker family in Rhode Island, active in the struggle against slavery. On a visit to England in 1824 he met with and studied the methods of William Wilberforce and other British antislavery leaders. He was the first president and a lecturing agent of the New England Anti-Slavery Society and was elected to the first Board of Managers of the American Anti-Slavery Society. Although he worked closely with William Lloyd Garrison, Buffum did not share Garrison's rejection of the political process. He believed that political action could be an effective method of working for abolition of slavery, and supported the Liberty, Free Soil, and Republican parties.

[24] Charles Brooks (1795-1872), minister of Third Unitarian Church in Hingham, Massachusetts, 1821-39, was an early advocate of normal schools, having seen teacher training schools in operation while traveling in Prussia. He was a supporter of peace reform as early as 1821. After his pastorate in Hingham, Brooks left parish work to become professor of natural history at the University of the City of New York. (Charles Brooks of Hingham is not to be confused with another Unitarian minister, Charles Timothy Brooks of Newport, Rhode Island, a Transcendentalist who translated many classics of German literature.)

[25] Benjamin Davenport (1780-1862) made his fortune as a merchant in Boston before returning at age 40 to Mendon, where he owned a large dairy farm. In 1831-32 he was serving in the Massachusetts state legislature.

[26] Edwin Stone's account of the conference and of the journey to and from Winchester is in the *Independent Messenger*, 27 September 1832.

27 Minutes of the meeting of the MAUR are in the *Independent Messenger*, 10 January 1833.

28 Ballou must be referring to the passage of the Constitution and Confession of Faith of the Massachusetts Association of Universal Restorationists. The Confession of Faith (*Independent Messenger*, 10 January 1833) is as follows:

> *Article 1.* We believe that the holy scriptures of the Old and the New Testament contain a revelation of the character of God and the duty, interest, and final destination of mankind.
>
> *Article 2.* We believe there is one God, whose nature is love, revealed in one Lord Jesus Christ, by one Holy Spirit; who will finally restore the whole human family to holiness and happiness.
>
> *Article 3.* We believe in a retribution beyond death, and in the necessity of faith and repentance; and that believers ought to be careful to maintain order and practice good works, for these things are good and profitable to men.

29 Dr. John G. Metcalf (1801-1892) practiced medicine in Mendon for sixty years, from 1826 to 1886. He served a term as vice president of the Massachusetts Medical Society and was active in medical societies at the county and local level. In 1843 he published a statistical study of abortion that was still being cited over a century later. See James C. Mohr, *Abortion in America* (Oxford University Press, 1978), pp. 44-45.

Dr. Metcalf was active in town affairs. Among many other offices, he was town treasurer for twenty-five years, and served on the school committee for forty years. He also served in the Massachusetts State Senate, 1858-59. He was a member of the Unitarian church and for many years the superintendent of the Sunday school. He was active in temperance and abolition societies. He was an enthusiastic amateur historian. After the Civil War he presented the American Antiquarian Society with a 56-volume "scrapbook" of newspaper clippings, letters, and other documents related to the war. He compiled the *Annals of the Town of Mendon*, 1880, and wrote the article on Mendon in the *History of Worcester County*, 1879. (Adin Ballou wrote the article on Milford.)

30 "Canker rash" and "scarlatina" are two alternate names for scarlet fever. Scarlet fever is caused by *Streptococcus pyogenes*, the same organism that causes common infections such as strep throat; the rash is a reaction to a toxin produced by certain strains of *S. pyogenes*, and is not clinically significant. Treatment of scarlet fever was the subject of lively debate in the nineteenth century. Common treatments included emetics, purgatives, quinine, and opium. None of these had any effect, except perhaps to weaken the patient. There was no effective treatment until the development of penicillin in the 1940s.

31 Mercy Paine Thayer (1796-1861) was the wife of Otis Thayer, a distant cousin of Adin Ballou. In the *Genealogy* Ballou wrote that Mercy and Otis "were both speakers among the Society of Friends, she quite regularly and frequently, he occasionally. She also ministered at numerous funerals." In the 1840s the Thayers left the Society of Friends to join a breakaway "Community of Friends" in Bellingham, Massachusetts.

32 Most infections caused by Group A *Streptococcus* are confined to the throat and skin, but life-threatening complications can occur if the bacteria invade parts of the body where they are not normally found. "Dropsy on the brain" was the name given to one of these complications, probably bacterial meningitis. A nineteenth-century doctor described the condition:

> The prominent symptoms are a pain in the head, rapidly increasing in acuteness with the increase of the disease, and denoted, in infants, by a restless movement of the head upon the

pillow and by moaning and occasional sudden screamings; by sickness and retching; impatience of light and noise; contraction of the pupils, and delirious terrors &c. (Joseph Ayre, M.D., *Researches into the Nature and Treatment of Dropsy*, 1825)

33 Samuel Clarke (1791-1859), a student of William Ellery Channing, came to Uxbridge in 1832 and remained for the rest of his life. He and Adin Ballou had regular pulpit exchanges and Ballou participated in the dedication of the new Uxbridge church in 1835. Clarke was a moderate Unitarian who tried to promote "practical piety, peace, and Christian unity" in his congregation (*Independent Messenger*, 2 January 1834).

34 These are the last two lines of "When Shall We All Meet Again," a hymn that first appeared in Joshua Leavitt's *The Christian Lyre* (1831). It is an example of a "farewell hymn," such as might be sung at the close of a camp meeting or revival, as the temporary congregation dispersed, "never to meet again in this world."

Chapter 13

1 Oxford, Massachusetts, was the home of one of the founding families of what would become the main stream of New England Universalism. According to Oxford tradition, Universalism was first introduced there by Isaac Davis (c.1715-1777), a physician from Connecticut. Dr. Davis was a distant cousin of the Davis family of Oxford, a number of whom became prominent local Universalists. Caleb Rich (1750-1821), a charismatic, unorthodox preacher also related to the Davis family, visited his cousins and evangelized there in 1775-76. A relative by marriage, Adams Streeter, was the first regular Universalist preacher in the Oxford vicinity in the late 1770s. These evangelists found a ready audience among people who had already distanced themselves from the troubled local Congregational church.

In 1785 the Universalists organized themselves as "the Second Religious Society in Oxford." They dedicated a meetinghouse in 1793. During the first decade of the nineteenth century, Oxford was part of the circuits of Hosea Ballou and Edward Turner. Oxford had irregular supply preaching until Lyman Maynard was engaged in 1828. The church became largely Restorationist during this period. When it voted to dismiss Maynard, the congregation specified that Seth Chandler or another Restorationist be called in his place.

2 Thomas J. Greenwood (1799-1874) was an overseer at a textile mill in Lowell, Massachusetts, who entered the ministry after being fired for holding Universalist views. He was the minister at Marlborough, Massachusetts, 1830-44. Greenwood's presence at Seth Chandler's ordination, among Restorationists and Unitarians, is interesting, as he later criticized Universalists who fraternized with Unitarians ("Liberal Christianity, No. 6," *Trumpet and Universalist Magazine*, 27 December 1856.)

3 John Goldsbury (1795-1890) is better known as an educator than as a minister. He taught at Taunton Academy for several years before serving the Unitarian church in North Bridgewater, Massachusetts, 1827-31. His longest pastorate was at Hardwick, Massachusetts, 1832-39, during a portion of which time he operated a high school there. Goldsbury resigned the pulpit in Hardwick in order to become master of the high school in Cambridge, Massachusetts. He wrote a number of widely-used textbooks: *The Common School Grammar* (1842), *The American Common-School Reader and Speaker* (1844, with William Russell), *Exercises and Illustrations on the Black-Board* (1846), and *New Theories of Grammar* (1846).

4 Seth Chandler's installation was reported in the *Independent Messenger*, 6 June 1833.

⁵ Stephen Albee (1811-1882), a painter and glazier, was a distant cousin of Lucy Hunt Ballou. Albee moved to Hopedale in 1852 and joined the Hopedale Community in 1853. He resigned from the Community in 1858, but lived in Hopedale for the rest of his life. In *History of the Town of Milford,* Adin Ballou wrote that Albee "took an early interest in the temperance, anti-slavery, and peace reforms, and has continued his faithful adherence to them till now."

⁶ *Friendly Letters to a Universalist on Divine Rewards and Punishments* (1833) was Bernard Whitman's reply to the series of letters addressed to him by Lucius Paige in the *Trumpet and Universalist Magazine* the year before.

⁷ Though he was not a Universalist, Bernard Whitman took an active part in the controversy between the Restorationists and the ultra Universalists. This was not just because of his friendship with Adin Ballou and other Restorationists, but because of his intense dislike of the no-future-punishment variety of Universalism. His 1832 newspaper debate with Lucius Paige, which led to the publication of his *Friendly Letters to a Universalist,* was one result of this opposition. Another was his controversy with Thomas Whittemore in the Unitarian and Universalist press in 1833.

After attending the dedication of the Universalist meetinghouse in Richmond, Virginia, in January 1833, Whitman wrote that ultra Universalists came to the church in Richmond "to find some justification in their sins, and to be assured of the certainty of entering heaven the moment they commenced the next conscious existence, let their conduct in this world be what it might" (*Christian Register,* 16 March 1833). Thomas Whittemore took great exception to this, and to Whitman's evaluation of the relative strength of Unitarianism and Universalism in the South and West. ("Rev. B. Whitman's Journey" and "Rev. B. Whitman," *Trumpet and Universalist Magazine,* 23 and 30 March 1833). On April 13 a letter was published in the *Trumpet* purporting to be from a resident of Richmond, criticizing the Restorationist minister J. B. Pitkin. Whitman and Pitkin were defended in an article entitled "Richmond Va." in the *Independent Messenger* (6 June 1833), which relied on information taken from a piece in the *Southern Pioneer,* discrediting the Richmond letter and supporting Whitman's original article.

In the meantime Whittemore used every opportunity to attack Whitman. Whitman was taken to task for using the term "ultra Universalists": "We request all men, particularly Mr. Whitman of Waltham, and his associates, to call us by our proper name" ("The Name Universalists," *Trumpet and Universalist Magazine,* 27 April 1833). In the same issue, reacting to the prospect of the publication of *Friendly Letters to a Universalist,* Whittemore wrote, "If it is the design of Mr. Whitman, as we suspect, to attempt to divide the Universalists, and bring on a controversy... we trust he will fail altogether" ("Mr. Whitman's Book," *Trumpet and Universalist Magazine,* 27 April 1833). Adin Ballou responded, "As to bringing on a controversy, that is impossible. It was long since brought on, and, what is pretty certain, will continue till the question of future or no future retribution is fairly settled." ("To Rev. Thomas Whittemore," *Independent Messenger,* 16 May 1833.)

⁸ Adin Ballou titled his review "New and Important Publication." In it he enthusiastically praised Whitman and his book:

> I expected from his pen an overwhelming refutation of Modern Universalism. My highest and most sanguine expectations are fully realized in the result. Mr. Whitman has rendered a service to Christianity, which not only entitles him to the profound esteem of all good men,

but of itself constitutes an imperishable memorial of well directed talent worthy of a whole life. It will remain a monument to his fame, when the errors it refutes shall be known only as the gleanings of ancient history. (*Independent Messenger*, 6 June 1833).

Thomas Whittemore responded to Whitman's *Friendly Letters to a Universalist* in two long articles ("Whitman's Letters," *Trumpet and Universalist Magazine*, 8 and 15 June 1833). The review proper, however, is very short:

> To say, in a few words, what ought to be said about this book, it is a weak and pitiable affair. Its mechanical execution is beautiful, and reflects credit upon the publishers. The work is indeed "beautiful outward, but within it is full of" – what? Ans. misrepresentation, sophistry and abuse. The doctrines of Universalists are caricatured, their arguments are misrepresented, their applications of scripture are misstated, and throughout there is a strain of contempt and bitterness towards them. Universalists bear all these things patiently because they are used to them. But there is one thing in this book that overcomes them, viz: the vanity of the author. There is a studied attempt throughout the work in him to show himself; he appears foremost on every page; and the reader finds him occupying a larger share of attention than the argument, which it requires somewhat of an effort to trace out and connect.

Whittemore then dismissed the argument of the book as not worth an answer. The bulk of the article was devoted to a recital of the story of the various stages of the Restorationist controversy, starting with the early 1820s.

In the second article, Whittemore rebutted a short passage from *Friendly Letters* that criticized his own *Notes and Illustrations of the Parables of the New Testament* (1832). Whitman, it turns out, had been no kinder in his treatment of Whittemore than Whittemore had been of him. For example:

> Of all ridiculous and absurd interpretations, this must be allowed to stand in the foremost rank. I have no doubt that many of my unitarian brethren, who never look into a universalist book, will think on reading this extract, that I am attempting to impose some nonsense of some ignoramus upon their credulity, for a genuine passage of some acknowledged writer ... To attempt a serious refutation of such burlesque would be useless. (*Friendly Letters*, p. 143)

[9] A reference to the Restorationist statement of faith adopted by the Universalist ministers in the Boston area in 1878 (see chapter 14, note 38).

[10] Edwin M. Stone's desire to turn over the editorship of the *Messenger* at this point was probably not because he "had become weary of the duties" of editorship, but because he had just been called to supply the pulpit in Beverly, Massachusetts, and wished to complete the transition from his earlier career in journalism to his later career in ministry.

[11] After being excommunicated by the Baptists of Grafton, Massachusetts, in 1823, Stephen Cutler (1799-1861) studied with Restorationist minister Jacob Wood. He became the first Universalist minister at Pawtucket, Rhode Island, 1827-28. He was a founding member of the Providence Association. Although he was not among the eight ministers who created the Massachusetts Association of Universal Restorationists, he served on the fellowship committee of the MAUR in 1833. Later that year he went into business with Ballou to publish the *Independent Messenger*. Shortly after this business relationship fell apart, in March 1834 Cutler was appointed Traveling Clerk for Restorationist Itineracy. He remained a member of the MAUR as late as the annual meeting of 1835. He was listed by the *Universalist Register and Almanac* as serving the society in Cumberland, Rhode Island, in 1836, after which time he disappeared from the ranks of Universalist preachers.

[12] This proverb appeared in Thomas Tusser, *A Hundred Points of Good Husbandry* (1557).

[13] Harm Jan Huidekoper (1776-1854), an immigrant from the Netherlands (not Germany as stated by Ballou), settled in Meadville, Pennsylvania, in 1804 as an agent for the Holland Land Company. While attending the local Presbyterian church, as a result of biblical study he became a Unitarian. Through his influence, and the preaching of the young Unitarian ministers that Huidekoper employed as tutors in his family, a Unitarian church grew up in the community. In 1844 a liberal theological school was established in Meadville, largely because of his sponsorship.

Ephraim Peabody, one of the first ministers to stay with Huidekoper, started a periodical, the *Unitarian Essayist* (1831-33), to which Huidekoper contributed eighteen essays. These articles, taken together, form a systematic expression of Huidekoper's theology: nine entries on the unity of God, two on original sin, one on election, one on redemption, two on atonement, one on eternal punishment, and two on the final destruction of the wicked. Huidekoper cautioned that the last two essays, called "On Man and His Destiny," were not to be understood as typical of Unitarians but were expressions of his own thinking on the topic.

In the 1840s Huidekoper expressed his dislike of the radical and Transcendentalist ideas that were sweeping through the denomination. In particular he criticized utopian experiments, socialism, and nonresistance.

[14] H. J. Huidekoper's "On Man and His Destiny" (*The Unitarian Essayist*, August 1832) was reprinted in the *Independent Messenger*, 14 and 21 November 1833. Huidekoper found Restorationism to be an insufficient deterrent to immorality. According to his way of thinking, if continued existence and ultimate happiness were assured, sinners would have no reason to be anxious about the prospect of a finite period of punishment. The true horror with which God threatens the impenitent, in Huidekoper's opinion, is non-existence.

[15] Meadville Theological School was founded by Harm Jan Huidekoper in 1844 as a school for both Unitarian and Christian Connexion ministers. The latter affiliation was dropped in the 1860s. In 1926 the school was moved to Chicago, where two years later it was merged with the Ryder Theological School of the Universalist-founded Lombard College (Galesburg, Illinois). Following the demise of Lombard College, the seminary became known as Meadville/Lombard Theological School.

[16] Adin Ballou's "Critical Examination of an Essay, 'On Man and His Destiny'" appeared in the *Independent Messenger*, 28 November 1833. Huidekoper's response was published as "Destructionism" (*Independent Messenger*, 5 and 12 July 1834). Ballou replied to this at length in five installments ("Destructionism: Reply to the Essayist," *Independent Messenger*, 2, 9, 16, and 30 August and 6 September 1834).

[17] Jonathan Farr (1790-1844) had a modest career as a Unitarian minister in Massachusetts, consisting of a series of brief settlements, and a period of pulpit supply. He spent his last years in his home town, Harvard, Massachusetts, where he served on the school committee, and engaged in temperance activities.

[18] *Independent Messenger*, 11 July 1833.

[19] Mark 8:24.

[20] Isaiah 60:2, Jeremiah 13:16, etc.

[21] Hosea 2:6.

[22] Leviticus 10:1; Numbers 3:4, 26:61.

[23] Galatians 5:1.

24 The controversy between Ballou and Farr began when Edwin M. Stone, acting in his capacity as resident editor of the *Independent Messenger*, responded to some passages from a collection of Farr's sermons, which had been reprinted in the Unitarian newspaper, the *Christian Register*. Farr objected to the construction put upon his words in Stone's articles (*Independent Messenger*, 9 and 23 May 1833), and sent a letter of complaint, which was published in the *Christian Register* (22 June 1833). Ballou apologized for his associate's inadvertent misunderstanding, then took up the debate in the letter excerpted in the *Autobiography* (*Independent Messenger*, 11 July 1833).

Farr did not respond immediately. On September 5 a correspondent to the *Independent Messenger* asked what had become of Farr, and hoped that he could be induced to answer Ballou in order that there might be a civil and non-polemical debate that would settle the issue of eternal punishment once and for all. It was fully a year after Ballou's first letter to Farr that the debate began. Farr's first letter, "To the Rev. Adin Ballou on the Subject of Exchanges between the Restorationists and Unitarians," appeared in the *Independent Messenger* on 19 July 1834, reprinted from Bernard Whitman's magazine, *The Unitarian* (1 July 1834). Ballou responded in the same issue. These two letters laid the foundation for the remainder of the discussion (in the *Independent Messenger* between 16 August and 15 November 1834 and in *The Unitarian* between August and December 1834). After Whitman's death in November 1834, Ballou lost interest in continuing the debate.

25 Matthew 11:25; Luke 10:21.

26 Although universal salvation was a logical consequence of their liberal theological ideas, at first Unitarians, not wishing to be associated with that particular heresy, held themselves aloof from Universalists. After their controversy with the orthodox Congregationalists had died down, some of the more radical Unitarians, such as Theodore Parker, began to espouse universalism. After the Civil War, the "Broad Church" Unitarians began to entertain the idea of a merger with the Universalists.

27 During the nineteenth century, several trends affected the attitude toward universal salvation among those belonging to the more liberal churches of mainstream Protestantism: a move away from the doctrine of predestination towards the idea that everyone has the potential to be saved; a tendency to revise upwards the proportion of the population that will be saved; and increasing dissatisfaction with the idea of eternal damnation. Although by the end of the century only a minority of theologians within these denominations openly preached universal salvation, a much larger number, like the Unitarians of a few generations earlier, simply chose to ignore the subject in their preaching.

28 See Psalms 103:16.

29 Isaiah 30:7.

30 Isaiah 1:18.

31 Daniel Drown Smith (1807-1878), son of Christian Connexion leader Elias Smith, was an ultra Universalist minister in the Boston area during the early 1830s. During this period he was the editor of *The Universalist and Ladies' Repository* and *The Child's Universalist Companion*. Smith served Universalist churches in Portland, Maine, 1836-38, and Gloucester, Massachusetts, 1838-40. Although his preaching in Gloucester attracted many new people to the church, the congregation split into two camps, leading to Smith's resignation in 1840.

Daniel Smith's troubles at this time were magnified by the scandals surrounding his brother, Matthew Hale Smith (1810-1879). Matthew Smith, who was prone to mental instability, renounced Universalism on three separate occasions. In 1842 Matthew published *Universalism Examined, Renounced, Exposed,* which Daniel called a "tissue of nonsense and misrepresentation." Soon afterward, when Daniel Smith resigned from the Massachusetts Convention, there was unfounded but understandable speculation that he, too, had ceased to be a Universalist.

After spending two years in Richmond, Virginia, Daniel Smith returned to Gloucester in 1844 to minister to the faction of his supporters who had separated from the original church. He left the ministry in 1848 to become a homeopathic physician. He later taught at the Homeopathic Medical College in New York for nine years.

[32] The correspondence accepting the challenge, negotiating, and agreeing to terms was printed in the *Independent Messenger,* 15 February 1834.

[33] Linus Smith Everett (1795-1870) was a Universalist minister and journalist. He served churches and edited Universalist newspapers in Buffalo and Auburn, New York, 1822-29; Charlestown, Massachusetts, 1829-34; Baltimore, 1834-39; and Middletown, Connecticut, 1839-41. He did less journalistic work during his settlement in Salem, Massachusetts, 1841-46, where his task was to repair the damage that had been done by the previous minister, Daniel D. Smith's sometimes demented brother, Matthew Hale Smith. Everett finished his career in the ministry where he had begun, in western New York State, as editor of two religious newspapers in Buffalo, 1846-48. After being suspended from fellowship by the Buffalo Association in 1848, he formally broke his connections with all Universalist organizations.

Everett held advanced views on many social issues, including temperance and women's rights, but counseled against abolitionism, not wishing to alienate southern Universalists. He preferred less radical measures such as colonization and improved treatment of slaves.

[34] Joshua Vaughan Himes (1805-1895) began his career as an itinerant preacher for the Christian Connexion in 1827. He was the minister at First Christian Church in Boston, 1830-37, then at Second Christian Church (Chardon Street Chapel) until 1842. Under his leadership, Second Christian Church became a center of antislavery, non-resistance, and other reform activity.

Himes is best remembered in connection with the Second Advent, or Millerite, movement. William Miller (1782-1849), a farmer from Low Hampton, New York, became convinced by study of the scriptures that the second advent of Christ would occur in 1843-44. After meeting Miller at a conference of Christian ministers in 1839, Himes, drawing upon his expertise as an organizer in reform causes, transformed Miller's prophecy into a national movement with provisions for fundraising, libraries and reading rooms, a newspaper, lecture tours, camp meetings, publication and distribution of literature, general and local conferences, and a network of local meetings and associations.

After the time predicted for the Second Advent passed, Himes was caricatured in the press as an unscrupulous charlatan who had exploited Miller's delusion for his own profit. He vehemently denied these charges, and no evidence was ever brought to support them. Following a bitter trial before the Second Christian Church in 1850, Himes left New England for the west. He continued to preach and to publish adventist newspapers in Michigan and Illinois. Late in life he returned to the Episcopal church in which he had grown up. At the time of his death, he was rector of an Episcopal church in South Dakota.

35 Richard Hildreth (1807-1865) was a journalist, philosopher, historian, and antislavery activist. He was trained as a lawyer (hence the title "Esq.") but never practiced law. At the time of the Ballou-Smith debate he was editor of the Boston *Daily Atlas*. The Universalists who engaged him to record the debate probably knew him as the author of a pamphlet defending Abner Kneeland.

In 1834 Hildreth, who suffered from tuberculosis, moved to Florida in hopes that the warm climate would benefit his health. During his two-year stay in Florida he wrote an antislavery novel, *The Slave, or Memoirs of Archy Moore*, and a nonfiction antislavery work. *The Slave*, which was published anonymously in 1836, is considered the first antislavery novel written in the United States, and the most popular until the publication of *Uncle Tom's Cabin*. Hildreth wrote for newspapers in Boston, 1836-40, and in British Guiana, 1840-44. In Guiana he wrote two volumes of a projected six-volume series on "The Science of Man," an attempt to apply the scientific method to an understanding of human nature.

Hildreth retired from journalism in 1844 in order to begin the major work of his life, his *History of the United States* (6 volumes, 1849-52). He was one of the first American historians to adopt the model of "scientific" history, attempting to present the past "exactly as it was" rather than as an edifying story with a patriotic moral. Less popular in its day than the work of romantic historians such as George Bancroft, it was greatly respected by the next generation of historians and remained a standard work for over forty years.

36 Adam Clarke (c.1762-1832) was a Wesleyan preacher and theological writer, originally from Northern Ireland. His most important work was *The Holy Bible: with a commentary and critical notes designed as a help to a better understanding of the sacred writings* (8 volumes,1810-26). Clarke's *Commentary* was widely popular in the early nineteenth century. It went through many editions both in Britain and the United States and has remained in print to the present time.

Clarke's theological viewpoint was for the most part typical of the evangelical Protestantism of his day, though he held some unorthodox opinions. His ideas on the trinity and on predestination, original sin, and atonement were influenced by English Unitarian theologians. Ballou would not have agreed with all of Clarke's interpretations; but in this work, with its combination of careful scholarship, evangelical piety, and the free exercise of individual judgment, he probably found much to admire.

37 Thomas Whittemore reviewed the debate in the *Trumpet and Universalist Magazine* ("Discussion in Boston," 29 March 1834). Whittemore contended that the discussion was an unimportant event, poorly attended, and largely disregarded by those ministers who counted. He claimed to be surprised by Smith's acceptance of Ballou's challenge; he thought the debate would encourage Universalists to divide themselves further over this unimportant doctrine. Having done his best to minimize the significance of the event, Whittemore gave his evaluation of the debate:

> The discussion was commenced by Mr. Ballou, who proceeded in the first place to adduce passages of Scripture to prove rewards in the future state ... The audience were waiting for Mr. Ballou's texts to prove the doctrine of punishment in the future state ... When Mr. B. brought forward a text, Mr. S.'s inquiry was, has he made any attempt to show that this refers to the future state?... But Mr. Ballou did not heed these questions... At length on Thursday noon the Moderators held a consultation, to decide whether or not it was Mr. Ballou's duty to show that the passages he adduced referred to the future state, and proved that men should be punished there for the sins of this life. They agreed at once that such was Mr. Ballou's duty. It was then that Mr. Ballou made the proposition to Mr. Smith to discontinue the discussion

> ... When it thus became impossible for Mr. Ballou any longer to evade the main point, he commenced on Thursday afternoon, with no small complaint, to show that the passages he had quoted referred to the subject of punishment and rewards after death for the sins of this life. Here, in our judgment, he utterly failed. He used the arguments we expected he would; but none were ever more unsound; and it seemed to us that the gentleman on this afternoon labored under the consciousness of inability to support his cause. We had no doubt that he was sorry to his inmost soul that he had brought himself into this debate.

Adin Ballou's criticism of this article was published as "Whittemore's Account of the Discussion" (*Independent Messenger*, 5 April 1834). Ballou denied that his arguments were irrelevant to the issue under discussion. He stated that he knew nothing of a reprimand delivered by a conclave of moderators; the request attributed by Whittemore to the group came from Linus Everett, Smith's chosen moderator. "As to Mr. Smith's reiterated demand for proof to the point we have only to say that, in our opinion, it was his most convenient pretext for keeping himself in countenance before the audience." Ballou maintained that it was Smith who made the first overtures for closure, and whose decision it was to end the discussion a day earlier than was originally planned. Ballou maintained that he had no regrets about entering into the debate, "except for one thing; viz. that he [Whittemore] instead of Mr. Smith was not our opponent."

On April 12 a short letter from Smith offering an additional argument was included in the *Messenger*, along with a rebuttal by Ballou. On the same day the *Trumpet* printed "A Correction," in which Smith took issue with Ballou's reporting of the debate. Ballou replied in the *Messenger* ("Mis 'Correction' Corrected," 19 April 1834). This exchange covered much of the same ground that had been already gone over by Whittemore and Ballou. One new point emerged: Smith claimed that Ballou would have been unable to sustain his arguments without aid from his friends in the audience:

> For though Mr. B. felt himself competent to meet the whole body of Universalists, yet, so poorly was he informed on many subjects, that Mr. Whitman had to inform him, and once in particular did he speak with an audible voice and give him information. And so ignorant was Mr. B. of the true sentiments of the venerable Murray that he would not have been able to proceed had not the Rev. Edwin M. Stone handed him a slip of paper, containing the information he needed. Several times did his brethren have pity on him and send him up arguments on slips of paper.

Ballou challenged the veracity of Smith's statements and threatened legal action. "We have stated several things as capable of proof in a court of law. If Mr. Smith takes it upon himself to contradict us again, we shall proceed to procure the testimony of competent witnesses."

In theory the most impartial witness of the proceedings was Joshua Himes, the neutral moderator. After the debate Himes sent a letter to Bernard Whitman, which was published in *The Unitarian* (1 May 1834) and reprinted in the *Independent Messenger*. Himes expressed surprise that Smith had claimed victory when he thought it obvious that Ballou had won:

> I supposed that the manifest and positive success of Mr. Ballou in sustaining the affirmative of the question would not be contested by the most ardent friends of ultra Universalism; especially as Mr. Smith failed to show that the proof-texts of Mr. Ballou might not, and did not, mean what he asserted and proved they did. It is true, Mr. Smith boldly asserted that the texts had no reference to a future state; but in applying them to the present state of existence he was under the necessity of giving explanations which, to say the least, were not very rational. (*Independent Messenger*, 10 May 1834)

An editorial in the *Boston Centinel*, replying to partisan letters claiming victory for each side in the Ballou-Smith discussion, expressed distaste for popular theological debates:

> The idea of Clergymen, professing to be the humble followers of the meek and lowly Jesus, putting forth in the public prints challenges to meet before public assemblies their brethren in the ministry and discuss the profound doctrines of theology, is revolting to men of sense. The truths of Christianity can never be brought to light or advanced by such means in excited mixed assemblies. The procedure is altogether too theatrical for good effect, and it is to be feared that those who take active part in them are more solicitous to triumph in verbal conflict than to advance the pure cause of Religion. Suppose a casual assembly thus attracted to gratify curiosity vote in favor of the one side or the other, what evidence is it that the majority is correct? None at all. (Quoted in the *Trumpet and Universalist Magazine*, 29 March 1834)

[38] *Report of a Public Discussion between the Revs. Adin Ballou and Daniel D. Smith; on the question, "Do the Holy Scriptures teach the doctrine, that men will be punished and rewarded subsequently to this life, or after death, for the deeds done in this life?"* (Boston, 1834).

[39] The 1896 edition of the *Autobiography* refers to this as a meeting of the Providence Association; however, according to the minutes in the *Independent Messenger* (26 September 1833), it was a meeting of the MAUR. Note also that the end of the chapter goes back to describe events earlier in the year 1833-34, before Ballou's purchase of the *Independent Messenger* and the debates with Jonathan Farr and Daniel Smith.

[40] This account of Edwin Stone's career contains a number of inaccuracies (see chapter 11, note 27, and chapter 13, note 10). Stone was not a native of Beverly, but had only just moved there from Boston during the summer of 1833 to supply the pulpit of the Second Congregational Church. While he may have "continued in fellowship" with the Restorationists until the denomination dissolved in 1841, it is inaccurate to say that he joined the Unitarians at that time, or that he served as pastor "in various places." Stone held only two pastorates in the course of his career, both under the auspices of the Unitarians: in Beverly, 1833-47, and as minister-at-large in Providence, 1847-77.

[41] Peter Corbett (1804-1858), a farmer, lived all his life in Milford. In addition to serving as colonel of the militia, he acted from time to time as selectman and as moderator of the town meeting. He was the brother of John Corbett Jr. (see chapter 7, note 7) and brother-in-law of Thomas Whittemore.

Horace Emerson (1801-c.1880), originally from Uxbridge, later settled in Douglas, Massachusetts. A history of Douglas describes him as "passionately found of military pursuits" and earnestly committed to his leadership role in the militia. It also mentions that he was a supporter of woman suffrage and of equality for all, without regard to race or gender.

Putnam W. Taft (c.1807-1881), originally from Mendon, later lived in Worcester. He was a Justice of the Peace and, in 1857, a candidate for mayor of Worcester. The Taft Public Library in Mendon is named in his honor.

Chapter 14

[1] Edmund Capron (1809-1837), a student of Adin Ballou, was ordained and installed as pastor of the First Restorationist Society in Millville, Massachusetts, in May, 1837. Weakened by tuberculosis, he died in a typhus epidemic the following September.

[2] Nathaniel W. Taylor was the long-time professor of theology at Yale Divinity School who helped to transform the "orthodox" Congregational church into one of the most liberal of Christian denominations (see chapter 11, note 24). Bennet Tyler (1783-1858)

was the foremost critic of the liberal theology of Taylor and the New Haven school. In 1833 Tyler was a founder of the conservative Connecticut Theological Institute in East Windsor. He was president of the school and professor of theology, 1834-57.

Ballou used the term "New School" for Taylor's liberal Congregational theology, and "Old School" to describe the Calvinist orthodoxy as preached by Tyler. However, it was Tyler, not Taylor, who belonged to the tradition known as the "New Divinity" – the evangelical Calvinist school associated with the teachings of Jonathan Edwards. Taylor, on the other hand, thought of himself as a descendant of the "Old Calvinists," those Congregationalists who, in the mid-eighteenth century, had opposed what they considered the excesses of the Great Awakening.

Ballou watched the controversy within Congregationalism with interest. Although Taylor's theology was closer to his own, he seems to have had more respect for Tyler, whose uncompromising logic and disciplined method of argument he found congenial (and whose conclusions he found it easier to refute). When Tyler spoke against Universalism, the *Independent Messenger* printed a detailed account of the lecture, with an introduction by Ballou in which he praised Tyler as "this able divine of the old Calvinistic school" and "a man of unquestionable talent and learning" (*Independent Messenger*, 17 May 1834). In a long "Reply to Dr. Tyler" (24 May; 7, 14, and 28 June; 5, 12, and 19 July 1834), Ballou undertook to respond to Tyler's critique and to argue, point by point, the case for Restorationism.

Ballou's writings on "new school" Congregationalism show impatience, and even contempt, for the liberals' attempts to reinterpret traditional Calvinist doctrines. In his articles on "Taylorism" for the *Independent Messenger* (4 and 25 April 1833), he agreed with Tyler's view that Taylor's explanations of Calvinist doctrines tended to undermine rather than to clarify those doctrines. He wrote, "It was incumbent upon him [Taylor] to show how the two parts of his professed faith are reconcilable . . . he labors under the disadvantage of endeavoring to be both a Calvinist and an Arminian at the same time" (25 April 1833). Yet Ballou predicted, accurately, that Taylor's thought represented the future direction of the Congregational church. The Taylorite compromise gave liberals a way to remain within the denomination while paving the way for the emergence of a new generation of Congregationalists who could honor their Calvinist forebears without feeling constrained to adopt their theology.

[3] Charles G. Finney (1792-1875) became a lay missionary following a conversion experience in 1821 and was ordained as a Presbyterian minister in 1824. From 1825 to 1832, he led successful revival campaigns throughout the mid-Atlantic states, attracting nationwide attention by his aggressive evangelistic style. In 1832 he was appointed to his first church settlement, at Second Free Presbyterian Church in New York City. But he was unable to work within the Presbyterian system of church governance, and left to found his own church, the Broadway Tabernacle. He became professor of theology at the liberal Oberlin College in Ohio in 1835 and was president of the college from 1851 to 1866.

Finney's great contribution was to introduce evangelistic techniques pioneered by the "sects" to the "respectable" Congregationalist and Presbyterian denominations. He not only incorporated the techniques of Methodists and Baptists but also adopted those used by politicians and advertisers: mass meetings, handbills, and newspaper advertising.

In spite of Ballou's assertion that he "measured swords" with Charles Finney in 1834, a search of the *Independent Messenger* for that year reveals no mention of Finney's name, nor anything that appears to be a direct reference to him or his activities. There are, however, a few articles on revivalism. Ballou could be quite critical of revivalism, though he took pains to disassociate himself from ultra Universalists who treated it with ridicule and scorn. He urged Restorationists to steer a middle course between these two extremes, "to set an example of religion without superstition – liberality without licentiousness – gravity without austerity, and practical godliness without fanaticism."

4   Orestes A. Brownson (1803-1876), subsequently known for his many changes of religious belief and affiliation, began his career as a Universalist minister and editor in central New York State. Driven from his pulpit in 1829 because of accusations (largely unfounded) that he had become an "infidel" in the mold of Abner Kneeland, he became a secular journalist and supporter of the Workingmen's Party before returning to the ministry as a Unitarian in 1832. He served three Unitarian churches: Walpole, New Hampshire, 1832-34; Canton, Massachusetts, 1834-36; and a new church in Boston, the Society for Christian Union and Progress, 1836-43, intended to make Unitarianism accessible to the working classes. His 1840 essay "The Laboring Classes," a proto-Marxist critique of industrial capitalism, marked the high-water mark of his political and religious radicalism. Shortly after this he adopted more traditional ideas of religion and society, culminating in his conversion to Catholicism in 1844. He became an important spokesman for American Catholicism, interpreting Catholicism for Americans, and American life for the largely immigrant Catholic population.

The major work of Brownson's later years was his autobiography, *The Convert* (1857). Though primarily a spiritual autobiography describing the process by which he found his Catholic faith, the book also includes sketches of characters with whom he came in contact along the way. Among these sketches is one of Adin Ballou:

> At the time of my ordination [as a Universalist minister, in 1826], those who believed in a future limited punishment, and those who denied all punishment after death, were associated together in one body, under the common name of Universalists. Subsequently, however, a division took place, and a portion of the former separated from the General Convention, as it was called, and took the name of Restorationists. This schism was formed mainly through the instrumentality of Adin Ballou, a distant relative of Hosea Ballou. He was a young convert from some evangelical sect – I forget what sect – and was full of zeal against the doctrine of no future punishment. He took with him Messrs. Dean, Turner, and Hudson, and several other ministers less known, and formed of them a distinct sect. But the majority even of those who held to a limited punishment after death, remained with the General Convention, and the Restorationist sect, after a few years of a fitful existence, became extinct. Its members for the most part have coalesced, I believe, with the Unitarians. I never went with the sect, though I was never one of those Universalists who restrict the consequences of our acts done in the body, whether good or bad, to this life ... Mr. Adin Ballou did not expire with his sect. He became a socialist, and founded the community of Hopedale; and when I heard last from him, he was a spiritualist, spiritist, or devil-worshipper, conversing with spirits, and believing in Andrew Jackson Davis and the Fox girls.

Although not always accurate in detail (for example, Edward Turner did not join the MAUR), and although it puts the worst possible construction on Ballou's interest in spiritualism, this passage does provide a rare neutral evaluation of Ballou's role in the Restorationist schism. By 1857 Brownson had no stake in the internal conflicts of the Universalists, and could afford to describe the situation as he saw it – and he saw Ballou as the primary instigator of the split. Ballou himself never made so strong a claim for his own importance. The ultra Universalist viewpoint, as represented by Thomas Whittemore, held that Adin Ballou was a minor figure, a puppet in the hands of Paul Dean.

⁵ George Ripley (1802-1880) was the minister at the Purchase Street Unitarian church in Boston, 1826-41. He was a leading member of the "Transcendental Club," which held its first meeting at his house in September 1836. In November of that year, Ripley wrote a review of James Martineau's *The Rationale of Religious Inquiry* for the *Christian Examiner* that set aside miracles as proof of Christian teaching, and substituted intuition for reason as the true source of religious truth. The subsequent debate with the Unitarian scholar Andrews Norton grew into the "miracles controversy." Beginning in 1837 Ripley edited a series of translations of French and German philosophers, theologians, and biblical scholars, whose work had been influential on the thinking of the Transcendentalists. In 1840 he became co-editor, with Margaret Fuller, of the Transcendentalists' journal, the *Dial*.

In 1841 Ripley resigned his pulpit out of frustration that his congregation did not share his interest in Transcendentalism and social reform. In partnership with his wife, Sophia, he organized the experimental community, the Brook Farm Institute of Agriculture and Education, in West Roxbury, Massachusetts, 1841-47 (see chapter 17, note 15).

During the last decades of his life Ripley had a successful career as a writer and editor. He succeeded Margaret Fuller as literary critic for the New York *Tribune*, 1849-80. Beginning in 1850, he was the editor of the literary department of *Harper's New Monthly Magazine*. Late in life he traveled to Europe, making himself known to the intellectual world that he had earlier helped to introduce to America.

⁶ The notice of Brownson's installation, including the complete list of participants, is in the *Independent Messenger*, 24 May 1834. Adin Ballou gave the address to the society. Ripley's sermon, "Jesus Christ, the Same Yesterday, Today, and Forever," is a famous one, which he subsequently repeated many times. Along with Theodore Parker's "The Transient and Permanent in Christianity" (1841), it is considered one of the definitive statements of Transcendentalist Christianity. Like Parker, Ripley portrayed Christianity as a system of timeless religious and moral truths rather than a miraculous intervention of God into human history.

⁷ The notice of Russell's installation is in the *Independent Messenger*, 31 May 1834.

⁸ Joseph Allen (1790-1873) was called to the First Congregational Church in Northborough, Massachusetts, in 1816, and remained there for the rest of his life. In 1832 the more orthodox of his parishioners left his church to form the Evangelical Congregational Church, an event that Allen regarded as the most painful of his life. Although he personally was a unitarian, and although the church grew and prospered after the split, he never ceased to regret "the multiplication of sects and places of worship ... the breaking up of a once harmonious society."

⁹ Peter Osgood (1793-1865) was the minister of the First Parish Church (Unitarian) in Sterling, Massachusetts, from 1819 until he retired in 1840 for health reasons.

¹⁰ David Rich Lamson (1806-1886), a native of Charlton, Massachusetts, worked in a textile mill in Woonsocket, Rhode Island. After losing a leg in an industrial accident, he became a schoolteacher and then a Restorationist minister. He served the Unitarian church in Berlin, Massachusetts, 1834-39. He was one of Adin Ballou's closest associates in the early days of the Hopedale Community, but quickly became disillusioned with the Community's joint-stock system of ownership, which he believed gave undue power to the richer members. When the Community amended its constitution in November 1842 to allow members to own property and transact business on their own, Lamson and his family went to live

in the Hancock Shaker Village at Pittsfield, Massachusetts. Six weeks later he wrote to his former associates at Hopedale, praising the Shakers as "the only united body of practical christians I have ever found." (These events are discussed in Chapter 18.)

Despite his initial enthusiasm for the Shakers' community of property and "personal equality," Lamson came to see them as a "tyranny" whose leadership controlled every aspect of the life of the lay members. After two years with the Shakers, he returned to "the world" with a new appreciation of individualism. In his exposé, *Two Years' Experience Among the Shakers*, 1848, he wrote, "[Any] community which seeks to bind itself by a common property, or any means which shall encroach upon the ... individual interests of its members, will be found to be attended with more evils than benefits." For the last forty years of his life, he lived quietly as a bootmaker in West Boylston, Massachusetts, making no further efforts to reform society.

Two Years' Experience also included what Lamson termed "a rap" at Adin Ballou and the Hopedale Community. He claimed that he had not resigned from Hopedale, but had been "excommunicated" for the mercenary reason that "[the Lamsons] have withdrawn their joint stock from the community; they may spend it, become poor, and return upon us to be maintained." Adin Ballou replied indignantly, "If no more reliance can be placed on his statements regarding matters and things among the Shakers than on those relating to Hopedale, his book is an imposition on the public credulity." ("Lamson vs. the Shakers," *Practical Christian*, 10 June 1848)

Two Years' Experience Among the Shakers – which is generally conceded to be an accurate, though hostile, portrayal of Shaker life of the period – has been reprinted, along with Lamson's other writings, in Peter Hoehnle, ed., *A Bruised Idealist: David Lamson, Hopedale, and the Shakers* (Clinton, NY: Richard W. Couper Press, 2010).

[11] The notice of Lamson's ordination is in the *Independent Messenger*, 28 June 1834.

[12] William Morse (b. 1798) was the minister of Second Universalist Church in Philadelphia, 1824-26. While in Philadelphia he married the daughter of Abner Kneeland, who was then also in Philadelphia. After serving as minister to the First Universalist Church of Nantucket, 1826-31, Morse moved to East Milton, Massachusetts, where he attracted the attention of a group of Universalists who were forming a church in neighboring Quincy. Morse accepted the call to Quincy on condition that he could participate in pulpit exchanges with both Universalists and Restorationists. However, in 1834 he was dismissed under pressure from ultra Universalists, who objected to his exchanging with Restorationists. He was then called to the Second Congregational Society in Marlborough, where he remained for ten years. In 1835 he became one of the corresponding editors of the *Independent Messenger*, a position he held until the demise of the paper in 1839. In his later years he served Unitarian churches in Tyngsborough, 1844-54, and Chelmsford, Massachusetts, 1854-56.

[13] James Walker (1794-1874) was the minister of the Unitarian church in Charlestown, Massachusetts, 1818-39, and a founding member of the American Unitarian Association. He was, along with Lewis Tappan and Ezra Gannett, one of the authors of its constitution. He was co-editor of the *Christian Examiner*, 1831-39. In 1839 Walker left Charlestown to become professor of Natural Theology, Moral Philosophy, and Civil Polity at Harvard. He served as president of Harvard from 1853 to 1860.

[14] Isaac Allen (1771-1844) originally intended to become a carpenter, but opted for a sedentary career after he was disabled by an accident. In 1803 he became minister at Bolton,

Massachusetts, a position he held for the rest of his life. Allen was not interested in the intellectual or theological side of ministry. A colleague recalled that he found writing "irksome and disagreeable." Another said, "Those who heard him preach for nearly forty years knew little about his theology." They remembered him instead as a kind and charitable man who loved nature, enjoyed being with people, and hated conflict, intolerance, and hypocrisy.

[15] John Davis Sweet (1807-1852) was the Unitarian minister at Southborough, 1833-35, and Kingston, Massachusetts, 1835-42. He then became principal of Bristol Academy in Taunton, Massachusetts.

[16] The notice of Morse's installation is in the *Independent Messenger*, 5 July 1834.

[17] Richard Stone (1798-c.1875) was, like Adin Ballou, a child of rural Rhode Island. Like Ballou, he was converted by an evangelical sect as a child, married a distant cousin at age nineteen, taught school while working his father's farm, and became a universalist after reading Elhanan Winchester.

Stone studied theology while working as a schoolteacher. In 1833 he was licensed to preach by the Worcester Association of Congregationalists. Although the Worcester Association was an association of Unitarian ministers, Stone himself was not a Unitarian. He considered himself orthodox, except for his views on universal salvation.

Stone served Unitarian churches in West Bridgewater, 1834-43, and Sherborn, Massachusetts, 1843-48. In 1848 he founded a nondenominational church in Sherborn and transferred his affiliation to the Methodists, whom he admired for their antislavery activity. After pastorates at a few small Methodist churches, he moved west in 1856. He spent most of the rest of his life in secular pursuits in the vicinity of St. Louis. At the age of seventy, he was called out of retirement to become acting pastor of a Congregational church in Bunker Hill, Illinois.

[18] Jason Whitman (1799-1848) was the first general secretary, or agent, of the American Unitarian Association, 1834-35. His brother Bernard, who had already undertaken several tours promoting Unitarianism, had been offered the job first, but had turned it down. During his year of service Whitman traveled throughout the country visiting small Unitarian societies, helping them to become self-sustaining. Because he opposed placing sectarianism above Christianity, he worked to suppress societies founded solely in opposition to other denominations. His mixed feelings about the apologetic and promotional aspects of this denominational posting led him to lay down the job after a single year.

In the midst of his engagement at the Second Unitarian Church in Portland, Maine, 1835-45, Whitman spent several months in Savannah, Georgia, hoping to improve his health. (Like his brother, Jason Whitman died relatively young, of tuberculosis.) He refused an invitation to settle in Savannah because he did not wish his children to grow up under the influence of Southern institutions. By the time he returned north he had become an abolitionist.

During his final pastorate, in Lexington, Massachusetts, 1845-48, Whitman had the opportunity to put into practice his views on Christian union. Shortly after his arrival the church building burned down. While a new church was being built, the Unitarians joined the local Baptists in worship, the two ministers alternating in the pulpit. Although the congregations differed in doctrine, they were able to find the common ground necessary to coexist in such an arrangement.

[19] The notice of Stone's installation is in the *Independent Messenger*, 30 August 1834.

[20] Minutes of the meeting of the MAUR are in the *Independent Messenger*, 20 September 1834.

[21] The beginning of this section is taken from Whitman's obituary in the *Independent Messenger* ("Rev. Bernard Whitman," 15 November 1834). Whitman's obituary in the *Messenger* is surrounded by a thick black border, not used for any other death notice.

The November 29 issue of the *Independent Messenger* reprinted the obituary from the *Christian Register* and the funeral address by Samuel Ripley, Whitman's colleague at First Parish in Waltham. A "Memoir of Rev. Bernard Whitman" from the Boston *Observer*, by "G. R." (George Ripley?), was reprinted in the *Messenger*, 3 January 1835.

Whitman's death was one of the turning points of Ballou's career. For several years his friendship with Whitman had been central in his life, and the ecumenical project they shared had been his greatest hope for the future. With Whitman perished Ballou's plans for Christian union based upon Unitarian-Restorationist rapprochement. Immediately after Whitman's death, Ballou began to lose interest in Restorationism, denominational rivalry, and the *Independent Messenger*. Following his deceased friend's lead, Ballou became increasingly interested in social reform. A few years later he would devote himself to pacifist socialist communitarianism, under a rubric that he adopted from a phrase Whitman often used, "Practical Christianity."

[22] Chloe Hunt's obituary is in the *Independent Messenger*, 6 December 1834.

[23] Edilda Ballou's obituary is in the *Independent Messenger*, 3 January 1835.

[24] Acts 9:36.

[25] See Philippians 2:5.

[26] See Matthew 25:35-40.

[27] This is an adaptation of a popular memorial verse found in obituaries and on gravestones to this day. The full verse is:
> To sect or party [his/her] large soul
> Disclaimed to be confined.
> The good [he/she] loved of every name,
> And prayed for all mankind.

[28] Ballou published his stock offering in the *Independent Messenger* on 20 December 1834. He valued the business at $2000, offering 400 shares at five dollars apiece. The first proprietors' meeting was held on January 7, 1835. Ballou agreed to continue to operate the paper, with Paul Dean, Charles Hudson, William Morse, and Philemon Russell as his associates, until the next meeting (scheduled for May) (*Independent Messenger*, 10 January 1835).

[29] Aaron Bancroft (1755-1839) was the minister of Second Congregational Church in Worcester, Massachusetts, for fifty years. The church was formed when the Congregational church in Worcester split in 1785, the more liberal members forming Second Congregational Church. The formation of Second Congregational Church was only the second case of secession from a Congregational church in Massachusetts due to doctrinal differences. (It is often called the first, but a similar event had taken place in Leominster in 1762.)

With the outbreak of the Unitarian controversy, Bancroft and Second Congregational Church found natural allies. Bancroft published *Sermons on Christian Doctrine* (1822), an early formulation of Unitarian theology. His leadership was influential in the spread of Unitarianism into central Massachusetts. Although he had doubts about the wisdom of forming an organization for the propagation of Unitarianism, believing that new religious ideas should be allowed to develop gradually as they had in Worcester, he participated in the formation of the American Unitarian Association and became its first president, 1825-36, taking office at the age of seventy.

[30] The dedication at Uxbridge is reported in the *Independent Messenger*, 17 January 1835.

[31] Minutes of the conference are in the *Independent Messenger*, 15 May 1835.

[32] Minutes of the meeting of the Providence Association are in the *Independent Messenger*, 12 June 1835.

[33] Minutes of the meeting of the MAUR are in the *Independent Messenger*, 25 September 1835. In his article on the meeting, Edwin M. Stone described Ballou's sermon as "powerful" and the prayers by Brownson and Dean as "thrillingly eloquent exhortations."

[34] William H. Fish (1812-c.1895) joined the Universalist Church in Providence, Rhode Island, during the ministry of David Pickering. His friendship with Adin Ballou began with a visit to Mendon in 1834. Shortly afterward he left Providence to begin training for the ministry. His first settlement, as both a Restorationist and a Unitarian, was at Millville, Massachusetts, 1838-41. He was one of the original members of the Hopedale Community in 1841, but not a resident until 1846. From 1842 to 1845 he served the Unitarian church in Gardner, Massachusetts. Shortly before the demise of the Hopedale Community, Fish was sent as a missionary into central New York State, where he remained as a circuit preacher for ten years. From 1865 to 1885 he was at First Parish in South Scituate (Norwell), Massachusetts.

[35] Henry B. Brewster was a partner in the printing firm H. B. & J. Brewster of Boston. Though he was ordained, it does not appear that he ever served a church or society.

[36] See chapter 11, note 25.

[37] "Omega" appeared in the *Independent Messenger*, 7 February 1835. What appears in the *Autobiography* is a substantial revision of the version in the newspaper.

[38] In 1878 the Boston area Universalist ministers issued a statement of faith (adopted by a vote of 33-2), saying, "We believe that repentance and salvation are not limited to this life" and that "death ... has no saving power. Salvation ... whether effected here, or in the future life, is salvation by Christ, and gives no warrant to the imputation to us of the 'death and glory' theory, alike repudiated by all." The statement (printed in *The Universalist*, 2 March 1878), represents a complete reversion to the Restorationist point of view. It could have been endorsed, had he lived to witness it, by Paul Dean.

[39] William P. Apthorp (1806-1883) spent most of his career as a Congregational home missionary, first in Raleigh, North Carolina, 1832-33, and then at various newly settled towns in Iowa. From 1838 to 1848 he taught at a missionary school in Quincy, Illinois. His short stay in Mendon in 1835-36 was one of a series of interim settlements in Massachusetts and New Hampshire in 1834-36 and 1853-58.

[40] The description of the debate with Apthorp is taken almost verbatim from Ballou's contemporary account, "Discussion at Mendon," *Independent Messenger*, 20 November 1835.

[41] Apthorp disputed much of Ballou's account of the origin and course of these debates. He denied meddling with Ballou's parishioners, saying he had called on very few, almost always

by invitation, and that his visit to Ballou had also been by invitation. Ballou responded that he had, as a matter of course, invited Apthorp to visit him when he first came to town, but that he was not seeking religious controversy. Each of the disputants blamed the other for turning a private conversation into a public debate. After Ballou marshaled and published various corroborating testimonies, Apthorp conceded that the debate was "as unexpected and unsought by [Ballou], as it certainly was by me."

Each, of course, put his own interpretation upon the outcome of the debate. Ballou claimed that Apthorp became agitated during Ballou's concluding address and insisted that he had to continue in order to win the contest, but was persuaded by others not to pursue a fruitless course. Apthorp, however, said that it was Ballou who had asked, "rather despondingly, as it appeared to me," for another session. An orthodox lay witness to the debate, whose certificate vindicated Ballou in matters of procedural detail, left the following evaluation of the debate, which is perhaps the fairest that can be found: "I consider the parties equally engaged in vindicating their respective doctrines, and refuting each other's reasoning."

The *Independent Messenger* articles that followed Ballou's original report are: Apthorp's rebuttal, printed with an introduction by Paul Dean under the heading "The Mendon Controversy," 4 December 1835; Ballou's defense against Apthorp's criticism, including the depositions of witnesses, "The Mendon Discussion Again," 25 December 1835; and "Rev. Mr. Apthorp's Reply," 15 January 1836.

[42] Ebenezer Daggett Draper (1813-1887) worked in a cotton mill in Uxbridge, Massachusetts, before joining his father, Ira Draper, in the manufacture of machinery for textile mills. Ira Draper had earlier invented the self-acting temple, a device that regulated the extension of cloth on a power loom, allowing for more efficient weaving. The patent on this invention provided the Draper family with an increasing source of revenue.

Although Ebenezer Draper and his wife, Anna Thwing Draper, lived in Uxbridge during the 1830s, they attended Adin Ballou's church in Mendon. They remained close friends of the Ballou family all their lives. The Drapers were charter members of the Hopedale Community, making major contributions to the communal assets. Manufacture of the loom temple and royalties on this invention provided the financial backbone of the Community. Draper became Hopedale's second president after Ballou stepped down in 1852.

In 1853 Ebenezer Draper and his brother George (see chapter 20, note 32) went into business together to manufacture the loom temple at Hopedale. In 1856 the brothers, who together owned three-quarters of the stock in the Hopedale Community, ended the utopian experiment when they assumed the debts of the Community in order to convert its industry back into private enterprise. These events are discussed in chapter 20 of the *Autobiography*.

After the Drapers gained control of most the Community's assets, they divided the property in such a way that Ebenezer owned most of the land. He tried to keep the spirit of the Community alive by selling land to "persons of liberal and reformatory ideas and tendencies."

The firm of E. D. and G. Draper flourished. By 1868, when they terminated the partnership, each brother had over $100,000, a fortune in those days. George carried on the business in partnership with his son, while Ebenezer invested his share in the "American Steam Fire-Proof Safe Company." That venture was unsuccessful, and Ebenezer ended his life as he began it, in modest circumstances.

[43] 2 Corinthians 12:9.

Chapter 15

[1] Ezra Ripley (1751-1841) was the minister of First Parish in Concord for sixty-three years, from 1778 until his death. He was an early peace advocate, a proponent of public education, and an organizer of one of the earliest temperance societies. Unlike most liberal Congregationalists of his day, he was not an Arminian; it was solely his opposition to the Trinity that connected him with Unitarians.

[2] David Damon (1787-1843) was a liberal Congregationalist. His theological views were Arian and Arminian, but not entirely unitarian. During his first settlement, at Lunenburg, Massachusetts, 1815-27, he endeavored to unite contending Unitarian, Universalist, and orthodox factions. His next settlement, at Salisbury and Amesbury, Massachusetts, 1828-33, was over two Unitarian churches, in one of which he shared the pulpit with the minister of the town's (non-Unitarian) Congregational church. He served the Unitarian church in West Cambridge (now Arlington), Massachusetts, from 1835 until his death.

[3] William Andrews (1810-1838) was the minister at Chelmsford, Massachusetts, from 1836 until he died, aged 28, two years later.

[4] William Hunt White (1798-1853) served the Unitarian congregation at Littleton, Massachusetts, from his ordination in 1828 until his death. Theologically moderate, he was for many years successful in keeping controversies out of his parish.

[5] The "Lowell system" of manufacturing was developed by Boston merchant Francis Cabot Lowell (1775-1817). While most mills in New England, like the one in which Ballou worked for a short time as a child, used the Slater system, which employed families, Lowell decided to hire young women, and set out to design a factory town that would provide housing, supervision, and wages adequate to satisfy the girls and their parents. Most of the "Lowell girls" were between 16 and 25 years old and worked for an average of 4-5 years before leaving for marriage or other work. Lowell's other innovation was to combine spinning, weaving, and finishing in a single factory that would take in raw cotton and turn out finished cloth (Slater mills produced thread only).

The first Lowell system factory opened in Waltham, Massachusetts, in 1815. After Lowell's death in 1817, his business associates decided to reproduce the system on a larger scale. They selected a site on the Merrimack River near Chelmsford, where sufficient water power was available, and in 1824 opened a large complex of mills. In 1826 the area was incorporated as the town of Lowell. By 1833 the town of Lowell had a population of 12,000, of whom 5,000 worked in the mills.

Ballou's visit to Lowell took place at the height of the town's success, when it seemed the model of a new, mutually beneficial relationship between owners and workers. Wages and working conditions declined in later years, as the mills became less of an experiment and more of a regular feature of the New England economy. In the late 1840s the presence of a large pool of Irish immigrant labor completed the transition from paternalism to outright exploitation of the mill workers.

[6] Imprisonment for debt had been on the decline in Massachusetts for well over a century. Required by a 1672 law to pay the expenses of keeping their debtors in confinement, Massachusetts creditors received little benefit from the system. After 1787 prisoners whose unpaid debts were small were released after a few months upon swearing an oath of poverty. In 1811 the state legislature passed a law prohibiting imprisonment for debts of five dollars or less.

Although debtors' prison was not entirely abolished until 1857, by the 1830s imprisonment for debt was largely confined to cases involving personal animus.

[7] Hersey Bradford Goodwin (1805-1836), a student and friend of Bernard Whitman, was ordained and installed at Concord, Massachusetts, in 1830 as the colleague and intended successor of the elderly Dr. Ezra Ripley. However, he died at the age of thirty-one; Ripley outlived him by five years.

[8] Thomas à Kempis (c.1380-1471) was the author of devotional and mystical works, of which the most well-known is *The Imitation of Christ*.

[9] A hymn text from Isaac Watts, *Hymns and Spiritual Songs* (c.1700).

[10] The mid-1830s was a time of persecution, and occasionally martyrdom, for abolitionists. In 1833 a mob broke up the organizational meeting of the New York City Anti-Slavery Society. In 1835 William Lloyd Garrison was dragged through the streets of Boston with a halter around his neck, until the mayor had him incarcerated for his own protection. On the same day a mob temporarily halted the formation of the New York State Anti-Slavery Society in Utica, New York. Other victims of mob violence included James G. Birney, a former Southern slaveholder whose printing press was repeatedly subject to attack; George S. Thompson, a British antislavery lecturer who was hounded out of the country under threat of assassination; and Amos Dresser, a seminary student publicly flogged in Nashville for being caught with abolitionist literature in 1835. The murder of the editor Elijah Lovejoy in 1837 (see chapter 15, note 38) was the climactic incident in this period of anti-abolitionist violence. By the late 1830s, a substantial minority of the people in the North had become convinced that the effects of the injustice of slavery could not remain confined to the South, but would continue to threaten life, property, and liberty throughout the nation.

[11] "That execrable sum of all villainies, commonly called the Slave Trade." John Wesley, *Journal*, 12 February 1772.

[12] Thomas Jefferson to Jean Nicolas Démeunier, 26 June 1786. Though Jefferson himself owned slaves, he considered slavery a "great moral and political evil" that would call down upon the United States the wrath of an outraged God.

[13] Article 4, Section 2 of the Constitution states, "No Person held to Service or Labour in one State, under the Laws thereof, escaping into another, shall, in consequence of any Law or Regulation therein, be discharged from such Service or Labour, but shall be delivered up on Claim of the Party to whom such Service or Labour may be due."

[14] Ballou's sense that he was a latecomer to the antislavery movement is borne out to a certain extent by comparison with some of his colleagues in the ministry. The list of clergy who publicly opposed slavery earlier than 1837 includes Aaron Bancroft, David Lamson, Alanson St. Clair, Philemon Russell, David Grosvenor, and Ballou's orthodox colleague in Mendon, John Perry.

[15] Rumors about a separation between Ballou and the Mendon church persisted for months after these events. In early 1838 Ballou felt compelled to publish a notice informing the editors of other newspapers that he had not been dismissed from his pulpit because of his abolitionist views (or, in some variations, because of the lack thereof). The notice read: "I am a thorough going abolitionist, and shall retain my pastoral charge over a united Church and a faithful and generous Parish, with all my rights and privileges as a christian freeman in full and unrestricted exercise" (*Independent Messenger*, 16 February 1838).

[16] In this speech Ballou took a stand against both racism and colonization. Colonization was a plan to encourage voluntary manumission by slaveowners, and then to resettle the freed slaves in a specially created colony, Liberia, on the west coast of Africa. An organization devoted to this purpose, the American Colonization Society, had been founded in 1816. It administered the colony and paid its expenses.

William Lloyd Garrison, who at one time had endorsed the society, began to denounce its program in 1830. He argued that, since plantation owners had no intention of emancipating the great majority of their slaves, colonization was merely a ploy to rid the South of free African Americans, whom the planters feared. Thus, colonization functioned not as a means of abolishing slavery, but, rather, as a prop to support the existing system.

Between 1833 and 1835 many prominent colonizationists were converted to immediate emancipation. By 1837 the society was in low repute, divided, debt-ridden, and ineffective. Nevertheless the idea that colonization was, in theory, a good solution to the problems of race and slavery remained popular until the Civil War.

[17] *A Discourse on the Subject of American Slavery, delivered in the First Congregational Meeting House, in Mendon, Mass., July 4, 1837* (Boston, 1837).

Here are some excerpts from Ballou's remarks:

> Let all laws, which make any distinction between men, on account of their color, or any similar imaginary incapacitation, be immediately abolished. And let there be one common level of merit and demerit, of qualification and disqualification, for all ...
>
> I pity the man who can seriously urge [that the negroes are an inferior race]. I must deem his head or his heart, or both, seriously disordered. It is but the groundless assertion of men, who themselves need a guardian, or a keeper. A thousand historical facts, a thousand facts of our own times, the contrivances of the slave system to prevent the rise of its victims, reason, revelation, and observation, are all against this insane conclusion. The Africans are men – created by the same God, and of one blood with ourselves ...
>
> [African Americans] are not Aboriginal Americans; neither are we. Their ancestors came from Africa, ours from Europe; and here, we are in the red man's country. If there is to be any shipping off without consent, we had better let the Indian say who shall be sent home. I dare say he would colonize Europe quite as liberally as we would Africa ... There is something quite as ludicrous as there is wicked, in this notion of transporting the colored people to their own country. No man can reflect a moment, without seeing that this is as much their country as ours; that Europe is as much our home as Africa is theirs; and that there is no more justice in shipping them to their father land, than in shipping their masters to theirs.

[18] The antislavery society in Mendon was formed at a time when abolitionist activity was increasing in central Massachusetts. Although the New England Anti-Slavery Society had existed since 1831, at first it operated primarily in and around Boston. In the mid-1830s, abolitionists began a campaign to establish local societies in other parts of the state. An antislavery society was organized for northern Worcester County in December 1835, and for southern Worcester County in February 1836. The Mendon society was an affiliate of the Massachusetts Anti-Slavery Society (the successor to the New England Anti-Slavery Society) and of the American Anti-Slavery Society, founded in Philadelphia in 1833.

In October 1838 Ballou represented Mendon at the state Young Men's Anti-Slavery convention. In May 1839 he was appointed delegate from Mendon to the annual meeting of the American Anti-Slavery Society in New York, but was unable to attend.

[19] Leviticus 25:10. "Proclaim Liberty throughout the land to all the inhabitants thereof" is the inscription on the Liberty Bell.

20 Millville separated from Blackstone and became a separate town in 1916.

21 Alanson St. Clair (1804-1877), who studied for the Universalist ministry under Sylvanus Cobb in Maine, became an active Restorationist in 1834. That same year he succeeded Nathaniel Wright at the Universalist church in Attleboro, Massachusetts. As a Restorationist he served the Unitarian church in West Boylston, Massachusetts, 1837-38, and co-edited the "Genius of Reform" section of the *Independent Messenger*.

St. Clair resigned from the MAUR in 1838. In his letter of resignation (*Independent Messenger*, 28 September 1838), he explained that he was resigning because of the Association's failure to take action in the causes of temperance, antislavery, and moral reform. He also cited theological differences: unlike the other Restorationists, he was a revivalist, "regarding conversion as indispensable to salvation." (In response to St. Clair's letter, Daniel Whitney, Isaac Pitman, and William Fish replied that they, too, were revivalists.)

Around the same time he resigned from the MAUR, St. Clair broke with the Garrisonian abolitionists, joining the American and Foreign Anti-Slavery Society and the Liberty Party. In 1845 he went west as an antislavery lecturer and publisher in Illinois and Iowa. From 1860 he was a Congregationalist minister in Michigan.

22 Emmons Partridge (1799-1873) was a blacksmith who became a teacher, Sunday school superintendent, and ministry student at the First Universalist Church in Providence, Rhode Island, 1831-36. He was ordained as an evangelist by the Providence church in 1838. He went on to a successful career as a Universalist minister in various towns in Massachusetts. His most significant settlement was his last, in Natick, Massachusetts, 1851-70.

23 Daniel Sanderson Whitney (1810-1894) studied for the ministry under Paul Dean and was ordained by the MAUR, but was never settled as minister of a church. Before joining the Hopedale Community he was an itinerant evangelist and lecturer in the area of Berlin and West Boylston, Massachusetts. He was one of the earliest residents in Hopedale, and one of the most beloved. In *History of the Hopedale Community* Ballou described him as "a kind of Purveyor of Amusements, providing ways and means of interesting and pleasing both young and old, getting up entertainments, festivals, and gala-days." He designed the May Day and Christmas festivals, both of which became Hopedale institutions.

Like George Stacy before him (see chapter 10, note 20), Whitney left Hopedale in consequence of one of the Community's periodic reorganizations. In late 1849 the Community's business interests, which had been substantially privatized in 1847, were brought back under direct Community control. At the same time, non-member workers were expelled, and a "Council of Religion, Conciliation, and Justice" was established "to maintain a scrupulous watchfulness over the morals and manners" of the Community. The new restrictions led to the resignation of six members, including Whitney.

After leaving Hopedale, Whitney continued to work for the antislavery and temperance causes, affiliating with the Republican party and later with the Prohibition Party. He was a delegate to the Massachusetts constitutional convention in 1853, where he distinguished himself as a champion of woman suffrage.

24 Paul Dean's circular letter is in the *Independent Messenger*, 30 September 1836.

25 Jacob Ide (1785-1880) settled in 1814 as Congregational minister at West Medway, Massachusetts, a position he retained for the rest of his long life. He was married to the daughter of Nathanael Emmons of Franklin (see chapter 7, note 1), and edited Dr. Emmons's collected works. Ide prepared more than forty students for the ministry, including Thomas Edwards.

[26] David Grosvenor (1802-1866) was called to the First Congregational Church and Society in Uxbridge in 1831, as colleague to the ailing minister, Samuel Judson. When Judson resigned the following year, the Unitarian controversy came to Uxbridge. Grosvenor was called by the church, but rejected by the society. He withdrew, along with the conservative element, to form the First Evangelical Congregational Church. The old First Congregational Church then called the Unitarian Samuel Clarke. Grosvenor remained at Uxbridge until 1842.

[27] Edmund Capron's installation was reported in the *Independent Messenger*, 12 May 1837. Ballou's sermon was printed in the *Independent Messenger* on 19 May 1837, and Samuel Clarke's address to the congregation on 9 June 1837.

[28] Capron's obituary is in the *Independent Messenger*, 13 October 1837. According to the obituary, the "fearful pestilence" that caused his death was typhus.

[29] William H. Kinsley (d. 1851) supplied the pulpit at First Congregational Church (Unitarian) in Hubbardston, Massachusetts, 1837-39, and was the minister of First Parish in Stow, Massachusetts, 1839-46.

[30] Those present but not signing the resolutions were Paul Dean, Edwin M. Stone, William Morse, Philemon R. Russell, and two others, named Coe and Banfield.

[31] *Independent Messenger*, 6 October 1837.

[32] Samuel W. Wheeler (1790-1857) was a bookkeeper for the firm of Pitman & Dorrance, jewelry manufacturers in Providence. Ballou described him as "one of our nervous sanguine outspoken uncompromising go-ahead sort of men; and consequently though he bears in his own bosom a really pure and benevolent heart, is not unfrequently disliked and denounced by persons of an easier temperament" (*Practical Christian*, 26 November 1842).

[33] *The Touchstone, exhibiting Universalism and Restorationism as they are, moral contraries*, American Unitarian Association Tracts 42 (Boston, 1837). In this pamphlet Ballou sought to demonstrate that Universalists (i.e. ultra Universalists) and Restorationists were so far apart in belief that they could not co-exist in the same denomination. Using the works of Hosea Ballou as a reference, he developed the contrasts in theology in twelve points. He argued that Restorationism represented a moderate version of the doctrine of universal salvation that could appeal to a broad range of Christians: "The better class of minds in all denominations are feeling their way to the middle ground – the long disregarded zone of truth. They hunger and thirst after a system of doctrine which combines the theory and practice of unbounded love, with the theory and practice of perfect moral restraint."

[34] The critique of *The Touchstone* in the *Christian Advocate and Journal* was reprinted, accompanied by Ballou's response, in the *Independent Messenger*, 21 April 1837.

[35] From the Latin of Thomas Brooks, *The Crown and Glory of Christianity* (1662): "Magna est Veritas et praevalebit."

[36] 1 Corinthians 9:16-17 – an important passage for Ballou, invoked at each major turning point in his life.

[37] Isaiah 58:1.

[38] The death of Elijah Lovejoy was a turning point in the fight against slavery. It convinced many moderate Northerners of the impossibility of reaching a compromise solution to the problem. The abolitionist leader Wendell Phillips, looking back in 1867, wrote, "I can never forget the quick, sharp agony of that hour which brought us the news of Lovejoy's death ... The gun fired at Lovejoy was like that of Sumter – it scattered a world of dreams."

In addition to drawing former moderates into the ranks of the abolitionists, Lovejoy's death changed the character of the abolitionist movement. By adopting Lovejoy as a martyr for the cause and refusing to condemn his armed defense of his printing press, pacifist abolitionists such as William Lloyd Garrison signaled their willingness to compromise on their commitment to nonviolence. It was the first hint of a rift between abolitionists and nonresistants, which would become acute at the time of the John Brown raid in 1859.

The second page of the *Independent Messenger* was set aside starting in November 1837 for a publication called "Genius of Reform," edited by Adin Ballou, David Lamson, and Alanson St. Clair. The Lovejoy murder provided its principal material for the following several months. Here is a sample:

> The Rev. E. P. Lovejoy, of Alton, Ill., the fearless and unconquerable champion of human rights in the West, has been shot down by the side of his printing press, while vainly endeavoring to prevent its destruction for the fourth time, by a gang of grog-paid Goths and Vandals. Now pour forth your faint regrets, ye mob-exciting scribblers of the land, and smooth the ruffled waters of public indignation by wily palliations of this outrage! Lament the mad fanaticism that made poor Lovejoy a martyr on the altar of defensive rights! ... How long is the Vilest of all tyrannies, this iron-hoofed, ten-horned monster of mobocracy, to dance in the blood and gore of the just? Where are our Constitutional rights? Ah! they are in the keeping of murderers – the banditti of slave holders and their northern whipsters.
>
> It is now plain that negro slavery in one half of the States of this union is a Cancer on the breast of our liberties ... The enslavement of the whites is in progress. Their inalienable rights and liberties, nay, even their lives, are under the slave seller's auction hammer. They are "going," "going," – and if not speedily rescued, will soon have "gone" for ever. (*Independent Messenger*, 8 December 1837.)

Chapter 16

[1] Charles Ballou (1796-1838) worked as a tailor in Milford, Massachusetts, and Woonsocket, Rhode Island. Adin Ballou wrote of him in the *Genealogy* that "teetotalism would have saved him from dangerous habits and consequent disasters. But he failed in that direction, like many a promising candidate for distinctive prizes in life."

[2] New England Village is the name of a section of the town of Grafton, Massachusetts. It was named for the New England Manufacturing Company, which built a complex of textile mills and workers' housing there in the 1820s. The mills were sold to another company in 1831, but the area is called New England Village to this day.

[3] Lyman Maynard's installation was reported in the *Independent Messenger*, 1 June 1838.

[4] Jonathan Russell (1771-1832) was ambassador to Great Britain, 1811-14. He conveyed the American declaration of hostilities in the War of 1812, and was one of five commissioners who negotiated the Treaty of Ghent that ended the war in 1814. From 1814 to 1818 he was the American minister to Norway and Sweden. On his return to the United States, he settled in Mendon, where he entered local politics. He served as a delegate to the Massachusetts constitutional convention of 1820 and represented his district in Congress, 1821-25.

[5] Luther Bailey (1783-1861) was the minister of the First Church of Christ in Medway, Massachusetts, 1816-35. He was active in the temperance movement and was on the American Peace Society's list of "ministers who are pledged to preach at least once a year in favor of peace."

During Bailey's pastorate, First Church, like many other town churches in Massachusetts, became Unitarian. Bailey, however, while not entirely orthodox in his theological views, was conservative by Unitarian standards. In 1835 he resigned from First Church and became the pastor of a newly organized Congregational church in Medway. The new church flourished for a few years, but did not survive after Bailey retired in 1843.

[6] Moses Buffum (1800-1874), a distant cousin of Adin Ballou, rose from an impoverished childhood to become a well-to-do woolen manufacturer and a colonel in the Massachusetts militia. He and his wife were prominent members of the Restorationist church and the Anti-Slavery Society in Millville.

[7] Paul Dean wrote an account of the conference at Millville ("Conference," *Independent Messenger*, 6 July 1838), making only a passing reference to the ordination. Charles Hudson's ordination sermon is featured in the issue of 7 September 1838.

[8] 2 Timothy 2:15; 1 Timothy 4:6.

[9] In addition to the stated Bible text, this sermon summary incorporates language from Ezekiel 18:32; Philippians 3:21; Romans 14:17; Matthew 6:10.

[10] This sermon summary incorporates language from Micah 7:18 and Matthew 6:12.

[11] This sermon summary incorporates a quotation from Jeremiah 2:19 and language from Proverbs 1:25, 30; Lamentations 3:19; Genesis 50:20.

[12] Before coming to America from England, Matthew Harding was an itinerant unitarian General Baptist minister, based in Kent and Cornwall. When he arrived in Montreal in 1832, his extemporaneous style of preaching did not appeal to the Unitarians there. He was therefore passed along to the American Unitarian Association in Boston. (Montreal asked for a more learned-sounding New England preacher in return.) Coming to the United States, Harding held a few brief pastorates in Massachusetts and served as a Unitarian missionary in Maine.

[13] Sylvanus Cobb (1798-1866) began his career as an itinerant Universalist preacher based in Waterville, Maine. During his second pastorate, in Malden, Massachusetts, 1828-37, Cobb was engaged as Lecturing Agent for the Middlesex County Temperance Society. He resigned from the Malden pulpit in 1837 in order to devote himself more fully to temperance work. When he accepted a call from Waltham, Massachusetts, the following year, he did so on the understanding that it would be not much more than pulpit supply. In Waltham, Cobb began his major life-work, as editor of an abolitionist and temperance newspaper, the *Christian Freeman and Family Visiter* (see appendix G, note 17). His last pastorate was in East Boston, 1849-52.

[14] The 1838 meeting was the high-water mark of the Massachusetts Association of Universal Restorationists. In his report of this meeting ("Association," *Independent Messenger*, 28 September 1838), Paul Dean mentioned the names of nineteen ministers who were present, more than in any other year. This high attendance may have been a response to the sharp division between reform and conservative camps that had emerged at the previous session of the MAUR. In the event, the issue did not come up at the 1838 meeting, though it would lead to a shattering of fellowship within three years.

The following table charts the growth and collapse of the denomination (numbers with asterisks are estimated):

	Clergy in fellowship with the MAUR	Clergy present at the Annual Meeting
1831	8	8
1832	8	8
1833	13	11
1834	12	11
1835	14	12
1836	15*	12*
1837	18	14
1838	23	19
1839	16*	12
1840	15*	10*

These figures, drawn from minutes and accounts in the *Independent Messenger*, suggest that, rather than fading away slowly for lack of interest, as its Universalist critics claimed, the MAUR collapsed rather suddenly. It was lack of consensus on social issues, especially abolition, that caused the denomination to expire.

[15] Joshua Stanton (1782-1856) and John Calkins (1790-1857) were Restorationists, non-resistants, and abolitionists from South Wilbraham (now Hampden), Massachusetts. Stanton was a farmer and Calkins was a shoemaker. Both are reputed to have been active in the Underground Railroad. Calkins and his wife joined the Hopedale Community as non-resident members in 1843.

[16] William S. Hastings (see chapter 11, note 28) was elected to the U.S. House of Representatives in 1836, not 1838 as Ballou reported.

[17] Alexander H. Everett (1790-1847) studied law in the office of John Quincy Adams. When Adams became ambassador to Russia, Everett accompanied him as attaché, 1809-11. During the War of 1812, Everett made a name for himself as a pro-war speaker and writer. He continued his diplomatic career in the Netherlands, 1815-16; France, 1818-24; and as ambassador to Spain, 1825-29. On his return to the United States he became editor of the *North American Review*, 1829-34. He served in the Massachusetts State Senate, 1830-35, and ran unsuccessfully for Congress in 1838. In 1840 he undertook a diplomatic mission to Cuba, then accepted the presidency of Jefferson College in Louisiana. In 1845 he was appointed commissioner to China, where he died.

[18] Ballou's Restorationist colleague Paul Dean was a pioneer of Christmas celebration. Nativity services were advertised for his church in Bulfinch Street, Boston, in 1835 and 1836. In a notice for the 1835 service Dean asked, "Why then should this day be any longer considered as the exclusive property of the Catholic or Episcopal Church when all denominations and people have the same reason, with them, to rejoice in the coming of Christ, and to be glad in the Lord?" (*Independent Messenger*, 25 December 1835)

[19] Ballou was probably thinking here principally of his close friend Samuel J. May, an early convert to the peace movement and, in 1838, one of the organizers of the New England Non-Resistance Society.

[20] See Mark 9:35, 10:44; 1 Corinthians 9:19.

21 The Standard of Practical Christianity was printed in the first issue of the *Practical Christian*, 1 April 1840.

22 Romans 14:17; John 18:36.

23 See Jeremiah 17:5.

24 See 2 Corinthians 10:4.

25 1 Peter 3:9.

26 Romans 12:21.

27 Matthew 5:44.

28 Romans 3:8.

29 See Matthew 25:35-36.

30 Exodus 23:2.

31 Deuteronomy 1:17; Proverbs 24:23; James 2:9, etc.

32 See Mark 9:38-40; Luke 9:49-50.

33 Acts 20:35.

34 2 Corinthians 5:10.

35 Matthew 5:48.

36 Matthew 3:8. See also Luke 3:8.

37 2 Corinthians 3:5.

38 Galatians 1:5; Philippians 4:20; 1 Timothy 1:17; 2 Timothy 4:18.

39 George W. Stacy's name was omitted from the list of signatories to the Standard as printed in the *Autobiography*. It is restored here, based on the *Practical Christian* and the *History of the Hopedale Community*.

40 Charles Gladding (c.1810-1855) was one of the earliest converts to Practical Christianity, but also one of the first to resign from the Hopedale Community. When the Community's constitution was amended in November 1842 to allow members to own property and transact business on their own, Gladding and his wife resigned in protest. However, even after his resignation, he remained in "fraternity and cordial fellowship" with the Community. It was understood that, as William H. Fish put it, "he left us as conscientiously as he came to us." Indeed, his scrupulous conscience was notable even by Hopedale standards. A tailor, he refused to make military garments, or even fashions that he considered too frivolous.

Though austere in his personal life, Gladding was generous and compassionate to those in need. In recognition of his special ministry to the sick and dying, the Hopedale Community cared for him in his own last illness. William H. Fish, Adin Ballou, E. D. Draper, and other Community members spoke at his funeral.

41 William W. Cook (1820-c.1900) belonged to one of Hopedale's leading extended families, the Draper/Thwing/Cook family. He was one of the most loyal and reliable members of the Hopedale Community. In the Community's early days he served as secretary, auditor, and lay preacher, and had charge of the garden. In later years he often held a leadership position such as Trustee or Director. He remained loyal to the Community after the defection of his brothers-in-law, George and Ebenezer Draper. He served as the Community's last Vice President, 1863-68.

⁴² Exodus 14:13.

⁴³ Middlesex Village was a built-up area at the head of the Middlesex Canal, a barge canal built in 1803 to connect the Merrimack River with the port of Boston. Since 1874 Middlesex Village has been part of the city of Lowell.

⁴⁴ Minutes of the meeting of the MAUR appear in the *Independent Messenger*, 11 October 1839. The main event at this conference was a series of debates upon theological topics. There is no mention in the minutes of any "differences between the two wings" of the denomination. Enthusiastic notice is taken of the presence of ladies, "a custom which has been gradually gaining ground among us."

⁴⁵ In December 1838 control of the *Independent Messenger* passed from Paul Dean to John Thornton. Under the new arrangement the "Religious Department" was edited by Paul Dean, Charles Hudson, and William Morse, while Thornton edited the "Miscellaneous Department." The "Genius of Reform" section was dropped. In September 1839 the paper was purchased by S. R. Hart, publisher of a secular newspaper, the *Daily Bostonian*. For the final months of its life, it was published as the *Independent Messenger and Weekly Bostonian*.

Chapter 17

¹ Movements to eliminate sectarian divisions and return to the condition of the primitive Christian church arise from time to time; Ballou's childhood church, the Christian Connexion, was the product of such a movement. The Christian Union movement of the 1830s was promoted largely by abolitionists as an alternative to national denominational bodies that refused to condemn slavery. A Christian Union Convention was held at Syracuse, New York, in 1838. Additional sessions were held in 1839 elsewhere in western New York and Pennsylvania.

² Gerrit Smith (1797-1874), an immensely wealthy landowner from New York State, was active in social reform, particularly as an abolitionist. In 1840 he helped to organize the Liberty Party. In 1846 he donated some 2000 forty-acre farms in North Elba, New York, to African Americans. The unsuitability of the land (in the Adirondack Mountains), the inexperience of the farmers, and opposition from white neighbors caused the venture to fail. During the 1850s Smith became increasingly willing to support violent resistance to slavery. He supplied funds for the defense of those prosecuted under the Fugitive Slave Law, for the support of antislavery settlers in Kansas, and, finally, to finance John Brown's raid at Harpers Ferry.

³ Silas Hawley (1815-1888) was a Congregational minister from Cazenovia, New York, about ten miles from Gerrit Smith's estate at Peterboro. He worked closely with Smith in antislavery and Christian Union causes in New York. In 1839, on Smith's recommendation, he came to Groton for three months as an agent of the Massachusetts Anti-Slavery Society. At the end of this period he was persuaded to stay on in Groton as pastor of a Union Church open to all who professed Christianity "as understood by the Evangelical Communions." It was in this capacity that he organized the Groton convention. He left Groton in 1841 to become minister of the Christian Connexion church in New Bedford, Massachusetts.

⁴ A short announcement of the upcoming convention appeared in the *Practical Christian*, 1 July 1840, with the note, "[We] should be obliged to any friend who would inform us

whether the call comprehended in its scope *heterodox* friends of the Redeemer." George Stacy wrote to Groton to inquire, and received replies from Luther Boutelle and Silas Hawley, which were printed in the *Practical Christian* on 1 August. Hawley wrote, "It is not among the objects of the proposed Convention, *to decide who are Christians, or what constitutes Christian Character* ... we cannot, as a matter of course, refuse the admission of those as members who claim to be Christians." The *Practical Christian* printed excerpts from Gerrit Smith's speech to the Syracuse convention (1 August) and from the Declaration of Sentiments composed by Silas Hawley (15 August and 1 September).

5   Amos Farnsworth (1788-1861) was a retired physician and a vice president of the Massachusetts Anti-Slavery Society. He contributed most of the funds to start the *National Anti-Slavery Standard* newspaper in 1840.

Edmund Quincy (1808-1877) was an author, editor, and reformer, active in the Massachusetts Anti-Slavery Society, the American Anti-Slavery Society, and the Non-Resistance Society. With William Lloyd Garrison and Maria Weston Chapman, he edited the *Non-Resistant*, 1839-40.

Oliver Johnson (1809-1880) was an antislavery lecturer and editor, one of the founders of the New England Anti-Slavery Society. Late in life he edited a newspaper called the *Christian Union*.

"Lucius M. Burleigh" is probably either Rev. Lucian R. Burleigh (1817-1884), Congregational minister of Plainfield, Connecticut, or his brother Cyrus M. Burleigh (1820-1855). Both were brothers of Charles C. Burleigh, the well-known abolitionist orator and editor.

6   The Groton gathering was intended as an "Evangelical Unity" convention, similar to those previously held in Syracuse and Cazenovia, New York. Though attended by people representing a wide range of religious perspectives, in the end the convention resolved "by a most decisive vote" that "the movement contemplated only a union on the Evangelical Basis ... that it was broad in this sense, and no broader."

Ballou reported on the convention in the *Practical Christian*, 1 September 1840. He noted that the broad terms of the invitation resulted in "one of the most motley and unique assemblies ever bro't together for the promotion of a Christian object," but could not comment on the outcome because he left before the final vote.

7   Acts 26:19.

8   The article "Communities" is printed in its entirety in chapter 1 of *History of the Hopedale Community*.

9   Ephesians 6:4.

10   Nathan Harris (1805-1850) and his wife, Martha Blood Harris, were among the charter members of the Hopedale Community – the thirty-two signers of the Constitution of Fraternal Community No. 1 in 1841. The Harrises were one of the first families to take up residence in Hopedale. Their son, Adin Ballou Harris, was the second child born in the Community.

Nathan Harris was one of the more entrepreneurial members of the Hopedale Community. When the Community amended its constitution in 1842 to allow more individual enterprise, he set up his own carpentry business, which constructed the first few private dwelling houses in Hopedale. He resigned from membership in 1844, when the pendulum swung back in the direction of community ownership of businesses. In partnership with Adin Ballou's nephew Cyrus Ballou Jr. and Lucy Ballou's brother Hiram Hunt, he established a lumber mill in Milford. He died in 1850 as a result of an accident at the mill.

[11] Henry Lillie (1803-1863) and his wife Caroline Hayden Lillie were charter members of the Hopedale Community. The Lillies were the first family to move into the "Old House" in October 1841. Their daughter, Lucy Ballou Lillie, was the first child born in Hopedale. Like Nathan Harris, Henry Lillie was a carpenter. Unlike the Harrises, who were among the first to leave the Community, the Lillies stayed to the end. The family remained in Hopedale until Henry's death, after which the widow and younger children moved to California.

[12] George W. Benson (1808–1879) came from a family of antislavery and peace activists. His father, George W. Benson Sr., had been an abolitionist since the 1790s. When the family settled in Brooklyn, Connecticut, in 1824, George Sr. joined the Unitarian minister Samuel J. May in founding the Windham County Peace Society. George Benson's sister Helen married William Lloyd Garrison in 1834.

In 1841 George Benson sold the farm in Brooklyn and moved to Northampton, Massachusetts, where he planned to invest in the manufacture of silk, then being promoted as an alternative to slave-produced cotton. By 1842 the proposed business venture had developed into the Northampton Association of Education and Industry. The Northampton Association began operations in April 1842, the same month as Hopedale. Both communities were committed to nonresistance, temperance, economic justice, and the abolition of slavery, though nonresistance was more important at Hopedale and opposition to slavery was more central at Northampton. Sojourner Truth, the African American abolitionist and feminist, was a member of the Northampton Association. The collapse of the Northampton Association after only four years was due largely to the failure of the silk-manufacturing venture.

[13] Charles Fourier (1772-1837) was a French businessman and self-taught philosopher who developed a highly idiosyncratic theory of social reform. He envisioned a society composed of self-supporting, self-perpetuating communities, or "phalanxes." In the ideal phalanx – made up of 1620 persons, each representing a different personality type – happiness would be maximized because each individual's passions, talents, and affinities would be used to the fullest extent. Fourier's ideas were less a serious proposal for restructuring society than a springboard for a critique of accepted ideas about such matters as work, wealth, gender, and sexuality.

Albert Brisbane (1809-1890), an American who spent two years studying with Fourier in Paris, returned to the United States in 1834 to publicize his own version of Fourier's system. He ignored the more sensational aspects of Fourier's thought and concentrated instead on promoting the idea of scientifically planned cooperative communities as an alternative to the tyranny of the marketplace. Horace Greeley (1811-1872), editor of the New York *Tribune*, and Parke Godwin (1816-1904) were journalists who used their influence to advance the cause of Associationism, as the American form of Fourierism was called.

The North American Phalanx in Red Bank, New Jersey, the longest-lived of the Fourier-inspired communities in the United States, lasted from 1843 to 1854. Albert Brisbane, Horace Greeley, and Parke Godwin all invested in and helped to organize the North American Phalanx, though none were residents.

[14] A number of short-lived Fourierist communities were founded in the midwestern states during the 1840s. Robert P. Sutton, *Heartland Utopias* (Northern Illinois University Press, 2009) lists six in Ohio, six in Illinois, two in Iowa, two in Wisconsin, and one each in Indiana and Michigan. Only two, the Marlborough Association in Alliance, Ohio, 1841-45, and the Wisconsin Phalanx, 1843-49, lasted longer than three years.

¹⁵ Brook Farm, the most famous of the communitarian experiments of the 1840s, was founded by Unitarian minister George Ripley in 1841. The idea for the community grew out of conversations among the Transcendentalists about the nature of the ideal society. Like Adin Ballou, Ripley was not content with theorizing, but determined to put his ideas into practical operation.

Ripley was particularly concerned about inequality of opportunities for intellectual and spiritual growth. He envisioned a community in which mental and manual labor would be equally valued, and where disagreeable tasks, rather than being heaped upon those least able to escape them, would be shared by all and lightened by companionship. Thus, at Brook Farm, George Ripley shovelled manure as well as teaching moral philosophy and mathematics, and Sophia Ripley taught history and languages and worked in the laundry.

Most participants found life at Brook Farm both educational and entertaining, and remembered it fondly in later life. However, the community never became financially self-supporting. In 1844 Brook Farm was reorganized as a Fourierist phalanx (see chapter 17, note 13). The leaders hoped that Fourierist discipline would help to control their expenses and that participation in the larger Associationist movement would give them access to more resources. The change did attract new members from the Associationist movement, but drove away others for whom Brook Farm's spontaneity and informality had been part of its appeal. The financial situation did not improve. A smallpox outbreak in 1845 and a fire in 1846 dashed any remaining hopes of success. Brook Farm declared bankruptcy in 1847. Ripley turned to journalism to support his family and pay the community's debts. The last creditor was paid in 1862.

¹⁶ In *Practical Christian Socialism*, written in 1854 at the height of the success of the Hopedale Community, Ballou argued for the superiority of Practical Christianity over Robert Owen's socialism, Charles Fourier's Associationism, the Perfectionism of John Humphrey Noyes and the Oneida Community, the individualist anarchism of Josiah Warren and Stephen Pearl Andrews, the communitarianism of the Shakers, and "the old and prevailing order of society."

¹⁷ The proceedings of the first meeting of the Community were printed in the *Practical Christian*, 15 February 1841, and in chapter 2 of *History of the Hopedale Community*.

¹⁸ The Constitution of the Fraternal Communion is printed in its entirety in chapter 1 of *History of the Hopedale Community*. The Constitution was printed in the *Practical Christian*, 15 February 1841, along with an "Exposition" containing a detailed commentary on the Preamble and the first five articles of the Constitution.

¹⁹ The proceedings of the second meeting of the Community are printed in chapter 2 of *History of the Hopedale Community*. This meeting was not reported in the *Practical Christian*. Ballou explained in the *History*, "It was regarded as good policy for us to keep our own counsels and noise our doings abroad as little as possible, until something definite was decided upon and we were prepared to go forward with our work in a well-ordered, systematic, effective way… the fact of our organization was known only to those immediately concerned and a few of our more deeply interested and intimate friends."

²⁰ William Ellery Channing (1780-1842) was the minister of the Federal Street Church in Boston for nearly forty years, 1803-42. He was the leading Unitarian minister during the Unitarian Controversy, the separation of the liberal Congregationalists from their more

conservative and evangelical brethren resulting in the formation of the American Unitarian Association in 1825. Though Channing deplored the necessity for the Unitarians to establish a new denomination, his sermon *Unitarian Christianity*, 1819, helped to articulate the distinctive features of Unitarianism: belief in the goodness and dignity of human nature, the benevolence of God, and the use of reason in religion.

Channing was ahead of his time on the issues of peace, class, and race, though he at first held back from the abolitionists because of a distaste for their rhetoric. His support of pacifism began during the War of 1812. In 1815 he helped Noah Worcester found the Massachusetts Peace Society. His opposition to slavery dated back to his time as a tutor in Virginia in 1798-99. Although William Lloyd Garrison was disappointed with the moderation of Channing's antislavery efforts, his advocacy gave the movement increased respectability. Similarly, radical socialists criticized Channing's emphasis on individual self-improvement as a means to social reform. However, Adin Ballou would have appreciated Channing's faith in the human capacity for moral self-improvement, which he expressed in his sermon *Self-Culture*, 1838.

[21] The officers elected were: Adin Ballou, President; William W. Cook, Secretary and Auditor; Lemuel Munyan, Intendant of Finance and Exchange; Ebenezer D. Draper, Intendant of Agriculture and Animals; Henry Lillie, Intendant of Manufactures and Mechanical Industry; David R. Lamson, Intendant of Health and Domestic Economy; Daniel S. Whitney, Intendant of Education, Arts, and Sciences; William H. Fish, Intendant of Religion, Morals, and Missions.

[22] The proceedings of the third meeting of the Community are printed in chapter 2 of *History of the Hopedale Community*. A report on the Quarterly Conference at Millville was printed in the *Practical Christian*, 5 September 1841. The meeting of the Fraternal Communion was noted but no details given.

[23] Cyrus Ballou Jr. (1812-1852) was the son of Adin Ballou's older brother Cyrus. This was the brother whose spirit had appeared to Ballou in a vision and demanded in the name of God that he become a preacher of the Gospel (see chapter 4). Cyrus Ballou Jr. and his wife were farmers in Milford and also served as keepers of the Milford Poor Asylum.

[24] The proceedings of the first annual meeting of the Community are printed in chapter 2 of *History of the Hopedale Community*. The Report of the Executive Council is printed in full, along with the minutes of the Annual Meeting, in the *Practical Christian*, 22 January 1842.

[25] Lemuel Munyan (1810-1886) was one of the most trusted members of the Hopedale Community. He was Intendant of Finance and Exchange in the early years of the Hopedale Community. In later years he was Auditor and Treasurer. Adin Ballou wrote in *History of The Town of Milford*, "[The Munyans] were among the best members of our Community at Hopedale during its best years. Fortune has seemed to frown on their pecuniary weal at times, but no blight ever touched their moral and social excellence."

[26] Butler Wilmarth (1798-1853) accepted the Standard of Practical Christianity shortly after it was published and became a member of the Hopedale Community in 1842. He became Intendant of Health and Domestic Economy while still living and practicing medicine in Leverett, Massachusetts. He moved to Hopedale in 1844 after training a young doctor to take over his practice.

Wilmarth began his career practicing the mainstream medicine of the day. However, he was, as Ballou wrote in *History of the Town of Milford*, "constitutionally a free inquirer and an independent thinker in all the departments of human concern, physical, intellectual, religious, and social ... The result was an ever expanding eclecticism and reformatory progression, chastened continually by a salutary cautiousness against extremism and erratic extravagance." On the basis of his experience at Hopedale, he became a convert to the water cure. In addition to baths, showers, hot and cold packs, and other forms of hydropathic treatment, the water cure regimen included rest, exercise, fresh air, and a simple vegetarian diet. Since regular, or "allopathic," medicine at the time relied heavily on blood-letting and on powerful, often poisonous drugs, alternatives such as homeopathy and the water cure often produced better results.

The Hopedale Community opened a water-cure infirmary in 1850, but it closed after only a few months of operation. Bidding farewell to his friends and patients "for a season," Wilmarth left Hopedale to become the medical director of the large water-cure establishment of New Graefenberg, in Herkimer County, New York. After about a year at New Graefenberg, and a few months at a similar establishment in New Lebanon, New York, he and another doctor opened their own water-cure infirmary in Westboro, Massachusetts. In 1851 Wilmarth was elected president of the American Hygienic and Hydropathic Association. He was returning from a meeting of this body in May 1853 when he was killed in a train wreck in Norwalk, Connecticut (see chapter 20, note 3).

[27] 1 Corinthians 9:16-17. See chapter 15, note 36.

[28] Minutes of the meeting of the MAUR are in the *Practical Christian*, 1 November 1840.

[29] Norwood Damon (1816-1884), the son of Rev. David Damon (see chapter 15, note 2), began his ministerial career as assistant to his father in West Cambridge (now Arlington), Massachusetts. He joined the MAUR in 1839. After his father's death he served a united Unitarian-Universalist church in Hardwick, Massachusetts, 1843-45. He subsequently went on to serve Unitarian churches in various places in Massachusetts.

[30] Samuel Hoar (1778-1856) was a prominent lawyer and politician from Concord, Massachusetts. He was one of the organizers of the Massachusetts Free Soil and Republican parties and served briefly in the U.S. House of Representatives, 1835-37. He was active in many civic and charitable organizations including the American Unitarian Association, the Massachusetts Temperance Society, and the Massachusetts and American Peace Societies.

George F. Hoar (1826-1904) served in the Massachusetts House of Representatives, the Massachusetts State Senate, the U.S. House of Representatives, and the U.S. Senate. During his long tenure as a U.S. senator, 1877-1904, he championed the rights of women, Indians, African Americans, and immigrants. Late in life he was an outspoken critic of American expansionism in Cuba and the Philippines.

[31] Ralph Waldo Emerson (1803-1882) had been on the lecture circuit for eight years by the time Adin Ballou met him. He had given some of his most well-known addresses, such as "The American Scholar," 1837, and the Divinity School Address, 1838, as well as lecture series on such broad topics as "The Philosophy of History," "Human Culture," and "Human Life." However, he had as yet few published works to his credit. His celebrated first series of essays was published a few months after his meeting with Adin Ballou.

[32] John Dale (1802-1841), a Methodist preacher, lived in Milford for two years before his death at age 38. Though he never formally joined the Restorationists, he held restorationist

views, attended the Quarterly Conferences of the MAUR, and occasionally preached from Ballou's pulpit. His obituary is in the *Practical Christian*, 1 February 1841.

[33] Abigail Scott Sayles's obituary is in the *Practical Christian*, 15 March 1841. Ballou had remained close to his former mother-in-law; he visited her a few weeks before she died. Her role in his conversion to Universalism is described in chapter 5.

[34] Channing's letter was printed in the *Practical Christian* on 25 December 1841. It is reprinted in chapter 2 of *History of the Hopedale Community*. Within the first few months of Community life, Ballou would have reason to remember Channing's words of warning about "the difficulty of reconciling so many wills, of bringing so many individuals to such a unity of feeling and judgment as is necessary to the management of an extensive common concern" and especially about "the loss of individual energy in consequence of dependence on the Community, the increased facility given to the sluggish of throwing the burden of toil on their better-disposed brethren."

[35] This is a slight misquotation of Channing's letter. Channing wrote, "I have for a very long time dreamed of an association, in which the members, instead of preying on one another and seeking to put one another down, after the fashion of this world, should live together as brothers, seeking one another's elevation and spiritual growth." The version of the letter in *History of the Hopedale Community* is more accurate.

[36] Ballou discussed "Mr. Dean's Letter" in the *Practical Christian*, 28 May 1842. He explained that in August 1841 he had received a letter from Dean "of so peculiar a character, that we could hardly determine whether the author meant it for a public or private communication, or whether he would expect an answer to it in any way." He mentioned it because he had heard that Dean was telling people that the letter "contained arguments and objections against the Community plan which we felt unable to answer." He had therefore decided to publish and answer the letter unless Dean objected. On 25 June Ballou reported that Dean did not wish his letter to be made public.

[37] Frederick Douglass (c.1818-1895) was twenty-four years old in 1842, and at the very beginning of his distinguished career as an antislavery speaker, editor, and author. After escaping from slavery in 1838 he settled in New Bedford, Massachusetts. He spoke in public for the first time at an antislavery convention in the summer of 1841 and was invited afterward to become an agent of the Massachusetts Anti-Slavery Society. Within three months he had become such a powerful speaker that some listeners refused to believe he had ever been a slave.

[38] The Washington Temperance Society, or Washingtonians, began in April 1840 as a self-help group for a half-dozen problem drinkers in Baltimore. As in the later Alcoholics Anonymous, members met to share their personal stories and support each other in their efforts to stay sober. By the end of the year, there were about a hundred members in the Baltimore-Washington area. In November 1840 the Washingtonians began to hold public meetings modeled on religious revivals. In these "experience meetings" speakers such as John Hawkins (1797-1858) told stories of their addiction and recovery. Audience members were then invited to share their stories and to come forward and take the pledge. The movement spread rapidly throughout the country, from New England to the Carolinas and west to Ohio. It reached the peak of its popularity in 1842 and 1843, but declined just as quickly. By 1850 it had disappeared in most places, or had been absorbed by other temperance, reform, or fraternal organizations.

Chapter 18

[1] Anna Thwing Draper (1814-1870) was a key member of the Hopedale Community. She served Hopedale in a variety of capacities: at first informally, as described in this chapter, and later as a member of the Relief Committee; the Council of Religion, Conciliation, and Justice; and the Promulgation Committee. She was a member of one of Hopedale's most prominent families, the Thwings. She had two sisters and a brother at Hopedale: Hannah Thwing Draper, Sylvia Thwing Bancroft, and Almon Thwing.

Anna and her husband, Ebenezer Draper, had no children of their own, but they took in several orphaned children. When they came to Hopedale they were accompanied by a teenaged foster son, William T. Stacy. In 1866 they adopted the orphaned children of Milford minister Henry Eaton (1826-1861). One of these children, Charles Henry Eaton (1852-1902), became a prominent Universalist minister in New York City (see chapter 24, note 19).

[2] The seven amendments to the original Community constitution are printed in the *Practical Christian*, 26 November 1842, and reprinted in chapter 3 of *History of the Hopedale Community*.

The amendments made a number of changes designed to transfer responsibility from the Community to the individual members. Members were allowed to own their own houses and businesses; education and poor relief were to be financed by voluntary contributions rather than by Community funds; and dividends were no longer to be paid on contributions of labor. The original uniform rate of pay for all members was replaced by "a fair compensation according to the nature and productiveness of the service." Instead of supplying the members with food, lodging, and other necessities, the Community would sell these items at cost.

[3] These six points are reprinted from the *Practical Christian*, 29 October 1842.

[4] An account of the second annual meeting is in the *Practical Christian*, 4 February 1843.

[5] Amos Jencks Ballou (1800-1869) is described in the *Genealogy* as a man of "common sense, sound judgment, a kind heart, moral integrity, and rational religion." Despite having been brought up "in a rum-dispensing Inn, in which he was for some time a knight of the toddy-stick," he was active in the temperance movement. His wife, Joanna Kelley Ballou, was the sister of the well-known antislavery lecturer Abby Kelley Foster.

[6] Ballou's account of his lecturing excursions to Grafton and New England Village is in the *Practical Christian*, 12 November 1842.

[7] In 1842 Rhode Island was still governed under the colonial charter granted by King Charles II in 1663, which included a property requirement for voting. The previous year, supporters of suffrage reform had held a convention at which they adopted a "People's Charter" that gave the vote to all white men with one year's residence in the state. In March 1842 elections were held under both charters, resulting in the election of two rival governors: Samuel Ward King under the old charter and Thomas Wilson Dorr under the People's Charter. A brief armed rebellion ensued. After the rebellion was suppressed, the state legislature adopted a new constitution that mandated universal male suffrage. Dorr was convicted of treason in 1844 and sentenced to life imprisonment, but was released the following year. His conviction was overturned shortly before he died in 1854.

[8] Ballou's account of his trip to Providence is in the *Practical Christian*, 26 November 1842.

⁹ Elder Benjamin Taylor (see chapter 2, note 9) and his brothers James (c.1790-1862) and John (1805-1872) were all ministers of the Christian Connexion. James A. McKenzie (1812-after 1857) and Martin Cheney (1792-1852) were Free Will Baptist ministers: McKenzie in Providence and Cheney in Olneyville, Rhode Island. The *Practical Christian* (3 September 1842) mentions Elder Cheney addressing a peace meeting in Providence in place of Adin Ballou, who was unable to attend.

¹⁰ The Pawtuxet Street Christian Society was founded in 1840 with Benjamin Taylor as minister. From 1841 to 1852 the minister was John Taylor, the youngest of the three brothers. Ballou's original text erroneously identified him as James Taylor.

¹¹ Ballou's account of this part of his lecture tour is in the *Practical Christian*, 26 November and 10 December 1842. His description of a further tour in the Boston area, including a railroad accident en route to Framingham, is in the *Practical Christian*, 4 February 1843.

¹² On the Millerite excitement, see chapter 13, note 34.

¹³ Maxcy Whipple Burlingame (1805-1879) was a well-known Free Will Baptist minister who during his career served numerous societies in Rhode Island, Massachusetts, and New Hampshire. At this time he was engaged in his longest pastorate, at a Baptist church in Blackstone, Massachusetts, 1830-46.

Willard Holbrook (1792-1860) studied theology with Nathanael Emmons (see chapter 7, note 1). He was the minister of the Congregational church in Rowley, Massachusetts, 1818-40. At the time of the Second Advent debate he was the minister of the Congregational church in Millville. In 1850 he retired to Rowley and did pulpit supply in the surrounding area.

¹⁴ The Second Advent debates at Millville took place on February 16 and 23, 1843. Ballou's articles on the discussions (*Practical Christian*, 4 and 18 March 1843) are largely taken up with criticism of his opponents' debating tactics. Ballou's own view is stated in one paragraph:
> I believe that the Second Coming, or appearance of Christ in his regal and judicial glory, took place about the time of the final dispersion of the Jewish nation, at the end of the Mosaic age. That the general resurrection of the dead, and *day* or *age* of Judgment, then commenced in the invisible world, denoted to mortals only by the terrors, calamities, and dreadful events attendant on the destruction of Jerusalem. That then all departed souls in Hades came forth before the judgment seat of Christ, they that had done good to the resurrection of life, and they that had done evil unto the resurrection of condemnation. That then the prophets, apostles and saints of past ages were glorified with Christ in the resurrection of the just. That thenceforth all who died passed immediately into the resurrection state and the judgment. That this is now and will continue to be the case with all who die, till death shall be no more. That the kingdom and judicial authority of Christ having thus been established, he will continue to judge the quick and the dead in righteousness, until he shall have subdued and reconciled the whole human race to God the Father – who shall finally be all in all.

Ballou was here following a common Universalist interpretation of the second coming. Similar arguments are found in Hosea Ballou's *Treatise on Atonement*.

¹⁵ Amos W. Pitts (1804-1858) was a charter member of the Hopedale Community. His wife, Mary Ann Ballou Pitts, was a distant cousin of Adin Ballou.

Francis Kelly (1799-1879) was a teacher in Blackstone, Massachusetts, for forty years.

¹⁶ An extract from *The True Scriptural Doctrine of the Second Advent* appears in the *Practical Christian*, 15 April 1843.

[17] Edmund Price (1808-c.1890), a hatter, and his wife Abby Hills Price (1814-1878) came to Hopedale in 1842. In *History of the Town of Milford*, Adin Ballou described Edmund Price as honest and industrious, but unsuccessful at managing money. Abby Price was the Community's resident poet, a frequent contributor to the *Practical Christian*, and a well-known speaker on the subject of women's rights. Because Abby dreaded being forced into the role of housewife, the Price family always lived in some sort of communal situation, where at least one other woman could share the "endless routine of domestic drudgery." After leaving Hopedale in 1853, the Prices went to another intentional community, the Raritan Bay Union in New Jersey. When that broke up in 1856, they shared a house in Brooklyn with another Raritan Bay family.

[18] Andrew H. Ernst (1796-1860) of Cincinnati had corresponded with Adin Ballou since 1831 and visited him several times. On one of his visits, he met and married Sarah H. Otis, one of Ballou's parishioners in Mendon. After making a fortune in land speculation, Ernst retired to the country to pursue his interest in horticulture. He became a nationally known horticulturist specializing in fruit trees. He is credited with introducing over a thousand varieties of apple and pear trees to the American midwest. In 1844, shortly after making his gift to Hopedale, Ernst joined a community, the Clermont Phalanx near Cincinnati, to which he donated a thousand fruit trees. Debts, dissension, and floods caused the community to fail after less than three years.

Sarah Otis Ernst (1809-1882) became a prominent Garrisonian abolitionist in the Cincinnati area. She established the Cincinnati Anti-Slavery Sewing Circle, which raised funds for the Western Anti-Slavery Society. From 1851 to 1855 she organized an annual Cincinnati Anti-Slavery Convention and Bazaar, which featured speakers such as Frederick Douglass and William Lloyd Garrison.

[19] Commenting on the conflict within the temperance movement between those who advocated strict adherence to moral suasion and those who favored legal prohibition of alcohol, Ballou noted that he opposed legal coercion, but cautioned, "We would say to both parties, keep cool; reason the matter kindly … there is no need of your imputing the worst motives to each other." ("The Temperance Controversy," *Practical Christian*, 14 October 1843)

Ballou's colleague George W. Stacy, however, was harshly critical of Washingtonian leader John Hawkins for calling on the protection of the law against an egg-throwing heckler. "Alas for the Washingtonians if they approbate this," he wrote. "It bears the mark of the beast." ("John H. W. Hawkins," *Practical Christian*, 16 September 1843)

[20] In 1840 there was a split between radicals and conservatives within the antislavery movement. As Ballou noted, one of the issues between them was participation in electoral politics: the conservatives wanted to form an antislavery political party, the Liberty Party, whereas Garrisonian radicals thought the necessity to win votes would compromise the movement's moral integrity. The conservatives also wanted to focus narrowly on the abolition of slavery while otherwise preserving the status quo, while the radicals were interested in other reform causes such as nonresistance and women's rights. At the annual meeting of the American Anti-Slavery Society in 1840, the conservatives walked out (ostensibly in protest against including the female activist Abby Kelley on the business committee) and formed a new organization, the American and Foreign Anti-Slavery Society.

[21] Ballou stated his beliefs about the Sabbath in his "Review of 'A Plea for Sunday Freedom'"(*Practical Christian*, 29 March and 12 April 1845). It was written in response to an anonymous pamphlet that complained that, for many working people, a Sunday spent

in traditional religious observance provides neither refreshment nor edification, but merely imposes a "yoke of ceremonial bondage." Ballou disagreed, arguing that it is "a principle of duty, an absolute moral requirement of God" that one day a week should be devoted to cultivation of "man's religious and moral sentiment, as the great life-regulating portion of his nature, which if right will set his entire being right, or if wrong will disorder his entire being, and render happiness an impossible attainment." If worship is not meaningful, he thought it should be reformed, not abandoned. Nor should it be treated, as the author of the pamphlet seemed to treat it, as a form of amusement, all right for those who enjoy it, but no more valuable than the alternatives of horse-racing, cock-fighting, gambling, drinking, or the ceaseless pursuit of wealth.

In 1848 the *Practical Christian* carried an announcement of an Anti-Sabbath Convention supported by William Lloyd Garrison and other prominent reformers. Ballou commented, "We are in a sort of *betweenity* on this controversy – having sympathies and repugnancies both ways." He deplored the hypocrisy, bigotry, and austerity of some Sabbatarians but still felt that the institution of a Sabbath, properly observed, was a valuable religious exercise. ("Anti-Sabbath Convention," *Practical Christian*, 19 February 1848)

[22] In Greek mythology, Scylla and Charybdis were monsters found on opposite sides of the Strait of Messina between Sicily and the mainland of Italy. As described in the *Odyssey*, Scylla had six heads on six long necks; as a ship passed through the strait, each head would devour a sailor. Charybdis created a whirlpool capable of swallowing up whole ships. Attempting to avoid Scylla meant passing closer to Charybdis, and vice versa. Ballou used the metaphor of Scylla and Charybdis several times in *History of the Hopedale Community* in reference to the Community's difficulty in finding a workable economic system.

Chapter 19

[1] James 1:17.

[2] Stacy's decision to leave Hopedale was precipitated by the most recent round of changes to the Community's economic system. Under the system adopted in December 1844, workers were organized into Bands and Sections under the supervision of Monitors and Directors. Work hours were increased. Children were expected to work four hours per day. A detailed system of record-keeping kept close track of each worker's attendance and adjusted pay accordingly. As Ballou admitted in *History of the Hopedale Community*, the new arrangement "did not work so harmoniously and advantageously as was confidently anticipated." It would, in fact, bring the Community to the brink of collapse by mid-1847.

In his farewell message ("Reply to C. O. R. and Withdrawal from Hopedale, " *Practical Christian*, 27 December 1845), Stacy objected to the new system as "artificial and burdensome," and an unwarranted intrusion on parental and family rights. He charged that "the capitalist" (presumably he was referring to E. D. Draper) had imposed this factory-like supervision of the work force by threatening to withdraw his money. The same issue of the *Practical Christian* carried a long reply by Adin Ballou ("Reply to Br. Stacy"), defending the system and airing a number of petty grievances against Stacy, for example, that he came to work late and failed to supervise his apprentices adequately. Both Stacy and Ballou agreed in the next issue ("Reply to Br. Adin Ballou" and "Omega with Br. G. W. Stacy," 10 January 1846) that the discussion should not have taken place in the public press, though both continued the argument about Stacy's management of the Hopedale printing office.

³ Robert Owen (1771-1858) was an influential British social reformer who is credited with initiating the nineteenth-century communitarian movement. At his model textile mill in New Lanark, Scotland, he pioneered humane treatment of workers, including the education of child laborers. As a result of his success at New Lanark, he developed the idea that character is completely determined by circumstances. In 1825 he attempted to put his ideas into practice by establishing the model community of New Harmony in Indiana, but the community failed after two years. Owen returned to England in 1827, having lost 80% of his wealth and much of his prestige. He devoted the rest of his life to the development of trade unions, workers' cooperatives, and social theory (he is credited with coining the word "socialism"). His ideas of equality and cooperation were popular and influential in the United States, though he aroused much opposition by speaking out against private property, marriage, and religion. A long article on Owen and his visit, "Robert Owen at Hopedale," appeared in the *Practical Christian*, 29 November 1845.

⁴ The President's Address and financial report from the 1846 annual meeting are printed in the *Practical Christian*, 24 January 1846.

⁵ The new arrangements are set forth in "Alteration of the Community Constitution," *Practical Christian*, 7 August 1847. The rules and regulations adopted in December 1844 were scrapped in their entirety. Members were not required to adopt any particular economic arrangements. Within the limits of the Declaration they had signed on entering, they were free to make any arrangements by mutual agreement.

⁶ David Davenport, a surveyor from Mendon, Massachusetts, was active in local politics, holding a number of offices in Mendon and in Worcester County during the 1840s and 50s. In 1867 a former resident of Mendon remembered him as a "broad-minded man and most excellent citizen" and one of "the best and most honored of the town." See Samuel P. Bates, letter in *An Address ... and other proceedings in commemoration of the two hundredth anniversary of the incorporation of Mendon, Massachusetts* (Worcester, MA, 1868), 88.

⁷ By "foreign help" Ballou meant, not workers from outside the United States, but those from outside the Hopedale Community. He explained in the *Practical Christian* that "it is extremely desirable with us that all who reside on our domain should be hearty advocates of the principles which lie at the foundation of our enterprise, or at least so far interested in them as to be conscientious enquirers after the truth of these principles. For we well know that our rising generation must be influenced to some extent by those who disregard or undervalue our principles, if they associate intimately with such" ("Our Affairs at Hopedale," *Practical Christian*, 30 September 1848).

⁸ Ellis Gray Loring (1803-1858) was a prominent Boston attorney active in the antislavery cause. He was one of the original twelve members of the New England Anti-Slavery Society, a financial supporter of the antislavery newspaper, the *Liberator*, and one of the lawyers in the famous case of the revolt of African captives on the ship *Amistad*. His most notable legal triumph was in the 1836 case of the slave child "Med," which established that the claims of out-of-state slaveholders would not be recognized in the state of Massachusetts. Loring's law student Robert Morris became the second African American attorney in the United States.

⁹ The real estate transactions performed at this time are described in full in *History of the Hopedale Community*, chapter 6. The purpose of these transactions was to change the form of ownership of the Hopedale property from "tenancy in common" to "joint tenancy." Under tenancy in common, each member would have the right to dispose of his or her

share individually. On the death of any member, a member's share would pass to his or her heirs, making it impossible for the Community to retain control over its property. The change to joint tenancy collected all of the land into a single legal entity administered by a Board of Trustees, so that real estate transactions would be performed by the Community as a whole rather than by the individual shareholders.

[10] No letter from Whitney or reply from Ballou appears in the *Practical Christian*.

[11] William Lloyd Garrison used this expression, taken from Isaiah 28:15, to refer to the United States Constitution. In 1843 the American Anti-Slavery Society passed a resolution, written by Garrison, "that the compact which exists between the North and the South is a covenant with death and an agreement with hell – involving both parties in atrocious criminality – and should be immediately annulled."

[12] The Prohibition Party was founded in 1869. Its greatest success was the passage in 1919 of the Eighteenth Amendment to the United States Constitution, which outlawed the production, sale, transportation, import, and export of alcohol. The party, which calls itself "the oldest third party in the United States," declined in popularity after the repeal of Prohibition in 1933, but it still exists. Its candidate received some 500 votes in the presidential election in 2012.

[13] In 1853 a constitutional convention was held to consider revising the Massachusetts state constitution of 1780. The convention proposed a number of reforms, including elimination of property requirements for voting and holding office; the secret ballot; term limits for judges; abolition of imprisonment for debt; prohibition of state funding for religious schools; and a constitutional convention every twenty years. When the convention's recommendations were presented to the electorate, every provision was voted down; however, many of them were subsequently adopted as amendments.

[14] Ebenezer D. Draper was elected president at the annual meeting in January 1852.

[15] The report of the annual meeting, Ballou's Valedictory Address, and the committee's response are in the *Practical Christian*, 31 January 1852. They are printed in full in *History of the Hopedale Community*, chapter 7. The version of the committee's letter printed here differs in numerous small ways from the version in the *History of the Hopedale Community*.

[16] Edmund Soward (1803-1855) was Hopedale's resident horticulturist, overseeing the Community's vegetable gardens and fruit trees. He was particularly interested in the welfare of the Community's children. He helped to organize the Hopedale school and served for many years on the Community's Board of Education. When he died he bequeathed his property to establish a fund for the education and amusement of the children. (One contributor to *Hopedale Reminiscences* remembered being taken to Boston to see "trained seals and mice," courtesy of the Soward Fund.) The Soward Fund outlived the Hopedale Community. It was transferred to the care of the Hopedale Parish in 1875.

[17] Susan (or Susanna) Fish (1793-1852) lived in Hopedale from 1843 to 1846. She remained a loyal supporter of the Hopedale experiment. When she died, leaving her property to the Community, resident poet Abby Price wrote an elegy containing these lines:

> The cause we here cherish was dear to her heart;
> Her prayer oft ascended that we might be blest;
> Though absent at last and dwelling apart,
> She longed in the peace of our valley to rest.

In accordance with her last wishes, Susan Fish was buried in the Hopedale Cemetery.

[18] These quotations are from the parable of the sower, Matthew 13:3-8,18-23; Mark 4:3-8,13-20; Luke 8:5-15.

[19] James Miller McKim (1810-1874) was a Presbyterian minister and abolitionist from Philadelphia. From 1836 he worked full time as an agent of the American Anti-Slavery Society and editor of an abolitionist newspaper, the *Pennsylvania Freeman*. After the Civil War he was active in promoting the welfare of former slaves.

[20] Hudson's review was published in a pamphlet called *Non-Resistance* (Boston, 1848). Hudson's major objection was to Ballou's refusal to participate in government. He cited scripture and history to show that government is necessary and supporting it is a duty. Ballou's reply, "Hudson on Non-Resistance," extended over five issues of the *Practical Christian* (13 May, 27 May, 10 June, 24 June, and 8 July 1848).

[21] On Ballou's previous encounters with Origen Bacheler, see chapter 8, notes 12-14.

[22] There were several Congregational ministers named Thomas Williams who served at one time or another in Providence. Ballou was probably referring to Thomas Williams (c.1779-c.1870), who served the Richmond Street Congregational Church, 1807-16.

[23] John Orcutt (1807-1879) was a Congregational minister and a pillar of the American Colonization Society. His interest in settling African Americans in Liberia appears to have been motivated by missionary zeal. He remained active in the Colonization Society until shortly before his death, long after American slavery had been abolished.

[24] From Isaac Watts, *Hymns and Spiritual Songs* (c.1700):
> Broad is the road that leads to death,
> And thousands walk together there;
> But wisdom shows a narrower path,
> With here and there a traveller.

[25] The belief that the spirits of the dead can communicate with the living is as old as humanity, but encounters with the deceased are usually private, subjective experiences, like Adin Ballou's vision of his dead brother Cyrus. A new era in spiritualism began in 1848, when Kate and Margaret Fox of Hydesville, New York, 12 and 15 years old, demonstrated their ability to hold conversations with spirits, who replied to questions with "rappings" audible to everyone in the room. Instead of private, unpredictable experiences, spirit communications became public events, capable of being produced by the use of certain techniques. This appeared to open the way to scientific investigation of the afterlife.

Widespread interest in the subject ensued. The Fox sisters, and many other mediums, were able to make a living on the lecture circuit or by holding séances in private homes. In 1888, forty years after their first public appearance, the sisters confessed to producing the rapping by cracking the joints of their toes, though they later recanted their confession. By that time it hardly mattered; people had long since drawn their own conclusions, pro and con, about spirit communication, often on the basis of personal experience.

[26] The Sadducees were one of three major Jewish groups around the time of Christ (the others were the Pharisees and the Essenes). A priestly group closely tied to the Temple at Jerusalem, they disappeared after the destruction of the Temple in 70 CE. The Sadducees did not believe in an afterlife, hence Ballou's characterization of skepticism about spiritualism as "modern Sadduceeism."

[27] *Hamlet* 1.5.

²⁸ In 1851 the *Practical Christian* carried an article by Hopedale's physician, Dr. Butler Wilmarth, debunking spirit communications, with a reply by Adin Ballou explaining why he disagreed. Wilmarth thought the phenomena could be accounted for by a combination of fraud, wishful thinking, the power of suggestion, and "animal magnetism" (hypnosis), with perhaps a bit of telepathy. He disbelieved that the messages came from spirits, "Not because we are unbelievers in 'angels and spirits' and a conscious, progressive and ultimate happy existence in a brighter world than this. But because it is contrary to reason, to the natural constitution of the human mind, and to all precedent, to give or receive any communication in this manner." He thought the messages were "trivial, and demonstrate retrogression rather than progression." Further, the communications "partake of the theology and literature of the Mediums." Ballou, on the other hand, thought that "there is an absolute reality to most of the phenomena," despite "incidental imitations, counterfeits, and deceptions here and there." ("'Mysterious Rappings' Explained," *Practical Christian*, 26 April 1851)

²⁹ Cyrus Peirce (1790-1860) began his career as a Unitarian minister, 1818-27, but soon discovered his true calling as an educator. In 1839 Horace Mann, the educational reformer and first secretary of the Massachusetts Board of Education, recruited Peirce as principal of the new state Normal School, or teachers' training school, the first such institution in the United States. From 1839 to 1849 (except for a hiatus of two years, 1842-44, caused by ill health) Peirce served as director and teacher of the Normal School, and also as principal of the model school where the students did their practice teaching.

The Normal School was originally located in Lexington. It moved to West Newton, 1843-53, and then to Framingham, where it still exists, as Framingham State College.

³⁰ William Sweetser Heywood (1824-1905) came to Hopedale in 1848. He studied with Adin Ballou for the Practical Christian ministry, became associate editor of the *Practical Christian*, and was ordained in 1849. In 1851 he married the Ballous' daughter Abbie. William and Abbie Heywood were co-principals of the Hopedale Home School, 1856-63. They left Hopedale in 1864. Heywood served several small Unitarian churches in Massachusetts. His last settlement was as Minister to the Poor in Boston. After Adin Ballou died, Heywood completed and published Ballou's *Autobiography* and other posthumous works.

³¹ Nicholas Tillinghast (1804-1856) began his career as an army officer. After leaving the army in 1836 he settled in Boston as a teacher. In 1840 he was recruited by Horace Mann as first principal of the Normal School at Bridgewater. He retired due to ill health in 1853.

³² The *Mammoth* ran from November 1845 to December 1848.

³³ The *Prospectus* was printed in the *Practical Christian* – not as a featured article, but in small print among the advertisements – on 6 and 20 December 1851 and 3 January 1852.

³⁴ Henry C. Wright (1797-1870), a radical abolitionist and pacifist, was one of the founders of the New England Non-Resistance Society. During the 1850s, however, he abandoned Christian non-resistance, saying, "Christ, as represented by those who are called by his name, has proved a dead failure, as a power to free the slaves." In his "Natick Resolution," 1859, he proclaimed, "It is the right and duty of the slaves to resist their masters, and the right and duty of the people of the North to incite them to resistance, and to aid them in it." Ballou's praise of Wright's "devotion to the cause" of non-resistance suggests that he was not aware of Wright's change of heart.

[35] "The sleep which knows no waking" was a well-known and widely quoted phrase in the nineteenth century, used by such popular writers as Henry Wadsworth Longfellow ("The Poor Student: A Dramatic Sketch," 1824) and Charles Dickens (*The Old Curiosity Shop*, 1841). It appears to be a variant of "Sleep the sleep that knows not breaking / Morn of toil, nor night of waking," from Sir Walter Scott's poem *The Lady of the Lake* (1810).

[36] Psalms 90:10: "The days of our years are three score and ten."

[37] Theodore Parker (1810-1860) was one of the most influential, and controversial, Unitarian ministers of the nineteenth century. In writings such as his famous sermon *The Transient and Permanent in Christianity*, 1841, he argued that the truth of the Bible was mythic and symbolic rather than literal, and that the inspiration of Jesus was of the same kind as that available to any person. Because of his radical ideas, other Unitarian ministers refused to exchange pulpits with him, a virtual excommunication. However, Parker's ideas attracted passionate admirers as well as detractors. In 1845 he began preaching to large audiences at the Melodeon Theater in Boston. By the time Adin Ballou preached to his congregation, Parker was speaking to audiences of 2000 people. Shortly after this the congregation moved to an even larger theater, the Music Hall.

[38] William Lloyd Garrison (1805-1879), editor of the antislavery newspaper, the *Liberator*, and one of the founders of the American Anti-Slavery Society, was the foremost champion of immediate abolition of slavery. He was so identified with this cause that "Garrisonian" became a synonym for "radical abolitionist." Believing that only moral power could defeat the entrenched power supporting the institution of slavery, he articulated a theory of nonviolent resistance that was influential on Adin Ballou and on later generations of nonviolent activists.

[39] Though Theodore Parker was a militant abolitionist who sheltered fugitive slaves, sent guns to Kansas, and helped to finance John Brown's raid, he opened his pulpit to non-resistants. William Lloyd Garrison preached a non-resistant sermon from Parker's pulpit in 1858, in which he said, "I pray you, abolitionists... do not make yourselves familiar with the idea that blood must flow. Perhaps blood will flow... but it shall not flow through any counsel of mine."

Chapter 20

[1] The expression "staff of accomplishment" became a catch-phrase at the time of the schism in the antislavery movement in 1839-40 (see chapter 18, note 20). When the more conservative abolitionists withdrew from the American Anti-Slavery Society they charged that, by embracing radical causes unrelated to the abolition of slavery, William Lloyd Garrison and his followers had "thrown away the staff of accomplishment." The expression was widely quoted and ridiculed in the Garrisonian camp.

[2] *An Exposition of Views Respecting the Principal Facts, Causes, and Peculiarities involved in Spirit Manifestations; Together with interesting phenomenal statements and communications* (Boston, 1852). Ballou argued that spirit communications, though real, are less reliable than scripture and reason. "Any attempt... to build up a religion or moral philosophy, radically contradictory to that of the genuine Christian Testament, on what is being disclosed to the world through Dreamers, Somnambulists, Impressibles, Clairvoyants, Spirit Media, the Rappings, etc., is irrational, and must prove mischievous rather than beneficial to the human race."

3   In 1853 the rail line between New York and Boston crossed an inlet of Long Island Sound at Norwalk, Connecticut, by means of a drawbridge. When the train reached the crossing on the morning of May 6, 1853, the bridge was open to allow a steamship to pass. The engineer, who was unfamiliar with the route, failed to notice the signal that the drawbridge was open. The first two passenger cars plunged into the water, killing about 50 of the 150 passengers on board.

4   William H. Fish, *Memoir of Butler Wilmarth, M.D.; One of the Victims of the late terrible Railroad Catastrophe at Norwalk Bridge, Ct.; with extracts from his correspondence and manuscripts* (Boston, 1854).

5   What Ballou described here as "an incoherent Transcendentalism" is probably "Individual Sovereignty," a libertarian philosophy espoused by Josiah Warren and Stephen Pearl Andrews, and put into practice at the Modern Times community in Long Island, New York. In *History of the Hopedale Community*, Ballou wrote that Individual Sovereignty "made every man and woman not only his own prophet, priest, and king, but virtually his own lawgiver and lawmaker – his own God in fact." Ballou had particular reason for hostility to Modern Times: in 1853 a couple expelled from Hopedale for adultery took refuge in Modern Times, claiming that they were practicing "free love." The full story of the incident is in *History of the Hopedale Community*, chapter 17.

6   Ballou engaged in extensive debate on the Bible in 1853. It began with an invitation from spiritualists Andrew Jackson Davis, William Green, and William P. Donaldson to participate in a convention "for the purpose of freely and fully canvassing the origin, authority, and influence of the Jewish and Christian scriptures." Ballou declined, in part because "I occupy ground respecting the merits of the Bible *between* the conservative and progressive *extremes*, which would require much discriminating exposition to set forth properly" ("Bible Convention," *Practical Christian*, 7 May 1853). In a longer article ("The Bible," 16 July 1853) he explained that he valued and venerated the Bible, but rejected "the doctrine of its plenary divine inspiration, *verbatim et literatim*." This called forth a reply from a correspondent identified as "B. A." who argued, on rationalist grounds, against according the Bible a higher status than any other book ("Article on the Bible Reviewed," 30 July 1853). Ballou replied, and the debate continued through eleven further installments between 13 August 1853 and 14 January 1854.

7   The proper method of keeping the Sabbath does not seem to have been a major concern during the time covered by this chapter. For Ballou's views on this subject, see chapter 18, note 21.

8   *Practical Christian Socialism* is written in the form of a dialogue between "the Inquirer" and "the Expositor." Part I contains Ballou's clearest and most systematic statement of his theological beliefs. Part II is a commentary on the Constitution of the Practical Christian Republic. Part III compares Practical Christianity with other competing systems (see chapter 17, note 16). An abridged version of *Practical Christian Socialism*, omitting Part III and presenting the arguments of Parts I and II without the dialogue form, was published in 2002 as *Practical Christianity* (Providence: Blackstone Editions, 2002).

9   Ballou's letters home were printed in the *Practical Christian* as "Editorial Correspondence," 20 May, 3 June, and 17 June 1854; "The Editor's Tour – Continued," 1 July, 15 July, 29 July, and 12 August 1854; and "Letter to the Inductive Communion," 29 July 1854.

[10] At this time Morgan and Sophia Bloom worked at the Five Points Mission. The following fall they moved to Hopedale as principals of the Hopedale Home School. Ballou reported in *History of the Town of Milford* that, after selling the Hopedale Home School to William and Abbie Heywood in 1856, the Blooms joined the Oneida Community.

[11] In the mid-nineteenth century, Five Points, a neighborhood in lower Manhattan occupied primarily by Irish and Jewish immigrants and African Americans, was one of the most notorious slums in New York. Five Points Mission and Five Points House of Industry were rival Protestant missionary and anti-poverty organizations serving this area. In addition to attempting to inculcate Protestant beliefs and values, they provided employment, housing for women and children, schools, and an orphanage.

[12] The Crystal Palace was an exhibition building (on the site of present-day Bryant Park) built for New York's first World's Fair, the 1853 Exhibition of the Industry of All Nations. It was constructed of iron and glass in imitation of the Crystal Palace built in London's Hyde Park for the Great Exhibition of 1851.

[13] The North American Phalanx, founded in 1843, was the longest-lived of the American Fourierist communities (see chapter 17, note 13). It was a project of the Fourierist Society, which was founded in New York in 1839 to popularize Fourier's theories and, eventually, to establish a model Phalanx. In 1843 ten enthusiastic Associationists in Albany, New York, put the plan into practical operation by adopting a constitution, raising funds, and buying a piece of property in Monmouth County, New Jersey. Although the Society had not planned to act until more people and more funds were committed to the project, they backed the venture. Horace Greeley, though not a resident, became the vice-president and the largest shareholder.

The Phalanx was largely an agricultural community, producing fruit, vegetables, and cereals for the New York market. In many ways it succeeded in realizing the Associationists' social program. Workers were organized into "groups" and "series" according to Fourier's theories. Men and women received equal pay, with the highest wages paid for the most disagreeable jobs. Education was offered for all ages, from infants to adults. The community was non-sectarian and committed to religious toleration.

Alongside these achievements there were some significant problems. Like the Hopedale Community, the Phalanx struggled to find the right balance between individual and community property. Some members felt that there was too much buying, selling, and record-keeping – for example, members were charged for each item eaten in the communal dining room. There was controversy over the authority of the leaders, the role of religion in the community, and the quality of the schools. In 1853 the Phalanx split, with some members leaving to form a more individualistic, more Christian, and more education-oriented community, the Raritan Bay Union.

Adin Ballou described his trip to the Phalanx in "Editorial Correspondence," *Practical Christian*, 3 June 1854, noting in particular the lush orchards and gardens. He thought the Unitary Mansion with its communal dining room "most economical" but noted, "I cannot think I should like to be confined to this manner of living."

Like Hopedale, in 1854 the North American Phalanx was approaching the end of its life. A fire in September 1854 destroyed the flour mill, sawmill, and other shops. Rather than rebuilding after the fire, the stockholders, most of whom were non-residents, chose to dissolve the community. The property was sold in 1856.

[14] Charles Sears (1810-1890) was a flour merchant in Albany, New York. There he met Horace Greeley, who was editing a Whig campaign newspaper based in Albany. Sears and Greeley became close friends, with a shared interest in Associationism. In 1842 Sears sent his two oldest children to be educated at Brook Farm. (His son, John Van Der Zee Sears, wrote a memoir of his childhood, *My Friends at Brook Farm*, 1912.)

In 1843 the North American Phalanx was established, with funds largely raised by Sears and his fellow Associationists from Albany. Sears was a leading member of the Phalanx until it was dissolved in 1855. His mother and two sisters were also members of the Phalanx.

In 1875 Sears moved to Kansas to work on another communitarian venture: the cooperative community of Silkville, near Williamsburg, Kansas. Silkville had been established in 1869 by the French émigré philanthropist Ernest Valeton de Boissière. Sears managed the silk industry, while his son, Charles T. Sears, took charge of the commune's farm, orchards, and vineyards. For a time Silkville prospered. But in the long run Kansas silk could not compete with imported silk from Asia. Nor could communal living compete with the lure of free land available under the Homestead Act.

Sears remained in Kansas, where he continued to write articles on socialist and cooperative topics for the rest of his life. De Boissière returned to France in 1892.

[15] The Fairmount Waterworks in Philadelphia was the first large-scale municipal water supply project in the United States. Housed in a complex of Greek revival-style buildings on the bank of the Schuylkill River, the Waterworks was a tourist attraction from the time it was opened in 1822.

Laurel Hill Cemetery is an early example of the "garden-style" cemetery. With their acres of landscaped parkland dotted with elaborate tombs and monuments, these cemeteries doubled as public parks and outdoor art galleries.

[16] During the half-century before the Civil War, one of the most contentious issues in American politics was the expansion of slavery into new territories. Tension rose particularly high when the territories of Kansas and Nebraska were organized in 1854. The Kansas-Nebraska Act established the principle of "popular sovereignty," that is, that the question of slavery would be left up to the residents of the new states. Because slavery had been prohibited in this area by the Missouri Compromise of 1820 (see chapter 3, note 10), popular sovereignty was actually a victory for the proponents of slavery. In addition, it led to violence between pro- and anti-slavery settlers in "Bleeding Kansas." Like the Fugitive Slave Law of 1850, the Kansas-Nebraska Act moved the nation a step closer to civil war.

[17] Charles Sumner (1811-1874), senator from Massachusetts, and Joshua Giddings (1795-1864), representative from Ohio, were leaders of the antislavery forces in Congress and outspoken opponents of the Kansas-Nebraska Act. Thomas Davis (1806-1895) of Rhode Island and Gerrit Smith of New York (see chapter 17, note 2) were each serving a first and, as it turned out, only term in the House of Representatives.

[18] The Baltimore & Ohio railroad reached Wheeling, Virginia (now West Virginia), in 1853, the first rail link between the Atlantic Ocean and the Ohio River. The "mighty and amazing constructions" along the route included eleven tunnels and 113 bridges. The other railroad lines used by the Ballou/Draper party were also quite new in 1854: the Cincinnati to Cleveland line was finished in 1850, and the Grand Trunk from Montreal to Portland, Maine, was completed in 1853.

[19] Abial Abbot Livermore (1811-1892) served as a Unitarian minister in Keene, New Hampshire, 1836-50; Cincinnati, Ohio, 1850-57; and Yonkers, New York, 1857-63. While in Cincinnati he was one of the organizers of the Western Unitarian Conference and served as its first secretary. While in New York he edited the *Christian Enquirer.* He was president of Meadville Theological School from 1863 to 1890. His major work was a six-volume commentary on the New Testament, published over a period of forty years, 1842-81. Among his "other meritorious works" is a much-reprinted essay on the evils of tobacco. Late in life he wrote a history of his home town, Wilton, New Hampshire.

[20] Daniel Parker (1781-1861), a self-taught lay preacher, was one of the first to preach Universalism in Ohio. He corresponded with Adin Ballou and was an agent for the *Independent Messenger*. In 1839 he founded Parker Academy, the first racially integrated school in Ohio.

[21] "Canada" in 1854 meant the United Province of Canada, consisting of Canada West (present-day Ontario) and Canada East (Québec). Commenting on speculation that the provinces would join the United States, Ballou wrote, "From what I heard said by intelligent Canadians on this subject, there is very little desire among the Provincialists to belong to our Slavocratic Union ... the chances are five to one for the ultimate formation of an independent Canadian Nation in close alliance with Great Britain. Time will show whether I guess right" ("The Editor's Tour – Continued," *Practical Christian*, 12 August 1854). His guess was a good one; in 1867 the provinces of Canada, New Brunswick, and Nova Scotia became the independent Dominion of Canada.

[22] The Queenston-Lewiston Suspension Bridge was completed in 1851. As Ballou said, it was at that time the longest suspension bridge in the world. However, its fame was eclipsed in 1855 by the construction of the world's first suspension railroad bridge, a mile or so upstream. The Queenston-Lewiston bridge was destroyed by wind in 1864. It was not rebuilt until 1899.

[23] A detailed description of this part of the trip may be found in a guidebook, *The Great Northern Route: The Ontario and St. Lawrence Steamboat Company's Hand-Book for Travelers* (1853). The trip from Niagara Falls to Montreal took three days: one day by stagecoach from Niagara Falls to Lewiston, New York, with sightseeing stops along the way; one day by lake steamer from Lewiston to Ogdensburg, New York; and the third day by river steamer to Montreal, "passing the Thousand Islands and all the Rapids by daylight." (The rapids were included for their entertainment value; commercial traffic used canals.)

[24] On his return Ballou received a touching tribute from the Inductive Communion, the young adults' group he led on Monday evenings. The students had had their daguerreotypes taken, and presented Ballou with a group portrait with the caption, "We know the loved are not all here," a reference to the deceased Adin Augustus Ballou. On receiving this gift, Ballou wrote, "the father's heart heaved with emotions too deep for utterance" ("Hopedale Inductive Communion," *Practical Christian*, 1 July 1854).

[25] Beginning in late 1854 William H. Fish wrote about a dozen articles for the *Practical Christian*, urging the desirability of establishing a new community in one of the western states (for example, "Westward, Ho!" 4 November 1854; "The West Once More," 2 December 1854; "What of the West?" 27 January 1855; "The Western Movement," 10 February 1855).

[26] The story of the emigrants to Minnesota is told in *History of the Hopedale Community*, chapter 8.

[27] Ballou described his trip in "Visit to Mystic and Vicinity, Ct." *Practical Christian*, 28 July 1855.

The Seventh Day Baptists observe the Sabbath on Saturday. Their beliefs are otherwise similar to those of other evangelical Christians.

Sherman Saxton Griswold (1805-1882) was pastor of Seventh-Day Baptist churches in New York State, 1842-47; Hopkinton, Rhode Island, 1847-50; and Greenmanville, Connecticut, 1850-65. He then returned to Hopkinton for a pastorate that lasted the rest of his life, 1865-82. In Hopkinton he served as superintendent of schools, c.1874-80, and wrote *An Historical Sketch of the Town of Hopkinton*, 1876. He served in denominational leadership roles, including a term as president of the Seventh Day Baptist General Conference. He was active in the temperance, antislavery, and women's rights movements.

[28] Passmore Williamson (1822-1895) was imprisoned from July to November 1855 for his part in helping Jane Johnson and her two children escape from slavery. The case focused attention on the extent to which the Fugitive Slave Law could be enforced even in a state like Pennsylvania, which did not recognize slavery. Williamson's imprisonment was extensively covered by the antislavery press. With the cooperation of sympathetic prison officials, his cell became a sort of tourist attraction. Adin Ballou was one of several hundred visitors; others included Frederick Douglass and Harriet Tubman.

[29] Robert Hare (1781-1858) was a professor of chemistry at the University of Pennsylvania. In 1853 he conducted a series of experiments designed to debunk "the gross delusion called spiritualism." Instead, he became a believer in the reality of spirit communications. He published his findings in *Experimental Investigation of the Spirit Manifestations*, 1854. The *Practical Christian* printed a brief excerpt from the book ("Professor Hare on Spiritualism," 15 December 1855).

[30] Gerrit Smith was a major donor to New York Central College (1849-1860), a coeducational and racially integrated college in McGrawville, Cortland County, New York.

[31] A report on the annual meeting was printed in the *Practical Christian*, 26 January 1856. The next issue included the President's address by E. D. Draper and the report of the Board of Education ("The Annual Papers," *Practical Christian*, 9 February 1856).

[32] George Draper (1817-1887), the younger brother of Community leader Ebenezer D. Draper, is generally considered the person most responsible for the demise of the Hopedale Community.

From 1832, when he was fifteen years old, to 1853, George Draper worked in various textile mills, rising from operative to overseer and then to manager. During this time he patented some improvements to the loom temple that had been invented by his father and was being manufactured by Ebenezer Draper at Hopedale. In 1853 George came to Hopedale to go into business with his brother. Though he had "only dubious faith in Community life," George joined the Community in 1854 and quickly became one of its major shareholders. His wife, Hannah Thwing Draper, refused to join, on the grounds, according to her son, that "she did not believe all questions should be decided by a majority vote or that there should be no rewards for pre-eminent ability and services."

In 1855 George Draper brought into the business (and into the Community) Warren Dutcher of Vermont, who held the patent on an improved version of the loom temple.

With Dutcher as a partner instead of a rival, the Drapers' business was in a position to become much more profitable. This could not happen, however, within the confines of the Hopedale Community, with its restricted, carefully screened work force, its standard rate of pay for all hands, and its limitation of profit to four percent. Taking advantage of the Community's unsophisticated accounting system, the Drapers created the financial crisis of 1856, thus freeing their capital from the joint-stock community. George Draper remained a nominal member of the Hopedale Community until 1863, when he resigned in order to participate actively in raising money and troops for the Union army.

Under the leadership of George and his son William, the Drapers' business prospered. By the turn of the century, tiny Hopedale was the leading manufacturer of textile machinery in the United States. George Draper was a leader in the effort to establish Hopedale as a separate town in 1886, and donated the funds to build the town hall.

[33] Ballou did not publish an account of the changes at Hopedale until November 1856, more than six months after the "fatal crisis," when he wrote, "Important changes were made last Spring in the property arrangements of this Community… These changes have transformed the Hopedale Community from a Joint-Stock to a kind of Rural Community." He wrote that he was now reconciled "in a good degree" to his disappointment, and consoled himself with the reflection that he would have more time for preaching the principles of Practical Christianity without being encumbered by secular Community business ("Social Position of Hopedale," *Practical Christian*, 15 November 1856).

[34] *History of the Hopedale Community* (1897) and volumes 2 and 3 of *Primitive Christianity and its Corruptions* (1899, 1900) were published posthumously, edited by William S. Heywood.

[35] The enactment establishing Communes was printed in the *Practical Christian*, 29 December 1855. Beginning on 9 February 1856, several issues carried an announcement of the formation of Commune No. 1 and an advertisement for its principal product, "Whipple's Patent Self-Acting Nipper Block," invented by Commune member Jonathan Whipple. The "Compact of Commune No. 1" was printed on 8 March 1856.

[36] Thomas Lake Harris (1823-1906) was the minister of the Fourth Universalist Society in New York City for a few years early in his career, 1844-47. He was one of several spiritualist Universalist ministers who resigned from fellowship when the New York Association of Universalists insisted that all members accept a creedal statement, "I sincerely declare that I receive the Bible as containing a special and sufficient revelation from God."

It was fortunate for Adin Ballou's peace of mind that he does not appear to have been familiar with Harris's career after leaving the ministry. In their community at Mountain Cove, Virginia, 1851-53, Harris and his partner James Leander Scott declared that they were the "two witnesses" mentioned in Revelation 11:3-13. They required their followers to sign over all their possessions and claimed the right to initiate the women into "spiritual intercourse." When Ballou visited him in 1856, Harris was back in New York as a Swedenborgian preacher. After 1860 he led a series of communities in New York and California, in which his followers lived in virtual slavery.

On the complex relationships between Universalism and spiritualism, including analyses of the careers of Thomas Lake Harris and Adin Ballou, see John B. Buescher, *The Other Side of Salvation: Spiritualism and the Nineteenth-Century Religious Experience* (Boston: Skinner House, 2004).

37 Ballou described his trip in "Excursion to Southold, N.Y.," *Practical Christian*, 4 October 1856. The Southold Universalist church, which had a series of spiritualist ministers dating back to the 1840s, was unusually hospitable to spiritualism. Ballou preached there during his visit. On the same occasion Thomas Lake Harris spoke "in his superior state" (i.e., while in a trance).

38 Zaccheus Goldsmith (1766-1835) and Joseph Hull Goldsmith (1799-1877) were descendants of a family with roots in Southold going back to the mid-seventeenth century. Joseph Goldsmith was an attorney, a founder of the Southold Savings Bank, and later treasurer of Suffolk Country. He was a spiritualist and an active member of the Universalist church in Southold. He had been a member of the Prince Street Universalist Church at the time that Adin Ballou was the minister there.

Chapter 21

1 Some memories of the Hopedale Home School are preserved in *Home School Memorial*, a commemorative booklet produced on the occasion of the Home School Reunion in 1867. It is reprinted in *Hopedale Reminiscences: Childhood Memories of the Hopedale Community and the Hopedale Home School* (Providence: Blackstone Editions, 2006).

2 See Isaiah 9:6; Matthew 5:39; Romans 12:21.

3 Ballou's lecture was published as *Lecture on the inspiration of the Bible: delivered in the town hall, Milford, Mass., Sunday evening, January 16, 1859*.

The five classes of "professed friends of the Bible" were: (1) those who admire its religious and literary merit, but lack a profound spiritual appreciation of it; (2) those, like Theodore Parker, who view it as one of many imperfect expressions of the universal human religious impulse; (3) those, like most Unitarians and Universalists, who see it as a subject for critical examination and study, on the grounds that this is the best way to rescue it from the attacks of unbelievers; (4) those, like the Swedenborgians, who believe that every word is inspired, but in an "internal" and "spiritual" sense that differs from the apparent sense; and (5) those who believe that every word is literally true, and that anyone who doubts this is an infidel.

4 Possibly the well-known Philadelphia clockmaker John Child (1789-1876).

5 The Hicksite-Orthodox split was a schism in the Society of Friends that took place around 1827. The Hicksites were followers of Elias Hicks (1748-1830), a liberal Quaker who opposed slavery and questioned (or at least attached little importance to) the divinity of Christ. The Hicksites were opposed by the Orthodox, who were more evangelical in religion and less interested in social issues.

6 Matthew 6:33.

7 Possibly Korlingen, a small village in western Germany near Trier.

8 Samuel Henry (1783-1860) was a Methodist minister until, as Adin Ballou wrote in his obituary, "his fidelity to divine principles rendered him unsuitable to work in a sectarian harness." He was active in the antislavery, temperance, and peace movements.

9 Effingham L. Capron (1791-1859), a textile manufacturer from Uxbridge, Massachusetts, was an a Garrisonian abolitionist and participated in the Underground Railroad. In 1838 he became the first president of the New England Non-Resistance Society.

[10] Stephen S. Foster (1809-1881) was one of the more radical of the abolitionists. Though he had once studied for the ministry, he came to believe that the churches were abettors of slavery. He wrote *The Brotherhood of Thieves; or A True Picture of the American Church and Clergy*, 1843. In 1845 Foster married fellow abolitionist and women's rights advocate Abby Kelley. Though generally a non-resistant, he wrote *Revolution the Only Remedy for Slavery*, 1855, in which he advocated slave rebellion and overthrow of the United States government.

[11] Andrew T. Foss, Charles L. Remond, and Thomas W. Higginson were abolitionists who advocated disunion, or the separation of the slave and free states into two separate nations, as a way of preventing the slaveholding south from imposing its will on the northern states.

Andrew T. Foss (1803-1875) was a Baptist minister who left the ministry to devote full time to the antislavery movement. In the late 1850s he became an outspoken advocate of disunion, calling the government of the United States "blasphemous and infamous" and the nation a "disgrace to humanity [that] should be dashed to pieces for ever."

Charles L. Remond (1810-1873) was one of the first African American antislavery speakers, on the lecture circuit beginning in the 1830s. In the late 1850s he called for all northerners to "buckle on our knapsacks and shoulder our muskets" in defense of freedom. "If the result... must be bloodshed, so be it! If it must be the dissolution of the Union, so be it!"

Thomas W. Higginson (1823-1911) was a Unitarian minister who advocated violent resistance against slavery. He organized the Worcester Disunion Convention in 1857. He was one of the "Secret Six" who financed John Brown's raid.

[12] This is a paraphrase of Garrison's speech on December 16, 1859. The speech included the following:

> A word upon the subject of Peace. I am a non-resistant – a believer in the inviolability of human life, under all circumstances; I, therefore, in the name of God, disarm John Brown, and every slave at the South. But I do not stop there ... I also disarm, in the name of God, every slaveholder and tyrant in the world ... I am a non-resistant, and I not only desire, but have labored unremittingly to effect the peaceful abolition of slavery, by an appeal to the reason and conscience of the slaveholder; yet, as a peace man – an "ultra" peace man – I am prepared to say, "Success to every slave insurrection at the South, and in every slave country." And I do not see how I compromise or stain my peace profession in making that declaration ... I thank God when men who believe in the right and duty of wielding carnal weapons are so far advanced that they will take those weapons out of the scale of despotism, and throw them into the scale of freedom. It is an indication of progress, and a positive moral growth; it is one way to get up to the sublime platform of non-resistance; and it is God's method of dealing retribution upon the head of the tyrant.

[13] From the Declaration of Sentiments adopted by the Peace Convention, 1838.

[14] John 18:36.

[15] John Boyden (1809-1869) was the Universalist minister in Woonsocket, Rhode Island, 1840-69. He was a champion of public education, temperance, antislavery, women's rights, labor reform, and alternative medicine.

Samuel May Jr. (1810-1899), the cousin of Ballou's close friend Samuel J. May, was the first minister of the Unitarian church in Leicester, Massachusetts, 1835-1846. He then resigned to work full time for the antislavery movement, but continued to live in Leicester.

Robert Hassall (1821-1900) was the Unitarian minister in Mendon, 1852-56. He served as a chaplain during the Civil War. He moved to Iowa in 1863.

George Hill (1825-1896) was a Universalist minister, active in reform causes. He served Universalist churches in three Massachusetts towns: West Cambridge (now Arlington), 1850-60; Milford, 1860-65; and Norwood, 1865-83. In 1885-86 he edited the *Universalist Register*.

[16] The Hutchinson Family Singers were popular performers from the 1840s to the 1880s. Originally composed of three brothers and a sister from Milford, New Hampshire, the group later included other brothers and sisters, and the children and grandchildren of the original members. Because their songs often dealt with social issues such as abolition, temperance, and women's rights, the Hutchinsons are sometimes considered forerunners of the twentieth century's "protest" singer-songwriters.

[17] George W. Burnham (1810-c.1895) was one of the organizers of the Universalist church in Willimantic, Connecticut, in the 1840s. During the 1860s the church was transformed into the First Spiritualist Church of Willimantic (still in existence in 2016). Burnham was one of the leaders of this church and served as president of the Connecticut Spiritualist Society.

[18] Miles Grant (1819-1911) was converted to belief in the Second Advent during the Millerite excitement in 1842 (see chapter 13, note 34). Although the date predicted by William Miller came and went, Grant continued to believe in and to preach the imminent second advent. In 1850 he gave up his job as a teacher to devote himself full time to preaching. He became one of the most prominent adventist preachers, and an active participant in controversies with leaders of other adventist sects.

[19] Lucy Florence Heywood graduated from New York Teachers College in 1892. The same year she married John Holden, a New York attorney. They had two children, Heywood and Constance Holden.

[20] Bryan Butts joined the Hopedale Community in 1852 and worked as a writer and printer for the *Practical Christian*. After the *Practical Christian* ceased publication, Butts and his wife, Harriet N. Greene, bought the press. Between 1860 and 1866 they issued a series of periodicals with names like *The Spiritual Reformer*, *The Progressive Age*, and *The Modern Age*.

[21] Charles H. Foster (1838-1888) had great success as a medium, especially around the time of Ballou's visit. In 1861, he toured Europe and Australia, appearing before eminent people such as Dickens, Thackeray, Tennyson, and Napoleon III. In 1863, however, the editor of *Spiritual* magazine claimed to have such "sickening details of his criminality ... that we should no longer soil our pages with his mediumship."

Foster's "pellet reading" has been explained as a conjuring trick; one exposé detailed how he surreptitiously read the paper pellets while pretending to light his cigar. His "skin writing" remains mysterious. It has been suggested that he had a skin condition known as dermographic urticaria, in which pressure on the skin causes raised red welts.

[22] Emanuel Newton Paine (1813-1860) was the husband of Adin Ballou's cousin Rachel E. Ballou, daughter of Rev. Barton Ballou (see chapter 1, note 31). In the *Genealogy*, Adin Ballou described the Paines as "choice personal friends."

[23] David Stearns Godfrey (1811-1853) was a leading citizen of Milford, instrumental in bringing the railroad to Milford in 1848. In *History of the Town of Milford*, Ballou remembered Godfrey for "his friendly regard for myself from his boyhood to the close of life" and

for "procuring a valuable portrait of me... which, just before his death, he donated to the Hopedale Community." Hence the choice of the code-word "Portrait."

24 1 Corinthians 7:22; Romans 13:8.

Chapter 22

1 The 1896 edition of the *Autobiography* has 1862. The Home School actually closed in 1863, as attested by *Home School Memorial: A Reunion of Teachers and Pupils of the Hopedale Home School* (1868).

2 Committee members Jerome Wilmarth (1831-1890) and Nancy Whipple Lewers (c.1830-1894) were both members of prominent Hopedale families. Jerome Wilmarth was the son of Hopedale's beloved physician, Butler Wilmarth, whose death in a train accident in 1853 had been such a blow to the Community (see chapter 20). Jerome was married to Abby Munyan, daughter of charter member Lemuel Munyan. Nancy Lewers had two sisters, two first cousins, and an uncle at Hopedale, as well as other, more distant relatives.

3 Garrison's opposition to the Sabbath was twofold: he objected to it as hypocritical and legalistic, but he also disliked it on the grounds that it encouraged the "mischievous delusion ... that we are to give one-seventh portion of our time to God, and the rest we may devote to 'secular' matters!" (Letter to Edward Morris Davis, 1848).

4 Mark 2:27.

5 Note that, although this text is in quotation marks, is taken not from Garrison's address, but from Adin Ballou's paraphrase in Ballou's own letter of July 9. We do not know what Garrison actually said in Hopedale, but presumably it was similar to his recorded speeches on the subjects in question. One clue is Ballou's use of the phrase "all the other books in the world." In his speech "The Divine Authority of the Bible," published in *Selections from the Writings and Speeches of William Lloyd Garrison* (Boston, 1852), Garrison said, "Truth ... would still exist, though a universal conflagration should consume all the books in the world." In the same speech, Garrison said that the Bible was "written nobody knows by whom" – another phrase that Ballou remembered. It is probable, therefore, that his talk in Hopedale was a version of "The Divine Authority of the Bible."

Though Garrison expressed himself in a forceful and provocative manner, his views, as expressed in "The Divine Authority of the Bible," are less hostile to the Bible than Ballou's summary would suggest. His major point is that the Bible is not one work but a composite of many, capable of being cited in support of a wide variety of views (including support of slavery), and that therefore "it is the province of reason to 'search the scriptures' and determine what in them is true and what false" – a proposition with which Adin Ballou would not disagree. The speech ends with an expression of respect and admiration for the Bible:

> I am fully aware how grievously the priesthood have perverted the Bible, and wielded it both as an instrument of spiritual despotism and in opposition to the sacred cause of humanity; still, to no other volume do I turn with so much interest, no other do I consult or refer to so frequently, to no other am I so indebted for light and strength, no other is so identified with the growth of human freedom and progress ... it embodies an amount of excellence so great as to make it, in my estimation, THE BOOK OF BOOKS.

6 The summer of 1862, when Ballou took Garrison to task for his willingness to "petition, advise, and strenuously urge a pro-war government to abolish slavery by the war power," was a particularly critical moment in the fight against slavery. After more than a year of

war, the abolition of slavery had not been accomplished, or even accepted as a war aim. "My paramount object," President Lincoln wrote that summer, "is to save the Union ... If I could save the union without freeing any slave I would do it, and if I could save it by freeing all the slaves I would do it; and if I could save it by freeing some and leaving others alone, I would also do that." The abolitionists' task, therefore, was to convince the government that emancipation was a military necessity.

Ballou saw any cooperation with the war effort as a betrayal of the principles of non-resistance. Garrison saw it differently. He did not advocate war, but once the war had begun, he accepted it as divine retribution for the sin of slavery. He quoted Jeremiah 34:17: "Ye have not hearkened unto me in proclaiming liberty every one to his brother ... behold I proclaim a liberty for you, saith the Lord, to the sword, to the pestilence, and to the famine." It was too late to avoid war; all that remained was to redeem the suffering by using the war to abolish slavery. Garrison was prepared do whatever he could to bring about this result, even if it meant speaking the language of politics and war instead of the language of moral suasion.

The fortunes of war and politics kept the issue in doubt throughout the summer. After the hard-fought Union victory in the battle of Antietam, the President felt that the time was right. He issued the Emancipation Proclamation on September 22, 1862. As of January 1, 1863, all slaves in the rebellious states would be "thenceforth and forever free."

[7] In accusing Garrison of "Jesuitical" reasoning, Ballou was reviving an old conflict between case-based and rule-based moral reasoning. The Jesuits were known for case-based reasoning, or "casuistry," which is based on the idea that right and wrong can only be evaluated in a specific context, taking into account such factors as the intent of the actors and the outcome of the action. Expressions similar to "the end sanctifies the means" are found in the work of seventeenth-century Jesuit casuists such as Vincenzo Filliucci (1566-1622), who wrote *finis comparando media* (the end should establish the means), and Hermann Busenbaum (1600-1668), who wrote *cum finis est licitus, etiam media sunt licita* (if the end is lawful, then the means are lawful).

Though casuistry can be a valid form of moral reasoning (it is the basis of English common law, which is built up from precedents rather than deduced from first principles), it is often associated with specious but unsound special pleading. The idea of Jesuits as masters of casuistry, in this negative sense, was popularized by Blaise Pascal in *Les Provinciales* (1656-57), and was widely shared by Protestants.

[8] *Julius Caesar* 3.1.

[9] John 18:36.

[10] The color red has long been associated with revolution, especially in France. In the 1790s French revolutionaries wore the *bonnet rouge*. The red flag was used by the more radical revolutionaries in 1830 and 1848. In 1871 it was the banner of the Paris Commune, which Karl Marx and Friedrich Engels considered to be the first "dictatorship of the proletariat." After 1871 the term "red revolution" began to take on its modern connotation of a specifically Communist revolution. Here, however, Ballou was probably using it in its older sense, as a general term for any attempt to achieve social change by violent means.

[11] Romans 12:14.

[12] The Enrollment Act of 1863, the first conscription law in the history of the United States, permitted draftees to supply a substitute or pay a "commutation fee" of $300 in lieu of serving. There was no formal provision for conscientious objectors. In 1864 the act was

amended to allow members of historic peace churches, such as the Quakers and Mennonites, to perform alternative service such as nursing in military hospitals. At the same time, the option of paying a commutation fee was restricted to members of these churches.

[13] John Lowell Heywood (1830-c.1900), one of five younger brothers of Ballou's son-in-law William S. Heywood, joined the Hopedale Community in 1854. In 1855 he was one of four men from Hopedale who went to Union Grove, Minnesota, in an ill-fated effort to establish a new community there. His wife joined him there the next spring. At some point between 1857 and 1860 the Heywoods returned to Hopedale. Around 1870 they went west again and settled in Aurora, Illinois.

[14] According to the terms of the Enrollment Act, a draftee who failed to report for duty or provide an acceptable substitute "shall be deemed a deserter, and shall be arrested by the provost-marshal and sent to the nearest military post for trial by court-martial." In practice, this rarely happened. Men who claimed conscientious scruples against fighting were usually exempted informally by their local enrollment boards. Even those who simply failed to respond to the draft notice were rarely prosecuted. The seriousness of the threat explains why Ballou counseled Heywood to pay the commutation fee, while the laxness of the enforcement explains why he later regretted having done so.

[15] Romans 13:1.

[16] Henry T. Child (1816-1890) was a Quaker physician, active in the temperance and antislavery movements beginning in the 1830s. In the 1850s he became interested in spiritualism. His enthusiasm cooled after he helped to expose two fraudulent mediums, though he retained his belief in the possibility of communication between the living and the dead. During the Civil War he helped to recruit volunteer doctors and nurses and to organize medical supplies. After the war he was active in disaster relief, providing medical care to victims of floods, earthquakes, and epidemics. He was one of the organizers of the Universal Peace Union and was for many years its secretary.

[17] Thomas Green Wiggins (1849-1908) was a blind African American pianist and composer. Born in slavery, at an early age he showed precocious musical talent and a remarkable auditory memory. When he was still a child, his owner began to exhibit him as "The Marvelous Musical Prodigy, Blind Tom." His act was immensely lucrative, but the proceeds all went to others. After the Civil War, though no longer enslaved, Tom was declared mentally incompetent and placed under the guardianship of various members of his former owner's family. His actual mental status is unclear. He is sometimes described as an autistic savant, whose performance was mostly a matter of mimicry. He was, however, capable of writing original compositions and improvising variations on popular tunes, which suggests that he was more than just a mimic.

Forgotten for nearly a century, in recent years the story of Blind Tom has attracted renewed attention because of the perplexing and disturbing questions it raises about race, class, and disability. He has been the subject of two biographies, a film, and a play. A recording of some of his compositions, *John Davis Plays Blind Tom*, was released in 1999.

[18] Andrew Leighton (c.1815-1877), a Liverpool merchant, was a prominent British spiritualist. In addition to many contributions to spiritualist journals, he wrote the introduction to the British edition of Ballou's *Spirit Manifestations*. His obituary in the *Spiritual Magazine* mentions "an interesting conversation he and other friends of [Adin Ballou] had with Mr. Ballou's son in spirit-life, Adin Augustus Ballou, through the mediumship of Mrs. Tappan"

(Cora Scott Hatch Tappan, a well-known medium who had lived in Hopedale for a short time as a child). After the trip on which he had made Ballou's acquaintance, Leighton wrote a series of articles entitled "Notes on Spiritualism and Spiritualists in the United States in 1866."

[19] Hopedale Unitarian Parish is still in existence as a member congregation of the Unitarian Universalist Association. Its current building dates from 1898 and was a gift of Eben S. Draper and George Albert Draper, two of the sons of George and Hannah Thwing Draper.

[20] *The Milford Directory: Containing a directory of the citizens, a business directory, and the town record: to which is added a history of Milford by Rev. Adin Ballou* (Milford, 1869).

[21] Volumes 2 and 3 of *Primitive Christianity and its Corruptions* were published posthumously in 1899 and 1900.

[22] The full text of "The Restorationist Secession," as printed in *The Universalist* (11 and 25 February 1871), is given in Appendix G.

[23] The late nineteenth century was a time of extraordinary theological diversity among Unitarians. Although most Unitarians thought of the denomination as Christian, there were some who did not identify as Christians and wanted to see Unitarianism redefined in purely ethical terms.

In moving beyond Christianity, these "radicals" were drawing on ideas in the Unitarian tradition as well as in the larger culture. One inspiration was Theodore Parker's idea of Christianity as one of many manifestations of Absolute Religion – a perception that was heightened by historical criticism of the Bible and by a growing awareness of other world religions. The theory of evolution put humankind in perspective as one species among many, and also displayed the impressive ability of science to explain natural phenomena. All of these factors combined to make science seem potent and exciting, while religion seemed to be a spent force.

At the time the radicals were a rather marginalized minority in Unitarianism. Frustrated by the lukewarm reception of their ideas by the National Conference of Unitarian Churches, they formed their own organization, the Free Religious Association, in 1867. But if the Unitarians, as a body, did not embrace the radicals' ideas, neither did they exclude them. Like Theodore Parker before them, the radicals challenged the Unitarian establishment to widen the circle of their inclusiveness. Eventually the ideas that had seemed so radical in the 1860s became the mainstream of twentieth-century Unitarianism and Unitarian Universalism.

[24] See Luke 2:49.

[25] The Universal Peace Society (after 1868, the Universal Peace Union) was founded at a Peace Convention held in Boston in 1866. The organizing committee included Adin Ballou, William S. Heywood, and Anna T. Draper. In contrast to the American Peace Society, which focused on the prevention of international war and had supported the Union cause in the Civil War, the new organization rejected any use of deadly force, offensive or defensive, by individuals or by nations.

The UPU had a broad definition of peace that included the elimination of all forms of inequality and injustice. It supported a broad range of peace and justice initiatives, including disarmament, international courts and arbitration, equal rights for women and minorities, temperance, and prison reform. An important focus in the postwar years was the struggle to secure justice for Native Americans. The "Moral Aid Department" offered counselling to families at risk for domestic violence. It also tried, with less success, to mediate labor disputes.

Most of the members of the UPU were Christian perfectionists: besides the Practical Christians, many belonged to pacifist sects such as the Shakers and the Progressive Friends. However, the organization voted, over Adin Ballou's objections, not to adopt any creedal test for membership (this may be what he meant by "objectionable complications").

Membership in the UPU peaked in the 1880s. By 1900 it was in decline, partly because of the unpopularity of its opposition to the Spanish-American War, and partly because the generation of pre-Civil War reformers was passing away. The UPU was disbanded in 1920.

[26] With the passage of the Fifteenth Amendment in 1870, the American Anti-Slavery Society declared its work done and voted to disband. However, many abolitionists continued to work on behalf of former slaves, particularly in the area of education. In the early postwar years, secular freedmen's aid associations worked alongside orthodox and evangelical missionary societies to establish elementary schools for African Americans throughout the South. These schools were eventually absorbed into state public school systems, leaving less need for small-scale educational philanthropy. By 1880 most secular and liberal reformers had redirected their energies to other reform movements such as women's rights and the labor movement. The missionary societies of the Congregationalists, Presbyterians, Baptists, and Methodists remained important contributors to higher education for African Americans, well into the twentieth century.

[27] The post-Civil War period saw the rise of several anti-alcohol organizations: the Prohibition Party in 1869 (see chapter 19, note 12); the Catholic Total Abstention Union in 1872; and the Women's Christian Temperance Union in 1874. Though moral suasion and education continued to be important, increasingly the emphasis was on legal prohibition of the manufacture and sale of alcoholic beverages.

[28] When the National Women's Rights Convention, which had met annually from 1850 to 1860, began meeting again in 1866, hopes were high that the Fifteenth Amendment to the Constitution would extend voting rights to women as well as to men of all races. To express its commitment to universal suffrage, the organization changed its name to the American Equal Rights Association. When the amendment turned out to prohibit the restriction of voting rights on the basis of "race, color, or previous condition of servitude" – but not on the basis of gender – advocates of women's rights faced a difficult decision. The Equal Rights Association split into two bodies: the American Woman Suffrage Association (AWSA), which reluctantly supported the amendment, and the National Woman Suffrage Association (NWSA), led by Elizabeth Cady Stanton and Susan B. Anthony, which opposed it. (The two merged in 1890 to form the National American Woman Suffrage Association.)

During the 1870s and 1880s the AWSA carried on a state-by-state campaign for changes to the voting laws. The more radical NWSA continued to press for a constitutional amendment. It also took on social issues such as liberalization of the laws governing marriage and divorce. None of these developments appealed to Ballou, since he did not believe in voting and was horrified by anything that reminded him of "free love."

[29] When he said that working people's "trust was in legislation and governmental coercion," Ballou was probably thinking of the National Labor Union (NLU), a coalition of unions and other workers' groups that was organized in 1866. Less a labor union than a political action group, the NLU campaigned for the eight-hour day, child labor laws, and other workplace reforms. In 1872 the NLU sponsored a political party, the National Labor Reform party, which nominated a candidate for president. The NLU was dissolved in 1873 without having achieved any of its goals.

Chapter 23

[1] Albert St. John Chambré (c.1830-1911) was born in England and immigrated to the United States around 1850. He studied for the Universalist ministry with Sylvanus Cobb, 1853-54. He served the Universalist church in Newark, New Jersey, 1856-62, and was a chaplain in a New Jersey regiment during the Civil War. He served Universalist churches in Stoughton, 1864-72, and Franklin, Massachusetts, 1872-80. He wrote *A Gospel Catechism for Sunday Schools*, 1869, and lectured on ecclesiastical history at Tufts College, 1875-76. He received an honorary Doctor of Divinity degree from Tufts in 1878. In 1881 he left the Universalist fellowship and joined the Episcopal Church. He served St. Anne's Church (Episcopal) in Lowell, Massachusetts, from 1883 until his death in 1911.

[2] Chambré's review certainly treated Ballou's work severely. The final sentence of the review is, "As a whole, and as designed in behalf of Christianity, to exhibit the corruptions of theology, and to present Christian truth, this volume is one of the most unsatisfactory we have ever examined." While conceding that "a good deal of research is manifested on the part of the author, and no little reading upon the general topics treated," Chambré criticized Ballou for being both too credulous and too skeptical – too credulous as regards spiritualism and spiritual entities, and too skeptical with regard to the miraculous birth of Jesus.

In his introduction Ballou explained that, although he considered the scriptures of the New Testament reliable as to essentials, he placed the birth narratives in Matthew and Luke among the inessentials that he felt free to disregard. "The supernatural is suspiciously excessive in them, and they are strongly mythical in their remarkable aspects. They have the air of exaggerated and uncertain traditions, or of apocryphal stories, designed – piously perhaps – to make or strengthen converts." Chambré objected to this on the grounds that any attempt to "dismember the gospels" would end by destroying the credibility of the Bible and Christianity generally.

When it came to Ballou's section on "angelology and demonology," however, it was Chambré who reinterpreted the Bible along rationalistic lines, and Ballou who insisted that it ought to be taken at face value. As in his writings on spiritualism, Ballou tried to find a middle ground between the extremes of credulity and skepticism. He was critical of some spiritualists (and some Catholics) for attaching too much importance to spiritual entities, but he thought it just as irrational categorically to deny their existence. To believe in a range of spiritual intelligences, some higher and some lower than humankind, seemed most consistent both with the teachings of Bible and with his own experiences.

[3] The Immaculate Conception is a dogma of the Catholic Church maintaining that, from the moment when she was conceived in the womb, the Virgin Mary was free of original sin. Ballou was aware of this when he wrote *Primitive Christianity and its Corruptions*, for he wrote: "The Council of Trent, held in the sixteenth century, decreed that 'the blessed and immaculate Mary, the Mother of God, is exempt from all sin, actual and original.' The present Pope, Pius IX, in 1854, proclaimed the immaculate conception of the Virgin Mary to be an established doctrine of the Roman Catholic Church." Yet when he wrote the *Autobiography* he seemed to have forgotten this, using the term "immaculate conception" as a synonym for the virgin birth of Jesus.

[4] Matthew 5:14, 5:13, 10:16; John 15:19; Matthew 5:15, 5:13; see also Luke 11:33, 14:34.

[5] See Matthew 6:1-18.

NOTES TO CHAPTER 23

⁶ Matthew 23:8. The phrase translated as "even Christ," which more properly belongs in verse 10, is not included in the best manuscripts and is usually omitted today.

⁷ Matthew 5:34, 37; see also James 5:12.

⁸ Luke 6:46.

⁹ Quotations and references to Matthew 6:33; Hebrews 13:5 (quoting Deuteronomy 31:6, 8; Joshua 1:5, etc.); 2 Corinthians 12:9; Psalms 113:2, 23:4.

¹⁰ Adin Ballou Underwood (1828-1888) was born in Milford and named for Adin Ballou, who was the minister of the Universalist church in Milford at the time of Underwood's birth. At the outbreak of the Civil War, Underwood was practicing law in Boston. In May 1861 he was commissioned as a captain. By 1863 he had risen to the rank of colonel, commanding the 33rd Massachusetts Infantry in the battle of Gettysburg. After being wounded in the battle of Lookout Mountain in November 1863, he joined the staff of General Joseph Hooker and was eventually awarded the rank of Brevet Major General of Volunteers. After the war he was appointed Surveyor of the Port of Boston, a position he held until his death. He wrote a regimental history, *The Three Years' Service of the Thirty-third Mass. Infantry Regiment 1862-1865* (1881).

¹¹ George Thompson (1804-1878) first heard about the horrors of the slave trade from his father, who had been a clerk on a slave-trading ship. In 1831 he became an agent of the British Anti-Slavery Society. After slavery was abolished in the British Empire in 1833, he turned his attention to speaking out against slavery in the United States. He toured the United States in 1834-35, eventually having to flee for his life. Back in England he continued agitating for antislavery, peace, and other reform causes. From 1847 to 1852 he was Member of Parliament for Tower Hamlets (a borough of London). He made two more trips to the United States, in 1850 and 1864-65. Through his speaking engagements and his personal relationships with American abolitionists such as William Lloyd Garrison and Frederick Douglass, he formed an important link between the British and American antislavery movements.

¹² See Ephesians 6:12.

¹³ 2 Timothy 4:2.

¹⁴ The last words of John Quincy Adams in 1848: "This is the last of Earth. I am content." These words seem to have made a great impression at the time. They were used as the title of the chapter describing the death of Little Eva in *Uncle Tom's Cabin*.

¹⁵ The Grand Army of the Republic (G. A. R.) was a fraternal organization for veterans of the Union armed forces during the Civil War. At its peak in 1890 it had almost 500,000 members. It was dissolved in 1956 when the last member died.

The G. A. R. was organized into state Departments and local Posts. Major E. F. Fletcher Post 22 in Milford, organized in 1867, was named in honor of Major Emmons F. Fletcher (1835-1867). Fletcher enlisted in June 1861 as a private in a Milford company that formed part of the 40th New York Infantry. He was promoted rapidly, becoming an officer in November 1861 and reaching the rank of major in July 1863. He was wounded at the battle of Spottsylvania in May 1864 and mustered out of the service two months later. He died in 1867, at the age of 32, as a result of disease contracted during his military service.

[16] From "Hush the Loud Cannon's Roar," a hymn text by the British Unitarian minister John Johns (1801-1847).

[17] Jerome Wilmarth (1831-1890) was the son of doctors Butler Wilmarth and Phila Osgood Wilmarth. He was an 1866 graduate of Harvard Medical School, belonged to the Massachusetts Medical Society, and occasionally published a case history in the *New England Journal of Medicine*. In *History of the Town of Milford*, Ballou wrote of him:

> Dr. Jerome inherited the medical genius, taste, and aptitudes of his parents... He has established himself in Upton as a physician by over 15 years of acceptable practice. He is deservedly popular there, and throughout a wide circuit in this general vicinity. For, besides eminent skill, he carries into every sick-room a gentle and soothing magnetism, no less salutary and agreeable than medical competence. He is greatly beloved and trusted by his numerous patients.

[18] William Denton (1823-1883), a geologist, psychical researcher, writer, and lecturer, was the kind of "anti-Christian Spiritualist" that Ballou deplored. He was harshly critical of Christianity, maintaining that not even Jesus could (or should) live in accordance with the teachings of Jesus. He was a vigorous exponent of spiritualism, clairvoyance, and other psychic phenomena. His particular interest was "psychometry," the ability to sense information about the history of an object by handling it. His researches in this area are detailed in a three-volume work, *The Soul of Things*, written with his sister. He died in 1883 while conducting geological exploration in New Guinea.

[19] James A. Garfield (1831-1881) was elected President of the United States in 1880 and was assassinated after serving only four months of his term. Though Ballou disagreed with some of his policies, such as his championship of conscription during the Civil War and his harsh approach to "civilizing" the Indians, he probably admired Garfield's commitment to civil rights and education for African Americans. Racial justice and inclusiveness was a consistent theme of Garfield's nine terms in Congress and his short presidency. As president, he appointed several African Americans to public office, including Frederick Douglass as recorder of deeds in Washington.

Garfield was a member of the Ballou family (his mother, Eliza Ballou Garfield, was Adin Ballou's second cousin). In the *Genealogy*, Adin Ballou wrote:

> James Abram Garfield, late illustrious, martyred, and universally lamented President of the United States, needs no historic glorification from our pen. The nation, and we might almost say, the whole civilized world is familiar with his name, character and biography. It would seem little better than ostentatious affectation to attempt adorning these pages with a sketch of what he was, did and suffered. It is indelibly chronicled on thousands of public tablets, and in millions of memories.

[20] Charles Burlingame Waite (1824-1909) was an Illinois lawyer who served as associate justice of the Utah Supreme Court and as district attorney of Idaho. In 1866 he retired from the law to devote himself to historical research and writing. *History of the Christian Religion to the Year A. D. 200* (1881) is his best-known work.

[21] Latimer Whipple Ballou (1812-1900) was born in the "Ballou Neighborhood" in Cumberland, Rhode Island. When Adin taught at the district school in 1821-22 (see chapter 4), Latimer was one of his students. The "bright, docile, and lovable lad" grew up to be one of the leading citizens of Woonsocket, Rhode Island: a successful banker, a pillar of the Universalist church, and a prominent member of the Rhode Island Republican party. He served three terms in Congress, 1875-81, and received an honorary degree from Tufts College in 1887.

Chapter 24

[1] Ira Ballou Peck (1805-1888) was a well-to-do cotton manufacturer in Woonsocket, Rhode Island. He began work on the Ballou genealogy in 1846, but put it aside in 1850 to work on the Peck genealogy, which he completed in 1868.

[2] Adin Ballou noted in the preface to the *Genealogy* that Peck turned over his materials to Ariel and Latimer Ballou on condition that they "include, so far as practicable, the female branches of descent along with the male lineages."

[3] Adin Ballou used the same expression (not otherwise traced) in writing about the Hopedale cemetery in *History of the Hopedale Community*.

> Although no death had as yet occurred on our territory, yet it was deemed advisable early in the year 1845 that a suitable tract of land somewhere within our borders should be selected for burial purposes ... where, as time went on, all that was mortal of our dearly beloved was to be consigned ... and where we ourselves, or so many of us as continued to reside in Hopedale to the end of our days, should finally, as to our material frames, sleep the last long sleep of earth and time.

[4] *Oahspe: A New Bible* was written in 1881-82 by an American dentist and spiritualist medium, John Ballou Newbrough (1828-1891). (He was named in honor of Hosea Ballou but not related to the Ballou family.) Newbrough explained that *Oahspe* was "mechanically written [that is, written on a typewriter, then a new invention] through my hands by some other intelligence than my own." Its full name is *OAHSPE: A New Bible in the Words of Jehovih [sic] and His Angel Ambassadors. A Sacred History of the Dominions of the Higher and Lower Heavens on the Earth for the Past Twenty-Four Thousand Years together with a Synopsis of the Cosmogony of the Universe; the Creation of Planets; the Creation of Man; the Unseen Worlds; the Labor and Glory of Gods and Goddesses in the Etherean Heavens; with the New Commandments of Jehovih to Man of the Present Day*. Today there are a number of small groups of believers, called Faithists, who continue to draw inspiration from *Oahspe*.

[5] Hosea Ballou's *Treatise on Atonement* was hardly a topic of current interest. It had been eighty years since *Treatise on Atonement* was published, and fifty years since Adin Ballou had declared "Omega" to controversy with the ultra Universalists (see chapter 14). In all likelihood the subject was recalled to his mind by his correspondence with Richard Eddy about the Restorationist Controversy.

As is described later in this chapter, Eddy consulted Ballou while researching the subject for the second volume of his *Universalism in America*. The structure of the chapter somewhat obscures the sequence of events, since it places the section "Dr. Richard Eddy and the Restorationist Schism" between the dedication of the Hopedale town hall in 1887 and Ballou's correspondence with Tolstoy in 1889-90. However, since the two volumes of *Universalism in America* were published in 1884 and 1886, Eddy probably corresponded with Ballou in 1884-85, around the same time Ballou was writing about *Treatise on Atonement*.

[6] From John Milton's sonnet "To the Lord General Cromwell, on the Proposals of Certain Ministers at the Committee for the Propagation of the Gospel" (1652).

[7] This was probably a response to "The Mistakes of Christ Corrected," an essay in the freethought journal *The Truth Seeker* (November 1884). Its author, Washington Gladden (see Appendix C, note 1), was not a freethinker, but a well-known Congregational minister and leader of the Social Gospel movement.

⁸ Charles King Whipple (1808-1900) was an abolitionist, non-resistant, and advocate of women's rights. He held leadership roles in many reform organizations, including the New England Non-Resistance Society, American Missionary Association, New England Woman Suffrage Association, American Anti-Slavery Society, and Freedman's Union Commission. He was an important contributor to the *Liberator*, the *Anti-Slavery Standard*, and the *Non-Resistant*. He was particularly interested in Adin Ballou's idea of non-injurious force, and elaborated it in pamphlets such as *Non-Resistance Applied to the Internal Defense of the Community* (1860). However, even before the Civil War, Whipple showed willingness to compromise his non-resistance principles in the interest of freeing the slaves. In this he may have been influenced by his minister, Theodore Parker, a founder of the Boston Vigilance Committee and a supporter of John Brown. Whipple was a member of the Vigilance Committee and wrote a pamphlet in which he urged non-resistance but refused to condemn John Brown's actions.

⁹ The expression "peaceably if we can, forcibly if we must" had its origin in the Congressional debate over the admission of Louisiana as a state in 1811. New states had been created before, but this would be the first to extend the territorial limits of the United States established at the end of the Revolutionary War. Josiah Quincy III of Massachusetts, concerned about the extension of slavery, took the position that such expansion was unconstitutional – that it would, in fact, invalidate the existing compact among the states. He said "that if this bill passes, the bonds of this Union are virtually dissolved; that the States that compose it are free from their moral obligations; and that, as it will be the right of all, so it will be the duty of some, to prepare definitely for a separation, amicably if they can, violently if they must."

Two years later, the words reappeared in a Congressional debate on an entirely different subject: the raising of troops for War of 1812. Speaker of the House Henry Clay, a leading "war hawk," made a speech denouncing opponents of the war as unprincipled opportunists who put their own interests above the nation's. He singled out Josiah Quincy for particular censure, accusing him of being part of "a plot that aims at the dismemberment of our union." To back up this claim, Clay reminded the House of Quincy's secessionist speech: "The gentleman cannot have forgotten his own sentiment, uttered even on the floor of this House, 'Peaceably if we can, forcibly if we must.'"

Thus Quincy's formulation, polished by Clay's eloquence, entered American political discourse. It proved to be remarkably versatile. It could be used, as Quincy had used it, to threaten disunion – but it could also express determination to preserve the union at all costs. It could be applied to one's opponents, as Clay had applied it to Quincy, to portray them as irresponsible and dangerous extremists – but it could also be applied to one's own party, to express seriousness and resolve. Adin Ballou, of course, entirely rejected the idea that violence is justified if milder means have failed. He wrote in *Christian Non-Resistance*, "The truth is, that what cannot be done uninjuriously can scarcely ever be done at all."

¹⁰ D. Hamilton Hurd, ed., *History of Worcester County, Massachusetts: with biographical sketches of many of its pioneers and prominent men* (1889).

¹¹ George D. Robinson (1834-1896) was a lawyer and politician from Chicopee, Massachusetts. After serving four terms in Congress, 1877-84, he was elected Governor of Massachusetts, 1884-87. Upon retiring from politics he returned to his law practice. He achieved some notoriety as one of the defense lawyers in the famous Lizzie Borden murder trial in 1892.

[12] John D. Long (1838-1915) was Governor of Massachusetts, 1880-83. He later served as Secretary of the Navy under President William McKinley, a period that included the Spanish-American War.

[13] Richard Eddy (1828-1906) was a Universalist minister and historian. Over his fifty-year career he served Universalist churches in New York, Pennsylvania, Ohio, and Massachusetts. His longest pastorates were at Gloucester, 1870-77, and Melrose, Massachusetts, 1881-89. His interest in Universalist history dated to his student days. He was president of the Universalist Historical Society for nearly 30 years, 1877-1906. His major work, *Universalism in America* (2 volumes, 1884 and 1886), was the standard work on the subject until the publication of Russell Miller's *The Larger Hope* in 1970. Eddy's chapter on the Restorationist Controversy, over 80 pages long, was the first detailed, non-partisan account of the event and its significance.

[14] The book that Adin Ballou read, *My Religion* (also known as *What I Believe*), was the first of Tolstoy's works to be published in English, in 1885. His major novels, *War and Peace* (published in Russia in 1869) and *Anna Karenina* (1875), were both published in English in 1886.

[15] Lewis Gilbert Wilson (1858-1928) was the Unitarian minister in Leicester, Massachusetts, 1883-85, then in Hopedale, 1885-1904. After leaving Hopedale he served as Secretary of the American Unitarian Association, 1908-15, and as its Editorial Secretary, 1915-20. He returned to parish ministry in Westboro, Massachusetts, 1920-24.

[16] Tolstoy admired Adin Ballou more than Ballou admired him. Andrew Dickson White, who served as the United States Minister to Russia, 1892-94, related in his autobiography this conversation with Tolstoy:

> I then asked who, in the whole range of American literature, he thought the foremost. To this he made an answer which amazed me, as it would have astonished my countrymen. Indeed, did the eternal salvation of all our eighty millions depend upon some one of them guessing the person he named, we should all go to perdition together. That greatest of American writers was – Adin Ballou! Evidently, some of the philanthropic writings of that excellent Massachusetts country clergyman and religious communist had pleased him, and hence came the answer.

[17] The complete correspondence between Ballou and Tolstoy is given in Appendix H.

[18] William H. Humphrey (1805-1883), a carpenter, and his wife, Almira Brown Humphrey (1810-1880), joined the Hopedale Community in 1849. Both held many responsible offices in the Community. William Humphrey was the Community's last president, serving from 1863 to 1868.

The Humphreys were known for being generous and hospitable. In *Hopedale Reminiscences*, Susan Thwing Whitney recalled, "In the early Hopedale days, when a stranger came to the place, he was directed to Mr. William Humphrey's for food and lodging." She related a charming story about the night the Humphreys found a prowler in their house: a "poor, half-witted fellow, whom the Humphreys had recently fed, doctored, and otherwise befriended," and who had returned to steal the dining-room silver.

> Later, when some one asked Mrs. Humphrey if she didn't feel real provoked with him for returning all their kindness in that way, she, the dear, kind-hearted woman, replied, "Why, no; I felt as if I wanted to take him right in my arms."

[19] Charles Henry Eaton (1852-1902), a prominent Universalist minister, was the son of Rev. Henry A. Eaton (1826-1861), minister of the Universalist church in Milford, 1849-53. Henry Eaton and his wife Susan both died young, of tuberculosis. Charles and his twin sister Mary Anna were cared for in Hopedale, first in the family of Ichabod Davis, 1861-66, then adopted by Ebenezer and Anna Draper. Charles attended Tufts College and divinity school. He served as minister to the Universalist church in Palmer, Massachusetts, 1877-81, and the Church of the Divine Paternity (Fourth Universalist Church) in New York City, 1881-1902. In 1908 Eaton Hall, the first library building at Tufts, was endowed in Eaton's memory by his parishioner Andrew Carnegie.

[20] Emil Otto Grundmann (1844-1890) was a German-American artist and art educator. In 1876 he became the first director of the School of the Boston Museum of Fine Arts.

[21] Grundmann's portrait of Adin Ballou is still displayed in the Howard Smith Trustees' Room of the Bancroft Memorial Library in Hopedale. The frontispiece of this book shows a photograph of the painting.

[22] John 9:4.

[23] Ballou's birthday reflection includes quotations from or references to Psalms 103:2, 23:6; Hebrews 13:5; James 1:17; Romans 11:36.

[24] The original edition has "John the Evangelist." Freemasons honor St. John the Baptist on June 24 and St. John the Evangelist on December 27. Since Ballou's last public appearance took place in June, it must have been associated with John the Baptist, not John the Evangelist.

[25] Translation of *Mens sana in corpore sano*, from *Satire X* of the Roman poet Juvenal.

[26] On Thomas Lake Harris, see chapter 20, note 36.

[27] Sarah Jane Farnum Hatch (1831-1906) joined the Hopedale Community in January 1856. She and her husband, George O. Hatch, were among the 15 members of Commune No. 1 (see chapter 20, note 35).

[28] Possibly a reference to Hebrews 4:9-10: "There remaineth therefore a rest to the people of God. For he that is entered into his rest, he also hath ceased from his own works, as God did from his."

[29] William F. Draper (1842-1910) was the son of George and Hannah Thwing Draper. He was educated in the Hopedale Community but, like his father, he was not a pacifist. He enlisted in the Union army as a private in 1861 and rose to the rank of lieutenant colonel. At the end of the war he was awarded the rank of Brevet Brigadier General of Volunteers. After the war he went into business with his father and patented over fifty improvements to textile manufacturing machinery. He became president of the Draper Corporation in 1896. He was elected to Congress, 1893-97, and was appointed U. S. Ambassador to Italy, 1897-99.

[30] Eben Draper Bancroft (1847-1925) was the son of Joseph and Sylvia Thwing Bancroft, one of the leading families of the Hopedale Community. Beginning as an accountant in the firm of his uncles, George and Ebenezer Draper, he eventually became a director and held several offices in the corporation. When Hopedale became a town in 1886, he was its first treasurer. He was an active member of the Freemasons and of the Hopedale Unitarian Parish, which he served as treasurer. He was the campaign manager for the Congressional campaigns of his cousin, Gen. William F. Draper.

[31] Origen B. Young (1837-c.1920) was an organist and music teacher in Milford. He had a long association with Hopedale, including a stint as a music teacher at the Hopedale Home School. One of the contributors to *Hopedale Reminiscences*, Nellie T. Gifford, remembered him as a teenager in the mid-1850s, playing the melodeon to accompany a vocal trio that included Nellie's brother Charles and Origen's brother George.

[32] John Greenleaf Whittier's poem "The Eternal Goodness" (1865) presents an argument for the goodness and mercy of God, in the form of an imagined debate with an orthodox Calvinist opponent. "I trace your lines of argument / Your logic linked and strong," the poet says. "But still my human hands are weak / To hold your iron creeds. / Against the words ye bid me speak / My heart within me pleads."

Whittier once explained that he was not a universalist, because he believed in "the possibility of the perpetual loss of the soul that persistently turns away from God." But he did believe "that the divine love and compassion follow us in all worlds, and that the heavenly Father will do the best that is possible for every creature that he has made." Presumably the reading at the funeral would have been taken from the verses expressing this faith, rather than from the more argumentative passages.

[33] George S. Ball (1822-1902) was the Unitarian minister in Upton, Massachusetts, for more than forty years, 1850-92. His pastorate was interrupted by service as interim minister in Plymouth, Massachusetts, 1855-57, and as a chaplain in the Civil War, 1861-62. He was also active in state politics. As a member of the Republican party, he served in the Massachusetts House of Representatives, 1865-66 and 1891-92, and the State Senate, 1866-67. In 1870 he was the Prohibition Party's candidate for Massachusetts Secretary of State.

[34] Not Ballou's close friend Samuel J. May, but his cousin Samuel May Jr. See chapter 21, note 15.

[35] Hebrews 12:1.

[36] Carlton A. Staples (1827-1904) had a 50-year career as a Unitarian minister, much of it in the Midwest: at Meadville, Pennsylvania, 1854-57; as assistant to W. G. Eliot in St. Louis, 1857-61; as chaplain in a Missouri regiment, 1861-62; and in Milwaukee, 1862-68. From 1866 to 1869, as Secretary of the Western Unitarian Conference, he presided over the founding of 28 Unitarian churches. He was the first minister of Third Unitarian Church in Chicago, 1869-72. He returned to New England when he was called to the First Unitarian Church of Providence, 1872-81. His final pastorate was his longest: 23 years in Lexington, Massachusetts, 1881-1904. In Lexington he developed a strong interest in local history: he was a founder of the Lexington Historical Society, led the campaign to preserve John Hancock's house and install historical markers throughout the town, and organized the celebration of the 125th anniversary of the Battle of Lexington.

[37] Frank E. Mathewson (1848-c.1920) was Master of Montgomery Lodge, 1889-90. Elbert W. Whitney (1849-c.1930), the minister of the Universalist church in Milford, was chaplain of Montgomery Lodge, 1893-1908.

[38] John Greenleaf Whittier, "In Remembrance of Joseph Sturge" (1859).

Appendix A

[1] Job 5:26.

[2] See Psalms 126:6.

3   2 Timothy 4:6-8.

4   Possibly a reference to Felicia Hemans, "Gertrude, or Fidelity Till Death" (1828): "I have been with thee in thine hour / Of glory and of bliss; / Doubt not its memory's living power / To strengthen me thro' *this*!"

5   See Hebrews 11:4.

6   Acts 17:28.

7   John 14:6.

8   See Proverbs 3:3, 7:3; Jeremiah 17:1; 2 Corinthians 3:3.

9   1 Thessalonians 5:21.

10 See John 14:2.

11 Matthew 13:46.

12 See 1 Corinthians 13:13.

13 Acts 28:22.

14 Hebrews 12:1, 22.

15 Matthew 6:10.

16 Luke 2:14.

17 Matthew 11:26; Luke 10:21.

18 Frances Laughton Mace, "Only Waiting" (1854). The poem was set to music as a popular song in the 1860s and as a hymn in the 1870s.

19 1 Corinthians 2:9.

20 John Tyndall (1820-1893) was a British physicist and author who aimed to make the latest scientific discoveries accessible to nonspecialist readers. The quotation is from Tyndall's 1868 biography of the scientist Michael Faraday (1791-1867). Tyndall admired Faraday despite their differing views on the relationship between science and religion: Tyndall was concerned to maintain a clear distinction between the two, whereas Faraday was an evangelical Christian who considered his faith an integral part of his scientific work.

21 Philippians 1:21.

22 Psalms 95:4.

23 Reference to Percy Bysshe Shelley, *Prometheus Unbound* (1820): "from Heaven's star-fretted domes / To the dull weed some sea-worm battens on."

24 Philippians 4:8.

25 Numbers 23:10.

26 George Lovell Cary (1830-1910) was born and brought up in Medway, Massachusetts. After graduating from Harvard in 1852, he became professor of Greek and Latin at Antioch College, 1856-62. He was professor of New Testament Literature at Meadville Theological School, 1862-1902, and president of Meadville Theological School, 1890-1902. During his tenure as president, Meadville instituted the Adin Ballou Lectureship (see appendix C).

27 Charles J. White (1836-1906) was the minister of the Universalist church in Woonsocket, Rhode Island, for 34 years, 1870-1904. Prior to entering the ministry he was a schoolteacher, and he retained a strong interest in education. He was Superintendent of

Schools in Woonsocket, 1871-86, and served on the Rhode Island Board of Education. He was instrumental in founding the Woonsocket Day Nursery to care for the children of factory workers.

[28] Reference to *Henry V* 4.3: "Then shall our names / Familiar in his mouth as household words / ... [be] freshly remembered."

[29] Paraphrase of Jesus's prayer in Gethsemane; see Matthew 26:39, 42.

[30] Psalms 116:15; Job 5:26.

[31] See John 4:38.

[32] James Shirley (1596-1666), "Death the Leveller."

[33] Alvin Freeman Bailey (1840-1918) was born in Illinois and grew up in western New York State. Following Civil War service, 1861-62, he attended Meadville Theological School. He served small churches in western New York, 1867-74, and Indianapolis, 1875-78. His thirty-year pastorate in Barre, Massachusetts, was his first and only settlement in the East.

[34] Austin Samuel Garver (1849-1918) went to a Lutheran college and a Calvinist seminary, and served an orthodox Congregational church before becoming a Unitarian in 1880. His first settlement as a Unitarian was as Adin Ballou's successor as minister in Hopedale, 1881-85. After leaving Hopedale he spent the remainder of his career at First Unitarian Church in Worcester, Massachusetts, 1885-1910. He was interested in art, art education, and the relationship between art and spirituality. In Worcester he gave lectures on art and helped found the city's art museum.

[35] Grindall Reynolds (1822-1894) was secretary of the American Unitarian Association, 1881-94. Before that he was the Unitarian minister in Concord, Massachusetts, 1858-81. He was an amateur historian and wrote articles on the history of Concord, the American Revolution, and the history of American Unitarianism.

[36] In the York Rite (also known as the American Rite) form of Freemasonry, the Knights Templar is the highest ranking order. It is open to Masons who have attained the Royal Arch degree and who profess a belief in the Christian religion (unlike most Masonic bodies, which require only belief in a Supreme Being). A Commandery is a local division of Knights Templar.

[37] *Julius Caesar* 5.5.

[38] *Romeo and Juliet* 3.1.

[39] These are five of the eight "Principles of Theological Truth" set forth in *Practical Christian Socialism* (part 1, conversation 4).

[40] The Christian Socialism movement in mid-nineteenth-century Britain arose in response to the failure of Chartism, a working-class movement that advocated political reforms such as universal manhood suffrage, the secret ballot, and equal representation in Parliament. The Christian Socialists argued that the issues raised by the Chartists were moral issues calling for a Christian response.

The leader of the group was Frederick Denison Maurice (1805-1872). Although Maurice was the son of a Unitarian minister, he was ordained in the Church of England. He taught history, literature, and theology at Kings College London until he was dismissed in 1853 because of his unorthodox religious beliefs, including belief in universal salvation. A champion of liberal education for the working class, in 1848 he helped to found a teachers' training school, Queen's College. In the 1850s he worked with Thomas Hughes, Charles Kingsley, and other Christian Socialists to found the Working Men's College and became its first principal, 1854-72. In 1874 he co-founded a sister institution, the Working Women's College. In addition to his achievements as an educator, he is remembered today as an important theologian and a pioneer in the study of world religions.

Thomas Hughes (1822-1896) was a lawyer and a Liberal Member of Parliament, 1865-74. He succeeded F. D. Maurice as principal of the Working Men's College, 1872-83. He is best remembered for his novel *Tom Brown's School Days*, set at Rugby School. In 1880 he founded a utopian community, also called Rugby, in Tennessee, which lasted until 1887.

Charles Kingsley (1819-1875) was an Anglican clergyman, a professor of history at Cambridge University, and a chaplain to Queen Victoria. He acted as a spokesman for the Christian Socialist movement and published its journals, *Politics for the People* (1848-49) and *The Christian Socialist* (1850-51). During the last years of his life he was principal of the Birmingham and Midland Institute, a scientific and technical school for adults. Kingsley was also a novelist, best known for his historical novels *Westward Ho!* and *Hypatia*, and a moral fable, *The Water-Babies*.

[41] The *Banner of Light* was the best known spiritualist periodical in late nineteenth-century America. It was published weekly from 1857 to 1910.

[42] The *Christian Leader* was the principal Universalist publication during the late nineteenth century. It was the result of the merger of several Universalist newspapers and magazines, including the oldest, Hosea Ballou's *Universalist Magazine*, founded in 1819. After the consolidation of the Unitarians and Universalists in 1961, the *Leader* merged with the *Unitarian Register* to become the *Unitarian-Universalist Register-Leader*, which in turn developed into its current incarnation, the *UU World*.

[43] The *Christian Register* was the Unitarian counterpart of the Universalists' *Christian Leader*. It was published continuously from 1821 (four years before the founding of the American Unitarian Association) to 1961. The name was changed to the *Unitarian Register* in 1957.

[44] Adelaide Ann Procter, "A Tomb in Ghent" (1858).

[45] Combination of Matthew 25:40 and Matthew 25:21, 23.

Appendix B

[1] See 2 Corinthians 5:4.

[2] James 1:17.

[3] John 7:16.

[4] See Matthew 22:37-39.

[5] John 4:23-24.

[6] Luke 6:35.

[7] See Romans 12:17; 1 Thessalonians 5:15; 1 Peter 3:9.

[8] See Matthew 5:39.

[9] See Romans 12:21.

[10] 1 Peter 1:20.

[11] See Galatians 4:4.

[12] 2 Corinthians 5:19.

[13] 1 Corinthians 15:28.

[14] See Philippians 2:9-11.

[15] 1 John 4:1.

[16] See 1 Corinthians 12:31.

[17] Reference to the commentary on Acts 20:17-27 by the English Presbyterian minister Matthew Henry (1662-1714): "Believing that this was the last time [the elders of the church] should see him, [Paul] appeals concerning his integrity. He had preached to them the whole counsel of God. As he had preached to them the gospel purely, so he had preached it to them entire; he faithfully did his work, whether men would bear or forbear."

[18] See 2 Corinthians 5:1; 2 Peter 1:13-14.

[19] See Matthew 3:10; Luke 3:9. On the upas tree, see chapter 7, note 10.

[20] Luke 22:26.

[21] Matthew 25:30.

[22] See Revelation 3:19; John 8:11.

[23] Alexander Pope, "The Universal Prayer" (1738).

[24] Acts 20:24; see also 2 Timothy 4:7.

[25] See Psalms 31:5; Luke 23:46.

[26] See John 14:2.

[27] Reference to the hymn text "Reunion of Friends After Death" by British Unitarian minister Pendlebury Houghton (1758-1824):
> Blest be the hour when friends shall meet,
> Shall meet to part no more,
> And with celestial welcome greet,
> On an immortal shore.

"On that bright immortal shore / We shall meet to part no more" was, and is, a popular inscription on tombstones.

Appendix C

[1] Washington Gladden (1836-1918) was a Congregational minister and an early leader of the Social Gospel movement. He believed that the church's task was to bring about the Kingdom of God in this world by applying Christian ethics to social problems. To this end he supported labor unions, opposed unbridled capitalism, and spoke out against political corruption and racial discrimination. A liberal Congregationalist, he denied that the Bible was inerrant, either literally, historically, scientifically, or morally, and urged Christians to come to terms with Darwin's theory of evolution.

After early pastorates in Brooklyn, New York, 1860-66, and North Adams, Massachusetts, 1866-71, Gladden became religious editor of the New York *Independent*, 1871-75. For part of this time he served as acting editor of the newspaper, using the position to oppose the corrupt political machine of New York's "Boss" William M. Tweed. He returned to parish ministry in Springfield, Massachusetts, 1875-82, then moved to his longest pastorate: over 30 years at the First Congregational Church in Columbus, Ohio, 1882-1914. While in Columbus he served for two years on the city council, where he advocated public ownership of municipal utilities.

[2] Francis Greenwood Peabody (1847-1936) was a Unitarian minister and a highly respected professor of theology and ethics at Harvard Divinity School, 1880-1912. He was Preacher to the University, 1886-1906, and Dean of the Faculty of Divinity, 1901-06. He was a leader in the effort to transform the Divinity School from a training school for Unitarian ministers to a modern nonsectarian school of theology and religious studies.

Peabody was a pioneer in the field of social ethics, seeking to combine Christian ethical teachings with the scientific study of social problems. In addition to introducing social ethics to the Divinity School, he founded the Department of Social Ethics and the Social Museum, a repository for a large collection of photographs intended to document social problems and facilitate the study of their solutions. He wrote: "The facts of philanthropy, industry, poor-relief, housing, insurance, cooperation, alcoholism and penology are as capable of graphic representation as the lives and habits of beetles or plants."

[3] Edward Everett Hale (1822-1909) was a prominent Unitarian minister and author. He was the minister of the Church of the Unity in Worcester, Massachusetts, 1846-56, and of South Congregational Church in Boston, 1856-99. After retiring from parish ministry he was chaplain of the United States Senate, 1903-09.

Hale was a staunch opponent of slavery and supporter of the Union cause in the Civil War. When the Kansas-Nebraska Act of 1854 established that a vote by the settlers would determine whether slavery would be allowed in Kansas, Hale was one of three founders of the New England Emigrant Aid Company, which arranged to send antislavery settlers to the territory.

Hale was a prolific author of short stories, novels, and many articles and books on history, autobiography, religion, and travel. His most well-known work is the patriotic short story "The Man Without a Country" (1863). The most influential was "Ten Times One is Ten" (1870), which popularized the motto "Look up and not down, look forward and not back, look out and not in, and lend a hand," and inspired the formation of hundreds of "Lend A Hand" clubs. There is still a Lend A Hand Society in Boston, which "lends a hand" with emergency housing assistance, medical equipment, libraries for schools and prisons, and camperships for inner-city children.

[4] E. B. (Elisha Benjamin) Andrews (1844-1917) was an ordained Baptist minister, but spent most of his career in higher education. Before coming to Brown University as professor of history and political economy in 1883, he was president of Denison College in Ohio, taught at the Baptist seminary where he had studied for the ministry, and spent a year studying in Germany. He became president of Brown in 1889. During his administration the number of undergraduates at Brown more than doubled; the variety of course offerings was greatly increased; the graduate school was established; and women were admitted as candidates for all degrees. Andrews left Brown in 1898 to become superintendent of the Chicago Public Schools, 1898-1900, and then chancellor of the University of Nebraska, 1900-08.

[5] Lyman Abbott (1835-1922) was a Congregational minister, theologian, and editor. He was a religious liberal who sought an accommodation between religion and the theory of evolution. As a proponent of the Social Gospel, he envisioned the church as a community center, offering health, recreational, educational, and other services. At the same time he

hoped to see the United States develop into a Christian commonwealth with a "fraternal" government based on mutual responsibility and cooperation.

Abbott publicized his views in *Outlook*, a weekly magazine that he edited for more than forty years, from 1881 to his death in 1922. *Outlook* was a successor to *Christian Union*, a religious magazine edited by Henry Ward Beecher. Under Abbott's leadership, it developed into one of the nation's leading "family" publications, offering fiction, essays, sermons, and articles on news and current affairs.

[6] Samuel W. Dike (1839-1913), a Congregational minister from Vermont, was secretary of the National Divorce Reform League (after 1897 the National League for the Protection of the Family) from 1884 until his death in 1913. Divorce began to be perceived as a social problem in the late nineteenth century as the divorce rate more than doubled, from 3% to 7%, between 1865 and 1900. (The divorce rate continued to rise during the twentieth century; by the 1980s, approximately 50% of American marriages ended in divorce.) Unlike many opponents of divorce, Dike did not believe that stricter laws would solve the problem. Instead he called for research into the causes of divorce and better education for marriage and family life.

[7] John Graham Brooks (1846-1938) was a Unitarian minister in Roxbury, 1875-82, and Brockton, Massachusetts, 1885-91. Between the two settlements he spent three years traveling and studying social and economic issues in Europe. In 1891 he left the ministry to become an investigator for the U. S. Department of Labor. He was the first president of the National Consumers' League, an advocacy organization to protect workers from exploitation and to ensure the safety and quality of consumer goods.

[8] Benjamin Franklin Trueblood (1847-1916) was secretary of the American Peace Society, 1892-1915, and editor of the Society's journal, *The Advocate of Peace*. He was a professor of classics and served as president of two Quaker colleges, Wilmington College in Ohio and Penn College in Iowa. He retired from academic life in his forties to devote himself to the cause of peace. He attended the 1899 Hague Peace Conference and organized peace congresses in the United States. He was a charter member of the American Society of International Law. His Adin Ballou lectures, "The Federation of the World," reflect his interest in world government as a means to international peace.

Appendix D

[1] Peter Bulkeley (1583-1659) was rector of Odell in Bedfordshire until he was ejected from his parish for nonconformity in 1634. He emigrated to New England in 1635 and in 1636 became the first minister of the new town of Concord. Cotton Mather described him as "conscientious, even to a degree of scrupulosity." His book of sermons, *The Gospel Covenant, or the Covenant of Grace Opened*, was one of the first books published in New England. In 1638 he was one of the ministers at the trial that excommunicated and banished Anne Hutchinson from the Massachusetts Bay colony.

Simon Willard (1605-1676) was a major in the English army before coming to Massachusetts in 1634 to establish himself as a merchant in the fur trade. When Concord was established in 1635, Willard, who had earned the respect of the Indians for his fair dealing, arranged the purchase of land for the new settlement. He was town clerk of Concord, 1635-53. From 1636 to 1654 he represented Concord in the General Court (the colonial legislature and court of appeals). For the last 22 years of his life he was a member of the Court of Assistants (the governor's council).

Among the earliest settlers in Concord were two sets of Wheeler brothers: Thomas, Ephraim, and Obadiah Wheeler, and their cousins George, Thomas, Joseph, and Timothy Wheeler. The Wheelers were from the same part of Bedfordshire as Rev. Peter Bulkeley, and probably came to America with him.

2   Ephesians 6:4.

3   The unattributed quotations in this paragraph are adapted from Adin Ballou's sketch of Pearley Hunt in *History of the Town of Milford*. The original text reads: "[Pearley Hunt] entered on the responsibilities of adult life in comparatively humble circumstances, but with superior natural abilities, aptitudes, and qualifications to make a respectable mark in society... In the domestic and social circles of life he was justly beloved and esteemed for kindness, urbanity, generosity, hospitality, and the kindred virtues... So he ended his days, notwithstanding his share of human infirmities and adversities, in honor and peace."

4   Alfred H. Love (1830-1913), a woolens merchant in Philadelphia, was president of the Universal Peace Union (see chapter 22, note 25) for 47 years, from its founding in 1866 until his death in 1913.

Before the Civil War, Love's major interests were antislavery and prison reform. The war led him to focus on the issue of peace. When he was drafted in 1863, he declared himself willing to be executed for conscience' sake rather than bear arms or hire a substitute. (A sympathetic draft board exempted him from service because of poor eyesight.)

Love was from a Quaker background but was not a member of any Friends meeting. He considered himself a Christian, but held out for freedom of conscience within the UPU, believing that truth emerged from the interaction of people with different views. His own version of Christianity rejected the idea of atonement based on the blood of Christ, on the grounds that God's plan for salvation would never involve a violent death.

Love was an advocate for women's rights and encouraged women to take leadership roles in the UPU. Women leaders included Julia Ward Howe, Lucretia Mott, and attorney Belva Lockwood. When Lockwood ran for president in 1888 as the candidate of the National Equal Rights Party, she named Love as her running mate. Love declined the nomination, as his peace principles did not permit him to vote, much less hold office, but his name nevertheless appeared on the ballot in several states.

5   These lines are from John Greenleaf Whittier's poem "Channing," written in memory of William Ellery Channing.

6   Proverbs 19:14.

Appendix F

1   Luke 1:70; Acts 3:21.

2   Jacob Wood (1793-1853), the Universalist minister in Charlton, Massachusetts, was one of the principal instigators of the Restorationist Controversy. In 1817 Wood published a pamphlet, *A Brief Essay on the Doctrine of Future Retribution*, in which he attacked Hosea Ballou's theory of immediate universal salvation as unjust, absurd, "productive of immoral effects," and "deleterious in its effects upon society." He envisioned his Brief Essay as the opening move in a campaign to have the Universalist General Convention adopt belief in limited future punishment as an article of faith. He planned to bring a resolution to this effect before the Convention at its annual meeting in 1817. In case this failed, he sounded out some of his colleagues about the possibility of withdrawing from Universalist fellow-

ship and forming a "Restorationist Association." In the end, finding little support for either of these proposals, he did neither. He continued to maintain that Restorationism and immediate universal salvation were irreconcilable and could not exist together in the same denomination. In 1822 he was the principal author of the so-called "Appeal and Declaration," the Restorationist manifesto that brought the conflict into the open (see chapter 5, note 13).

Wood was formally reconciled with the Southern Association of Universalists in June 1824. In 1828 he left Massachusetts to serve the Universalist church in Saco, Maine. A few years later he left the ministry and settled in Troy, New York.

3   The expression "cold and bitter as the dregs of death" was used, in a somewhat different context, four years later in a published sermon by Universalist minister Isaac Dowd Williamson. Williamson wrote that visions of misery in the afterlife "are open fountains of misery, and cold and bitter as the dregs of death they go down into the soul, and poison the engagements of life" ("Dedication Sermon," *Religious Inquirer and Gospel Anchor* [Brattleboro, Vermont], 3 October 1835). Since Ballou and Williamson do not appear to have known each other, this points to a common source, not as yet identified, that was current in Universalist circles at the time.

4   See Matthew 20:12.

5   Walter Balfour (1775-1852) was born in Scotland and educated there for the Presbyterian ministry. In 1807 he came to New England with a letter of introduction to Jedidiah Morse, the Congregational minister at Charlestown, Massachusetts. Balfour, however, had his own ideas about the sacraments of baptism and communion, which made him unwelcome among the Congregationalists. Beginning about 1810 he preached to a small independent congregation in Charlestown.

Balfour's conversion to Universalism came as an indirect consequence of the Unitarian controversy. In an orthodox response to William Ellery Channing's "Unitarian Christianity," Rev. Moses Stuart cited Biblical passages in which Jesus is worshiped by every creature "in heaven and on earth and under the earth." Although Stuart was making an entirely different point, Balfour was struck by the phrase, which he interpreted as a proclamation of universal salvation. During 1820-21 Balfour expressed his doubts and questions in ten anonymous "Letters to Stuart," which were published in the *Universalist Magazine*. In 1823 he announced his conversion to Universalism and revealed himself as the author of the letters.

After his conversion, Balfour became a Universalist preacher, lecturer, and writer. Being better educated than most of his Universalist colleagues, he was able to argue the case for a Universalist interpretation of the scriptures based on the meaning of key words in the original Biblical languages. He presented his views in the form of "letters" and "replies" to various opponents; usually these were orthodox defenders of endless punishment, but two of his books were replies to the Restorationist teachings of Charles Hudson. All of his major works were written between 1824 and 1835. He continued to preach until disabled by a stroke in the early 1840s and wrote occasionally for the press until 1850.

6   Walter Balfour, *Inquiry Into the Scriptural Import of the Words Sheol, Hades, Tartarus and Gehenna: All Translated Hell* (Charlestown, MA, 1824).

7   Ultra universalists cited passages such as Matthew 16:28 and Mark 9:1 to show that Jesus's predictions of wrath and judgment referred to events that were to take place within the lifetime of his hearers, and not to a future Day of Judgment. See, for example, Thomas Whittemore, "Dialogue Concerning Mat. XXV," *Universalist Magazine*, 7 July 1827.

[8] Acts 24:15; see also Matthew 5:45.

[9] John 5:29.

[10] The ultra Universalist position was inferred from passages such as 1 Corinthians 15:51-53: "we shall all be changed ... and the dead shall be raised incorruptible." See, for example, Thomas Whittemore, "Dialogue between a Parent and Child," *Universalist Magazine*, 11 August 1827.

[11] This description applies specifically to the theology of Walter Balfour, which was not shared by most of his ultra colleagues. Balfour believed that all were predestined to salvation, but that this would take place at the final resurrection of the dead following the day of judgment. He disbelieved in the survival of the individual soul after death.

[12] Charles Hudson, *A Series of Letters Addressed to Rev. Hosea Ballou of Boston: Being a Vindication of the Doctrine of Future Retribution* (Woodstock, VT, 1827).

[13] Walter Balfour, *Three Essays on the Intermediate State of the Dead ... With Remarks on Mr. Hudson's Letters in Vindication of a Future Retribution* (Charlestown, MA, 1828).

[14] Adin Ballou's letter, printed in the *Trumpet and Universalist Magazine*, 4 April 1829, asked four questions, of which the fourth (referring to Matthew 12:32) was, "Did those Pharisees, who blasphemed against the Holy Ghost, live till both those ages had passed away, in neither of which their sin was to be forgiven? or did they die in the end of the age, that then was?" Whittemore responded at some length to the other three questions, but replied to the fourth, "To this question you will perceive it is impossible for any person to give an answer."

[15] Whittemore's review of Charles Hudson's *Reply to Mr. Balfour's Essays, Touching the State of the Dead, and a Future Retribution* appeared in the *Trumpet and Universalist Magazine*, 28 February 1829. Whittemore's review of Walter Balfour's *Letters on the Immortality of the Soul, the Intermediate State of the Dead, and a Future Retribution, in Reply to Mr. Charles Hudson* appeared in the *Trumpet and Universalist Magazine*, 12 December 1829.

[16] William I. Reese (1799-1834) was a Universalist minister in West Bloomfield, New York, 1824-29; Portland, Maine, 1829-31; East Bloomfield, New York, 1831-34; and Buffalo, New York, 1834. He died of cholera four months after beginning his pastorate in Buffalo.

[17] A quotation from John Adams's remarks on signing the Declaration of Independence: "Sink or swim, live or die, survive or perish, I give my hand and my heart to this vote ... All that I have, and all that I am, and all that I hope, in this life, I am now ready here to stake upon it ... Independence now, and Independence forever."

[18] See Hosea 2:6.

[19] See Isaiah 2:3; 1 Peter 2:5.

[20] Clement of Alexandria (c.150-215), Origen (c.185-254), and Gregory of Nyssa (c.335-c.395) are among the early Christians discussed in Hosea Ballou 2d's *Ancient History of Universalism*.

[21] These represent the forerunners of Universalism, as retrospectively adopted by both ultra Universalists and Restorationists. All of these names are included in a list of 97 notable early universalists or proto-universalists assembled by Thomas Whittemore (*Universalist Magazine*, 23 June 1827).

John Tillotson (1630-1694), chaplain to Charles II and Archbishop of Canterbury from 1691 to 1694, was a champion of the Enlightenment and a "latitudinarian." Sir Isaac Newton (1643-1727) was claimed as a universalist in Whittemore's *Modern History of Universalism*. William Law (1686-1761), an English mystic, said that heaven and hell were not places, but conditions of the soul. David Hartley (1705-1757) was a British philosopher and psychologist whose *Observations on Man* (1749) argued for universal salvation on the basis of scripture and reason. Andrew Michael "Chevalier" Ramsay (1686-1743) was a Scottish Roman Catholic whose *Philosophical Principles of Natural and Revealed Religion* and *The Travels of Cyrus* (1727) showed universalist leanings. Ferdinand Oliver Petitpierre (1722-1790), expelled by his church in Switzerland for universalist preaching, wrote *Thoughts on Divine Goodness* (1786), which became popular among American Universalists. Petitpierre's optimistic determinism was an important influence on the theology of Hosea Ballou.

[22] 1 Corinthians 15:28.

[23] See Matthew 16:27; Revelation 21:1.

[24] In *Foxe's Book of Martyrs* (1563), the expression "follow them as they followed Christ" is attributed to Hugh Latimer, one of the "Oxford Martyrs" executed under Mary Tudor in 1555. It was widely used in Protestant preaching and writing.

[25] The story of the rich man and the beggar Lazarus is in Luke 16:19-31. The description of the rich man's torments in hell was often quoted against Universalists, especially ultra Universalists, as providing clear scriptural evidence of punishment in the afterlife.

[26] 1 Corinthians 13:13.

[27] Joshua 24:15.

Appendix G

[1] Hosea Ballou began to preach against future punishment following his debate with Edward Turner in the *Gospel Visitant* in 1817. See chapter 1, note 7.

[2] "Without fear or favour" is a phrase from the judicial oath sworn by judges in England since the seventeenth century. A version of this oath is used in many countries whose legal system is descended from English common law, including the United States.

[3] See Acts 26:9.

[4] A proverbial expression dating back to the eighteenth century. A related expression, "more kicks than halfpence," appears in Francis Grose, *A Classical Dictionary of the Vulgar Tongue* (1785).

[5] Reference to 1 Kings 18:17-18, where King Ahab asks the prophet Elijah, "Art thou he that troubleth Israel?"

[6] This summary of the career of Edward Turner is incorrect. See chapter 5, note 15.

[7] Genesis 18:25.

[8] On Hudson's and Balfour's books, see Appendix F, notes 12 and 13.

[9] Matthew 16:26.

[10] On Ballou's use of 1 Peter 3:18-20 and 4:6 in the Medway sermon, see chapter 10, note 8.

[11] Thomas Whittemore, *Notes and Illustrations of the Parables of the New Testament* (1832).

[12] James H. Sayward (1808-1844) was a Unitarian minister. There is no indication that he was ever a Universalist or a Restorationist. He studied for the ministry at Harvard Divinity School but had only two short pastorates: in Mansfield, Massachusetts, 1835-37, and in Fitzwilliam, New Hampshire, 1842-43. He died of lung disease at the age of 35.

[13] Samuel Loveland (1787-1858) was a Universalist minister, editor, and educator, based for most of his career in Reading, Vermont. Here he established a "theological and classical school" to prepare young men for careers in law and medicine as well as training about a dozen Universalist ministers. In 1820, only a year after Hosea Ballou started the *Universalist Magazine*, Loveland began publishing a bimonthly magazine, the *Christian Repository*. Seven of his students went on to edit Universalist periodicals.

A self-taught linguist and scholar, Loveland claimed a reading knowledge of eleven ancient and modern languages, including Hebrew, Arabic, and Anglo-Saxon. In 1828 he published a Greek lexicon of New Testament, for which he received an M.A. from Middlebury College, the first honorary degree ever awarded to a Universalist minister.

Loveland was a believer in future punishment, but he tried to stay on good terms with Universalists on both sides of the Restorationist controversy. He printed the "Appeal and Declaration" in the *Christian Repository*, but took no part in the Restorationist schism (see chapter 5, note 13).

[14] Dolphus Skinner (1800-1869) studied for the Universalist ministry with Samuel Loveland. After a few years as an itinerant preacher in New Hampshire and Vermont, he became the first minister of the Universalist church in Saratoga Springs, New York, 1825-27. In 1827 he was settled at the Universalist church in Utica, New York, where he remained for the rest of his life.

Throughout his career Skinner was devoted to the progress of Universalism. He was a founding member of the New York State Convention of Universalists and the Universalist Historical Society, and a great supporter of Universalist education at all levels. He edited the *Evangelical Magazine and Gospel Advocate*, the largest-circulation Universalist newspaper of its time. Like his mentor Loveland, he was a restorationist, but he deplored controversy within the denomination and tried to remain on good terms with both sides. His neutrality, along with his unquestioned loyalty and commitment to the Universalist cause, gave him the moral authority necessary to bring the controversy to a close.

[15] Dolphus Skinner, "The Universalist Controversy," *Evangelical Magazine and Gospel Advocate*, 25 January 1834. Skinner identified the authors of the offensive articles as Theophilus Fisk, editor of the *New Haven Examiner*, and Henry J. Grew, editor of the *Gospel Anchor* (Troy, New York).

[16] On the beliefs of Universalists in the 1870s, see chapter 14, note 38.

[17] The *Christian Freeman and Family Visiter* was an antislavery and temperance newspaper owned and edited by the Universalist minister Sylvanus Cobb. According to Cobb's son, in the early part of his career Cobb had been "battling with what he sincerely believed to be false and dangerous systems of religion" (that is, engaging in theological debate about the doctrine of universal salvation). When he founded the *Christian Freeman*, however, he "stepped forth into a new field, and set himself about the work of battling against errors that were winked at, if not directly upheld, by many of his own denomination." As Cobb wrote in his autobiography:

> In my travels over the country ... I had observed the lack of a weekly paper in the patronage of the Universalist denomination, more considerably devoted, than any then in circulation, to interesting miscellany for the younger members of the families, and more decidedly committed to the moral reforms of the day, such as Anti-Slavery and Temperance ... The elder representatives of the denominational press [including] Rev. T. Whittemore, of the *Trumpet and Universalist Magazine* ... gave my bantling the cold shoulder ... [for fear of] harm to the Universalist denomination, from the introduction of the exciting topics of Slavery and Temperance.

Ironically, in 1862 the *Christian Freeman* merged with the *Trumpet and Universalist Magazine*, whose editor had given it the "cold shoulder" a quarter-century earlier.

Appendix H

1. John 5:25.
2. Luke 9:23.
3. Luke 12:49.
4. Matthew 6:32.
5. Matthew 6:33.
6. Paraphrase of Matthew 16:18.
7. Tolstoy was referring to his *Synthesis and Translation of the Four Gospels*, which he began in 1880-81 and never entirely finished. It consisted of his own translation of the gospels, arranged thematically into twelve chapters, omitting or reinterpreting the supernatural elements. The work exists in several different abridged versions, in French, English, and Russian, but was not published in its entirety until 1957.
8. John 14:6.
9. See 1 Corinthians 1:19-25.
10. Psalms 118:22; quoted in Matthew 21:42; Mark 12:10; Luke 20:17; Acts 4:11; 1 Peter 2:7.

Index

Note: A number in square brackets following a person's name, such as **Arnold, Rosina Ballou [769]**, indicates a member of the Ballou family, and is a cross-reference to the person's entry in the *History and Genealogy of the Ballous in America*. A number followed by an asterisk, such as **Arnold, Nathan [769*]**, indicates the spouse of a member of the family.

Abbot, Lyman, 389, 548n.5
abolitionists. *See* antislavery movement
Adams, John, 24, 552n.17
Adams, John Quincy, 213, 504n.17, 537n.14
Adams, Laura Ann, 90, 457n.7
Adams, Sylvanus, 94
Albee, Stephen, 164, 481n.5
alcohol, alcoholism, 15-16, 437nn.24-25. *See also* temperance movement
Alcott, A. Bronson, 80, 456n.24, 475n.30
Aldrich, Jabez, 147, 159, 191, 474n.28
Aldrich, Nathaniel, 63-64
Alexander, Asa, 160
Allen, Isaac, 179, 492n.14
Allen, Joseph, 178-179, 491n.8
Andrews, E. B., 389, 548n.4
Andrews, Stephen P., 509n.16, 522n.5
Andrews, William, 189, 190, 497n.3
antislavery movement, 159, 193-197, 205, 209, 213, 235, 256, 321, 498-499nn.10-18, 515n.20, 521n.1. *See also* antislavery organizations; colonization; slavery; Brown, John; Garrison, William Lloyd; other individual abolitionists
antislavery organizations
 American and Foreign Anti-Slavery Society, 473n.26, 500n.21, 515n.20
 American Anti-Slavery Society, 197, 256, 272, 289-290, 471n.11, 473n.26,
475n.32, 478n.23, 499n.18, 507n.5, 515n.20, 519n.19, 535n.26. *See also* Garrison, William Lloyd
 Massachusetts Anti-Slavery Society, 475n.30, 499n.18, 506n.3, 507n.5, 512n.37
 Mendon Anti-Slavery Society, 197, 499n.18
 New England Anti-Slavery Society, 478n.23, 499n.18, 507n.5, 517n.8
 Worcester County Anti-Slavery Society, 290, 499n.18
 other antislavery organizations, 498n.10, 503n.6, 515n.18, 537n.11
Apthorp, William P., 184-187, 495nn.39-41
Arnold, Nathan [769*], 8
Arnold, Rosina Ballou [769], 8, 88, 433n.4
Associationism. *See* Fourierist communities (phalanxes)
Assonet, MA. *See* Freetown, MA
Attleboro, MA, 441n.2; meeting of MAUR, 179. *See also* St. Clair, Alanson; Wright, Nathaniel
Austin, Daniel, 149, 475n.31

Bacheler, Origen, 107-108, 257, 455n.21, 462nn.12-14
Bailey, Alvin F., 374, 545n.33
Bailey, Luther, 209, 502n.5
Balch, William S., 458n.11, 471n.10

Balfour, Walter, 551n.5, 552n.11; controversy with Restorationists, 140-142, 144, 406, 416, 469n.28; *Inquiry into the Scriptural Import of the Words... Translated Hell*, 403, 465n.6, 551n.6; *Essays on the Intermediate State of the Dead* and controversy with Charles Hudson, 406-407, 409, 417-418, 461n.6, 472n.16, 552n.13, 552n.15

Ball, George S., 363, 366-367, 543n.33

Ballou, Abigail [770]. See Cook, Abigail Ballou

Ballou, Abigail Sayles [775*] (wife): engagement, 44-45, 48-49; wedding, 53-55; married life, 55-56, 61-62, 73, 74, 93, 95, 102; illness and death, 106, 107, 108-110

Ballou, Abigail Sayles [2378] (daughter). See Heywood, Abbie Ballou

Ballou, Abner [72], 10, 15, 435n.9, 436n.12

Ballou, Adin Augustus [2380] (son), 165, 206, 260-261; death and mourning, 255, 262-263, 265, 270, 343, 364, 525n.24; spirit communications, 300, 533n.18

Ballou, Adin Jr. [2377] (son), 73, 74, 93, 95-96, 102, 116, 159; death, 161-163

Ballou, Alfred [774], 8, 10, 11, 25, 35, 433n.4

Ballou, Amos J. [1089], 242, 245, 513n.5

Ballou, Ariel [56] (grandfather), 7-8

Ballou, Ariel [191] (father): family life, 7, 10-12, 14-15, 21-22, 24, 31, 35, 49; religion, 25-26, 30, 33-34, 62-64; conflict and reconciliation with AB, 32, 158, 181, 188; death, 220

Ballou, Ariel Jr. [776] (brother), 8, 12, 114, 159, 340, 341, 434n.5; death, 356-357

Ballou, Arnold [772], 8, 31, 433n.4

Ballou, Barton [1214], 21, 397, 438n.31, 446n.4, 450n.17, 530n.22

Ballou, Charles [1129], 207, 502n.1

Ballou, Cyrus [771], 8, 22, 25, 30-31, 433n.4; AB's vision of, 46-47

Ballou, Cyrus Jr. [2361], 229-230, 507n.10, 510n.23

Ballou, Darius [1192], 446n.3

Ballou, Edilda Tower [191*] (mother), 7, 8, 10-12, 13, 15, 19, 25, 39, 63, 69, 114, 158; death, 180-181; spirit communication, 300

Ballou, Eli [3253], 10, 437n.18

Ballou, Frederick M. [3917], 434n.6

Ballou, Hannah Horton [776*], 8, 159

Ballou, Hosea [163], 68, 103-104, 435n.7, 453nn.10, 465n.4; family/genealogy, 8, 68, 448n.12; *The New Birth* and AB review, 52-53, 443-444nn.4-6; pulpit exchange, 78, 94, 59n.15; Prince Street church, 94, 95, 99-101, 107, 460n.2; controversy with Restorationists, 113, 121-122, 132-133, 140-144, 402-403, 406, 410, 415-418, 443n.3, 448n.13, 461nn.6-7, 466nn.8-9, 469n.28, 472n.19; *Treatise on Atonement*, 344, 445n.1, 514n.14; ministerial students, 438n.31, 446n.5, 477n.15; Freemasonry, 456n.22. See also Restorationist controversy; *Universalist Magazine* (*under* newspapers)

Ballou, Hosea Faxon [648], 68, 448n.12

Ballou, Hosea 2d [1856], 59, 62, 67, 109-110, 116, 339, 446n.5, 453n.10, 465n.3; pulpit exchange, 78, 94; *Ancient History of Universalism*, 447n.7

Ballou, James [3], 8-9

Ballou, James [14] ("the Cumberland patriarch"), 8-10, 435n.9

Ballou, James [59] (of Richmond, NH), 10, 436nn.14-15

Ballou, James [219] ("the astrologer"), 10, 437n.16

Ballou, Jerusha Slack [56*] (grandmother), 7-8, 433n.3

Ballou, Jesse [358], 436n.15

Ballou, Latimer W. [3714], 340, 341, 370, 538n.21

Ballou, Levi [1212], 58, 59, 69, 446n.2

Ballou, Lorinda Bates [772*], 8, 31

Ballou, Lucina Comstock [191*], 8

Ballou, Lucy Hunt [775*] (wife): introduced, 90, 457n.7; courtship and marriage, 114, 115-116; early married life, 158, 159, 160, 206, 223; in Hopedale Community, 226, 230, 237, 250-251, 271-274; later married life, 282, 287, 314, 329, 337-339, 343, 357, 361-362; spiritualism, 299-300; as collaborator on histories, 328, 342; biographical sketch, 391-394

Ballou, Massena Berthier [649], 68, 113, 448n.12

Ballou, Matilda Cook [774*], 8

Ballou, Maturin [1], 7, 8, 433n.1, 434n.6

Ballou, Maturin [42] (father of Hosea Ballou), 436n.15

Ballou, Maturin Murray [655], 68, 448n.12

Ballou, Nathaniel [15], 8-10

Ballou, Nehemiah [20], 8

Ballou, Obadiah [16], 8-10

Ballou, Olney [1213], 69, 450n.17

Ballou, Pearley Hunt [2379] (son), 131-132; death, 162-163

Ballou, Rosina [769]. *See* Arnold, Rosina Ballou

Ballou, Samuel [17], 8

Ballou, Sarah [773], 8, 433n.4

Ballou, Silas [215], 10, 437n.17

Ballou, Susanna [771*, 1112], 8, 31

Ballou, William [305], 15-16, 437n.23

Bancroft, Aaron, 182, 494n.29, 498n.14

Bancroft, Eben D., 363, 542n.30

Bancroft, Sylvia Thwing, 513n.1, 542n.30

Baptists, 441nn.8-10, 529n.11, 548n.4; in Ballou family, 8, 433n.3, 435n.7, 435n.9, 436n.12, 436n.14;
Free Will Baptists, 244, 514n.9, 514n.13
Six Principle Baptists, 10, 13, 436n.11, 436n.13
Seventh Day Baptists, 276, 526n.27
and Universalists, 70-72, 117, 451n.1, 452nn. 3-5, 493n.18; Baptists who became Universalist, 166, 439n.2, 445n.1, 458n.11, 482n.11, 503n.12; AB speaks in Baptist meetinghouses, 208, 209, 242

Barre, MA. *See* Bailey, Alvin F.

Barre, VT, meeting of UGC, 145

Barrett, Samuel, 150, 476n.1

Bates, Pearley Ballou [1289.5], 437n.23

Bellingham, MA, 67, 70-73, 94, 97, 157, 159, 207, 208, 441n.2, 451n.1, 452nn.3-5

Benson, George W., 227, 508n.12

Berlin, CT, meeting of Southern Association, 144-145, 410

Berlin, MA, 178-179. *See also* Lamson, David; Whitney, Daniel

Bible: AB's views and interpretations, 35, 57, 58-60, 167-169, 186, 208-209, 284-287, 292-293, 322-323, 522n.6, 528n.3, 536n.2; William Lloyd Garrison's views, 304, 309-310, 531n.5

Blackstone, MA, 70, 94, 131, 468n.5

Bloom, Morgan and Sophia, 272, 283, 523n.10

Boston, MA, 52, 67-68
Central Universalist Society (Bulfinch Street), 73, 113, 208, 453n.7, 504n.18; meeting of MAUR, 161, 212. *See also* Dean, Paul
First Universalist Society (Hanover Street), 69, 73-74, 94, 174, 451n.18, 453n.7. *See also* Murray, John; Streeter, Sebastian
Second Universalist Society (School Street), 94, 453n.7. *See also* Ballou, Hosea
Twenty-eighth Congregational Society, 265. *See* Parker, Theodore

Bottom, Frederick W., 158

Bowen, Henry, 435n.7, 461n.4

Boyden, John, 296, 374, 462n.14, 529n.15

Boyden, Lewis, 157

Boylston, MA, meeting of Fraternal Communion, 228. *See also* Stacy, George; Whitney, Daniel

Bradburn, George, 139, 471n.11

Bragg, Arial, 75, 77, 101-102, 127, 454n.17, 454n.17, 455n.19

Brewster, Henry B., 182, 183, 495n.35

Bridgewater, MA. *See* Normal School

Briggs, Levi, 448n.13

Brisbane, Albert, 227, 508n.13

Brook Farm, 227-228, 491n.5, 509n.15, 524n.14
Brookfield, MA, meeting of Worcester Unitarian Conference, 323
Brooklyn, CT. *See* Benson, George W.; May, Samuel J.
Brooks, Charles, 159, 478n.24
Brooks, John G., 390, 549n.7
Brown, John, 288-292, 506n.2, 521n.39, 529nn.11-12, 540n.8
Brown University, 19, 32, 389, 438n.31, 441n.10, 563n.16, 548n.4
Brownson, Orestes A., 178, 183, 490n.4, 495n.33
Buffum, Arnold, 159, 478n.23
Buffum, Moses [1558], 210, 503n.6
Bulkeley, Peter, 391, 549n.1
Bullard, Dexter [787*], 37, 42-44, 442n.6
Bullard, Juliana Sayles [787], 37, 40, 42-44, 442n.6
Bullard, Leonard, 204
Burdon, Aaron, 70, 451n.2
Burleigh, Lucius, 233, 507n.5
Burlingame, Maxcy W., 243-245, 514n.13
Burnham, George W., 296, 530n.17
Butts, Bryan J., 298, 530n.20

Calkins, John, 212-213, 504n.15
Canada, 274, 525n.21
Canton, MA, 178
Capron, Edmund, 177, 183, 201-202, 420, 488n.1, 501nn.27-28
Capron, Effingham L., 290, 528n.9
Carlisle, MA, 189-190. *See also* Stacy, George
Carrique, Richard, 453nn.10-11
Cary, George L., 373, 544n.26
Catholics, Catholicism, 144, 213, 274, 418, 535n.27, 536nn.2-3. *See also* Brownson, Orestes
Chambré, A. St. John, 322, 536nn.1-2
Chandler, Seth, 111-112, 113, 114, 119, 128, 137, 144, 162, 410n.1, 463n.1; installations, 138-139, 164, 178; MAUR, 420, 471n.10

Channing, William Ellery, 228, 233-234, 248, 474n.29, 509n.20, 512nn.34-35
Charlestown, MA, pulpit exchange, 94-95. *See also* Balfour, Walter; Smith, Linus; Thompson, John; Turner, Edward; Walker, James
Charlton, MA, 113. *See also* Turner, Edward; Wood, Jacob
Chauncy, Charles, 122, 138, 140, 414, 445n.1, 466n.10, 467n.11
Cheney, Martin, 242, 514n.9
Cheney, Wales and Alexander, 88
Chepachet, RI, 113
Child, Henry T., 314, 533n.16
Child, John and Rachel, 287, 528n.4
cholera, 154, 158, 478n.21, 552n.16
Christian Connexion, 25-29, 483n.15; ministers of, 30, 37-38, 178, 242-243, 439n.2, 440-441nn.6-9, 442nn.5-7, 443n.2, 471n.6, 485n.34, 506n.3, 514nn.9-10; meetings of, 30, 51-52; theology of, 35-36, 440n.3; AB ministry, 49-51, 62-64, 448n.9; history of, 440n.3, 440n.6
Christian Non-Resistance. See under works of AB
Christian Socialism (Britain), 378, 545n.40
Christian Union, 151; convention at Groton, 222-223, 506n.1, 506nn.3-4, 507n.6
Christmas, 213, 500n.23, 504n.18
Cincinnati, OH. *See* Ernst, Andrew and Sarah
Civil War 297-298; conscription, 312-313, 532n.12, 533n.14, 550n.4; emancipation of slaves, 531n.6; veterans of, 333-337, 537n.15
Claflin, John, 76
Clark, Thatcher, 267-268
Clarke, Adam, *Complete Commentary upon the Scriptures*, 174, 486n.36
Clarke, Samuel, 162, 182, 187, 201, 210, 480n.33, 501n.26
Clermont Phalanx, 515n.18
Cobb, Sylvanus, 212, 500n.21, 503n.13, 536n.1, 554n.17

colonization (of freed slaves in Africa), 485n.33, 499n.16, 519n.23
communities, 223-228. *See also* Hopedale Community; Brook Farm; Fourierist communities (phalanxes); North American Phalanx; Northampton Association; Raritan Bay Union
Concord, MA, 189-190, 233; early history, 391, 549n.1. *See also* Goodwin, Hersey; Reynolds, Grindall; Ripley, Ezra
Congregationalists, 79, 130; in Milford, 75-76; in Mendon, 146, 153-154, 184-187, 201, 470n.2; liberalizing tendency, 473nn.24-25, 488n.2
Cook, Abigail Ballou [770], 8, 433n.4
Cook, Amos [853], 16, 437n.24
Cook, Clark, 113
Cook, Davis [770*], 8
Cook, Joanna, 95
Cook, Josiah, 435n.9, 436n.12
Cook, Matilda [774*]. *See* Ballou, Matilda Cook
Cook, Nathaniel, 435n.9, 436n.12
Cook, Noah, 34, 102
Cook, William W., 218, 230, 505n.41, 510n.21
Corbett, John Jr., 90, 457n.7
Corbett, Peter, 176, 488n.41
Corbett, Polly, 160-161
Crandall, Prudence, 442n.6, 475n.30
Crossman, Zephaniah, 25-26, 27, 37, 439n.2, 446n.4
Cumberland, RI: AB childhood home, 7, 10-13, 14-15, 35; Ballou neighborhood, 8-9, 15-16; Elder Ballou meetinghouse, 9-10, 13-14, 435n.9, 436n.10, 436n.13. *See also* Christian Connexion; schools
Cushman, Martin, 157-158
Cutler, Stephen, 165-166, 482n.11

Dale, John, 233, 511n.32
Damon, David, 189, 497n.2
Damon, Norwood, 232, 511n.29
Dartmouth, MA, 52. *See also* Hix, Daniel

Davenport, Benjamin, 159, 191, 478n.25
Davenport, David, 253, 517n.6
Davenport, Isaac, 90, 457n.7
Davis, Andrew Jackson, 490n.4, 522n.6
Davis, Ichabod, 542n.19
Davis, Isaac, 480n.1
Davis, Thomas, 273, 524n.17
Dean, Paul, 73, 449n.14, 51n.18, 453n.7, 504n.18; as Restorationist, 68, 113, 132-134, 144, 402, 410, 416, 420-422, 448n.13, 463n.3, 469n.27; pulpit exchanges, 78, 113, 208, 455n.20; *Independent Messenger*, 128, 182, 494n.28, 506n.45; Providence Association, 137, 467n.18; MAUR, 138, 160, 161, 179, 182-183, 199-200, 202, 220, 471n.10, 495n.33; ordinations and installations, 39, 150-151, 178-179, 189, 208, 210, 219; ministerial students, 189, 219, 468n.20, 471n.5, 474n.27, 500n.23; opposition to social reform, 234, 501n.30, 512n.36; Freemasonry, 456nn.22-23
Denton, William, 339-340, 538n.18
Dialogical Instructer. See under newspapers
diary entries, 112-113, 157-161, 188, 207-210, 337-338, 346-348, 354, 359, 360-361
Dike, Samuel W., 390, 549n.6
Dodge, Nehemiah, 458n.11
Doggett, Simeon, 135, 470nn.1-2
Donaldson, William P., 522n.6
Dorr Rebellion, 242, 513n.7
Douglass, Frederick, 235, 512n.37, 515n.18, 526n.28, 537n.11, 538n.19
Dow, Lorenzo, 38-39, 442-443nn.8-9
Draper, Anna Thwing, 237, 271-274, 299, 355-356, 496n.42, 513n.1, 534n.25; funeral sermon, 399
Draper, Eben S., 534n.19
Draper, Ebenezer D., 187, 189, 204, 299, 351, 355-356, 496n.42; in Hopedale Community, 226, 230, 277-279, 510n.21, 516n.2, 518n.14; journey to the West, 271-274

Draper, George, 278-279, 297-298, 329, 349, 350-351, 355, 496n.42, 526n.32
Draper, George A. (son of George Draper), 534n.19
Draper, Hannah Thwing, 513n.1, 526n.32
Draper, William F., 363, 370, 526n.32, 542n.29-30
Dresser, Amos, 498n.10
Dutcher, Warren, 526n.32

East Medway, MA (now Millis), 209; meeting of MAUR, 183
Eaton, Charles H., 356, 369-370, 513n.1, 542n.19
Eddy, Richard, 351-352, 463n.1, 539n.5, 541n.13
education: in Rhode Island, 16-17, 438n.26; in AB childhood, 17-21, 32, 40-42; of AB's children, 259-260. *See also* schools
Edwards, Thomas, 201, 500n.25
Elder Ballou Meetinghouse. *See under* Cumberland, RI
Emerson, Horace, 176, 488n.41
Emerson, Ralph Waldo, 233, 346, 511n.31
Emmons, Nathanael, 84-85, 457n.1, 500n.25, 514n.13
Episcopalians, 213. *See also* Ballou, Ariel Jr.; Chambré, A. St. John; Himes, Joshua
Ernst, Andrew and Sarah Otis, 246, 273-274, 288, 515n.18
Everett, Alexander H., 213, 504n.17
Everett, Linus Smith, 174-175, 485n.33, 486n.37

Farnsworth, Amos, 223, 507n.5
Farr, Jonathan, 167-171, 483n.17, 484n.24
Fay, Allen, 76, 455n.18
Fernald, Mark, 38, 442n.7
Finney, Charles G., 177, 489n.3
Fish, Susan, 255, 518n.17
Fish, William H., 495n.34; as Restorationist, 183, 209-210, 232, 243, 420, 500n.21; in Hopedale Community, 218, 226, 230, 255, 275, 505n.40, 510n.21, 525n.25; at AB's funeral, 363-364, 369; *Memoir of Butler Wilmarth, M.D.*, 269, 522n.4
Fisher, Abial, 71-73, 451n.1, 452nn.3-5
Fisk, Theophilus, 554n.15
Fitz, Henry, 99, 458n.11, 460n.1
Flagg, Joshua, 453n.11
Flagg, Zebediah, 75, 454n.16
Fletcher, Emmons F., 537n.15
Follett,— (Second Advent debate), 243-244
Forest, Samuel, 33
Foss, Andrew T., 291, 529n.11
Foster, Abby Kelley, 513n.5, 515n.20, 529n.10
Foster, Charles H., 299-301, 530n.21
Foster, Stephen S., 291, 529n.10
Fourier, Charles, 227, 468n.20, 508n.13, 509n.16
Fourierist communities (phalanxes), 227, 508n.14. *See also* Brook Farm, North American Phalanx, Clermont Phalanx
Fourth of July: in AB's childhood, 25; in Milford, 89-91, 331-332, 457-458 nn.6-9; in Blackstone, 131, 468n.25; in Mendon, 197
Fox sisters, 490n.4, 519n.25
Franklin, MA, 67, 84-85. *See also* Chambré, A. St. John; Emmons, Nathanael; schools
Fraternal Communion (forerunner to Hopedale Community), 226, 227, 232, 242; constitution, 509n.18
Fraternal Community No. 1. *See* Hopedale Community
Freemasonry, 78-79, 359, 434n.5, 456nn.22-23, 474n.29, 477n.15, 542n.24, 542n.30, 545n.36; AB funeral service, 363, 365, 374, 543n.37
Freetown, MA, meeting of Christian Connexion, 30
Frieze, Jacob, 74, 75, 107, 446n.4, 454n.13, 456nn.22-23
Fugitive Slave Law. *See under* slavery
funerals: performed by AB, 51, 67, 75, 78, 84-88, 105, 111, 116-119, 136, 157-160, 165, 176, 187, 207, 209, 235, 239, 269, 281, 320, 342, 355-356, 357,

358, 359-360; of family members, 109, 162, 220; of AB, 363-365, 366-369, 379-386
Furious Priest Reproved. See under works of AB

Gallagher, Charles, 212
Garfield, Eliza Ballou [949], 538n.19
Garfield, James A. [2939], 340, 538n.19
Garrison, William Lloyd, 332-333, 498n.10, 508n.12, 518n.11, 521n.38; non-resistance, 266, 291-292, 310, 501n.38, 507n.5, 529n.12, 531n.6; discourses in Hopedale, 303-311, 531nn.3-6; views on the Sabbath, 304, 308-309, 515n.21, 531n.3; views on the Bible, 309, 531n.5. *See also* antislavery movement; American Anti-Slavery Society (*under* antislavery organizations)
Garver, Austin S., 374, 545n.34
Gaskill, Lebbeus, 79
Giddings, Joshua R., 273, 524n.17
Gladden, Washington, 389-390, 539n.7, 547n.1
Gladding, Charles, 218, 505n.40
Gloucester, MA. *See* Eddy, Richard; Murray, John; Smith, Daniel D.
Godfrey, David Stearns, 530n.23; spirit communication, 300-301
Godwin, Parke, 227, 508n.13
Goldsbury, John, 164, 178, 480n.3
Goldsmith, Joseph H. and Zaccheus, 282, 314-315, 528n.38
Goodwin, Hersey B., 190, 498n.7
Grafton, MA, 209, 242, 513n.6; New England Village, 207, 502n.2
Grant, Miles, 297, 530n.18
Grant, William, 116
Greeley, Horace, 227, 508n.13, 523-524nn.13-14
Green, John, 190
Green, William, 522n.6
Greene, Harriet N., 530n.20
Greenwood, Thomas J., 164, 480n.2
Grew, Henry J., 554n.15

Griswold, Sherman S., 276, 526n.27
Grosvenor, David, 201, 498n.14, 501n.26
Groton, MA. *See* Christian Union; Stacy, George W.
Grundmann, Emil Otto, 358, 542nn.20-21

Hale, Edward Everett, 389, 548n.3
Hall, James, 99
Hampden, MA. *See* South Wilbraham, MA
Hampton, CT, 51, 243
Harding, Matthew, 212, 503n.12
Hare, Robert, 276, 526n.29
Harris, Nathan, 226, 230, 507n.10
Harris, Thomas Lake, 281-282, 362, 527n.36, 528n.37
Hart, S. R., 506n.45
Harvard University, 152, 389, 446n.5
Hassall, Robert, 296, 529n.15
Hastings, William S., 147, 191, 213, 474n.28, 477n.17, 504n.16
hat business, 45, 56
Hatch, Sarah Jane, 363, 542n.27
Hawkins, John, 235, 512n.38, 515n.19
Hawley, Silas, 222, 506nn.3-4
Hayward, Mary Hastings, 158, 477n.17
Henry, Samuel, 288, 528n.8
Heywood, Abbie Ballou [2378] (daughter), 108, 116, 158, 159, 260, 298, 338-339, 361, 362; as principal of Hopedale Home School, 283, 303; as heir of AB, 387-389
Heywood, John L., 312-313, 533nn.13-14
Heywood, Lucy Florence [6271] (granddaughter), 298, 530n.19
Heywood, William S. [2378*] (son-in-law), 260, 295, 298, 302, 362, 389, 520n.30, 534n.25; as principal of Hopedale Home School, 283, 303; as editor of AB works, 1-3, 330-331, 434n.6, 447n.7, 527n.34
Higginson, Thomas W., 291, 529n.11
Hildreth, Richard, 174-175, 486n.35
Hill, George, 296, 529n.15
Hillsborough, NH, 206

Himes, Joshua V., 174-175, 485n.34, 486n.37
Hingham, MA, 208, 220. *See also* Brooks, Charles; Maynard, Lyman
History and Genealogy of the Ballous in America. *See under* works of AB
History of the Hopedale Community. *See under* works of AB
History of the Town of Milford. *See under* works of AB
History of Worcester County. *See under* works of AB
Hix, Daniel, 30, 52, 441n.8
Hoar, George and Samuel, 233, 511n.30
Holbrook, Willard, 244, 514n.13
Holden, Asa, 91-93, 95-96, 97
Holden, Lucy Heywood. *See* Heywood, Lucy Florence
Holden, MA, 78, 297
Hopedale cemetery, 253, 326, 539n.3; Ballou plot, 109, 343, 365; burials, 269, 356, 518n.17
Hopedale Community: planning, 225-230, 509nn.17-19, 510nn.21-25; constitutions and regulations, 228, 240-241, 252, 509n.18, 513n.2, 516n.2, 517n.5; Community life, 230-231, 235, 237-242, 245-248, 250-255, 268-269; real estate, 253, 517n.9; Commune No. 1, 279-280, 527n.35; dissolution, 277-279, 280-281; post-Community life, 283-284, 287-288, 295-296, 302-303, 325-326
Hopedale Educational Home, 261-262, 267
Hopedale Home School, 260, 283, 303, 528n.1, 531n.1. *See also* Bloom, Morgan and Sophia; Heywood, Abbie Ballou; Heywood, William
Hopedale, town of, 348-351
Hopedale Unitarian Parish, 315-318, 324-325, 329-330, 373, 534n.19. *See also* Wilson, Lewis
Hopkinton, MA, 94, 97. *See also* Phelps, Amos; Stacy, George
Horton, Hannah [776*]. *See* Ballou, Hannah Horton

Hoskins, James W., 159, 478n.22
Hudson, Charles, 450n.16; as Restorationist, 68, 132-133, 145, 416, 448n.13; *Letters to Hosea Ballou* and controversy with Walter Balfour, 104, 406-409, 417-418, 461nn.6-7, 552n.12, 552n.15; *Independent Messenger*, 128, 182, 468n.19, 494n.28, 506n.45; Providence Association, 137; MAUR, 138, 160, 176, 199, 202-204, 232, 420, 471n.10; ordinations and installations, 139, 150, 164, 179, 210, 503n.7; review of *Christian Non-Resistance*, 257, 519n.20
Hughes, Thomas, 545n.40
Huidekoper, Harm Jan, 167, 483nn.13-16
Human Progress in Respect to Religion. *See under* works of AB
Humphrey, William H. and Almina B., 354-355, 541n.18
Hunt, Chloe Albee (mother-in-law), 158, 264-265; spirit communication, 299-300
Hunt, Chloe Albee (sister-in-law), 180
Hunt, Harriet, 90, 457n.7
Hunt, Hiram, 457n.7, 507n.10
Hunt, Lucy [775*] (wife). *See* Ballou, Lucy Hunt
Hunt, Pearley (father-in-law), 90-91, 158, 159, 248-249, 454n.17, 456n.22, 457n.7, 550n.3; leadership role in Milford church, 75, 76, 97-98, 101, 453n.11; spirit communication, 299
Hutchinson Family Singers, 296, 530n.16

Ide, Jacob, 201, 500n.25
Independent Messenger. *See under* newspapers
Inestimable Value of Souls. *See under* works of AB

Jefferson, Thomas, 24, 194, 498n.12
Jenckes, Luke, 58, 69, 446nn.2-3
Johnson, Oliver, 223, 264, 507n.5
Jones, Abner, 30, 36, 440n.6

Kansas-Nebraska Act. *See under* slavery
Kelley, Abby. *See* Foster, Abby Kelley
Kelly, Francis, 245, 514n.15
Kingsley, Charles, 545n.40
Kinsley, William H., 202, 204, 210, 501n.29
Kneeland, Abner, 92, 96, 105, 407, 455n.21, 458nn.11-12, 461n.8, 486n.35

Lamson, David R., 491n.10, 498n.14; as Restorationist, 178-179, 202, 204, 420; *Independent Messenger,* 501n.38; in Hopedale community, 218, 226, 230, 240-241, 510n.21
Lathe, Zephaniah, 444n.6, 453n.11
Lebanon, NH, meeting of UGC, 412
lectures (by AB), 70, 78, 94, 111, 119, 136, 153-154, 156, 157, 178, 184, 190, 197, 207-209, 210, 232, 233, 242, 243, 256, 268, 275-276, 284-287, 296, 357
Leicester, MA, 160. *See also* May, Samuel Jr.; Wilson, Lewis
Leominster, MA, 243, 494n.29
Lewers, Nancy W., 304-305, 531n.2
Lexington, MA. See Staples, Carlton; Whitman, Jason
Lillie, Henry, 226, 229-230, 508n.11, 510n.21
Lincoln, Abraham, 296, 531n.6
Livermore, Abial Abbot, 273, 525n.19
Long, David, 75, 77-78, 454n.14
Long, John D., 349-350, 541n.12
Loring, Ellis Gray, 253, 517n.8
Love, Alfred H., 393, 550n.4
Lovejoy, Elijah P., 205, 498n.10, 501n.38
Loveland, Samuel C., 420, 554nn.13-14
Lowell, MA, 189, 497n.5. *See also* Chambré, A. St. John

Mace, Fayette, 446n.4
Mann, Horace, 520n.29, 520n.31
Mann, Thomas, 55, 445n.9
Marlborough, MA, 113, 179. *See also* Frieze, Jacob; Greenwood, Thomas; Morse, William
marriage. *See* weddings; Ballou, Abigail Sayles; Ballou, Lucy Hunt
Mason, Abraham, 11-12
Mason, Otis, 40, 443n.11
Massachusetts Association of Universal Restorationists (MAUR): founding of, 138, 419-420; Universalist reaction to, 139-145, 472n.22; meetings of, 161, 176, 179, 183, 199-200, 202-204, 212, 220, 506n.44; and reform, 203-204, 220, 421; end of, 231-232, 420-421; confession of faith, 479n.28; membership table, 503n.14
Mathewson, Frank E., 365, 543n.37
Maurice, Frederick Denison, 545n.40
May, Charles, 475n.30
May, Samuel J., 148-149, 150-152, 159-160, 164, 276, 475n.30, 504n.19, 508n.12
May, Samuel Jr. (of Leicester), 296, 363-364, 367-368, 529n.15, 543n.34
Mayers, — (Second Advent debate), 243
Maynard, Lyman, 470n.4; *Independent Messenger,* 128; Providence Association, 137; MAUR, 160, 183, 199, 202, 204, 220, 232, 420, 471n.10; ordinations and installations, 189, 208
McKenzie, James A., 242, 514n.9
McKim, James Miller, 256, 519n.19
Meadville Theological School, 273, 373, 483n.15, 525n.19, 544n.26; Adin Ballou Lectureship, 388-390
medicine: Thomsonian, 37, 441n.7, 442n.4; homeopathic, 484n.31; hydropathic (water cure), 510n.26. *See also* Ballou, Ariel Jr.; Metcalf, John; Peck, Gustavus; Thurber, Daniel; Wilmarth, Butler; Wilmarth, Jerome
Medway, MA, 70, 78, 97, 119, 127-128, 138-139, 207, 208, 243, 464n.10. *See also* Bailey, Luther; Chandler, Seth; Ide, Jacob; Maynard, Lyman
Medway sermon. See *Inestimable Value of Souls* (*under* works of AB)

Mendon, MA: AB preaching, 70, 97, 113; militia muster, 79; Ballou family home, 135, 182; arbitration of boundary dispute, 197-199
   First Congregational Parish (Unitarian): ministry of Simeon Doggett, 470n.1; ministry of AB, 131, 135-136, 146-148, 187, 188, 191-192, 213, 234-235, 470n.3, 498n.15; AB installation, 150-151; AB diary, 157-161, 207-209
   meetings: MAUR, 138; Restorationist conference, 182-183; Fraternal Communion/Hopedale Community, 226-227, 230; Providence Association, 419-420
   North Congregational Church, 153, 184-185, 201, 470n.2. *See also* Perry, John M. S.
   reform movements: antislavery, 196-197, 499n.18; temperance, 152-154, 156, 192, 235
Messer, Asa, 32, 441n.10
Metcalf, John G., 161, 479n.29
Metcalf, Lewis, 58, 446nn.2-3
Methodists, 75, 77, 187, 204, 233, 493n.17. *See also* Dow, Lorenzo
Milford, MA: meeting of Southern Association (AB ordination), 74; Ballou family home, 75, 83-84
   Congregational society, 75-76. *See also* Long, David
   Methodist society, 75
   spiritualist societies, 283, 287, 298
   Universalist Society, 441n.2, 453n.11; ministry of AB, 74-78, 81-82, 94, 97-98, 101-103, 106-107, 119, 127-128, 130-131, 407-408, 464n.10; AB diary, 112-113; pulpit supply, 357. *See also* Eaton, Charles Henry; Frieze, Jacob; Hill, George; Whitney, Elbert; Whittemore, Thomas
   See also Fourth of July; *History of the Town of Milford* (*under* works of AB); schools
militia, 16; AB chaplaincy, 79-80, 176
Miller, William. *See* Second Advent

Millis, MA. *See* East Medway, MA
Millville, MA, 113; meeting of MAUR, 199-200, 232; ordinations and installations, 201-202, 209-210; meeting of Hopedale Community, 229-230; Second Advent discussion, 243-245, 514nn.13-14. *See also* Capron, Edmund; Fish, William
Milton, MA, meeting of MAUR, 202-204
Minnesota, Union Grove colony, 275, 526n.26, 533n.13
Missouri Compromise. *See under* slavery
Mitchell, Edward, 105, 407, 458n.11, 461n.8
Modern Times (community), 522n.5
Monitorial Guide. See under works of AB
Morse, Cyrus, 187
Morse, Darius, 84
Morse, William, 179, 182, 189, 199, 202, 212, 220, 420, 453n.9, 492n.12, 494n.28, 501n.30, 506n.45
Munyan, Lemuel, 230, 510n.21, 510n.25
Murray, John, 73, 451n.18, 452n.6, 456n.22, 464n.1; cited in Restorationist controversy, 122, 138, 140-141, 143, 415, 443n.3, 467n.11
Myers, John F., 458n.11
Mystic, CT, 276, 526n.27

Nelson, Newell, 91, 229, 457n.7
New Bedford, MA, meeting of Christian Connexion, 52
New England Non-Resistance Society. *See under* peace organizations
New York City, 93, 95-96, 272, 459n.14, 460n.18, 523nn.11-12
   First Universalist Society (Prince Street), 91-93, 96, 99-103, 105-106, 407, 458nn.11
   Second Universalist Society, 458n.11
   Fourth Universalist Society. *See* Eaton, Charles Henry; Harris, Thomas Lake
   United Christian Friends. *See* Mitchell, Edward

newspapers
  Anti-Slavery Standard, 507n.5, 540n.8
  Anti-Universalist, 107-108, 462nn.12-14
  Banner of Light, 377, 546n.41
  Boston Centinel, 486n.37
  Boston Commonwealth, 345
  Boston Herald, 375-376
  Boston Journal, 376
  Boston Recorder, 130, 132, 419
  Christian Freeman and Family Visiter, 421, 503n.13, 554n.17
  Christian Leader, 377, 546n.42
  Christian Register, 318, 377-378, 393-394, 476n.1, 484n.24, 494n.21, 546n.43
  Christian Repository, 437n.18, 448n.13, 554n.13
  Christian Telescope, 455n.21, 462n.13
  Columbian Phenix; or Providence Patriot, 24, 439n.1
  Dialogical Instructer, 96, 102, 460n.19, 461n.5
  Evangelical Magazine and Gospel Advocate, 420-421, 554nn.14-15
  Gospel Anchor, 420, 554n.15
  Gospel Visitant, 435n.7, 466n.8
  Independent Messenger, 128-129, 135-137, 146, 165-166, 181-182, 221, 468n.19, 482n.10, 494n.28, 506n.45; "Genius of Reform" section, 500n.21, 501n.38, 506n.45
  Liberator, 517n.8, 521n.38, 540n.8
  Mammoth, 261, 520n.32
  Milford Gazette, 375
  Milford Journal, 331-332, 364, 375, 393
  New Haven Examiner, 420, 554n.15
  New York Tribune, 178, 491n.5, 508n.13
  Non-Resistant, 263-264, 507n.5, 540n.8
  Practical Christian, 221, 222, 264, 281, 283, 293-295, 530n.20
  Trumpet and Universalist Magazine, 102, 121-122, 126-127, 132, 139-145, 294, 408-413, 454n.12, 461nn.4-5, 554n.17
  Unitarian, 474n.29, 484n.24, 486n.37
  Universalist, 319-320, 415-422
  Universalist Magazine, 67, 444n.6, 461n.4, 546n.42. See also Ballou, Hosea; Whittemore, Thomas
non-resistance, 209, 213-215, 233, 242-243, 265-266, 276, 345; and John Brown raid, 288-292; and Civil War, 297-298. See also Christian Non-Resistance (under works of AB); Garrison, William Lloyd; Non-Resistant (under newspapers); peace organizations; Tolstoy, Leo N.
Normal School, 260-261, 478n.24, 520n.29, 520n.31; death of Adin Augustus Ballou, 262
North American Phalanx, 227, 272, 508n.13, 523n.13, 524n.14
Northampton Association for Education and Industry, 227, 508n.12
Northbridge, MA, 209, 243
Norton, MA, 257
Noyes, John Humphrey. See Oneida Community

Oberlin College. See Finney, Charles G.
Olney, Christopher, 19-20
Oneida Community, 509n.16, 523n.10
Orcutt, John, 257, 519n.23
Osgood, Peter, 178, 491n.9
Otis, Sarah. See Ernst, Sarah Otis
Owen, Robert, 252, 509n.16, 517n.3. See also Kneeland, Abner
Oxford, MA, 164, 441n.2, 472n.17, 480n.1; meeting of Providence Association, 128. See also Chandler, Seth; Maynard, Lyman

Paige, Lucius R., 158, 453n.9, 477nn.15-16, 481nn.6-7
Paine, Emanuel N. [3722*], 530n.22; spirit communication, 300
Parker, Daniel, 273, 525n.20
Parker, Theodore, 265-266, 484n.26, 521n.37, 521n.39, 534n.23, 540n.8
Parkhurst, Otis, 130
Partridge, Emmons, 199, 500n.22

Pawtucket, RI, 21, 107, 454n.13
Peabody, Francis G., 389, 548n.2
peace movement. *See* Non-Resistance
peace organizations
American Peace Society, 321, 390, 471n.6, 502n.5, 511n.30, 534n.25, 549n.8
Massachusetts Peace Society, 475n.30, 509n.20, 511n.30
New England Non-Resistance Society, 220-221, 247, 263-264, 291, 504n.19, 520n.34, 528n.9, 540n.8
Universal Peace Union, 321, 375, 393, 533n.16, 534n.25, 550n.4
Windham County Peace Society, 508n.12
Peck, Gustavus D., 109, 114, 455n.18, 463n.15
Peck, Ira Ballou [1118], 341-342, 539nn.1-2
Peirce, Cyrus, 260, 520n.29
Perry, Adams, 111
Perry, John M. S., 153-154, 162, 477n.12, 498n.14
Phelps, Amos A., 146, 473n.26
Philadelphia, PA, 272, 276, 287, 314, 524n.15
Pickering, Benjamin, 158
Pickering, David, 78, 93, 187-188, 455n.21; as Restorationist, 113, 132-133, 144, 410, 462nn.13-14, 463n.3; *Independent Messenger*, 128; Providence Association, 137, 467n.18; MAUR, 138, 420, 471n.10; ordinations and installations, 150-151, 164; Freemasonry, 456n.22
Pierce, George B., 83
Pitman, Isaac, 210, 500n.21
Pitts, Amos W., 245, 514n.15
Place, Stephen, 10, 13, 436n.13
Plummer, Frederick, 30, 441n.7
political parties
Anti-Masonic Party, 456n.23
Liberty Party, 146, 500n.21, 506n.2, 515n.20
National Equal Rights Party, 550n.4

National Labor Reform Party, 535n.29
Prohibition Party, 254, 500n.23, 518n.12, 535n.27, 543n.33
Portland, ME, 274. *See also* Reese, William; Smith, Daniel D.; Streeter, Russell; Whitman, Jason
Potter, Reuben, 37, 51, 54, 442nn.5-6
Practical Christian Republic, 270-271, 275, 277, 298, 522n.8
Practical Christian Socialism. See under works of AB
Practical Christian. See under newspapers
Price, Abby Hills, 515n.17, 518n.17
Price, Edmund, 245, 515n.17
Primitive Christianity and its Corruptions. See under works of AB
Providence Association. *See under* Universalist organizations
Providence, RI, 38-39, 57, 67, 78, 93, 95, 103, 183, 242; early history, 7, 433n.1. See also Bacheler, Origen; Pickering, David; Stone, Edwin M.
Purchase, Reuben, 12-13

Quakers, 162, 479n.31, 528n.5, 532n.12. *See also* Buffum, Arnold; Child, Henry; Child, John and Rachel; Crandall, Prudence; Trueblood, B. F.
Quincy, Edmund, 223, 228, 507n.5

railroads, 273, 524n.18, 530n.23; railroad accidents, 269, 514n.11, 522n.3
Raritan Bay Union, 515n.17, 523n.13
Rawson, Warren, 158, 159, 477n.18
Ray, Joseph, 70, 451n.2
Reese, William I., 410, 552n.16
Remond, Charles L., 291, 529n.11
Restorationist controversy, 68, 120-130, 132-134, 139-145, 183-184, 319, 351-352, 443n.3, 448n.13, 465n.3; "Epistle General to Restorationists," 401-414; "The Restorationist Secession," 415-422. *See also* Ballou, Hosea; Dean, Paul; Hudson, Charles; Turner, Edward; Wood, Jacob; Massachusetts Association of Universal Restorationists

Revolutionary War, 9, 190, 433n.2, 439n.1; veterans of, 25, 158; and slavery, 193-194, 290-291
Reynolds, Grindall, 374, 545n.35
Rich, Caleb, 443n.3, 445n.1, 453n.11, 480n.1
Richmond, NH, 10, 436nn.14-15, 437n.17
Richmond, VA, 481n.7. *See also* Smith, Daniel D.
Ripley, Ezra, 189-190, 497n.1, 498n.7
Ripley, George, 178, 491nn.5-6, 494n.21. *See also* Brook Farm
Ripley, Samuel, 494n.21
Robinson, Ebenezer, 52, 164, 178, 443n.2
Robinson, George D., 348, 540n.11
Roxbury, MA, 67, 78, 94. *See also* Ballou, Hosea 2d; Brooks, John G.
Russell, Abigail, 209
Russell, Jonathan, 209, 502n.4
Russell, Philemon R., 128, 137, 138, 144, 178, 182, 202, 420, 471n.6, 471n.10, 494n.28, 498n.14, 501n.30

Sabbath, 202, 531; AB views on, 270, 308-309, 515n.21
Sayles, Abigail [775*] (wife). *See* Ballou, Abigail Sayles
Sayles, Abigail Scott (mother-in-law), 44, 57, 63, 159, 233, 512n.33
Sayles, Ariel [788], 40
Sayles, Avilda [782], 40
Sayles, Daniel [192*], 40, 67
Sayles, Juliana [787]. See Bullard, Juliana Sayles
Sayles, Orin [789], 40
Sayles, Smith (father-in-law), 44, 63, 159
Sayward, James H., 420, 554n.12
scarlet fever, 161-163, 206, 479n.30, 479n.32
schools
 attended by AB: Cumberland, RI, 16-18, 19-21, 32, 34; West Wrentham, MA, 18-19; Franklin, MA, 40-42
 taught by AB: Cumberland, RI, 53-55, 57; West Wentham, MA, 69; North Purchase (Milford), MA, 80-81, 108; Milford, MA, 83, 89, 115
 See also Hopedale Educational Home, Hopedale Home School
Sears, Charles, 272, 524n.14
Second Advent, 178, 243-245, 297, 485n.34, 514n.14, 530n.18
sermons (by AB), 49-50, 67, 74, 84, 85-87, 94, 114-115, 117, 121, 127, 139, 158-161, 183, 187, 189, 196, 201, 207-212, 213, 235, 243, 265-266, 315, 318, 325, 334-337, 359, 410-411
Seventh Day Baptists. *See under* Baptists
Sewall, Charles C., 149, 150, 475n.32
Shakers, 241, 491n.10, 509n.16
singing school, 33-34
Six Principle Baptists. *See under* Baptists
Skinner, Dolphus, 420-421, 554nn.14-15
Slater, Samuel, 21, 438n.32, 438n.36
slavery
 Fugitive Slave Law, 506n.2, 526n.28
 Kansas-Nebraska Act, 272, 524nn.16-17, 548n.3
 Missouri Compromise, 40, 443n.10, 524n.16
 See also antislavery movement, antislavery organizations
Smith, Daniel D., 172-176, 484n.31, 486n.37
Smith, Elias, 30, 36, 37, 440n.6, 441n.7, 441-442nn.3-4, 484n.31
Smith, Gerrit, 222, 228, 273, 276-277, 506nn.2-4, 524n.17, 526n.30
Smith, Matthew Hale, 484n.31, 485n.33
Smith, Sabin, 113
Smithfield, RI, 54-55, 93, 103
Snow, Josiah, 158, 477n.20
Social Gospel, 539n.7, 547n.1, 548n.5
Social Manufacturing Company, 22, 438n.36
South Wilbraham, MA (now Hampden), 212-213
Southborough, MA, 223. *See also* Sweet, John; Whitney, Daniel
Southbridge, MA, 158

Southern Association. *See under* Universalist organizations
Southold, NY, 282, 314-315, 528nn.37-38
Soward, Edmund, 255, 518n.16; Soward fund, 326
Sparrell, William, 204
spiritualism, 258-259, 268, 276, 281-282, 283-284, 296, 298, 299-301, 320, 340, 347, 362, 377, 382, 519nn.25-26, 520n.28, 521n.2, 526n.29, 527-528nn.36-38, 530n.17, 530n.21, 533n.16, 533n.18, 538n.18. See also *Spirit Manifestations (under* works of AB)
Springfield, MA, 272
St. Clair, Alanson, 199, 204, 210, 498n.14, 500n.21, 501n.38
Stacy, George W., 183, 189-190, 199, 204, 420, 468n.20, 515n.19; *Independent Messenger*, 128-129; in Hopedale Community, 218, 226, 228, 245, 251-252, 505n.39, 516n.2; at AB's funeral, 374
Stacy, Nathaniel, 456nn.22-23
Stafford, CT, 74. *See also* Ballou, Hosea 2d
Standard of Practical Christianity, 215-218 (text), 219, 221, 223-225, 228, 231, 236, 256
Stanton, Joshua, 212-213, 504n.15
Staples, Carlton A., 364, 368, 371-372, 543n.36
steamboats, 93, 95, 103, 273, 274, 459n.13, 460n.17, 525n.23
Stetson, Seth, 446n.4
Stone, Edwin M., 160, 201, 474n.27, 478n.22, 486n.37, 488n.40; *Independent Messenger*, 146, 158, 482n.10, 484n.24; MAUR, 176, 199, 202, 220, 420, 495n.33, 501n.30
Stone, Richard, 179, 493n.17
Streeter, Adams, 164, 453n.11, 480n.1
Streeter, Barzillai, 446n.4, 448n.13
Streeter, Russell, 102, 461nn.3-4
Streeter, Sebastian, 74, 94, 449n.14, 453n.8, 456nn.22-23
Sumner, Charles, 273, 524n.17

Sumner, Clark, 90, 116, 457n.7
Sumner, Sullivan, 75, 77, 83-84, 90, 454n.17
Sweet, Joanna Sayles, 88-89
Sweet, John D., 179, 493n.15
Syracuse, NY, 276. *See also* May, Samuel J.

Taft, Amariah, 147, 474n.28
Taft, Putnam W., 176, 488n.41
Taylor, Benjamin, 30, 37, 64, 242-243, 441n.9, 514nn.9-10
Taylor, James, 242, 514n.9
Taylor, John, 243, 514nn.9-10
Taylor, Nathaniel W., 146, 177, 473n.24, 488n.2
temperance movement, 152-157, 176, 178, 190, 192-193, 203-205, 207, 209, 235, 243, 247, 314-315, 321, 383, 437n.25, 476n.11, 477n.12, 515n.19. *See also* alcohol
temperance organizations
American Temperance Society, 476n.11
Mendon Temperance Society, 153, 192
Prohibition Party. *See under* political parties
Washington Temperance Society (Washingtonians), 235, 247, 512n.38, 515n.19
other temperance organizations, 497n.1, 503n.13, 511n.30, 535n.27
Temple, Alexander T., 202, 204
textile manufacturing, 21-22, 438-439nn.32-38, 497n.5. *See also* Draper, Ebenezer; Draper, George; Draper, William; Social Manufacturing Co.
Thayer, Henry, 70, 451n.2
Thayer, Mercy [877*], 162, 479n.31
Thompson, CT, 160
Thompson, George S., 333, 498n.10, 537n.11
Thompson, John S., 94-95, 460n.16
Thomson, Samuel. *See under* medicine
Thornton, John, 506n.45
Thurber, Daniel, 109, 114, 161, 463nn.15-16

INDEX 571

Tillinghast, Nicholas, 260, 520n.31
tobacco, 112, 383, 525n.19
Tolstoy, Leo N., 352-354, 423-429, 541n.14, 541n.16, 555n.7
Torrey, Elizabeth Mellen, 158
Touchstone. See *under* works of AB
Tower, Levi and Mary (grandparents), 7, 433n.2
Troy, NY, 267-268
Trueblood, Benjamin F., 390, 549n.8
Tubman, Harriet, 526n.28
Tufts College, 446n.5, 536n.1, 538n.21, 542n.19
Turner, Edward, 450n.15, 469n.28, 480n.1; debate with Hosea Ballou, 143, 435n.7, 466n.8, 472n.19; as Restorationist, 68, 402, 416-417, 448n.13; Freemasonry, 456n.22
Tyler, Bennet, 177, 488n.2
Tyler, Fisher Ames, 158, 477n.14

Underwood, Adin Ballou, 332, 537n.10
Unitarians, Unitarianism, 484n.26, 534n.23; views on universal salvation, 124, 166-172; cooperation with Restorationists, 148-149, 150-152, 164, 178-179, 208, 420-421; AB in fellowship with, 146-147, 317-318, 320, 323
Unitarian organizations
  American Unitarian Association, 179, 374, 476n.1, 492n.13, 493n.18, 494n.29, 509n.20, 541n.15, 545n.35
  Free Religious Association, 534n.23
  National Conference of Unitarian Churches, 534n.23
  Western Unitarian Conference, 525n.19, 543n.36
  Worcester Conference of Congregational and Other Christian Societies (Unitarian), 317, 320, 323, 357, 374, 493n.17
Universalists, Universalism, 495n.38; AB: early impressions of Universalism, 36, 52-53, 65; conversion to, 57-62; welcomed to ministry, 65-68, 74; prejudice against Restorationists, 36, 68, 82, 103-104, 401-404; Universalist sermon, 116-119; becomes a Restorationist, 120-128, 405-411. *See also* Restorationist controversy
Universalist organizations, 467n.18
  Boston Association, 144
  Buffalo Association, 485n.33
  Eastern Association, 144
  Hudson River Association, 459n.15
  Maine Convention of Universalists, 145, 419, 478n.22
  New York State Convention of Universalists, 145, 419, 554n.14
  Providence Association, 128, 136-138, 144-145, 157, 183, 410, 412, 419-420, 467n.18
  Southern Association, 59, 74, 144-145, 410, 419, 446n.4, 453n.9, 467n.18
  Southern Convention of Universalists, 454n.13
  Universalist General Convention (UGC), 113, 120, 128, 140, 142-143, 144-145, 409-410, 412, 415, 419, 448n.13, 452n.6, 453n.11, 459n.15, 463n.3, 464n.1, 465n.2, 467n.18, 472n.17, 472n.22, 550n.2
Universalist Historical Society, 446n.5, 454n.12, 463n.1, 541n.13, 554n.14
Upton, MA, 97, 209, 243, 257-258, 357. *See also* Ball, George; Wilmarth, Jerome
Uxbridge, MA, 97, 113, 159, 176, 182, 187, 257. *See also* Clarke, Samuel; Draper, Ebenezer; Grosvenor, David

Varney, Belle A., 362
veterans, AB address to, 333-337

Waite, Charles B., 340, 538n.20
Walker, James, 179, 492n.13
Walker, Timothy, 91, 458n.9
War of 1812, 22-23, 24, 91, 209, 502n.4, 504n.17, 509n.20
Warren, Josiah, 509n.16, 522n.5

Washingtonians. *See under* temperance organizations
Washington, DC, 272-273
Watertown, MA, 165. *See also* Russell, Philemon
weddings: AB and Abigail Sayles, 44-45, 53-55; AB and Lucy Hunt, 115-116; Dexter Bullard and Juliana Sayles, 42-44; performed by AB, 74, 75, 94, 105-106, 111, 159, 281, 319, 329, 357, 359, 360
Wesley, John, 194, 498n.11
West Boylston, MA, 178. *See also* Lamson, David; Russell, Philemon; St. Clair, Alanson; Whitney, Daniel
West Bridgewater, MA, 179. *See also* Stone, Richard
West Medway, MA. *See* Medway, MA
West Newton, MA. *See* Normal School
West Wrentham, MA. *See* Wrentham, MA
Westminster, MA, 160; meeting of Providence Association, 137; meeting of MAUR, 176, 232. *See also* Hudson, Charles
Wheeler, Samuel W., 204, 242, 501n.32
Whipple, Charles K., 345, 540n.8
Whipple, Jonathan, 527n.35
White, Charles J., 373-374, 544n.27
White, William H., 189, 497n.4
Whitman, Bernard, 148-149, 150-152, 161, 164-165, 167, 174-175, 180, 474n.29, 477n.16, 481nn.6-8, 486n.37, 494n.21
Whitman, Jason, 179, 493n.18
Whitney, Daniel S., 500n.23; as Restorationist, 199, 219, 220, 420, 500n.21; in Hopedale community, 218, 226, 230, 235, 253-254, 510n.21
Whitney, Elbert W., 365, 543n.37
Whitney, Susan Thwing, 541n.18
Whittemore, Benjamin [651*], 446n.4, 448n.12
Whittemore, Thomas, 74-75, 102, 294, 453n.11, 454n.12; controversy with Restorationists, 121-122, 126-127, 130, 132-134, 139-145, 408-412, 416, 443n.3, 444n.6, 446nn.3-4, 461nn.4-5, 463n.3, 464n.10, 466n.9, 467n.13, 468n.26, 469n.27, 481nn.7-8, 486n.37; *Modern History of Universalism*, 465nn.3-4, 472n.19, 552n.21
Whittier, John G., 363, 543n.32, 543n.38, 550n.5
Wiggins, Thomas G. ("Blind Tom"), 314, 533n.17
will: of Adin Ballou, 387; of Lucy Hunt Ballou, 393
Willard, Simon, 391, 549n.1
Williams, Roger, 7, 433n.1, 445n.8
Williams, Thomas, 257, 519n.22
Williamson, Isaac Dowd, 551n.3
Williamson, Passmore, 276, 526n.28
Wilmarth, Butler, 230, 269, 510n.26, 520n.28, 522nn.3-4; spirit communication, 300
Wilmarth, Jerome, 304-305, 337-338, 362, 531n.2, 538n.17
Wilson, Caleb Ward, 40-41, 443n.12
Wilson, Lewis G., 353-354, 355, 358, 370, 393-394, 423-429, 541n.15
Winchester, Elhanan, 445n.1, 447n.8, 472n.18; *Dialogues on Universal Restoration*, 57-59; cited in Restorationist controversy, 122, 138, 140, 143, 414, 415, 443n.3, 467n.11
Winchester, New Hampshire, 113, 160; meeting of UGC, 144, 410. *See also* Balch, William; Maynard, Lyman; Russell, Philemon
Winchester Profession, 472n.22
women's rights, 321, 515n.17, 535n.28; in Christian Connexion, 440n.3; in antislavery movement, 471n.11, 473n.26, 475n.30, 515n.20; in Universal Peace Union, 534n.25, 550n.4; National Equal Rights Party (*see under* political parties)
Wood, Jacob, 402, 416, 448n.13, 456n.22, 550n.2
Woonsocket, RI, 22, 67, 207, 222, 373-374, 462n.14. *See also* Boyden, John; White, Charles

Worcester, MA, 160, 222, 290-291, 297. *See also* Bancroft, Aaron; Garver, Austin; Hale, Edward Everett
Worcester, Noah, 475n.30, 509n.20
workers' rights movement, 321, 475n.30, 535n.29
works of Adin Ballou
   Autobiography of Adin Ballou, 341, 358-359, 361-362
   Christian Non-Resistance, 256-257
   Furious Priest Reproved, 72-73
   History and Genealogy of the Ballous in America, 340, 341-342, 357, 434n.6
   History of the Hopedale Community, 279, 317, 328, 527n.34
   History of the Town of Milford, 319, 328-329, 331-332, 339, 341
   History of Worcester County, 345-346, 350-351
   Human Progress in Respect to Religion, 315
   Inestimable Value of Souls, 121-122, 127, 410-411, 419, 465-466nn.7-9
   Lecture on the Inspiration of the Bible, 284-287, 528n.3
   Memoir of Adin Augustus Ballou, 263, 270
   Monitorial Guide, 298-299
   Non-resistance in Relation to Human Governments, 221
   Non-Resistant Catechism, 397
   Practical Christian Socialism, 271, 509n.16, 522n.8
   Primitive Christianity and its Corruptions, 279, 319, 322-323, 325, 326-327, 387, 527n.34, 536nn.2-3
   Review of a lecture sermon ... by Hosea Ballou, 52-53, 56, 58, 443-444nn.4-6
   Spirit Manifestations, 263, 521n.2, 533n.18
   Touchstone, 204, 501nn.33-34
   True Scriptural Doctrine of the Second Advent, 245, 514n.16
   Violations of the Federal Constitution, 296-297
   See also Appendix E, 395-400

Wrentham, MA, 67, 116-117, 243, 446n.3; meeting of Southern Association, 59, 446n.4. *See also* schools
Wright, Henry C., 264, 520n.34
Wright, Nathaniel, 137, 138, 139, 150, 164, 179, 420, 471n.5, 471n.10

Yale Divinity School. *See* Taylor, Nathaniel W.
Young, Origen B., 363, 543n.31

www.ingramcontent.com/pod-product-compliance
Ingram Content Group UK Ltd.
Pitfield, Milton Keynes, MK11 3LW, UK
UKHW022229230426